CHARLES
SUMNER

CHARLES SUMNER

CONSCIENCE OF A NATION

ZAAKIR TAMEEZ

HENRY HOLT AND COMPANY
NEW YORK

Henry Holt and Company
Publishers since 1866
120 Broadway
New York, New York 10271
www.henryholt.com

Henry Holt® and ⓗ® are registered trademarks of Macmillan Publishing
Group, LLC.

Distributed in Canada by Raincoast Book Distribution Limited

Library of Congress Cataloging-in-Publication Data

Names: Tameez, Zaakir, author.
Title: Charles Sumner : conscience of a nation / Zaakir Tameez.
Other titles: Conscience of a nation
Description: First edition. | New York : Henry Holt and Company, 2025. | Includes
bibliographical references and index.
Identifiers: LCCN 2024047167 | ISBN 9781250362551 (hardcover) | ISBN 9781250362568
(ebook)
Subjects: LCSH: Sumner, Charles, 1811–1874. | Legislators—United States—Biography. |
United States. Congress. Senate—Biography. | Slavery—Political aspects—United
States—History—19th century. | Antislavery movements—United States—History—
19th century. | Free Soil Party (U.S.) | Reconstruction (U.S. history, 1865–1877) |
United States—Politics and government—1849–1877. | Boston (Mass.)—Biography.
Classification: LCC E415.9.S9 T36 2025 | DDC 973.7/114092 [B]—dc23/eng/20250203
LC record available at https://lccn.loc.gov/2024047167

Our books may be purchased in bulk for promotional, educational,
or business use. Please contact your local bookseller or the Macmillan
Corporate and Premium Sales Department at (800) 221-7945, extension
5442, or by e-mail at MacmillanSpecialMarkets@macmillan.com.

First Edition 2025

Designed by Meryl Sussman Levavi

Printed in the United States of America

1 3 5 7 9 10 8 6 4 2

This book is dedicated to the memory
of two beloved family members:

Asra Adeela Hussain

July 14, 1998 – January 29, 2025
American Airlines Flight 5342

AND

Mohammed Shafi Ghafoor

March 25, 1937 – August 19, 1980
Saudia Flight 163

We await our reunion with you in the
"gardens beneath which rivers flow," *inshallah.*

Mr. Sumner is a remarkable man. . . .
The man speaks like a prophet.

—Alexis de Tocqueville, 1857

*

I have never had much to do with bishops down where we live;
but, do you know, Sumner is just my idea of a bishop.

—Abraham Lincoln, 1861

*

There is now a man at Washington who represents the future,
and is a majority in himself. . . . That man is Charles Sumner.

—Frederick Douglass, 1872

CONTENTS

INTRODUCTION

Charles Sumner was described by the poet Henry Longfellow as "a *colossus* holding his burning heart in his hand," a burning heart that bled for abolition, racial justice, and constitutional democracy. He was a six-foot-four Bostonian lawyer with a wild mane of chestnut hair, thick sideburns, broad shoulders, and a sonorous voice that could roar like a lion. He was a polyglot who knew six languages and a worldly man who counted Charles Dickens, Ralph Waldo Emerson, and Alexis de Tocqueville among his friends. He possessed a towering presence and intellectual prowess, even as he dealt with childhood poverty, suicidal thoughts, depression, and heartbreak. A controversial and hypersensitive man who craved praise, he often cried in front of his friends when he didn't receive the gratitude he thought he deserved for his service to his country.[1]

Born in 1811, Sumner was the most famous civil rights leader of the nineteenth century, much like Martin Luther King Jr. in the twentieth century. He was a household name in his era. He began earning national fame and notoriety for his civil rights work in the fall of 1849, when he joined a Black lawyer on the first case argued by an interracial legal team in American history. Together, they represented a young Black girl who tried to attend one of Boston's white-only public schools. More than a century before *Brown v. Board of Education*, Sumner thundered against the "arbitrary discrimination of color" in a Massachusetts courtroom.

In this forgotten case, *Roberts v. City of Boston*, Sumner coined a phrase that had never before been heard in American jurisprudence: "equality before the law." Believing that equality should be the cornerstone of constitutional democracy, Sumner said that the Declaration of Independence's promise that "all men are created equal" should be legally concretized, such that no American would suffer discrimination for being born white or Black. "The equality which was declared by our fathers in 1776," he asserted, ". . . was *equality before the law*."[2]

While he lost the case, Sumner won an election to the U.S. Senate as a third-party candidate in 1851, succeeding the renowned Daniel Webster. There, he confronted the cadre of proslavery senators who dominated America, whom he described as being members of a "slave oligarchy." The slave oligarchs insisted on the inherent superiority of whites and sought to expand their rich society premised on the exploitation of Blacks.

Loudly, Sumner denounced his Senate colleagues for imposing repressive fugitive slave laws on the North and expanding the South's slavery into the western territories. He often did so by cloaking himself in the American Founding. Pointing out that he was mentored by John Quincy Adams, he charged enslavers of committing treason against the Declaration of Independence, which Adams's father had helped write. He also popularized the argument—later adopted by Abraham Lincoln—that Congress should ban slavery within the territories, even if it was still permitted within the states, to fulfill the aspirations of the Founding Fathers.

Sumner presented as a modern Cicero, accusing proslavery colleagues of being threats to the survival of the republic. He blamed the growth and spread of slavery for destabilizing the country and its democracy. With grand rhetoric, he showcased his mastery of Latin and Greek as he compared proslavery politicians to traitors of Ancient Rome who were executed for treason. He also cast himself as a biblical prophet. Speaking in parables, he warned that God would one day smite the oppressors of African Americans.

Proslavery senators were outraged, baffled, and exasperated by this man who had the gall to compare himself to Founding Fathers, Roman orators, and biblical prophets. They couldn't shut him down despite an endless torrent of taunts. "Until that moment slavery had not seen in public life the man whom it truly feared," a *Harper's Weekly* editor observed. "Here was a spirit as resolute and haughty as its own."[3]

Sumner was haughty, as well as heartbroken. He stood out like a sore thumb as one of the Senate's two bachelors in a time when men his age were expected to be married or widowed. While in Washington, he missed the kinship of a male friend back home in Boston. He was likely a gay man who didn't understand his sexuality. Southerners taunted him as "eunuch Sumner," an "unsexed creature," and even a pedophile whose abolitionism suggested he had a "weakness for young negroes." Once, southern senator Andrew Butler—who allegedly sired two children from an enslaved mistress—mocked Sumner's chastity in a drunken speech while other senators hooted, hollered, and snickered. That night, like many nights, Sumner may have cried.[4]

* * *

SUMNER WROUGHT HIS revenge in 1856 in "The Crime Against Kansas," one of the most consequential speeches in American history. For five hours stretched across two days, entirely from memory, Sumner roared against his proslavery colleagues, accusing them of turning America into a dictatorship ruled by slave oligarchs. He focused on the crisis in Kansas, where proslavery politicians helped to manipulate ballots, destroy newspaper offices, and seize polling stations at gunpoint to ensure the territory became a slave state.

Sumner singled out Senator Butler, one of the architects of the Kansas crisis. He denounced Butler as a threat to democracy and implied that he was a rapist who violated enslaved women. Butler's nephew Congressman Preston Brooks resolved to avenge his family's honor. With a gutta-percha cane, he beat Sumner in a similar manner as he beat his own slaves, until Sumner was bloody and unconscious on the Senate floor. "I struck him with my cane and gave him about 30 first rate stripes," Brooks bragged. "Towards the last he bellowed like a calf."[5]

The caning shattered the false image that many white northerners had of southern enslavers as gentlemen who treated their slaves kindly. Northerners were alarmed that so many southerners approved of the attack. Even the stately Senator Butler celebrated his nephew's choice "to whip" and "disgrace" Sumner. The language of whipping evoked the image of slavery. In the words of Black journalist Mary Ann Shadd, slavery had spread "from the black man to the white." If a leading senator could be lashed into silence, northerners reasoned, no one was safe until the slave oligarchs were stopped. Across the South, enslavers had already banned abolitionist speech and criminalized dissent against their rule. Just as Sumner had warned, slavery seemed to be a threat to the republic: so long as there was slavery, there was no freedom, not even for whites.

The caning breathed life into the Republican Party, a new political party that had emerged only a few years earlier that was premised on stopping slavery's expansion. At the next party convention, Republicans shouted and chanted Sumner's name in unison, and they made his empty chair the emblem of their party's campaign. "Every friend of freedom," Ralph Waldo Emerson said, "thinks him the friend of freedom." Having played a key role in the party's founding, Sumner effectively became the Republican party's mascot and symbolic leader. The party distributed as many as three million copies of "The Crime Against Kansas."[6]

While Republicans paraded his speech and his name, Sumner suffered the long-lasting physical and psychological trauma that came with being beaten nearly to death. For three years, he traveled in search of recovery, hoping to soon rejoin the struggle. His pursuit of justice, even from his sickbed, solidified his reputation as a martyr. "I never received such an impression of holiness from mortal man," novelist Lydia Maria Child said after meeting Sumner. Traveling to Europe, Sumner spent time at Alexis de Tocqueville's chateau. "The man speaks like a prophet," Tocqueville recalled with amazement. "He says that slavery will soon entirely disappear in the United States. He does not know how, he does not know when, but he feels it, he is perfectly sure of it."[7]

* * *

SUMNER WAS BACK in Washington by the time Republicans won their first election, bringing President Lincoln to the nation's capital. Now, there were at least two men in the city who were six foot four. When they first met to discuss southern secession, Lincoln suggested they put their backs up against each other to see who was taller. Sumner grunted, declaring that "this was a time for uniting our fronts and not our backs before the enemies of our country." Lincoln chuckled, while Sumner was confused about what was so funny. "I have never had much to do with bishops down where we live," Lincoln later said. "But, do you know, Sumner is just my idea of a bishop." They ended up being close friends. When Lincoln was shot, he held Sumner's hand as he died.[8]

During the Civil War, Sumner was a key adviser to Lincoln. In his capacity as chair of the Senate Foreign Relations Committee, he worked with Lincoln to manage America's fraught relationship with the British Empire, which profited enormously from southern cotton and nearly joined the conflict to help the Confederacy. Leveraging his deep relationships with British aristocrats and knowledge of international law, Sumner helped to avert two British interventions that would have been disastrous for the Union cause. He later succeeded in holding Britain financially and morally accountable for constructing warships for the South.

Sumner was the first major political leader to realize that the Civil War could lead to abolition and equal rights. While others sought compromise with the South to avoid war, Sumner insisted that the Union should wage its fight to the very end in order to bring the nation back together on the terms of equality for all. From the earliest days of the war, Sumner would frequent the White House and insist that Lincoln issue a unilateral declaration of freedom for southern slaves. "Slavery is the very Goliath of the Rebellion," Sumner explained. "But a stone from a simple sling will make the giant fall upon his face to the earth."

That stone became the Emancipation Proclamation. After Lincoln finally took Sumner's advice by signing the Proclamation, he gave his pen to Sumner. Lincoln also worked with Sumner and others to recruit nearly 200,000 Black soldiers to fight for their liberation in the Union Army. He often debated with Sumner about the prospect of redistributing land to freedpeople and granting them the right to vote after the war. As Frederick Douglass put it, "Mr. Lincoln and Mr. Sumner were leaders of the colored people."[9]

After Lincoln's death, Sumner pushed President Johnson to adopt an ambitious project of racial reparations and enfranchisement. When Johnson refused to do so, Sumner tried to remove Johnson and helped lead Congress in passing groundbreaking statutes that overrode Johnson's vetoes—including bills to create the Freedmen's Bureau, integrate Washington streetcars, and enfranchise Black men across the South.

As Sumner worked to inaugurate America's first experiment in multiracial democracy, he grappled with his own aching loneliness. Desperate for love and belonging, he rushed into a marriage with a young widow whose personality clashed with his own. After they separated, his wife began spreading rumors that Sumner was sexually impotent, adding to his sense of humiliation and exacerbating his battle with depression.

Sumner's depression was partly eased by a group of Black entrepreneurs who were among his closest friends during the Reconstruction period, a short-lived era of astonishing Black prosperity after the Civil War. Sumner enjoyed fine wine and oysters at dinner parties with African American caterers, hotel owners, and even lawyers in Boston and Washington. Tired of being relegated to second-class status, these Black businessmen helped to persuade Sumner to spearhead the most ambitious campaign for racial equality in the nineteenth century.

That campaign began in 1870, when Sumner collaborated with John Mercer

Langston, a Black professor and law dean at Howard University, to draft the bill that became the blueprint of modern-day civil rights law. The bill said that everyone should be able to access schools, colleges, hotels, restaurants, churches, juries, and public transportation on a nondiscriminatory basis. Sumner called on America to embark on a national project of racial integration, articulating the very same dream that Martin Luther King Jr. would express nearly one hundred years later at the 1963 March on Washington.

* * *

THERE ARE MANY parallels to draw between King and Sumner, two towering historical visionaries who briefly commanded national attention and tried to use their soaring oratory, along with their sharp political instincts, to drive a stake through the heart of America's racial caste system by invoking America's highest ideals.

For example, Sumner grew up in a Black neighborhood in Boston, an astonishing and critical fact overlooked by almost every past biography of Sumner's life. Though separated by time and place, Black Boston in the early 1800s had striking similarities to Black Atlanta in the early 1900s, where King grew up. Both communities were vibrant hotbeds of Black intellectualism, as preachers, activists, and writers debated the best path forward for African Americans. Both communities also endured the crushing weight of American racism, suffering from forced poverty, discrimination, and the daily brunt of white brutality.

From childhood, Sumner passed by Black churches, schools, charities, and storefronts, and he would cut his hair at a Black barbershop near his home. There, he would hear stories of racial injustice and learn to empathize with African Americans despite his white skin. "In my feelings and sympathies, I am a colored man," Sumner told a southern Black pastor, "and feel most deeply all the wrongs that your people suffer."[10]

Like King, Sumner battled depression, death threats, and a martyr complex. He longed to die for the abolitionist cause, rather than live in what he called the "dreary world." As one friend put it, Sumner's "instinctive love of life was weaker than with most men." That weak love of life prompted him to make poor decisions regarding his health, which may have led to a premature heart attack at the age of sixty-three. It also made it hard for his loved ones to protect his safety. Once, Sumner's best friend Dr. Samuel Howe tried to persuade Sumner's mother to buy him a pistol. "Oh, doctor," she replied, "he would only shoot himself with it."[11]

Like King, Sumner wrestled with the question of how African Americans should approach politics. As a radical who spent much of his career in third parties, Sumner believed Blacks should never swear loyalty to either Republicans or Democrats. He celebrated when two million Black men gained the suffrage, a feat he helped to inaugurate. "Make allegiance to you the measure of your support," he told Black voters. "So doing, all parties will seek your vote." In the 1872 election, Sumner shocked the nation by endorsing the candidate Horace Greeley, a known racist, to punish President Grant for failing to support the civil rights bill. He asked the Black community to adopt the same strategy of bullish realpolitik. "Above all, never vote for any man who is not true to you," he advised.[12]

Like King, Sumner spent his final years as an ardent anti-war activist who expanded his advocacy for the freedom of Black and brown people to the international sphere. When Grant tried to annex the modern-day Dominican Republic and threatened war against Haiti, Sumner broke with many civil rights leaders by waging a nearly single man fight against the president. While Grant's actions were more complicated than Sumner construed them, his dogged advocacy for Caribbean independence made him a role model for future anti-imperialist activists.

For all his moral grandeur, like King, Sumner had blind spots. After helping to ratify a treaty to buy a Russian territory in 1867, Sumner popularized the term "Alaska" and wrote a book about the region. His book failed to acknowledge the ongoing slaughter of Native people that was taking place in Alaska and across the American West. He was decidedly an American expansionist, who believed that a free America should stretch from sea to shining sea. Also, in 1864, Sumner collaborated with Susan B. Anthony and Elizabeth Cady Stanton in a petition movement for abolishing slavery. But he ignored these women's suffrage activists afterward. While privately admitting that women should be able to vote, he could not muster a public word in favor of female suffrage.

In addition, Sumner could be hot-tempered, insecure, combative, and egotistical. He often conflated himself with his movement, letting his personal feelings toward others get the best of him. "Sumner uses words as boys do stones," a friend said, "[to] break windows and knock down flowerpots, while he all the time plays the offended." Much like King, Sumner was an admirable, farsighted, flawed, and all-too-human leader.[13]

* * *

THE SIMILARITIES BETWEEN King's and Sumner's lives are uncanny. They are also tragic. For if Sumner's advocacy had been successful, King's mission would never have been needed. Toward the end of his life, Sumner's dream of racial equality fell out of reach. After the liberation of more than four million enslaved people who secured for themselves equal citizenship, the Ku Klux Klan and other white supremacist groups began terrorizing African Americans in the South. Black freedpeople lost access to almost every acre of land that had been promised to them. Sumner couldn't persuade the Senate to pass the civil rights bill for nationwide integration. "I wish I could do more," Sumner confessed to a group of Black activists. "I wish I was stronger. I wish I had more influence."[14]

After Grant's reelection, Sumner lost his influence within the Republican Party, despite being one of the party's symbolic founders. Republicans ostracized Sumner, expelled him from their caucus, and ignored his impassioned pleas for racial justice. That only changed after Sumner's death, which spurred an outpouring of national mourning. More than 50,000 people attended his funeral events, and some attendees launched a new movement to pass his civil rights bill in his honor. According to an entry in an 1886 encyclopedia, "no American, unless Washington and Lincoln, ever received such respect as was paid Mr. Sumner's memory."[15]

In this atmosphere of grief, Republicans honored Sumner's death by passing a watered-down version of his integration bill in the Civil Rights Act of 1875. But the party let the act fall into desuetude and hardly complained when the Supreme Court struck it down eight years later. Sumner's law was then tossed into the dustbin of history, where it remained until the drafters of the Civil Rights Act of 1964 relied on it as a model.

In the decades after Reconstruction, white Americans brutally imposed a system of racial apartheid in the South called "Jim Crow." Whites in both the North and the South also reinterpreted the story of the Civil War. The war became a tragedy, rather than a success story. The war was no longer a glorious revolution for freedom, as Sumner understood it. Instead, the war was treated—as it is often still treated today—as a national tragedy and needless conflict that had little to do with slavery and could have been avoided if cooler heads had prevailed.

White historians aided in this reimagining of the past during the Jim Crow era, distorting the memory of political abolitionists whom a prior generation of white northerners had venerated. As one writer put it, they "played curious pranks with the reputations of America's statesmen." They blamed northern agitators like Sumner, rather than the obstinance of southern enslavers, for the Civil War. "Few men contributed more to national tragedy" than Sumner, declared the historian Avery Craven. "He spoke with venom and bitterness of the Southern people," said W. E. Woodward. In the words of James Truslow Adams, "the fanaticism and egotism of Sumner combined to despoil the nation of that peace which Lincoln would have brought."[16]

Meanwhile, early twentieth-century Black writers tried to protect Sumner's memory and legacy. "To the chosen disciples of Civil Liberty throughout the world, he was the morning sun," explained a group of Black lawyers in the turn-of-the-century book *Justice and Jurisprudence*. An article in the *Journal of Negro History* said in 1928 that "to Sumner, as much as to Lincoln, the Negro owed his freedom." In his famous 1935 book *Black Reconstruction*, W. E. B. Du Bois decried that Sumner's "magnificent figure" has "been besmirched almost beyond recognition." He cited Sumner by name nearly 200 times and called him a "seer of democracy."[17]

The last major scholarly biography of Sumner's full life repeated and codified many of the negative claims that Jim Crow–era historians made about this seer of democracy. Published by David Donald in 1960 and 1970, the two-volume book overemphasized Sumner's egotism, framed him as a lawless and ineffective agitator, and ignored his relationships with Black civic leaders. The book ridiculed and minimized the majesty of Sumner's political project, going so far as to describe his activism as "inflexible zeal" and "moral terrorism."[18]

Expertly written and researched, Donald's biography of Sumner was an impressive scholarly work that historians should still read. But it was also a character assassination of a monumental figure in the history of civil rights. "The subversion of the character of a founding father of American civil equality should not be taken lightly," one critical book review noted in 1961, "especially during the era of the Freedom Riders."[19]

Today, Freedom Riders and civil rights heroes like Martin Luther King Jr. are rightly celebrated in history classes in high schools and colleges. Yet Sumner is still not celebrated, even though he is included in standard American history textbooks. In these textbooks, Sumner is generally treated as a brash provocateur whose incendiary language provoked Preston Brooks to attack him on the Senate floor. Textbooks present the caning as an illustration of partisan rancor gone to the extreme. That framing fails to capture the moral depth behind the raw and violent partisanship: Brooks fought for slavery, while Sumner called for freedom.[20]

* * *

THIS BIOGRAPHY BRINGS Sumner back to life, returning him to the place he deserves in the pantheon of American heroes. That said, this book is no hagiography. It presents Sumner in his full complexity with a fair portrait that emphasizes his heroism without ignoring his flaws. The book depicts Sumner in the flesh and bones, so that readers can picture him as a living, breathing person, who struggled with moral dilemmas, family crises, romantic longing, poor health, financial hardship, psychological trauma, tough friendships, and hard political conflicts.

While written for ordinary readers, this book is a scholarly work for historians as well. Relying on long-neglected archival material and rigorous research, the book directly quotes from over 600 of Sumner's personal letters and nearly 400 contemporary newspaper articles. In so doing, the book recounts Sumner's lifelong advocacy for civil rights in more depth than any book ever written. It explores Sumner's rich social life with Black activists, whose fascinating stories have been neglected. And it presents some never before published letters, including letters by a Haitian minister to Sumner during the Dominican annexation crisis.

This book is also a work of constitutional law. Written by a lawyer, the book connects Sumner's innovative legal ideas to the current debates taking place in the legal academy and the courts. It explores Sumner's role in precipitating the constitutional revolution of the late 1860s and his work to embed freedom and equality into the bedrock of American law. Based on deep engagement with contemporary legal scholarship, the book also touches on Sumner's contributions to international law, legal codification, civil service reform, and legal education.

A graduate of Harvard Law School, Sumner was trained by Joseph Story, a Supreme Court justice in early America who wrote the nation's most celebrated treatise on constitutional law. Story taught Sumner that the Constitution had established a strong national government that answered to the people, not to the states. Soon after graduating, Sumner met retired president John Quincy Adams. An ardent antislavery man, Adams taught Sumner that America made a promise in the Declaration of Independence's phrase "all men are created equal." Adams said that one day, the

Constitution—which both he and Sumner believed allowed slavery in the states—should be amended to abolish slavery and fulfill the Declaration's promise of equality.

Adopting the views of his teachers, Sumner advocated for the *nationalist* Constitution and the *promissory* Declaration. He defended these two ideas against proslavery politicians, many of whom resented America's founding charters, ardently supported states' rights, and celebrated white supremacy. For example, soon after caning Sumner, Representative Preston Brooks said the Constitution "should be torn to fragments" so that the South could create a new charter in which "every State should be a slave state." Sumner often noted that proslavery senator John Pettit once ridiculed the Declaration's promise of equality as "a self-evident lie."[21]

During the Civil War, Sumner believed the fighting wasn't just about bayonets and blood. It was a battle of ideas, a battle about the principles of America's founding charters. He went as far as to say that a "great rule of interpretation" was "conquered at Appomattox," the final battle. He declared a new rule, a rule so radical that it has never been put into practice in American law, not even today. "Every clause and every line and every word" of the Constitution, Sumner said, "is to be interpreted uniformly for human rights."[22]

After the Civil War, "human rights" was Sumner's watchword whenever he discussed the Declaration or the Constitution. The term "human rights" captured Sumner's sweeping vision of equality, which went far beyond that of many white abolitionists who were content with just ending slavery. To Sumner, America was bound—per its promise in the Declaration—to guarantee racial equality on every civil, social, and political plane of public life that was governed by law. To fulfill this duty, he wanted the Constitution amended and reinterpreted so that equality could become its grundnorm. "Equality in rights is the first of rights," he said.[23]

* * *

SUMNER'S TRIUMPH CAME in the late 1860s, an epoch that scholars now call the Second Founding. In this re-founding, Americans ratified the Thirteenth, Fourteenth, and Fifteenth Amendments. These changes abolished slavery, guaranteed equal protection, established birthright citizenship and the privileges that come with it, and recognized a right to vote regardless of race. In many ways, these amendments codified into law the principles that Sumner had first articulated nearly two decades earlier, when he tried to integrate Boston schools. "No person can be *born*, with civil or political privileges, not enjoyed equally by all his fellow-citizens," Sumner had argued in 1849. "He may be poor, weak, humble, black—he may be of Caucasian, of Jewish, of Indian, or of Ethiopian race—he may be of French, of German, of English, of Irish extraction."

The Second Founding inaugurated America's first multiracial democracy, a democracy governed by a new constitutional order. With constitutional amendments and reinterpretation, Second Founders like Sumner increased the national government's powers over the states and embedded the Declaration's principles of equality into the Constitution. They passed scores of laws to promote racial justice in the states that would have once been treated as unconstitutional. From then on, according to Sumner, "anything for human rights is constitutional."[24]

As Sumner helped to bring forth this human rights–based Second Founding, he constantly hearkened back to the First Founding. The words of Founding Fathers like Washington, Jefferson, and Hamilton were readily on Sumner's lips. While many Founding Fathers were slaveholders themselves, Sumner insisted that their ideals were pure. He studied them voraciously and sang their praises in public and private. He always believed that his era's constitutional transformations reaffirmed the aspirations of the original Founders. In the words of his friend Carl Schurz, Sumner tried "to revolutionize the Constitution in its own name."[25]

That constitutional revolution waned toward the end of Sumner's life, as Reconstruction gradually met its demise. The constitutional legacy of Reconstruction was then mostly erased from public memory. But in recent years, historians and legal scholars have embarked on a fresh study of Reconstruction's impact on the law. Even the Supreme Court has lately described the epoch as America's "Second Founding." To shed light on current legal questions about the Constitution and the Second Founding, this book examines Sumner's views on federalism, the separation of powers, judicial review, and other key issues. The book also explores his farsighted understanding of terms like equality, civil rights, human rights, and republican government.[26]

During the Second Founding, Sumner used a form of constitutionalism akin to many liberal jurists today. He argued that "the Constitution is not mean, stingy, and pettifogging, but open-handed, liberal, and just, inclining always in favor of Freedom." He decried the idea of states' rights, saying that "*there can be no State Rights against Human Rights.*" That said, much more like conservative jurists today, Sumner used history as a key tool for constitutional interpretation. He connected to America's founding values and the historical record. As his friend Ebenezer Hoar, the first head of the Department of Justice, put it, "[Sumner] had drunk deep from the sources of American institutions, in the writings and lives of our Revolutionary fathers."[27]

Sumner believed that the Constitution belonged to the people, not just to judges or lawyers. To this end, he wrote his speeches on the law in digestible, accessible form. He published them in newspapers and in pamphlets for constituents. He presented constitutional ideas to "the farmer in the field, the mechanic in his shop, the traveller by the way," according to one *Harper's Weekly* editor. Relatedly, he believed Congress—the people's democratic voice and temple—had a unique ability to interpret the Constitution on its own. In his interpretation, the Constitution, especially after being amended, empowered Congress to legislate freely for human rights without interference from the courts or what he once called the "swarm of technicalities, devices, and quibbles" of lawyers. "The Supreme Court is not arbiter of Acts of Congress," he argued. "Give me a lawyer to betray a great cause," he complained. While speaking to the first graduating class of law students at Howard University, he explained that "you cannot be a good lawyer unless you are a good man."[28]

Sumner was one of the most innovative, famous, progressive, and influential constitutional thinkers of his day. But his constitutional ideas have been neglected by historians and legal scholars, to the detriment of scholarship on the Second Founding. This book addresses that dearth. In his lifetime, Sumner was dubbed the "great defender of the constitution" by Harriet Beecher Stowe, author of the novel *Uncle Tom's Cabin*. "It is Sumner's first and not least glory that he saved us the fathers and the Constitution," the abolitionist bishop Gilbert Haven said. In Haven's words, Sumner treated the Constitution as "an object of love, not fear."[29]

Sumner had immense love and faith in constitutional democracy, where the people decide core constitutional questions out of loyalty to the Founding *and* to make a better world. To him, the Constitution offered America's best hope for racial justice. He was heroic in his legal imagination, in his capacity to convey what constitutional law could become in order to fulfill the promises of equality in the Declaration of Independence. Sumner saw what the egalitarian future of America could be, even as America continued to prolong, within his lifetime and perhaps to this day, the racial inequalities that started with slavery.

* * *

SUMNER'S CONSTITUTIONAL ENDEAVORS during the Second Founding have proved prescient over the years. In a quiet town in eastern Kansas in the winter of 1950, for example, a young girl embarked every morning on a two-mile journey to school, braving a harsh wind so cold it would freeze the tears on her face. She was so broken by her daily sojourn that her father, the mild-mannered Black pastor Oliver Brown, had had enough. He took his daughter by the hand and marched straight up the steps of Sumner Elementary, a nearby white school that was coincidentally named after the senator, and demanded that his daughter be enrolled. When she was denied, Pastor Brown and other Black families sued the school district for violating the Fourteenth Amendment.

The case was *Brown v. Board of Education*, which led to the integration of American public schools. When Brown's case had reached the Supreme Court, the justices asked the segregationist lawyers and the NAACP lawyers, led by Thurgood Marshall, to submit historical briefs about what the drafters of the Fourteenth Amendment really meant when they said that no state shall "deny to any person within its jurisdiction the equal protection of the laws." The Court wanted to know if "equal protection" prohibited school segregation, as Sumner had once argued.

In the NAACP's brief, Marshall cited Sumner more than forty times by name. He traced the intellectual lineage of the Equal Protection Clause back to Sumner's argument in *Roberts v. City of Boston* more than one century earlier. "It was one thing, and a very important one, to declare as a political abstraction that 'all men are created equal,' and quite another to attach concrete rights to this state of equality," Marshall said. "The Declaration of Independence did the former. The latter was Charles Sumner's outstanding contribution to American law."[30]

This book retells Sumner's story—in its fullness, complexity, drama, and importance.

PART I

BRAHMIN OUTCAST

CHAPTER 1

A BLEMISHED FAMILY

L ONG BEFORE HE EMERGED AS ONE OF THE MOST CONSEQUENTIAL statesmen in American history, Charles Sumner was born on January 6, 1811, in his family's residence on Boston's Beacon Hill, a place that would shape his early views on race and justice. Featuring gaslit lamps, steep cobblestone roads, and redbrick sidewalks, Beacon Hill was home to the city's wealthy, cultured, and high-born elite, who lived on the hill's South Slope. But the Sumners' small wood-frame home, unlike the South Slope's adorned mansions and lofty row houses, stood on the North Slope. The Black slope.

Boston's first Black residents arrived almost two hundred years before Sumner's birth, forcibly brought to American shores to be enslaved by the Puritans who settled the city. Not all Black Bostonians were free until the 1780s, when Quock Walker, an enslaved African American, hired a lawyer and sued for his freedom. Walker's lawyer successfully convinced the state supreme court that slavery was incompatible with the state constitution, which declared that "all men are born free and equal." The case effectively ended slavery in Massachusetts, also known as the "Bay State."

In search of opportunity and community, Black Bostonians gradually converged upon the North Slope of Beacon Hill in modest homes overlooking the Charles River. Bearing the brunt of the icy winds and the noxious smells coming from the river's tidal salt flats, they were not as fortunate as their rich white neighbors, who enjoyed the warmer South Slope that descended into the snowy fields of Boston Common. By the turn of the century, though, these Beacon Hill Blacks, only a few hundred in number, were making the most of their circumstances. To worship, they built a small redbrick church they affectionately called the African Meeting House. To take care of one another, they formed the African Society, a mutual aid group to help families, widows, and orphans. To fraternize, the men organized the African Lodge, a Masonic temple. For the children, they created the African School. Their community grew vibrant and full of life, even as they endured the poverty and persecution that came with being Black in early America.[1]

By the time of Sumner's birth, his neighborhood was a busy, bustling ethnic enclave in predominantly white Boston. Black men were sailors, laborers, sweepers, butlers, and window cleaners. Other Black men learned trades, becoming soap makers, shoemakers, caulkers, and barbers. Women worked, too, often as servants and laundresses for the mansions on the South Slope, carrying up and down baskets of white people's clothes to scrub, wash, and dry.

Sumner did not write down his childhood memories of the Black neighbors who walked along the alleyways of Beacon Hill, which zigzagged to form a dense labyrinth no bigger than a square mile. But as a young boy, he surely interacted with the children who marched each morning to the African School; the women who commonly wore long, bright dresses and multicolored bandanas; the men who chopped hair and twisted leather into shoes. These people, free but certainly not equal, constituted the community of his upbringing.[2]

How did Charles Sumner, a white boy from a line of countryside farmers, come to be born in a Black neighborhood in the city of Boston? His story, like every person's story, begins long before his birth.

* * *

WHILE CHARLES SUMNER never knew his grandfather, Job Sumner played an important role in the American Revolution, serving alongside the revolutionary heroes who would come to shape his grandson's views on freedom and equality.

Job Sumner descended from a family of farmers who migrated from England to the Blue Hills of Massachusetts in the 1630s, less than two decades after the Pilgrims landed at Plymouth Rock. A smart, adventurous teenager who wanted to make a name for himself, Job grew restless tilling soil for a local landlord. In the fall of 1774, he foreswore farming forever, saved what money he could, moved to the small town of Cambridge— across the Charles River from Boston—and enrolled himself at Harvard College.[3]

Almost as soon as Job left, the farm owner he worked for, Daniel Vose, planted one of the seeds of the American Revolution. A local civic leader in rural Massachusetts, Vose convened delegates from nearby towns who were furious with Great Britain, which had imposed a blockade on Boston Harbor to punish the whole colony for the actions of a few rabble-rousing protesters who had thrown British tea into the sea. These delegates signed the Suffolk Resolves, a pledge to boycott British goods, withhold taxes, and pay no obedience to repressive laws like the Stamp Act and Tea Act.

Paul Revere, a local silversmith, rode on horseback to Philadelphia with the Suffolk Resolves in hand to deliver them to the Continental Congress, a new convention of delegates from twelve of the thirteen American colonies, which endorsed them as its first action. Feeling emboldened, Massachusetts then armed its town militias and declared itself an autonomous zone, notwithstanding the thousands of British redcoats stationed in Boston. On April 19, 1775, these redcoats marched into the countryside and confronted the ragtag militias composed mostly of local farmers. There was a long, tense, quiet standoff . . . until somebody fired a bullet, the first shot of the American Revolution, what became known as "the shot heard round the world."[4]

Job felt uneasy about being buried in the Latin textbooks that Harvard made him memorize while a revolution was taking place in the Massachusetts countryside he called home. Craving adventure, he didn't have to leave Harvard to get involved in the war—the revolution came to him. After the Battle of Lexington, Massachusetts militiamen converged upon Cambridge with hopes to lay siege to Boston, which was held by the British. Needing somewhere to sleep, they demanded that Harvard College dismiss its students and hand over its dormitories to the revolutionaries. By May, Harvard obliged the rebels, sending its students into the countryside to continue their studies, while the militias formed an encampment on the college campus.[5]

For adventure, for glory, for freedom, Job Sumner told Harvard he wouldn't keep studying amid a great revolution, and he enlisted in what became the Continental Army. After fighting in the Battle of Bunker Hill, the Siege of Boston, and the retreat from Quebec, he had so impressed Generals Benedict Arnold and Philip Schuyler that he was made captain at the age of twenty-two. Job was then put in charge of a gunboat at Lake Champlain, and he led an infantry company at West Point. Even Gen. Henry Knox came across Job, calling him "a gallant, and intelligent officer." By the time the war was over in September 1783, Job was a major, a rank so high that he even corresponded with Gen. George Washington himself on some administrative matters.[6]

* * *

IN NOVEMBER 1773, Job Sumner was in New York City, second in command of the last military act of the Revolutionary War. He had served in the army from nearly the beginning, signing up within days of the Battle of Lexington. Now, at the very end, he was charged with supervising the expulsion of the redcoats who had been occupying New York for seven years. By November 25, the last redcoat was on a ship back to England, traveling home in humiliating defeat. Soon after, Job and his cavalcade escorted a triumphant General Washington into the city, as New Yorkers waved plumes and tossed flowers, crying tears of joy. These New Yorkers were free at last, free along with all the other white Americans of the thirteen colonies.[7]

Nine days later, Job Sumner basked in the presence of General Washington one last time, having been invited to the general's farewell party at Fraunces Tavern in New York. It was Washington's last day of work, so to speak—the commander in chief was about to board a ship for Annapolis, where he famously resigned his commission, relinquishing military control so that democracy might flourish in this new republic.

When Washington strode in, Job and the other thirty or forty soldiers stood up respectfully. The great, stoic commander in chief spoke some words of goodbye to these men until he broke down, crying. Job and the other men started sobbing, too, as they reflected on the eight years of life-and-death struggle with Great Britain that it had taken to reach this moment. As each officer came forward, Washington embraced them one at a time, kissed them on the cheek, and bade them a tearful farewell. After getting his kiss, Job led his infantry in escorting General Washington to his barge. He saluted Washington as the general waved his hat to say goodbye.[8]

With the war over, Job was on to his next adventure, seeking to make a name for himself and reap the fruits of eight years of wartime toil. He scored big when Congress appointed him as a federal commissioner to Georgia to manage the state's war debts. Moving to Savannah on his government mission, Job began a lavish lifestyle. Once a meager farmer, now he was a planter. Once a freedom fighter, now he owned at least one slave, bought a horse, lived on an estate, and hobnobbed with the state's wealthy enslavers. These planters loved Job's jovial, happy-go-lucky personality; they liked him so much that they almost elected him governor of the state. But then Job tumbled into terrible debt after purchasing some fraudulent landholdings. Catching a bad fever, he set sail for New York in search of better health. While on board, he ate the meat of a dolphin caught in the Outer Banks, which gave him food poisoning. On September 16, 1788, he died shortly after landing.[9]

Word spread that the valiant major Job Sumner, who had helped liberate New York, had died in the city. "Recollecting the protection afforded them on the evacuation," said a newspaper, the citizens of New York "gave a sigh to his memory, and generously paid the last friendly tribute to his virtues." Vice President John Adams, General Knox, and some senators and representatives—at the time, New York was America's capital—"shed the tear of sorrow on his grave." They watched solemnly as Col. Alexander Hamilton and other soldiers picked up the pall and buried it in the center of St. Paul's Churchyard. An earth-colored tombstone was later installed that commemorated Job and his "unblemished Character through Life as the Soldier Citizen and Friend."[10]

Probably unbeknownst to Washington, Schuyler, Arnold, Adams, Knox, and Hamilton, unbeknownst to the press and to the public and to the planters with whom he was so popular in New York and Georgia, Job Sumner wasn't just a soldier, citizen, and friend. He was a father.

A *blemished* father.

* * *

AROUND THE TIME the revolutionaries were battling redcoats at Lexington, Job Sumner impregnated a farm girl. Her name was Esther Holmes. History has left little trace of what she was like, what her aspirations were, or how she felt about Job. She gave birth to their son in Milton, Massachusetts, on January 20, 1776. She named him Job, after his father. But Job Senior didn't want this bastard son carrying his first name, so he renamed him Charles Pinckney, after the prominent South Carolina enslaver and Founding Father who had helped draft the U.S. Constitution. To Job Senior, being named after this rich southern planter (who believed God had "probably intended" to make Africans serve "the whites") was a high honor.[11]

Raised by his mother, Charles Pinckney Sumner grew up fatherless, spending his days laboring in the fields north of the Blue Hills and his nights herding cows in the square mile around his home. He didn't recall having friends as a child; he was busy toiling to survive in the poverty that came with being the bastard son of a war hero. Job Sumner visited his son a few times, regaling him with stories about General Washington and the American Revolution. But these were the only memories that Pinckney Sumner seemed to have of his gallant, renowned father—or at least the only memories he was willing to share.

During the winter months, Pinckney Sumner attended the local parish school, until his father, Job, felt sufficiently guilty about his son's prospects that he coughed up the funds to send him to Phillips Academy, in Andover, Massachusetts. Starting at the age of eleven, Pinckney Sumner was tutored by the school's principal, Ebenezer Pemberton, a respected educator who had taught many children of the emerging American elite— including James Madison, Aaron Burr, Ezra Stiles, and Josiah Quincy. Job Sumner begged Principal Pemberton "from my heart" to teach his boy Latin, to prepare him for the life of "a gentleman and scholar." Pemberton obliged, teaching the boy willingly at the academy—so long as his father could afford to pay.

As soon as his father fell into debt, Pinckney Sumner was kicked out of the academy. Desperate for his son to resume his education, Job beseeched a couple of friends for loans and managed to scrounge the money for Pinckney Sumner to finish his schooling and graduate. By the time the boy finished, though, his father had died. Far from New York City, Pinckney Sumner did not attend Job's funeral—possibly, he did not even know of his father's death until long after he was gone. For the rest of his life, Pinckney Sumner would live in the shadow of this great American revolutionary whom he barely knew.[12]

Many years later, Charles Sumner wrote a brief history of his family. While reflecting at some length on his father, Pinckney Sumner, he devoted only two lines to his grandfather, whom he never talked about. "My father's father, Major Job Sumner, [was] of the army of the Revolution," he wrote. "It seems to me better to leave it all unsaid."[13]

* * *

When Pinckney Sumner turned sixteen, he wisely spent his small inheritance from his father to pay for fees at Harvard College. Lost and confused and looking for direction as an orphan produced by sin, he may have fallen under the spell of the stern, dogmatic, puritanical professor

of the Hebrew language Eliphalet Pearson. Professor Pearson was so adamant about his Calvinism that he once tried to stop Harvard from hiring
a man who had committed the crime of being a Unitarian. Professor Pearson was also an adamant abolitionist, once insisting to everybody in the
college at a commencement ceremony that all people, even "unhappy *Africans*," were "son[s] of Adam," entitled to liberty. When Pinckney Sumner
attended the first day of class, Pearson began by warning the freshmen,
hissing at them in Latin, "Procul o, procul este, profani." ("If ye are unholy,
begone, begone.") Pinckney Sumner was enthralled.[14]

Pinckney Sumner found clarity in the moral strictness that Professor
Pearson embodied. He never dabbled in his father's lechery, and he never
sought the fame of a hero, either. Instead, he studied poetry, observing the
strict disciplines of rhyme and meter while writing his poems. In his third
year, he befriended Joseph Story, a freshman who also loved poetry. Pinckney Sumner became Story's mentor, guiding the boy through Harvard and
blossoming a friendship that became very important to their adult lives.[15]

By graduation, Pinckney Sumner was a poet and an abolitionist, inspired
by men like Professor Pearson. At commencement, he was chosen to recite
an original valediction poem. He called it "The Compass," and it included
a quartet about the future, about a time better than the one they lived in:
"More true inspir'd, we antedate the time, when futile war shall cease throa
every clime; no sanction'd slavery Afric's sons degrade, but equal rights shall
equal earth pervade." Equal rights, equal earth. These were twenty-year-old
Pinckney Sumner's values.[16]

After an unsuccessful stint at teaching, Pinckney Sumner embarked
on a trip to the West Indies—probably to earn some money as a seaman.
In February 1798, his ship stopped on Santo Domingo Island, in modern-
day Haiti. At the time, the Haitians were waging a long, messy revolution
against France, England, and Spain. All three colonial empires had subjected roughly half a million Haitians to the brutality of chattel slavery on
the island's lucrative sugar plantations. Asserting the ideals of the French
Revolution for themselves, enslaved Haitians threw down their chains,
killed their masters, and finally won their battle for freedom in 1804, thus
making Haiti the first nation in history to fully abolish slavery.

To most white Americans, the Haitian Revolution was an appalling,
grotesque outpouring of violence that scared them out of their wits. Few
white Americans connected the dots between their revolution against
the British and the Haitians' quest for freedom from European empires.

But Pinckney Sumner recognized that these two revolutions had much in common. In childhood, he had eagerly listened to his father's tales of killing redcoats to become free. While in Haiti, he marveled at what he believed was the enslaved's godly fight for liberty.

As it so happened, the Haitian revolutionary general Jean-Pierre Boyer was organizing a public celebration for George Washington's birthday when Pinckney Sumner and a handful of other Americans on the ship were docked in the Haitian capital, Port-au-Prince. General Boyer invited these Americans to partake in a banquet to honor the hero they collectively admired. When asked to give a toast, Pinckney Sumner raised his glass. "Liberty, Equality and Happiness, to all men," he said. Boyer was so impressed that he asked his aide-de-camp to bring Pinckney Sumner to the front to sit near the head of the table. "The day the negroes in british West Indies are all free," Pinckney Sumner wrote in his diary, "[they] stand a good chance for social equality & happiness."[17]

* * *

WHEN GEORGE WASHINGTON died in December 1799, Pinckney Sumner gave a eulogy in his hometown of Milton that revealed his own insecurity at being raised fatherless by his mother. After paying homage to his father's "last friendly, impassioned embrace" with Washington, Pinckney Sumner used the opportunity of this eulogy—of all places—to scold his father's "dalliance in the lap of ease" and "reverse of fortune." He also spent time in his eulogy honoring Martha Washington, whom many other Washington eulogists completely forgot. She was "the worthy disconsolate partner of his heart," whom "we thank for the life-long smile with which she smoothed his brow." He prayed that "future generations rise up and call her blessed." Pinckney Sumner knew—like anyone raised solely by their mother knows—that so much credit for great men belonged to the great women beside them.

Pinckney Sumner's eulogy alluded to his belief that whites should have no monopoly on freedom. He told his listeners that they should be filled with gratitude to Washington. If not for him, you "might have reposed in the tranquil despair of subjugated India." Thanks to him, you can "kiss the children that throng around your knee, and teach them to bless God, that they are not born to the inheritance of slavery." And because of him, "smaller luminaries" who lived "in other climes" were "attempting to move in his orbit" to affirm "the dignity of man." He was probably thinking of General Boyer in Haiti, a Black revolutionary who honored General Washington just as much as he did. While eulogizing a white revolutionary, Pinckney Sumner chose to pay homage to Black revolutionaries, too.[18]

A passionate writer, speaker, thinker, and believer in freedom and equality, Pinckney Sumner decided to pursue a career in law. After apprenticing with the local attorneys George Minot and Josiah Quincy, he was admitted in 1801 to practice before Chief Justice Shearjashub Bourne at the Court of Common Pleas in Suffolk County. But his career floundered. Despite his credentials as a graduate of Phillips Academy and Harvard, Pinckney Sumner lacked an interest in the daily routine of law and, perhaps more important, the familial connections from which others benefited: his father had never introduced his bastard son to any of the generals, senators, representatives, Cabinet members, and presidents he personally knew.[19]

Pinckney Sumner grew both proud and resentful as he watched his younger friend Joseph Story also pursue law and become a wild success. An extremely hard worker with a razor-sharp mind, Story was admitted to the bar at the same time as Pinckney Sumner, and he rapidly climbed the career ladder. By 1805, just four years into practice, he was serving as a representative in the Massachusetts State House. Probably with Story's help, Pinckney Sumner then applied to be and was named clerk of the House, a somewhat prestigious but low-paying secretarial role for the state lawmakers. This work lasted only two years. Although he served a second stint in 1810–11, Pinckney Sumner spent most of his life in relative poverty, scrounging for legal work.

For cheap housing, he rented a room in a boardinghouse. There, he met Relief Jacobs—the woman who would become his wife, and mother to Charles Sumner.[20]

* * *

RELIEF JACOBS SEWED clothes to survive. Having grown up comfortably in a large countryside home in Hanover, Massachusetts, she expected an easy life. But in 1799, at the age of fourteen, she lost her father, mother, and younger sister to a typhus-like disease. Afterward, she and her older sister, Hannah, moved to Boston to fend for themselves. Hannah became a teacher, and Relief became a seamstress.[21]

These two sisters, alone in Boston, seemed to have been abandoned by their paternal grandfather. David Jacobs Sr. came from a wealthy family that had lived in Massachusetts since nearly the beginning of the English migration to the United States. According to one contemporary, the family was "a mixture of the Hebrew and the Puritan," who "belonged in fact to a Christianized Jewish family." During the Revolution, Jacobs sat on the local committee of public safety, a body that enforced revolutionary ideology and governed the community in the absence of the British. In Hanover, he owned a sawmill and a gristmill, which had been in the family for sixty years, and a tavern. He also owned two slaves prior to the abolition of slavery in the state. While his granddaughters Relief and Hannah were poor, he certainly was not.[22]

David Jacobs Sr. had many grandchildren. Perhaps there wasn't enough money to go around to provide for Relief and Hannah. Perhaps he was stingy. Perhaps his second wife, whom he married after the sisters' grandmother had died, refused to let him give money to any grandchildren who weren't hers. Most likely, he scorned the two girls because their parents had committed a terrible sin: they had conceived Hannah, who was born three months after their marriage, out of wedlock. And so, Hannah and Relief were damned to poverty.[23]

When Pinckney Sumner met Relief at the boardinghouse where they both stayed, he fell in love. Around twenty-five years old, she was quiet, religious, kind, and practical, and she scrupulously managed her finances to make the most of her meager circumstances. At the time, Pinckney Sumner was thirty-four-years old, overeducated, farm-born, poor, an orphan, and a bastard. He wasn't said to be handsome, and he was only of medium height. Quiet and reserved, he had few friends. Yet he carried himself with dignity. Polite to everyone, he was known to dress well, and those who knew him trusted him, for he was loyal to the bone.

After deciding to marry Relief, Pinckney Sumner picked out a home across the street from the boardinghouse. This modest wood-frame house was in the heart of Black Boston. While many poor whites chose to live on the North Slope of Beacon Hill because it was affordable, these whites preferred to stay on its edges. Pinckney Sumner chose instead to live deep within this Black neighborhood—on South Russell Street, only a block away from the African Meeting House. Other whites had qualms about living here; he apparently did not. Preferring to call his neighbors "people of color" rather than "negroes," he was known to tip his hat whenever he passed a Black person. "The best thing the abolitionists can do for the people of color," he once said, "is to make their freedom a blessing to them in the states where they are free."[24]

On April 25, 1810, the couple moved in together, solemnizing their marriage on the same day in a small ceremony inside their new home. Eight months and eleven days later, Relief gave birth to twins.

CHAPTER 2

GAWKY SUMNER

Two neighbors eagerly chatted with each other upon learning that Relief Jacobs Sumner had given birth three days earlier. "Let us go over and see Mrs. Sumner's babies," one said to the other. When they strutted into the Sumner home, their excitement turned to horror. One neighbor said "they were the smallest infants she had ever seen, weighing but three pounds and a half each."

Relief and Pinckney Sumner were filled with dread. They were convinced their two babies were too sickly to survive. They weren't entirely wrong—Matilda, one of the twins, had consistently poor health and would die of consumption (tuberculosis) at twenty-one. But Charles grew up to be a healthy and energetic, if slightly scrawny, child.

As a toddler, Charles loved sledding down the slopes of Beacon Hill, which made for nice, steep, fast rides thanks to the cold, snowy Boston winters. In the summers, he would cross over into the white side of Beacon Hill, hike down the slope, and march up to the shallow Frog Pond at Boston Common to sail small mimic boats for fun. Charles also loved swimming, but he hated dancing. When his parents enrolled him in a dancing school, he refused to participate. Still, he was happy to sit and quietly watch the other children dance.

Charles wasn't very talkative. Yet he was very respectful to his parents and other elders. Whenever he was asked to do chores, he did them diligently. He also never complained about the food on the table, which was, given his father's teetering law practice, meager at best. To his parents' astonishment, Charles rarely got sick, and he was surprisingly strong, despite his bony build.

From an early age, Charles was bullied. On one occasion, a group of boys tried to grab a stick he was holding. They kept pulling on the stick while Charles tightened his fists around it, refusing to let go. One boy then picked up a rock. Bashing the rock against Charles's clenched fists, the boy pounded and pounded. But Charles wouldn't give in. Alarmed by Charles's sheer sense of will, the bully fled the scene.

Blood had spattered all over Charles's white knuckles. But he didn't care: he had kept his stick.[1]

* * *

CHARLES TOOK LITTLE interest in other children, including his twin sister, Matilda, and other siblings. Over the years, Relief gave birth to seven more children—in order, Albert, Henry, George, Jane, Mary, Horace, and Julia. But Charles barely paid any attention to any of them in childhood, and it was only in adulthood that he developed meaningful relationships with George and Mary. Tragically, most of these siblings would die before the age of forty, and two (Horace and Albert) would be lost at sea in shipwrecks.[2]

By the age of nine or so, Charles was a headstrong, determined boy. From an early age, he had been begging his parents to let him learn Latin. But his father did not see the point in a highfalutin classical education. After all, such an education seemed to have accomplished very little for him in his life. He and his family were poor. They needed their eldest son to enter the workforce quickly. After gaining a rudimentary education at a small school that his mother's sister, Hannah, operated on the upper floor of the Sumner house, Charles was sent to the ordinary public school.

Young Charles wasn't satisfied with the education his parents were providing him. He quietly collected enough coins to buy himself two Latin books from an older student. At home, on his own, he studied both books while hiding them from his parents. After learning as much Latin as he could muster, he went down the stairs one morning to surprise his father during his morning shave. He recited a few sentences of Latin that he had memorized from the books and reiterated his request to learn the language. Astonished by his son's relentlessness, Pinckney Sumner finally agreed to give Latin a chance.[3]

Pinckney Sumner sent Charles and his brother Albert to take the enrollment exam at the Boston Latin School, one of New England's most prestigious day schools. Founded in 1635, the school had taught generations of the regional elite, including Samuel Adams, Benjamin Franklin, and John Hancock. Ostensibly, Boston Latin was a public school, and open to any white male student who passed the exam. But in practice, its students were the children of wealthy elites. The school absorbed a far greater per-pupil proportion of taxpayer dollars than the rest of the common schools in Boston, and it excluded Black students completely.[4]

Pinckney Sumner resented the system of private schools and the Latin School. A graduate of Phillips Academy, he saw firsthand how elite schools created class divisions in the young republic, undermining the egalitarian values of the American Revolution. He also remembered being kicked out of Phillips briefly because his father had missed tuition payments. In a series of anonymous letters to the Boston *Yankee*, a local paper, Pinckney Sumner vented his frustration. "*The Town Schools . . . are the poor man's best birthright,*" he asserted in one letter. "In the country . . . they make no invidious distinction between an English and a Latin school," he pointed out in another. These were "the feelings of a parent, whose humble means allow him not to look to any other source of instruction for an infant numerous family than what is afforded by the Town Schools."[5]

Yet Charles was determined to earn for himself the elite education his father couldn't afford. To Pinckney Sumner's surprise, both Charles and Albert passed the entrance exam to the Latin School and were admitted. Together, they would join Boston's elite in school, attending for free. Pinckney Sumner would now get to share the blessings of an aristocrat's education with at least two sons. These sons, he certainly hoped, would use that classical education to obtain more upward mobility than he ever had.

* * *

By the time Charles started at the Latin School in the fall of 1821, he was going by his last name "Sumner" rather than "Charles." He preferred being called "Sumner" for the rest of his life. But the rich boys at the Latin School had a better idea.

They called him "Gawky Sumner." At ten years old, he was lanky, awkward, and clearly poor. He wore coarse, chunky shoes and cheap clothing made of satin that was probably sewn by his mother. He stood out like a sore thumb. One classmate, Wendell Phillips, refused even to speak to Sumner because he came from the Black side of Beacon Hill. Phillips was a politician's son—his father was about to become mayor of Boston—at the top of the school's pecking order, asserting himself against commoners like Sumner. (Many years later, Phillips would become an abolitionist, and Sumner became one of his best friends.)[6]

The differences between Phillips and Sumner were unmistakable. According to a novel by Oliver Wendell Holmes, a Boston doctor whose son later served on the U.S. Supreme Court, there were two kinds of Boston schoolchildren. "The first youth," Holmes declared, "is the common country boy, whose race has been bred to bodily labor." He was typically inelegant, clumsy, ill-dressed, and unmusical. One cannot "expect too much" of this country boy, for "very few of them ever become great scholars." The second youth was slender, smooth, with bright, quick eyes and a musical ear. He "will take to his books" immediately, for he was the "son of scholars or scholarly persons," and "he comes of the *Brahmin caste of New England*."[7]

The Brahmins were a small class of patrician families who played a significant role in early America, a role so outsized that many Brahmins are household names today. Descended from the Puritans who settled the city in the 1630s, Brahmin families included figures like Abigail Adams, Paul Revere, John Hancock, and others who spearheaded the American Revolution. The Brahmins also boasted literary talents, from Ralph Waldo Emerson to T. S. Eliot, and inventors, including Eli Whitney. They were—according to Holmes, who coined the term—a quasi-aristocratic caste that passed its talents down to each subsequent generation.

Unlike Wendell Phillips, Sumner was no Brahmin. At the Latin School, where so many Brahmins attended, he was like Holmes's "country-boy": a skinny kid who got bullied for coming from the Black part of town. His parents were poor and had come from the countryside. Children like Phillips, the crème de la crème of Boston society, were born to succeed. Young boys like Sumner were little more than runts.

Undeterred, Sumner dove into the books to which his eager young mind was exposed. Years later, one of his classmates bitterly remembered spending the first year being "wholly occupied in committing to memory the most abstract formulas of Adam's Latin Grammar." But Sumner loved studying Latin grammar. Over the next few years, he also loved Caesar, Tacitus, Sallust, Virgil, Horace, and his favorite, Cicero. He memorized full passages from these classical authors and won prizes at school for his translations. On some mornings, he even read the English historians Hume and Gibbon, calling himself an "ardent student of *history*."

By the time of his graduation at the age of fifteen, Sumner was regarded by his teachers as one of their smartest students. "I used to look at him with wonder as I heard him talk on subjects I knew nothing of," a classmate recalled with astonishment. Although Sumner did not receive particularly high grades—probably because he was focused on reading what *he* wanted to read, rather than his assignments—he was honored along with a classmate to deliver the closing speech at commencement to several notable guests, which included President John Quincy Adams.[8]

There is no record of how Sumner felt about speaking to the president or being bullied by his richer classmates. All he did was read, read, *read*, a sponge so absorbed in soaking in his books that he seemed to have hardly paused to stop, look around, and share his thoughts with others. At least one historian has suggested that Sumner was possibly on the autism spectrum, noting that his "ability to hyperfocus on a specific topic," among other personality traits, was a classic sign of what some psychologists have categorized as Asperger syndrome. While any attempt to diagnose Sumner retroactively is foolhardy, it is difficult to think that such a diagnosis would be completely unmerited given some of his childhood behaviors. For example, at the age of fourteen, Sumner made an eighty-six-page chronological list of major events in English history—not for school, but for fun.[9]

If Sumner showed one aspiration, it was to join the historical and intellectual chorus of the men he read about. Around the time of his graduation, Boston held a commemoration for Thomas Jefferson and John Adams, who had recently died of illness only hours apart on July 4, 1826. In their honor, Boston asked the state lawmaker and soon to be senator Daniel Webster, a rising local celebrity, to deliver the eulogy inside Faneuil Hall, an event space in the city that had been a hotbed for town halls and public speeches during the American Revolution.

Sumner badly wanted to listen to Webster, but he didn't have a ticket to go inside. When the doors to the event opened, he scurried as quickly as he could into the building, using his short, wiry body to weasel his way through the thick crowd. Then he dove to the ground. On his hands and knees, he crawled through the maze of men's legs until he came out into the very front of the crowd. There, he watched in gaping rapture as Webster's sonorous voice rumbled in the ballroom. He was especially enthralled when Webster transitioned into Latin, thundering, "Felix, Jefferson, non vitae tantum claritate, sed etiam opportunitate mortis!" ("You were lucky, Jefferson, not only with the renown of your life, but with the timeliness of your death.")

Afterward, Sumner rushed home and eagerly told his father that Webster had quoted the *Agricola* by Tacitus. His father went straight to the bookcase, took down the *Agricola*, and turned to chapter forty-five. He asked Sumner to repeat what he remembered Webster saying. When Sumner recited the sentence exactly right, his father was amazed; Charles had remembered it verbatim. "Then I felt proud," Charles Sumner recalled. "For I understood the sentence; and I felt that I too belonged to the brotherhood of scholars."[10]

* * *

DESPITE CHARLES SUMNER'S obvious desire to be a scholar, Pinckney Sumner had no plans to send his son to Harvard College, where the graduates of the Boston Latin School tended to go. Initially, he had enjoyed sharing his classical education with his son, but he grew alarmed at what seemed to be his son's obsession with memorizing passages in Latin, reading history books, and dwelling on other subjects that were mostly useless in real life. He also felt that his son was spending far too much time indoors, hunched over texts. "He had no interest in games and athletic sports; never, so far as I know, fished or shot or rowed," one friend recalled. Like many worried fathers in his situation would, Pinckney Sumner decided to ship his son off to military school.

Pinckney Sumner saw an advertisement in a magazine for a military academy based in Middletown, Connecticut, on the campus that Wesleyan University now occupies. He jumped at the chance to get Charles admitted, but he was afraid that his Latin-trained son would come across as overqualified. And so, he wrote to the school's principal, Captain Alden Partridge, a military instructor whose program became the model for what is now the Reserve Officers' Training Corps (ROTC).

"I have a son, named Charles Sumner," Pinckney Sumner wrote. He explained that he wished to give his son "a useful, but not what is commonly called a learned, education. My means enable me only to think of usefulness." Confessing that his son was qualified to attend Harvard, Pinckney Sumner explained that "the life of a scholar would be too sedentary and inactive for him" and that his body was "not so firm and solid" as it should be. He asked the captain to write back and explain if his son was eligible for the military school. A few weeks later, he wrote a similar letter to Secretary of War James Barbour to inquire about sending his son to the U.S. Military Academy at West Point. In that letter, he dubiously claimed that his son wanted to go to West Point. Fortunately for Charles Sumner, who almost certainly hated the idea, neither academy accepted him as an admit.

Around the same time, Pinckney Sumner's financial status improved considerably. On September 6, 1825, he was made high sheriff of Suffolk County, leading public safety for the region. The job was not prestigious for someone of his schooling, but it offered a respectable place in society and a modest, stable salary that far exceeded what he was earning as a deputy sheriff, a position he had taken some years earlier.

With the money in hand, Pinckney Sumner had little reason to deny Charles an opportunity to study at Harvard. Despite his skepticism that Harvard would give Charles what he needed, he let his son go.[11]

* * *

ON SEPTEMBER 1, 1826, Charles Sumner eagerly moved to Cambridge, like his father and grandfather before him, to begin his studies at Harvard College. He was fifteen years old, a typical age for a Harvard freshman at the time. There, unlike at the Latin School, Sumner found his place among the thirty-five classmates and fit in well. Though not a Brahmin, he had the advantage of having attended the local preparatory school and entering with a wide circle of acquaintances. At Harvard, he made several friends, with whom he would travel and explore nearby areas in New England. They even started a harmless secret society, which they dubbed "the Nine," to meet and discuss literature.

Sumner was no longer called "Gawky Sumner." Now his classmates nicknamed him "the Chatterbox" because he would ramble endlessly to them about all the things he was reading. Every so often, he would even pop into the rooms of his dormmates and break into Latin, reciting the latest classical speech he had just memorized. When the students had to conduct their declamations (recitals in Latin and Greek in front of their professors), Sumner excelled, while other students struggled. "It always seemed a mystery to me how he could be so cool," one classmate recalled, "while I trembled like an aspen-leaf."

Sumner also joined the Hasty Pudding Club, a social group that hosted mock trial competitions. He was a fierce competitor. Foreshadowing the stinging, perspicacious oratory style that would propel his future activism, he became known, according to a classmate, for his ability to deliver "not only the formidable engine of legal argument, but the two-edged sword of satire, the poisoned darts of irony, and the barbed shafts of ridicule." Talkative, quick-witted, and hardworking, he impressed everyone.[12]

Even as he excelled in literature and debate, Sumner struggled in mathematics. Rather than learn algebra and geometry, he resorted to memorizing problems in the textbooks. On exams, he simply guessed the answers. He was often right, because the tests frequently repeated textbook problems, and Sumner most likely had a photographic memory. However, professors knew he was skirting by. "Sumner, I can't whittle a mathematical idea small enough to get it into your brain," one of his teachers complained.

As Sumner grew acclimated to Harvard, he also grew restless. He was exasperated by the strict schedule Harvard imposed on its students. One of his classmates explained the daily routine in a letter to his parents: "Prayers in the morning about seven o'clock. Breakfast at ½ past eight. Dinner at one. Evening prayers at ½ past four. Tea immediately after. Study bell in the morning at nine o'clock, in the afternoon at two, and in the evening at eight o'clock. All of course attend chapel (on Sundays) except such as are (or feign to be) sick." All the while, students spent most of their free time memorizing passages in Greek and Latin for their declamations. "We were expected to wade through Homer," one classmate complained, "as if the *Iliad* were a bog."[13]

Sumner felt that the routine deprived him of intellectual exploration, starving his voracious appetite for knowledge. "Every thing here is always the same," he complained. "The same invariable round of bells and recitations, of diggings and of deads! Mathematics piled on mathematics! Metaphysics murdered and mangled! Prayer-bells after prayer-bells; but, worse than all, commons upon commons! Clean, handsome plates and poor food!" When he grew older, he held the same view. "I am not aware that *any one single thing* is well taught to the Undergraduates of Harvard College," he later wrote. "Certainly I left it without knowing anything."[14]

* * *

AFTER GRADUATING IN the summer of 1830, Sumner returned home to the North Slope of Beacon Hill. Almost as soon as he arrived, his father decided to move the family to a new home. Although Pinckney Sumner could now afford many areas in Boston with his new income, he wanted to stay close to Black Boston. He picked a house on the far edge of a white neighborhood that had recently emerged on the North Slope, just one block away from the African Meeting House. Located at 20 Hancock Street, where the building still stands, the Sumner house was a four-story brownstone with thirteen rooms and a nice low-pitched Greek Revival portico that was installed later. Though the brilliant young Sumner, frustrated as he was by his academic stagnation, likely did not fully appreciate it, his neighborhood was bursting with the abolitionist ideas that would later propel him into the ranks of the luminaries he so admired.[15]

Black Boston was an exciting place to live. By this time, the small Black community had only around a thousand members, but it was teeming with part-time musicians, writers, and activists who contributed to a bubbling movement of Black abolitionism. It was quickly gaining a national reputation as a place that had culturally flourished despite suffering from discrimination, oppression, and forced poverty by white Bostonians. "The name of Boston always had a musical and joyous sound to the colored people of the South," one free African American recalled. Black Boston's Beacon Hill was a beacon of hope.[16]

Every fall, Black Freemasons in the neighborhood organized a parade to celebrate the independence of Haiti, the world's first so-called Black Republic: a constitutional government run by Black people for Black people. Pinckney Sumner probably attended these annual parades, either in his personal or police capacity, given that they took place within minutes of his home. He may even have brought his children along to them, which would have interested him considerably. In 1824, when Charles Sumner was thirteen, for example, the Baptist minister of the African Meeting House, Rev. Thomas Paul, spoke at the parade about his recent trip to Haiti, where he had met the revolutionary general Jean-Pierre Boyer, whom Pinckney Sumner had met decades ago and who was now in the sixth year of his term as president of Haiti.

Four years later, another exciting event took place when Prince Abdul Rahman Ibrahima ibn Sori joined the Haitian independence parade. Born to rule a Muslim kingdom among the Fulani people in West Africa, Prince Abdul Rahman had been kidnapped in the late 1780s, forced into slavery, and shipped to the United States. After roughly thirty years of lobbying for himself, he had persuaded Secretary of State Henry Clay to arrange his return trip home with the Moroccan embassy. Before his departure, he passed through the Sumners' neighborhood as part of a speaking tour to raise funds to buy the freedom of his enslaved children and grandchildren in Mississippi.

Prince Abdul Rahman proved to Black Americans that Haiti wasn't the only Black-run nation. He told long stories to the Bostonians about Africa, proving it had cultures, kingdoms, and religions that many Americans had never heard of. Tall, charismatic, dark-skinned, and fluent in many languages, including Arabic, the prince dressed in what Americans perceived to be Moorish garb in order to impress them. He marched through the streets of Beacon Hill with a blue cape, a crimson sash, and a green silk Turkish cap with a crescent on it, beseeching white and Black Bostonians alike to give him money to free his family.

Astonished and impressed, Black Freemasons asked the prince to join their annual parade and invited him to a celebratory dinner at their Masonic lodge. "The day of my anticipation has arrived, and I now have the pleasure of being in the company of an African prince," one Black Bostonian said, beaming.[17]

While there is no record of whether Pinckney Sumner or his children ever met Prince Abdul Rahman, who must have walked right past their home on the North Slope during the parade, or Reverend Paul, whose church was only one block away, Sumner's childhood and early life were certainly shaped by this thriving Black community and the ideas and aspirations of these Black leaders. Pinckney Sumner, with his abolitionist politics, stern Christianity, and Haitian sympathies, also encouraged his children to relate more deeply to their Black neighbors than did almost any other whites of the period.

* * *

WHEN CHARLES WAS eighteen, the Sumner household probably received a copy of David Walker's *Appeal to the Colored Citizens*, a popular pamphlet being passed around on the North Slope of Beacon Hill that was later published as a book. Born a free man in North Carolina, David Walker moved to Boston in 1825, settling into a home only blocks from where the Sumners lived. He set up a used clothing store and joined the Black Freemasons of Beacon Hill. An active community member, he commonly marshaled the Haitian parades, including the parade that featured Prince Abdul Rahman. In his free time, Walker wrote. A deep thinker who had seen slavery up close, he published his *Appeal* in 1829 and directed it to both Black and white audiences.

To Black people who contemplated migrating to Haiti or Africa, Walker's pamphlet insisted that they stay in the United States. "The greatest riches in all America have arisen from our blood and tears," Walker pointed out. "Will they drive us from our property and homes, which we have earned with our *blood*?" He argued that Black Americans should stay in the country and demand their rights. This was their home, he argued.

To white readers, Walker spared no words. "The whites have always been an unjust, jealous, unmerciful, avaricious and blood-thirsty set of beings, always seeking after power and authority," he declared. He pointed out the hypocrisy of American revolutionaries—men like Job Sumner—for claiming to fight for freedom during the war and then enslaving other human beings afterward. "Was your sufferings under Great Britain, one hundredth part as cruel and tyranical as you have rendered ours under you?" Walker asked. Invoking ideas that would echo in Sumner's own later writings, Walker also argued that white people directly contradicted the phrase "all men are created equal" in the Declaration of Independence. "See your Declaration Americans!!! Do you understand your own language?" he wondered.

Walker prophetically warned that if slavery were not abolished, America would one day suffer from a terrible war. He wasn't sure whether the war would arise from slaves revolting—as had happened in Haiti—or some other form, but he was convinced that God wouldn't let Black people in America suffer much longer. "O Americans! Americans!! I call God—I call angels—I call men, to witness," he warned, "that your DESTRUCTION *is at hand*, and will be speedily consummated unless you REPENT."

Pinckney Sumner shuddered at the prospect of what God might do to his country, for he knew that men like his father were hypocrites who had preached revolutionary ideals of human equality but enslaved other human beings. With nine children, he worried about the fate of the country that his father had helped to create. When he was born in 1776, the United States had an enslaved population of roughly 450,000 people. By 1830, that population had quadrupled to nearly two million. Having been to Haiti, Pinckney Sumner knew that enslaved people were capable of revolting. In fact, he believed they had a *right* to revolt. Moreover, he also believed that free states like Massachusetts might one day end up in a conflict with the slave states of the South, for liberty and bondage could not mix together forever.

Often, Pinckney Sumner told stories to his children about his journey to Haiti and his meeting with General Boyer. He also told them stories about their grandfather's interactions with General Washington. To him, the American revolutionaries and Haitian revolutionaries had fought for the same ideals, whether they practiced them or not—liberty, justice, equality, and the like. Probably to his consternation, though, his eldest son, Charles, was so buried in books that he didn't seem to care much about his father's stories. Only many years later would his son begin to invoke them.

Believing his own elite education had been mostly worthless, Pinckney Sumner tried to impart to his children moral teachings, rather than academic ones. "Let others to teach *their* children to abhor naughty words," he wrote in his diary. "I will try to teach *mine* to abhor naughty deeds." He insisted that his children treat everyone, white or Black, with kindness, respect, and justice. If white people learned to treat African Americans with respect, he hoped, perhaps a future crisis could be averted.

And yet—Pinckney Sumner was scared. While speaking to a neighbor about the question of slavery one day, he shared his anxieties about what Charles and his siblings might one day experience in a country that subjected millions to unjust bondage. Probably with dread in his eyes, hoping his prescient words wouldn't turn out to be true, he correctly predicted the future. "Our children's heads," he remarked, "will some day be broken on a cannon-ball on this question."[18]

CHAPTER 3

I AM ENAMORED OF THE LAW

IN THEIR NEW HOME ON HANCOCK STREET, CHARLES SUMNER decided to spend his time engaging in self-study, rather than find employment. Determined to learn all the things that Harvard didn't teach him, he dedicated himself to reattempting mathematics and reading scores of additional books. "I have doomed myself for this year at least to hard labor," he boasted to a college friend, Jonathan Stearns, about this plan. "I intend to diet on study—go to bed late & get up early & leave none of my time unemployed."

Sure enough, Sumner found it impossible to self-study. There was too much "little chaos around," he grumbled. With eight siblings, he couldn't focus amid the "children and chairs, boxes and books, and irons and paper, sunlight and Sumners" filling the house. And so, as the year came to a close, he decided to go back to Harvard to attend law school.[1]

This was an unconventional choice, given that Harvard Law School, founded in 1817, had hardly any students by the late 1820s. In fact, in the early nineteenth century, professional legal education barely existed. The conventional way to become a lawyer was to be an apprentice who learned on the job. Practically, it made more sense to apprentice with a senior lawyer, who could acculturate his protégés to their state's specific laws and legal culture, than to study the law as an academic discipline.

But Sumner had insider knowledge that Harvard Law School would be different, for his father's college best friend, Joseph Story, had become the school's lead professor—in part due to Sumner's father's advice.

* * *

WHILE PINCKNEY SUMNER's legal career had floundered, his old friend Story's had soared. In 1811, Story was appointed to the Supreme Court of the United States—the very year that Pinckney Sumner was poor and living in a small wood-frame house raising two tiny twins. Four years later, in 1815, Pinckney Sumner waited outside a courthouse in Boston to try to catch up with Story, with whom he had been gradually falling out of touch. But Judge Story (who preferred to be called "Judge" rather than "Justice") was so engrossed in a conversation with a few lawyers that he didn't notice Pinckney Sumner standing nearby waiting to talk to him. After eight to ten minutes, Judge Story walked away with these lawyers, leaving Pinckney Sumner feeling dejected and overlooked.

Afterward, Pinckney Sumner wrote a long, plaintive letter to Judge Story. "I do not & I cannot, see you quite so often & so familiarly as I was once accustomed to," he confessed. "The more a man is elevated by the just award of his country, tho' his admirers are to be found every where, his friends must be looked for almost exclusively in the circle of the great," he said. "I bow to the unalterable nature of things." Apologizing for his "cowardly bashfulness," he then made Judge Story a proposal: come back to Boston to teach law.

Pinckney Sumner had at least once before proposed to Story that he start teaching classes in Boston, where students would pay for each course. He now reiterated his proposal, suggesting that now would be a good time to start. "You would be thereby rendering a very great & needed service to your country," he explained. "Whatever be the price, I will be one of your disciples."

In reply, Judge Story said that he had in fact been thinking about teaching ever since Pinckney Sumner first raised the possibility. Noting that Harvard was exploring the idea of creating legal classes, Judge Story said he would "await the decision of the college" rather than start on his own. He then ended by promising that he appreciated his old friend. "At all times, be assured that I shall be happy to see you and to converse with you," he vowed. "I shall always remember the kind notice with which you honored me at college."[2]

Fourteen years later, in 1829, Judge Story started teaching legal classes in Cambridge, Massachusetts, just as the young Charles Sumner was deciding his first career steps. When Story arrived, Boston hosted a celebratory dinner for the Supreme Court Justice that Pinckney Sumner proudly attended. Perhaps in honor of being one of the first men to suggest the idea of Story teaching in Cambridge, Pinckney Sumner was asked to give a toast. Everybody raised their glasses as he began to speak.

"Law just as 'tis, wrong or rightly understood," he said, "Our greatest evil or our greatest good."[3]

Judge Story had a transformative vision for Harvard Law, seeing the program as a lever to impact American politics, legal studies, and society at large. After joining the Supreme Court, Story had been quickly persuaded by his Federalist friend and mentor Chief Justice John Marshall that the U.S. Constitution had established a strong national government and a strong judicial branch. Both men developed a jurisprudential philosophy that is now known as constitutional nationalism. The basic premise, as Story explained it in one opinion, is that the Constitution "was ordained and established, *not* by the United States in their sovereign capacities, but emphatically, as the preamble of the Constitution declares, by '*the people of the United States.*'" Marshall and Story hoped to protect this vision of a strong national government during the Jacksonian era, a time when southerners and others strongly pushed for more power to be given to the states rather than to the nation.

At Harvard, Story would further develop his nationalist views, teach them to his students, and transform the school into a fixture of American law. Story was considered the law school's de facto founder, and his marble statue sits imposingly at the entrance of the school's main building to this day. At a time when few lawyers received formal training, he trained more than six hundred students over a multidecade-long teaching career. On top of his work as a professor, Story would continue serving on the Supreme Court and would author a prodigious number of legal treatises, many of which are still studied today. "He was in himself a whole triumvirate," Charles Sumner later recalled, explaining that Story treated his students "as if they were all members of one family with him."

This fatherly professor, like many parents who would never admit it, had a favorite child.[4]

* * *

DURING STORY'S SECOND year at Harvard Law, Sumner became one of his students. Sumner was thrilled to escape his large, poor, chaotic family in the dense neighborhood of the North Slope. "I have left Boston & the profitless thoughts which its streets, its inhabitants, its politics & its newspapers ever excite," the twenty-year-old Sumner said exuberantly. "I find myself again in [be]loved Cam[bridge] where is sociality & retirement."

Sumner quickly fell in love with his law studies, which began in September 1831. "[I] have read a Vol & a half of Blackstone & am enamored of the Law," he declared after a mere four weeks of school. "We have struck the true profession," he also decided. "The one, in which the mind is the most sharpened & quickened; & the duties of which, properly discharged, are most vital to the interests of the country."[5]

Sumner's newfound fixation with the law can be partly explained by his admiration for his teacher. After years of being taught to memorize and regurgitate, Sumner finally found an instructor who intellectually engaged with his students. Story lectured with contagious enthusiasm, inviting students to ask questions and to push back on his arguments. Story also tested students on the reading material, asking them on the fly to explain their understanding. Then he responded with his own commentary and additional questions. Today, law students describe this as "cold calling." In Sumner's time, the method had never been used before in the teaching of law, in neither England nor the United States. Story and his colleagues invented the system of cold calling, and Sumner was among the first students to benefit from it.

At long last, Sumner had found the intensive intellectual environment he had been seeking all his life. Once a week, students participated in a moot court. They debated unsettled issues of law, and Story chimed in with his own opinions about each side's argument. Students also wrote essays, to which Story provided feedback. All this occurred over an intense eighteen-month period during which students were expected to master the fundamentals of real and personal property law, commercial and maritime law, equity law, criminal law, civil law, the law of nations, and constitutional law.[6]

Sumner dove into the reading material Story and his other professors assigned to him. "In my studies," he later boasted, "[I] never relied upon the textbooks, but went to the original sources, read all the authorities and references, whether treatises or decided cases." A classmate remembered that "his room was piled with books: the shelves overflowed and the floor was littered with them." By the end of his time at Harvard Law, he was "universally acknowledged to be the best scholar in the school," according to the diary of another student, "& was by many said to be the most learned in legal literature of any man that ever left the school."[7]

Unsurpassed in his studiousness, Sumner scoffed at those who knew less than he. He saw them as lazy. "The fact is I look upon a *mere* lawyer, a reader of cases & cases alone, as one of the veriest wretches in the world," he once wrote. "A lawyer must be a man of polish—with an *omnium gatherum* of knowledge." Lawyers "must know law, history, philosophy, human nature," he asserted on another occasion. "And, if he covets the fame of an advocate, he must drink of all the springs of literature." Putting his belief into practice, Sumner claimed to a friend that he spent every "forenoon wholly and solely to law; afternoon to classics; evening to history, subjects collateral and assistant to law, &c." His regimen left no time for a social life. "I wish no acquaintances," he declared, "for they eat up time like locusts."[8]

Judge Story was so impressed with this ridiculously hardworking prodigy that he pulled Sumner under his wing. Soon after the term began, Story wrote a gushing letter to his boss, Harvard president Josiah Quincy, about Sumner. "He has a wonderful memory; he keeps all his knowledge in order, and can put his hand on it in a moment," Story beamed. Perhaps to test his abilities, Story wrote to Sumner to ask him to review a draft of his new treatise, *The Conflict of Laws*, and to verify all quotes and citations for him. Over time, Judge Story began to treat Sumner as far more than just his student. "I feel proud to think that . . . I have, in some sort, as the Scotch would say, a heritable right to your friendship," the judge wrote to his disciple. Story's son William later said of Sumner that his "father was very fond of him and treated him almost as if he were a son."

Several times per week, Sumner spent his evenings at Judge Story's home. William recalled that his father always welcomed Sumner "with a beaming face" and enjoyed his "ever-flowing stream of questions." Sumner loved Story. "Who can forget his bounding step, his contagious laugh, his exhilarating voice, his beaming smile, his countenance that shone like a benediction?" he wrote after Judge Story's death. Even during Story's lifetime, Sumner showered his mentor with heaps of praise. "Not a day—not an hour passes without some perception of your kindness coming into my mind," Sumner wrote Story once. He described his mentor as his "best friend" in one letter; in another he told Story that he could "never express towards you the fullness of my feelings."[9]

While impressed by Sumner's genius, Story worried about the young scholar's obsessive nature. "You must begin to be chary of your intellectual as well as physical strength," the judge once advised him, "or it may be exhausted before you reach the fair maturity of life." One classmate described Sumner in law school as a "tall, thin, bent, ungainly law-student; his eyes were inflamed by late reading, and his complexion showed that he was careless of exercise." Reportedly, he was six foot two, but only 120 pounds. "You are studying law with all the zeal and ardor of a lover," a college friend wrote to him. This was good, his friend believed, but he worried that Sumner might "kill himself prematurely" if he continued to "sacrifice his health."[10]

Regardless, Sumner's stirring enthusiasm for the law was infectious. Even children noticed the shine on the scrawny scholar's face. "He was, as a young man, singularly plain," according to William Story. "Nothing saved his face from ugliness but his white gleaming teeth and his expression of bright intelligence and entire amiability." The daughter of Harvard president Josiah Quincy recalled a similar appearance. "This youth, though not in the least handsome," she remembered, "is so good-hearted, clever, and real, that it is impossible not to like him and believe in him." As Harvard's favorite student, Sumner was often invited to his professors' homes, even at times simply to keep their wives and children company when they were away.[11]

When Sumner approached graduation, Story encouraged him to stay at Harvard. His colleague, Professor Simon Greenleaf, agreed. They offered Sumner the honor of serving as the law school's first librarian. Over the past few years, Greenleaf and Story had amassed a collection of 3,500 law books for Harvard. "The library is, perhaps, the largest and most valuable, relating to law, in the country," Greenleaf boasted. But the problem was that the library was not organized. Sumner, with his photographic memory and voracious appetite for books, was the man for the job.

Provided with lavish accommodation, far larger than his law school dormitory, Sumner was paid a modest salary to arrange the thousands of texts. "I made myself acquainted with every work of the common law, from the Year Books in uncouth Norman down to the latest reports," he recalled. William Story remembered that Sumner knew the books so well that he could go into the library at night and find any book in the dark. Sumner wrote the first catalogue of the Harvard Law Library in history.[12]

A few months after his time as librarian, Sumner's residence at Harvard Law School came to a natural end. Story and Greenleaf recognized that as much as they wished to keep their protégé near them, Sumner needed to practice law and gain life experience outside the academy before he could become the true scholar they wanted him to be. Story arranged for Sumner to work at the law practice of Benjamin Rand, a respected lawyer, beginning around the start of 1834. "Sumner . . . has left me," Greenleaf wrote to Story when their pupil finally crossed the river and returned to Boston. "I stoutly refused *ever* to bid him farewell."[13]

* * *

MEANWHILE, PINCKNEY SUMNER—NOW *Sheriff* Sumner—took his new profession with incredible seriousness. He proudly marched the streets of Boston in a blue coat with military regalia, yellow breeches, white tipped boots, a tricornered hat, and a sword worn at his side. He was the last sheriff in Boston history to wear the antique English dress. Putting his Harvard training to use, Sheriff Sumner even authored a journal article with original research on the history of English sheriffs dating back to King Henry III. There are many reports of the dignified, polite, and respectful demeanor with which this scholar-cop carried himself. "Good learning and good manners; two good companions," he once said. "Happy when they meet, they ought never to part."[14]

Sheriff Sumner had a keen sense of right and wrong—which he applied with absolute, unbending justice to himself and others. For example, he conducted his own executions. When asked why he didn't delegate such a disagreeable task, he replied, "Simply because it is disagreeable." At one execution, he accidentally stepped on the foot of his prisoner, took off his hat, and apologized before hanging him. After another execution, he donated all the income he earned from the hanging to the widow whose husband had been killed by the prisoner. At a third execution, he told the thousand-person crowd watching that he would perform "the severest duty that the law imposes upon any of its servants." Sinking the platform, he killed the prisoner by hanging. Then he explained that the criminal had been blessed to talk to clergy before meeting his fate. Religion can "soften the bed of death," he reassured his audience.[15]

The execution was a classic example of Old Testament justice. But Pinckney Sumner also believed firmly in the biblical teaching of human equality. He usually attended King's Chapel, a magnificent Unitarian church near the old Massachusetts State House.[16] Unitarians preached the oneness of God, rejecting the Trinity but affirming the special spiritual significance of Jesus Christ. They saw God as loving and benign and not, like their Puritan ancestors, as harsh and punishing. They also taught the Bible as a book "written for mankind" that could be interpreted "in the same manner as that of other books," as one theologian put it.

Unitarians emphasized a direct relationship between humans and God.

They held an optimistic faith in human nature and "the progress of mankind onward and upward forever." They preached that God had placed a moral conscience in every human being, a conscience that humans ought to follow. With a doctrinal worldview that easily lent itself to progressive views, or perhaps even commanded them, many Boston Unitarians would become active abolitionists in the decades ahead, though the institutional church never endorsed it.[17]

As a Unitarian who believed in following his conscience and honoring the equality of humankind before God, Sheriff Sumner treated Black residents of Boston with respect. "The people of color cannot be christianized until they are equalized," he once said. Noting that he would be "entirely willing to sit on the bench with a negro judge," Sheriff Sumner did his best to ensure fair trials for Black prisoners and to reduce his complicity in the system of racial injustice. Once, during his tenure, two Black women were put on trial for allegedly being fugitives from slavery. Some free Black citizens stormed the courtroom and prematurely helped the women escape before the conclusion of their trial. When Sheriff Sumner was accused of tacitly allowing the women to take flight, he did not deny the charge. "I should be ashamed of myself if I did not wish that every person claimed as a slave might be proved to be a freeman," he told a newspaper.[18]

The sheriff also mistrusted white elites, having suffered exclusion and derision due to his poverty and bastard status from the very people with whom he had once attended school. After graduating from Harvard, he and his friend Joseph Story had joined the Democratic-Republican Party. Led by Thomas Jefferson and James Madison, the Democratic-Republicans championed agrarian farmers, derided New England elites, and were skeptical of big government. Like most wealthy or intellectually minded Bostonians, Story gradually drifted away from the agrarian party and toward the nationally minded, pro-manufacturing Whigs.

Sheriff Sumner stuck to his anti-elite roots. Sometime in the late 1820s, he had joined the Anti-Masonic Party, a new political party that emerged over growing fears by voters that a small cadre of elites was controlling American democracy. These voters blamed the Freemasons for being the culprits of this conspiracy. After all, many Founding Fathers—George Washington, Benjamin Franklin, and John Hancock, for example—were Freemasons. The sheriff, himself a Freemason, wasn't nearly as conspiratorial as most people in the party. But he was outraged with how wealthy Bostonians were using Freemasonry to benefit one another with special political and economic privileges that most ordinary people weren't getting.

Joining other Masons who had long felt uncomfortable with the exclusive and secretive society, Sheriff Sumner had announced that he was "seceding" from Freemasonry. He wrote a sixteen-page public letter explaining himself. "Some think that Masonry does no harm," he declared. "But I believe it does no good." Masons were furious that a public official had left the organization and tarnished its name. And so, for months, they spread rumors about the sheriff in local papers for committing various acts of misconduct.[19]

Sheriff Sumner's lifelong suspicion of the white, wealthy, educated elite made sense, despite his education at Phillips Andover and Harvard. His own father, Job, had neglected him, fighting far-flung battles for the Revolutionary Army and earning repute as a federal commissioner while he and his unmarried mother lived separately in Massachusetts. Now, the sheriff probably hoped to be a better father to his own children and to pass along a better set of moral principles to them.

But alas, Sheriff Sumner's relationship with his eldest son was rocky at best. While he was principled and polite, the sheriff was quiet, melancholy, and rarely known to smile. He was a stern, harsh father who expected far more from his children than he had achieved in his own life. Accordingly, Charles kept his distance from him and preferred not to live at home. He also assiduously avoided discussing his father in writing, both now and for the rest of his life, leaving only a few traces behind about their relationship. "What your father has been to you, you have not disguised from me," a friend wrote to Sumner once. Sumner later told another friend that his "childhood & youth passed in unhappiness, such as I pray may not be the lot of others."[20]

Despite their cool relationship, Charles Sumner still followed in his father's footsteps in studying law. He always admired his father for bravely questioning the morality of the establishment, vocally speaking out against it, and enduring the price of social exclusion, harassment, and slander. Like his father, he would spend much of his life as a social outsider in elite circles, despite his crème de la crème credentials. But he was not yet an aspiring social reformer. At the age of twenty-three, having left his position as librarian at Harvard Law School, Sumner attempted to start his career as just an ordinary lawyer.

* * *

IN JANUARY 1834, Charles Sumner moved into a private boardinghouse in central Boston and began his career on Court Street as an apprentice to Benjamin Rand, a well-respected and learned commercial lawyer. From the moment he started, his heart was not in the work. "I had rather be a toad and live upon a dungeon's vapor," he once wrote to a friend, "than one of those lumps of flesh that are christened lawyers." He reviled lawyers "who know only how to wring from quibbles and obscurities . . . who have no idea of law beyond its letter." Unlike them, he wished to "dwell upon the vast heaps of law-matter . . . at the spirit,—the broad spirit of the law," and to "bring to his aid a liberal and cultivated mind."[21]

In pursuit of a liberal and cultivated mind, Sumner preferred reading books in Rand's library over helping his master with his practice. Rand and his colleagues, amused by Sumner's earnestness, did not seem to mind. Devouring books, Sumner also took time to write. Staying up late, until "that witching hour when ghosts and goblins walk," he penned journal articles on the most obscure topics and submitted them to *The American Jurist*. Soon, the *Jurist*, the star legal publication of its time, appointed him as an editor, where he authored hundreds of pages of content. "There is an agreeable, romantic feeling in sitting up and trimming your solitary lamp when the whole world are stretched in repose," he wrote to his old law professor Simon Greenleaf. "And this romantic feeling is especially heightened when one is writing law."[22]

After a few months of apprenticeship, Sumner opened his own law practice with his classmate George Hillard. He quickly discovered that reading and writing law was not the same as *practicing* law. Preferring to spend swaths of each day reading or in intellectual conversation with friends, Sumner struggled with "vulgar contracts, dealing with magnified trifles, inhaling bad air, moiling in formal documents, trudging, drudging, where scarce a breath from Heaven can reach me."

Sumner also performed poorly in front of juries, who were turned off by his illustrious learning and penchant for pedantry. Though he was praised by a local newspaper as "more deeply read in the law than any other individual of similar age," his erudition came with costs. Potential clients were wary of hiring the brilliant but impractical scholar-lawyer. "Your article on 'Replevin' was learned, and well and logically expressed," one lawyer once wrote to Sumner about a piece in the *Jurist*. "It was an extraordinary article for a young man; but it is not practical. You seem to delight in the speculative in the choices of your articles."[23]

For the next three years, Sumner's legal career would fail to take off and achieve the high expectations everybody placed on him. "I cannot disguise from my self the sense of weakness, inferiority, & incompetence which I feel," he wrote to Greenleaf. Sumner also considered himself out of sync with the profit-seeking mind-set of his colleagues at the bar. "What are the world's goods, the dross of gold & silver," he once wrote to a friend, "compared with the priceless treasures of the mind." Most other lawyers lacked his big-brain sensibilities. "Great learning is not necessary in order to make money at the bar," he sorrowfully observed. "Indeed, the most ignorant are often among the wealthiest lawyers."[24]

Even as Sumner's practice waned, his success as a scholar was unparalleled. "In what may be called the literature of the law . . . he has no rival among us," one legal publisher wrote. In January 1835, Judge Story asked Sumner to return to Harvard Law School to teach while the judge had Supreme Court duties in Washington. For three months, the twenty-four-year-old taught in the stead of the country's preeminent jurist. Sumner's students, who were upset about Story's absence, nevertheless found Sumner to be impressive. Having done fairly well as a teacher, he was invited back to teach the following year.

Judge Story also asked Sumner to serve as his reporter when he heard cases. Dutifully, Sumner would attend arguments where Story served in his capacity as a circuit judge, take his notes, and publish them as pamphlets. In all, he published three volumes of *Sumner's Reports*, which earned him some money.

In 1837, at the age of twenty-six, Sumner was the sole professor at Harvard Law School because both Story and Greenleaf had to take absences. "I hope that this is but the beginning," Story wrote to him in 1835, "and that one day you may fill the chair which he or I occupy." Both men had incredibly high opinions of Sumner's abilities. "Our earnest desire is to have you occupy an additional professor's chair," Greenleaf wrote him in 1838, "bringing into our institution all that power and all the affluence of your mind."[25]

CHAPTER 4

MAD DEMOCRATIC TENDENCIES

Through the course of his mid- to late twenties, Sumner traveled, cultivated mentorships, and read books that set the intellectual tone for his life.

The first major formative experience for him was a trip to Washington, D.C., in March 1834, when he was twenty-three, upon the invitation of Judge Story. Currently in the country's capital to hear arguments at the Supreme Court, Story wanted his protégé to see firsthand the happenings of the U.S. government and to groom Sumner for his future as a leading scholar of American law.

Almost as soon as he arrived, Sumner hated the city. "I probably shall never come here again," he wrote to his father. "Nothing that I have seen of politics has made me look upon them with any feeling other than loathing," he continued. Watching debates in Congress, he was disappointed by most politicians. "He is no orator," he complained about John Calhoun, South Carolina's rabid proslavery senator. "Very rugged in his language, unstudied in style, marching directly to the main points of his subject without stopping for parley or introduction." Sumner was equally unimpressed with President Jackson, whom he met in a brief visit to the White House that Story probably arranged. "I have seen General Jackson (the old tyrant)," he wrote to one of his younger sisters. "He seemed to have hardly nerve enough to keep his bones together."[1]

Sumner's negative impression of politics stuck with him for the rest of his life. But there were other fields, ideas, philosophies, and movements that would come to truly inspire him.

* * *

MOST OF ALL, Sumner loved the law. Almost every day in Washington, he attended arguments at the Supreme Court, which at the time was located in the lower level of the Capitol Building.

Beneath the vaulted marble-white ceiling of this small, dark, intimate semicircular chamber, sitting in one of the wooden chairs on the red velvet carpet, Sumner watched attorneys passionately argue their cases before Judge Story and six other black-robed justices, who sat in the front, expressionless and inquisitive. On one of his first days, he was absorbed in an argument by Francis Scott Key, a respected commercial litigator who wrote a famous poem called "The Star-Spangled Banner." Soon after, he listened to Key's co-counsel, Daniel Webster, in the same case. While still practicing law, Webster was also now a Massachusetts senator—one whose dramatic, expressive, soaring oratory skills had enthralled Sumner ever since he was fifteen.

Craning his neck to hear every single one of Key's and Webster's words, this gaunt young scholar quickly detected the defects in their arguments, or at least he thought he did. After hearing the case, Sumner wrote to Professor Greenleaf to say that Key had relied on his "quickness and facility of language rather than upon research." As for Webster, Sumner was even harsher. He told Greenleaf that Webster, despite his great rhetoric and confident style, had seemed unprepared, "doing the labor in court which should have been done out of court." Sitting in the back, listening and critiquing these two world-famous attorneys, Sumner wondered whether *he* should be the one standing up front, talking and arguing, instead.[2]

As if the universe were designed to inflate his ego, Sumner found himself being assigned one of the most important jobs in the Supreme Court after just a few days of sitting in the back of the courtroom. During every case, an official reporter was tasked with taking notes on each lawyer's arguments and each judge's oral decisions. Those notes were privately published in reports that became the official record. Recently, the previous reporter, Henry Wheaton, had sued the current reporter, Richard Peters, for copyright infringement. When the case was heard at the Court, Peters asked Sumner to take the notes for the case, probably because it seemed like a conflict of interest for Peters to do it himself. Sumner's notes were then published by Peters in his report for *Wheaton v. Peters*, one of the leading American copyright cases of the nineteenth century.[3]

On most evenings, Sumner came home to have dinner with the other justices after their busy days in the chamber. At the time, the justices lived together in the same boardinghouse—a practice put into place by Chief Justice John Marshall, who believed that an intimate, shared living environment would foster comradery between the team of seven justices who didn't always agree with one another.

After one such dinner with four of the Court's justices, Sumner eagerly wrote to his parents about the experience. "I supped and dined with them once *en famille*, as it were,—if I may apply that term where there is no family," he wrote. "No conversation is forbidden, and nothing which goes to cause cheerfulness, if not hilarity. The world and all its things are talked of as much as on any other day." He took note of some of the justices' personalities—describing Justice Smith Thompson as "a kind-hearted man, now somewhat depressed from the loss of his wife," and Justice Gabriel Duvall as "eighty-two years old, and is so deaf as to be unable to participate in conversation."

Most of all, Sumner enjoyed spending time with Chief Justice Marshall, a good-humored, jovial old man who still boasted a thick head of hair and a tall, thin, athletic body. Marshall took a liking to Sumner from the start, inviting the young man to join him on his morning walks from the boardinghouse to the Court. At dinners with his colleagues, Marshall fondly enjoyed telling stories and cracking jokes, which delighted Sumner to no end whenever he had a chance to sit at the table. "Judge Marshall a model of simplicity . . . naturally taciturn, and yet ready to laugh; to joke and be joked with," Sumner eagerly told his parents. Quoting Alexander Pope, Sumner said that Marshall "is '*in wit a man, simplicity a child*.'"[4]

* * *

WHILE SUMNER SAT and listened to Chief Justice Marshall tell stories, he may have heard about Marshall's young adulthood fighting in the American Revolution. Like Sumner's grandfather Job, Marshall was a poor farm boy who signed up to fight for his country's freedom shortly after the Battles of Lexington and Concord. While enduring the long, difficult years of war, Marshall lifted himself from obscurity into a life of fame and significance by catching the attention of General Washington. Marshall's most formative wartime experience was spending a cold, dreary winter with the general at Valley Forge, where many soldiers nearly starved to death because the Continental Army couldn't afford to buy much food. That winter taught Marshall a valuable lesson: if the United States was going to succeed, its government needed to be big, strong, and financially sustainable.

Not all Americans agreed. While Marshall, Job Sumner, and other revolutionaries toiled for their survival in General Washington's cash-strapped army, delegates at the Continental Congress hemmed and hawed about creating a national government with too much power. Most delegates wanted to keep power within the thirteen states, which had heretofore been their homes and their identities. Rather than create a *nation* to represent all Americans, these delegates decided to create a *confederacy*, what was effectively an alliance between the states. That alliance was established in the Articles of Confederation, a governing charter for the United States that didn't let the national government raise money even to fund basic things like food for the revolutionary soldiers. Instead, everything was dependent on the generosity of the states.

After independence, states realized that the Articles weren't creating a government strong enough to ensure the survival of America. People in the states were also increasingly seeing themselves as part of a single nation, with a single identity. In 1787, delegates came together again to draft a new governing charter, the U.S. Constitution. This charter established a strong, sovereign national government that didn't answer to the states. Instead, the new American government answered to the *people*. Beginning with the words "We the People," the Constitution was sent to the states for people to discuss, debate, and ratify. Millions of voters around the nation had an opportunity to decide whether to ratify this text. When they did so, these American citizens ordained the U.S. government as it is known today.

Exponents of states' rights didn't disappear at the Founding. Instead, for the next several decades, politicians primarily in the South continued to argue that states were sovereign and endowed with large powers, while the national government had to be limited and constrained. Whenever these debates spilled into the courts, Chief Justice Marshall almost always sided with the national government, advocating for a liberally interpreted Constitution that gave broad powers to the government to do as the people desired.

Marshall's friend, colleague, and protégé Joseph Story also believed in a strong national government, which he spelled out in a book called *The Commentaries of the Constitution*. On the very first page, Story dedicated the treatise to Marshall, "whose youth was engaged in the arduous enterprises of the Revolution; whose manhood assisted in framing and supporting the national Constitution." The treatise described "the decline and fall of the Confederation" and the "origin and adoption of the Constitution." Story said his treatise was based solely on Marshall's opinions and on the *Federalist Papers*, a body of work primarily written by another famous nationalist, Alexander Hamilton. The idea that "the Constitution created a national government," William Story later wrote about his father, "was the keystone to all his constitutional opinions."[5]

Judge Story was particularly anxious to protect the ideas of constitutional nationalism, which were under threat by the time Sumner was studying law. Fearing that the national government might one day interfere with slavery, southern leaders like John Calhoun had been arguing that states could nullify national laws they didn't believe were constitutional. The idea of "nullification" frightened Story to no end, for it had the possibility to unravel the entire U.S. government.

Story's fear wasn't misplaced. Some southern states, especially South Carolina, regularly threatened to secede from the Union if the national government interfered with their practice of slavery. The threat of disunion was so serious that many Americans who disliked slavery were willing to tolerate it. "Great as the evil of slavery is," one of the Founding Fathers had said, "a dismemberment of the Union would be worse." Judge Story agreed with this view. In decisions like *Prigg v. Pennsylvania*, he ruled that states—even states that had internally abolished slavery—had a legal obligation to return fugitives back into bondage, based on the Constitution's Fugitive Slave Clause.

Fearing any talk of disunion, Story wanted to ensure that whoever succeeded him as the main professor at Harvard Law School would vigorously defend constitutional nationalism and all constitutional provisions, including the Fugitive Slave Clause. He believed that man was Sumner— with whom he had often chatted in the classroom and at home while writing the *Commentaries*. "I shall die content, so far as my professorship is concerned," Story once said, "if Charles Sumner is to succeed me."[6]

* * *

SUMNER FOUND MARSHALL's and Story's life experiences, ideas, and philosophy inspiring. In one set of his lecture notes as a law professor, he wrote down and underlined "*Nation not Confederacy.*" He also found Story's dense, beastly three-volume *Commentaries* to be a delicious read, which he devoured and shared with others. Writing to one of his college friends, Sumner called the *Commentaries* "a light law-book, and a most instructive work as to the government under which we live, which shall be more entertaining and informing." He was, from the very beginning, a believer in constitutional nationalism.[7]

Sumner also took to heart Judge Story's passion for equity jurisprudence, a branch of law that would inspire the rest of his intellectual life. Equity jurists were concerned about ethics, fairness, and justice in the law. They believed that the law had an underlying moral core that wasn't always reflected in precedents or statutes. This moral core arose from natural law, a philosophy that suggested that all laws ultimately come from God, who decreed principles that humankind could discern by reason and should strive to follow. A core concept in natural law was that God had endowed "certain inalienable rights," as the Declaration of Independence put it, such as the right to "Life, Liberty and the pursuit of Happiness."

Equity jurists believed that judges needed to be flexible sometimes in deciding their cases and specifying remedies, in order to avoid morally repugnant outcomes. On the very first page of his reference notebook, Sumner wrote that all laws "were grounded upon nature." On the next page, he wrote down the story of an equity jurist who didn't always enforce statutory law when it sat in tension with natural law, for he "would never suffer the strictness of law to prevail against conscience."[8]

Inspired by the idea of moral law, Sumner annotated a major report of English cases on equity jurisprudence that introduced to American readers some of the principles that English chancellors followed to decide when, why, and how to apply ethically minded remedies in cases. Sumner dedicated the reports to Joseph Story, who had written one of the two leading American treatises on equity. Story was most pleased to see his name on the front page of Sumner's annotated reports. "We may swim down the stream of time together," he eagerly told his protégé. "I am rejoiced to have my name united with yours in this manner, so that the public may know how long and how intimate our friendship has been."

Sumner also struck up a friendship with the head of the New York Court of Chancery, James Kent, author of the other leading equity treatise in America. At first, Sumner was so cocky that he wasn't impressed with the world-famous jurist when he visited Kent's home in New York as a stopover during his trip from Boston to Washington. "Kent's conversation is lively and instructive, but grossly ungrammatical," Sumner wrote to his parents. "It is a wonder which I cannot solve, that he is so correct a writer . . . so incorrect a converser."[9]

Over time, Sumner grew to admire Chancellor Kent, who spent many hours with the young man graciously showing him many of the books in the large, stately library in his suburban New York home. Kent was stunned by the power of Sumner's mind, once remarking that he was "the only person in the country competent to succeed Story." Once, Kent hosted Sumner for the night. As he showed Sumner his home, Kent told him about being mentored by Alexander Hamilton as a young man. Getting emotional, he explained that Hamilton used to host him in his Poughkeepsie home. Sumner was thus linked to one of America's Founding Fathers.[10]

* * *

WHEN SUMNER RETURNED to Boston in late spring 1834, he continued to struggle with his law practice. By August, he told a friend that he was experiencing the first headache of his life while doing work for one of his few clients. Rather than practice, Sumner much preferred reading, reading, and *reading*, anything and everything he could get his hands on. Sometime in 1835, he discovered a local newspaper, printed in a shop on the same city his block as his office, that was unlike anything he had ever read before: the *Liberator*.

Founded by William Lloyd Garrison, a tall, thin, unassuming white journalist with wiry glasses, the *Liberator* was an intense, fiery newspaper that demanded the immediate abolition of slavery. "I am in earnest—I will not equivocate—I will not excuse—I will not retreat a single inch," Garrison wrote in his paper's first edition, "AND I WIL BE HEARD." Garrison's searing hatred of slavery impressed many Black Bostonians, who gravitated toward him and became contributors to the *Liberator*, which had a subscriber base that was three-quarters African American.[11]

Sumner was so amazed by the *Liberator*'s contents, which he must have found intellectually invigorating and fresh, that he became one of the paper's monthly subscribers. As he began to read Garrison's writing, he was perpetually shocked by the sharpness of its tone, believing it was "often vindictive, bitter & unchristian." At the same time, he was emotionally moved by the deep moral impulse that undergirded Garrison's outrage over the slave system. The *Liberator* also provided him with an outlook to better understand his neighbors in Black Boston and keep in touch with the happenings of the community.

Inspired but turned off by Garrison's radicalism, Sumner befriended Rev. William Channing, a more mild-mannered antislavery man. An aging, frail minister who would wear thick scarves and enormous hats to brave the cold Boston winters, Channing was a Unitarian moral philosopher. Around the same time that Sumner had started reading Garrison's *Liberator*, Channing published *Slavery*, a very gentle book that politely suggested that slavery might be incompatible with the precepts of Christianity. Men like Garrison believed that Channing didn't appreciate the sheer scale of slavery's evil. Yet by being so cautious, measured, and nonthreatening, Channing was able to lend more credibility to the antislavery movement in elite Boston Brahmin circles, credibility that abolitionists such as Garrison and his followers badly needed to get their message across.[12]

Most white northerners nominally thought that slavery was immoral; few cared all that much. Many who did care were self-described colonizers, who wanted the country's enslaved Black population to be freed and deported to Africa. Others thought that free Blacks should continue living in the country in a degraded, second-class status. Nearly all who believed in emancipation thought it should be gradually carried out via taxpayer compensation to white slaveholders in exchange for their freeing the people they brutalized.

Almost no white American, not even Channing, wanted what Garrison's followers *demanded*: that slavery be abolished unalterably, immediately, and without compensation to enslavers and that the full political and civil rights, privileges, and immunities of citizenship be awarded to Black freedpeople at the same status as whites. The idea was so radical that Garrison was mocked and reviled for his fanciful and fanatical dreams.

To many white people, abolition meant the death of the United States. Any attempt at nationwide abolition would lead to states like South Carolina seceding from the Union, potentially causing a civil war. Garrison openly embraced the possibility. Despite being an avowed pacifist, Garrison proclaimed that the United States should pursue abolition no matter what the secessionists would do, even if the country broke apart. In the alternative, Garrison proposed that the abolitionists should themselves secede.

For many white people, abolition also meant violence. The mere idea of Black freedom evoked images of the Haitian Revolution, where thousands of white families were killed or exiled by Black ex-slaves who were in the process of liberating themselves. White Americans couldn't seem to draw the obvious parallels between the Haitian Revolution and the American Revolution, where terrible acts of violence also took place. Fearing that any actions that gave Black people the hope of freedom could lead to potential rebellions, many white people roundly denounced abolitionists as agitators who desired mass bloodshed.

Most abolitionists desired a peaceful (but immediate) end to slavery. Many abolitionists, notwithstanding Garrison, believed the United States should hold together. But that didn't change the reputation that abolitionists had in the country. All abolitionists were effectively branded as disunionists and terrorists. To be an abolitionist was to incur the wrath, scorn, and fear of white society.

Sumner knew this was wrong. He knew from his father that the Haitian Revolution very much resembled the American Revolution and that his grandfather's role in fighting for white freedom in America was very similar to what Haitian ex-slaves had done in their own country. He also knew that men like his father could be abolitionists but *not* Garrisonian disunionists. As a young man, Sumner watched as his father quietly served the Garrisonians, in small but important ways, even if he wasn't one of them.

* * *

On October 21, 1835, Sheriff Sumner tried to quell a mob of a thousand white Bostonians who stormed the offices of the Massachusetts Anti-Slavery Society, an organization founded by Garrison. The mob tore down an antislavery banner, smashed the window in the office door, threw a projectile into the meeting room, lobbed hoots and howls at the people inside, and shoved a few attendees. They grabbed Garrison, dragged him out into the open, wrapped a rope around his neck, and nearly tarred and feathered him before he was rescued by city officials. Garrison, who believed in nonviolence, calmly permitted the mob to seize him without fighting back. "Never," an onlooker reported, "have I seen him in better spirits."

By sheer force of will, Sheriff Sumner and a few deputies managed to save Garrison's life, notwithstanding Garrison's lack of effort to save his own. After some time recovering, he paid a visit to Charles Sumner's home to thank his father. "The Sumners were, as usual, quite polite and chatty," Garrison wrote to his wife afterward. "They . . . declared that I was too good a man to be mobbed."[13]

It is unclear whether Charles Sumner was at his family's home when Garrison visited in the fall of 1835. But in early 1836, Sumner's life began to intersect indirectly with Garrison's via another man, who would become one of Garrison's most loyal disciples: Wendell Phillips. A tall, athletic, good-looking Boston Brahmin whose father had previously served as mayor of the city, Phillips had predictably despised abolitionism. As a young boy in the Boston Latin School, he had even bullied his classmate Sumner for being from the Black part of town. Over the years, as they attended college and law school together, Phillips mellowed and eventually befriended Sumner.

On one stormy morning, Phillips and Sumner were scheduled for a carriage ride to court an eligible girl. Sumner, at the last minute, canceled. This left Phillips alone with Ann Terry Greene, a wealthy young heiress who had been inspired by Garrison to join the abolitionist movement. She was once described as "the aurora borealis in human form—the cleverest, loveliest girl," despite being "a rabid Abolitionist." On the ride with Miss Greene, Phillips fell in love. She taught this blue-blooded white man about the evils of slavery and the necessity of joining the movement. While courting her, Phillips visited Greene's home and coincidentally met Garrison there. The ferocity of Garrison's beliefs blew Phillips away and changed his life. He quit his law practice, married Greene, converted to the cause, and joined forces with Garrison.[14]

For the next few years, Phillips would try to pull Sumner into the Garrisonian movement. But Sumner would go only so far. In addition to being turned off by Garrison's rhetoric, he couldn't come to terms with Garrison's scorching contempt for the Constitution. Despite the soaring ideals of liberty and equality in the Declaration of Independence, the Founding Fathers wrote the Constitution to protect slavery in the states where it existed. To Garrison and his followers, this was proof that the Constitution was "dripping . . . with human blood."

Sumner couldn't shake his affection for the Constitution, which had established one of the first nations in the history of the world based on the written law of a single democratic text. "In my view, every constitutional effort ought to be made to restrain and abolish slavery," he explained to a friend. "In this I am quite in earnest; but I am disturbed not a little by those who attack the Constitution and Union." Referring to the *Liberator*, Sumner told someone else, "I have been openly opposed to the doctrines on the Union & the Constitution which [the paper] has advocated for several years."

Perhaps for this reason, Garrisonian abolitionists tried to draw Sumner into their fold by using the Constitution as their carrot. In February 1837, he was invited to give a lecture on constitutional law to a Black audience. He eagerly agreed. Walking through the narrow, windy cobblestone streets of his neighborhood, he needed only take around three hundred steps to get from his family's house to the Abiel Smith School. At this all-Black school, now a museum, Sumner methodically taught each provision of the Constitution with an eye toward being simple and clear. Yet his notes were also acutely tone-deaf, delineating the various rights Americans enjoyed without acknowledging how rarely those rights were applied in practice to his Black audience members.

While clearly naïve, Sumner was making a genuine effort to engage with the Black community of his upbringing. He showed up to this small lecture room dressed in his best attire, as if he were speaking to the wealthiest white audience in Boston. Somebody asked him why he had taken so much care to dress before an African American audience. "If I would teach them to respect themselves, I must myself respect them," he replied.[15]

To learn more about his neighbors, Sumner read Lydia Maria Child's *An Appeal in Favor of That Class of Americans Called Africans*, the first antislavery book in the United States written by a white person. Influenced by David Walker's *Appeal*, Child exposed both the brutality of slavery in the South and the inhumane experiences to which Black Bostonians were being subjected. "In Boston, we continually meet colored people in the streets," she noted. "They generally appear neat and respectable." Yet Black Bostonians were often assaulted on street corners and denied housing, jobs, and education for no reason other than being "children of the same Heavenly Father, who careth alike for all."

Sumner was so emotionally moved by Child's book that he told her, nearly two decades later, that it was among the most influential works of his life. As he walked the streets of Black Boston, he continued to reflect on the privileges of being a white man, whose life contrasted sharply with the daily struggles his neighbors experienced. "We are becoming abolitionists at the North fast," Sumner explained to a friend. "The riots, the attempts to abridge the freedom of discussion . . . the conduct of the South generally have caused many to think favorably of immediate emancipation who never before inclined to it."

The next step on Sumner's intellectual journey took place a few months after the Smith School lecture, in the fall of 1837, when he decided to cross the pond and explore Europe.[16]

* * *

SUMNER'S MENTORS THOUGHT it was ludicrous that he wanted to go to Europe. "You will come home with a cane, moustaches and an additional stock of vanity," the president of Harvard, Josiah Quincy, warned the alumnus upon learning of his plans. Sumner had neither the time nor the funds to travel. Abandoning his clients for a European rendezvous would be a disaster for his already flailing legal practice. And despite saving as much as he could, he still had to borrow three thousand dollars from three men (including Story) to finance the adventure. Many friends and mentors, including Sumner's aging father, thought the expensive trip harebrained and brash.

But Sumner was adamant. Since boyhood, he had fantasized about visiting the places of antiquity he loved. At ten years old, he had taught himself some Latin to impress his father. At fourteen, he had listed in his diary eighty-six pages' worth of major events in English history. Through college and law school, he had read classical and modern literature from France, Italy, England, and elsewhere. "The thought of Europe fills me with the most tumultuous emotions—there, it seems, my heart is garnered up," he told his friend Francis Lieber.[17]

Sumner believed his trip would be educational in nature, a kind of nineteenth-century study abroad experience. "The knowledge derived from such a tour, I regard as a kind of *intellectual capital*," he told Judge Story. "I go for purposes of education, and to gratify longings which prey upon my mind and time. . . . I make a present sacrifice for a future gain; that I shall return with increased abilities for doing good, and acting well my part in life," he wrote in his travel diary.

To this end, Sumner asked community elders like Judge Story and Josiah Quincy to write letters on his behalf addressed to respected Europeans, encouraging them to meet with the young scholar. After arriving in Europe, he continued to write home to seek more letters, even somehow managing to obtain one from the Kentucky senator Henry Clay—who, despite having never met Sumner, called him "a young gentleman of fine talents, high promise, and good connections."

With letters in hand, the twenty-six-year-old embarked on his grand adventure at New York Harbor on December 8, 1837. "May God grant that I may return from Europe with increased knowledge and added capacity for usefulness," he told Judge Story ahead of his departure. "If I do not, then, indeed, shall I have travelled in vain." Writing to a friend, Sumner explained the plan for his trip: "I shall aim to see *society* in all its forms which are accessible to me; to see men of all characters; to observe institutions & laws; to go circuits & attend terms & parliaments; & then come home and be happy."[18]

* * *

SUMNER'S FIRST STOP was France. "Houses were older than my country," he wrote excitedly to one friend upon his arrival in Paris. He was quickly mortified to discover that he could barely speak French, despite having studied the language in college. "I shall renounce every thing until I learn to speak French," he declared to a friend back home. Rather than explore the country as a normal tourist would, Sumner spent his first two months as a social recluse on the Left Bank, practicing French with two tutors whom he had hired. He also attended lectures at local universities, listening silently to French professors as he tried to understand them. "I generally hear two or three lectures of an hour or more each before breakfast," Sumner wrote to Judge Story. In a letter to Professor Greenleaf, he estimated having attended "one hundred and fifty or two hundred lectures in all branches of jurisprudence (droit), belles-lettres, and philosophy."[19]

Sumner expected to learn French and perhaps the subject matters being taught. But he learned something unexpected, too. At one of his first lectures, in an experience mirrored a century later by James Baldwin's formative travels in France, Sumner observed relationships among Blacks and whites that were at once startling and eye-opening for the young American. He saw Black students attending classes side by side with white students.

Describing the Black classmates in his diary, Sumner noted that they "dressed quite *á la mode*, and having the easy, jaunty air of young men of fashion, who were well received by their fellow-students." Sumner was shocked to see that "their color seemed to be no objection" to the white students. "I was glad to see this, though, with American impressions, it seemed very strange," he confessed. "It must be, then, that the distance between free blacks and whites among us is derived from education, and does not exist in the nature of things."[20]

Growing up, Sumner lived near a Black school and saw Black schoolchildren getting an education. Recently, he had even delivered a lecture at that school, on constitutional law, to an adult Black audience. But he had never seen Black students attending a white educational institution. Neither had he ever seen Black students sitting side by side with white ones, the two learning the same subjects *together*.

There, in France, far removed from the system of racial apartheid in his own country, Sumner grasped the possibility of a better world. He finally perceived how cruel and stupid American racial segregation really was. "The prejudice of color," he later noted, "is peculiar to our country." When he came home, he would champion integration with unprecedented clarity, grounded in the conviction that Blacks and whites should share the same public spaces, just as they did in France.[21]

After two months of study, Sumner delivered the letters of introduction he had brought with him to the Old World. Attending parties and soirees, wining and dining with the French elite, he became much beloved. Those he met were impressed by this young American who seemed so culturally refined and spoke French so well. To Frenchmen, America was an irrelevant backwater—hardly on the map. Sumner told friends that well-educated Parisians asked him "if the people of Massachusetts spoke English," and one "very intelligent" gentleman "asked me, with the greatest gravity, if the aristocratic families among us were not descended from Montezuma & the Mexican Emperors!" He was humbled rather than offended by their ignorance of America. "Since I have been here, I have felt my insignificance," he told Professor Greenleaf. "It is a good lesson."[22]

Those who did know about America asked Sumner about slavery. Four decades earlier, French revolutionaries had abolished slavery in all French colonies and "decreed that all men, without distinction of color . . . are French citizens, and entitled to the enjoyment of all the rights secured by the Constitution." While Napoléon reintroduced some forms of slavery after seizing power, an egalitarian spirit still animated Paris. Frenchmen often asked Sumner to explain how Americans could hold people in cruel bondage. One French historian, Jean Sismondi, expressed to Sumner astonishment "that our country will not take a lesson from the ample page of the past & eradicate slavery, as the civilized parts of Europe have done." The more conversations Sumner had, the more he rethought his role as a citizen of a country that protected the institution of slavery.[23]

* * *

WHEN SUMNER LEFT France for the United Kingdom, he took his questions about social reform with him. Arriving in England at the end of May 1838, he first introduced himself to members of the English bar and of several prominent gentlemen's clubs. These Englishmen found the young tourist delightful and fascinating. Chatty and full of stories to tell, Sumner found himself being invited to nearly everything. "He was wondrously popular, almost like a meteor passing through the country," an English lady recounted forty years later. "Young, agreeable, full of information and animation, he enchanted every one." Another Englishman recalled the young Sumner's "legal attainments, his scholarship, his extensive knowledge of English literature, his genial and unaffected manners, but above all the enthusiasm and simplicity of his character." These attributes, he remembered, "opened to him at once not only the doors but the hearts of a large circle of persons eminent in this country."[24]

As Sumner spent the year mingling with British elites, he privately questioned the system of aristocracy he was enjoying. Admitting that English society was "better educated, more refined, and more civilized than what is called society in our country," he asserted in one letter that "the true pride of America is in her middle and poorer classes, in their general health and happiness, and freedom from poverty, in their facilities for being educated, and in the opportunities to them of rising in the scale there." Disturbed by how in England "wealth flaunts by the side of the most squalid poverty," he praised "the health, education, happiness, & freedom from poverty of the humbler classes" in America. He was so troubled by the English aristocracy's desire "for a round of pleasure, of balls, & of rides" that he longed "for the enjoyment of the affections, & the doing good."[25]

When Sumner wrote letters home sharing his reflections, his teachers worried about the young man's emerging interest in social reform. "See *quite through* the jacobism & radicalism & atheism of modern Europe, & all its other *isms*," Professor Greenleaf pleaded with his former student, "& come home a sound & liberal conservative, as God made you." Judge Story urged Sumner to tell his "conservative Friends we are not all Demagogues, or mad conceited Democrats. We dread Radicalism quite as much as they do." A friend joked that Greenleaf was "very much afraid you will become too *principled* and too *unprecedented*."[26]

Their fears were not misplaced. Though spending time with people across the spectrum—"whigs, tories, radicals, judges, literary men of all grades and classes, scientific, professional men"—Sumner admitted to Story that he had found himself identifying as a "moderate Radical." Like classical liberals, radicals believed in liberty as a premier political value: people should generally be able to do as they please without government interference.

But radicals also put more weight on another political value: *equality*. Recognizing the misery endured by the poor, radicals wanted to break aristocracies and monarchies and create a world where nearly everyone could work for wages, own their own property, and participate in elections. In 1830s England, radicalism was a bold, visionary ideal stuck on the edges of the political spectrum in a world where only wealthy white landholders could vote. In France, radicalism had swept the country during the Revolution but had fallen into decline when monarchic rule was reestablished.[27]

Sumner, from now and until his final days, would identify as a radical. "You will not believe me influenced by any mad democratic tendencies," he reassured Story while in London. But he confessed that his experience in England had convinced him that "representation should be equalized" in a country where wealthy lords had more voting power than anyone else. He further thought that "the law of primogeniture" should be abolished in order "to break the aristocracy, to reduce estates, and to divide them." "I have always enjoyed the refinement of the best society," he recalled a few years later. "But I have never sat in the palaces of England, without being pained by the inequality of which the inordinate luxury was a token." France, meanwhile, had opened Sumner's eyes to the urgency of ending slavery. "My intercourse with men in Europe convinces me," he wrote to another friend, "of the necessity of . . . abolishing slavery."[28]

Sumner didn't reveal his radicalism to the largely conservative British aristocrats who were so gracious to welcome this young, sprightly American into their high society. "I have been received with a kindness, hospitality, and distinction of which I truly felt my unworthiness," Sumner blushed in a letter to a friend. "I am not what my hosts & English friends suppose me to be. Who am I?—A poor lawyer, hardly recognized at home, or if recognized, only received as a young man." Traveling through the United Kingdom, Sumner became a celebrity. While fraternizing with wealthy aristocrats, powerful politicians, and literary talents—including William Wordsworth, Mary and Percy Shelley, and Thomas Carlyle—he received more flattering attention than any other visitor from the United States of the time.[29]

* * *

AFTER A BRIEF stop in Paris, Sumner's journey continued in Italy in May 1839. Here, he saw another sight that impressed upon him the possibility of a better world. While touring a Catholic monastery in the Italian countryside, Sumner met an Ethiopian monk who served side by side with the Italian monks at the convent. "To one, accustomed to the prejudices of color which prevail in America," Sumner later explained, "it was beautiful to witness the freedom, gentleness & equality with which he mingled with his brethren." He was disturbed to think that churches back home in Boston typically excluded Blacks or forced them to sit in separate pews, denying them the equal "participation in the privileges of worshipping the common God."

Exhausted from the social revelry of the past year, he spent most of his time in Italy in intense self-study. Every day in Rome he followed a rigid schedule: "Rose at 6 ½ o'clk, threw myself on my sofa, with a little round table near well-covered with books,—read undisturbed till about 10, when the servant brought on a tray my breakfast . . . the breakfast was concluded without quitting the sofa—rang the bill, & my table was put to rights, & my reading went on—often till 5 & 6 o'clock in the evening, without my once raising from the sofa." After having spent the day reading Italian and Latin works, he would usually go for a walk and dinner at night.[30]

Sumner's relentless pursuit of knowledge inspired a similar interest in art. Having never taken art lessons and unfamiliar with art history and criticism, he desperately wanted to improve his eye for beauty. He visited museums, read books on art history and criticism, and met many Italy-based artists. As he did so, he improved, but he could never develop the skill of discernment that other art critics seemed to have for high art. "The world of art, as art purely, was to him always a half-opened, if not a locked world," recalled Judge Story's son William, who became a sculptor. "He longed to enter into it, and feel it as an artist does; but the keys were never given to him."[31]

Thomas Crawford, a poor American sculptor who lived in Rome, offered to take Sumner on a tour of the Vatican. The two became fast friends, and Sumner took an interest in Crawford's art. At the time, Crawford was working on a sculpture of Orpheus, a figure from Greek mythology—but he couldn't find a buyer. "He is poor & I feel anxious to do something for him," Sumner wrote to William Story. "If I could convince any body to order this large piece he is now engaged upon, *his fortune would be made.*" Writing dozens of letters to friends in Boston and beyond, Sumner spread the word about Crawford's potential as an artist. Eventually, through his efforts, Crawford found a purchaser—the Boston Athenaeum, one of the country's oldest libraries—and his career catapulted. Decades later, with Sumner's help, Crawford designed his most famous work, the *Statue of Freedom*, the monumental (twenty-foot-tall) figure of a woman representing liberty that stands atop the U.S. Capitol Dome to this day.[32]

* * *

WHILE CHARLES SUMNER frolicked through Europe, Sheriff Sumner fell ill. Within just a few weeks, the sheriff succumbed, dying at the age of sixty-three on April 24, 1839. He would be remembered by Bostonians as a polite, honorable man who treated everyone with respect and was extremely mindful of his duties. But as a father, he was cold and imposing. Grave in tone and rarely known to smile, the sheriff had an especially distant relationship with his eldest son, Charles.

As soon as he learned about his father's death while in Rome, Charles wrote to his friend and law partner George Hillard. "[It is] an event which has caused me many painful emotions," he said. "Not the less painful because beyond the reach of ordinary sympathy. To you, who so well understand my situation, I need say nothing." Another close friend said in his condolence letter, "That you are not as deeply afflicted by his death as you would have been if he had been *like a father* to you I cannot suppose."

Charles almost never talked about his father again. Neither did he leave behind evidence of much of their relationship: he or his executors probably destroyed any letters that discussed his father. Whatever life was like inside the Sumner house, it was not happy for him. Once, Sumner was asked to write about his family history. He described his father as "a person of literary taste & knowledge, of remarkable independence & sterling integrity." That was pretty much all he said.

Nonetheless, Sumner would quote from his father's poems, fondly recount his father's stories of Haiti, and keep in touch with his father's friends. Sumner never ceased to respect his father's commitment to justice and his willingness to endure social exclusion. He also often repeated his father's favorite saying, which became, in many ways, the motto of Sumner's life:

"The duties of life are more than life."[33]

CHAPTER 5

SUMNER OUGHT TO HAVE BEEN A WOMAN

TRANGE CONTRAST AWAITS ME!" CHARLES SUMNER WROTE TO Judge Story shortly before his return in May 1840. "To quit these iris-colored visions for the stern realities of American life! To throw aside the dreamy morning-gown and slippers, and pull on the boots of hard work! Let it come! I am content. But who will employ me?"

As it turned out, everybody would employ him. Word spread among Boston's Brahmin elite that Sumner had met spectacular social success in Europe, wining and dining with aristocrats across Britain, France, Italy, and elsewhere. Nothing excited Boston elite more. "Boston takes a sort of pride in you," one of Sumner's friends alerted him. "You will be caressed, fêted, and feasted. You will be the lion of the season."[1]

A lion he was. As soon as he returned to his fatherless home on the North Slope of Beacon Hill, Sumner received an invitation to the best mansion on the other slope. Eagerly, he marched uphill, to the top of his cobblestone street, circled around the majestic State House with its gleaming copper dome, and went down to the very first house on Park Street. Constructed atop the ruins of a dismantled almshouse for the poor, the Park Street mansion had been home to some of Boston's wealthiest men and had even hosted the French general Marquis de Lafayette when he visited the city. Now it belonged to George Ticknor, a retired Harvard professor who had taught Sumner when he was in college. Welcoming Sumner inside, Ticknor walked his guest past a magnificent portrait of Sir Walter Scott into his private library, one of the largest on the Eastern Seaboard. In the confines of this gorgeous room with its overflowing shelves of rare books, Ticknor asked Sumner to tell him about every aristocrat he had met in Europe. Having spent some years on the Continent himself,

Ticknor wanted names, stories, locations, and more. Night after night, Sumner returned to Ticknor's mansion, dutifully informing him about all his adventures over the past few years.

Professor Ticknor was amazed by his former student, for he saw himself in Sumner. The grandson of a farmer and son of a grocer, Ticknor had earned the admiration of Boston's elite through the sheer power of his mind and his wonderful social graces. After becoming a professor of languages at Harvard, he had married a Brahmin heiress who inherited the modern-day equivalent of roughly two million dollars. Despite his humble origins, he now operated as the self-appointed guardian of the Boston aristocracy, along with his wife, who "ruled as a social queen," according to one of her friends. The Ticknors were so impressed with Sumner that they decided to train him to join Boston's high society.[2]

The fact that Boston had a working aristocracy startled Europeans who visited the city. When Alexis de Tocqueville explored Boston, his companion Gustave de Beaumont observed "a superior class with the tone and manners of European society." Beaumont said it was a "strange anomaly" to see a high social caste in "the midst of a republican society founded on the principle of absolute equality." Tocqueville himself said Boston's elite acted "almost exactly like the upper classes of Europe."

Boston society was described by a contemporary as a "two-year-old aristocracy," for its wealth had arisen only over the past two generations or so. The genesis of their wealth was textile manufacturing, which came to New England in 1790. Loyal to their Puritan and revolutionary heritage, Boston manufacturers patronized the city's religious and scholarly society, leading to many mixed marriages and creating a small, tight-knit, incestuous web of ministers, professors, novelists, lawyers, merchants, businessmen, poets, and politicians. "It's quite the fashion for our rich girls to buy themselves a professor," one contemporary journalist explained.

These patrician Boston families saw themselves as custodians for American intellectual life. With mentors like Professor Ticknor and Judge Story, Sumner seemed eligible to join their ranks. "A life of happiness, distinction, and success is before you," one of his friends predicted. "Eminently fortunate you have been, and eminently fortunate you are destined to be."[3]

* * *

DURING HIS TIME in England, Sumner had felt uneasy about his presence among aristocrats while he saw poverty and oppression on the streets.

Back home in Boston, he must have felt similarly uncomfortable as he left the Black neighborhood of his birth every day to go to work on Court Street, or to attend dinners at the Ticknor mansion on Park Street.

For several years, Sumner tried to forget his discomfort while enjoying lavish meals with the Ticknors and other Brahmin families. He must have ogled the bowls of hot stewed oysters, the poultry platters, and the fresh cakes with icing that were commonly served at these homes by teams of Black waiters. Thanks to these dinners, Sumner not only ate well but became friendly with many of Boston's leading men. These men brought Sumner business. During his first year back home, he was hired to serve on no fewer than thirty litigation matters involving Boston mercantile interests and won most of them.[4]

"Business calls," he told a friend. "I charged one client yesterday, as *part* of my fee in one case, six hundred dollars"—the equivalent of more than twenty thousand dollars today. Sumner worked hard to please his wealthy clients and co-counsels. "Pocket that, ye croakers!" he boasted to a friend. "Who said that Europe would spoil me for office-work." His law partner, George Hillard, was impressed by his new work ethic. "Sumner is behaving like a very good boy," Hillard observed. "Nailed to his desk like a bad cent to a grocer's counter."[5]

Hillard and other friends began calling Sumner "Don Carlos," for he looked stronger, manlier, and far better dressed at the age of twenty-nine than he had before his trip to Europe. "His appearance had been very materially improved under the hands of a London tailor," one friend beamed. "He had lost, too, some of the leanness and lankness of face and figure which he carried through his school and college days."[6]

Every weekend, Sumner and Hillard got together with some friends for what was ostensibly a reading group dubbed the "Five of Clubs." Rather than read, Sumner would tell stories about Europe. On one Sunday, Hillard recalled Sumner speaking "in one continuous flow" about his trip for seven hours straight. He joked that hearing Sumner's nonstop stories was "like being under Niagara," as the traveler gushed on and on. "Sumner is full of life and soul and anecdote," one of the other friends in the group, Henry Longfellow, wrote in his diary. "Only a little too much Anglomania about him, which will wear off."[7]

Sumner had met Longfellow while both were teaching at Harvard, for Longfellow had succeeded Ticknor as a languages professor there. He adored Longfellow, a good-humored romantic who seemed to put him at ease, helping him to forget the perils of the world that bothered him. "He cares not at all for politics or statistics, for the Syrian question, or the disasters of Afghanistan," Sumner said of Longfellow. "But to him the magnificent world of literature and Nature is open."

Almost every weekend after his return, Sumner would trek down Beacon Hill, cross the Charles River, and head to the Cambridge suburbs to stay with Longfellow. By some marvelous stroke of luck, Longfellow had rented an available apartment inside the Craigie House, a yellow mansion that had hosted General Washington while his troops, including Job Sumner, were in the encampment at Harvard during the Revolution. (Longfellow later purchased the house.) Here, in what Sumner fondly called "the headquarters of our great chief," Longfellow and Sumner lazily read poetry to each other, shared nostalgic travel stories of Europe, and discussed their aspirations and searches for love.

When a shower was installed in the Craigie House, an exciting innovation that was rarely seen in private homes at the time, Sumner eagerly tried it out. Standing nude under the showerhead, ready to pull the string to release the water, he said to Longfellow, "This is a kind of Paradise." Longfellow laughed, responding, "And you a kind of Adam!" As the droplets began descending, Sumner said playfully, "With all my ribs!"[8]

*　*　*

MORE THAN HIS career, his aspirations, and perhaps even his family and himself, Sumner loved Longfellow and his other friends. They were his constant source of emotional support, affirmation, and a cure for boredom, for he realized that he had no passion for the commercial work he did at Professor Ticknor and Judge Story's encouragement. When Story asked Sumner to employ his son William as an apprentice, he obliged. Rather than put William to work, he rambled endlessly to William, using him as a distraction from his work. "He would talk to me by the hour of the great jurists, and their lives, and habits of thought . . . of poetry and general literature and authors," William Story said of his boss. "After the flush of those exciting days abroad, his office and daily occupations seemed dull and gray."[9]

Forgetting his clients, Sumner volunteered himself to anyone who needed assistance doing legal research, editing articles, locating books, and finding publishers for their work. His friend Francis Lieber took special advantage of Sumner's time. A Prussian-born academic who came to the United States and befriended Judge Story, Lieber, a law professor and political scientist, became one of Sumner's most intense correspondents.

They wrote hundreds of letters to each other over the years, especially after Lieber moved to South Carolina for a teaching position. Sumner devoted himself to advancing Lieber's academic career, particularly by sending him books and papers that weren't readily available in the South.

Sumner also freely offered himself to anyone from Europe who needed a Boston tour guide, as if he had all the free time in the world. When Charles Dickens came in January 1842, Sumner eagerly took him around for weeks. A celebrity for his beloved English novels and short stories, Dickens was just shy of thirty, a year younger than Sumner. Sumner introduced him to the Ticknors and other elites, reminding him of people's names, keeping his calendar, and ensuring that his days were well spent. "Sumner is of great service to me," Dickens wrote. "He is a most delightful person," Sumner told Judge Story. "Overflowing with genius, cordiality & kindness."[10]

Sumner brought Longfellow along on his city tours with Dickens, in a clever bid to bolster his young poet friend's career. Together, the trio embarked on a midnight oyster crawl at the Boston Wharf, attended church services, and hiked for ten miles to Bunker Hill, the Revolutionary War site where Sumner's grandfather had fought. When Longfellow later traveled to England, Dickens returned the favor by taking him around London, which helped to establish Longfellow's literary reputation. Sumner also assiduously pitched Longfellow's poems to publishers in both Britain and the United States. He was so adept at wooing publishers that he helped establish Longfellow as one of America's leading poets.

Dickens was so touched by Sumner's hospitality that he told many friends to rely on him in their travels. Sumner became known as the "Encyclopedia of Boston" for his knowledge of the city, its people, and its history. As more European aristocrats came to Boston, they asked Sumner to be their guide. When Lord Ashburton visited Boston while negotiating the Webster-Ashburton Treaty (settling some of the boundaries between the United States and Canada), Sumner gave him a tour. And when Lord Morpeth arrived, Sumner suspended almost all legal business for several weeks to entertain him. "Charles Sumner's friends are like other men's brothers," Francis Lieber said of Sumner's generosity.

Sumner wasn't just being generous with his time out of the kindness of his heart. He was also looking for distractions, because he began to hate his commercial work. "Though I earn my daily bread, I lay up none of the bread of life," he confessed to Lieber. "My mind, soul, heart, are not improved or invigorated by the practice of my profession; by overhauling papers, old letters, and sifting accounts in order to see if there be any thing on which to plant an action." After the remarkably successful year of 1841, Sumner appeared in only three circuit cases in 1842. By 1843, that was down to two. By 1844, it was down to one. When Judge Story fell ill in 1843, he asked Sumner to teach classes at the law school. But the salary for teaching part-time wasn't very high.

In 1843, Sumner's friend the Supreme Court reporter Richard Peters had retired. Hoping the position might be ideal for him, Sumner sought Judge Story's help to be appointed as Peters's successor. But Story's illness prevented him from lobbying for the appointment in Washington. On top of this, Sumner tried to get appointed as a clerk in the State Department, enlisting the help of a friend who had influence with the Polk administration. That failed to materialize, too.[11]

Despite continuing to publish articles and teach at the law school, Sumner could not focus on any remunerative work. People began calling him "the briefless barrister," a learned lawyer with no cases. As his career plummeted, his debts rose. His mother, Relief Sumner, eventually paid off his European travel debts. By 1843, at the age of thirty-two, Sumner could think only of the irony of his situation: he enjoyed the company of Boston elite; remained famous among aristocrats in Europe; attended dinners at the Ticknor house, where General Lafayette used to live; and spent the weekends at Longfellow's, where Washington had slept. Yet he was a broke bachelor living in his mother's house on the North Slope of Beacon Hill.[12]

* * *

WHILE SUMNER'S CAREER was tanking, another, deeper suffering ripped at his heart. In 1837, he had met a man: Samuel Gridley Howe, a muscular, agile man with sharp features, flowing black hair, and intense blue eyes. Howe was ten years older than Sumner and very different in personality. Howe didn't care much for books or society, and his favorite hobbies were horseback riding and sword fighting. Born to a prim family, Howe rebelled after getting his medical degree by fleeing the country to go to Europe in search of adventure—*real* adventure, unlike Sumner's wining and dining with aristocrats. Donning a Greek uniform, he served as a part-time army doctor and part-time warrior in the Greek Revolution, savoring every mighty moment fighting Turks, foraging grubs, and sawing off limbs during the gory war. By the time he was done, he looked like "an Arab in figure and in horsemanship," according to a contemporary.

After his exciting European escapade, Howe came to Boston to start a normal life. Inspired by the moral reformers he met in Europe, he took over a school for the blind (the Perkins Institute), teaching young women like Laura Bridgman, who could not see, hear, or speak, how to communicate. But he was always longing for new adventures, constantly following the news of European revolutions. "I am a poor devil of a Chevalier!" he liked to say, believing his destiny lay on the fields of glory.[13]

Sumner met Howe shortly before his own European trip, when a riot broke out on Broad Street near the Long Wharf. Having seen his father quell riots, Sumner foolishly plunged into the crowd and tried to stop the violence. He was hit by a projectile and might have gotten himself killed, if not for the chivalrous Howe, who heroically jumped into the fight to save Sumner, a stranger. Awed by Howe's courage, Sumner befriended this guardian angel and was even more impressed to learn that he was a social reformer.[14]

Sumner and Howe reconnected after Sumner's return from Europe. Fast friends, they talked often about their values and aspirations. Sumner marveled at Howe's passion for helping the blind and his past life as a Greek revolutionary. Howe, in turn, was attracted to Sumner's inner spirit. He believed Sumner was too good a man to spend his life as a commercial litigator. A reformer at heart, Howe pushed Sumner to use his career to serve humankind.

Both men bonded over their sorry condition as lonely bachelors. They sometimes wandered aimlessly through Boston together on a carriage, chatting about the women they passed by on the streets, hoping one would finally catch their eye. They sometimes courted women together, telling jokes to each other about the ladies after they had left. They both felt incredible pressure to get married, a pressure they internalized. When urged by one older lady to settle down, Sumner replied defensively, "I am married to Europa." To his closest friends, however, he confessed his deep desire for matrimony. "I am very much alone, and altogether a poor creature," he admitted in one letter. Howe felt the exact same pit of loneliness and longing as Sumner. He once remarked to his best friend, "You, you dog, are *malgré moi* my *alter ego!*"[15]

As the two men grew closer, they became inseparable, so much so that Bostonians noticed. The "wags of Boston" called the two friends "the 'Dioscuri, or Immortal Twins,' like Pleasure and Pain," according to their friend Cornelius Felton. "If you see one, the other is sure to be near," he noted. Sumner freely admitted that he was "with Howe a great deal," and he started to bring Howe along to the Five of Clubs reading group. Sometimes, Howe would pop into Sumner's law office and surprise him. Other times, they would make plans. They even started taking singing lessons together. (Sumner proved to be atrocious at singing.)

During one summer, Sumner and Howe were spending time once or twice a week together. "Bachelors both," Sumner explained to a friend, "we drive and ride together—pass our evenings far into the watches of the night in free and warm communion." On these evenings, Sumner would gallivant with Howe on horseback into the countryside for hours. When they returned at night, they would find a pub, order strawberries and cream, and chat about "remembered things, experiences, and hopes of all sorts."

Retiring to Howe's apartment in South Boston, Sumner would undress, unstrapping his buttons and waistband. Then he would step into Howe's red slippers and, holding a glass of his favorite wine, Orvieto, sit in Howe's easy chair, while Howe intently stared into what he called Sumner's "sweet smile on his lips." When it was time to sleep, the men would get into their separate beds, in two rooms separated by a door left ajar, and spend all night talking about their dreams, aspirations, and their long, aching search for women to love.

"He is quite in love with Howe," Sumner's law partner, George Hillard, jested, ". . . and spends so much time with him that I begin to feel the shooting pains of jealousy."[16]

* * *

JEALOUSY HIT SUMNER, too. In the summer of 1841, Howe met Julia Ward, a beautiful, wealthy, literary twenty-two-year-old from New York. Sumner and Longfellow had arranged the match. They brought Julia, whose older brother, Sam, was one of Sumner's friends, to Howe's school for the blind while she was in Boston. There, she watched Howe ride up on a black horse as if he were a knight. Her heart fluttered. For months, Howe wooed this girl nearly half his age with flirtatious notes that emphasized his manliness, telling her that she was "the captive of his bow and spear" who would be kept "prisoner in [his] arms." Julia was smitten from the start.[17]

Initially, Sumner was thrilled. "Howe is more restless, if possible than you or I," he told Longfellow. "How it would delight me to see his perturbed spirit find repose at last on such a bosom!" But thrill turned to dread as their courtship became serious. "I think, however, he will be married very soon," he said. "What then will become of me? It is a dreary world to travel in alone." When Howe proposed to Julia, Sumner wrote the bride-to-be and her brother with earnest enthusiasm. "A truer heart was never offered to woman. I know the depth, strength, and constancy of his affections," Sumner reassured Julia. Yet he also feared his own lonely fate. "I feel sometimes that I am about to lose a dear friend," he admitted to Julia's brother, Sam.[18]

Sumner was stricken with grief after the couple's engagement. "Where are you?" he wrote Howe. "I never see you; I never expect to see you more. Like two ships that have sailed together over many seas, we are at last parting company; Western breezes are floating you away to Happy Isles, while I, weltering on stagnant waters, can scarcely discern your pennan far off against the sky." Sumner felt that he was being left out to dry. "I sit alone in my office, finding as much comfort as possible in books," he told Howe. Perhaps even more painfully, Sumner served as Howe's best man at their wedding. When the Howes went to Europe for a honeymoon, he felt fully alone. As he left with Julia, Howe felt guilty about leaving Sumner behind.[19]

Howe's guilt grew even worse when Sumner's second best friend, Henry Longfellow, got engaged to Fanny Appleton, the beautiful daughter of the textile magnate Nathan Appleton. "Howe has gone, & now you have gone," Sumner complained to Longfellow. "Nobody is left with whom I can have sweet sympathy. My days will pass away." So perturbed by Sumner's depression, Fanny decided to invite him to crash part of her honeymoon with Longfellow. Although he joined, he still felt an aching loneliness.[20]

Feeling like he had "got into paradise & left my best friend outside," Howe urged Sumner to find a woman who would fill his heart's void. It was to no avail. "I never had enjoyed the choicest experience of life—that no lips responsive to my own had ever said to me—'I love you,'" Sumner told Howe. "You cannot fathom the yawning depths of my soul," he wrote another friend. When Howe eagerly heard that Sumner finally took an interest in a woman, Sumner dispelled the rumor mournfully. "Never in my life have I been less in love than at this moment. You are much mistaken. *I am not in love.* My heart does not flutter at the mention of a single name."[21]

But Sumner *was* in love. Sumner loved *Howe*, whose name would flutter in his heart for the rest of his long, lonely life as he grappled uneasily with the fact that he shared his best friend with a wife.

* * *

THE WORD HOMOSEXUALITY did not exist in the English language at the time. Living without definition, Sumner battled with his aching loneliness, confused about who he was. He didn't understand why his friends seemed capable of falling in love while he was left in the dust. He thought something was wrong with him.

Americans did not categorize people into immutable sexual identities, such as "homosexual" or "gay," until after the work of psychologists Sigmund Freud and Havelock Ellis. Before then, no man feared being labeled a homosexual for expressing his love to another man, for such a label did not exist. Although sodomy was generally illegal and frowned upon, there was little stigma attached to most other intimate acts between men, such as holding hands, hugging at length, kissing on the face or lips, or sleeping in one another's embrace.

In this world without gayness as such, men freely enjoyed physically and emotionally intimate bonds that transcend what characterizes male-male best friendships today. Historians have labeled these relationships "romantic friendships." They developed in early adulthood, as young men sought partners to help navigate the difficult terrain of finding love, careers, and their place in society. When men married, their romantic friendships tended to wither away as the men focused on their wives. The early nineteenth century is replete with examples of romantic friendships. Most famously, Abraham Lincoln and Joshua Speed shared a bed together for nearly three years while riding circuit as young lawyers. Other examples include Alexander Hamilton and John Laurens; Nathaniel Hawthorne and Franklin Pierce; and Daniel Webster and James Bingham.[22]

Sumner enjoyed romantic friendships with Longfellow and Howe. While the latter two fell in love with women and married, Sumner did not. He never let go, clinging as tightly as he could all his life, long after romantic friendships were expected to take a back seat to men's marriages.[23]

The evidence suggests that Sumner was probably gay, insofar as a modern term means much when applied retroactively to the past. From the day Howe was married, friends were alarmed by the scale of Sumner's heartbreak. They tried to find him a wife who could heal his wounds in the wake of Howe's departure. Cornelius Felton declared that the Five of Clubs reading group was now going to be a "committee" on domestic relations solely devoted to finding Sumner a spouse. Its members kept pitching possible matches for him, including Julia's younger sister Louisa. Sumner genuinely enjoyed Louisa's company, but as soon as she bought him a birthday gift, he stopped speaking to her.[24]

All his life, Sumner resisted flirting with women, even when male friends encouraged him to try it. "He would at once desert the most blooming beauty to talk to the plainest of men," William Story recalled. "This was a constant source of amusement to us, and we used to lay wagers with the pretty girls, that with all their art they could not keep him at their side a quarter of an hour." His friends were vexed that he couldn't seem to find love, for he would openly "bewail his celibacy," according to George Hillard.[25]

Howe was perturbed that Sumner couldn't redirect his love to a woman, as he could. "You have more of love in you than any man I ever knew," he told Sumner, instructing him to "bring your affections to the right focus." But Sumner couldn't refocus himself away from Howe and toward a woman. "There is something at the bottom of my heart & on my lips always for *you*," he later explained to Howe.[26]

* * *

MOREOVER, HOWE GRAPPLED with the challenge of being in love with two people, for both Julia and Sumner tore at his heartstrings. During his honeymoon, Howe wrote frequently to Sumner rather than talk to his new wife. "You complain of your lonely lot, & seem to think your friends will lose their sympathy with you as they form new ties of love," he wrote in one letter. "But dearest Sumner, it is not so with me." He confessed that "hardly a day passes but I think of you & long to have you by my side." In letter after letter, Howe reassured Sumner. "You are my only friend—you and Julia; may I preserve you as long as I live," he said. "I love thee not less because I love her more," he promised.[27]

Julia resented how Sumner tugged at her husband's heart. "Sumner ought to have been a woman and you to have married her," she complained to him. As Julia grew older, Howe grew controlling, refusing to let her pursue the literary career of her dreams. Sumner reaffirmed Howe's attempts to keep Julia in the house. Lonely and isolated, she would spend much of her life discreetly writing poems and novels, publishing them under pseudonyms for many years until Howe finally let her be more open about her work.[28]

One of Julia's novels is especially revealing about her possible perspective on Howe and Sumner's sexuality. A few years into her marriage, she wrote a sensational story about a hermaphrodite who oscillated between loving males and females in deeply emotional and physical ways. The hermaphrodite seemed to be her impression of her husband, Howe, who oscillated between loving her and loving Sumner. She left this story behind in a four-hundred-page manuscript. Long after her death, the manuscript was discovered in a big stack of her papers bequeathed to Harvard University, and was published in 2004.[29]

Julia's book—if taken to be a commentary on her husband's sexuality—confirms that Howe and Sumner enjoyed an emotionally close, passionate, and possibly sensuous relationship. Sumner once said he had a "special intimacy" with Howe. Years later, when he was elected to the Senate, Howe informed him that he had burned many of their letters out of caution, for fear they might be seen "by unfriendly eyes" and harm Sumner's career. "It cost me something to burn a piece of paper that has been hallowed to my eye by the impress of your hand, but I do it. I have no confidant for such things—no! not one," Howe explained. Throughout his life, he regularly burned or shredded parts of his letters to and from Sumner. After his death, Julia burned even more letters exchanged between her late husband and Sumner.[30]

Even in the truncated historical record, it is clear that Sumner loved Howe, and Howe loved him. They loved each other deeply and *passionately*, whatever that might have meant or looked like to them in the mid-nineteenth century. Once, Howe wrote to Sumner to promise his eternal love, a love that would animate and complicate the rest of their lives. "In hope or fear, in fortune or adversity, in joy & in sorrow," he promised Sumner, "I am, forever will be, your affectionate Howe."[31]

* * *

No MATTER HOW much Howe insisted to Sumner that he loved him, that he wouldn't forget about him, Sumner felt isolated, broken, and abandoned by Howe's departure for a long European honeymoon. "I am all *alone,—alone.* My friends fall away from me," he wrote. "What then will become of me? It is a dreary world to travel in alone."[32]

Heartbroken and dejected, Sumner did what he always did in bouts of melancholy: turn to books. But rather than dive into literature, as he normally did, he signed up to annotate a twenty-volume set of law reports for a prestigious American publisher. The work would provide him with the compensation his dismal law practice no longer earned. Expected to complete one volume every two weeks, he anticipated finishing in ten months for a handsome salary. But the project devolved into a disaster after only two months. The constant, unrelenting, day-and-night tedious toil failed to distract Sumner from the brokenness inside him.[33]

In the summer of 1844, Sumner's despair reached a breaking point. Getting into bed on the upstairs floor of his mother's home in early June, caught with a light fever, he spent the next two months struggling to get out. Doctors diagnosed him with consumption (tuberculosis), though he showed few signs of it. When they told him he was unlikely to recover, he was not in the least disturbed.

Fancying death, staring at the ceiling for most of every night as an insomniac, hallucinating a visit from Howe on at least one occasion, Sumner spent weeks in this sorry condition. As friends visited, they were struck by how little he seemed to care if he survived. "There are so few like him upon earth," mourned Samuel Ward, Julia's brother, "that I cannot believe God really means to deprive humanity of so noble an example of all that is good and high-minded and pure."

Sumner seemed to know that his illness was mental more than physical. "I do not think . . . that they comprehended my case," he explained to his brother George, referring to the doctors who diagnosed him with tuberculosis. "I consider my disease to have been a slow, nervous fever." After a few weeks in bed, Sumner mustered the strength to step outside once a day, which he regarded as his daily accomplishment. "It has been with inexpressible delight that during my drives I have looked on the green trees, and the sky, and the beauties of Nature,—from which, for several weeks, I have been quite shut out," he told George.[34]

The breakdown of 1844 was an inflection point, but it was also part of a pattern—an aspect of Sumner's lifelong battle with depression. He once told Howe about how his "childhood & youth passed in unhappiness, such as I pray, may not be the lot of others." Some years later, when he was a controversial abolitionist whose life was in danger, Howe—a trained doctor—told Sumner's mother to buy him a pistol so that he could keep himself safe. "Oh doctor," she replied. "He would only shoot himself with it."

Sumner had little "instinctive love of life," according to a friend. He always rejected pleas from others to take caution when he became a public figure. He was often pickpocketed on the street or at train stations, which he never seemed to notice or care about, even if he did. "I never locked a door in my life, not when sleeping in the wildest place," he once claimed. Julia Ward Howe recounted how Sumner's mind was "occupied with things far away" and gave "little heed to what went on around him." Once, Sumner lost two hundred dollars while traveling on a train. He seemed to think being robbed was an inevitable aspect of life that wasn't worth preventing. "If I had million," he said afterward, "it would slip through my open fingers."[35]

While he gradually regained his will to live after the breakdown, Sumner continued to feel that his life was meaningless. His legal career had failed to take off, and his intimate friends had abandoned him (or so he felt). Even worse, he faced another heart-wrenching challenge: while he was ill, his eighteen-year-old sister Mary contracted tuberculosis. "She is fading like a flower which will never bloom again, except in Paradise," he wrote to George. "She enjoys life," he wrote to Howe, "and I often wish that I could pour into her veins the redundant health which has been wasted on one, who is ungrateful for the blessings he enjoys." Shortly after Sumner's recovery, Mary died. "Why was I spared?" he asked Howe.[36]

Sumner wished it had been *him*, and not *her*, whom God took. As he suffered his breakdown, grieved his sister's death, and regained the will to live, he came to a realization. "Let me extract from my illness a moral," he told George. "It may not be unprofitable, if it serves to . . . inspire love and attachment for my fellow-men."[37]

* * *

EFFECTIVELY ABANDONING BOTH his scholarly and commercial legal career, Sumner invested his time in the radical social reform work that had inspired him in Europe. Initially, he directed most of his attention to education. Like his father before him, he believed that common schools were the bedrock of a republican democracy. With the blessing of his friend Horace Mann, often considered the father of American public schools, Sumner ran for the Boston School Committee. Despite losing, he worked to raise money for Mann's vision of building a "normal school" in Boston—a school designed specifically for training schoolteachers. Collecting pledges, he naïvely advanced the five thousand dollars up front to the school system and assumed other donors would pay him back over time. When pledgees backed out, Sumner fell deeper into debt and grew frustrated with how little his goodwill was matched by that of others.

Howe cheered on Sumner as he found humanitarian causes to which to dedicate himself. "No matter what motives may be ascribed to you; no matter if your best friends do not duly appreciate them . . . you have secured what fate cannot take from you,—self-approval," Howe wrote to Sumner after the latter expressed hurt over the other pledgees failing to meet their promises. "I must say I envy you for what you have been *trying* to do," Howe went on. "I love you, dear Sumner, and am only vexed with you because you will not love yourself a little more."

Howe repeatedly pushed Sumner to stretch his political imagination and urged him to devote his life to serving the public good and committing to a public life. As Sumner followed his best friend's instruction, he grew healthier and happier. "Sumner's appearance was curiously metamorphosed," Julia Howe recalled. "After his recovery, he gained much in flesh. . . . He now became a man of strikingly fine presence, his great height being offset by a corresponding fullness of figure."[38]

Sumner began contributing to several social causes. Serving on a construction committee for the Boston Athenaeum, Sumner helped design the library's current building. He attended meetings of the Prison Discipline Society, which advocated for incarcerating criminals rather than inflicting corporal punishment. The thinking at the time was that prisons could contribute to a criminal's moral reformation. Sumner also attended events and wrote many letters expressing his growing interest in the abolition of slavery. And he joined the Peace Society, an organization that called for the end of war.[39]

The specter of war hung over the United States in 1845. Ten years earlier, mostly white ranchers and farmers in northern Mexico had revolted, founded the independent Republic of Texas, and sought admission into the union as a slave state. While sympathetic to the Texans, Presidents Andrew Jackson and Martin Van Buren rebuffed Texas annexation requests out of fear that admitting a new slave state would inflame national politics. But in 1844, a dark horse Democratic candidate, James Polk, ran on a platform that included annexing Texas, and won.

Sumner joined other antislavery activists, including the abolitionists Wendell Phillips and William Lloyd Garrison, in protesting Polk's effort to annex Texas. They also feared that Polk wanted to annex land from

Mexico—which, at the time, spanned from the top of modern-day California to the bottom of New Mexico. If Mexico would not sell, it was
widely speculated, Polk would start a war.

* * *

"A WAR WITH Mexico would be mean and cowardly," Sumner maintained.
It was his belief that wars of aggression to claim new land violated international law. In Europe, he had seen firsthand the destruction that war
wrought in places like France and Austria. "All his study of history," one
journalist later observed, "had impressed him with a horror of war." He
was horrified that Polk wanted to violently take western land.

For decades, Americans had believed in a kind of divine right, a Manifest Destiny, to spread their nation from sea to sea. Manifest Destiny
encompassed many fantasies—spreading Christianity to Native people,
exploring far-flung frontier lands for the simple joy of discovery, developing
the United States into a country with global legitimacy, creating new farm-
land for the everyday poor yeoman, and expanding the reach of slavery for
the wealthy slaveholders, whose insatiable desire for growing cotton and
other cash crops required new, fresh land. The last fantasy is what Sumner
feared was the core desire that lurked beneath Polk's calls for buying—or,
in the alternative, conquering—Mexican territory. He saw it as insidious.

In April 1845, Sumner was invited by the Boston Board of Aldermen
to deliver the keynote oration at the city's annual Fourth of July celebration on a topic of his choice. He decided that he couldn't stay silent over a
potential war with Mexico. For years, he had participated in various progressive causes. But his involvement was most often on the sidelines, or
half-hearted, or in private fundraising, at best. Howe pushed him to pursue social advocacy more forcefully. Sumner had resisted, feeling a need to
show respect to the conservative Whigs who had nurtured his career and
to focus on his fickle law practice. But now, having suffered a breakdown
and finally finding his footing, he decided to make his life more meaningful by using his platform to speak out against war.[40]

Annual Fourth of July celebrations had a storied tradition in Boston.
Every year, a parade of thousands would celebrate on Boston Common
before moving to an indoor hall for an oration. Each year's oration was
delivered by an up-and-coming man, usually a young Brahmin, who was
thought to represent Boston's future. "There are few men of consequence
among us who did not commence their career by an oration," John Adams

once recalled. So many great Bostonians had started their careers with this July 4 oration, from John Quincy Adams to Josiah Quincy.[41]

Traditionally, the orators recounted great stories of literature or history to their audiences. But in recent years, they had taken the opportunity to advance modest political messages—Horace Mann, for example, delivered Boston's Fourth of July oration in 1842 and spoke about the importance of public education. Now it would be Sumner's turn to speak. Though his legal career had been lagging, Boston Brahmins still expected great things from the Harvard Law School–trained and European-traveled prodigy. They did not anticipate that the topic of his speech would be far more radical, far more *insulting*, than any before: pacifism.

The day of festivities started early in the morning. Eight hundred children bearing bouquets, wreaths, and evergreens led the July 4 procession from Boston Common toward the Public Garden, as thousands cheered them on, waving American flags. Massachusetts militiamen proceeded after the children, escorting a retinue of city officials and the guest of honor, Charles Sumner, to Tremont Temple. As he took his seat onstage, while two thousand people filled the audience, a choir of one hundred schoolgirls clad in white sang the national anthem.

After a prayer and a reading of the Declaration of Independence, Sumner rose to speak. He wore a blue dress coat with gilt buttons, a white waistcoat, and trousers. "Sumner's appearance, style, and manner were very fine indeed," one attendee recalled. "That is such a man as I would like for a husband," one young lady in the audience whispered to her friend.[42]

"All hearts first turn to the Fathers of the Republic," Sumner began. After extolling their virtues, he said that each generation had a duty to add to their legacy by doing even better than they had. He then presented the topic of his address: "I propose to inquire *What, in our age, are the true objects of national ambition—what is truly national glory—national honor—*WHAT IS THE TRUE GRANDEUR OF NATIONS."[43]

Sumner argued that peace was the true grandeur of nations; war was not. He then squarely focused on Mexico. "By an act of unjust legislation," he declared, America had extended "our power over Texas" and "endangered Peace with Mexico." He warned that annexing any part of Mexico would be an attempt to spread slavery. "Who believes that the *national honor* will be promoted by a war with Mexico . . . ?" he asked. "The heart sickens at the murderous attack upon an enemy," he argued. Then, he boomed, "IN OUR AGE THERE CAN BE NO PEACE THAT IS NOT

HONORABLE; THERE CAN BE NO WAR THAT IS NOT DISHONOR-ABLE."

Sumner's audience was horrified. More than one hundred army and naval officers were the distinguished guests of the program that day. With "almost child-like innocence," according to one observer, "he went on dealing stab after stab to estimable servants of the United States." As one paper put it, "everything went off beautifully and harmoniously" that day "until the orator . . . had ascended the tribune."[44]

In a speech that lasted two hours, nearly one hundred pages in print, delivered straight from memory except for the occasional recitation of statistics, Sumner showed off his remarkable learning, his faith in high ethical ideals, and his utter disdain for the soldiers in the audience. Recounting story after story about great wars from history, he then condemned historians for failing to reckon with the evil of the past. "The horrors of these redden every page of history," he declared, "while, to the disgrace of humanity, the historian has rarely applied to their brutal authors the condemnation they deserve." He also slammed Constantine and the Catholic Church for having "failed to discern the peculiar spiritual beauty of the faith" and for finding "new incentives to war in the religion of Peace." War was in fact pagan, Sumner decried. "Who is the God of Battles?" he asked. "It is Mars; man-slaying, blood-polluting, city-smiting Mars!"

Departing from abstractions, Sumner turned his attention to the officers before him. "There is now floating in this harbor a ship of the line of our country," he observed, referring to the naval ship *Ohio*, docked at Boston Harbor and decked in flags. Describing it as an "armament of blood," he pointed out the irony that every Sabbath, a Christian preacher "addresses the officers and crew" of the ship, who were likely sitting in the crowd, even though "*Christianity forbids war in all cases*." Sumner then declared the army to be "an utterly useless branch of the public service," West Point to be "a seminary of idleness and vice," the navy to be "a vain and most expensive TOY!" and the militia to be "clearly inadequate" for protecting public safety. "No person, who has seen them in an actual riot," he insisted, "can hesitate in this judgment."

One military officer was so outraged during Sumner's speech that he stood up and called on the other soldiers to storm out in protest. When another officer replied that it would look like cowardice, a characteristic that Sumner had accused them of, the officers stayed seated.

Sumner closed by proposing that "Arbitration" or "a Congress of

Nations" peacefully address future grievances between nations. As if his speech weren't far-fetched enough, he then suggested that America ought to guarantee "the peaceful emancipation of three million of our fellow-men, 'guilty of a skin not colored as our own.'" He said emancipation, if it ever came, would be a victory far greater than "that of Bunker Hill."[45]

* * *

SUMNER'S AUDIENCE WAS shell-shocked. "Here was a spectacle worth beholding," one attendee remarked. "A gifted son of Massachusetts standing for peace against the whole influence of Boston." Somebody in the audience called "the whole scene so deliciously humorous," because Sumner had prepared an oration that was "studiously framed so as to be utterly *in*appropriate to the occasion."

After the speech, a private dinner was hosted at Faneuil Hall. Thirteen men stood up to give toasts, and each toast blasted Sumner while military officers at the dinner applauded. Some toasts were full of scorn, while others were gentle roasts. Boston was "a city of notions," one speaker sarcastically remarked, "but the strangest notion of all was the orator's." The most startling toast came at the end, when Congressman John Winthrop, a conservative Whig who had opposed the annexation of Texas as a slave state, rose to imply that he now patriotically supported it because America was "still *our* country."[46]

As people censured him, Sumner sat quietly—until it was his turn to give a toast. When he stood up, the other dinner guests expected fighting words from the orator who had been so feisty that morning. Instead, raising his glass, Sumner spoke cheerfully, ignoring the vicious remarks. He toasted "the youthful choristers of the day," wishing that "their future lives be filled with happiness, as they have filled our hearts to-day with the delights of their music." Everyone was pleasantly relieved that he let himself be attacked without fighting back. "No man could have behaved with more exact and refined courtesy," one officer admitted.

Over the next few days, Sumner worked to make amends with Boston society, but without compromising on his position. He privately spoke to one military officer, reassuring him that "his allusions in the address were to principles, and not to men." He also included a conciliatory letter of introduction in the pamphlet edition of his speech, published a few days later. And as he received letters criticizing the speech, he wrote back cordially. But he didn't back down from his controversial stance on war. In fact, he personally mailed copies of his speech to nearly all his friends and mentors, especially those who could not attend, in order to spread his message and solicit reactions.[47]

While Sumner now had many critics, there were others who admired his remarks. "I could never love you more than I did yesterday morning," Howe wrote to him, beaming with pride. "You have done a noble work, even though ridicule and sarcasm should follow you through life." "You will be assailed by many," another friend wrote, "but truth is on your side." "How did the old 'gray fathers' look . . . startled? I dare say," chortled Wendell Phillips. Even Chancellor Kent, conceding that the speech took him "quite by surprise," acknowledged that he agreed "on all essential points, though not with the same fervor and force." And the prominent abolitionist Rev. Theodore Parker, who had not yet met Sumner, reached out to praise his speech and ask him to publish a cheap edition so that he could spread Sumner's words.

Taking Parker's advice, Sumner published multiple editions of the speech. He also did not copyright the work, so that it could be distributed as widely as possible. As far as he was concerned, the feisty speech was a success, for it stirred a conversation on pacifism and the possible war against Mexico. Peace societies around the country distributed the speech. When one copy reached London in December, English peace societies also began distributing copies, including one sent to Queen Victoria. All in all, the speech was printed at least fourteen thousand times. It was "the most noble contribution of any modern writer to the cause of peace," wrote Richard Cobden, a prominent English Radical politician, to Sumner. Even the poet Samuel Rogers caught wind of Sumner's speech. "Every pulse of my heart beats in accordance with yours on the subject," he wrote to the orator.

While Sumner incited an important conversation, he severely harmed his reputation among Boston aristocrats in the process. "He has committed a social *felo de se*," one Bostonian observed, referring to the Latin term for the felony of suicide. Friends and critics alike flooded Sumner's law office in the days ahead to interrogate him about his speech and what on earth he was thinking. In his diary, Francis Lieber called Sumner's speech "the worst advised, and one of the worst reasoned speeches I have ever heard."[48]

Sumner had insulted Boston. Granted the honor to speak to the entire city, to an audience of many distinguished guests and out-of-town military officials, he had embarrassed the city with his topic and tone. Also, despite the best efforts of his conservative teachers, he had embraced the radicalism so many feared he developed in Europe. And though he was polite to his critics in the aftermath, Sumner never apologized. In fact, from this point forward, he would never mince his words again.[49]

*　*　*

AS SUMNER NAVIGATED this precarious moment, he was hit with a devastating blow: on September 10, 1845, Judge Story passed away from illness at the age of sixty-six. Sumner was broken. Crying at his mentor's funeral, he spent hours afterward walking alone among the graves at Mount Auburn Cemetery, visiting the tombstones of other mentors and old professors who had passed away. He stayed until there was no one left but the "humble gardeners, smoothing the sod over the fresh earth" above Story's casket. "His death makes a chasm which I shrink from contemplating," he wrote in a eulogy for the local paper. Without Story's keen guidance, he was now alone in the world—alone in the sense that he no longer had anyone to fall back on. "The voice of the Teacher is mute," he mourned.

In his final letter to his beloved student, Story had written to Sumner about the Fourth of July speech he delivered. Praising its "elegance of diction and classical beauty," Story admitted that he was "compelled to dissent" from its radical outlook. The conservative teacher had long feared his student's liberal bent. Now it was out in full view. But he didn't wish to discuss it further. "I am too old to desire . . . controversy," he told Sumner. The judge then concluded his letter with the last words he would ever write to his student before dying:

"I have spoken in all frankness to you . . . but be assured that no one cherishes with more fond and affectionate pride the continual advancement of your professional and literary fame than myself, and no one has a deeper reverence for your character and virtues. Believe me, as ever, most truly and affectionately, your friend, Joseph Story."[50]

CHAPTER 6

HE IS OUTSIDE THE PALE OF SOCIETY

I HOPE YOU WILL PARDON THE FRANKNESS OF THIS COMMUNICATION," Sumner wrote to the chairman of the New Bedford Lyceum in November 1845. The Lyceum had invited him to deliver an address, offering him a chance to redeem himself from the Fourth of July oration. Given how badly his recent oration had been received by Boston's high society, this was an opportunity he could not refuse. But refuse he did.

"I have read in the public prints a protest," he continued, "that at the present time tickets are refused to colored persons." The Lyceum, previously open to Black members and attendees, now prohibited them from sitting downstairs in the ticketed seats closest to the stage. This prejudice of color "does not exist in other civilized countries," Sumner asserted. "In France colored youths at college have gained the highest honors, and been welcomed as if they were white. At the Law School there I have sat with them on the same benches. In Italy I have seen an Abyssinian mingling with monks, and there was no apparent suspicion on either side of anything open to question." By accepting their invitation, Sumner felt that he "might seem to sanction what is most alien to his soul"—namely, the "distinction of *Caste*."

Boston's elite society was astonished by Sumner's recent behavior. Dashing, charming, and wildly intelligent, Sumner had once been the star graduate of Harvard Law School, a man who traveled across Europe and returned to Boston as one of its most promising sons. But he was throwing his social prestige away. From their perspective, he was grandstanding on the issue of racial injustice, which did not directly concern him.[1]

The Boston Brahmins detected an element of self-destruction in Sumner's readiness to provoke. Rather than moderate his political stances and make amends with high society after the Fourth of July, Sumner continued to dig in his heels. They could not dismiss his behavior as youthful rebelliousness; he was thirty-four years old. And yet he was acting like a brash provocateur, embracing that role as a part of his identity. To many Bostonians, Sumner's brashness made him seem like a tactless, and perhaps even egotistical, fool. They didn't recognize the modest, obeisant, ever-so-talkative scholar they used to know.

To others, the broke bachelor's brashness was increasingly seen as a sign of deep moral courage. After his major speech, he began to live by the ethical values of pacifism, abolition, and antiracism openly and proudly. That slowly earned him respect and even admiration across Massachusetts. Within a few short years, Sumner earned back in new social circles all the social standing he had lost in the old.

*　*　*

At first, Sumner struggled. The Fourth of July oration had wrecked his reputation. An anonymous thirty-page rebuttal was published as a pamphlet that attacked him and his speech in cruel, scathing terms. "He is a theorist; and there is perhaps, no man more useless in society than the theorist," the pamphlet declared. "Unlike the silkworm," it continued, "he spins his web out of his brains instead of his bowels." The pamphlet decried Sumner's choice in delivering this incendiary speech on the country's birthday and from a pulpit granted him by the city of Boston. The *Boston Post* called his speech a "mixture of monomania, sophistry and presumption" that was "appropriate perhaps for an insane Quaker in his dotage." Former Boston mayor Samuel Eliot rebuked Sumner for sacrificing his "reputation for good judgment and civility." Speaking to a friend, Mayor Eliot declared that "the young man has cut his own throat."[2]

Even worse, the Harvard Board of Governors refused to let Sumner succeed the late Judge Story as Dane Professor of Law. They denied him the position that had been practically promised to him by Story and Professor Simon Greenleaf. Rather than advocate for his protégé, Greenleaf persuaded Harvard to hire William Kent, son of Chancellor James Kent. Ironically, Chancellor Kent—another one of Sumner's mentors—had once said Sumner was "the only person in the country competent to succeed Story." But when his own son received the offer instead, Kent was pleased and relieved. He and Greenleaf now understood that Sumner wouldn't become the conservative jurist they had trained him to be.[3]

To cope with his defeat, Sumner convinced himself that he didn't want the professorship anyway. "I have my doubts whether I should accept it, even if it were offered to me," he claimed to his brother George. "In office, my opinions will be restrained, & I shall no longer be a free man." Two years later, Sumner's name was again turned down for a new opening when Professor William Kent resigned. "You ought to succeed me, Sumner," Professor Kent wrote him. He explained to Sumner that he could have been "a great lawyer, adding to the fields of jurisprudence," if he weren't becoming so controversial in his views so quickly.

In a private letter to somebody else, Professor Kent explained that the Harvard Board of Governors rejected Sumner twice in a row because of his political views. "Sumner has become an outrageous Philanthropist—neglecting his Law, to patch up the world—to reform prisoners and convicts—put down soldiers and war—and keep the solar system in harmonious action," Kent scoffed. "The conservative Corporation of Harvard College . . . consider Sumner in the Law-school, as unsuitable as a Bull in a china-shop."[4]

* * *

IN THE MONTHS after Sumner's oration, the United States steadily pursued the project of annexing the Republic of Texas into the union. Desiring to be annexed, Texas proposed a state constitution to Congress that protected slavery and banned its legislature from ever abolishing slavery by statute. Antislavery activists and abolitionists across the North were outraged by the draft Texas constitution and campaigned to stop its annexation. Joining the movement, Sumner became an editor for a short-lived journal, *The Free State Rally and Texan-Chain Breaker*, and wrote regular articles denouncing the effort to accept Texas as a slave state.

Sumner joined a local coalition of young organizers, the State Anti-Texas Committee, to hold events against annexation. That committee brought him in touch with people whose views radically diverged from his own. As he attended meetings, he was startled at the hatred that many other activists felt toward the United States and the Constitution. These radical activists pointed out that the Constitution had been written by a set of Founding Fathers that included many brutal enslavers. One of Sumner's fellow anti-Texas committee members, William Lloyd Garrison, later famously denounced the Constitution as "a covenant with death and an agreement with hell." Some years later, he would also stand onstage with Sojourner Truth and Henry David Thoreau at a Fourth of July celebration and light the Constitution on fire as an act of protest.[5]

To many Americans, including Sumner, the Constitution was the shining example of democracy at work. Born through a set of compromises by delegates who shared very different values, the Constitution formed a government where citizens could peacefully deliberate to make decisions for their nation and remain unified despite differences. After being amended with ten amendments, the Constitution protected basic liberties such as the right to bear arms, speak freely, and not be deprived of property without due process of law. It was a magnificent charter for freedom, unlike anything the world had ever seen before—at least for white men.

To enslaved people, the Constitution was an instrument of brutal oppression. Abolitionists noted that the Constitution implicitly codified the right of white men to own Black people as property and stopped Congress from ever regulating slavery within the states. For many abolitionists, the Constitution was to be reviled and eventually destroyed. As long as the Constitution governed America, they feared, there could be no emancipation. In particular, Garrison wanted northern free states to abandon the Constitution and secede from the union. Alternatively, he said that southern slave states should secede. That way, the North could wipe its hands clean of slavery in a new independent country where freedom was the national rule, while the South would have to contend alone with a large slave population that, he hoped, would one day revolt.

Sumner debated Garrison's provocative ideas with Wendell Phillips, another anti-Texas committee member, who had been his undergraduate and law classmate at Harvard. A key lieutenant of Garrison, Phillips tried to persuade Sumner to see the Constitution for what he believed it truly was: a demonic text, rather than the charter of freedom that Judge Story had taught them both to venerate in law school. But Sumner couldn't accept Phillips's arguments. "You already support the Constitution of the U.S. by continuing to live under its jurisdiction," he once explained to Phillips. "You receive its protection & owe it a corresponding allegiance."

Sumner argued that the Constitution, despite its flaws, was the best charter of its kind. "With all its imperfections, [it] secures a larger proportion of happiness to a larger proportion of men, than any other Government," he told Phillips. "I know of no Constitution or form of Government, in the world, from the ancient rule of China to the most newly-fashioned republic of our hemisphere, which does not sanction what I consider injustice & wrong. But because Governments lend their sanction to what I consider unjust, shall I cease to be a citizen?"

Sumner couldn't fathom turning against his government. "I am a Constitutionalist & a Unionist, & have always been," he once said. He also didn't understand the tactics of Garrisonian abolitionists, who generally refused to vote or participate in politics because they believed the system was too corrupted to be redeemed. "Shall I not rather," he once asked Phillips, "exercise any influence among my fellow-men, by speech, by the pen, by *my vote* . . . ?" In spite of their differences, abolitionists collaborated with Sumner to resist Texas annexation.[6]

On November 7, 1845, Sumner joined Phillips, Garrison, and a host of other activists for a large anti-Texas rally at Faneuil Hall. Speaking onstage, delivering the first political speech of his life, Sumner tried to articulate an alternative course to resisting slavery than that of Garrisonian abolitionists. He instructed his audience to demand not the *abolition* of slavery, which was unconstitutional, but to stop the *expansion* of slavery, through the democratic process. He wanted activists to campaign to persuade Congress to never admit another slave state again, such that slavery would remain only where it currently existed. Gradually, Sumner hoped, slavery would die. "By the present movement, we propose no measure of change," he said. "Our movement is conservative," he continued. "It is to preserve existing supports of Freedom."[7]

* * *

DESPITE THE BEST efforts of northern antislavery activists, Texas was admitted into the union in December 1845. This came as no surprise, for Congress was dominated by proslavery lawmakers. Thanks in part to the Three-Fifths Clause of the Constitution, slave states had outsize political control in Washington because their nonvoting slaves were counted as partial persons for apportioning congressional seats. In the South, voters were rabidly proslavery. Even in the North, most voters were sympathetic to slaveholders or apathetic about the moral and economic problem of slavery. Yet this was beginning to change.

Thanks to abolitionist agitation and the growing fears that slavery might spread northward, voters in states like Massachusetts were increasingly worried about the policies being pursued by Congress. In Washington, the vast majority of lawmakers supported the expansion of slavery. Among Democrats, most lawmakers thought slavery should keep expanding and be allowed in all territories. Among Whigs, most lawmakers were content to let slavery expand, but only in southern territories. Almost no one said that slavery should stop expanding entirely. To keep a numerical balance between free and slave states, and resolve disputes between Democrats and Whigs, Congress followed the Missouri Compromise: a deal codified in 1820 that allowed slavery in territories in the southern half of the country, but required freedom in the north.

Taking advantage of the Missouri Compromise, Democrats in Congress led the charge on May 12, 1846, to recognize a state of war between the United States and Mexico, which owned vast southern lands that they hoped to seize and turn into future slave states. A handful of Whigs voted against the Mexican War on the grounds that it was an unjust war of aggression and would lead to the expansion of slavery. But most congressional Whigs supported it to avoid appearing antipatriotic and against American troops.

Congressman Robert Winthrop, who was one of Sumner's friends and former classmates, voted in favor of the war. A Massachusetts Whig who aspired to become Speaker of the House, Winthrop had deep moral qualms about a war to expand slavery but believed that his political future depended on supporting the fight. After he took his vote, antislavery activists pounded on him for becoming an abettor of violence.

Writing under a pseudonym, Sumner denounced Winthrop for being a bloody warmonger in a series of articles published in a local newspaper. "Away beyond the current of the Rio Grande, on a foreign soil, your name will be invoked as a supporter of the war," Sumner pronounced in one article. "Surely this is no common act. It cannot be forgotten on earth; it must be remembered in heaven." Charging his congressman with having blood on his hands, Sumner declared that "not all great Neptune's ocean can wash them clean."

Reading these biting articles, Winthrop was furious at their anonymous nature. Believing the writer had to be one of Boston's educated men, given the flurry of literary references used, Winthrop began to ask around to figure out who was the author. When Sumner learned that people were suspecting him, he wrote to Winthrop directly to confess to being the writer. With total naïveté, he said that he hoped to stay friends with Winthrop despite disagreeing with him on the war. But Winthrop wouldn't have it. "My hand, is not at the service of any one, who has denounced it, with such ferocity, as being stained with blood," he scoffed.[8]

* * *

CONGRESSMAN WINTHROP WAS in his mid-thirties at the time, like Sumner, and he roamed in the same social circles of Boston. Winthrop told friends, mentors, and acquaintances among the city's social elite about Sumner's vicious articles and their underhanded nature. "That a man who but yesterday professed to be my friend," Winthrop ranted, "should turn upon me with such ferocity, denounce me so publicly and grossly, and pursue me with such relentless malignity . . . is almost inconceivable." Many Boston Brahmins weren't as surprised as Winthrop. They had already been alarmed by Sumner's rabid pacifism from the previous year. To them, Sumner's fight with Winthrop was just confirmation that one of their most promising young men was going rogue.

Boston elites were infuriated with Sumner. In the months after his fight with Winthrop, Sumner found himself disinvited from countless social events and struggled to get wealthy clients for his law practice. By going after Winthrop, Sumner had challenged the prevailing social order. But he didn't attempt to calm the waters. Whenever he discussed politics with friends and elders, he rambled about current events and pleaded with Boston elites to stand against Winthrop and in favor of peace and justice. He went out of his way to write long pedantic letters to his mentors and elders demanding them to speak out against the Mexican war. He would also ask them to consider becoming abolitionists. "In Sumner's alphabet just now there are only two words: Slavery and the Mexican War," his law partner George Hillard complained.[9]

Troubled by the strength of Sumner's pacifism and antislavery views, Hillard distanced himself from Sumner. He wished Sumner would spend more time on law rather than politics. It was hard to come to the office every day and hear Sumner's rants. He also worried that being associated with Sumner was costing him clients and hurting his practice, especially after the Winthrop fight. Soon enough, he moved out of the office he had shared with Sumner for over a decade. While they stayed friends, their friendship would never be the same.[10]

Sumner also ended up fighting with one of his closest friends, Harvard professor Cornelius Felton. When Felton married into a merchant family that earned its wealth from southern cotton, Sumner accused him of being complicit in slavery. Felton, in turn, charged Sumner of preaching "nothing more nor less than old fashioned Jacobinism . . . insidious appeal to class prejudices—an attempt to rouse the hatred of the poor against the rich, and to organize the vulgar passions of envy and jealousy into political action." Angrily, Sumner minced no words back. "You stand pledged to sustain before the world a system of slave-catching, more cruel & vindictive than any the world has yet seen," he accused Felton. They wouldn't reconcile for years.[11]

Worst of all, Sumner had a falling out with George Ticknor, the retired Harvard professor and aristocrat who had been inviting Sumner to his exclusive parties for years. Having helped to groom Sumner for a life in Boston aristocracy, Ticknor decided to shun him after they had a heated argument on some political matter. "In a society where public opinion governs, unsound opinions must be rebuked," Ticknor declared. When asked by a guest if Sumner would be present at a party, Ticknor grew indignant at even the *idea* of welcoming Sumner into his house again. "He is outside the pale of society," he scoffed.

The wives of Sumner's two closest friends, both wealthy heiresses, felt sorry that their husbands' best friend was being thrown out of the social circles they grew up in. "He has destroyed his social position in Boston," Fanny Appleton Longfellow wrote to a friend. "Altho' he has gained hosts of friends elsewhere, he is there almost a Pariah." Fanny tried to persuade her father, the wealthy textile magnate Nathan Appleton, to stay on good terms with Sumner. But Appleton wouldn't budge. "I have regretted to see talents so brilliant as yours, and from which I had hoped so much for our country, take a course in which I consider them worse than thrown away," Appleton wrote to Sumner. "Oh! how the old Whigs do hate us!" Julia Ward Howe wrote to her sister. "They will hardly speak to Sumner, or invite him to their homes."[12]

Sumner seemed ready to debate politics with anyone, anywhere, no matter their age or status. "One by one he is outraging his friends and driving them away," Felton complained. "You have taken hold of this one idea of slavery," a rich socialite who once admired Sumner rebuked him. "I could name scores and scores of men whom you have honored your whole life who regret and condemn the course you have taken."

Confiding in Samuel Howe, Sumner confessed to being hotheaded and wondered if he deserved the exclusion. He mourned about "the wreck of my past life, with friends leaving me." He said he wished that conservatives extended more charity to his views. "I need charity & candour; God grant that I may always shew them to others," he noted. While passing through

Beacon Street one day, he recalled a time "when there was hardly a house within two miles of this place where I was not a welcome guest. Now, hardly one is open to me."[13]

* * *

IN THE VERY days that Sumner was losing his chummy relationships with conservative Boston elites, he was developing new friendships and networks across Massachusetts and greater New England. Spending less and less time within the city and in the office of his failing law practice, he traveled through the region for paid speaking engagements. People loved hearing him speak, whether they agreed with his views or not. He had a booming, sonorous voice that could command the attention of large crowds in a world without microphones. He filled his speeches with allusions to Greek antiquity and English history, drawing from the rich mental repertoire he had cultivated at Harvard. And he chose to discuss radical ideas that reflected an almost total lack of regard for the Brahmins who had ostracized him, which made him an exciting orator.

The opportunities for Sumner to speak publicly were endless after he made his name in the Fourth of July oration. A new social movement, sometimes described as the Lyceum Movement, took root in New England around this time. Loosely affiliated societies across the region were inviting interesting speakers to give Lyceum talks, public addresses on various social topics that were delivered to guests who paid a small subscription fee to attend. Lyceum addresses were, in a nutshell, nineteenth-century TEDx Talks.[14]

Lyceum subscribers enjoyed hearing from speakers who were both intellectually gifted and willing to challenge prevailing social norms. Characters as diverse as Ralph Waldo Emerson and Frederick Douglass made their name in part due to Lyceum lectures. Sumner did, too. He delivered dozens of paid lectures at Lyceums around the region, which helped him pay his bills and compensated for his meager legal income.[15]

One of Sumner's best Lyceum addresses was "White Slavery in the Barbary States." In the speech, he examined the enslavement of white Christians by Muslims in the Barbary states of North Africa. From the 1500s to the 1700s, the Barbary states had acquired slaves from Europe and the Americas by capturing vessels in the Atlantic. Sumner told the awful stories of many of these slaves, including that of one American colonist from Quinnipiac—now New Haven, Connecticut—who was abducted by Turks on his return voyage to England and sold into slavery in North Africa in 1640. Sumner noted that by 1793, at least 115 white Americans were enslaved in Algeria. Early Americans were so outraged by the capture and enslavement of their fellow citizens that George Washington made it a priority of his administration to bring them home.[16]

To justify slavery, Sumner noted, Muslims in the Barbary states claimed that slavery was relatively benign under Islamic law. He conceded the point, insisting it was not relevant. "Whatever deductions we may make from the current stories of White Slavery in the Barbary States,—admitting that it was mitigated by the genial influence of Mahometanism," Sumner said that the institution of white slavery was "hardly less hateful in our eyes." It didn't matter that the slaves of Muslim enslavers "were well clad and well fed . . . often treated with lenity and affectionate care,—that they were sometimes advanced to posts of responsibility and honor." He said slavery was still "a violation of the law of nature and of God," a "usurpation of rights not granted to man."

Sumner delivered this talk to countless audiences of white Christians in the late 1840s. Listeners found the idea of white Americans being enslaved in the Barbary states appalling. Just as white slavery in Africa was abhorrent, he argued, so, too, was Black slavery in the American South. Even if chattel slavery were benign—a ludicrous claim that southern enslavers would make—he said it made no difference. He challenged listeners to see the equivalence between Christians enslaved by Muslims and Blacks enslaved by whites: "*Is there any difference between the two cases than this, viz. that the American slaves at Algiers are WHITE people, whereas the African slaves at New York were BLACK people?*"

This would become a recurring strategy for Sumner: telling stories about history to make arguments about the current day. He was far from the first activist to adopt this approach, but he was unique in being able to do so in a manner that raised a groundswell of popular support. He drew from the works of abolitionists who were reviled, mocked, and cast out by popular society—abolitionists like Garrison, Phillips, and William Cooper Nell. Sumner knew them, read them, and spread their arguments to the public. He was effective because he was charming, eloquent, and fun to watch. The same speeches that distanced him from Boston's privileged financial and intellectual circles won him a far larger social network among the Massachusetts masses.

Young people especially loved hearing Sumner deliver Lyceum orations.

If they didn't come for his views, they came for his looks. At six foot four, with muscular shoulders, wild blue eyes, a thick mane of chestnut hair, and long curly sideburns, he presented a striking figure. "He seemed to me a new Demosthenes or Cicero, even like a Grecian god, as he stood on the platform," one woman recalled at a speech that Sumner delivered to the Phi Beta Kappa Society at Harvard. "I thought him the handsomest and the finest looking man I had ever seen. His presence was superb, a trifle haughty perhaps; but that only added to his grandeur. I remember the remark of a lady who was sitting beside me, that she was already in love with his hair."[17]

* * *

THERE WAS AN old man who came to love Sumner, too. Former president John Quincy Adams had reveled in Sumner's controversial Fourth of July oration. "You set all the vipers of Alecto a-hissing by proclaiming the Christian law of universal peace and love," Adams commended Sumner. A man of many controversies himself, Adams admired Sumner's willingness to challenge prevailing social norms. He told Sumner that "no man is abused whose influence is not felt," a phrase that Sumner would repeat to himself all his life.[18]

Sumner had befriended the retired president by accident. An elderly man who lived in a countryside suburb of Boston, Adams invited Sumner to his home one day because he mistakenly thought Sumner had been to Russia. Adams, who had once served as a diplomat in Russia, wanted to learn about Sumner's trip and recount his own memories of the country. While disappointed to discover that Sumner had never been there, he took a keen interest in Sumner's travels to other parts of Europe. He continued to invite Sumner to his country home from time to time, enjoying the young man's company and offering him life's wisdom.[19]

In his retirement from the presidency, Adams had become a member of Congress. He was now the leading congressional opponent to the Mexican War and seemed to have had a guilty conscience about being complicit in slavery for most of his political career. As if to make amends, Adams had been passionately arguing in the House against the addition of new slave states. He had also made it a point to introduce antislavery petitions from his constituents on the House floor. That practice irked his proslavery colleagues, who were so upset about the petitions that Congress passed a "gag rule" to ban any petitions that protested slavery from being introduced on the floor. The rule infuriated Adams so much that, for the first time in his life, he considered himself to be an antislavery activist and champion of the free speech rights of abolitionists.

Even as he opposed the Mexican War, Adams believed that Sumner's idealistic pacifism was too naïve. He recognized that war often led to important social goods. The American Revolution that his father helped to lead, after all, had liberated the thirteen colonies from British tyranny. While speaking to an audience of free Blacks, Adams suggested that enslaved people might get their own revolution someday, too. "The day of your redemption must come," he promised. "It may come in peace, or it may come in blood."

Sumner appreciated Adams's wisdom and learned from it over time. For example, during one of his speaking engagements to a peace society, Sumner admitted that enslaved people might be justified to use violence in ways that free people weren't. "Shall a people endure political oppression or the denial of Freedom, without resistance?" he asked the audience rhetorically. While insisting that peace was usually a better avenue for freedom, he confessed that there may be certain moments where his pacifistic ideals wouldn't apply. "These three millions of fellow-men, into whose souls we thrust the iron of the deadliest bondage the world has yet witnessed," Sumner decided, "must be justified in resisting to death the power that holds them in fetters."

Sumner gathered from Adams that a slave insurrection wouldn't just be morally justified but possibly the most practical solution to the problem of slavery. While speaking on the House floor one day, Adams admitted that the Constitution protected slavery within the states. But he suggested that this legal protection would expire if the South ever fell into a state of "servile, civil, or foreign" war. During a state of war, Adams explained, the President and Congress would be able to exercise their "war powers," which are legal powers that a government can only exercise in extreme circumstances in order to restore peace. Throughout history, nations had seized enemy property, such as slaves, and freed them during wars. Civil war, Adams suggested, might pave a viable and legal path to abolition. Decades later, Sumner recalled this lesson keenly.[20]

Sumner learned another key lesson from Adams. Even more than the Constitution, Adams admired the Declaration of Independence and its principles of equality and freedom. The Declaration was the lodestar that informed his entire political philosophy. The Declaration, which his father helped to write, said that "all men are created equal." John Quincy Adams saw this eloquent phrase as a binding promise—a promise that ought to be legally enforced. He argued that everything in the Constitution should be construed, to the extent feasible, under the liberty and equality principles of the Declaration. Just as John Marshall and Joseph Story taught Sumner about the *nationalist* Constitution, Adams taught Sumner about the *promissory* Declaration.[21]

During his many visits to the Boston countryside, Sumner listened with reverent attention to Adams's advice. He affectionately called Adams "Old Man Eloquent," a nickname the retired president acquired. The old man, who suffered from poor health, often lay down in the white sheets of his bed, telling Sumner stories while he sat obeisantly in a nearby chair. He encouraged Sumner to take to heart these lessons on pacifism, war, abolition, and the Declaration of Independence. And he pushed Sumner to pursue politics. "Be not Atticus," Adams once sternly told Sumner, referring to a Roman banker who stood on the sidelines while his best friend, Cicero, served in the Roman senate. "You have a mission to perform," Adams explained.[22]

* * *

AT ADAMS'S ADVICE, Sumner befriended a group of young Whigs who had become politically active in the mid- to late 1840s. The group's informal leader was Charles Francis Adams, one of John Quincy's sons. Sumner and the younger Adams dined often at the retired president's house or at the younger Adams's own home. Between dinners and other activities, they discussed the state of their country and what they should do.

Sumner, Adams, and other young Whigs began meeting at Sumner's law office, conveniently located centrally in Boston on Court Street. There, they developed strategies to challenge the power of the city's older Whigs. During these regular meetups, Sumner and Adams befriended Richard Henry Dana, a young Brahmin lawyer who was frustrated with the conservative politics of his social circle. They also met Henry Wilson, a humble shoemaker who worked hard and had ambitions to one day run for political office. Along with a few others, these young men adopted a new label for themselves. They called themselves the "Conscience Whigs."

The Conscience Whigs were disturbed that Boston, a manufacturing power in early America, had an economy fueled by the raw material most tied to slavery: cotton. Thanks to cotton, slavery had expanded after the time of the Founding, instead of declining as the Founders had thought.

"Nothing is more clearly written in the book of destiny than the emancipation of the blacks," Thomas Jefferson once wrote. One of Jefferson's best friends, the French general Marquis de Lafayette, also believed that slavery wouldn't last much longer after the American Revolution. "I would never have raised my sword in the cause of America," he explained decades later, "if I could have conceived that thereby I was founding a land of slavery."

Only a few years after the ratification of the Constitution, slavery began to expand. In 1793, Boston Brahmin Eli Whitney invented the cotton gin, a machine that increased the speed of deseeding cotton by a factor of ten. Seizing on the gin's promise, slaveholders transformed southern land into lucrative cotton fields that eventually stretched across two million acres. On these cotton plantations, slaveholders and their overseers brutalized men, women, and children, forcing them to plant, pick, deseed, and pack cotton, which the gin had made so easy to produce.

At first, southern slave-produced cotton was shipped solely to British textile mills. But in the 1810s, Boston Brahmins Francis Cabot Lowell and Nathan Appleton had traveled to England, learned the ins and outs of textile production, and returned to Boston to start their own textile mills. Then they formed relationships with southern enslavers and established trading routes to bring raw cotton from the South into Massachusetts for refining. By the middle of the century, textiles were the leading engines of economic growth in New England. Cotton now benefited the South and North alike. After decades of refining slave-produced cotton, Lowell, Appleton, and other textile mill owners became the most powerful men in Massachusetts, controlling two-fifths of Boston's banking capital and one-third of the state's railroad tracks.

New England textile mills, along with their counterparts in Great Britain, played a key role in driving the growth of southern slavery. In Sumner's youth in the 1810s, cotton represented just a quarter of America's exports. By the time he practiced law in the 1830s, cotton had expanded to nearly half of America's exports. Even more cotton was remaining within the country and being shipped to New England. As the cotton and textile industry grew, the country's enslaved population doubled. In the 1810s, there were around one million enslaved people in America; by the 1830s, there were two million. Thanks to cotton, the gin, and textile mills, American slavery was growing rather than shrinking. As one slaveholder famously boasted, "Cotton is king."

Boston's cotton gin inventors and textile magnates came from the city's premier Brahmin families. Whitney, Appleton, Lowell, and their peers were the philanthropists of the city, building its young museums, schools, and literary societies. They served in high-level political positions. They fueled Boston's remarkable economic vibrancy, a vibrancy that made possible the careers of Boston's bankers, lawyers, merchants, railroad barons, and other businessmen. And their wealth, all of it, in one way or another, was directly tied to the cotton plantations of the South. Thanks to them, Boston was in a symbiotic relationship with slavery.

Sumner and the other Conscience Whigs denounced the supporters of Boston's lucrative textile factories as "Cotton Whigs." Led by Senator Daniel Webster and Congressman Winthrop, Cotton Whigs believed that textile and other manufacturing industries formed the basis of American prosperity. They wanted high tariffs to protect domestic factories, large investments in infrastructure to make it easier to transport goods along roads and canals, and a strong national bank to provide credit for indus-trialization.[23]

Sumner had no more patience for Cotton Whigs, many of whom had mentored him for years and welcomed him into their homes. At political ral-lies, he accused Cotton Whigs of being abettors of chattel slavery. "There is an unhallowed union conspiracy," he declared at one rally, "between the cotton-planters and flesh-mongers of Louisiana and Mississippi, and the cotton-spinners and traffickers of New England,—between the lords of the lash and the lords of the loom." Sumner accused the so-called lords of the loom for being "selfish, grasping, subtle, tyrannical," and for unit-ing their "money-power" with "the slave-power."

Sumner helped Charles Francis Adams launch a journal, *The Daily Whig*, to speak for the Conscience Whigs against the Cotton Whigs. The journal criticized Webster, Winthrop, and others for having allowed the addition of Texas as a slave state. In one article, Adams accused Cotton Whigs of "thinking more of sheep and cotton than of Man." They were willing to do anything and everything, Adams said, for "the sake of slaveholding gold." It was time for new leadership—time for Whigs who wouldn't admit new slave states.[24]

* * *

IN SEPTEMBER 1846, Sumner, Adams, and other Conscience Whigs attended the state Whig Party convention as delegates. There, they faced off with the Cotton Whigs. While unable to defeat the Cotton Whigs in drafting the political platform, the Conscience Whigs still won a chance to be heard. Knowing that Congressman Winthrop would get to address the crowd, Conscience Whigs demanded that Sumner get an opportunity to speak as well. They chanted Sumner's name until he was permitted to give a short address.

Onstage, Sumner explained the political agenda of the Conscience Whig movement to the crowd. As he laid out their vision, he tried to straddle a line between the competing currents of antislavery thought and the tensions within his own mind. While sharing the moral fervor of rabid abolitionists like Garrison and Phillips, Sumner tried to stay within the bounds of the law, as Judge Story and John Quincy Adams had taught him.

Sumner distanced the Conscience Whigs from abolitionists and radicals in his speech. "The Whigs have been called . . . *conservatives*," he noted. He said that "conservative" was the right word to describe themselves. "The Whigs should be conservators of the ancestral spirit, conservators of the animating ideas in which our institutions were born," he continued. What did this conservativism look like? "It is the conservatism of '76."

Sumner hearkened to the Founding Fathers, who, in 1776, "sealed with their blood" the principle "that all men are created equal" in the Declaration of Independence. To carry out their conservative vision, Sumner said the Whigs should rely on another document the Founders wrote: the Constitution. "The Constitution contains an article pointing out how, at any time, amendments may be made," he said. "This is an important element, giving to the Constitution a *progressive* character." He explained that the Founders didn't have a problem making compromises with slavery because they thought it was gradually declining. Since this did not happen, it was time to amend the Constitution to eliminate those compromises in order to fulfill the Founders' moral vision.

Combining *conservative* and *progressive* rhetoric and ideas, Sumner pitched a democratic means to fulfill the Founders' mission and bring the Constitution into alignment with the Declaration. The idea was so inconceivable that few antislavery men had ever bothered to suggest an amendment to the Constitution to abolish slavery and declare equality. For roughly forty years, the Constitution had remained the same. Much like today, the Constitution was treated in the mid-1840s as a near-sacred text that was nearly impossible to amend. Yet beginning now, and for the next two decades, Sumner would advocate for an abolition amendment. He got the idea from John Quincy Adams, who had recently proposed one in the House.[25]

Adams wasn't the only former president who was troubled by the growth of slavery. In New York, former president Martin Van Buren had also taken a stand against annexing Texas because it was a slave state. His stance had cost him the Democratic nomination to James Polk in the most recent election, in 1844. Ever since, Van Buren had been stewing with anger against Polk and fellow Democrats who favored slavery's expansion. In the winter of 1847 to 1848, he plotted a new political movement to combat proslavery Democrats.

Unlike Sumner, Van Buren was no racial egalitarian. He was racist to the bone, and he couldn't care less about the rights of Black Americans. Yet he still opposed slavery. To him, slavery hurt poor northern white people the most. He surmised that many northern whites shared similar views but lacked the political avenue to express them. Taking to his pen, he drafted a memorandum and gave it to his protégé, the young lawyer Samuel Tilden. "If you wish to be immortal," he told Tilden, "take this home with you, complete it, revise it, put it into proper shape, and give it to the public." He called it the "Barnburner Manifesto."

Sumner surely read the Barnburner Manifesto and recognized the political power of its reasoning. Van Buren had managed to lay out a new political agenda—by and for the poor white man—that put antislavery at its center. "We invite to our shores the children of labor and the votaries of liberty from every clime," the manifesto said, "by holding out to them the promise of an equal participation in the blessings of free institutions." The manifesto argued that this promise of equality was incompatible with slavery. Thanks to slavery, wealthy slaveowners lived in luxury and forced Black people to work for free. That made it harder for poor white people to get well-paying jobs. It also degraded the value of manual labor, denying poor white laborers the respectability they deserved. Slavery, in short, made society unequal for white people.[26]

* * *

SHORTLY AFTER THE manifesto's release, Sumner began corresponding with John Van Buren, the former president's son, to explore the idea of a new political party that aligned antislavery Democrats and Conscience

Whigs in a single coalition. In early August 1848, Sumner traveled with Charles Francis Adams to Buffalo, New York, for a convention with John Van Buren and other political antislavery men. These ambitious men felt confident that a party premised on stopping slavery's expansion could be viable on the national scene. After all, they had the sons of two former presidents on their side. They called themselves the Free-Soil Party.

The architect of the Free-Soil convention in Buffalo was Salmon Chase, a hardworking Ohio-born lawyer and devout Christian who became one of Sumner's closest lifelong friends. Chase had a deep moral aversion to slavery. He was so disgusted by slavery's expansion that he became involved in the Liberty Party, a fringe abolitionist party that demanded immediate, unconditional, uncompromising national emancipation. For years, Chase tried to persuade the radical party to broaden its appeal by becoming more ideologically flexible. He suggested that rather than demand national abolition, which alienated and frightened most white voters, the party should ask for something more specific, feasible, and appealing: to stop adding new slave states.

In 1848, Chase and a few others organized a new political party based on this core principle. He asked Sumner, Adams, Van Buren, and other key leaders around the nation to attend. They came to witness a spectacle: tens of thousands of ordinary Americans gathered under a giant tent in Buffalo in the summer heat, demanding new leadership in Washington to stop the growth of slavery. In between the large cookouts and rallies that Chase had organized, key leaders attended a smaller gathering where actual decisions were made.

In this smaller room, Chase explained his vision for a united front that combined disgruntled Whigs, Democrats, and Liberty voters into a single party. "Free Soil, Free Speech, Free Labor, and Free Men," he wrote into the party's platform. The phrase "Free Soil" captured the idea of making all future states and all territories free land. "Free Speech" pointed to the problem that John Quincy Adams and others had faced of having their voices silenced for speaking out against war and slavery. "Free Labor" spoke to poor whites who worked hard in manual labor jobs and didn't like to be underpaid because of slave labor. "Free Men" was a nod to Blacks and abolitionists, suggesting the party desired universal emancipation even if it didn't demand it. With a catchy and pithy phrase, Chase had formed a big-tent antislavery movement.[27]

The Free Soilers decided to participate in the presidential contest in the fall of 1848, naming former president Martin Van Buren as their candidate and Charles Francis Adams as their vice-presidential nominee. With these big names on their ticket, Sumner felt tremendous excitement for the election. Along with virtually all Conscience Whigs in Massachusetts, he abandoned the Whigs and eagerly joined the new Free-Soil Party. "I never supposed that I should belong to a successful party," he told a friend. "Truly, success seems to be within our reach."

After the convention and a tourist visit to Niagara Falls, Sumner returned to Boston full of energy. At the encouragement of friends like Samuel Howe, he even agreed to be named as the Free-Soil candidate to run against Robert Winthrop for his local congressional district. He spoke across the city and state about the free-soil vision for America. Even in the smallest venues, his voice thundered with gusto and conviction. His friend Henry Longfellow attended one of these small events and was amused at how out of place Sumner's booming voice seemed. "It was like one of Beethoven's symphonies played in a saw-mill," Longfellow jested.[28]

Sumner handily lost the election against Winthrop, and Van Buren and Adams failed to win the White House in November. But the Free-Soil Party still did far better than critics expected, claiming almost 30 percent of the vote in the northern states of New York, Massachusetts, and Vermont. "Our friends feel happy at the result," Sumner wrote to his brother George. "The Free Soil movement is destined to triumph," he predicted, expecting success in the next election, of 1852. "I do hope that at last there will be a party that does believe in God," he said to someone else, "or at least in some better devil than Mammon."[29]

* * *

Unfortunately for Sumner, the year 1848 also came with tragedy. After the close of the Mexican War, the United States annexed the land that encompassed modern-day California, Nevada, Utah, and parts of Colorado, Arizona, and New Mexico, with the intention to create new slave states. When the House entertained a resolution to honor the veterans of the Mexican War, the eighty-year-old congressman John Quincy Adams stood up to cast his vote. "NO!" Adams yelled. He then collapsed to the ground and several other representatives rushed to his aid. A young Whig congressman who was sitting just a few feet away, Abraham Lincoln, watched in stunned silence as Adams suffered a debilitating stroke on the House floor.

Two days later, Adams died of brain hemorrhage. "That lifeless body, wherever it is carried, will preach for freedom," Sumner told a friend sadly as he mourned his mentor's sudden death. Charles Francis Adams, after gathering his late father's belongings, gifted Sumner one of the former president's silver rings. Sumner kept the ring, engraved with the initials J.Q.A., on his pocket-watch chain for the rest of his life.[30]

CHAPTER 7

FROM PISGAH TO
THE PROMISED LAND

PREOCCUPIED WITH HIS EFFORTS TO MOBILIZE THE FREE-SOIL
Party, caught up in delivering orations across Massachusetts, and navigating the difficult terrain of love and loss, Sumner may have forgotten at times that he was a lawyer with a law practice. Still very much broke despite his increasing renown, Sumner focused his meager practice on small claims, wills and estates, and, when he was lucky, the occasional more high-paying patent or insurance case. Due to his lack of focus and controversial politics, wealthy clients rarely hired him. Many boycotted him because he was a radical. "They thought they could starve me into silence," he recalled.

In 1849, the young Black Bostonian lawyer Robert Morris entered Sumner's office and gave him a reason to take more pride in his profession. Morris was an extraordinary twenty-six-year-old man. Born to parents who had escaped slavery in the South, he grew up in freedom in Massachusetts but still endured the daily toll of racism by white New Englanders. At fifteen, he worked as a servant in the home of Ellis Gray Loring, an abolitionist and lawyer to Ralph Waldo Emerson. He impressed Loring so much with his beaming intellect that Loring offered to teach him law. For the next decade, he worked as Loring's legal apprentice until he was ready to take the bar himself. In 1847, Morris passed the bar and became the second Black attorney in American history. That same year, he became the first Black attorney to win a jury trial. "There was something in the courtroom that morning," he said after his victory, "that made me feel like a giant."[1]

Sitting in Sumner's office, Morris explained the case of Sarah Roberts, a young Black girl who had briefly attended a white-only public school until a police officer, operating under instructions from the Boston School Committee, was sent into the school to force her out of the building. "The less the colored and white people become intermingled," the School Committee declared, "the better it will be for both races." Sarah's father, Benjamin Roberts, was incensed. He didn't want his daughter going to the Smith School, which was far away from their home and the only school in the city open to Black schoolchildren.[2]

To help the Roberts family, Morris had formulated an innovative legal argument that had never before been made in American history. He argued that the Massachusetts Constitution, which said "all men are born free and equal," compelled equal access to public schools regardless of race. After losing in district court, Morris decided that a more experienced white attorney should argue his appeal before the Supreme Judicial Court of Massachusetts. Sumner agreed to do so and offered to represent Roberts for free. "Sumner was considered the whitest lawyer in Boston," a friend recalled. "A man for whom money had no value."[3]

* * *

BENJAMIN ROBERTS MAY have been hesitant about Sumner representing his daughter due to past negative experiences with white abolitionists. Years ago, Roberts had been a newspaper printer who worked for the abolitionist William Lloyd Garrison at the *Liberator*. While politically committed to racial equality, Garrison often ran up against local African American leaders who felt that he had a superiority complex and still harbored some racial prejudices. They were frustrated that Garrison seemed to think of himself as the leader of Black activism in the city. Roberts found it especially alarming that Garrison, a visionary but highly opinionated activist, had full discretion on what views to publish, whom to elevate, and which local Black events to highlight.

Roberts believed Black Bostonians should have a newspaper of their own. So he created the *Anti-Slavery Herald*, a radical abolitionist journal that, in addition to discussing local events and issues, was laced with militant language demanding absolute emancipation immediately. Unfortunately, the white benefactors who had financed Roberts withdrew their support after they grew troubled by his rhetoric. He suspected Garrison had something to do with it. "There has been and *now is*, a combined effort on the part of certain *professed* abolitionists to muzzle, exterminate and put down the efforts of certain colored individuals," he vented.[4]

Roberts had little patience for putative white allies who refused to let

African Americans lead the abolitionist movement. His experience was partly informed by what had happened at the only Black school in Boston, which Roberts did not want his daughter to attend. Founded in 1798, the Smith School was located a few blocks from the Sumner family's house on the North Slope of Beacon Hill. Over the years, Boston had chronically undermined and underfunded the school that was once the pride of the local Black community.[5]

In the early 1840s, the Boston School Committee chose a domineering white headmaster to teach the Black schoolchildren at the Smith School. The headmaster was presumed to be a racial progressive who, after all, was willing to teach Black children when hardly any other white man would. Yet he flogged, beat, and whipped his Black students, believing they were dumber than white schoolchildren. "The colored people manifest but little . . . interest in the education of their children," he apparently believed. When dozens of Black parents informed the committee about his brutality, the committee ignored them and kept him in charge.

In the mid-1840s, a group of Black community leaders announced a boycott. So long as the School Committee refused to let Black schoolchildren attend neighboring white schools, they would not attend the Smith School, either. These Black Bostonians demanded an integrated school system for all. "We are satisfied that we never shall have a . . . flourishing school under this system," one petition declared. Instead, there must be a "system of allowing the white and colored children to attend the same schools." Once educating more than a hundred students, by 1849, the Smith School saw its daily attendance collapse by half.[6]

In the late 1840s, Black integrationists sought redress from the Massachusetts Legislature. Joined by the abolitionists Wendell Phillips and Ellis Gray Loring, these Black civic leaders petitioned for a bill that would require Boston to permit Black schoolchildren to attend white schools. Phillips and Loring may have felt optimistic about their proposal. After all, Boston was the *only* city in the state that segregated its schools. The rest of the state's schools had no formal rules excluding Black schoolchildren. Many white lawmakers in New England considered themselves egalitarians who approved of public education for African Americans. But permitting Black children near their own white kids on a wide scale in the city of Boston was a bridge too far. "Give the negro his liberty," one newspaper declared, "but KEEP HIM IN HIS PLACE." The bill failed.

The next step for integrationists was to turn to the judiciary in 1849. In an atmosphere of great distrust, where Black community leaders in Boston had been stymied by whites at every corner, Robert Morris and his client Benjamin Roberts still sought the help of Charles Sumner to argue before the Supreme Judicial Court of Massachusetts. Their collaboration would help forge a deep relationship between Sumner and the local Black Boston community, a relationship that would endure for the rest of Sumner's life. Together, Morris and Sumner represented Sarah Roberts. They were the first Black and white lawyers in history to file an appellate brief together and argue a case side by side before an American court.[7]

* * *

SUMNER AND MORRIS argued their case on September 7, 1849. Inside the stately courtroom, they stood before Chief Justice Lemuel Shaw, a giant of the common law. To this day, every American law student has likely come across one of Shaw's famous opinions, such as *Brown v. Kendall*, where he was among the first to apply a negligence standard to tort law. Shaw was sharp, cynical, and ever so willing to interrupt lawyers with aggressive and downright hostile questions. Famously ugly, his hair shaggy, his spectacles always tipped down to the edge of his nose, Shaw had often been described by peers as looking like an unpleasant lion.[8]

Morris stood up first. A young Black man in his mid-twenties, he may have felt nervous standing before Shaw and the other justices. He mustered up the courage to begin speaking, telling Sarah Roberts's story. He explained the long walk she would take every day to the unpleasant Smith School, and how her father was so frustrated by that experience that he enrolled her at a white-only school to see what would happen. He described her expulsion and explained that her father now sought justice before this court. Then he sat down.

Sumner rose to give the legal argument. He, too, may have felt nervous, for he probably knew that Shaw had quietly played a role in preventing him from being hired as a full-time professor at Harvard Law School. Nevertheless, he projected his booming voice and presented a lengthy speech before Shaw and the other justices. "May it please your Honors," he began. "Can any discrimination, on account of color or race, be made, under the Constitution and Laws of Massachusetts, among the children entitled to the benefit of our public schools?" he asked. "This is the question which the Court is now to hear, to consider, and to decide."

Sumner may have turned to his side, pointing to young Sarah Roberts, who was likely present in the courtroom. "This little child asks at your hands her *personal rights*," Sumner said. "So doing, she calls upon you to decide a question which concerns the personal rights of other colored children." He declared that "on the one side is the city of Boston, strong in its wealth, in its influence, in its character." Then, "on the other side is a little child, of a degraded color, of humble parents, still within the period of natural infancy, but strong from her very weakness."[9]

Sumner's advocacy on behalf of young Sarah's personal rights took place more than a century before *Brown v. Board of Education*, the 1954 Supreme Court decision that integrated American schools. Long before the modern civil rights movement, Sumner delivered an argument in this Massachusetts courtroom invoking words that included *discrimination, color, race, entitlements, benefits, public schools*, and *personal rights*, words that few people—and certainly no lawyers—used in court in the mid-nineteenth century.

While Sumner's argument was prescient and visionary, he tied it to history. "The equality which was declared by our fathers in 1776, and which was made the fundamental law of Massachusetts in 1780," he argued, "was *equality before the law.*" Translating the phrase from the French Revolution *égalité devant la loi* into English, Sumner effectively coined this now-famous expression that had never been used in an American courtroom before. He argued that the principle of "equality before the law" meant that "no person can be *created*, no person can be *born*, with civil or political privileges, not enjoyed equally by all his fellow-citizens." It was time "to efface all political or civil distinctions, and to abolish all institutions founded upon birth."[10]

Sumner argued that equality was impossible in a system of separate schools. White schoolchildren had dozens of schools available; Black schoolchildren did not. White schoolchildren could walk to schools close to their homes; Black schoolchildren had to walk across town simply to get to one. The white schools were better funded, better resourced, and of better quality than the Black school. Even if they had been of the same quality, even if that were true, Sumner said it would not be enough: separate schools imposed a stigma that only integration could erase. "The Jews in Rome are confined to a particular district, called the Ghetto," he observed. Even if the ghetto was somehow equally pleasant to any other part of Rome, "this compulsory segregation from the mass of citizens is of itself an *inequality* which we condemn with our whole souls."

In a ruling in March 1850, Chief Justice Shaw and his colleagues conceded the "broad general principle" that "all persons without distinction of age or sex, birth or color, origin or condition, are equal before the law." But he said people's actual rights "must depend on laws adapted to their respective relations and conditions." Just as it was proper to separate girls from boys, it was "expedient to organize [Blacks] into a separate school, to receive the special training, adapted to their condition." If segregation were "to deepen and perpetuate the odious distinction of caste," Shaw reasoned, so be it. "This prejudice, if it exists, is not created by law, and probably cannot be changed by law." His ruling would be cited nearly fifty years later in *Plessy v. Ferguson*, an infamous Supreme Court decision that established the doctrine of "separate but equal."[11]

The defeat in *Roberts* devastated Sumner's client and the Black community he had been working with. Benjamin Roberts expressed his shock at how "blind and deaf" the court was, how it approved of a "great injustice against the colored people perpetrated by those agents in the public service." He and others had anticipated winning. So much hope had been placed in this court decision, in this expectation that a new leaf might be turned by the judiciary. Yet hope in judges ended up being, as so often in history, utterly misplaced.

The community didn't give up. "We pledge to each other our unceasing efforts, till the struggle results in victory," a group of Black community members swore. For six more years, Roberts, Morris, and other Black leaders continued their boycotts and pushed their lobbying efforts in the Massachusetts Legislature to pass a law mandating integration in Boston. The effort was largely driven by African Americans, and white activists like Sumner played only a small role. In early 1855, the state legislature finally integrated Boston schools. It was "the greatest *boon* ever bestowed upon our people," Roberts celebrated. Morris was more muted. In a letter thanking Sumner many years later, he simply called desegregation a "great blessing."[12]

But all was not well for Sumner and Black Boston. The loss at the Supreme Judicial Court of Massachusetts only foreshadowed far greater dangers to come at the hands of judges and the law.

* * *

BACK IN 1846, Morris had attended a large meeting at Faneuil Hall organized largely by Sumner and Samuel Howe. Standing on the stage with a few other activists, Sumner and Howe explained to the crowd that Boston needed a new interracial organization to provide charity, legal advice, and armed protection to fugitive slaves who were at risk of being recaptured. They wanted funding and volunteers to get the organization going. To give themselves legitimacy in their new endeavor, Sumner and Howe had persuaded John Quincy Adams to give brief remarks at the start of the event. By the end, forty men—including Morris—were so inspired by Adams's words that they signed up to join the initiative. They called it the Boston Vigilance Committee.[13]

The two best friends, Sumner and Howe, shared a belief that citizens had a moral duty to disobey the law sometimes in order to protect their neighbors from oppression. In Boston, many of their Black neighbors were people who had escaped slavery over the years. They lived in perpetual fear of being identified, arrested, and deported back to the South. To protect them, Sumner and other lawyers developed legal strategies to slow down possible arrests and try to win back arrestees' freedom. They also advised volunteers on how to safely protest and encouraged conscientious government officers to openly refuse to enforce fugitive slave laws.

Sumner and Howe recognized that civil disobedience sometimes required violence. While Sumner was too squeamish to ever partake, Howe had plenty of experience with arms, having served in the Greek and Polish revolutions. He collaborated with fellow militant abolitionists on the Vigilance Committee to gather pistols, gunpowder, and other arms to stop potential arrests. One man who praised the committee's militancy was Henry David Thoreau, author of the famous tract *On Civil Disobedience*. Commonly misinterpreted today, Thoreau did not think passive nonviolent resistance was the only proper means to oppose unjust American laws. Breaking with pacifists like Garrison, Thoreau thought abolitionists should be ready to resort to guns.[14]

Morris, Sumner, Howe, Thoreau, and others did not need to rely on violence to protect fugitives from slavery for the first few years of the Vigilance Committee's existence. That changed in 1850.

During the California Gold Rush, northern U.S. senators wanted to admit California, a territory, into the union as a free state. They knew that their constituents, many of whom had joined the Free-Soil Party, would not tolerate more slave states. But southerners objected to adding a free state without making concessions to slavery. In January 1850, Kentucky senator Henry Clay pitched a compromise between North and South to permit California's admission. That compromise was debated all year until a deal was hashed out in September, thanks to a collaboration between senators Clay, Daniel Webster, and John Calhoun.

The final deal was explained to the public as a necessary compromise to preserve the union, which had become increasingly unstable as some southern states threatened to secede over the California issue. In exchange for accepting California as a free state and banning the slave trade in Washington, D.C., northern senators agreed to form territorial governments in New Mexico and Utah as slave territories. Since the deal allowed the spread of slavery, Sumner was horrified. "From the beginning of our history," he later said, "the country has been afflicted with compromise. It is by compromise that human rights have been abandoned."[15]

The deal had a fifth provision, which proved to be the most controversial of all. To placate enslavers who had long complained about the Underground Railroad, which helped enslaved people escape to freedom in the North, Congress passed the Fugitive Slave Act of 1850. Widely considered one of the most repressive and totalitarian laws in American history, the Fugitive Slave Act empowered enslavers, bounty hunters, and law enforcement officers to arrest any Black person accused of being a slave. To send an accused person into slavery, all a white person effectively had to do was sign an affidavit claiming the arrestee was their slave. Moreover, anyone who tried to help an alleged fugitive avoid recapture could be fined or sent to prison for up to six months. Even a simple act of Christian charity, like giving shelter for the night, was punishable.

Until this point, white northerners could pretend slavery didn't affect them. Most of them had never seen the brutality of slavery up close. But there was no *not seeing* anymore. After the passage of the act, bounty hunters prowled the streets of Boston, New York, Cincinnati, and other cities in search of Black people to accuse of being slaves. White northerners feared their own arrest or jail time for helping a Black person hide or run away. They also feared a provision in the law that allowed law enforcement officers to *force* civilians to assist in making arrests. Every northerner—free or fugitive, rich or poor, white or Black—was implicated.

Sumner called the Fugitive Slave Act the "most cruel, unchristian, devilish law." Thanks to the law, many ordinary white northerners who had felt ambivalent about slavery now felt complicit in, and afraid of, the regime of oppression that prevailed in the South. Like their Black neighbors, they could feel the seeming expansion of southern slavery into free northern land. They were outraged, terrified, and galvanized.[16]

* * *

WITHIN THE FIRST three days of the act's passage, an estimated forty Black Bostonians fled for Canada. As the city stood on the precipice of a mass exodus of local Blacks, the Boston Vigilance Committee came together to discuss. Rather than shrink out of fear of being arrested, the committee had doubled in size to eighty members. These men resolved to do everything in their power to protect the city's African American residents.[17]

The first two Black runaways in Boston who faced the threat of deportation were William and Ellen Craft. Born to a slave mother in Georgia who was impregnated by her white master, Ellen was so light-skinned that she could pass as a white person. Her husband, William, had a dark complexion. In 1848, the couple escaped slavery through a remarkable trick. Ellen dressed up as a southern white gentleman by dyeing her hair and donning a top hat, jacket, and trousers. William posed as her slave. The couple traveled by train and steamboat and made it safely into freedom in time for Christmas. Since then, they had enjoyed a free life in Boston and went on a speaking tour to share their dramatic escape story.[18]

At first, the Crafts weren't worried about being recaptured in Boston, which had been considered a sanctuary of freedom and was the home of more than six hundred fugitives from slavery. But the Fugitive Slave Act jeopardized the safety of Boston Blacks. It tied the hands of local officials who had conscientiously objected to enforcing preexisting fugitive slave laws in the past. Facing enormous pressure from the national government, local officials started issuing warrants for the arrest of fugitive slaves after receiving affidavits.

When three Georgia bounty hunters submitted affidavits claiming the Crafts were slaves, local officers reluctantly gave them warrants for arrest. But they were so disgusted by the Fugitive Slave Act that they refused to help carry out the capture, telling the bounty hunters that they had to abduct the Crafts on their own. The bounty hunters were eager to do it, as the Crafts' owner back in Georgia was paying them top dollar. Many abolitionists called bounty hunters like these "bloodhounds." Sumner called them "dogs."[19]

In late October 1849, these three dogs barked along the streets of Boston on the hunt for the Crafts. Discovering their presence, the Vigilance Committee held an emergency meeting. Some timid members said that the Crafts should flee to Canada right away. But one member, Lewis Hayden, didn't want the Crafts to abandon their home. Sumner backed up Hayden. He argued that the Crafts should stand their ground and let conscientious Bostonians protect them. "I counsel no violence," Sumner said around this time. Yet he surely knew that violence might be necessary. "Like the flaming sword of the cherubim at the gates of Paradise," he declared, the committee would "prevent any SLAVE-HUNTER from ever setting foot in this Commonwealth."

Lewis Hayden, himself a fugitive slave, offered up his home to protect the Crafts. Born in Kentucky, Hayden had once been married to Esther, an enslaved woman who was owned by Senator Henry Clay. In spite of Hayden's begging and pleading, Clay had sold Esther to a plantation far away from their home to pay off some of his debts. While Clay made an enormous profit, Hayden never saw his wife again. Heartbroken and devastated, Hayden escaped slavery and made it safely to Boston. There, he remarried and forged a decent life for himself as a store owner. But he never gave up his search for his first wife, and his heart burned with hatred for Senator Clay. He was determined to resist the Fugitive Slave Act that Clay helped to write.[20]

The Vigilance Committee decided that William Craft would stay in Hayden's home while Ellen Craft would hide elsewhere. They obtained sketches of the hunters' faces and plastered them all over the streets. On the North Slope of Beacon Hill, where Hayden lived, Black residents fortified the streets, stood guard on the lookout for the hunters, and armed themselves with guns, swords, and knives in preparation for a fight.

Meanwhile, Sumner and other lawyers on the committee connived several creative legal tricks to slow down the hunters. They drafted bogus legal petitions against the hunters, charging them with various crimes including intent to kidnap. While the petitions had little chance of succeeding, they hoped to persuade local officers to arrest the hunters and charge them bail prior to release on the pretense of these charges. They also came up with plans to keep the Crafts in the city. For example, they floated the idea of accusing the Crafts of committing illegal fornication, since they weren't legally married. If city officers arrested the Crafts for being fornicators, they reasoned, the bounty hunters wouldn't be able to send them back into slavery pending trial.

Sometime around October 25, the Vigilance Committee attorneys deployed their strategy. They managed to persuade local officers to arrest the hunters, and they were detained for several hours before being released. When the hunters left the courthouse, an interracial crowd of thousands of protesters stood outside hissing and flashing pistols, then followed them to their lodgings. For the next week or so, the hunters tried to escape the attention of protesters and learn where the Crafts were hiding.

When the bounty hunters finally approached Hayden's house on Phillips Street, only around six blocks from the Sumner house, they met Hayden and a posse of armed Black men outside. To protect William Craft, Hayden had double locked the doors and barred the windows. Reportedly, he informed the hunters that there were kegs of gunpowder underneath the front of his home. Holding a torch, Hayden declared that if the bounty hunters didn't leave, he would blow everybody up. They left in disbelief.[21]

On October 30, a group of Vigilance Committee men visited the bounty hunters at their hotel. The group leader was Reverend Theodore Parker, a Unitarian theologian who had befriended Sumner and Howe some years earlier. Reverend Parker preached a kind of fiery Christianity, a Christianity that didn't advocate for turning the other cheek in the face of oppression. "The fugitive has the same natural right to defend himself against the slave-catcher," he once said, "that he has against a murderer or a wolf." Reverend Parker warned the hunters that they would be killed if they didn't leave the city. A few days later, the hunters left Boston, and the Crafts, after raising some money from the committee, moved to England for their safety.[22]

* * *

BAY STATERS WERE furious at the Fugitive Slave Act for wreaking havoc on the city of Boston and threatening the freedom of white and Black people alike across the state. They directed their ire especially at Senator Daniel Webster, who had endorsed the act as part of the compromise measures of 1850. As if in gratitude, President Millard Fillmore nominated Webster for the position of Secretary of State shortly afterward. To many voters, Webster had betrayed Massachusetts to advance his own political career. Looking to run for president soon, Webster knew he needed support from the South before he could launch his candidacy.

Sumner was especially disgusted by Webster, who was one of his childhood heroes. As a young boy, Sumner had been mesmerized while listening to one of Webster's spellbinding speeches. Not anymore. "With all his majestic powers, he is a traitor to a holy cause," Sumner told his brother George. "Webster has placed himself in the dark list of apostates," he wrote to a friend. "He reminds me very much of Strafford, or of the archangel ruined. In other moods, I might call him Judas Iscariot, or Benedict Arnold." Sumner believed that Webster's "ignorant ambition" had led him to forget about "freedom." He had made "the cunningest and best bid for the Presidency," a bid that Sumner hoped would soon crumble before his eyes.

Sumner believed that the Fugitive Slave Act, horrible as it was, provided a valuable chance to channel northern rage toward the Free-Soil Party in the upcoming election. He also recognized an opportunity in the vacancy that Webster had created. Shortly after Webster's rise to the president's cabinet, Congressman Robert Winthrop was appointed to fill his vacant senate seat for the time being. After the November 1850 election, however, the Massachusetts State House would get to decide who would become the permanent senator for a full six-year term. (At the time, unlike today, state legislatures, rather than voters, chose U.S. senators. That only changed with the ratification of the Seventeenth Amendment to the Constitution in 1913.)

Thanks to the Free-Soil Party, Democrats and Whigs weren't the only players in the upcoming election. If they won just enough seats in the state legislature, no single political party would hold a majority in the State House. Then, Sumner reasoned, Democrats and Whigs would be forced to negotiate with the Free Soilers for control over the State House. In exchange for support, the Free Soilers would have a chance to convince one of the two parties to oust Winthrop and award them the Senate seat. Here was a chance, he hoped, for political antislavery to take over Massachusetts politics and get onto the national scene.

Almost daily, Sumner met with other Free-Soil leaders in his law office on Court Street to discuss the upcoming election and potential political coalitions. He also agreed to run as the Free-Soil candidate to take Winthrop's now-vacant congressional seat. But he didn't expect to win, because Boston remained a Whig stronghold that was economically interdependent with southern cotton and loyal to Webster. It was in the rest of Massachusetts that Sumner believed the Free Soilers could earn substantial gains. And it was in the Senate—not the House—that Sumner ultimately hoped Free

Soilers could get a seat. "The antislavery agitation which it was hoped to hush by the recent laws is breaking out afresh," he explained to his brother George. "It will not be hushed. Mr. Webster is strong in Boston, but not in Massachusetts. Out of the city he is weak. . . . I think that everywhere the antislavery sentiment will get real strength."[23]

Across the state, Sumner campaigned vigorously for the Free Soilers, centering his message around Webster's fated endorsement of the Fugitive Slave Act. He needed his party to win as many seats in the state legislature as possible to influence the Senate pick. Addressing a packed crowd at Faneuil Hall, he said voters should look for three things in choosing whom to support. "The first is *backbone*; the second is *backbone*; and the third is *backbone*," he declared. "When I see a person talking loudly against Slavery in private, but hesitating in public, and failing in the time of trial, I say, *He wants backbone.* When I see a person who coöperated with Antislavery men, and then deserted them, I say, *He wants backbone.*" The audience thundered with applause.[24]

* * *

WHEN THE ELECTION took place on November 11, 1850, the Whigs suffered historic losses across the state. Losing their majority in both chambers of the Massachusetts Legislature, Whigs were forced to reckon with the Free Soilers, who had now gained more than one hundred seats in the State House and a dozen in the State Senate. If the Free Soilers aligned with Democrats, as Sumner had been contemplating, they could take the majority in the legislature and influence the choice of senator. "You have whipped Webster," an ecstatic friend told Sumner.[25]

At first, Free Soilers couldn't decide whether to form a coalition. Charles Francis Adams—possibly the most prominent Free Soiler in the state, even more so than Sumner—felt affinity for his former party, the Whigs, and was horrified by the idea of working with Democrats. Unlike the educated Anglo and Protestant elite, who tended to be Whigs, Democrats were the party of immigrants, Catholics, working-class men, and farmers. They favored things that Adams found intolerable, such as breaking up the state's large corporations, granting subsidized land to farmers, and decentralizing the banking system. Adams had an aristocratic disdain for the Democrats. "To join with them," Adams believed, "strikes me as a renunciation of all moral character."[26]

By contrast, Henry Wilson, another leading Free Soiler, favored a coalition. Raised in poverty to a drunkard father, Wilson had worked his way up through the shoemaking business. He naturally sympathized with the working-class reforms that Democrats advocated. He also wasn't an ideological purist like Adams. Extremely ambitious and hardworking, he thrived in the wheeling and dealing that came with state politics. He didn't waste time with writing speeches and formulating ideas. Without the consent of Adams, who arguably served as the Free-Soil Party's symbolic leader, he began hobnobbing with Democrats to form a coalition.

Wilson proposed a grand deal: in exchange for giving Democrats the governorship, which had to be decided by the legislature because no candidate had won a majority, Free Soilers would get their choice for the next U.S. senator. To both sides, this was an excellent proposal. Massachusetts Democrats cared relatively little about national politics, focusing on various economic reforms within the state. Meanwhile, Free Soilers cared almost exclusively about the slavery issue in Washington. A similar alliance between state Democrats and Free Soilers had already been formed in Ohio, which propelled Sumner's close friend and the Free-Soil Party's leader, Salmon Chase, to the Senate two years earlier. Another alliance had also been formed in New Hampshire.

A third prominent Free Soiler, Francis Bird, backed up Wilson against Adams. A shrewd campaigner and wealthy businessman, Bird had been so disgusted by slavery's expansion that he had been funneling all his financial resources into the Free-Soil Party. For the past few years, he had been organizing regular dinners at his personal expense, inviting politicians across the state to meet and discuss antislavery ideas. A tall, friendly man with noble manners, Bird proved just as good as Wilson in bringing unlikely coalitions together. "He enjoyed manipulating the secret wires that moved the puppets of politics," Bird's children recalled.[27]

Wilson and Bird were workhorses and pragmatists who expected *results* rather than sticking to ideological purity. Against the will of Adams, they spent all of November and December meeting with Democrats to hash out the contours of a political coalition. As they did so, they pushed aside Adams, who was repulsed by the backroom arrangement they were negotiating. Given Adams's lack of interest, Wilson and Bird pitched the party's second-most prominent member as their candidate for the open Senate seat: Charles Sumner.

* * *

As the prospect of a coalition became more real, Sumner felt reluctant about the deal that Wilson and Bird had been crafting. He was uncomfortable with being their favored choice for the Senate. "I have searched my heart, & have its response. I do not desire to be Senator," he wrote to his brother George. He had also long resented the dealmaking that came with politics and politicians. "It is *money, money, money,*" he once complained about politics to his best friend Henry Longfellow. "Put not your faith in *politicians,*" he vented to his other best friend, Samuel Howe. "They may talk fairly, but they will *ACT always as politicians.*"[28]

Despite his aversion to politics, Sumner realized that there was no way to challenge slavery's dominance over the country without it. That prompted him to change his mind. Slavery "must be opposed not only by all the influences of morals and religion, but directly by every instrument of Political Power. As it is sustained by law, it can be overthrown only by law," he decided. "I am sorry to confess that this can be done, only through the machinery of politics. The politician, then, must be summoned," he said in one speech. "The moralist and the philanthropist must become for this purpose politicians."[29]

Sumner recognized that the paramount goal of the Free-Soil Party was to place a politician in the Senate. "Websterized Whiggery must be defeated," he observed. If that required a coalition with the Democrats and his own name on the ticket, so be it. "When I think of the importance of Senator, to our cause, I confess the strength of the temptation," he confided in Howe. "Nothing seems clearer to me than our duty, in utter disregard of all state issues, & placing our Anti-Slavery above all other things," he explained, than "to try to obtain the *balance of power* in the Legislature, at least in the Senate, so that we may influence *potentially* the choice of a senator in Congress." Howe and others were stunned at Sumner's willingness to ally with the other side and abandon the Whig Party in which they had grown up. He believed it was necessary.

With Sumner's consent, Wilson and Bird negotiated a final deal between Democrats and Free Soilers. The parties agreed to elect Democrat Nathaniel Banks, a former bobbin boy in the textile mills, as Speaker of the State House. They put the Free Soiler Wilson, who had been elected to the State Senate, as president of the body. Democratic shopkeepers, blacksmiths, cobblers, and other ordinary working people were chosen for high state offices. Democrat George Boutwell was named governor. No Whigs would have any role in Massachusetts governance. As one aristocratic Harvard lawyer put it, "This state is to be 'shoemakerized.'"[30]

After the legislature carried out the various procedural votes to put the coalition members into their respective offices, the final part of the deal was to elect Sumner to the U.S. Senate. That process began on January 4, 1851, when lawmakers cast ballots for their desired senator, choosing between the main candidates of Sumner and Winthrop. Sumner was expected to be the winner. But when the votes were the counted in the House, he came out five short of the majority he needed. There was a deadlock, leading to no one being elected. A core group of Democrats, led by the Boston lawyer Caleb Cushing, refused to honor the deal.

For the next several months, Cushing and his small posse blocked Sumner's election to the Senate in ballot after ballot, despite the pleadings of state Democratic party leaders to honor their agreement with the Free Soilers. These disgruntled Democrats were outraged that their state party leaders were willing to send an antislavery man to Washington, given that the national Democratic Party had embraced slavery's expansion. Every time a ballot was taken to elect the next senator, Cushing and his allies refused to pick Sumner. In desperation, some Democrats tried to extract a promise from Sumner not to agitate on slavery for the first few years of his potential Senate term. "I would not move across the room to take the post," Sumner replied. "It must seek me—and . . . if it finds me, it will find me an absolutely independent man, without any pledge or promise."[31]

*　*　*

WHILE SUMNER'S ELECTION hung in the balance, two extraordinary events took place in Boston that were so explosive that they transformed the political calculus of state lawmakers and forever changed Massachusetts history. First, in February 1851, the Vigilance Committee defended Shadrach Minkins, a fugitive slave, from recapture. The committee even silently condoned the actions of a mass of Black protesters who stormed the courthouse at gunpoint, rescued Minkins, and transported him along the Underground Railroad to Canada.

Southerners and their allies in the North watched Minkins's rescue with horror as Boston fell into a state of utter lawlessness in their eyes. There was a "negro insurrection in Boston," declared one newspaper. Decrying the situation in Massachusetts, Senator Henry Clay demanded to know whether a "government of white men was to be yielded to a government by blacks." To enforce the Fugitive Slave Act and put Boston Blacks in their place, President Fillmore decided to act. In an executive order cosigned by Secretary of State Daniel Webster, Fillmore called for prosecutions against everyone who played a role in Minkins's rescue. He also authorized the American military to intervene to ensure that no more fugitive slaves escaped recapture.[32]

Second, on April 3, the Vigilance Committee learned about the arrest of Thomas Sims, a fugitive who had escaped enslavement at a rice plantation in Georgia. A thin, wiry young man who may have been as young as seventeen, Sims was snatched by two police officers only weeks after he arrived in Boston. While Sims was awaiting a summary proceeding at a courthouse to deport him back to Georgia, Reverend Theodore Parker and other committee members visited the court and demanded to see him to offer their legal services. They were refused, and after a heated argument with a police officer, one lawyer was arrested and locked up, too.

The next morning, abolitionists rushed to the courthouse to protest Sims's detainment. They were met by the sight of hundreds of federal troops and local officers—possibly more than five hundred in all—who had gathered overnight. The guards had wrapped the perimeter of the courthouse in iron chains, which reminded Bostonians of the fetters used on the arms and legs of slaves. The chains weren't high enough to walk under or low enough to step over. To get past them and enter the courthouse, one had to crawl.

Even Chief Justice Lemuel Shaw, when he arrived for work that day, had to squirm through the mighty blockade of armed officers and crawl underneath the iron fetters to enter his own court, a so-called temple of justice. In the days ahead, Sumner collaborated with Richard Dana and other attorneys to plead with numerous judges for Sims's freedom. That effort stopped with Shaw, who denied their petition for habeas corpus to release Sims. Shaw also upheld the constitutionality of the Fugitive Slave Act, declaring that it "behooves all persons, bound to obey the laws of the United States," to support the recapture of fugitives.

In the early dawn of April 12, Boston police and federal troops stepped into formation outside the courthouse they had been guarding for nearly ten days. Clad in chains, Thomas Sims was shoved out of the court and ordered to march toward Boston Harbor with an escort of roughly three hundred guards. Tears were flowing down the young man's cheeks as he was ushered onto a ship, while abolitionist protesters screamed and hollered, demanding his freedom. "Sims, preach Liberty to the Slaves!" somebody shouted as the ship began to leave. "And is this Massachusetts liberty?" he exclaimed back. Minutes later, he was gone.

By then, hundreds of Bostonians had converged on the dock to watch in tearful horror. At the direction of a local preacher, the mass of Bostonians knelt and collectively prayed for Sims. It wasn't lost on anyone that he was being sent to slavery from the very harbor where, nearly eighty years earlier, colonists had thrown tea into the sea to call for freedom. Here, in this symbolic cradle of liberty, Sims was sent back into slavery. On his arrival in Georgia, he was whipped thirty-nine times in a public square, imprisoned, and then resold to a Louisiana slave broker.[33]

* * *

TWELVE DAYS AFTER the Sims affair, on April 24, the Massachusetts House held the twenty-fifth ballot to decide whether Sumner would become their senator. The tide was turning as public fury erupted across the state, demanding that Sumner be chosen given his leading opposition to the hated Fugitive Slave Act. Once again, Sumner came up short—but this time, only a couple of conservative Democrats dissented. Then, a Whig lawmaker proposed that the House cast secret ballots rather than public ones to decide the senatorial election. Figuring that Sumner was less likely to win under secrecy, lawmakers passed the motion. The plan backfired. On the very next ballot, the twenty-sixth, Sumner earned 193 votes. That was the exact number he needed.

At the time, Sumner was having dinner at the home of Charles Francis Adams. The Adams family had sent their young boy Henry to the State House to monitor the ballots and report back. When Henry returned, interrupted dinner, and announced his victory, Sumner took the news quietly. He gathered his things and left the Adams home just as everybody else was getting ready to celebrate. As thousands of Free Soilers entered the streets ringing bells, firing cannons, and dancing in jubilee, Sumner rushed out of the city.[34]

As fast as he could, Sumner ran through the Boston streets, crossed the Charles River, and went straight to the reclusive home of Henry Longfellow in Cambridge. While on his way, he stumbled into Lewis Hayden, the fugitive slave who had protected the Crafts. "I am doing what you did once—running away," Sumner told Hayden. "I am a fugitive—from my friends."

Avoiding Wilson, Bird, and everyone else who played a key role in his election, Sumner spent the rest of the evening with the Longfellows. According to Fanny Longfellow, Sumner didn't look happy at all. He was "depressed," she recalled. "He really did not want the office," Sumner's Free-Soil friend John Greenleaf Whittier later claimed. "But we forced it upon him."[35]

In this moment of mixed feelings, perhaps Sumner was thinking about the enormous burden he was about to take on in Washington. Perhaps he was reflecting on how much he was going to miss Samuel Howe, Longfellow, and others in Boston. Most likely, he may have been struck by the extraordinary coincidence that the date of his election, April 24, coincided with the anniversary of his father, Charles Pinckney Sumner's, death.

For the past few years, Sumner had been mocked, reviled, ostracized, and abandoned by friends and mentors for his antislavery politics. Now, he was bound to become one of the most famous and influential men in the North. A new dawn was rising, a dawn with great promise. Years ago, the late John Quincy Adams had seen it coming, predicting that Sumner would one day inherit his mantle after his death. "You will enter public life . . . in spite of yourself," he had once prophesized to Sumner. "I see you have a mission to perform. . . . I look from Pisgah to the Promised Land; you must enter upon it."[36]

PART II

THE
SLAVE POWER

CHAPTER 8

THE SENATE IS A DIRTY HOUSE

"THREE TIMES YESTERDAY I WEPT, LIKE A CHILD," CHARLES SUMNER wrote to Samuel Gridley Howe during his journey down to Washington, D.C., in November 1851. "First, in parting with Longfellow, next in parting with you, & lastly, as I left my mother & sister." Sumner was anguished at losing the people closest to him as he settled in a new city, burdened by great public responsibility. "I now move away from those who have been more than brothers to me," he continued. "My soul is wrung, and my eyes are bleared with tears."[1]

In Washington, Sumner found more to frighten him: he had never lived side by side with slavery before. The nation's capital, squished between two slave states, was a southern city. After the site for the capital was chosen in 1790, enslaved laborers had built the town's infrastructure and its two temples of democracy: the White House and the Capitol Building. By 1850, more than four thousand people were enslaved within the district. Another ten thousand Black individuals lived free. Together, they constituted one of every four people in town. The remaining three fourths were demographically mixed: enslavers who held land straddling the city's periphery, Irish immigrants who had come for work, federal employees (mostly white southerners) staffing the government, and nearly three hundred members of Congress, including sixty-two U.S. senators.[2]

Sumner was now one of them. Forty years old, he was in his prime. Not a gray hair on his head, he looked every inch a classical Roman senator: barrel-chested, tall in stature, well dressed. His deep, melodious voice was "resonant, not without gentle tones, but capable of a lionlike roar," as one future senator recalled. He stood with poise, often with his left hand on his hip and his right toying with an eyeglass. When excited, he would toss his hair. When he sat, he was mindful of posture. When he spoke, he did so with dignity and absolute conviction—never swearing, never admitting fault. And he dressed like a self-possessed and somewhat flamboyant aristocrat: preferring English tweeds over the more common black frock coats, he was typically seen in brown coats, light waistcoats, lavender or checkered trousers, and shoes with English gaiters.

"There is an Arabian proverb that no man is called of God till the age of forty," the abolitionist Thomas Wentworth Higginson once remarked, "and Sumner was just that age when he entered the Senate." Forty he may have been, but Sumner was still a rookie who merely looked like a statesman. Confused and unprepared, he was often up until midnight drafting his floor speeches; sometimes he would spend a whole night in preparation, pacing back and forth in the lonely bedroom he rented in a private home.

Despite his novice status, Sumner's supporters expected him to be the nation's leading antislavery lawmaker. It wasn't an easy bar to clear. "You see, my dear Sumner, that I expect much of you, that I expect heroism of the most heroic kind," the abolitionist Rev. Theodore Parker had sternly explained to him. "I hope you will be the senator *with a conscience*."[3]

* * *

ALMOST AS SOON as Sumner arrived in Washington, he received a warning. Warmly grasping his hand, Senator Thomas Hart Benton grunted that "he had come to the Senate too late." Benton told Sumner that "all the great issues and all the great men were gone. There was nothing left but snarling over slavery, and no chance whatever for a career." Benton, the longest-serving senator of the time, had just lost his reelection. While a slaveholder himself, he opposed slavery's expansion into the western territories America had conquered from Mexico. After taking a principled vote against the Compromise of 1850, he was ousted by the Missouri legislature. Horace Mann, who had replaced John Quincy Adams in Congress, called Sumner "the greatest constitutional lawyer in the country, except Col. Benton."[4]

Several other great statesmen of the past decade had also reached their sunsets. Secretary of State Daniel Webster, despite all his efforts to promote the Fugitive Slave Act and set the stage for a presidential campaign, fell into bad health and died suddenly the next year. John Calhoun, the nation's leading proslavery senator, would also die in 1852. Senator Henry Clay, architect of the Compromise of 1850 and of the Whig Party, was sick as well. As it happened, Sumner's first day in the Senate was Clay's last day of attendance. By coincidence, he had also chosen for himself the seat that had been formerly occupied by Calhoun (and Mississippi's senator Jefferson Davis) in order to sit next to his Free-Soil friend, Senator Salmon Chase.[5]

With the power brokers gone or going, few senators wanted to revisit the slavery question. The Senate was a powerful place where any wrong step had the potential to upend the country. "In the twenty years before the Civil War the Senate was the dominant force in the Government," one respected early twentieth-century historian observed, "and 'the fate of the country was largely settled in the Senate.'" After the grueling compromise of 1850, any new political fights regarding slavery's expansion risked the stability of the Union and the prospects of any officeholder. Yet Sumner had been elected precisely to upset the unhappy status quo.

At first, most colleagues found him nonthreatening. Although the Free-Soil movement had taken Massachusetts by storm, politicians in many parts of the country thought it a laughably hopeless cause. Sumner was clearly intelligent and beamed with sincerity. But senators fully expected the buttoned-up, Harvard-educated New England scholar to get chewed up in the dog-eat-dog world of national politics.[6]

When Sumner stepped into the Senate Chamber, he discovered a strikingly intimate and imposing place. Covered by a richly ornamented low-vaulted dome with apertures to let in sunlight, the semicircular room had excellent acoustics that allowed senators to hear their words reverberate around the chamber. They sat on luxurious Moroccan leather chairs and used mahogany desks arranged on nicely curved platforms that gradually descended toward the room's center. Sumner was in awe.[7]

His awe gradually evaporated in the foul, punishingly humid air of the badly ventilated room. He discovered that senators were often drunk by afternoon supper because committee rooms were stocked with free liquor. He was horrified to learn that senators chewed tobacco and spat its juice directly onto the opulent red carpet, even though dozens of spittoons were available around the room. They did it simply because they could. When his friend Charles Dickens had visited the Senate Chamber, he noted that it was so strange "to see an honourable gentleman . . . shooting [tobacco] from his mouth, as from a pop-gun." Writing to Charles Francis Adams, Sumner confessed that the Senate wasn't what he had expected. "The scenes of the Senate have disgusted me," he wrote.

At times, senators even brawled in the chamber. Only a year before

Sumner's arrival, Senator Benton had lunged at Mississippi senator Henry Foote, who responded by pulling a gun on Benton. Baring his chest, Benton boomed, "I have no pistols! Let him fire!" before Foote's gun was confiscated. The brawls, often about slavery, shocked Sumner. "The Southerners are in high quarrel," he told a friend in early December after one such occasion. "Foote & Butler at red-hot words. The scene was theatrical."

Raised in the land of Puritans, Sumner was appalled by this machismo behavior—what he called "plantation manners" (even though some northern senators partook). "Slavery is the source of all meanness here from national dishonesty down to tobacco-spitting," he explained to Howe. "The Senate [is] a *dirty* house," he told someone else. "Pah! The vulgarity, the swagger, the vileness—nobody knows who has not sat in it."[8]

* * *

FOR OVER A year, Sumner did not criticize the Fugitive Slave Act or speak about the expansion of slavery whatsoever in the Senate. He wanted to build a rapport with his colleagues and come across as a reasonable man before bringing his fire. He also didn't want to be perceived as a single-issue senator. "The time has not come for me to say what is in my heart on Slavery," he explained to a friend. "I am unwilling to be mixed up with . . . Southern extremists." And so, he hobnobbed with his colleagues, including the Senate's most fierce proslavery men.[9]

To his surprise, politicians were much more pleasant in social gatherings than at work. Sumner enjoyed a nice dinner with the rabidly pro-slavery congressman Henry Wise and New Hampshire senator Franklin Pierce (soon to be President Pierce). He befriended Louisiana's proslavery senator Pierre Soulé, a worldly man whose French upbringing appealed to Sumner. He even had lively conversations with Varina Davis, the future First Lady of the Confederacy, at several parties hosted by southern belles. "He never intruded his peculiar views upon us in any degree," Mrs. Davis recalled nearly forty years later. She delighted in listening to Sumner's melodious voice as he chatted about "the Indian mutiny, lace, Demosthenes, jewels, Seneca's morals, intaglios, the Platonian theory, and once gave . . . quite an interesting résumé on the history of dancing."[10]

Sumner's first floor speech involved whether Congress should invite a Hungarian revolutionary to an official reception. Sumner opposed the reception on isolationist grounds. But this seemingly mundane issue evoked an eruption from his closest friend, Samuel Howe. Before the two first met, Howe had served as an army doctor in the Greek and Polish revolutions. Sumner's lack of enthusiasm for the Hungarian Revolution of 1848 was crushing to Howe. "This is the speech of Lawyer Sumner, Senator Sumner," he complained in a letter. "Not of generous, chivalrous, high-souled Charles Sumner, who went with me into the Broad Street riot, and who, if need had been, would have defended the women and children in the houses by pitching their ruffian assailants down the stairs."[11]

Sumner was hurt by his best friend's mean words. While he and Howe quickly made up, they would continue to ruffle each other's feathers on political issues for the rest of their lives. These conflicts tore at Sumner, who discovered how lonely his life would now be. Every decision, every action, every speech, from now until his death, would be scrutinized, praised, or criticized by both the public and the people he loved most. This realization was jarring for a man who had never held public office before and who had now been thrust onto the national stage. "I feel heart-sick here," he wrote to his confidant Longfellow. "The Senate is a lone place."[12]

Seeking to help the antislavery cause quietly, Sumner visited Daniel Drayton in prison. Four years earlier, Drayton and his mate Edward Sayres had been caught attempting to transport more than seventy slaves to freedom on their schooner. After being represented at trial by Sumner's friend Horace Mann, they were fined ten thousand dollars and thrown into prison when they couldn't afford to pay the steep price. Visiting Drayton in jail, Sumner told him that he would try to earn him and his mate a pardon by talking to President Fillmore. They agreed that Drayton's best chance for freedom was for Sumner to lobby discreetly without publicly discussing the case. "I had been made enough of a martyr," Drayton thought.[13]

Abolitionists in Massachusetts didn't know much about Sumner's private efforts. They were instead furious at their senator for failing to speak publicly about Drayton and Sayres's confinement. In February 1852, they sent Sumner a petition of nearly three hundred signatures demanding presidential pardons for the pair. For two months, Sumner didn't even respond to the petition or present it to the Senate as requested. The great abolitionist William Lloyd Garrison furiously accused Sumner of lacking a backbone and betraying the cause. "If need be, I shall show *backbone* in resisting the pressure even of friends," Sumner said defensively to his ally Henry Wilson. He told Wilson confidentially of his private efforts. "Had I uttered a word for Drayton and Sayres in the Senate," he insisted, "I should have a dealt a blow at them which they well understood."[14]

In the end, Sumner's quiet diplomacy worked. After failing to win renomination by the Whigs over the summer, Fillmore decided he might as well do some good deeds. And so, he mailed Sumner a letter with a pardon for the pair. Sumner went straight to the jailhouse with the letter in hand, persuaded the jailers that the letter was credible, escorted Drayton and Sayres out of the jail, and put them on a private carriage toward Baltimore that very night before any angry proslavery mob discovered the news and tried to interfere.

To Sumner, the affair was a spectacular success. But his abolitionist base couldn't have cared less. They charged him with being a coward. Even when he explained all his private actions to the press, his supporters found the story hard to believe or credit. Sumner grew frustrated with his supporters for not appreciating his work. Over time, he learned a valuable lesson from the experience: in politics, publicity is everything.[15]

* * *

SUMNER'S SUPPORTERS GREW increasingly angry with him over the course of 1852, believing he had sold out by not delivering abolitionist speeches. One friend warned him against becoming "dry and big and pompous like some whom you will find your neighbors there." Sumner proudly rebuffed his detractors. "From the time I first came here I determined to speak on slavery some time at the end of June or in July, and not before," he insisted to one critic. Many voters didn't believe him. "Do you see what imminent deadly peril poor Sumner is in?" the abolitionist Rev. Theodore Parker wrote to Samuel Howe, urging the latter to convince Sumner to be more aggressive. "If he does not speak, then he is *dead—dead—dead!*"

Howe pleaded with Sumner to speak urgently. Recently, Howe and other Free Soilers had launched an antislavery newspaper, the *Boston Commonwealth*, to effectively serve as Sumner's propaganda arm. They were struggling to defend him while he was being so cautious. Despite Howe's pleas, Sumner doubled down. "I can claim the credit of having carried Anti-Slavery truth, & the ideas of Progress, not unsuccessfully, before audiences to which they had never been presented," he declared to Howe in April. "But in so doing I have always borrowed something from Prudence." Writing to John Whittier, Sumner explained that "the public should become submissive to the idea that I am a senator before they hear my voice. Unless this is so, I shall not secure a fair hearing from the country."[16]

Meanwhile, Boston Whigs jeered at Sumner for losing support from his base. Robert Winthrop, his rival of many years and his opponent in the Senate race, celebrated that "it was too late" for Sumner ever to earn back his reputation as an antislavery agitator. Winthrop and other Whigs believed Sumner was an aberration, an abolitionist fluke who had entered the Senate by a surprise deal. They eagerly awaited the day he would be replaced by a loyal Whig as soon as his term was complete. Believing he was unimportant, most Brahmin circles still shunned Sumner. Major conservative newspapers in Boston simply ignored his existence.[17]

Sumner's loneliness and political difficulties partly stemmed from the fact that he lacked staff support. At the time, only Senate committee chairs received funding for clerical assistance. Sumner didn't even have a private office. Compelled to work in the Senate library, at home, or at his desk on the Senate floor, and with his closest friends and political advisers far off in Massachusetts, Sumner had to develop political strategy completely on his own. Feeling worried for his friend, the Free Soiler Henry Wilson traveled to Washington to impress upon Sumner the urgency of speaking out. "You must not let the session close without speaking," Wilson practically begged. "Should you do so, you would be openly denounced by nine-tenths of our people."[18]

Convinced by Wilson, Sumner decided to give a big speech about slavery in the summer of 1852. He planned for it to be a decisive essay on slavery and the Constitution. To prepare, he decided to look at everything the Founding Fathers had said about slavery. And so, in addition to doing his own research, he wrote to John Adams's grandson. "Are there any special words of your grandfather against slavery anywhere on record, in tract or correspondence?" he asked Charles Francis Adams. "If there are, let me have them."

In addition to looking at the Founding Fathers, he wanted to review contemporary legal arguments being made by antislavery lawyers. To start, he drew on the work of his Ohio colleague Salmon Chase, who had effectively founded the Free-Soil Party. Five years earlier, Chase had argued a Supreme Court case articulating his position on the unconstitutionality of the Fugitive Slave Act of 1793. Sumner also revisited Martin Van Buren and Samuel Tilden's Barnburner Manifesto, which was one basis for the Free-Soil Party's political platform.

Sumner aimed to soak in every existent written word on constitutional antislavery ideas, synthesize those ideas, and spell them out in definitive form. He once described his mind as a "cistern, not a fountain." He believed his greatest strength was in summarizing and communicating ideas rather than developing and originating them. Writing to a friend, Congressman Horace Mann explained that Sumner's upcoming speech "will require not originality . . . but skill in using [materials], and this is his *forte*."[19]

Yet in preparing his epic address, Sumner made a near-fatal political mistake. He told too many politicos about his plan. When he was finally ready to present in late July, proslavery senators who knew his intentions voted against allowing him the floor. The norm at the time was to give freshmen senators one chance to deliver a lengthy oration on any topic of their choice. But political norms didn't apply to slavery. Even some of the Senate's moderately antislavery senators, who were not Free Soilers, were horrified that Sumner was denied a chance to speak. "The shutting of the doors against Sumner was wicked," New York's William Seward decried. "Indignation pervaded me to the finger-ends."

Sumner must have felt especially angry that his two neighbors contributed to silencing him. On one side sat South Carolina senator Andrew Butler, who said he was "extremely embarrassed" about breaking norms to muzzle his neighbor but believed it was necessary to stop Sumner from rocking the "angry waters of agitation." His other neighbor, Virginia senator James Mason, author of the Fugitive Slave Act, was more dismissive. "You may speak next term," Mason said glibly. "I must speak this term," Sumner insisted. When Mason taunted him, repeating, "You sha'n't," Sumner grew angry. "I will; and you can't prevent me," he shouted.[20]

While projecting outward confidence, Sumner grew nervous that he would fail to get to speak on the floor and would look like a sellout to his supporters. His days were numbered: It was now the end of July, and the final day of session was August 31. He had not spoken about slavery once. He was not turning out to be the vocal, fearless antislavery politician (in the image of John Quincy Adams) he had promised to be. Wendell Phillips had already warned Sumner that he had been "asked scores of times by free soilers as well as our folks" across Massachusetts whether their new senator was trustworthy. Phillips begged Sumner to find a way to address the Senate. "You will have to fight for it," Charles Francis Adams bluntly told him.

Sumner studied the Senate parliamentary rules in search of a way to win the floor. He finally settled on a plan. Catching wind that the Finance Committee planned to introduce an amendment to the civil appropriations bill ahead of its floor vote that would concern funding for the Fugitive Slave Act, Sumner decided to propose an amendment to the amendment (a trick he would use many times in the future). In so doing, he would be allowed, according to Senate rules, to speak without a time limit or the consent of others to explain his amendment. Seizing this time might jeopardize the fate of the entire bill—the most important bill of the session. "But I shall proceed," he wrote with determination to a friend. "Do not let this be known publicly."[21]

On August 26, 1852, Virginia senator Robert Hunter introduced an amendment on behalf of the Finance Committee. Rising to propose his amendment to Hunter's amendment, Sumner seized the floor. He pulled out his speech, which had been hidden in his desk. "Parliamentary courtesy may be forgotten, but parliamentary law must prevail," he declaimed. "Now, at last . . . I am to be heard; not as a favor, but as a right." The time for Sumner's pent-up silence on slavery was over. Soon, his friendships with proslavery senators would be over, too. But that was no matter— Sumner's nearly four-hour-long oration was a soaring success.[22]

*   *   *

"ACCORDING TO THE true spirit of the Constitution and the sentiment of the fathers [slavery] can find no place under our *National* Government," Sumner declared. This opening claim flew in the face of contemporary wisdom. The Constitution, which many enslavers had helped write, required Congress to permit the international slave trade until 1808. It had also awarded slave states with outsize political control by counting nonvoting slaves as three-fifths of a person for the purposes of deciding representation in the House and the Electoral College. Many Founding Fathers (e.g., Washington, Jefferson, Madison, Monroe, and Marshall) were enslavers. Most abolitionists believed the Constitution was a proslavery charter.

Sumner's constitutionalism stood apart for two reasons. First, he was an antislavery senator from Massachusetts. A lifelong resident of Boston's Black neighborhood and friend of its abolitionist community, he was the closest thing to a voice the anti-constitutionalist Garrisonians ever had in the Senate. Second, he was a Harvard-educated lawyer par excellence. Well reputed as the best student the law school had ever had, Sumner had the legal chops other Free Soilers did not. Few could question his affinity for the American Founding, either, considering his bona fides as the protégé of John Quincy

Adams and other key figures. "Among the memories of my youth are happy days in which I sat at the feet of [the Supreme Court]," Sumner boasted in his speech, "while Marshall presided, with Story by his side."

Sumner's speech presented a constitutional worldview grounded in the Founding era. He began by citing an English case, *Somerset v. Stewart* (1772), that was popular in abolitionist circles. *Somerset* held that an enslaved person cannot be forcibly removed from England and sold elsewhere because slavery "is so odious, that nothing can be suffered to support it but positive law." Because slavery was so profoundly amoral and contrary to nature, *Somerset* held that it was illegal by default and permissible only when man-made law explicitly permitted it. Sumner then declared an interpretive rule he would advocate for all his life: "In any question under the Constitution," he said, "*every word is to be construed in favor of liberty.*"

Critics would claim that Sumner's liberty-promoting vision of the Constitution was naïve idealism rather than hard-nosed law. But Sumner was serious about legal analysis. In modern terms, he might be called something akin to an originalist: a jurist who applies the Constitution as understood by those who drafted and ratified it. "I may seem to stand alone," he declared, "but all the Fathers of the Republic, are with me." Inheriting this method from Story and Marshall, Sumner marshaled impressive evidence from the Constitution's text, animating principles, and original understanding to illustrate its antislavery character.

Sumner's originalism came with a twist. Informed by John Quincy Adams and the abolitionists, he interpreted ambiguities in Founding-era thought toward liberty. He believed that Founding-era views on slavery and the Constitution—interpreted generously toward liberty—remained binding decades later irrespective of any legal precedents to the contrary that arose after the Constitution was ratified.[23]

Sumner examined the drafting of the Constitution's text. In reviewing the convention debates, he showed that the Founders had made concessions to slavery but had never sanctioned it. The Constitution's infamous Slave Trade Clause, for example, declared that Congress could not outlaw the forced migration of enslaved people into the country until 1808. That was a *compromise*, not a *sanction*, of the slave trade. An early draft of the clause described slaves as "imports" that could be taxed. But Roger Sherman opposed this language because it was "*acknowledging men to be property.*" James Madison similarly "*thought it wrong to admit in the Constitution the idea that there could be property in man.*" So, the Founders amended the language to charge a tax *"for each person."* Though states might recognize a slave's status as property, the nation could not. While enslaved *sectionally*, slaves were free *nationally*. In 1841, Sumner noted, the Supreme Court endorsed this idea: *"The Constitution acts upon slaves as* PERSONS, *and not as property."*[24]

Next, Sumner turned to three major events in the Founding era. The first was the signing of the Declaration of Independence, primarily authored by Adams and Jefferson, which declared "that all men are created equal." The second was a letter, penned by Madison, sent by the Continental Congress to the states at the end of the Revolution. It urged states to remember "that the rights for which [America] has contended were the rights of human nature" and "FORM THE BASIS" of state governments. The third was Washington's inauguration as president. "WHEN WASHINGTON TOOK HIS FIRST OATH TO SUPPORT THE CONSTITUTION OF THE UNITED STATES," Sumner declared, "THE NATIONAL ENSIGN, NOWHERE WITHIN THE NATIONAL TERRITORY, COVERED A SINGLE SLAVE." No federal territory had slavery until after the Founding; the slave city of Washington, D.C., did not yet exist.

As Sumner understood it, then, slavery was legal only *inside* a state at the time of the Founding. He believed that same rule was binding today, irrespective of how constitutional law's attitude toward slavery had transformed since then. Under Sumner's view, slavery was illegal nationwide. It was only in "the shelter of local laws," he contended, that "slavery unhappily found a home." Under this theory, a state could permit enslavement within its borders as a local law. But a slave state could not force a free state to aid in its evil by capturing fugitive slaves; neither could there be slavery in any national territory. Whatever happened within a state, freedom was the national policy. Sumner captured the idea in a slogan that, though coined by Salmon Chase, he effectively popularized: "freedom national, slavery sectional."[25]

The slogan captured more than just the topic of slavery. "Freedom national, slavery sectional" implied that people had a direct relationship with the national government, one unmediated by the states. Sumner's mentor Joseph Story had called this "general citizenship"—citizenship that emerged from the fact that the Constitution was "a compact, by which the federal government is bound . . . to every citizen of the United States." This was a bold, radical proposition at a time when most Americans were conceived as primarily citizens of their respective states. To Sumner, national citizenship was also a vehicle for equality and freedom. "The word 'person' in the Constitution embraces every human being within its sphere, whether Caucasian, Indian, or African, from the President to the slave," he declared. "Show me a person, no matter what his condition, or race, or color, within the national jurisdiction, and I confidently claim for him this protection."[26]

* * *

SUMNER'S ORATION WAS a master class in constitutional law. Pulling citations from the Declaration, the American Revolution, the Continental Congress, the Constitution, and the Founding Fathers, Sumner had articulated a coherent, compelling constitutional theory about slavery in the national jurisdiction that could siphon off its ever-growing expansion. But did he stop there? If he had, his speech may have been irrefutable—at least insofar as it claimed that slavery lacked any formal national legal status at the moment of the Constitution's ratification. But he pushed the envelope even farther, making tenuous arguments that were harder to square with the constitutional record. These arguments pertained to what Sumner called the "devilish law."

The Fugitive Slave Act of 1850 enforced a gruesome constitutional clause that said that any "person held to Service or Labour in one State" should be "delivered up" if they end up "escaping" into another. Sumner claimed that the clause, because it did not use the word *slave*, applied only to escaping people who worked for pay as hired servants—and therefore the act lacked authority. His argument was implausible on its face. The clause, though euphemistic, almost certainly referred to slavery. Slave states would not have agreed to the Constitution if it meant anything else. Madison even told Virginians that the indirect language was "expressly inserted, to enable owners of slaves to reclaim them." In making his claim that the clause was not what it almost obviously was, Sumner undermined the credibility of his otherwise compelling argument.[27]

Perhaps knowing this claim was weak, Sumner pivoted to other reasons to reject the act. He argued that Congress lacked authority to pass a law enforcing the clause. He also suggested that anything pertaining to slavery, including the reenslavement of people who escaped bondage, was the exclusive domain of state law. If states chose to disobey or undermine the Fugitive Slave Act, they constitutionally could do so. These arguments, on the whole, were also weak—and they strayed from Sumner's lifelong commitment to nationalism: the idea that states were inferior to the national government, which was supreme.[28]

Sumner's resolve to push arguments a bit too far reflected a deep moral impulse. Part of this impulse was his faith that the Founders simply could not have believed in anything abominable. Some abolitionists assumed Sumner harbored private doubts about the Founders. He certainly knew, for example, that Founders like Jefferson and Madison never freed their enslaved people and embraced strong proslavery views in old age. But Sumner never expressed misgivings about the moral core of the Founders—not once, in public or in private. Their faults aside, he credited Jefferson with the "immortal words" of the Declaration and Madison for not putting "slaves" into the Constitution. Sumner's willingness to extend the benefit of the doubt to slaveholding Founders was remarkable, a testament to his audacity, faith, and—as critics put it—naïveté.

Sumner defended George Washington, too. He told a story about when Washington sought to recapture an enslaved woman, Ona Judge, who fled the president's house (then in Pennsylvania). He then pulled out an original letter, signed by Washington himself, that had "never before seen the light," in which the president expressly instructed that he wanted Judge captured only if it could be done without the need to "excite a mob or riot." Sumner claimed this letter was a smoking gun that proved "the just forbearance of him whom we aptly call Father of his Country." Because Washington freed his enslaved people in his will, Sumner loudly proclaimed that he was an abolitionist. "From Washington on earth I appeal to Washington in heaven," he said. "However he may have appeared before man, he came to the presence of God only as the liberator of his slaves."[29]

Another aspect of Sumner's moral impulse was his conviction that the Fugitive Slave Act—so thoroughly against God's law and the Declaration's injunction that "all men are created equal"—needed to be destroyed, perhaps by any argument necessary. He seemed willing to skimp on constitutional rigor to address the moral crisis and to fulfill the Declaration's promise. "My principles are . . . 'to step to the *verge* of the Constitution to discourage every species of traffic in human flesh,'" he once said. Unlike the Garrisonians, he didn't ditch the Constitution wholesale. Neither did he adopt arguments that he deemed too far-fetched, such as those made by Lysander Spooner, an abolitionist who asserted that the Constitution somehow *prohibited* slavery, even in the states. Rather, Sumner balanced competing constitutional views within the abolitionist movement, articulated a clear middle path, provided it with an intellectual foundation, and tied it together in a neat political slogan. If some parts of his argument were a stretch, he reasoned, so be it. The crux was thoroughly constitutional.[30]

Reaching his oration's climax, Sumner declared that he was under no obligation to follow the act. In language that would be echoed one century later by Martin Luther King Jr., Sumner invoked a quote from St. Augustine that "an unjust law does not appear to be a law." The so-called law therefore deserved no obedience. Sumner cited the Founders as his example, because they disobeyed English laws, like the Stamp Act, that unfairly taxed colonists. "By the Supreme Law, which commands me to do no injustice; by the comprehensive Christian Law of Brotherhood; by the Constitution, *which I am sworn to respect*," Sumner thundered, his voice reverberating in the small chamber, "I AM BOUND TO DISOBEY THIS ACT."

Senators shuddered at Sumner's call for resistance against federal law. It hearkened back to the days when John Calhoun openly called on southern states to nullify national tariffs. Yet here was a northerner, an *abolitionist*, adopting a similarly belligerent strategy toward national law. Senators knew that Sumner meant it: only two years earlier, he had helped organize armed resistance against the slave catchers seeking to seize the Crafts and other fugitives from slavery.

Sumner's call for resistance against the Fugitive Slave Act mirrored that of his peer, the abolitionist Henry David Thoreau, who had recently published his *On Civil Disobedience*—if the law "is of such a nature that it requires you to be the agent of injustice to another, then, I say, break the law," Thoreau avowed. Sumner went a step farther than Thoreau by pulling the Founders into the fight with him. Declaring them to be on *his* side, reclaiming the American revolutionary spirit against the current American government, he flipped the narrative about who was patriotic and who wasn't. He didn't shy away from what he was advocating. "Beware of the groans of the wounded souls," he declared. "Oppress not to the utmost a single heart; for a solitary sigh has power to overturn a whole world."[31]

* * *

THE SENATE WAS stupefied. Alabama's Jeremiah Clemens—reportedly drunk—replied first. He urged colleagues to ignore Sumner so as not to give him undue attention. "The ravings of a maniac may sometimes be dangerous, but the barking of a puppy never did any harm," he scoffed. Other senators were too angry to be quiet. Decrying Sumner's "grand crusade for liberty, equality, and fraternity," Iowa's Augustus Dodge warned that Sumner might try to "introduce black-skinned, flat-nosed, and woolly-headed Senators and Representatives, in this Chamber and in the House of Representatives." While delivering a thoughtful rebuttal, North Carolina's George Badger sneered that he would refrain from using "an appropriate epithet" to describe Sumner out of respect for Senate decorum. Quoting Joseph Story's views on the Fugitive Slave Clause, Badger said he deemed "the authority of Justice Story of ten thousand times more value than that of the Senator from Massachusetts."[32]

California's John Weller claimed Sumner desired violence. Open rebellion to the Fugitive Slave Act would require bloodshed, making Sumner a murderer. "Are you prepared for that?" he asked. He went on to say that violence against slave catchers was unjustified, even by slaves. "I would rather be the lowest and humblest slave in all the land," he dubiously claimed, "than to have the blood of murdered men upon my hands." Moreover, Stephen Douglas rose to effectively call on Sumner to resign. Declaring that anyone who resisted the Fugitive Slave Act was disobeying the Constitution, Douglas pronounced that Sumner and others had "no right to hold office under this Government, or under the State governments, while the Constitution exists." Though Douglas stopped short of mocking Sumner by name, he would soon begin to taunt the senator endlessly. Eventually, Sumner would lash out. For now, though, the freshman senator listened quietly, refrained from any personal attacks, and occasionally interrupted other senators to defend his views gently.

Though most replies were vicious, a few senators were clearly impressed. "I did not know that it was possible that I could endure a speech for over three hours upon the subject of the abolition of slavery," Senator Weller began in his response to Sumner. "But this oration of the Senator from Massachusetts, today, has been so handsomely embellished with poetry, both Latin and English, so full of classical allusions and rhetorical flourishes, as to make it much more palatable than I supposed it could have been made." Catching wind of the oration, even Daniel Webster stopped by the Senate to hear Sumner's speech. Pacing from one side of the chamber to another, the so-called Defender of the Constitution tarried for an hour. He gazed upon Sumner with astonishment: Here stood the man who had condemned him for being a Judas Iscariot. Now that younger man sat in Webster's seat, claiming the mantle of the Constitution for himself. It was Webster's last visit to the Senate—two months later, he would die of illness.[33]

The response from the public invigorated Sumner. "Hundreds of thousands will read it," predicted Senator Salmon Chase, who said the speech marked "a new era in American history, when the anti-slavery idea ceased to stand on the defensive and was boldly advancing to the attack." Parts of the speech were instantly reported by telegraph to other parts of the nation. "I have read your speech with envious admiration," wrote Wendell Phillips. "You have exhausted the question," Henry Wilson concluded. "It will afford to any one the most complete view of the questions in dispute of anything ever published." The *London Examiner* declared it "one of the closest and most convincing arguments we have ever read on the [fugitive slave] policy."

Sumner's innovation was to present a dense legal analysis in a digestible, accessible form—a legal treatise presented to the Senate that read like a page-turning constitutional manifesto for laypeople. "Instructed by him, the farmer in the field, the mechanic in the shop, the traveler by the way—all law-loving Americans everywhere, could maintain the contest with their neighbors point by point upon the letter of the Constitution," *Harper's Weekly* editor George William Curtis recalled. Suddenly, hundreds of thousands of Americans were equipped with a constitutional argument for freedom. It was a watershed moment.[34]

Sumner also found support from unexpected places. The wives of both nominally antislavery New York senators eagerly wrote to him. Julia Fish, married to Hamilton Fish, predicted that his address would make "a lasting impression even here, where prejudice holds the common mind fast bound in ignorance and error." Frances Seward, the wife of William Seward, said she was "truly glad to see that Mrs. Fish has become so warm a convert to principles which have as yet failed to win her husband." And even one slaveholding congressman, William Polk, privately came up to Sumner to deliver a backhanded compliment afterward. "If you should make that speech in Tennessee," he joked, "you would compel me to emancipate my n——s."[35]

Sumner was now an international figure. Though his election to the Senate had already caused a stir, his fiery oration catapulted him into a spotlight that would shine on him until his death. One German historian described his speech as "as loud a call to battle as that which Garrison had uttered twenty years before." From now on, every major American newspaper followed Sumner's activities and speeches with either great interest or frustration. Several hundred thousand copies of his remarks were printed in the United States. The British edition of *Uncle Tom's Cabin*, a blockbuster antislavery novel by Harriet Beecher Stowe that Sumner had helped revise, referenced the speech in its preface. A German translation of Sumner's speech soon buzzed in Europe. Though it cost him standing in the Senate, the oration's public success raised Sumner's national and global profile by legions. There would be no private Charles Sumner anymore.[36]

* * *

THE SENATE ADJOURNED in September 1852 for the presidential election. Franklin Pierce, the proslavery Democratic nominee, was running against Winfield Scott, a Whig who had served as a general during the Mexican War. Because both parties endorsed the Compromise of 1850, the Free Soilers ran their own candidate: John Hale. Running a third-party candidate in a two-party country was a fool's errand. Yet the Free Soilers decided they needed to stick to principles. "The rising public opinion against Slavery cannot now flow in the old political channels. It is strangled, clogged, and dammed back," Sumner avowed at the state convention in mid-September. "But if not *through* the old parties, then *over* the old parties this irresistible current *shall* find its way," he swore to the raucous crowd. It was only a matter of time, he and others reasoned, before the burgeoning antislavery movement reached a critical, electable mass. Their time to sweep the nation would come, but not yet.[37]

Recognizing that the national election was a long shot, Massachusetts Free Soilers focused their energies on home turf. They aimed to win control of the state legislature and a few offices. Hope was high. Sumner's friends threw their names into the ring: Horace Mann for governor and Henry Wilson and Charles Francis Adams for Congress. When Sumner returned home, he arrived as a political celebrity. While completely ostracized by Boston's patrician elite, he was now adored by Free Soilers and voters across the state. They were impressed by the new senator's epic recent speech in Congress. Crowds gathered before his family's Hancock Street house to welcome him. Free Soilers expected Sumner to rally the public toward a victory in November, but to their righteous frustration, he didn't step up to the plate.[38]

Though accustomed to working hard, he never managed a consistent day job before joining the Senate. In his lawyer days, he would waste entire afternoons chatting with friends. Sometimes, he would let several week-long stretches go by without doing work before resuming intense labor. Yet for the past nine months, the freshman senator dutifully attended every single day and hour of session. He felt entitled to a break. "I am weary, and long for a vacation," he told a friend. While he may have earned it, it was patently selfish. "The party has claim upon you," Howe reminded his friend. He urged Sumner to show gratitude to those who had put him in the Senate. "You ought to take the stump," he sternly told Sumner.[39]

Sumner didn't listen. Leaving Boston almost as soon as he arrived, he rushed to Canada. A man he had met in London, the Earl of Elgin, James Bruce, was serving as governor-general of Canada for the British Empire. Sumner wished to spend time with him to escape the politicking that stressed him so much. On his way home, he stopped at his brother Albert's home in Newport. Returning only weeks before the election, he was practically useless in the critical final days. When the Whigs regained control of the State House, all three of his friends narrowly lost—Wilson by fewer than one hundred votes. People were rightly upset with Sumner. "He was not only not practical, but he was unpractical and impracticable," somebody later quipped.[40]

Remarkably, Sumner didn't accept any blame. He instead wrote letters to local papers insisting that he simply didn't have time to campaign for his partymen due to the busy obligations of his work as a senator. The letters were disingenuous at best. While he had reason to be exhausted, it was no excuse for a politician in such a high office. The man who had once been known to do anything for his friends, to spend his hours at their service, was growing in his sense of self-importance and vanity.

By this time, Sumner was also losing his patience with the enslavers whom he had considered personal friends. One friend, Francis Lieber, a German American political theorist who had known Sumner for years, took special umbrage. The intellectual compatriots rarely met, but they had exchanged more than a thousand letters over the course of their lives, assisting each other with their ideas and writing. In 1835, Lieber accepted a professorship at South Carolina College and became a slaveowner. From then on, the two debated slavery with gradually growing ferocity. Lieber told Sumner that he "did not rejoice" at the latter's election to the Senate on an antislavery platform. Afterward, Sumner pelted Lieber with letters enclosing gory articles about slavery.

Sumner's torrent of letters to Lieber was frightening him—South Carolinian authorities monitored the mail to snuff out and arrest antislav-ery sympathizers. When Lieber pleaded with him to stop sending letters, Sumner slammed him as an "apologist of slavery." Furious, Lieber cut off their correspondence. He wouldn't speak to Sumner again until the start of the Civil War. "Sumner uses words as boys do stones," to "break windows and knock down flowerpots, while he all the time plays the offended," Lieber once complained.[41]

* * *

FREE SOILERS FARED poorly in the national election of 1852. The Demo-crats and their presidential candidate, Franklin Pierce, resoundingly won the contest. When Sumner returned to the Senate in December 1852 for the next session, he was seen by everyone as part of a losing team. After two past cycles of modest success, the Free-Soil Party had been dismally defeated. Anticipating its demise, Democrats and Whigs snubbed the three Free Soilers—Sumner, Chase, and Hale—by denying them commit-tee memberships. Mean-spirited laughter rang through the Senate when leadership announced this decision. While Hale eventually received an appointment, Sumner and Chase spent the entire session feeling useless. They were righteously upset.[42]

That said, Sumner could still socially intermingle with southerners, who didn't perceive him yet as a real threat. "On the floor of the Sen-ate[,] I sit between Mr. Butler of South Carolina, the early suggester of the Fugitive Slave bill, and Mr. Mason of Virginia, its final author, with both of whom I have constant and cordial intercourse," Sumner wrote to the antislavery novelist Lydia Maria Child in January 1853. "This experience would teach me, if I needed the lesson, to shun harsh and personal criti-cism of those from whom I differ."[43]

After a few dull months in Washington, Sumner returned to Massa-chusetts in April. The Senate wouldn't meet again until December. In the meantime, Free Soilers set to work to break Whig dominance in the state. Having lost at the polls, the Free-Soil Party state chairman, Henry Wilson, connived a plan: changing the Bay State's voting process to make it more favorable to their cause. Allying with Democrats, the coalition won public support for a constitutional convention. At the convention, a new state constitution was drafted that would split up the voting districts around Boston, a Whig stronghold, and empower rural towns across the state with greater representation. In November, it would be put to a vote.

Initially, Sumner planned to stay out of the politicking. "My desire was to visit the West, which I have never seen, during the coming spring," he wrote to Wilson. But the party cleverly put his name on a ballot and elected him as a delegate without his knowledge. He was now honor-bound to attend the convention. "I dislike *politics & politicians,*" he complained in a letter. "And yet my duties are among them," Sumner sighed.

Sumner went the extra mile to show his partymen that he took his duties seriously. The senator chaired a committee that drafted a new bill of rights for Massachusetts and devoted his full attention to the dozens of meetings and sessions that took place in the summer of 1853. When the draft of the new state constitution was done, he took the stump, journeying across the state to advocate for its passage. Hitting seventeen towns in eighteen days, he spoke to crowds of thousands about the new constitution. He also took the opportunity to reaffirm his vision of "freedom national, slavery sectional."[44]

The daily two-and-a-half-hour-long speeches raised a groundswell of popular enthusiasm for the new senator. It also placated allies who had been frustrated with Sumner's unwillingness to cooperate with his party. Mixing populist Democratic rhetoric with the Free-Soil antislavery cause, Sumner called on the state to "break the back-bone of the Boston oligarchy" and destroy "the Boston cabal, whose home is State Street, & whose breath is Silver Grey Websterism." The anti-elitism stunned the Boston Brahmins who had raised Sumner as their own. Even some Free-Soil Bostonians, like Charles Francis Adams and John Palfrey, were disturbed by Sumner's rhetoric and reluctant to agree to, if not downright opposed to, constitutional reform.[45]

Ultimately, the effort failed at the November election. Boston's Irish immigrants, who were generally Democrats, followed the Catholic Church in voting against the new constitution because its nonsectarian clause would have banned state funding for religious schools. Boston Whigs, who feared labor laws and other reforms, voted against the new document, too; some Whig textile mill owners even forced their workers to vote no. Other voters simply resented the wheeling and dealing that went into the Free-Soil strategy of rewriting a constitution to win more votes. Even worse, the White House weighed in on the initiative. President Pierce's attorney general, a Massachusetts Democrat, issued a public letter calling on the state's Democrats to break their alliance with the Free-Soil

Party. Although the new constitution would have helped the Democrats, Pierce hated "abolitionism, under whatever guise or form it may present itself," and wanted it "crushed out."

Once again, the Free-Soil cause had been thwarted. As the year wrapped up, Sumner returned to Washington looking like a bigger loser than ever. All the tides were turning against Free Soil.[46]

CHAPTER 9

LET THE PULPITS
THUNDER AGAINST OPPRESSION

THIS CONGRESS IS THE WORST—OR RATHER PROMISES TO BE THE worst—since the Constitution was adopted," Sumner wrote at the start of the next Senate session in December 1853. "It is the 'Devil's own.'" The Free-Soil Party's decision to run third-party candidates, which split the vote, helped southern-sympathetic candidates gain many more seats in Congress. Once again, Sumner and Salmon Chase were denied committee appointments, even though most senators received at least two. (Chase eventually received assignments.) Among Senate committee chairmen, eleven of the fourteen men who were appointed were proslavery southerners or westerners. The twelfth was Illinois's Democratic senator Stephen Douglas, who was renamed chair of the powerful Territories Committee.[1]

For ten years, Douglas had been trying to create territorial governments in the land of Nebraska. Nebraska was a broad expanse of the Great Plains—485,000 square miles stretching from the Canadian border down to Texas and from the Missouri River to the Rocky Mountains. To many white Americans, it was an exciting, unexplored frontier. Almost no whites lived in these rolling hills and dry prairies, except in a southern part that became known as Kansas. Most of the rest of the land was Indian country, home to the Pawnee, Omaha, Osage, Kansas, and Wyandot nations, among other tribes—some indigenous to these plains, others forcibly resettled there.

At the start of the session, Douglas introduced yet another bill to organize the territory. This time, he was determined to pass it in order to unite the country from sea to shining sea: the United States had no incorporated land between the Mississippi River and California. To organize the Nebraska region, Douglas believed that "the Indian barrier" would need "to be removed"—a euphemism for potential ethnic cleansing. This didn't bother him at all. He hoped that the Nebraska region would be populated by white settlers.

Douglas had many reasons for pushing his bill. If Nebraska were incorporated, he could then try to pass a bill to build a transcontinental railroad across the United States through this region. That railroad would pass right through his home state of Illinois, pleasing his voters. Anticipating this possibility, Douglas and others started buying cheap land titles along the potential railroad path in the hope of making a killing. Douglas also hoped one day to run for president. If he could turn some of the Nebraska region into new slave states, southerners might support him in a future election even though he was a northerner.[2]

But Douglas had a problem: the Missouri Compromise. In 1820, the country had been nearly ripped apart over the debate on whether to admit Missouri as a slave state or a free state. After a grueling fight, Congress passed a law that many northerners and southerners alike considered necessary to protect the Union. While admitting Missouri as a slave state, it decreed that no future territory above the 36°30' parallel would ever permit slavery. The issue was that the Nebraska Territory, *almost all of Nebraska*, sat above the line.

To avoid dealing with the Missouri Compromise too soon, Douglas wrote in his bill that the territory would be organized "with or without slavery" so the issue could be debated later. But a group of southern senators gave him an ultimatum: to gain their support, his bill needed to explicitly overturn the Compromise by permitting slavery in the Nebraska region. It was an outrageous request—a request to shatter the impregnable border between slave and free territory that had existed for more than thirty years. Douglas himself had once said the Compromise was "a sacred thing, which no ruthless hand would ever be reckless enough to disturb."

These southerners were reckless enough to disturb it.[3]

* * *

AMERICA'S FIERCEST PROSLAVERY lawmakers were known as Fire-Eaters. In the Senate, Andrew Butler of South Carolina was the leading Fire-Eater. A protégé of John Calhoun, Butler had made his name after organizing a state convention to discuss Calhoun's nullification theory, which proposed that states could outright defy any national laws deemed unconstitutional. Butler's three closest colleagues were also Calhoun protégés: Missouri's David Atchison and Virginia's two senators, Robert Hunter and James

Mason. Together, they made a powerful quartet. Atchison was the Senate's president pro tempore; Hunter was the chair of the Finance Committee; Mason led the Foreign Relations Committee; and Butler led the Judiciary Committee.

Butler and his three colleagues didn't just plot together; they lived together. While most members of Congress, including Sumner, rented their lodgings, these men pooled their money and bought a home on F Street, between Ninth and Tenth Streets, around the corner from where Ford's Theatre sits. Taking advantage of the power vacuum left by the deaths of the famous senators Calhoun, Clay, and Webster, these four roommates dominated the Senate by coordinating their actions. In between eating meals and doing chores, they made decisions to effectively control the U.S. Senate—and, by extension, American democracy.[4]

Emboldened by the recent electoral success and fearing the rise of anti-slavery sentiment in the North, the F Street Mess, as they became known, decided that the Nebraska bill presented an opportunity to open up slavery across the expansive West and crush any glimmer of hope for Free Soilers' antislavery dreams. Atchison told Douglas that if he wanted their support, his bill needed to repeal the Missouri Compromise. "I will incorporate it into my bill," he relented, "though I know it will raise a hell of a storm."[5]

Douglas's acquiescence affirmed what many northerners had suspected for decades: a small class of slaveholders wielded outsize influence over American politics. Abolitionists dubbed the power of this cabal the Slave Power. Sumner fueled the conspiratorial rhetoric about the Slave Power with his own phraseology: he called it the slave oligarchy. To understand Sumner's response to the Nebraska bill, it is useful first to discuss a speech he gave sometime later, in November 1855, where he exposed the slave oligarchy's threat to American democracy.

* * *

"YES, FELLOW-CITIZENS, IT is an oligarchy," Sumner declared to a crowd at Faneuil Hall in Boston. "Odious beyond precedent; heartless, grasping, tyrannical; careless of humanity, right, or the Constitution." He pointed out that the last census had shown that even though there were nearly 350,000 slaveholders in the United States, only 92,000 of them enslaved more than two people. This "small company" of large slaveholders, roughly 1.5 percent of the American population, "dominates over the Republic, determines its national policy, disposes of its offices, and sways all to its absolute will." Sumner underscored what many abolitionists had long suspected about the Slave Power. He did so from his position in the Senate, providing an insider's look into how the Slave Power actually operated in controlling the levers of the American republic.[6]

"There is nothing in the National Government which the Slave Oligarchy does not appropriate," he declared. He claimed that these enslavers held the keys to every office, organized the Cabinet, directed the army and navy, and managed every department of public business. His conspiratorial rhetoric was grounded in much truth. For the Constitution's first seventy years, from the American Founding in 1789 until 1860, no president or Cabinet officer called for abolition—not even gradual, compensated abolition—while in office. It was a stunning and brutal fact that to be politically successful, one had to be either vocally supportive of or silent about slavery. "At Washington slavery rules everything," Sumner's colleague John Davis once told him.

Sumner offered details. The oligarchy "sits in the chair of the President of the Senate," he declared, referring to Atchison. They arrange "the Committees . . . placing at their head only the servitors of Slavery," he contended, referring to Hunter, Mason, Butler, and their allies like Douglas. They exclude "the friends of Freedom," he continued, referring to himself and Chase. And the oligarchy "subsidizes the national press," he accused. In 1854, Sumner even witnessed the Senate replace the moderately proslavery newspaper that officially reported on congressional business with a new media organ, endorsed by the F Street senators, that was even more vociferously proslavery.[7]

By describing slavery as an oligarchy, Sumner moved past mere moral criticism of individual acts of brutality. He was advancing arguments of political economy. For Sumner, the Founding was a radical attempt at self-governance in which anyone—"Caucasian, Indian, or African, from the President to the slave"—would eventually be able to participate. The slave oligarchy, Sumner argued, made democracy impossible by exerting undue control over the levers of political power and crushing the republican vision of the Founders. At the end of his address, he also called out bigotry against immigrants, who—much like the slaves—"filled our workshops, navigated our ships, and even tilled our fields." He believed all Americans should be able to work for pay and earn equal social respect. Informed by his time abroad, he was inspired by French and English radicals, who called for reordering society to reduce inequalities. In Europe, this meant breaking the aristocracy. In America, it meant breaking the slaveocracy.

Slaveocracy was not inevitable, Sumner believed. He hearkened back to the Founding, when, as he had explained in previous speeches, there was initially no legal recognition of slavery in any national territories. But unfortunately, "the original policy of the Government did not long prevail." Sumner narrated a compelling story of nefarious large slaveholders using their financial and institutional power to ruthlessly spread slavery and undermine the ideals of the Founding.

First, he claimed, they lobbied for the creation of the national capital in a slave region. Then they pushed President Thomas Jefferson to purchase the Louisiana Territory from France and Florida from Spain. Next, they dictated the terms of the Missouri Compromise—permitting slavery below the 36°30' parallel. Still hungry for slave territory, they urged America to annex Texas and invade Mexico to conquer large swaths of the West. After that, they passed the Fugitive Slave Act, making nowhere in the North safe from slavery's reach. And finally, they sought slavery's spread into the Nebraska Territory, including the land that became Kansas. "Our first political duty is . . . to oppose this Oligarchy," Sumner said, "and to bring the administration back to that character which it enjoyed when first organized under Washington."

The speech conveyed a palpable political message about the power of slavery and the impotence of past northern leaders to stand against it. Sumner presented himself and other antislavery politicians as the solution. They, unlike past leaders, would courageously take a stand and confront the behemoth head-on. "Prostrate the Slave Oligarchy, and the North will no longer be the vassal of the South," he declared. "Prostrate the Slave Oligarchy, and Liberty will become the universal law of all the national Territories." Sumner called out those who saw slavery as a secondary political issue. "In vain you seek economy in the Government, improvement of rivers and harbors, or dignity and peace in our foreign relations," he declared, "while this Power holds the national purse and the national sword." He urged political focus on slavery. "Prostrate the Slave Oligarchy, and the door will be wide open for all generous reforms."[8]

To protect slavery, slave oligarchs believed they needed the West. For the South to remain profitable, many slaveholders reasoned, there always needed to be new lands for enslaved workers to toil. That was because cash crops like cotton destroyed the soil. Rather than farm more sustainable crops, ambitious planters were constantly moving into the frontier in search of new soil to plant more cash crops. In turn, they would buy slaves from the established plantations of the East, providing a source of revenue to the sedentary slaveholders who stayed behind. The forced migration of enslaved people also prevented the South's enslaved population from growing too much, too fast. By this time, there were roughly four million southern slaves: nearly one in four people in the South. White southerners feared mass rebellion against their rule. The frontier was their safety valve to reduce the enslaved population, thereby reducing the risk of revolution.

Sumner and other antislavery thinkers believed the best way to end slavery was to stop its expansion. They colorfully called their plan "the scorpion's sting." Legend had it that when scorpions are surrounded by a cordon of fire, with nowhere to go, they would rather sting themselves than be killed by fire. Similarly, Sumner and others reasoned, if slavery were surrounded by a cordon of freedom, confined only to a few southern states, slaveholders would rather abolish slavery (gradually) than risk the experience of plunging profits and slave revolutions. The goal was to "put a cordon of fire around the Southern States," South Carolina Representative Preston Brooks once explained about his antislavery opponents, "and force slavery, scorpion-like, to sting itself to death."

The scorpion's sting theory could work only if expansion were prevented. To this end, Free Soilers were absolutely committed to stopping the expansion of slavery into the West. And the slave oligarchy was ready to fight tooth and nail to keep expansion going. They were caught in a zero-sum existential fight, a fight over the fate of America.[9]

* * *

THE F STREET senators didn't care much for most of Nebraska, which was too far north for cash crops to grow viably. But they believed the symbolic victory of opening Nebraska to slavery would assist in the broader project of spreading it westward. They also had their eye on a southern portion of the Nebraska Territory, already known as Kansas. Lush, fertile Kansas, bordering Missouri at the very same latitude, presented a tempting destination for new plantations. At slaveholders' insistence, Douglas devised a new plan that he hoped would please the southern Fire-Eaters without, ideally, losing northern senators and the northern public.

He called it the Kansas-Nebraska Bill. Quietly drafted in early January 1854, the bill proposed to organize two territories. Neither would be pro- or antislavery per se. Instead, they would be governed by a doctrine Douglas called "popular sovereignty," whereby voters would decide. When the territory was ready to apply for statehood, he surmised, its residents could democratically choose whether to permit or prohibit slavery.

Douglas thought "popular sovereignty" was a brilliant idea that would resonate with American sensibilities about republicanism. But his plan reeked of trouble. When he said "people," he of course meant *white men*, who would decide whether to enslave *Black people*, who had no say. And which white men? Kansas had few white settlers; Nebraska had nearly zero. In reality, Douglas had no plausible plan—he wanted a quick, palatable solution to rush his bill to a vote. Little did he know that he was providing the fuel that Free Soilers needed to reignite their movement.

Alarmed by the proposed expansion of slavery, Sumner and Chase devised a retaliatory ploy: they would leak Douglas's proposal and shape the narrative before he had a chance to sell his snake oil theory to the public. Although there had already been a trickle of leaks to the press about potential Nebraska action, awareness and outrage had not yet grown. Some abolitionists sensed an opportunity. "Do not, I beseech, wait for, but *make, seize* an opportunity; now, while public sentiment is not formed," Samuel Howe encouraged Sumner. "I wish to God you felt it to be your time & mission to send a blast through the land."

Sumner and Chase met with four antislavery congressmen to co-draft a pamphlet to expose the bill: *The Appeal of the Independent Democrats*. "It is our duty to warn our constituents," the *Appeal* began. It explained the plan to open the Nebraska Territory to slavery, traced the territory's borders, and illustrated the area's sheer scale: twelve times the size of Ohio, larger than all free states combined, excluding California. The *Appeal* decried the South's willingness to break the Missouri Compromise—calling it "a gross violation of a sacred pledge" and a desire to turn a whole swath of America into a "dreary region of despotism." After preemptively responding to every argument Douglas and southerners might raise, the *Appeal* closed with an open call for resistance.

"We appeal to the People," it exhorted. "The dearest interests of freedom and the Union are in imminent peril. . . . We entreat you to be mindful of that fundamental maxim of democracy, EQUAL RIGHTS AND EXACT JUSTICE FOR ALL MEN. Do not submit to become agents in extending legalized oppression and systematized injustice over a vast territory yet exempt from these terrible evils." Calling all to "protest, earnestly and emphatically, by correspondence, through the press, by memorials, by resolutions," the *Appeal* called for a mass uprising against Douglas's bill. "The cause of human freedom is the cause of God," it ended.[10]

The *Appeal* was set to be published in the *National Era*, an antislavery newspaper, on January 24, 1854. When Douglas reported the bill to the Senate floor on January 23, Chase casually, and disingenuously, asked him to postpone discussion of the bill for a day so that he would have time to read it. When Douglas politely agreed, Sumner took it farther by asking for a week. Douglas agreed again. On the following morning, he woke to the *Appeal* in circulation, with Chase and Sumner among its authors. Douglas's plan for popular sovereignty had been exposed before he had had time even to propose it. To add insult to injury, the *Appeal* personally accused him of drafting his bill to help in his "Presidential game." He was enraged.[11]

* * *

ON JANUARY 30, 1854, Douglas introduced his bill to the Senate floor and set off what one historian has called "perhaps to this day, America's fiercest congressional battle." When he rose to speak, he boomed in a loud voice with his finger wagging and his head shaking for emphasis. Quivering with rage, he tried to calmly explain how his bill would (dubiously) protect Indian tribes—as Sam Houston of Texas had urged—and aligned with the principles of the Compromise of 1850, which he said superseded the Missouri Compromise. But he couldn't contain his anger. "The Senator from Illinois lost his temper before he began," the *New York Times* reported.[12]

Douglas got personal. Directing his attention to "those two Senators," Douglas exploded on Chase and Sumner for acting deceptively, maligning his character, and exposing his bill "to the world" as the *Appeal* spread in outlets across the country. "These few names attached to it," his voice doubtless rising to a shout, are "the pure unadulterated representatives of Abolitionism, Free Soilism, N——ism in the Congress of the United States." Chase called for a point of order. "I DO NOT YIELD," Douglas shouted back. "A Senator who has violated all the rules of courtesy and propriety . . . has no right to my courtesy."

Douglas was so angry that one reporter remarked that he had a "terrific tornado raging within him." For several long minutes, the senator viciously hammered into Chase and Sumner, whom he called "abolition confederates," for serving "a negro movement" and engaging in "wicked fabrication" and "atrocious falsehood." Some remarks were so abusive and vulgar that newspapers did not even report them.[13]

Chase and Sumner responded carefully to Douglas's tirade. Chase addressed some factual claims with his corrections. Sumner replied by saying it wasn't personal. "In doing this, I judged the act, and not its author," he said. In the days ahead, shouting matches ensued between Chase and Douglas, and Chase delivered his formal rebuttal on February 1.[14]

Meanwhile, anger roiled the North after the release of the *Appeal*, which had lit such a powder keg that some historians have called it "one of the most effective pieces of political propaganda in our history." Abolitionists organized mass meetings to decry the Kansas-Nebraska Bill. Thousands of people who had never attended abolitionist circles before grew outraged, too. For these bystanders, this was the last straw. Uneasy about the Fugitive Slave Act, they had nonetheless accepted it as part of a needed compromise with the South to preserve the Union. Now they were being asked to enable the potential spread of slavery through all the remaining unexplored West. If that happened, free states could be trapped with the slaveocracy surrounding them to the west and south. For the vast majority of northerners, it was a bridge too far.

Ignoring the northern backlash, key power brokers on F Street made clear their intent to breach the Missouri Compromise no matter what. Every day, the Senate Democratic Caucus met to coordinate strategy. They couldn't risk too many northern Democrats defecting. They also hoped to bring Southern Whigs along, opening up their daily meetings to them. For years, Whigs opposed slavery's spread, fearing its potential to crack the Union. But southern leaders positioned the bill as a matter of southern honor. Facing pressure from voters, most southern Whig senators announced their support for Douglas's bill. As slaveholders themselves, they did not see it as a hard choice when push came to shove.

Northern Whigs were furious at their allies, and terrified. Their party was splitting apart on a high-profile issue nine months before the midterm elections. One Whig called it the "choking and stabbing of the National Whig Party—preparatory to the funeral." Senator William Seward sadly mourned that he had "no longer any bond to Southern Whigs." Southern Democratic leaders like Butler and Hunter relished watching the Whigs fall apart. Their hero, John Calhoun, had dreamed of the day when southern Whigs and Democrats united under one party banner.[15]

* * *

SUMNER WAS EXCITED, too. The political antislavery movement had been losing steam. Now it boiled like a cauldron. On February 21, 1854, he delivered "The Landmark of Freedom," his first formal remarks on the Kansas-Nebraska Bill. A crowd—including a "bright array of ladies," according to Seward—gathered in the gallery to watch. With typical thoroughness, Sumner offered a history of the Missouri Compromise. He then bemoaned how America had changed from "a Republic merely permitting, while regretting Slavery . . . to a mighty Propagandist, openly favoring and vindicating it."

Next, Sumner decried Douglas's doctrine of popular sovereignty. "The principle of self-government, when truly administered, secures equal rights to all, without distinction of race or color, and makes Slavery impossible." The idea that people could vote in a democracy to enslave others was "an inconsistency too flagrant . . . like saying *two* and *two* make *three*." He called Douglas's proposal a "*monstrum horrendum*."

Having kept his speech measured so far, Sumner finally aimed squarely at Douglas. "Slavery loosens and destroys the character of Northern men," he declared. Likely facing Douglas from his seat, Sumner called him a "human anomaly, *a Northern man with Southern principles*." The crowd in the gallery roared in applause. Cheering, booing, and jeering directed at Douglas continued steadily until the Senate was called to order.[16]

It was embarrassing for Douglas—having served in Congress for ten years—to be chastised by a freshman senator to thunderous applause. He was dreadfully realizing that he may have made a bad mistake in listening to the F Street senators and proposing to overturn the Missouri Compromise. Douglas was fast becoming the most hated politician in the North. Seven days after Sumner's speech, somebody hanged an effigy of Douglas on a flagpole in the center of Boston Common labeled "S. A. Douglas, the Benedict Arnold of 1854."

Sumner, by contrast, was popular at last in his hometown. Boston Whigs met at Faneuil Hall on George Washington's birthday to call southern Whigs traitors. Even reliably proslavery northern merchants were incensed. They had staked their reputations on the hated Fugitive Slave Act. Now they were being told to support an even *more* controversial law. The Brahmin establishment saw Sumner in new light. "You have my head, my heart, my conscience, and my cordial thanks," said one merchant. Even Sumner's old law partner, George Hillard—who had grown estranged due to his conservatism—liked his recent speech. "I read it with admiration, and generally with assent," Hillard wrote. "You have borne yourself well, and gained credit everywhere at the North."[17]

* * *

THREE DAYS LATER, on February 24, 1854, Senator Butler gave Sumner a taste of his own medicine—an experience of humiliation. Butler had heretofore been cordial to Sumner, who used to sit next to him and now sat behind him. But Sumner was threatening southern power and had just subjected their ally, Douglas, to deep indignation, going so far as to call his bill a "*monstrum horrendum.*" He needed to be put in his place.

Butler was the Senate's leading power broker. He looked like a disheveled old man, despite being just fifty-five years old. He had a massive head, expressive features, pinkish skin, and snow-white hair that he barely combed. A smart and energetic debater, he liked to prowl the floor rather than stick to his seat. Generally courteous when sober, he was caustic, aggressive, and bitingly satirical when drunk. This time, he was likely drunk.

In a rambling speech to the Senate, Butler mocked antislavery senators, declared that "inequality pervades the creation of this universe," and denigrated Sumner's favorite phrase—the Declaration's promise that all men are created equal—as purely "sentimental." Then Butler spoke directly about Sumner. Probably turning his wispy white head around so he could stare at Sumner dead in the face, so close that Sumner could likely smell the alcohol on his breath, Butler began dribbling one of the most egregious, hurtful, and—from Butler's perspective—deliciously humorous stories he had ever conceived on the Senate floor.

"Take the case of a young gentleman of a romantic disposition, of high imagination, with all the gifts that could be bestowed upon him by nature," he began. "Suppose it were proposed to him that, if he would consent, he could marry an empress or a princess whose dowry was . . . the Archipelago of the South." Senators cracked up and snickered. Nobody knew where this was going, but they were excited to find out. "Now suppose this young man never saw a black woman before, and therefore he has no prejudice at all," Butler continued. "She may have her ankles covered with pearls, and her fingers with rings of rubies and diamonds," and she has "white teeth . . . black skin and kinky hair."

Then came the punch line. Butler said the man, mortified by the sight of a kinky-haired, black-skinned woman decked in jewelry ready to marry him, would cry out in Latin: *"monstrum horrendum!"* The Senate burst into exuberant laughter and guffaws. "Equality! Equality!" Butler sneered. "I should like to see a play written on this matter. I have no doubt that the honorable Senator from Massachusetts, with his taste and talent, could draw up one." After laughing at his own joke, Butler continued with his speech.[18]

Though Sumner at no point called for a point of order and did not respond to Butler's caustic remarks, he must have been hot in the face. Not only did Butler draw on vulgar and racist themes about Black women. Not only did he, the senator who *sat in front of* Sumner, taunt Sumner unprovoked to the boisterous laughter of their colleagues. But Butler, an elderly, refined, respected, *powerful*, dominating presence in the Senate, went much farther: he snickered at Sumner's sexuality and chastity; he bullied him for his bachelorhood.

* * *

SUMNER WAS FORTY-THREE years old and one of only two men in the Senate who had never married. When he was young, bachelorhood was a sad, ordinary, mundane condition of life. But as he grew older, Victorian England heavily influenced American social culture into treating bachelordom as a condition that must be severely stigmatized and discouraged. To be a bachelor by one's forties or fifties—especially one who was not actively seeking marriage—was to invoke suspicion, scorn, and disgust. "It is the fashion to marry," a *Harper's Weekly* editorial noted in 1855. "It is the fashion to abuse those who do not."[19]

Mid-nineteenth-century Americans tended to suspect that middle-aged bachelors were potentially perverts, adulterers, or sexual degenerates of some kind. As one newspaper put it in 1856, bachelors had "crude and possibly gross tastes and experiences." Otherwise, they surely would have married. White bachelors were suspected of same-sex sodomy, sex with prostitutes, sex with Black women, and the like. Even chaste bachelors were suspected of harboring illicit sexual fantasies or engaging in masturbation.

Henry David Thoreau, a Transcendentalist poet and one of Sumner's friends, mourned his bachelordom and internalized the idea that he had deviant fantasies because of it. Like Sumner, Thoreau was probably gay.

"Our life without love is like coke and ashes,—like the cocoanut in which the milk is dried up," Thoreau wrote in his journal in 1852. "Like cuttlefish, we conceal ourselves, we darken the atmosphere in which we move. . . . Our sin and shame prevent our expressing even the innocent thoughts we have."[20]

Even worse, medical doctors warned against bachelorhood because they commonly believed in a now-debunked condition called "bachelor's disease," also known as spermatorrhea. Legitimate physicians thought that spermatorrhea, defined as the involuntary release of semen at night by men who didn't regularly engage in healthy sexual intercourse, could increase the likelihood of consumption, epilepsy, insanity, lifelong impotence, and even death. The solution, naturally, was to get married.[21]

Americans believed that many bachelors, but not all, were perverts. As he mocked Sumner's bachelordom, Senator Butler was implying that Sumner was one of the perverts. It was one of the worst insults he could possibly make and it struck directly at Sumner's deepest vulnerability, for Sumner felt incredible shame over what he called his "cage of celibacy." He mourned his aching feeling of loneliness, and he possibly feared premature death due to his condition. Raised in a strict puritan household, Sumner was also prudish by nature and very uncomfortable with lewd jokes and sexual innuendos.[22]

Senator Butler made a laughingstock of Sumner's bachelorhood, suggesting he fantasized about Black women. In so doing, Butler may have been a hypocrite. He was a wealthy planter who, like all southern slaveholders, had a legal right to unrestricted sexual access to his slaves. On his plantation in Edgefield, South Carolina, Butler enslaved more than seventy human beings who grew his cotton. One of these men, Henry Ryan, was interviewed in 1937 for a federal initiative to gather stories from ex-slaves. "Old Judge Butler was a good man," Ryan testified. "Master wouldn't let [his overseers] treat slaves cruel, just light whipping."

According to Ryan, his master, Senator Butler, had kept a mistress in the house and sired two children by her. Ryan didn't mention whether the mistress was free or enslaved, white or Black, a wife or a liaison. Perhaps he didn't remember. After all, he gave this testimony in his eighties, and was less than ten years old when Butler had died. But records indicate that Butler never remarried after the death of his second wife in 1832. According to the records, Butler had only sired one legal white daughter. If his former slave's recollection was true, Butler had quietly impregnated an unmarried woman at least twice. She was probably his slave.[23]

It wasn't uncommon for southern planters to keep an enslaved mistress after losing their wives. Most famously, Thomas Jefferson had a sexual relationship with Sally Hemings, an enslaved woman, for nearly four decades after his dying wife made him swear not to remarry. Jefferson even had children with Hemings, whom he kept enslaved. In Butler's hometown of Edgefield County, at least one white neighbor kept an enslaved Black mistress. Butler may have done so as well.

The brazen hypocrisy of enslavers infuriated Sumner. Enslavers often charged abolitionists with lusting after Black women, even though they themselves routinely engaged in rape and adultery over women they possessed. To Sumner, rape, adultery, and slavery were morally abhorrent acts, repugnant to God.[24]

After Butler's scathing, possibly hypocritical, heathen joke, Sumner was never interested in speaking to him again. In the past, they were relatively cordial with each other. Not anymore. From there on, Sumner would make no effort to interact with Butler or to socialize with almost any of the proslavery men in the Senate, who had laughed and jeered at his bachelorhood. Soon, he would get his revenge.[25]

But not yet. Sumner didn't need to go into attack mode again—the North was already surging in support for his cause as it was. "All the friends of freedom, in every State, and of every color, may claim you, just now, as their representatives," Frederick Douglass wrote him in a beaming letter. With a bit of ego and a feeling of triumph, Sumner paid New York's Senator Seward a visit to show him the letters of congratulations he was getting from across the North for his anti-Nebraska speeches. "I find myself a popular man," he bragged. "People had grown angry under the bullying of the South, and they leaped forward to me sympathetically. No papers in Massachusetts now mention my name except with kind words." Angry as he may have been by Butler's bullying, Sumner had no political incentive, yet, to respond. He steadily focused on Nebraska.[26]

* * *

THE FINAL DRAFT of the Kansas-Nebraska Bill reached the Senate for a vote in late May 1854. Though the bill was certain to pass, the debate raged late into the evening as many senators wished to speak. Toward midnight on May 25, Sumner got his turn. He had a massive stack of paper in his hands. "I now present the remonstrance of a large number of citizens," he started. Remonstrances were petitions with long explanations. For months, Sumner, Chase, and others had accumulated a dizzying array of anti-Nebraska petitions to present on the floor. One effort was spearheaded by Harriet Beecher Stowe, author of the famous 1852 antislavery novel *Uncle Tom's Cabin*. She had helped coordinate more than three thousand clergy members, from diverse denominations across the North, to write remonstrances against opening new territory to slavery. Sumner's fellow Massachusetts senator Edward Everett presented most of these letters, but a new batch had just arrived for Sumner to present.

"In the name of Almighty God, and in his presence," Sumner began, "these remonstrants protest against the Nebraska bill." He continued: "Believing in God, as I profoundly do, I cannot doubt that the opening of an immense region to so great an enormity as slavery is calculated to draw down upon our country His righteous judgments." He then named three senators—Butler, Mason, and Douglas—who, he said, "might learn something" from the example of the clergy. Next, quoting a saying of John Adams during the American Revolution, he roared: "Let the pulpits thunder against oppression!" Sumner concluded with an abrupt transition. "This is the best bill on which Congress ever acted." To the shock of other senators, he meant it. "It annuls all past compromises with slavery, and makes all future compromises impossible." Thus, "it puts freedom and slavery face to face, and bids them grapple."

Steeped in religious language, Sumner's speech fell into a genre of oratory that some literary scholars have called "the American jeremiad." In the Bible, the Prophet Jeremiah used sharp, warlike rhetoric to beseech his people to repent collectively for their moral decay and to return to traditional Jewish values to escape divine wrath. Starting with the Puritans, American preachers and social reformers similarly called on their people to redeem themselves of collective sins. These orators also promised something uniquely American, distinct from the biblical Jeremiah: they promised salvation here, on earth, if redemption were pursued.

While not a regular churchgoer, Sumner believed deeply in God's role in human affairs and God's hand in history. Like the biblical Jeremiah, he warned senators that God would punish them terribly for engaging in evil. In the fashion of the American jeremiad, he also raised the possibility of divine salvation on earth. To be saved, Americans had to go back to traditional values rather than embrace something new. Those values were liberty and equality, as embodied at the Founding in the Declaration of Independence. If Americans rejected political evil, repented for past crimes, and began attempting to return to these values, Sumner prophesized that God wouldn't wait until Judgment Day to deliver them. Rather, He would facilitate their success in the here and now—by rewarding them with a new birth of freedom, so to speak.

Channeling prophetic rhetoric, Sumner offered a parable. He compared proslavery senators with ostriches who bury their heads in the sand, becoming willfully blind to the predators coming their way. "The clergy have prayers to be feared by the upholders of wrong," Sumner warned. Those prayers would move the spirits of northern voters, who would act in the "spirit of the Lord" by an "involuntary inspiration" to bring down "righteous judgment" upon the ostrich senators. That judgment would come in the form of "the great Northern Hammer," which "will descend to smite the wrong." Then, "the Slave Power will be broken," and the "Flag of Freedom, undoubted, pure, and irresistible," would create "ripples in every breeze" again.[27]

Douglas fumed. Sumner was one of the last voices, and certainly the most messianic, to speak before the vote on the bill was called. In so doing, he stole the narrative from what should've been a happy night for Douglas. Sumner was the living harbinger of a new movement that was rising against Douglas's bill—a movement that Sumner professed was moving in the spirit of the Lord. Douglas angrily charged Sumner with trying to pull "northern Whigs, disaffected Democrats, Abolitionists, and Free-Soilers" into "a sectional party that is marshaled under the black flag of Abolitionism," a philosophy he regarded as a kind of dangerous religious cult.

Douglas unleashed a series of invectives against the clergymen. Confessing that most of God's preachers were fine people, he blasted those "who hypocritically assume to be the followers of our Saviour" and who "convert the pulpit into the hustings, and profane the holy Sabbath by stump speeches from the sacred desk." The startlingly distasteful language he directed at three thousand clergymen—who had committed the sin of merely signing petitions—probably converted many of these ministers to abolitionism overnight.[28]

It was fair game to be polemical against Sumner. But Douglas's angry tirade against clergymen clearly crossed a line. It was self-defeating, and he seemed to know it. Everywhere in the North, editorials were defaming Douglas as a traitor. He feared that the political tides were turning against him. Still, he believed he had no choice but to push his fateful bill to passage. Like the biblical Pharaoh, he was too deep in the water to turn back.

* * *

AFTER THE BILL passed around midnight, violence broke out in Boston the next day. A fugitive slave, Anthony Burns, had been arrested by federal authorities on May 24, 1854, the day before the bill came to a vote. On May 26, several thousand Bostonians met at Faneuil Hall to decide how to resist. Ever since the release of the *Appeal*, the small Boston Vigilance Committee had grown immensely popular in the radicalizing city. The committee—including Wendell Phillips, Samuel Howe, Robert Morris, Theodore Parker, and other white and Black abolitionists affiliated with Sumner—publicly deliberated between a violent plan to rescue Burns from jail and a nonviolent plan to block Boston's roads so that he could not be easily whisked out of the city. While the debate was ongoing, a man rushed into the hall to shout that a rescue mission had just started.

The Faneuil Hall crowd scrambled to the courthouse, where a massive throng of Black Bostonians had already come to protest. These demonstrators watched eagerly as a group of Black men, led by Lewis Hayden, pummeled a battering ram at the courthouse door to force it open. Demonstrators chanted, "TAKE HIM OUT! RESCUE HIM!" while throwing bricks at the courthouse. Hayden and another man, still trying to break in, fired pistols into the doorway. The door then heaved open, and they penetrated inside. Met by policemen with wooden clubs, Hayden's men and other demonstrators brawled with the cops for several minutes.

During the clashes at the courthouse door, an Irish American truckman who volunteered to help the police was inadvertently shot, and soon died. Meanwhile, Hayden's men weren't able to push past the police to free Anthony Burns. A few days later, Burns was deported to Virginia to be reenslaved.[29]

Back in Washington, the violent episode on Sumner's turf was blamed on Sumner himself. Tabloids declared that Sumner had "blood on his hands" for his extreme rhetoric and reckless calls for resistance against the Fugitive Slave Act, which had led to the death of the Irishman. "The masses look upon Sumner as responsible," the *Washington Star* seethed. The *Star* asked readers to confront Sumner wherever they saw him in the city, to put him into a state of perpetual fear, as he deserved. "Let public opinion condemn these men everywhere,—in the street, in the Capitol, in every place where men meet." Sumner "and his infamous gang," the *Star* continued, "[should] evince a little more circumspection in their walk, talk, and acts" in the city.

The *Washington Union* took things a step farther, openly calling on readers to nip Sumner in the bud. He was "the Abolition fanatic, the distant leader," who was inspiring the dangerous cult of abolitionism that was threatening to upend peace in America. The *Union* decried that Sumner walked "safe from the fire and the fagot" while inciting bloodshed. It was time to "encourage the assassin" to stop Sumner's agitating.[30]

Within a few days, while Sumner was walking along a Washington street, a gang of angry southerners confronted him. They threatened to find him again and put a bullet through his head for the violence he was instigating across the North. At a restaurant where Sumner often dined, a furious Washingtonian man was waiting for him. The man accosted and harassed him for a bit. Rumors spread that a proslavery posse in Alexandria planned to come to the city to seize Sumner and hold him hostage in exchange for fugitive slaves in the North.

Sumner's friends begged him to exercise some caution for a while. One of his friends from Connecticut even offered him physical protection. "I will come to Washington by the next train, and quietly *stay by*," the friend offered. "I have revolvers, and can use them." But Sumner would have none of it. "I was never for a moment disturbed," he insisted to Frances Seward, describing the death threats. "I am here to do my duty & shall continue to do it without regard to personal consequences," he declared. To Theodore Parker, Sumner bragged that "the howl of the press here against me has been the best homage I ever received."[31]

* * *

SUMNER CONTINUED WALKING the muddy avenues of Washington, alone, through the summer of 1854, as the humidity rose and the seasonal rainstorms drenched the city. Unfazed by the occasional death threats and recurring street confrontations, he was more bothered by the capital's warm, steamy weather. He much preferred the cool summers and the dry, frigid, salty winds he had braved growing up near the Charles River on the North Slope of Beacon Hill. "I am less prepared than many of my friends to endure the climate here," he once complained. "I feel perceptibly its sultry heats, and I long for the taste of salt in the atmosphere."

While the Washington atmosphere was saltless, Sumner could taste victory in the tumultuous swirl of the new political atmosphere of the North. "There is something strange and moving in the way this man," a Frenchman once said of Sumner, "exercises his most temporary influence in the midst of the most violent tempest and apparently enjoys braving them." With an oracle's confidence, Sumner believed an antislavery political storm was coming. That storm, as one newspaper put it, meant that "the single brigade of abolitionism will, like a great boa constrictor, swallow up the entire army of the Whig party North."

Standing on the steps of the U.S. Capitol one night, Sumner chatted with Senator Salmon Chase. Both men realized that they felt oddly jubilant that Douglas and the F Street senators had passed the Kansas-Nebraska Act. It gave Free Soilers enough fodder to ignite the North. "They celebrate a present victory," Chase whispered to Sumner. "But the echoes they awake will never rest till slavery itself shall die."[32]

CHAPTER 10

THE SLAVE OLIGARCHY IS MAD

D O YOU HEAR THAT MAN?" STEPHEN DOUGLAS ONCE REMARKED TO a friend while pacing behind the president's chair in the Senate Chamber, listening to another one of Charles Sumner's caustic remarks. "He may be a fool, but I tell you that man has pluck. I wonder whether he knows himself what he is doing."[1]

After mass violence at a Boston courthouse led to the death of an innocent Irishman, many senators expected Sumner to scale back his rhetoric and condemn the vigilantism that was taking place. But he wouldn't stand down. Even though people were already accusing him of having blood on his hands, on June 26, 1854, Sumner introduced yet another petition against the Fugitive Slave Act. The petition was signed by three thousand Bostonians, including some signatories who had participated in the courthouse rescue attempt. Sumner called on the North to keep disobeying the law, implying that he approved of the violent resistance.

Senator Butler was aghast at Sumner's seeming endorsement of lawlessness. Turning around to face him directly, staring him dead in the eye, Butler angrily demanded to know if Sumner would obey the Fugitive Slave Clause of the Constitution: a document that all senators had sworn an oath to support. "Does the honorable Senator ask me if I would personally join in sending a fellow-man into bondage?" Sumner snarled. He invoked a verse from the Second Book of Kings: "Is thy servant a dog, that he should do such a thing?"

Butler and other senators erupted in fury. "You rise and tell me that you regard it as the office of a dog to enforce it?" Butler shouted. "You stand in my presence, as a coequal Senator, and tell me that it is a dog's office to execute the Constitution of the United States?" He declared that

Sumner's "whole style, tone, and character does not become a Senate." Senator Mason denounced Sumner as "a fanatic" who was rousing people "to the very verge of treason." As if he were enjoying himself, Sumner stood up and sneered at both men. Mason had "an odious character" that came from "plantation manners," he snickered. He taunted Butler for "racy and exuberant speech" that "gurgles forth to defend what is obviously indefensible."[2]

Southerners often succeeded in using angry tirades to shut down northern politicians, but not so with Sumner. "Until that moment slavery had not seen in public life the man whom it truly feared," editorialist George William Curtis observed. "Here was a spirit as resolute and haughty as its own." Brazen and boastful, Sumner seemed to thrive on threats designed to silence him. He shot literary bullets from the arsenal of his mind to anyone who belittled him. "He could not be contemptuously dismissed by his brother Senators as a mere 'freedom screecher,'" literary critic Edwin Percy Whipple remarked. "For he screeched Grotius and Puffendorf, screeched L'Hôpital and Turgot, screeched Hale, Holt, Mansfield, Chatham, Camden, Burke, and Fox, screeched Washington, Jefferson, Hamilton, Madison, Jay, Marshall, Jackson, Story, and Webster."[3]

When Indiana senator John Pettit accused him of spitting on his senatorial oath, Sumner retorted that he was fiercely loyal to *his* view of the Constitution, not anyone else's. "Never! NEVER!" he retorted. "I swore to support [the Constitution] as I understand it; nor more, nor less," he explained. He cited Andrew Jackson and Thomas Jefferson as his precedents. Both had famously rejected the Supreme Court's ultimate interpretive authority by holding that "each public officer, who takes an oath to support the Constitution, swears that he will support it as he understands it." Writing to a friend of his late father's, Sumner explained that even John Quincy Adams, Jackson's longtime political opponent, shared the same view: anyone who takes an oath to the Constitution has an independent duty to interpret it. "I have not hastily adopted my views," Sumner said emphatically. "[It was] one of the most solemn counsels I received from John Quincy Adams, constituting a sort of legacy, given to me as he lay in his bed between the white sheets."[4]

Southerners believed that Sumner was being pompous, reckless, lawless, and irascibly imperious. How dare he quote from the Bible when interpreting the Constitution, as if he were a kind of prophet? How did he have the gall to equate himself to presidents like Jackson, Jefferson, and Quincy Adams? Frequently, Sumner even compared himself to the Founding Fathers who disobeyed the British Stamp Act.

Sumner's grandiosity angered his colleagues, but it electrified abolitionists in Massachusetts and across the North. His haughtiness reaffirmed their dignity, intelligence, and patriotism. For years, abolitionists had been spurned by mainstream society as rabble-rousing thugs. Now they had a bombastic, educated, unapologetic, charismatic, and frighteningly erudite champion in the Senate who boldly asserted that *they*, the abolitionists, were more tied to the American Founding than proslavery southerners ever would be. "It is Sumner's first and not least glory that he saved us the fathers and the Constitution," an abolitionist recalled. "His enemies expected him to assail that venerable document. . . . They never dreamed that he was going to snatch this very platform from beneath their feet, and make them . . . the violators of the Constitution itself."

Northerners who had once hated abolitionists were also buying into Sumner's message. The public rallied against the slave oligarchy and promised to vote out northern politicians who had betrayed the Missouri Compromise. One northerner enthusiastically wrote to Sumner to encourage him to keep going:

"Agitate! Agitate! Agitate! till the work is done."[5]

* * *

WHEN SOUTHERN WHIGS had voted in favor of the Kansas-Nebraska Act, northern Whigs were so furious that they began to abandon their party en masse. "We went to bed one night old fashioned, conservative, compromise Union Whigs," one wealthy merchant wrote to his friend, "and waked up stark mad Abolitionists." Realizing that their party was on the verge of collapse, southern Whigs fled to the Democrats in droves. Meanwhile, many northern Democrats were disgusted that their party had decided to embrace the expansion of slavery and were prepared to exit it. But where would these disgruntled Democrats and angry northern Whigs go? Sumner, Chase, and their allies were ready to offer the country a new alternative: the Republican Party.

Born in a series of organic town meetings in various localities, the Republican Party was essentially the Free-Soil Party refurbished, rebranded, and expanded to anyone under a big-tent umbrella who was angry about the Kansas-Nebraska Act. The Republicans weren't officially opposed to slavery per se. They were against its *expansion*, and against the wealthy enslavers who seemed to dominate Washington. The party's creed was captured by Sumner's two popular phrases: "freedom national, slavery sectional" and the "slave oligarchy."[6]

When the first Republican Party state convention took place, in September 1854 in Worcester, Massachusetts, the crowd went wild as Charles Sumner stepped onto the stage. He had just come back from Washington, after another fight against Douglas and the southern senators that much of the northern public deemed heroic. "From slave soil I have come to free soil," Sumner shouted to loud cheers. Less than ten years before, Sumner had been ostracized for a controversial Fourth of July speech. Now he was one of the most influential opposition leaders in the country, speaking to a boisterous crowd. And he loved it. "Sumner seemed never happy except on exhibition," one voter noticed. "He seemed to be as much in his place on the platform as a statue on its pedestal," novelist Lydia Maria Child said.[7]

Unfortunately, Sumner had a problem: another party had arisen from the ashes of the Whigs. Across the North and especially in Massachusetts, former Whigs met in secret lodges to blame recent events on the Irish. Over the past ten years, roughly 1.5 million Irish had come to America to escape the potato famine. The Irish mostly voted for Democrats, who were responsible for the Kansas-Nebraska Act. The Irish also supported social welfare programs, public funding for Catholic schools, more liberal policies for alcohol, looser immigration measures, and other things that most American-born Protestant Whigs despised.

For a long time, respectable Whigs had muted the anti-Irish sentiment in their party, believing it was driven by sheer racist bigotry. But when the Whigs collapsed, nativism was unleashed in full force. Keeping their affairs secret at first, lodge attendees, when asked about these groups, would say they "know nothing." Once they became public, bigots and critics alike were stunned to see their massive numbers. Formally called the American Party, the briefly ascendant political party was more often called the Know Nothings.[8]

The Know-Nothing cause exploded in Massachusetts, where millions of Anglo-Saxon Bay Staters resented Boston's new 400,000-strong Irish immigrant community. Even Sumner's friend Henry Wilson was ready to join it. Wilson was furious at the Irish community for voting against the Free-Soil constitutional reforms that failed the year before. (The failed constitution would have banned public funding for religious schools.) Having been raised in a poor family, and a shoemaker by profession, Wilson sympathized with people who blamed Irish immigrants for taking away their jobs. He was also extremely ambitious, and having given up economic security to work in politics to help men like Sumner, he felt it was his turn to get elected to office.

As the Republican nominee for governor heading into the November 1854 election, Wilson abruptly pulled out of the race only a few days before Election Day. Republicans were aghast. The Know Nothings then swept the election, in small part due to Wilson's defection. Nearly every seat in the new legislature was claimed by the nativist party. When lawmakers first met, one of their first orders of business was to choose a new senator to serve alongside Sumner in Washington. The new Know-Nothing governor—grateful to Wilson for pulling out of the race—threw in his support for Wilson. He had almost certainly formed a backroom deal with Wilson prior to the election. Wilson fed on anti-Irish bigotry by avowing to "revise the naturalization laws" and resist "foreign influence" by stopping "foreign paupers" and "alien criminals" from dominating the political scene. Impressed, the new nativist lawmakers chose Wilson for the Senate seat.

Sumner was uncomfortable with the bigoted statements his friend had made to win office. "I am ignorant enough; but I am not a Know Nothing," he once wrote. He believed America was a home for anyone, regardless of race, religion, or class. That said, he was happy to welcome Wilson to Washington and felt he couldn't complain too much, as Wilson had orchestrated the backroom deal that got him *his* Senate seat.

For months, Sumner kept quiet about rising bigotry in his home state. He hoped to redirect the popular sentiment toward the Republican Party in due time, when he believed it would be more tactful to do so. Wilson, for his part, privately assured Republicans like Sumner that his hateful remarks were just talk. He promised Theodore Parker that he would not "infringe upon the rights of any man, black or white, native or foreign." If he said racist things, Wilson claimed, he did so only to win the election. Frustrated, Massachusetts Republicans searched for opportunities to bolster the antislavery message to keep Wilson on course.[9]

The new Senate looked quite different from the old one. Many northern Democrats and Whigs lost their seats. Salmon Chase had left the Senate to serve as governor of Ohio. William Seward and Benjamin Wade had left the Whigs to join Sumner and Wilson in the Republican Party. Seward, Wade, and Wilson were deeply opposed to slavery's expansion, but they were mellow public speakers. Republicans needed their bullhorn, Sumner, to redirect attention away from the Know Nothings and squarely at the slave oligarchy.

* * *

IN EARLY 1855, Sumner tried to stir action over a new Senate bill to grant immunity from civil liability in state courts to federal commissioners who seized fugitive slaves. Republicans spoke loudly against the bill on the day it would get a vote. Toward midnight, Sumner delivered his own impassioned rebuke. But Andrew Butler interrupted Sumner repeatedly with rambling questions about the senator's fidelity to the Constitution, which cut off Sumner's steam. Butler was "shamefully drunk," according to a reporter. "It was very, very sad to see the representative of chivalrous South Carolina disgracing his State and the Senate by his maudlin incoherencies," the reporter said. The bill passed, and Sumner didn't really generate the public attention he had wanted.[10]

Meanwhile, one of Sumner's close supporters, the Bostonian lawyer John Andrew, sought his help in freeing the enslaved family of one of his clients, the ex-slave Henry Williams. After buying his own freedom and working for a while to earn money, Williams now had the funds to buy his enslaved wife, three children, and mother-in-law. He hired Andrew to make the transaction, and Andrew asked Sumner for help, because the family lived near Washington in Prince William County, Virginia. After receiving eight hundred dollars from Andrew by mail, Sumner met with the slaveholder's attorney and the family. He bought the property deeds for Williams's family members. While their paperwork was being arranged to declare them free, Sumner was technically their slaveholder.

When the paperwork was done, Sumner was delighted to tell the family the good news. "You are free, young man," he said to the eldest son, a ten-year-old boy named Oscar. "Do you know what that means?" Oscar replied with self-assurance, "I now belong to myself." Sumner laughed. "Well! There is a definition which philosophy might borrow."[11]

A bachelor with no family of his own, Sumner loved children. "He is a man to whom all children come," an Englishman once noted. Sumner spent many of his evenings in Lafayette Park on a bench watching youngsters play. It was not unusual for a child to come up and play with his fingers or stand between his knees. When he visited other homes, young children liked to sit next to him. He was fondly called the "harmless giant" by Samuel Howe's two daughters, whom Sumner adored. "I prefer daughters to boys," Sumner once wrote to Howe. "Boys are apt to be cubs—often unruly, ill mannered, making parents anxious—staying away from home, fighting, perhaps, in the trees; but girls are the delight of home—sitting in quiet near the mother & cherishing her look, her smile, her word. To see such a child grow up must be wonderful."

For a few weeks, Sumner kept the Williams family quartered near his home in Washington while he arranged for their journey to Boston. He spent time with them during this period. He was impressed by Oscar, whom he described as "bright and intelligent, with fine silken black hair, the eyes of an eagle, and a beautiful smile." He was even more impressed by Oscar's sister, Mary. Only seven years old, she may have evoked Sumner's memories of his beloved younger sister of the same name, who had died at the tender age of eighteen. Mary had "auburn hair, large eyes, and Caucasian features," Sumner recalled. She was "completely white."[12]

Mary's complexion startled Sumner. She reminded him of a girl from a recent novel, *Ida May: A Story of Things Actual and Possible*. In the story, a young white girl was abducted and sold into slavery. She spent eight years enslaved in South Carolina before being rescued and returned to her home in Pennsylvania. The book was meant to be a bestseller like Harriet Beecher Stowe's *Uncle Tom's Cabin*, an 1852 novel about slavery that sold hundreds of thousands of copies, stirring a national conversation. *Ida May* was not so famous yet, but Sumner had read it. Mary Williams fit his mental image of the protagonist.[13]

Ida May was a fictional account, speculating about a world where white girls were kidnapped and enslaved like Black girls. Mary Williams was real and grew up enslaved. Her mother looked white, as did her grandmother, and generations before her. Although her ostensible father, Henry Williams, asserted that Mary was his biological daughter, her complexion suggested that she was the product of rape at the hands of a white enslaver. And now, looking as white as any other white girl on the street, she was, in the logic of the slave system, a Black girl.

Mary Williams sparked Sumner's ambition, for he believed she could become a potent political symbol for the Republicans. Hardly waiting for permission from her father, Sumner acquired a daguerreotype photograph of Mary and decided to send her and her family on a public exhibition before they were reunited with Henry Williams in Boston. (Williams eventually gave permission, but he was hardly in a position to say no.)

Sumner wanted white Americans to see a formerly enslaved young girl who looked like *their* girls, to show them that *they*, too, could be implicated by slavery. He also wanted to prove that the entire idea of racial distinction made no sense. "I send you by the mail the daguerreotype of a child about seven years old, who only a few months ago was a slave in Virginia," Sumner wrote to a friend in a public letter, explaining that he "had the happiness of being entrusted with" securing her freedom. "She is bright and intelligent—another Ida May." Announcing that her picture would be exhibited, Sumner called out proslavery Democrats, known as Hunkers. "Let a hard-hearted Hunker look at it and be softened! Such is slavery! There it is! Should such things be allowed to continue?"

Here, Sumner was announcing one of the first photographs ever to be used for a political cause in American history. Across New England, exhibitions of Mary's photograph, a photograph of her and her brother Oscar, and of Mary herself took place. After creating "quite a sensation in Washington," according to the *New York Times*, Mary and her family were escorted on first-class tickets to New York by a lithographic publisher Sumner trusted. Upon their arrival, members of the public were invited to examine Mary like a specimen. Reporters for the *Times* said they couldn't find anything but "the slightest trace of Negro blood." They were amazed: "She was one of the fairest and most indisputable white children that we have ever seen."[14]

One can only imagine Mary's confusion at being exhibited like a zoo animal to white strangers on her journey toward freedom. Sumner's use of her was nothing short of manipulative: a seven-year-old girl being paraded for political ends. As his scheme unfolded, proslavery newspapers picked up on another obvious fact: Sumner used Mary because she was conventionally pretty, prettier than how other young Black girls were perceived by sympathetic whites. "Senator Sumner has a weakness," jeered one paper. "It is for young negroes." Whereas he had "heretofore worshipped the black, flat-nosed, thick-lipped sons and daughters of Africa," the paper continued, "he has now become fascinated with a most beautiful white girl." Another article claimed that it was "impossible to make a hero out of a big, black, odorous buck negro—or a heroine out of a thick-lipped, flat-nosed, nappy-headed negro wench." For that reason, the article said, Sumner had found a girl who "is *quite* white," like "a tender lily," to "render effective sympathy with African slaves."[15]

When Mary and her family made it to Boston in mid-March 1855, they were reunited at last with Mary's father, Henry Williams, after years apart. But they were kept from living in peace by self-righteous abolitionists who insisted on parading Mary around Boston, too. "She was taken to the State House soon after her arrival here," a newspaper reported. Alongside Solomon Northup, a freeborn Black who was abducted and spent twelve years a slave before regaining his freedom, Mary met with state lawmakers. "She was much caressed and flattered by members of the Legislature," who were astonished that the girl "would easily pass for 'white folk.'"

Mary was exhibited across the state, thanks to Sumner. One church even displayed her with five young white girls and invited attendees to figure out which one was Mary. Strangers played with the girls' hair, examined their fingernails, and debated who was the former slave. To the crowd's astonishment, they settled on the wrong girl as Mary. Sumner's point—that slavery could impact anyone—was clearly getting across.[16]

Black abolitionists, meanwhile, were exasperated by Sumner's ploy. "We see daily white fugitives," William Cooper Nell noted in a newspaper. Why was it any surprise? Blacks knew that white slave masters raped women and enslaved the half-white children of their seed. "The cupidity of a slaveholder would suffer him to keep anyone, even his mother, in slavery." It had taken many northern whites long enough to realize this. Now that they finally had, some, like Nell, acknowledged that it might contribute to meaningful policy change. But they remained skeptical, and they doubtless recognized the power imbalance of Sumner, a leading white politician, using Mary, a recently enslaved seven-year-old girl, to advance a political project. Mary's father, who had consented to her being paraded, could hardly say no to a man who held the keys to his family's freedom. Even a white observer felt it was an "injudicious practice" to allow strangers to gape at a young girl who had just been freed from slavery as if she were a circus act.[17]

When Sumner returned to Boston in March, he used Mary one last time. The senator arrived at a triumphant moment: only a couple of weeks earlier, abolitionists had raised enough money to buy the freedom of Anthony Burns, the fugitive who had been forced back into slavery the previous year. At a sold-out event at Tremont Temple, Sumner delivered a speech called "The Anti-Slavery Enterprise," with Burns and Mary sitting behind him on the stage. The talk—which he had already delivered several times to packed crowds in New York, including at the home of William

Seward—advocated for a unified political alliance against the slave oligar-chy. Sumner invited Mary to hop off her seat and join him at the podium. Astonished at her whiteness, the crowd was struck by her benefactor's confidence. Speaking of slavery, he challenged his audience: "Do not put it aside. Do not blink it out of sight. Do not dodge it. Approach it. Study it. Ponder it. Deal with it."[18]

Implicit in Sumner's speech was the fact that Mary's white complexion was the product of white male lust. Slavery was not only bondage; it was rape and sexual power. Rape confounded northern prejudices about race. Sympathetic to the plight of enslaved Black women, most northern whites still harbored deep prejudices about their mental and physical capacities. They assumed that Blackness was a fixed construct, an immutable cate-gory erected by God. With Mary Williams as his symbol, Sumner upended these preconceptions. He had long thought race was an illusion—what scholars today call a "social construct." Now he was showing it, proving it, with a young girl who served, consensually or not, as his prop.

* * *

SUMNER WAS ADDING to a racial reckoning that Boston whites had been facing for some time. One year before, in 1854, Robert Morris—the Black lawyer who served as Sumner's co-counsel in the *Roberts v. Boston* case—retained another Black client who wanted to attend a white school. With light-skinned parents of mixed Black, white, and Native American lineage, Edward Pindall was enrolled in a white elementary school without any administrator noticing his assigned race at first. When they did notice, he was kicked out.

After Pindall sued the school and lost in court, Morris took his case to the city council. To his surprise, a council committee agreed with Morris. "In no other city or town in the Commonwealth is any distinction made in admitting children to the public schools on the ground of color," the committee noted. They recommended "the *equal* right of *all* to participate in the benefits of a common school education."

Morris succeeded in part because Pindall's light skin was so confus-ing to the all-white committee. The committee's report set the stage for a massive lobbying campaign by Boston's Black community to integrate their schools. Going to the Massachusetts State House with Nell and oth-ers, Morris lobbied until they found a young Know-Nothing lawmaker who took interest in early 1855. Noting Sumner's "able and eloquent argument" some years before in *Roberts v. City of Boston*, the lawmaker issued a report that decried the debarring of "the colored race from these advantages" of the "common-school system." A few weeks after Mary visited the State House on Sumner's request, the legislature passed a law opening Boston's white public schools to Black children.[19]

The success represented the oddity of the Know-Nothing movement. Though informed by deep prejudices against Catholics, most Know-Nothing lawmakers were against slavery and caught up in the same anti-Nebraska whirlwind as the Republicans. Abolitionists heralded the victory in the legislature and saw it as a sign of good things to come. "Men were always asking," Wendell Phillips told a celebratory crowd, "what has the Anti-Slavery agitation done? . . . It has opened the schools!" He declared that "the best thing learned by these struggles is, how to prepare for another, to be in for the war." In the months ahead, abolitionists hoped to build on the momentum and to redirect the energy of the Know-Nothing movement toward antislavery.[20]

As abolitionists looked for the next big thing, Mary Williams and her family faded into anonymity. After her notoriety dissipated, Sumner paid for Mary's time. He and John Andrew raised money from friends, including Henry Longfellow, to give to her father, Henry, to buy the freedom of other family members still in slavery. They also arranged for the daguerreotypes of Mary and her brother Oscar to be sold in paper form, with the proceeds going to the family. And Sumner rebutted a bizarre request from the abolitionist Thomas Wentworth Higginson to adopt Mary as an act of charity, so that he could raise her as a white woman unmoored from her darker-skinned relatives. After settling up with Mary's family, Sumner left for New York to deliver a few lectures. Then, he embarked on a journey.[21]

The previous year, he had canceled a trip to the West when Free Soilers insisted that he stay home to assist in the constitutional reform effort. This year, Republicans doubtless wanted him to stay again to combat the Know-Nothing fever pitch. There were even fears that Henry Gardner, Massachusetts's Know-Nothing governor, would try to unseat Sumner and place himself in the Senate when the senator's term expired. But Sumner was determined to go on his trip. All year long, he had been fighting to protect the Missouri Compromise and stop slavery's expansion into the West. Now he would finally—for the first time in his life—see the far edge of the American frontier for himself. In the summer of 1855, Sumner embarked for the West.

* * *

LONG BEFORE THE Founding, Americans dreamed of the West. Thirteen colonies settled on the Eastern Shore could only imagine what lay beyond the Appalachian Mountains, out into the vast expanse of land the British had designated as Indian Territory, farther still to the lands claimed by Spain and France, and even beyond to the other sea, the great Pacific Ocean, where few had been. They were "scenes of visionary enchantment," as the explorer Meriwether Lewis described it, empty canvases for the American mind.

Never mind that the land was already populated. Indigenous tribes, some with settlements, some who roamed, and some who had been forced to live there after being expelled, claimed most of this land as theirs. But many presidents, especially Andrew Jackson, directed large-scale killing and resettling campaigns to take Native land. White settlers on the frontier also frequently massacred tribal people on their own, in their hunger for more land. Although many Americans objected to this violent acquisition of western lands, most recognized that expansion was inevitable, a kind of Manifest Destiny. "The whole continent of North America appears to be destined by Divine Providence," John Quincy Adams wrote, "to be peopled by one *nation*." The violent campaign westward gave birth to the idea of America the beautiful, from sea to shining sea.[22]

Visions of the American West differed largely along sectional lines between the North and South. Most northerners wanted free land populated by small farmers and pioneers who would till the soil and earn the fruits of their labor. Most white southerners wanted slave land filled with larger plantations that bought enslaved people from the South, where most arable land was already cultivated. In the summer of 1855, Sumner ventured westward right into the mix of the complicated imagery impressed upon the land.

Passing through New York and Pennsylvania, he made his first stop in Ohio. Ohio was the heart of the Northwest Territories, a land where buying and selling human beings had always been illegal. A bastion of Free Soilism, Ohio was home to many important antislavery politicians, including Joshua Giddings, John Bingham, and Salmon Chase. There, Sumner visited Horace Mann, who had moved to the state to serve as president of Antioch College, and spent time with Chase, who had completed his Senate term and was now running for governor. Then Sumner moved southward to Kentucky, a border state that straddled North and South with the Appalachian Mountains on one side and the Ohio River on the other. Apart from brief moments of transit through Pennsylvania and Maryland, this was Sumner's first time in a true slave state.[23]

In Kentucky, he stayed in a sprawling forty-five-room plantation house owned by the antislavery farmer Cassius Clay (a cousin of the famous senator Henry Clay, and the namesake of the famous boxer Muhammad Ali). There, he rode horses and enjoyed learning about Clay's breeding of cattle and sheep.

Clay had freed the enslaved people he inherited from his father and started his own antislavery newspaper in a Lexington office. The paper, "moderate enough," in Clay's own words, pitched gradual emancipation: that is, giving free Blacks some rights and forming a compromise between ex-slaves and enslavers where the latter kept "the Lion's share." But even that little was too much for the proslavery public. A mob stormed Clay's office, destroyed his printing equipment, and threatened to kill him. Relenting to pressure, he closed the office and financed a new paper across the Ohio River, in Cincinnati, while continuing to live in Kentucky.[24]

The suppression of abolitionism was even worse in other slave states. Virginia made it a crime for anyone to deny a slaveowner's right to own slaves. Maryland and Tennessee banned antislavery publications. North Carolina imposed the death penalty on anyone who circulated publications that encouraged slaves to resist. The lack of basic civil liberties was unsurprising given who governed these states. Large slaveholders were overrepresented in state legislatures, usually by a factor of five or more. They also dominated their economies: in many counties, the most common farm size exceeded a thousand acres. Public schools were nearly nonexistent, and the illiteracy rate for free adults in most slave states was more than double that in free states. These oligarchical regimes were run by small juntas of slaveowners who brutalized the people they owned and oppressed free whites, too; less than a third of white families in the South even owned slaves.[25]

Passing through any of those states would have been dangerous for Sumner, but he wanted to see a slave plantation with his own eyes. At his request, Clay took the senator to visit the plantation of his brother, who was still a slaveholder. Alone, the two walked through the farmlands where more than a hundred people were in bondage. Sumner asked many questions but made few comments. Clay tried to show him that his brother was among the more humane slaveholders, who provided his enslaved people with clean, warm cottages. "What is all this physical comfort?" Sumner thought to himself. "The child and others are still slaves." While passing by one young enslaved boy, he tossed the child a coin, muttering "poor boy" under his breath.

From the bluegrass countryside, Sumner went to the city of Lexington. On the way, his stagecoach was delayed so the driver could "help lick a n——r." In the city, he watched a slave auction where a man was "compelled to open his mouth and show his teeth, like a horse." At the hotel, he "witnessed the revolting spectacle of a poor slave, yet a child, almost felled to the floor by a blow on the head from a clenched fist." As an honored guest in a state that tolerated no one who spoke out, Sumner said nothing, despite being horrified. He was quietly galled by the contrast of the land: the rolling hills, the lush green pastures, the horse and cattle farms, tainted by the auction blocks, the cruel physical beatings, and the cracks of the whip.[26]

Sumner journeyed onward by stagecoach. In Louisville, he stopped by the grave of Andrew Jackson. In Nashville, a local paper caught wind of a "sly visit" by the "notorious Charles Sumner" after he had left. After passing incognito through St. Louis and St. Paul and recovering from a small accident with a horse in Iowa, he went on his way to Madison, Chicago, and Detroit. He then spent two weeks in isolation, lodging somewhere near Lake Superior without access to newspapers. Then he traveled toward New York by ship through the Great Lakes; spent some time in Saratoga; hiked the White Mountains in New Hampshire; stopped by his brother Albert's home in Newport; and returned to Boston in September 1855.[27]

All in all, Sumner had traversed eleven free states and three slave states in only a few months. Doubtless he had spent much time in reflection. What had his life come to? A younger Sumner had been eager to read books, impress and serve his mentors, and carve out a life for himself as a law professor. Here he was now, an activist, a senator, a hated and revered man. A younger Sumner had wanted love, looking for a woman and never finding one, taking solace in two friends who, he felt, had abandoned him when they married. And here he was now, a bachelor seeking solace in a life full of pain. All the while, his mind stayed focused on what became his life's purpose—ending slavery. "There is an old saying . . . that whoso the gods wish to destroy they first make mad," Sumner had written from Lake Superior. "The Slave Oligarchy is mad, and their overflowing madness runs through every agent and tool. . . . I rejoice to believe that there is unmistakable evidence of that madness which precedes a fall."[28]

Back home, Sumner caught up on political developments. "The K.N's here behave badly," he wrote to John Jay, referring to the Know Nothings. "Our contest seems to be with them. Still I think the Republicans will prevail. They *must* prevail. They *shall* prevail." Sumner finally denounced the Know Nothings publicly. "Ourselves the children of the Pilgrims of a former generation, let us not turn from the Pilgrims of the present," he declared in a speech to a Bostonian audience ahead of the November election. "The history of the country . . . testifies to the merits of foreigners," he continued, citing "Lafayette of France" and "Alexander Hamilton, who was born in the West Indies." Sumner urged northern unity. "Slave-masters are always united. Hence their strength. . . . The friends of Freedom have thus far been divided. They, too, must be united."

Alas, nativists swept the state election, with the governor, Henry Gardner, at the helm. "It is humiliating that this . . . faction should have thus triumphed," Sumner lamented to William Seward. Fortunately, unlike in Massachusetts, Republicans won control over state legislatures across the North. When he and Seward returned to Washington in December 1855, they came to a new session of the Senate where nearly one fourth of the seats were now Republican. Southerners were enraged and anxious by the growing presence of antislavery politicians.

The Senate was now more polarized than it had ever been, on starkly sectional terms. "Our bitter session commences soon—the bitterest ever held," Sumner believed. "The next Congress will be the most violent one in our history," Senator Henry Wilson predicted, thinking that duels and brawls might transpire. "If violence and bloodshed come, let us not falter, but do our duty, even if we fall upon the floors of Congress."[29]

CHAPTER 11

THE FIRST BLOW IN A CIVIL WAR

ON DECEMBER 25, 1855, SUMNER DISCUSSED POLITICAL STRATEGY over Christmas dinner with several major political actors, including Francis Blair, Salmon Chase, and Nathaniel Banks. Once upon a time, these three men were Democrats. They had each left the party at different points in time because they were disgusted by its increasingly proslavery bent. Along with Sumner, they agreed to use all their resources to stir every pot and work every channel in the North to delegitimize the northern Democrats as being irredeemably proslavery. They decided to gradually coalesce their various factions under the Republican banner, and they committed to focusing their messaging squarely on one issue and one issue alone: Kansas.[1]

* * *

AFTER THE PASSAGE of the Kansas-Nebraska Act, slaveholders in Missouri had rushed into the next-door territory of Kansas to claim the best land titles for themselves. Worried that these Missourians would turn Kansas into a slave state, northerners raised money to send free-state settlers to the new land, too. In their search for freedom, enslaved people in Missouri began crossing into Kansas as well.

Thus began a deluge of northerners and southerners coming to Kansas in a frenzy, seizing land and founding townships in a desperate bid to claim the majority of the land. Both sides took up arms, fearing possible attacks from the other. "Kansas is made the abode of an army of hired fanatics, recruited, transported, armed and paid for the special and sole purpose of abolitionizing Kansas," said one southern settler. A northern settler proclaimed Kansas "the great struggle between freedom and slavery."[2]

Northern and southern settlers fought over land, stole animals from each other, and burned down homes. Some settlers were even killed in the routine melees as gangs of antislavery and proslavery men prowled the streets looking for enemies to attack. Both sides hoped to scare off the other in order to guarantee that the territory would become free or enslaved. The nation watched in despair as violence unfolded, a sign that Stephen Douglas's idea of "popular sovereignty"—white men democratically deciding whether to be proslavery or antislavery—was a disaster. All the while, some northern antislavery men kept funneling arms into Kansas, while some proslavery men in the South did the same, fueling the conflict.

Sumner received scores of letters from Kansas settlers, begging him to do something to ease the violence and ensure the territory became free land. As he read these letters with dread, Sumner was especially horrified to learn about the actions of one of his former colleagues: David Atchison, the former Missouri senator and president pro tempore of the Senate.

Determined to secure a new slave state for the South, which would ensure two additional proslavery senators in the Senate, Atchison had quit his public office and moved back home to orchestrate a takeover of Kansas. He organized a large gang of Missourians and led them into Kansas, armed with bowie knives and guns. Instructing them to "hang a negro thief or Abolitionists, without Judge or Jury," Atchison had his gang of proslavery raiders seize townships at gunpoint. He taught his raiders that Kansas was just step one of a much larger aspiration: "If we win, we can carry slavery to the Pacific Ocean," Atchison declared.[3]

In January 1856, Atchison's ruffians violently took possession of polling locations, stuffed them with thousands of fraudulent ballots, and intimidated free-state voters in order to elect a proslavery legislature to run the territory of Kansas. Outraged free-state settlers created their own government in Topeka, which they said expressed the true will of the people. President Franklin Pierce threw his support behind the proslavery side and sent the U.S. Army to crush the Topeka resistance. With help from American soldiers, the proslavery Kansas government jailed Kansas free-state leaders, shut down antislavery newspapers, applied the death penalty in cases in which anyone engaged in helping runaway slaves, and declared it a felony for anyone to criticize slavery.[4]

Kansas had effectively become a proslavery dictatorship, thanks to soldiers acting at the direction of the President of the United States and armed gangs led by the former president pro tempore of the Senate. The future of American democracy itself was on the line. As Sumner put it, Kansas pushed America to "the brink of a fearful crisis."[5]

* * *

DESPITE THE URGENCY of the moment, Congress seemed completely ill-equipped to do anything about it. The legislature had never been more divided or incompetent in the wake of the Whig Party's collapse. For two months, the House squabbled over who to pick as the new Speaker. More than twenty congressmen tried to get elected. After 133 ballots, the House finally tapped Nathaniel Banks—a moderately antislavery man from Massachusetts who was one of the Christmas dinner guests from a few months prior—as speaker. Banks had managed to straggle together a loose northern coalition among Know Nothings, Republicans, ex-Whigs, and disgruntled northern Democrats. While the Senate remained firmly in the hands of proslavery forces, the House was now led by a moderately antislavery man for the first time in decades. Yet his coalition was weak.

Congress was getting more rancorous and dangerous in this climate. A congressman beat up influential *New York Tribune* editor Horace Greeley over a negative editorial. Another congressman shot and killed a waiter for failing to serve his breakfast. "Truly—truly—this is a godless place," Sumner said.[6]

Sumner was furious at the state of Congress and the bloodbath in Kansas. "In the House we are weak; in the Senate powerless. This Know Nothing madness has demoralized Northern representatives," Sumner explained. "The tyranny of slavery over us is complete. Will the people submit?" he asked a friend. He decided to deliver a major speech that would refocus the political arena on the crisis in Kansas. In doing so, he hoped to deflect Know-Nothing sentiment in the North and keep slavery at the top of voters' minds.

Sumner's speech needed to be powerful, passionate, and provocative for his ambitious strategy to succeed. "I shall deliver the most thorough philippic ever uttered in a legislative body," Sumner promised to Theodore Parker. It would be "the most thorough & complete speech of my life," he predicted to Salmon Chase. Parker wrote back to encourage Sumner to "strike a great blow," telling him that "the North is ready—if you err at all let it be on the side of going too fast & too far, not the other."[7]

Sumner also hoped to exact personal payback against his colleagues, who had long demeaned him and had orchestrated the current crisis. There was Andrew Butler, Atchison's former roommate at the F Street Mess and a key architect of the Kansas-Nebraska Act. Often drunk in the Senate Chamber, Butler regularly interrupted Sumner when he spoke, driveled in racist language, and had once ridiculed Sumner's chastity to a laughing Senate. Butler's housemate Virginia senator James Mason had authored the Fugitive Slave Act and had once mocked Sumner for not being able to deliver an antislavery speech on the Senate floor during his first term. And there was Stephen Douglas, who had authored the Kansas-Nebraska Act and had once screamed at him, maligning him as a "confederate" of "abolitionism, free soilism, n——ism."

Sumner believed that an invective speech could rally northern support for the antislavery cause, deflect Know-Nothing sentiment, vindicate the oppressed free-state settlers of Kansas, reunite northern members of Congress, and humiliate senators who had long berated him. It was a brilliant idea; it was also dangerous. Southerners had assaulted northern politicians who harangued them before. They said it was part of their code of honor, which bound them to defend their reputations in the face of personal attacks. Sumner hoped to make fun of this chivalrous code and to target especially the man who had mocked his bachelorhood: Andrew Butler.[8]

Sumner must have known that he would be putting himself in harm's way by mocking Butler and others. Less than two months earlier, he had watched Butler march up to Senator William Pitt Fessenden with clenched fists, nearly assaulting him after the latter asked a provocative question. He probably knew that Butler had impulsively challenged Senator Thomas Hart Benton to a duel several years earlier. Though the duel never materialized, Benton had once killed a man in a duel and could have easily handled Butler. Could Sumner? The buttoned-up scholar had never used a weapon of any kind before, let alone a gun.

Though big and strong, Sumner was no fighter. Despite the fact that there had been several recent acts of congressional violence, Sumner decided to make things even more dangerous for himself, as if the death threats he had been receiving over the past few years weren't enough to scare him already. "I am happy to learn that you intend to speak," Eli Thayer, an abolitionist and activist for a free Kansas, wrote him. "But there will be gnashing of teeth among the defenders of Slavery. Be prepared, therefore, for the worst of their endeavors."

After writing his provocative speech, Sumner practiced it in front of Senator Seward and his wife. The couple urged him to temper his message.

He didn't listen. "There is a time for everything," Sumner once explained. "When crime and criminals are thrust before us, they are to be met by all the energies that God has given us,—by argument, sarcasm, scorn, and denunciation. The whole arsenal of God is ours; and I will not renounce one of the weapons,—not one."⁹

* * *

On Monday, May 19, 1856, Sumner delivered the first part of "The Crime Against Kansas," one of the most important speeches in American history. While the Senate Chamber was almost as hot as ninety degrees on this humid day, a crowd of Washington locals came to watch, for Sumner was famous for his oratory skills. "There is something very seductive and thrilling in the full, rich, base voice of Mr. Sumner," a contemporary said. "Its variations are truly captivating, and its base tones thrill through one's whole frame like the blast of a bugle." The galleries were thronged to capacity with men and women; the floor brimmed with spectators who overflowed past the doorways; every journalist's desk was occupied; and many congressmen left the House to watch the speech in the Senate, including Georgia's Alexander Stephens, the future vice president of the Confederacy.

Throughout the speech, Sumner commanded attention, and only one point of order was raised. At first, Stephen Douglas chatted loudly with other senators to show how little he cared about Sumner's remarks. But he was shushed by the sergeant at arms at Sumner's request, and eventually even he fell silent, captivated. "No such scene has been witnessed since the days of Daniel Webster," reported the *New York Evening Post*.¹⁰

Sumner decried the potential admission of Kansas as a slave state as "the rape of a virgin Territory." He denounced it as "foreshadowing a . . . fratricidal, parricidal war." He ascribed the South's mission to admit Kansas to a "madness for Slavery which should disregard the Constitution, the laws, and all the great examples of our history." Declaring "the Slave Power of our Republic" to be "unmasked" at last, "heartless, grasping, and tyrannical," he proposed to reveal what he called "the crime against Kansas." He organized his speech under three headings: exposing the crime, rebutting apologies for the crime, and applying the remedy (admitting Kansas as a free state). Sumner spoke from memory for three hours on Monday and two hours on Tuesday.¹¹

The best way to understand Sumner's speech is through its allusions. His first major allusion compared Kansas under President Pierce to Sicily under the Roman territorial governor Gaius Verres. Verres had been exposed by the great Roman senator Marcus Tullius Cicero as an oppressive governor. Cicero accused Verres of whipping, killing, and crucifying a dissenter, even though the man cried out, *"I am a Roman citizen!"* Verres displayed the dead man's body on a Sicilian beach in eyeshot of Italy, where his rights would have been recognized. Pierce was just like Verres, denying the rights of American citizenship—such as free speech and gun ownership—to territorial residents that would have been available in an American state.

Cicero had charged Verres with stealing funds from Sicily's temples. Similarly, Sumner decried Pierce for plundering ballot boxes, what he called shrines "more sacred than any heathen altar." Cicero had also infamously accused Verres of being "a ravager of chastity" for engaging in sexual violence. Without mentioning Verres's impropriety, Sumner implied that Pierce was complicit in slaveholder debauchery. As soon as he finished his allusion, he described Kansas as "the rape of virgin Territory."[12]

Sumner's next main allusion mocked Senator Butler by comparing him to Don Quixote, an elderly man in a famous Spanish novel who deluded himself into thinking he was a chivalrous knight. To form his retinue, Don Quixote picked out a prostitute as his maiden and recruited his neighbor as his squire. Sumner mocked Senator Butler for believing himself to be "a chivalrous knight." He said that Butler had "chosen a mistress" who is "polluted in the sight of the world," but "is chaste in his sight." Who was Butler's mistress? Sumner said it was "the harlot, Slavery." And Butler's squire? Stephen Douglas.

Sumner's goal was to show that slavery was full of sexual depravity. It did not matter how gentlemanly a slaveholder might appear in Washington. A slaveholder could never be a chivalrous man, no matter how much he claimed to be, for he enslaved others and possibly raped women.

Butler wasn't there to hear Sumner's speech. He had recently survived a stroke, one of many he had suffered over the years. Butler was recovering back home on his plantation, which had more than seventy enslaved people. Mocking his absentee victim, Sumner sneered, "Even his white head ought not to protect from rebuke." Referring to Butler's frequent drunkenness and his speech impediment—he spat uncontrollably while speaking after a stroke—Sumner jeered at the "loose expectoration" of Butler's speech.

Butler would express shock at Sumner's vulgar allusions regarding his character—but they should have come as no surprise. Sumner had probably not forgotten the incident, two years earlier, when Butler had humiliated him on the Senate floor by using sexual innuendos, mocking his chastity, and depicting a scene where he met a Black princess, with the intention to marry her, and was revolted by her sight. Ironically, evidence suggests that Butler owned an enslaved mistress and sired two children by her.[13]

The sexual perversity of slavery had been front of Sumner's mind for months. When he freed the Williams family earlier in the year, he was instantly struck by the young girl Mary, whose white complexion high-lighted a legacy of exploitation. In his speech, Sumner also bemoaned a mother who was recently in the news for having "taken the life of her offspring," likely referring to Margaret Garner, a runaway slave who killed her daughter before being captured in order to spare her from a life of torture at the hands of southern men. (Garner's case would become the inspiration for Toni Morrison's award-winning novel *Beloved*.)

Sumner's next major allusion compared Missouri's former senator David Atchison to Rome's Lucius Sergius Catiline. Catiline contrived a plot to overthrow the Roman Senate. When Cicero exposed him, he fled Rome and raised a rebellious army in the countryside. Few believed at first that the senator was trying to unravel the Roman Republic, but when the plot finally became obvious, the Roman Senate sentenced their colleague to death for treason.

Sumner explicitly compared Atchison to Catiline. "Like Catiline, he stalked into this Chamber, reeking with conspiracy," Sumner declared. "And then like Catiline he skulked away . . . to join and provoke the con-spirators."

Though few but Sumner were wont to admit it, Atchison was actively sabotaging democracy and threatening to unravel the American experi-ment by using violent border raids to take over polling stations. Sumner didn't go so far as to call for Atchison's death for committing treason, but he did wrap himself in Cicero's mantle, plainly exposing Atchison as a threat to the American republic. Further, he accused Butler of being Atchison's "open compurgator"—after all, he was Atchison's close friend and former roommate.

While Sumner did not mention it, his allusion also implied sexual impropriety on the part of Atchison's men. Cicero had famously accused Catiline, like Verres, of sexual violence and debauchery. He arraigned Catiline's army of rebels for taking "no thought for anything but murder, arson, robbery, rape." Atchison's armed mobs were composed of enslavers. As far as Sumner was concerned, they were rapists.[14]

Sumner's final major allusion targeted Stephen Douglas. He described Douglas's doctrine of popular sovereignty as akin to "Sin" in the epic poem *Paradise Lost*. In the poem, Sin was a creature that "seemed a woman to the waist, and fair; but ended foul in many a scaly fold." Like Sin, popular sovereignty was fair at first glance: it permitted white settlers to democratically vote in elections. But the doctrine was foul below the waist, for it allowed *white* men to vote to enslave *Black* men and women who had no say. In Milton's epic, Sin is Satan's daughter. As popular sovereignty's father, Douglas was being characterized by Sumner as Lucifer incarnate.[15]

At this point, Sumner had breached every form of decorum with the most provocative speech in the history of the Senate. He had compared Douglas to Lucifer, Atchison to a Roman traitor, Butler to Don Quixote, and President Pierce to a Roman dictator. He characterized all of them as antidemocratic, treasonous scoundrels who were either complicit or active participants in sexual debauchery and rape.

Sumner didn't stop there. He ridiculed Butler's home state of South Carolina, declaring that civilization would lose little if his state's history were "blotted out of existence." He noted that the state constitution was "republican only in name," requiring state lawmakers to be men with "a settled freehold estate of five hundred acres of land and ten negroes." (Sumner left out that one could also qualify without possessing slaves, by owning a certain value of real estate.)

Sumner then attacked Virginia senator James Mason, another one of Atchison and Butler's F Street roommates and the author of the Fugitive Slave Act. Sumner declared that Mason "does not represent that early Virginia" of Jefferson and Washington, who believed in the "equality of men." Mason instead stood for "that other Virginia . . . where human beings are bred as cattle for the shambles."

While viciously denouncing his colleagues, Sumner presented himself as a modern-day Cicero who was the savior of the American republic. He called on America to renew its republican character by strangling the Slave Power and returning to its original Founding values. "I appeal to the great principle of American Institutions," he said. That principle was "embodied in the Declaration of Independence, by which Government is recognized as deriving its just powers only *from the consent of the governed*."

In closing, Sumner openly admitted that his provocative speech was intended for public arousal rather than persuading his colleagues. "From Congress to a broader stage . . . to the People . . . I appeal," he said. "Vindicate the electoral franchise in Kansas" and "help to guard the equal rights of distant fellow-citizens." At last, he sat down.

Senators were horrified and outraged by Sumner's remarks. Michigan senator Lewis Cass first rose to brand the oration "the most un-American and unpatriotic speech that ever grated on the ears of the members of this high body." Douglas spoke next. "We have had another dish of the classics served up, classic allusions, each one only distinguished for its lasciviousness and obscenity," he decried. "Is it his object to provoke some of us to kick him as we would a dog in the street, that he may get sympathy upon the just chastisement?" Douglas asked. Then rose Mason, who said Sumner did not possess "manhood in any form."

Saying little to Cass and Mason, Sumner delivered a final taunt to Douglas, as if he were trying to provoke him. "The noisome, squat, and nameless animal, to which I now refer, is not a proper model for an American Senator." Perhaps anticipating that he might receive an aggressive response, he added, "Let the Senator . . . remember hereafter that the bowie-knife and bludgeon are not the proper emblems of senatorial debate." He then closed. "On a former occasion I did something to exhibit on this floor the plantation manners which he displayed," he said. "I will not do any more now."

* * *

The fury, and fear, in Washington were palpable. Ohio congressman John Bingham rushed to Senator Henry Wilson to warn him that Sumner was probably in danger. Bingham interpreted Douglas's reference to a possible need to "kick him as we would a dog" as a call for violence against Sumner. Wilson took heed and arranged a patrol of Republican politicians to escort Sumner home. But Sumner sneaked out through a side door without them. For the next few days, he went about his business unguarded, rebuffing requests for protection. Meanwhile, some southerners hooted for an attack. One congressman said that "Mr. Sumner ought to be knocked down, and his face jumped into." A senator remarked that he wished he could hang Sumner on the spot. Another congressman said he hoped Andrew Butler "would whip him, and put his foot upon his face."[16]

Congressman Preston Brooks, whose father was Butler's first cousin, was especially enraged by Sumner's speech. A strong six-foot-tall man with wavy brown hair and a thick, curly goatee, Brooks had never met Sumner before. Yet he had been itching for a fight ever since Nathaniel Banks became the country's first antislavery Speaker of the House, in February. "I never could understand the magnanimity or chivalry of southern gentlemen," Brooks had pronounced on the House floor, referring to southerners who backed away from fighting their colleagues. "We are standing upon slave territory, surrounded by slave States," he had said. "Pride, honor, patriotism, all command us, if a battle is to be fought, to fight it here upon this floor."

A unremarkable congressman in his second term, Brooks was facing political troubles back home in his district in Edgefield County, South Carolina, where proslavery extremists charged him with being too moderate. They mocked him for his inglorious service during the Mexican-American War, where he had been discharged due to illness. They also knew he had achieved relatively little while in Congress, perhaps because he was burdened by a drinking problem. At last, Brooks had a reason for a fight—a fight that would avenge his home state, his kinsman, and his own political future, all in one fell swoop.[17]

Born to a wealthy slaveholding family, Brooks had fought many brawls in his youth. At nineteen, he nearly instigated a duel that ended in a fistfight. At twenty, he was expelled from South Carolina College for threatening to kill the town marshal. At twenty-one, he fought a duel that resulted in a bullet through his thigh, which obliged him to use a walking stick for the rest of his life. After the injury, Brooks forswore dueling. In addition to serving in the military, he became a lawyer and planter who was well liked by the white people of his community.

In Edgefield, Brooks was a man of high status, a planter who owned more than eighty slaves. "The institution of slavery, which it is so fashionable now to decry," he once declared, "has been the greatest of blessings to this entire country." Brooks saw slavery as the fuel that made American civilization possible. Like nearly all slaveholders, he was committed to the inherent inferiority of Blacks, who he believed needed guidance, discipline, and lordship from whites in order to rise above the savagery that was supposedly instinctual to their nature. He believed that slavery, in fact, "enlightened and ennobled" African Americans.[18]

Brooks had apparently learned, days before the oration, that Sumner planned to chastise South Carolina in his speech. He watched Sumner's speech on Monday, May 19. Though Sumner said nothing about the state on Monday, he did insult Butler. Brooks told Virginia senator Robert Hunter that he felt personally insulted by Sumner's remarks. It is unclear if Brooks watched on Tuesday, but he professed to have read the oration in full by Wednesday morning, seething with anger. To condemn slavery was to criticize everything he had been taught to believe, everything upon which his livelihood, sense of self, and community depended. To defame South Carolina was to mock the place he called home and to undermine its right to exist as a slave society. To accuse his own kinsman of sexual misconduct was practically to ask for blood.[19]

Brooks believed in what many scholars have described as the southern code of honor. The idea was simple: Gentlemen were entitled to protect their reputation against those who libeled them. They would also look like cowards if they didn't stand up for themselves when unjustly maligned. With Butler being elderly and out of town, Brooks felt it was his duty to stand up for the honor of his kinsman, his home state, and slavery. He resolved to attack Sumner if he did not apologize. But he would not challenge Sumner to a duel, as was the custom. Duels were illegal in Washington and would increase Brooks's potential legal liability. He also thought Sumner was not a gentleman who was appropriate for a duel. "To punish an insulting inferior," a southerner once explained, "one used not a pistol or a sword but a cane or horsewhip." The purpose was to *degrade* Sumner, to lower his social standing and show him who was boss: southern gentlemen.[20]

Thinking at first to use a "horse whip or a cowhide," Brooks settled on lashing Sumner with a cane. He feared that Sumner, "my superior in strength," might wrest a whip from his hand. (Brooks was also four inches shorter than Sumner, who was six foot four.) Brooks feared getting hurt or having to kill Sumner in self-defense (presumably, with another weapon, like a pocket pistol). He chose a thin cane, about one inch thick on the larger end and tapered to five-eighths of an inch on the other end. The hollow stick was made of gutta-percha, a rubberlike substance derived from tree sap, which is as hard as wood without being brittle. Made from the gutta-percha trees of East Asia, the material was used in just about everything at the time, from water pipes to transatlantic cable insulation and surgical instruments to the soles of shoes. Brooks's gutta-percha cane, gifted to him by a friend, was said to have the same gravity as a hickory or whalebone cane. It was topped with a thin gold head, which Brooks planned to hold as the handle while mauling Sumner with the other end.[21]

On Wednesday, at around 11 a.m., Brooks awaited Sumner on the Capitol stairs for more than an hour. When his friend Virginia congressman Henry Edmundson passed by, Brooks shared his plan with him. Around fifteen more minutes passed before he gave up, thinking Sumner had taken a carriage. At some point he and Edmundson were joined by South Carolina representative Laurence Keitt and Arkansas senator Robert Johnson. Though Brooks claimed he did not tell Johnson, he confessed to having informed Keitt at some point about his plans. He also told South Carolina representative James Orr.[22]

Around 6 p.m. Brooks was rumored to have visited a restaurant where Sumner frequently dined to see if he was inside. He was reportedly joined by Edmundson and Keitt, both of whom had condoned or participated in congressional violence before. One time, Edmundson nearly pulled a bowie knife on another congressman while drunk on the House floor; in 1860, he would attack another congressman with a cane. Keitt, for his part, once declared that if northerners blocked slavery in the West or repealed the Fugitive Slave Act, "it would be the duty of the South to take possession of the Capitol . . . and expel from it the traitors to the Constitution." When the trio failed to find Sumner, they went home. Brooks slept little that night, thinking of his next move.[23]

On Thursday, at around 11 a.m., Brooks waited an hour and a half for Sumner at the Pennsylvania Avenue entrance to the Capitol grounds. Edmundson claimed to have again run into Brooks by chance. Brooks told him he had chosen the spot to have maximum visibility over any of the likely paths Sumner could take to walk into the Capitol and over the road Sumner would need to use if he came by carriage. Edmundson advised that it was unwise to attack Sumner on the Capitol grounds because the Massachusetts senator was taller and possibly stronger than Brooks. Agreeing, Brooks walked with Edmundson to the Capitol when both the House and the Senate began their sessions at around 12:30 p.m.[24]

Brooks went straight to the Senate, where a eulogy was being delivered. The Senate adjourned, and most senators left afterward. But Sumner stayed—as did Brooks, who sat in an absent senator's seat. Sumner was busy signing copies of "The Crime Against Kansas," which he had prepared for publication before even delivering it. As Sumner focused on the autographs, Brooks waited for Henry Wilson, who sat near Sumner, to leave. He was also waiting for a group of twenty to thirty ladies, who were in the Senate for some reason, to exit.[25]

At some point, Edmundson arrived and saw Keitt. He suggested that they leave. "No," Keitt replied. "I cannot leave till Brooks does." Edmundson then talked to Brooks. Brooks told him he was going to call on Sumner to chat outside. Edmundson advised him that Sumner would insist on their talking near his desk. Agreeing, Brooks returned to the chamber. Edmundson then pulled aside Arkansas senator Robert Johnson to ask about the propriety of Brooks's attacking Sumner on the Senate floor.[26]

Meanwhile, the number of ladies dwindled to one, left in the lobby. Brooks asked an officer to get rid of her. (He may have also been trying to distract the officer.) "No; that would be ungallant; besides, she is very pretty," the officer replied. "Yes, she is pretty," Brooks responded, "but I wish she would go." Interrupted by a Senate page, the officer looked the other way. Brooks seized the moment and got out of his chair. (Although Brooks would deny it, the lady was probably still present.) Turning around, the officer saw Brooks rushing toward Sumner; in a panic, he called on a nearby army major. But it was too late. At roughly 1:15 p.m., Brooks attacked—without waiting for the apology he said he would request.[27]

"Mr. Sumner," Brooks was reported to have said as the senator looked up. "I have read your speech over twice carefully; it is a libel on South Carolina and Mr. Butler, who is a relative of mine." Perhaps without finishing his sentence, Brooks lunged forward onto the desk and swung his cane, smashing it into Sumner's head. The first blow so stunned Sumner that he temporarily lost his vision. Then came more blows, bludgeoning his skull, shoulders, arms, and neck, until he lost consciousness. In the heat of the moment, Sumner had neglected to pull his chair back, which was tucked deep under the desk and could be pulled back by rollers. His body convulsing, he instinctively tried to force himself upright, and on the second attempt to get up, he wrenched the mahogany desk (which sat atop three inches of wooden blocks that were attached to an iron plate, all of which was bolted to the ground) off the floor, badly bruising his thighs.[28]

The desk tumbled as Brooks thrashed Sumner with increasing severity. He wanted to impair Sumner as much as possible before facing the massive hulk of the senator at eye level. At some point, according to Brooks, Sumner "bellowed like a calf." The cane shattered into several pieces during Brooks's heavy strikes, which were loud enough for everyone in the room to hear. As Sumner flailed his arms uncontrollably, intercepting some of the blows, he gradually swayed toward the aisle. Brooks seized the upright senator by the lapel and pulled him close to keep attacking him with his shorter stick, which had reportedly lost around six inches from the tip. Another desk tumbled as Sumner spun around, with Brooks continuing to hit his arms and head. Brooks would recall striking Sumner thirty times; most other eyewitnesses said they saw between ten and twenty. However many times Sumner was hit, the rapid and heavy blows fell upon the senator in less than a minute. Brooks—an expert swordsman, fighter, and enslaver—knew how to flog someone.[29]

Well over a dozen witnesses, perhaps as many as twenty or thirty, watched in shock as Brooks bloodied Sumner in this surprise attack. Kentucky senator John Crittenden rushed toward the beating as South Carolina representative Laurence Keitt, who was standing behind the vice president's desk, brandished his own cane above his head in a menacing manner. "Let them alone!" Keitt was said to have shouted at Crittenden. "Let them alone, God damn you!" Georgia senator Robert Toombs, also rushing to the scene, urged Keitt not to harm Crittenden. Toombs later said he approved of Sumner's assault, but he did not want an elderly senator who had nothing to do with Sumner's speech to get hurt, too.[30]

Taking hold of Brooks, Crittenden reportedly urged, "Don't kill him," Brooks was said to have retorted back, "I do not intend to," even as he continued his assault and blood spurted everywhere. Brooks may have also muttered, "I only intend to flog him." New York representative Ambrose Murray scurried toward Brooks. Intercepting Brooks's right arm in mid-attack from behind, he pulled him back and around. Brooks managed one more blow before being fully restrained. Toombs and the Senate's assistant doorkeeper also took hold of Brooks. Meanwhile, New York representative Edwin Morgan jumped between them and caught Sumner, who was staggering backward. Stumbling into a desk, Sumner slumped to the ground as Morgan eased his fall. A pool of blood soaked invisibly into the Senate's tobacco-stained crimson carpet.[31]

Thick blood freely dripping into his collar, waistcoat, trousers, and broadcloth, Sumner looked dead. He was "covered with blood as I never saw man covered before," an eyewitness recalled. Morgan begged for a surgeon. Sumner regained consciousness after a few minutes as Senate officers, politicians, and even some journalists surrounded him. Senator Douglas, who rushed into the Senate after hearing what had occurred, said that "the crowd was so large that I could not see what happened." A page brought Sumner a glass of water. He muttered that he could walk and asked that the signed copies of his speech, still on his desk, be taken care of. Leaning against several men, Sumner was escorted into an anteroom, where he collapsed onto the sofa. His bloody head was placed in a water basin and washed. A surgeon, Dr. Cornelius Boyle, dressed his cuts by shaving some of his hair and putting four stitches into two head wounds. After some time, Sumner told a reporter what he recalled. He was then taken home in a carriage by Henry Wilson and Massachusetts representative James Buffington, who dressed him in a clean shirt as several worried men sat outside his bedroom.[32]

Sumner suffered two deep and ragged gashes, both roughly two inches in length, to his head. There was also a minor head gash by his right ear, a cut to the nose, and bruises on his arms, shoulders, hands, and thighs. The skin was lacerated in many places, turning black as the tissue died. One major head gash appeared toward the top of his forehead, two inches to the right of the median. The other major head gash was somewhere near his left ear, above and behind it. Both cut through the scalp to his skull. The left gash was nearly one inch deep, based on a probe Dr. Boyle tucked into the wound. He was stunned that Sumner survived. According to a witness, Boyle remarked that the head wounds were so bad he would have assumed that Sumner had been hit by a brick rather than a cane. "If one of these blows had been on the temple," the doctor was said to have remarked, Sumner would have been dead on the spot.[33]

* * *

MANY SOUTHERNERS THOUGHT Sumner had it coming. "No man ever did more to provoke an attack upon himself than did Mr. Sumner," declared Virginia lawyer John Sergeant Wise. Wise's father, Henry, was among the most physically aggressive congressmen of his era. Shortly after the attack, Henry Wise acquired Brooks's damaged gutta-percha cane, had it repaired, and proudly used it as a walking stick. The Wise family treated the cane as a family heirloom until it was donated in 1921 to a Boston historical society that now displays the cane in a museum. Other pieces of the cane were salvaged by the House sergeant at arms and ultimately found their way into the possession of a few southerners and the South Carolina State Museum. "The fragments of the stick are begged for as *sacred relicts,*" Brooks bragged to his brother.[34]

Many in the South were indeed thrilled. Throngs of people mailed

Brooks canes to replace the one he had shattered. Students at the University of Virginia sent him "a splendid cane . . . with a human head for the handle, badly cracked and broken." Edgefield constituents gifted him a cowhide "for future use." Brooks's brother, noting that he "might have substituted the cow-hide for the Gutta percha," was otherwise pleased. "I am more proud of you than ever! I believe I love you better!" he celebrated. "Hit him again!" urged an editorial in the *Edgefield Advertiser*. One paper felt bad for Brooks, not Sumner. "We are exceedingly sorry that Mr. Brooks dirties his cane by laying it athwart the shoulders of the blackguard, Sumner," exclaimed Virginia's *Petersburg Intelligencer*.[35]

A minority of southerners, mainly ex-Whigs, believed the brutal, unexpected act made a mockery of southern chivalry. "I, who have been principal and second in duels, engaged in so many street fights and mobs (however unwillingly), declare I never saw yet anything so utterly and atrociously craven as Brooks's conduct!" declared Sumner's friend Cassius Clay. "He attacked Sumner under very reprehensible circumstances," North Carolina's *Wilmington Herald* chastised. "Mr. Brooks should have sought a different time and place. . . . To attack him in the Senate Chamber and chastise him, while the latter was unprepared and in a defenceless position, was unjustifiable." Henry Wise's cousin Charlotte was also perturbed. "All agree that if Brooks had beaten him anywhere but *on the head & in the Senate*, he would but have served him right," she wrote. The Louisville *Journal* called the attack "monstrous."[36]

Although Brooks couched the rationale for his assault in the southern code of honor, he had indeed broken many norms that most southern congressmen observed. Fights in Congress usually broke out in the heat of the moment. In the alternative, there would be a duel challenge. If the aggrieved party worried about the legal costs of a duel, he would seek out a street brawl. Even then, it was customary for a combatant to give a warning to his future victim, so that he could arm himself and be ready at all times of day. And it was always recommended to seek an apology or retraction before resorting to physical force. To attack unprovoked, unannounced, with no opportunity for an apology, a victim that the aggressor had never even met before, was a clear sin.[37]

Unless, of course, the victim was worthy of no respect. The *New Orleans Courier* pronounced Sumner a "loathsome spectacle of a man who claims the name of an American Senator, and yet who acts as well as speaks the sentiments of a negro." Brooks's "design was not to kill, but to degrade," another paper declared. Sumner's "submission to your blows has now qualified him for the closest companionship with a degraded class," a group of eager southerners wrote to Brooks. "The vulgar abolitionists must be LASHED INTO SUBMISSION," concluded the *Richmond Enquirer*.

Brooks's use of a cane had the symbolic effect of pronouncing Sumner to be a "negro." The *Enquirer* said that "Sumner in particular ought to have nine and thirty early every morning," referring to the practice of whipping enslaved people thirty-nine lashes for infractions. Though whips are more popularly associated with slavery today, enslavers often used canes as their weapon of choice. Canes symbolized status. In many cities, the law prohibited Black men from carrying them. Canes belonged to the white man.[38]

News of the caning had reached major American cities by telegraph in less than forty-five minutes. It took a little longer for the news to make it to Edgefield County, where Andrew Butler lived. As soon as he heard a rumor about an assault in his honor, Butler rushed to the nearest city to learn more details and then headed straight to Washington. By the time he returned to his post in Congress, much had transpired.

Seward had asked the Senate to form an investigative committee to look into the caning. Breaking with contemporary norms, the Senate formed a committee of all Democrats and refused to put Seward on it. New Hampshire senator John Hale decried that "not a single political friend of Mr. Sumner" was chosen. The sham committee decided ambivalently that the Senate lacked jurisdiction to investigate an assault committed by a House member. The House, for its part, created its own investigative committee, with three Republicans and two Democrats. The House committee visited Sumner's home to gather testimony about what had happened. Sumner accused several senators by name of witnessing the caning with indifference and doing nothing to stop it or help him afterward.[39]

On Tuesday, May 27, Butler arrived in the Senate. That day, three senators that Sumner accused of watching the caning with ambivalence spoke out. First, Stephen Douglas expressed no sympathy for Sumner and denounced him for allegedly framing him. Probably speaking the truth, Douglas said he wasn't there until afterward. "How the idea got into Mr. Sumner's brain," Douglas fumed, "[is] impossible for me to conceive." By contrast, Louisiana senator John Slidell wouldn't deny being there. "I have not spoken to Sumner for two years," Slidell said with a shrug. "I did not think it necessary to express my sympathy." Finally, Toombs embraced the fact that he saw Sumner lying on the ground soaking in a pool of blood and did nothing to help. "I approved of it," he said smugly.

Senator Butler declared that Sumner had it coming. He commended his "gallant relative" Preston Brooks, defended the reputation of his Missourian friend David Atchison, and stated his intention to respond to every claim in "The Crime Against Kansas" in due time. Though some newspapers had assumed that Butler would be embarrassed by the behavior of his rambunctious nephew, Butler seemed perfectly pleased.

Senators Benjamin Wade and Henry Wilson expressed their horror at how little their colleagues cared—if not for Sumner, then at least for the dignity of the Senate. How could somebody beat another man senseless on the Senate floor without a word of condemnation by most senators? The fact that Sumner had used offensive language seemed to bother senators much more than open violence and near murder. Many senators also didn't seem bothered at all by Sumner's claim that a former U.S. senator was actively sabotaging the democratic process through violence in Kansas.

Many senators probably wanted to avoid offending Butler, the chair of the Judiciary Committee and one of the Senate's most powerful members. When Wilson described the caning as a "brutal, murderous, and cowardly assault," Butler shouted back. "You are a liar!" he screamed at Wilson. The Senate's presiding officer then called Wilson, not Butler, out of order. The pecking order was clear.[40]

* * *

ALL THE WHILE, Sumner writhed in pain. Did he want to be a martyr? One decade before, he was depressed and nearly suicidal, heartbroken and in despair, feeling that his life was worthless. Fighting against slavery had given his life meaning. Ten years later, he still had no children and no one to love, but he had a cause—a cause he may have been willing to die for. Sumner had once spoken at Plymouth Rock on the anniversary of the Pilgrims arriving in the new land. "These outcasts, despised in their own day by the proud and great," he said, "are the men whom we have met in this goodly number to celebrate." Popular in some circles, Sumner had been despised, belittled, isolated, and now, beaten, in Washington. One day, he imagined, perhaps long after he was gone, Americans would thank him for vindicating their democracy on this day.[41]

It seems to be the case that Sumner anticipated getting assaulted as a result of his speech. Before falling into a deep slumber on the night of the caning, Sumner allegedly whimpered, "I could not believe that a thing like this was possible." At the same time, though, he also reportedly told Seward that he was hopeful that the caning could benefit the antislavery cause. He had framed much of his speech around mocking southern ideals of chivalry. All his caustic comments were designed to goad other senators into a reaction. He had even warned that senators shouldn't resort to the "bowie-knife and bludgeon" against him, as if to set up the argument his supporters could make after a potential attack.[42]

By seeking out tragedy, Sumner had revealed his willingness to make the ultimate sacrifice to expose the ugliness of slavery. His solemn offer of death moved many Americans to tears. "When I lifted his bleeding body from the floor and laid him upon a lounge, and then washed his blood from my hands," said a weeping Senator Wilson, "I swore eternal vengeance to slavery, and consecrated my life anew to the cause of human freedom." Seward, for his part, felt the significance of the moment. "The blows that fell on the head of the Senator from Massachusetts have done more for the cause of human freedom in Kansas and in the Territories of the United States than all the eloquence . . . which has resounded in these halls," he declared. "You have torn the mask off the faces of traitors, and at last the spirit of the North is aroused," Longfellow wrote to Sumner.[43]

"The outrage upon Charles Sumner made me literally ill for several days," Lydia Maria Child wrote. "[A] tight ligature seemed to stop the flowing of my blood." People were nauseous, nerve-stricken, and heartbroken as they found out what had happened. "I think of you every hour of every day; you haunt me," Richard Henry Dana wrote him. His children had cried after the caning. Horace Mann was horrified. "We are wounded in your wounds, and bleed in your bleeding," he wrote. "Mrs. Mann read one account of the outrage, and could never read another. She said she felt the concussion of the blows all through her brain."[44]

Many northerners were so disturbed by the South's rush to justify the attack that they concluded the South was barbaric to its core. According to Frederick Douglass, "no one act did more to rouse the North to a comprehension of the infernal and barbarous spirit of slavery." Tens of thousands of northerners gathered in what they called "indignation meetings" for expressions of collective mourning and rage. At one gathering, Henry Ward Beecher said that "the symbol of the North is the pen. The symbol of the South is the bludgeon."

At another indignation meeting, Ralph Waldo Emerson spoke. He shed tears for Sumner in Concord, telling an audience that he "has the whitest soul I ever knew." Emerson resolutely defended the character of Sumner, whom he considered a friend. "His opponents accuse him neither of drunkenness, nor debauchery, nor job, nor peculation, nor rapacity, nor personal aims of any kind. No, but with what?" he asked. "Discourtesy. Then, that he is an abolitionist: as if every sane human being were not an abolitionist." The famed poet cloaked Sumner in a shroud of the whole New England. "Every man of worth in New England loves his virtues; that every mother thinks of him as the protector of families; that every friend of freedom thinks him the friend of freedom."[45]

Abolitionists felt a deep, nearly spiritual, significance to the caning. Sumner's blood was "sacred, a sacrament to Freedom, an offering to the altar of our God and our Country," one writer believed. "For they are holy, the wounds that the Southerner dealt thee: Count them blessed, and blessed the mother that bore thee," Julia Ward Howe rhapsodized in a poem. A Methodist bishop said that Sumner "bore in his body the marks of the Lord Jesus." Seward's wife, Frances, wrote to Sumner in similar terms. "You have made so many sacrifices and above all for the sake of the Son of God the suffering, meek, and patriot Jesus," she said. She believed that Sumner had shed "the blood of the martyrs."[46]

Countless Black Americans also wrote to Sumner. "No persons felt more keenly and sympathized with you more deeply and sincerely, than your colored constituents in Boston," the Black lawyer Robert Morris told Sumner. Prior to the caning, Sumner's correspondence with African Americans had been limited to a few Bay Staters and Frederick Douglass. The senator's relationships with ordinary Black folks multiplied in the aftermath. Many saw him as one of their own. "[The cane] fell upon the head of our beloved Sumner—aye ours," one Black writer declared, "for having stood for us, having suffered for giving voice to the thoughts & feelings that were ours." The Black political leader P. B. S. Pinchback recalled two decades later that "when they struck Charles Sumner, they struck through the body of every true colored man in the United States." The caning had spread slavery "from the black man to the white," the Black feminist Mary Ann Shadd wrote.[47]

Even antislavery whites couldn't help but make the comparison. "For the first time has the extreme discipline of the Plantation been introduced into the Senate of the United States," pronounced the *Albany Evening Journal*.

"Let him be beaten with rods . . . let America see her son die by the miserable and painful punishment commonly inflicted on slaves," Ohio's representative John Bingham declared. "White men themselves are becoming the slaves," Seward wrote in his diary. In their imaginations, Sumner had experienced the life of a figurative white slave, not unlike the girl in the fictional story of *Ida May* or seven-year-old Mary Williams, whom Sumner had recently exhibited. One editorial in the *Liberator* connected Sumner's pain to what was endured by those enslaved on Brooks's plantation. "I would not love him the less; but I think we would all do well to love Brooks's slaves a little more . . . who, unlike Mr. Sumner, are not loaded with sympathy and honors."[48]

* * *

ON THE DAY after Sumner concluded his speech, May 21, 1856, former senator David Atchison led his armed gang of ruffians into Lawrence, the largest town with antislavery settlers in the territory of Kansas. The town had been under siege for months by proslavery vigilante forces. Atchison ordered four cannons to batter the Free State Hotel, the largest building in town, and collapse it with four kegs of gunpowder. His men then destroyed the printing presses of abolitionist newspapers in Lawrence, looted stores, and burned down at least one home. The retired senator's terrorism was a serious escalation in his campaign to destroy democracy in Kansas.

One northern settler in Kansas, John Brown, decided to fight back. An intense, fiery abolitionist, Brown decided that the only way to end slavery was through revolutionary violence. "Though a white gentleman," Frederick Douglass once said of Brown, "he is in sympathy a black man, and as deeply interested in our cause, as though his own soul had been pierced with the iron of slavery." When Brown learned about the caning, it was the final straw for him, his children, and his men, who had already been preparing to shed southern blood. "A man came to us with the news of the assault upon Senator Sumner of Bully Brooks," recalled one of Brown's sons. "At that blow the men went crazy—*crazy*. It seemed to be the finishing, decisive touch." Brown ordered his sons to get their weapons together for a nighttime expedition into the woods.[49]

On the evening of May 24, Brown and his men kidnapped five proslavery settlers. Taking them to Pottawatomie Creek, he had them hacked to death. The news horrified the country. Brown's message was clear: If slavery continued, there would be no peace. Over the next few months, Kansas descended into more violence. The virgin territory that Sumner had eulogized was now soaked in blood.

When news of Sumner's assault and Brown's massacre reached Great Britain, a British statesman was so alarmed that he told the Duchess of Argyll that "in any country but America, I should think civil war must be impending." Another British statesman, George Cornewall Lewis, didn't think that America was so special or impervious to domestic conflict. He predicted that Sumner's caning would be "the first blow in a civil war."[50]

CHAPTER 12

SUMNER TAKES A BEATING BADLY

Ever since he had entered the Senate, Charles Sumner had the reputation of being a strong man, both emotionally and physically. He was perceived to be a stoic and rigid dogmatist, a fighter who knew no fear or anxieties. Though he exercised little, he was large, muscular, shockingly tall, and full of boundless energy. He almost never got sick. His thick hair, sonorous voice, and haughty attitude added to a sense of grandeur and invincibility that both friend and foe recognized. At last, he had been humbled. From this point forward, the senator was known to cry often. He was regarded by others as emotional, perhaps overly sentimental. Tears flowed frequently—when he was alone, with friends, even in public. He would look frail, almost elderly, aged beyond his years. Spasms of pain would rip through his body, sometimes without warning, for the rest of his life.

"Sumner is contending with death," Senator Seward feared. Though he seemed to be getting on all right at first, by Tuesday, May 27, 1856, he had developed a terrible fever. His skin was pale and hot to the touch; his eyes were suffused with blood; his head and neck were inflamed. A violent pain in the back of his head kept him sleepless, despite the help of opium. When his brother George arrived on Wednesday, he fired Dr. Cornelius Boyle and retained a friend, Dr. Marshall Perry, instead. Perry and a few other doctors reopened the gash on Sumner's forehead to discover tablespoonfuls of pus, which oozed out of his burning and inflamed scalp. Sumner had almost certainly caught a bad infection; Boyle had probably failed to correctly sterilize the wounds.[1]

Even after the infection subsided, Sumner could barely walk. At every wobbling step, he would feel searing pain in his head, to the point where he would sometimes nearly fall over. Neither could he read or write; trying to focus on a page was impossible. In the first five weeks of recovery, he mustered the energy to write only five letters. There was little respite in sleep, either. On some nights, he didn't sleep a wink, "literally hearing the clock strike every hour till daylight." Spending most of his hours in bed, Sumner was worried about living the rest of his life condemned as an invalid, which he feared more than death. "I sometimes am led to apprehend that I may yet be doomed to that heaviest of all afflictions," he told Joshua Giddings. "To spend my time on earth in a living sepulcher."[2]

All he wanted to do was get back into the action. "For three weeks of this session I would have given three years of any future public life," he told Giddings. "Gladly would I commence our campaign," he declared to Samuel Gridley Howe. "The war of liberation is begun." When he announced his desire to go back to the Senate to give a speech on the barbarism of slavery, friends urged him to be patient. "Your empty chair can make a more fervent appeal than even you," Wendell Phillips reassured him. "If you do it, it will be the last speech you make in this world," Seward warned. "If I am able to speak as I desire, I think that I shall be shot," Sumner conceded. "Very well, I am content. The cause will live."[3]

Fortunately for the sake of Sumner's life, he lacked the strength to prepare a speech. Deciding to get away from Washington, he traveled through New England to stay at the homes of friends. After some time with Francis Blair in Silver Spring, he ventured north to Philadelphia to escape the heat. Then he went to Cape May to be by the seaside, and by August, he had moved up to the Allegheny Mountains for fresh air.

Nothing helped, despite Sumner's desperate desire to get back to work. His head was at war with his ambition. Walking, talking, reading, writing, thinking—all of it sent icicles of pain up his skull. "His brain is throbbing with pent thunderbolts," one woman who visited him explained. "He described it as a fifty-six pounds weight upon his head," Dr. Perry wrote. "He had neuralgic pain in the back of the head, coming on in paroxysms." To his friend Edward Pierce, Sumner said that his "spinal cord continues morbidly sensitive, involving the whole back and shoulders, and finally the brain, from which it all proceeds." Doctors also worried he had some sort of brain problems. "The brain, as well as the spinal cord, has been the seat of some serious lesion," one doctor wrote. "There must have been either congestion, or concussion," another decided.[4]

Sumner suffered from several conditions. At minimum, even though his skull was probably not fractured, Sumner clearly had a severe concussion, which his mid-nineteenth-century doctors did not fully grasp. Concussions are traumatic brain injuries that can arise from bruising, damage to blood vessels, and injury to the nerves. Sumner's concussion caused debilitating headaches and inhibited concentration; it may have also caused dizziness and difficulty walking. The effects of a severe concussion can last several months.

Sumner's trouble with walking may also have been due to his brutal soft tissue injuries, which manifested in the many dark bruises he incurred on his back, shoulders, thighs, and neck. Those physical injuries may also have caused neuralgic pain, such as occipital neuralgia. A common condition that arises when nerves in the shoulders and neck are pinched by aggravated or injured muscles, occipital neuralgia can feel like shooting, electric pains in the neck and head, much like Sumner had described. At its worst, it can impair vision, balance, and concentration, and it can worsen if the aggravated muscles aren't given time to heal.

Possibly, Sumner suffered a subdural hematoma, a traumatic head injury that is far worse than a concussion. An injury that is sometimes fatal, subdural hematoma can involve severe memory loss, disorientation, nausea, and difficulty walking. That said, the symptoms of subdural hematoma left untreated usually get progressively worse over time, while Sumner's symptoms generally improved or stayed static.

Perhaps worst of all, Sumner almost certainly suffered from posttraumatic stress disorder (PTSD). PTSD is a psychosomatic disorder where memories of trauma can lead to intense emotional or physical reactions. These reactions can last years. They can even cause physical symptoms after physical wounds have healed. For the next few years, Sumner experienced what he once described as "torments" whenever he thought about political business or came close to the Capitol. The trauma of the caning was too intense to handle.[5]

By August 1856, three months after the caning, Sumner was finally improving somewhat. He had begun to write nearly ten letters a day, taking a break between each one to lie down. Despite barely being able to walk for lack of balance, he would go horseback riding for miles on end when he stayed in the Allegheny Mountains. People read his correspondence out loud to him, as hundreds of letters flowed in from all parts of the country. Strangers—young and old, white and Black—poured out their hearts to the senator in these letters. "Mr. Brooks is a very naughty man and if I had been there, I would have torn his eyes out," one young girl wrote him.

Sometimes, Sumner replied, either by handwriting or dictating his responses to others. He often said that his eyes were moistened with tears upon reading these notes. And he frequently chastised sympathizers for thinking too much of his difficulties. "Oh, no," he whimpered to one journalist who expressed shock at how badly he was injured. "The poorest slave is in danger of worse outrages every moment of his life."[6]

* * *

ALL THE WHILE, southerners believed Sumner was shamming his injuries. "Sumner takes a beating badly," Senator Toombs wrote to a friend. "He is said to be ill tho' I don't believe it." It didn't help Sumner's case that his initial doctor, Cornelius Boyle, testified to the House committee investigating his attack that Sumner was "doing very well" with "nothing but flesh wounds" and "no concussion." Boyle claimed that his patient was ready to return to work and that his friends "make Mr. Sumner out a great deal worse than he is." Proslavery papers ran the gamut on Boyle's comments, declaring that Sumner was "playing possum," a common idiom used to mock slaves who allegedly feigned illness to avoid work. "Sumner's sickness has been exaggerated," the Richmond Enquirer declared. "His confinement to his room is but part and parcel of the n——r game that he is playing to keep alive the Kansas excitement." For months, Boyle's testimony was used to accuse Sumner of shamming.[7]

When Dr. Boyle first made these claims in late May, George Sumner fired him. He paid Boyle in full and publicly denied that the doctor's testimony had anything to do with his dismissal. Months later, though, Charles Sumner admitted to a friend that George fired Boyle because he sympathized with slavery and had minimized his injuries. "I shuddered when I recovered consciousness, and found this man beside me," he recalled.

George and Charles Sumner had reason to suspect Dr. Boyle's motives. A private physician who was popular among Democrats, including Stephen Douglas and numerous southern politicians, Boyle was decidedly proslavery and lied to the House Committee when he said he was an apolitical ex-Whig. Two years before, in 1854, Boyle had created a secret pro-southern militia in Washington. (During the Civil War, he led this militia in an attempt to take over the capital. Over the course of the war, he became one of Robert E. Lee's most trusted spies. Boyle was even suspected of aiding in Lincoln's assassination.)

Dr. Boyle's testimony clearly minimized the damage done to Sumner.

Sumner's infection and the eruption of pus also suggest that Boyle improperly closed his wounds. After being dismissed, Boyle wrote to Senator Butler to restate his claim that Sumner's wounds were minor. When a trial against Brooks took place, Boyle offered himself as a defense witness. And when Brooks was later dying of an illness, Boyle served as his physician and attended his funeral.[8]

With Dr. Boyle's helpful testimony, Senator Butler pushed the narrative that Sumner was shamming. On June 12, 1856, Butler delivered a rebuttal to Sumner's speech. "Being rather a handsome man, perhaps he would not like to expose himself," Butler joked about Sumner. While calling Sumner a "degenerate son" who ought to "hang his head in shame," he celebrated Brooks as a hero. "He is one of the best tempered fellows I ever knew," Butler declared. He then claimed dubiously that Brooks had caned Sumner only after being harassed on the streets of Washington by South Carolinians demanding the assault. Defending Brooks, Butler declared that his nephew's design was merely "to whip him" and "to disgrace him," not to kill him.[9]

Thus emboldened, Preston Brooks stood triumphantly at the Circuit Court of the District of Columbia on charges of misdemeanor assault on July 7, the same day Sumner embarked for Philadelphia. (Sumner, having testified to the grand jury after a legal summons, voluntarily declined to participate in the trial.) Senators Butler and James Mason joined Brooks in a show of support. "I confess, Sir, and without shame," Brooks bragged to the judge. Likening himself to husbands who killed adulterous men who slept with their wives and to children who killed in defense of their parents, Brooks explained that he had been obliged to avenge "his political mother," South Carolina, which Sumner had slandered. Noting Sumner's "convenient and deliberate absence," Brooks sought the judge's mercy. The judge assigned no jail time and a fine of three hundred dollars, roughly eleven thousand dollars in today's money. Southerners fundraised to pay the fine so Brooks wouldn't have to.[10]

The House investigation committee interviewed nearly thirty people, laid out the facts of the caning, and determined that Brooks had engaged in disorderly behavior. The committee also decided that Brooks had violated the spirit of the Constitution's Speech or Debate Clause, which declares that a member of Congress "for any speech or Debate in either House . . . shall not be questioned in any other place." Harping on this language, two southern Democrats on the committee dissented with a long-winded and sophistic argument that no privilege existed for offensive speech and that the House somehow lacked jurisdiction over an assault that had taken place in the Senate.[11]

One week later, a majority of the House of Representatives voted to expel Brooks based on the committee's recommendation. But a majority wasn't enough: the Constitution requires two-thirds of the House to favor an expulsion for one to take place. Among 120 votes in favor, all but one were from representatives of free states. Among the 95 votes against, all but one were from southerners or northern Democrats. Soon after, Congress voted in favor of censuring Laurence Keitt, but against censuring Henry Edmundson, both of whom knew about Brooks's plans and may have aided him in carrying them out.

America had reached a stage of polarization where even a violent assault was quickly cast into sectional terms, decried by some politicians and celebrated by others. There would be no accountability.

Brooks spoke shortly after the expulsion vote. Explaining that the assault vindicated his "self-respect and constitutional rights," he cast the House's attempt to punish him as a slippery slope toward oppression against slaveholders. "How far does your authority extend . . . where do you stop?" he asked. Decrying that the House might punish him next for flogging his slaves, "which, by the common law and the constitutional laws of my country, I have the right to inflict," Brooks warned that the government might try to pursue him "into the Avenue—into the steamboat—to my plantation."

In his short speech, Brooks found the time to mock the "bald head" and "corporeal rotundity" of one antislavery congressman, another representative as "a feminine gentleman," and a third congressman as a "cock that crows and won't fight." After ridiculing his colleagues, he announced that he had already handed his resignation to the governor of South Carolina, long before the House voted on his expulsion. Declaring that his constituents would resoundingly reelect him, he dramatically stomped out of the chamber.[12]

"He would have killed him!" somebody shouted during Brooks's speech. Labeled "Bully Brooks," the rowdy congressman was treated by the northern press as the embodiment of all that was repugnant about slaveholders. "Persons bred up in slaveholding communities become accustomed" to violence, explained Congressman Joshua Giddings. "God's image is daily assailed, disfigured, and mutilated before their eyes."[13]

To the South, Bully Brooks was a hero, a man who had stood up for the character of the South, who had defended her honor before snobbish northerners who knew little about their culture. Brooks's reelection was scheduled for only a few weeks later, in late July. In the interim, Brooks challenged three northern politicians to duels (none of which materialized). He also defended himself in a public letter addressed to his constituents. "I resigned my seat, and kicking the black dust of a black republican majority from my feet . . . My appeal is to you. If I have represented you faithfully, then re-elect me with a unanimity which will thunder into the ears of fanaticism the terrors of the storm that is coming upon them." In late July, his constituents responded by reelecting Brooks almost unanimously.[14]

When Brooks returned home, an estimated ten thousand supporters gathered in Charleston to welcome him, in a massive event that included Orr, Butler, Toombs, and other proslavery politicians. Brooks declared that the "problem of slavery's utility, its morality, and its perpetuity, has yet to be settled, and that settlement must be soon. The crisis has arrived." Blaming the Founding Fathers for the "mistakes" of permitting a ban of the transatlantic slave trade in 1808 and outlawing slavery in the Northwest Territory, Brooks said it was time to dissolve the Union. "The Constitution of the United States should be torn to fragments," he shouted, "and a *Southern* Constitution formed in which every State should be a slave state!" The crowd roared as Brooks openly called for treason.[15]

* * *

HEADING INTO THE November election, America readied for a showdown on slavery. The Democrats nominated James Buchanan, a veteran politician from Pennsylvania who supported slavery even though he lacked the extremism of many of the southern Fire-Eaters. The Democrats embraced the Kansas-Nebraska Act in their platform as "the only sound and safe solution of the 'slavery question.'" The Know-Nothing Party nominated Millard Fillmore, a past U.S. president and former Whig from New York who had signed the Fugitive Slave Act of 1850.[16]

The Republican Party organized itself against these two abominable acts. At the national convention in Philadelphia, the party shrouded itself in the language of the American Founding. "Resolved," the platform declared, "that as our republican fathers, when they had abolished slavery in all our national territory, ordained that no person should be deprived of life, liberty, or property, without due process of law." The party listed the violations of the Bill of Rights that had been perpetrated in Kansas—the right to bear arms, to a speedy and public trial, and to freedom of speech—and said it opposed having any slavery in any territories.[17]

At the end of the first day, Henry Wilson spoke. Decrying that a civil war rages "beyond the Missouri [River]," Wilson deplored how "a Senator of a sovereign state on the floor of Congress, for denouncing the crime against Kansas, has been stricken senseless on the floor of the American Senate." Somebody shouted, "Three cheers for Sumner." Rounds of vociferous cheering roared through the hallway for some time. "Three groans for Brooks," somebody else exclaimed. A storm of groans and yells rippled through the crowd. "We are not only fighting . . . to save Kansas, to make a Free State beyond the Missouri [River]," Wilson resumed, "but we are fighting to vindicate the freedom of speech in the National Congress."[18]

Republicans cast the caning of Sumner as a free-speech issue. If Members of Congress couldn't speak against slavery, who could? Kansas was being run by a dictatorship with virtually no civil liberties for free-state settlers. Republicans feared a southern plot to spread anti-republicanism across the country. "Was not the villainous blow which fell upon the honored head of CHARLES SUMNER dealt by the infamous Brooks of South Carolina aimed at the free speech of the entire North?" asked one writer. A satirical newspaper story with a faux Democratic Party platform put it this way: "Freedom of speech is liable to abuses, abuses which can only be corrected by the application of the gutta percha to the naked head of the offending party." Republicans turned Preston Brooks into a caricature of Democrats and the South.[19]

At the close of the convention, the Republicans nominated John Frémont, a valorized Mexican-American War veteran and former California senator, for president. Frémont was modestly antislavery and lacked the radical baggage of politicos like Salmon Chase and William Seward, whose names were also floated.

To get Frémont's campaign going, Horace Greeley, the Republican newspaper editor of the *New York Tribune*, decided to mass-produce Sumner's speech "The Crime Against Kansas." Creating a cheap pamphlet version, Greeley ordered Republican organizers around the country to start reprinting it. "Supply every household in your county," he instructed. "There should be Three Million copies of that speech in circulation by the Fourth of July."

Perhaps as many as three million Americans read Sumner's provocative and salacious speech, wherein he accused his colleagues and ex-colleagues of a corrupt antidemocratic conspiracy and sexual debauchery. Sumner had claimed to be Cicero, warning his fellow citizens about a threat to the Republic. Then Sumner was nearly killed. To millions of Americans, the caning was confirmation that Sumner's warning was true. "Nothing is talked of anywhere I go, but Sumner, and Kansas, and Fremont," a woman told her husband. "If Fremont is elected," Frémont's opponent, Millard Filmore, said, "the Republicans ought to pension Brooks for life."[20]

* * *

AS THE ELECTION approached, Sumner came home to cast his ballot for Frémont. On November 3, 1856, the city of Boston organized a procession to return the martyr to his mother's house. Eighteen carriages escorted Sumner from Brookline through Roxbury toward the North End. At some point, seven hundred men on horseback joined the parade, which stopped near the southern boundary of the city. There, Josiah Quincy, past president of Harvard, introduced Sumner. Leaning against the side of his open carriage, Sumner spoke softly; even in the pin-drop silence, few could hear him. "You have made allusion to the suffering which I have undergone," he said, his voice barely above a whisper. "This is not small . . . but how little is it . . . compared with the suffering of fellow-citizens in Kansas? How small is it compared with that tale of woe which is perpetually coming to us from the house of bondage!"

Sumner's voice quivered and fell silent briefly. The crowd mourned; their bombastic senator had lost his swagger. Yet he had not lost his gall. "In the darkest days of the Revolution, [Washington] said: 'I see my duty; that of standing up for the liberty of my country,'" Sumner said with all the strength he could muster. Declaring that General Washington's words "apply to my own case," he promised, like Washington, "to persevere to the end." The crowd exploded in cheers.

Sumner's entourage continued toward Beacon Hill, passing by men who lifted their hats in respect. Women waved handkerchiefs. Flags, streamers, and wreaths of flowers lined the streets. Some people tossed bouquets into Sumner's carriage, with notes like "Welcome home!" and "If the ladies could vote, he would be the next president." All the while, Sumner looked pale and exhausted, meekly smiling to the jubilant masses until he arrived at last at the State House. At least fifteen thousand people were said to be present. Gov. Henry Gardner—a Know Nothing who had his eyes on Sumner's Senate seat—introduced him at the State House. "After I heard of that assault . . . I pledged Massachusetts to stand by you," he declared. Gardner had no chance of replacing the bloodied statesman anymore. "She does stand by you to-day. She will stand by you to-morrow; and she will stand by you, in her defence forever," he swore.

Standing up to speak again, Sumner felt so weak that he couldn't manage to address the crowd. He handed his manuscript to a reporter to ensure it would at least be read, if not heard. He stepped back into his carriage and proceeded to his mother's home on Hancock Street. Passing by a throng of onlookers, Sumner walked into the house, where he appeared at a window with his mother and waved to the crowd.[21]

In a few weeks' time, tragedy struck the Sumner family. Charles Sumner's younger brother Albert and his family were traveling to France on the *Lyonnais*. The steamer collided with another ship at night, killing more than one hundred people. While the family had boarded a lifeboat steered by Albert, they never made it to shore. Sumner learned of the shipwreck from two estranged friends, Cornelius Felton and George Hillard, who rushed to share the news at Longfellow's house, where Sumner was staying at the time. (The ship ruins were not discovered until August 2024.)

Sumner sped home and grieved quietly on Hancock Street with his family for the tragic loss. Although Albert and Charles Sumner were not close, and had rarely written to each other, Charles had frequently visited Albert's home in Newport, his favorite vacation spot. When Albert's wife's estate passed to the Sumners, Charles and his brother George relinquished their inheritance claims and gifted all their late sister-in-law's estate to the woman's relatives, who were immensely grateful.[22]

Meanwhile, the Republicans lost the election; the proslavery Democrat James Buchanan was elected president. But the party was triumphant even in defeat. Frémont had gained 33 percent of the vote and carried most of the northern states. If Fillmore's Know-Nothing votes had been combined with Frémont's, the North would have won. It was proof that a unified northern party could win an election. Desiring a united front, the Know Nothings disintegrated over the next few months and hopped onto the Republican bandwagon. "Our defeat is Bunker Hill again, full of great auguries," Sumner eagerly decided.[23]

* * *

By the time the victorious President Buchanan arrived in Washington, the South had learned terrible news. After catching a severe cold, Preston Brooks suffered a throat inflammation that kept getting worse until, on January 27, 1857, he heaved for air, clutched his throat, and began choking. His friend congressman Laurence Keitt and his doctor, Cornelius Boyle, watched helplessly as Brooks died of asphyxiation. Senator Butler rushed to the home, threw himself atop the still body, and wept like a child. At thirty-seven, Brooks was gone.

Buchanan attended Brooks's funeral ceremonies in Congress. Intent on showing civility, Representative Keitt and others spoke respectfully about their divisive colleague's sudden death in muted tones. Even Lewis Campbell, who had chaired the investigative committee on the caning and spearheaded Brooks's expulsion, gave a short, polite eulogy about Brooks. The eulogies ignored the elephant in the room, until one proslavery congressman took it upon himself to describe Brooks's caning of Sumner as an attack "the world has ever since approved and applauded," much like when "Brutus stabbed Caesar in the Capitol." Some Republicans stormed out of the chamber in disgust, appalled that a respectful commemoration of Brooks's life was being politicized.[24]

Many northerners saw Brooks's sudden death as divine intervention. The murderer had died; the martyr had lived. "I could not but feel today that God had avenged the blows of May last," Senator Henry Wilson wrote to Sumner. But Sumner felt ambivalent about Brooks's death. "What have I to do with him?" he once said. "It was slavery, not *he*, that struck the blow." Sumner had literally never spoken to Brooks except perhaps during the minute-long interval of his beating. When asked what he thought of his assailant, he replied, "only as to a brick that should fall upon my head from a chimney. He was the unconscious agent of a malign power." Over the years, Sumner rarely brought up Brooks and rarely said something negative about him. "Mr. Sumner never disclosed the least lingering personal animosity," recalled Senator Justin Morrill with amazement.[25]

After being unanimously reelected by the legislature, Sumner made an arduous trip back to Washington in late February. His injuries continued to debilitate him. Sumner wished he could've joined Brooks and Butler—who died of edema at sixty-seven a few months after Brooks—on the other side, rather than continue in his atrophied state. "Nothing I shall ever be able to do for this country will ever be of half the value that my death would have been," he wrote to a friend. Doctors advised him to go to

Europe, hoping that fresh air and distance from the problems of America might improve his condition. Republicans, who saw the political utility in Sumner's symbolic empty chair, urged him to take all the time he needed. "Sit in your seat if you can," John Andrew had written him. "If you can't, let it be vacant."[26]

Sumner did not need much convincing. For seventeen years, he had missed Europe. He wrote often to European friends he had not seen in years. And so, he decided to embark for Europe after a few weeks of Senate service. Aside from taking his oath of office and voting on a tariff bill important to Massachusetts businessmen, he attended no business at the Capitol. He seemed to be experiencing the traumatic effects of PTSD while inside the congressional building. "I have sat in my seat only on one day," he wrote to Parker. "After a short torment to my system became great, and a cloud began to gather over my brain, I tottered out and took to my bed. I long to speak, but I cannot."[27]

Leaving Washington almost as soon as he arrived, Sumner went to New York City to board a ship on March 7. After enjoying an evening with the presidential runner-up John Frémont, Frémont's wife, and a few other prominent Republicans, he set sail the next morning for Europe, where he would spend the rest of the year, with France as his first stop. After boarding the ship, he wrote one final letter from the harbor to a journalist for publication in the newspapers announcing his departure in search of health. "With a farewell to my country," he wrote, "I give my last thoughts to suffering Kansas, with devout prayers."[28]

* * *

LITTLE DID SUMNER know that on the day he left, news had hit New York by telegraph about a shocking Supreme Court decision that seemed to ruin any hope of freedom in suffering Kansas. While informed politicos were aware of this foreboding case at the nation's highest court, the decision took most of the public by surprise.

The Supreme Court rarely issued decisions of significant political importance in antebellum America. Those kinds of cases were few and far between. Cases that involved the constitutionality of national statutes were especially rare. In fact, before 1857, the Supreme Court had only once *ever* overturned an act of Congress, exercising what is now the common practice of "federal judicial review." In *Marbury v. Madison*, Chief Justice John Marshall had famously said that a small part of the federal Judiciary

Act of 1789 was unconstitutional. Though the case had some political importance, the section of the law that was invalidated was extremely minor. Few lawyers in antebellum America had ever used *Marbury* as a precedent, and it was rarely cited, if ever, to support federal judicial review. In practice, federal judicial review barely existed.

The Supreme Court decided to break from its long-standing practice, dating back to the Founding era, of judicial restraint and deference to Congress about the constitutionality of legislation. An enslaved man named Dred Scott had sued his enslaver, claiming that he was entitled to his freedom after living for several years in Wisconsin, where the law freed any slave who lived in the territory for an extended period. When the case reached the Court, Chief Justice Roger Taney jumped at the chance to force all American territories to become slave territories. He and a few other proslavery justices wanted a decisive blow, a final solution to stamp out hope among antislavery agitators.[29]

Writing for the Court, Chief Justice Taney held that any congressional legislation that banned slavery in northern territories was unconstitutional. He also held that no territory could ban slavery, such that Scott was still a slave despite having lived in Wisconsin. Taney declared that Black Americans "are not included, and were not intended to be included, under the word 'citizens' in the Constitution." Blacks—all of them, enslaved or free—were "an unfortunate race" and "a subordinate and inferior class of beings" who were "altogether unfit to associate with the white race either in social or political relations, and so far inferior that they had no rights which the white man was bound to respect." He also held that because Blacks were not citizens, men like Dred Scott could not legally sue their masters.

Throughout its opinion, the Supreme Court distorted facts about the Founding era to project its own racism. It claimed that "the enslaved African race were not intended to be included" by the Founders as citizens. But as the dissent noted, free native-born African Americans were citizens in New Hampshire, Massachusetts, New York, New Jersey, and North Carolina and may have voted on the Constitution when it was ratified. Even earlier, when the Articles of Confederation were drafted, the Framers voted *against* a motion to limit citizenship to "the free white inhabitants" of each state, opting instead to say "free inhabitants." And by 1789, the only state to explicitly limit voting by race was South Carolina.

The Court also claimed the Constitution required slavery in territories, even though the First Congress banned it in the Northwest Territories. And the Court said Blacks could not bring lawsuits, even though they often did in the Founding era, particularly in Massachusetts, where enslaved people like Elizabeth Freeman and Quock Walker sued their masters in the early 1780s and won their freedom.[30]

Dred Scott caused mass hysteria in the North. All Free-Soil constitutionalism had been declared unconstitutional. All of Kansas and Nebraska now had to be slave territory. Almost the entire Republican Party platform, which centered on banning slavery in the West, had now been ruled defunct. "SLAVERY, AND NOT FREEDOM IS NATIONAL," exclaimed the *Poughkeepsie Journal*, inverting the words of Sumner's famous slogan. "COLORED MEN ARE NOT CITIZENS," the *Journal* decried. Across the country, newspapers reported the decision and printed swaths of Taney's lengthy, arduous opinion in their pages.

News of *Dred Scott* followed Sumner across the pond, where European observers were horrified by what took place and nervous about what might happen to America in its wake. As the English abolitionist Harriet Martineau predicted at the time, "*Dred Scott* will, in all probability, be renowned hereafter as the occasion, though not specifically the cause, of the outbreak of the second great American Revolution."[31]

CHAPTER 13

THE MAN SPEAKS
LIKE A PROPHET

ARRIVING IN PARIS IN LATE MARCH 1857, SUMNER WAS SPARED THE judicial dynamite that had exploded back home. At last, he had found respite. "The sea air, or sea sickness, or absolute separation from politics at home, or all combined, have given me much of my old strength," he wrote on the first day in a diary—the first diary he had kept since his time abroad two decades prior. Sumner whiled away his days with a tight schedule of morning drives, scrumptious dinners, visits to museums and churches and opera houses, and similar delights.

After some time in Paris and the French countryside, he stayed at length in the United Kingdom and made trips to Switzerland, Germany, Holland, and Belgium, socializing everywhere he went. "The lapse of nineteen years is very plain in the shrunk forms and feeble steps of some whom I had left round and erect," he wrote to Longfellow about the many old friends he had seen. Old and new associates included Harriet Martineau, the Earl of Carlisle, the Duchess of Sutherland, the Duchess of Argyll, Lord Palmerston, Lord Gladstone, Samuel Wilberforce, William Thackeray, Thomas Macaulay, John Russell, Richard Cobden, John Bright, Alphonse de Lamartine, and François Guizot, among others.[1]

European friends must have marveled at the change in Sumner. Those who had met him before recalled a scrawny but energetic scholar in his late twenties, a jobless prodigy who could talk for hours about his studies and who ogled every little new sight with his innocent American eyes. Years after his leaving Europe, as news hit that the jovial Sumner had been elected to the U.S. Senate, European friends followed his meteoric rise and controversial reputation with keen interest, writing letters often and excitedly to him and other Americans they knew about his unfolding political drama with proslavery politicians. They were aghast at his brutal beating.

And now he was back—tall, muscular, and statesmanlike; important and self-important; still learned and still talkative but older, wiser, and sadder. The senator sometimes squealed with pain at headaches and other pangs triggered by his irritated nerves. He could walk only a few hours a day, at most. He looked far older than his years, feeble and weak, as if the caning had broken his spirit and soul.

One companion lifted Sumner's spirits more than anyone else. Alexis de Tocqueville had first met Sumner when the latter traveled to France in 1838. Their brief encounter led to a handful of letters exchanged between the two, mostly discussing prison reform. Now their friendship blossomed. They dined at least six times in Paris—sometimes alone, sometimes with others—talking most often about politics and slavery. When Tocqueville left for London in June, Sumner followed shortly after, dining with him again at least twice. When Tocqueville crossed the channel to stay at his Normandy chateau, Sumner saw him once again, spending three nights with him at his famous countryside manor.[2]

The French aristocrat is best remembered as a political theorist. At the spry age of twenty-five, he embarked on a nine-month tour of America. His extensive notes turned into the bestselling *Democracy in America*, a tour de force about life in the young republic. The book observed *two* Americas. There was the North, which traced back to the Pilgrims of New England and had escaped the shackles of aristocracy with a radical form of government where everyone could participate and see one another as equals, regardless of wealth or status. And there was the South, which from its inception was defined by slavery. Though the South featured some of the same republican tendencies of the North, it was also a quasi-oligarchy not unlike England. "The citizen of the southern states of the Union is invested with a sort of domestic dictatorship," Tocqueville wrote, explaining that southern enslavers were in many ways operating in conflict with core American values.[3]

To Tocqueville, the remarkable feature of American republicanism was its twin emphasis on liberty and equality. Although tensions existed between these virtues, democracy needed both. So long as slavery survived, the South had neither. Tocqueville's primary concern was not the "good of the negroes." He thought slavery should primarily be abolished *for the good of the whites*. Until that happened, slaveholders—tied up in a system that required them to torture other humans and suppress speech—could never sustain true democratic habits like respect for the rule of law and treating others as equals. For American democracy to survive, even for white people, Tocqueville believed that slavery had to die.[4]

Sumner respected Tocqueville's view that white democracy required freedom for Blacks, although he was far more racially egalitarian than Tocqueville ever was. Sumner also shared Tocqueville's recognition that liberty *and* equality were the twin virtues of republicanism, twin virtues that depended on each other. To Sumner, abolition was more than just a charitable cause that emanated from pity for poor, oppressed people. Abolition was central to the democratic project, necessary for the American experiment to survive.

For the rest of his life, Sumner built on Tocqueville's ideas and helped popularize them in America. "In the years following the Civil War," Tocqueville's biographer wrote, "Sumner did much to cement Tocqueville's reputation as a visionary." Tocqueville, for his part, believed that Sumner was playing an essential role in fulfilling the promise of America. Without men like Sumner, he thought, American democracy had no future. "Mr. Sumner is a remarkable man," Tocqueville later remarked. "He says that slavery will soon entirely disappear in the United States. He does not know how, he does not know when; but he feels it, he is perfectly sure of it. The man speaks like a prophet."[5]

* * *

RETURNING HOME IN November 1857, Sumner felt that his health had improved. Though his time in Europe was marked by some fatigue, occasional headaches, back strain, and difficulty walking, his symptoms were far better than when he had left. He decided it was time to resume a career in politics. He declared his intention to make a speech about the barbarism of slavery, a speech that he admitted might get him shot, because it "would be like first proof brandy to molasses and water" as compared with "The Crime Against Kansas" speech.[6]

Sumner was tired of being a martyr—at least a living one. He feared being a lifelong invalid, useless to the cause and forgotten to history. He wanted to plunge back into the action. In December, he returned to Washington believing he was ready to restart his crusade against slavery. But the psychological trauma of being back in the place where he had been beaten was too difficult to bear. Shortly after entering the Senate Chamber, he scurried out and went home as fast as he could, crying to himself after getting to his room. "Then this is the end. It is all over with me now," he thought. He didn't understand what was wrong with him, but he knew that his head throbbed too painfully whenever he tried to enter the Capitol. He felt crushed, defeated, and agonized.

Sumner sought consolation from his friends, explaining to them what appear to have been symptoms of post-traumatic stress disorder (PTSD). "Yesterday, after sitting in the Senate, I felt like a man of ninety," he wrote to Theodore Parker. "At times I feel almost well, and then after a little writing or a little sitting in the Senate[,] I feel the weight spreading over my brain," he told Howe. "This is hard—very hard. It is hard to be so near complete recovery and still be kept back," he confided to the Duchess of Argyll. All he wanted was to escape from his trauma.

Spending two weeks in Washington, mostly avoiding work by reading newspapers at home, Sumner gave up resuming his participation in the Senate. He left the city feeling absolutely dejected. For the next five months, he was in low spirits, living variously in Boston, Philadelphia, and New York among caring friends, going to Washington only occasionally to brave the Senate Chamber in order to participate in critical votes where the party needed him.[7]

"Two years have gone already! How much more!" he cried out in one letter to Howe. While studying in the Library of Congress one day in April 1858, Sumner collapsed to the floor and suffered some kind of back spasm. For weeks he stayed at home, enduring debilitating pain and hardly able to walk. Blaming his suffering on his brain, he also contracted a urinary illness at the same time. His doctors again advised him to travel abroad. "Where shall I go? What do? Europe? where in Europe? baths there? water-cure there? extensive travel there? . . . Where shall I go and what do?" he wrote in a long rant to Longfellow. "I grow old, inactive, and the future is dreary." He was getting desperate.[8]

As the maladies continued, Sumner found a new obsession: collecting engravings. Engravings are made by cutting grooves and adding ink to a flat metal surface that can be pressed onto pages. It was a popular form of image making at the time, a way to make photograph-like pictures or to replicate paintings. For months at the Smithsonian, the Library of Congress, the Astor Library, and private collections, Sumner pored over engravings and amassed his own collection. "Sumner is insatiable," Longfellow wrote in his diary, groaning about the many hours he would be dragged by his friend to Harvard Library to flip through engravings. "I cannot take in so much at once; it fatigues my brain and body." Sumner, for his part, had found a lifelong hobby. "Other invalids, seeking occupation without burden, may find in them the solace that I did," he hoped.[9]

While Sumner distracted himself, politics grew even more inflamed. Stephen Douglas shocked everyone by denouncing the dictatorial government in Kansas after the territory sent a proposed proslavery constitution to Congress for approval. He said that enslavers had gone too far, even for him, by denying free and fair elections that contradicted his philosophy of popular sovereignty. Southern Democrats furiously threatened to excommunicate Douglas from the party. But some Republicans were pleasantly surprised by his pivot and wanted to collaborate with him, thinking that his potential defection might help seal the deal for a politically unified North. Sumner urged colleagues not to trust Douglas, thinking it was all a desperate ruse to regain support at home after becoming one of the most hated politicians in the North.[10]

Douglas's about-face was motivated by an insurgent threat from his own home state of Illinois. A folksy, middle-aged lawyer and aspiring politician was rumored to be eyeing Douglas's seat. That lawyer, who earned regional fame after nearly winning a Senate election two years earlier, started out as a nobody. He had grown up in Kentucky and Indiana as a child laborer, constantly loaned out by his father, before moving to Illinois in early adulthood to educate himself and earn a paycheck as a lawyer. Though he had served one term in Congress as a Whig, where he saw with his own eyes the dramatic collapse of John Quincy Adams, his political stature did not even remotely compare to that of the eminent Douglas. Yet Douglas was afraid.

Abraham Lincoln gave one of his first speeches in response to Douglas after the latter praised *Dred Scott*. Lincoln assailed the Court's ruling and hinted that Congress and the president had no obligation to obey it. He then argued that America had become *more* racist since the Founding— claiming that back then, the "Declaration of Independence was held sacred by all, and thought to include all," including free Blacks.

Lincoln positioned himself as a man who wanted to restore the promise of the American Founding that had been grossly distorted by the slave oligarchy. But he was no racial egalitarian, at least not yet. Responding to the claim that Republicans favored interracial marriage, Lincoln suggested that he opposed it. "In some respects, she certainly is not my equal," Lincoln declared, referring to Black women. "But in her natural right to eat the bread she earns with her own hands without asking leave of anyone else, she is my equal, and the equal of all others." Lincoln also said that if slavery were ever abolished, America ought to forcibly send Black people to Africa through a process called "colonization," not unlike the mass migration of the Israelites from Egypt. He simply could not imagine Blacks and whites living peacefully as equals.[11]

Lincoln's odd mix of beliefs made him a powerfully compelling Republican political candidate. Here was a man who hated slavery almost as much as any radical like Sumner. Yet he abhorred racial integration almost as much as any conservative like Douglas. And he endorsed colonization, a popular idealistic fantasy of many moderate antislavery men. Everybody in the North could find something to like in Lincoln. Douglas, fearing a potential political upset by this savvy newcomer, scrambled to reposition himself before the election.

Although many politicos foreshadowed a showdown between Lincoln and Douglas, Sumner was not paying attention. He had been almost entirely removed from politics, avoiding it for the sake of his health by feeding his urge for intellectual stimulation with other things, such as engravings. He had also been preparing to return to Europe for another trip, as doctors advised. "It is with real reluctance that I proceed on this pilgrimage," he wrote. "But it is the surest way to regain my health. The ghost of two years already dead haunts me."

On May 22, 1858, exactly two years after his caning, Sumner embarked again for France. There was a sense among friends and allies that he ought to give recovery one more chance and, if it was unsuccessful, resign his post in the Senate. Sumner prayed that he would find his elixir so that he could resume his career in the national spotlight. "If health ever returns," he soon swore to Howe, "I will repay to slavery and the whole crew of its supporters every wound, burn . . . ache, pain, trouble, grief which I have suffered. That vow is registered."[12]

* * *

WHEN SUMNER ARRIVED in France in early June, he was introduced to a world-famous physician now recognized as a pioneer in modern neurology. Born of mixed-race heritage in Mauritius, Charles-Édouard Brown-Séquard studied medicine in Paris and loved experimenting with his patients. A brilliant physician, Brown-Séquard understood the human nervous system better than nearly anyone alive at the time, albeit far less than doctors today do. He was also eccentric: toward the end of his career, the doctor started injecting mashed-up animal testicles into elderly men, including himself, in the belief that this treatment might slow down human aging and bring back sexual virility. He was, unsurprisingly, wrong.[13]

Brown-Séquard spent three hours examining Sumner before concluding that his patient suffered from a contrecoup brain injury, an injury that damaged both the impact site in the skull and a more distant place, in this case the spinal cord, via an effusion of fluid about the brain and some degree of congestion. (Contrecoup injuries are real, but they are still not well understood by modern medicine.) Sumner must have been impressed by the doctor's detailed diagnosis (which was, in retrospect, not quite right). "What then shall be the remedy?" he asked the eccentric doctor. "Fire," the physician replied.[14]

Sumner asked to begin the fire treatment right away. Brown-Séquard placed pieces of fungi or cottonwood on Sumner's bare neck and spine as the patient leaned over a chair. He then lit them ablaze. Sumner likely screamed in agony, gripping the back of the chair so tightly that it broke. Though he was offered chloroform, he declined on the doctor's advice that "the greater is the pain you have suffered . . . the greater also is your chance of being cured." For seven days spread across two weeks, Sumner endured the scalding flames on his skin, which left burn wounds and blisters so painful he could barely sleep. Sumner's assent to this excoriation was a sign of his desperation and of his conviction that conventional medical advice would no longer suffice. He was prepared to endure anything, painful as it might be, for the chance to return to his abolitionist mission.

Brown-Séquard never tried his excruciating experiment on any patient ever again. Though he insisted to a reporter that his bizarre therapy worked, he confessed (decades later) that he had subjected Sumner "to the martyrdom of the greatest suffering that can be inflicted on mortal man." The treatment was loosely based on an ancient Chinese therapy called moxibustion, which involves burning dried mugwort on pain points in the body. Today, it is typically administered without direct contact and with less heat than Brown-Séquard seems to have used. No modern moxibustion done correctly would create the wounds Sumner had. For forty-five days straight, the doctor visited Sumner to help dress the wounds he had inflicted.[15]

"The doctor is clear that without this cruel treatment I should have been a permanent invalid," Sumner wrote defensively to Longfellow about his insane ordeal. Friends back home were horrified to learn about the eccentric experimental therapy an unsupervised Sumner had agreed to undergo. "I thought the furnace you lived in was hot enough at Washington; but to be roasted after this extra-fashion is awful," Charles Francis Adams wrote him. Adams despised "this fiery trial" and "medical butchery." (Sumner replied to him with a long and defensive letter about why he had opted in to the treatment.) One Boston doctor called Brown-Séquard's treatment "the most barbarous practice of superstition," a kind of "torture." Salmon Chase noted that his friend's endurance "would have sustained a martyr at the stake." When rumors hit the press about his treatment, southerners found it hilarious that Sumner was in so much pain after voluntarily signing up for an exotic therapy. "God knows Mr. Sumner is no fire-eater," a southern newspaper quipped.[16]

Brown-Séquard's experiment destroyed much of the progress Sumner had made in his health. For months, he struggled to walk, complained about terrible headaches, and suffered terrible back and neck pain. Then, one night in late July 1858, he felt a severe tightening pain in his chest. He endured extreme agony through the night, confused about what was going on, and as he tossed and turned, the burn wounds across his back stung him even more. He was suffering from angina pectoris, a chest pain that occurs when the heart does not get enough blood and oxygen. For the rest of his life, he would battle angina attacks, which he said were so bad that they "make the fire seem pleasant."[17]

⋆ ⋆ ⋆

WHILE SUMNER UNDERWENT his fire treatment, America was also being lit ablaze. In the fall of 1858, Lincoln ran a nationally watched political campaign against Douglas in Illinois. The two sparred in seven hot debates across the state, and the transcripts were distributed across the country. Douglas filled his speeches with racist drivel and depicted Republicans as trying to break up the union. Lincoln portrayed Democrats as the real extremists who had departed from true American values by embracing slavery's expansion. Lincoln even cited Preston Brooks several times as an example of a southerner who actively disrespected the Founders. Though Douglas won reelection, Lincoln became a nationally prominent figure. He was invited to the East Coast to go on a speaking tour and was regarded as a potential candidate for the presidential nomination in two years' time.[18]

The country seemed to know the upcoming 1860 election would be an existential one, an all-out showdown between antislavery and proslavery candidates. Only a year before the election, in October 1859, John Brown and his men seized a federal arsenal at Harpers Ferry, Virginia (now West Virginia), attempting to arm enslaved people across Appalachia with thousands of guns in order to ignite a national slave revolution. When the raid failed, Brown was captured and tried for treason. At his trial, he embraced the fact that his blood was to mingle "with the blood of millions in this slave country whose rights are disregarded." He terrified southerners, who feared greater violence if Republicans won the 1860 election. While most white northerners were also horrified by Brown's raid, many abolitionists and younger Republicans grew increasingly militant in its wake, deciding that Brown was right: a slave revolution or a war against the South was the only viable path to freedom.[19]

Brown had crossed paths with Sumner, in more ways than one. According to the abolitionist preacher James Freeman Clarke, Brown had paid Sumner a visit while he was recovering from the caning in his mother's home in early 1857. Clarke said that Sumner invited Brown to open his closet to examine the blood stains on the coat from the day of his attack. "John Brown . . . looked at it for a few minutes with the reverence with which a Roman Catholic regards the relics of a saint," Clarke recalled. Years later, Sumner's secretary Arnold Johnson said that Clarke's story about the bloody coat was false because the coat had been cleaned after the assault. Regardless, Brown's visit to Sumner's home certainly took place. It must have been a deeply emotional visit for the freedom fighter to meet freedom's martyr.

During his time in Boston, Brown convened with Sumner's friends Samuel Howe and Theodore Parker. All three were radical abolitionists. Brown explained his conviction that peace would never lead to justice for the enslaved. Violence, mass violence, was needed. Howe and Parker reportedly concurred. The two, alongside Sumner, had often tacitly endorsed or actively participated in violent resistance to the Fugitive Slave Act. Brown wanted to engage in a far greater scale of bloodshed than Howe or Parker had ever imagined. Although they knew few details about Brown's plans, they nevertheless helped raise money for his epic expedition. After Brown was caught, federal officials investigated Howe, Parker, and others (including Frederick Douglass) for their alleged participation in Brown's insurrection. Most so-called conspirators, including Douglass and Howe, fled the country and stayed in Canada for a while, disclaiming any involvement.

While Brown plotted and conducted his raid, Sumner had been enjoying himself in the south of France. Beginning in the fall of 1858, he finally found some peace. "I am now comfortable, and enjoy my baths, my walks, and the repose and *incognito* which I find here," he wrote. A new doctor prescribed daily baths, interchangeably hot and cold, in the mornings. After each bath, Sumner would wrap himself in a bedsheet and lie for hours, which no doubt healed the burn wounds. Loving this therapy, he did his best to abstain from reading the news. Onward to Germany and Italy, Sumner continued to enjoy blissful ignorance. In Rome, he stayed several weeks with William Story, son of the late Joseph Story, who had long ago moved to Italy to become a sculptor. Story indulged Sumner's new love for engravings, and the two spent long evenings chatting. They also met mutual acquaintances who were in Italy at the time, such as the novelist Nathaniel Hawthorne.

Sumner was getting better now that he had learned to find joy in his rest. Taking delight in engravings, sweet relaxing baths, and lying down, he found the strength he couldn't get by looking for quick and easy solutions, such as the fire experiment. "For more than three months I have seen no Massachusetts newspaper except a solitary *Liberator* kindly sent to me from Paris," he proudly told a friend. After Italy, he went to Switzerland, enjoying "every moment, in every mountain, hill, lake, river, valley, and field," which "filled me with delight." Returning to southern France, he spent most of his time in bed reading, and he "devoured books with his ancient ardor" for the first time in decades. "No prisoner in the Bastille ever read more!" he boasted to Edward Pierce.

But Sumner knew he would eventually have to leave Europe. Writing to Story, he noted that the day was coming soon when he would have to be "in another place, in scenes very different, amidst tobacco-spitting, swearing slave-drivers, abused by the press, insulted so far as is possible, pained and racked by insensibility about me to human rights."[20]

* * *

SUMNER CAME HOME to a nation on the brink, as the 1860 election approached in an atmosphere of fear, violence, and uncertainty. In the South, enslavers were terrified that Republicans would win the election and ban slavery in the territories. They kept threatening secession. If Republicans were to pursue any antislavery policies, South Carolina congressman Laurence Keitt warned, "it would be the duty of the South to take possession of the Capitol . . . and expel from it the traitors to the Constitution."[21]

Most Republicans treated the secessionist threats as a bluff by angry southerners who didn't really mean it. But the party's most radical abolitionists dreamed of disunion and welcomed secession by enslavers. They didn't have any interest in sharing a country with the South, which they thought was beyond redemption. They declared that a permanent separation between North and South would effectively leave slaveholders out to dry, because a massive oppressed population could easily overthrow their masters in due time in the absence of help from American troops in Washington. A separation would also create a new border of freedom for slaves to escape to, bringing freedom five hundred miles closer than distant Canada.

To the South's consternation, abolitionists were now in a genuine political coalition alongside Free Soilers, ex–Know Nothings, and ex-Whigs. They were all unified under the antislavery Republican banner. At the convention in May 1860, Republican delegates embraced the central principle of Sumner's 1852 speech "Freedom National, Slavery Sectional." Ignoring threats from southerners to secede from the Union if any antislavery legislation was attempted, Republicans declared their intent to pass laws to ban slavery in all territories if the party was elected. They also debated several potential nominees, including two passionate antislavery men whom southerners deeply feared: William Seward and Salmon Chase. Both Seward and Chase had worked closely with Sumner for many years. He would have been happy with either candidate.

Neither won. Instead, the Republican delegates ended up choosing the dark horse candidate Abraham Lincoln. Though he was almost nobody's favorite choice, Lincoln was recognized as wildly eloquent, erudite, and outstanding in character. After he won the nomination, the party rallied behind Lincoln with an enthusiasm that drowned out Seward and Chase's woeful resentment. Sumner accepted the nomination happily despite knowing little about this Illinois man whom he had never met. He wrote consoling letters to his friends Chase and Seward and then turned his focus to the dramatic saga unfolding before his eyes. At last, slavery and antislavery were on the ballot.[22]

Lincoln's opponents were in total disarray. Northern and southern Democrats fought viciously among themselves, as northern party members were disturbed by the autocratic government in Kansas while many southern party members celebrated slavery's dominance in Kansas and openly threatened secession if Republicans won the election. In the end, northern Democrats decided to host their own convention to nominate Douglas, while southern Democrats chose Kentucky's John Breckinridge as their nominee. Breckinridge and his supporters implied that the South would create its own independent country if he lost the election. Some southerners, largely ex-Whigs, were so disturbed by the talk of secession in their communities that they formed a fourth political group, the Constitutional Union Party, endorsing Tennessee's John Bell.

Arguably, southerners were right to be afraid of Lincoln and the Republicans. Though moderate in tone and eclectic in views, Lincoln hated slavery with a fiery passion that inflamed the North. His rhetoric stoked the existential dread of the South. "A house divided against itself cannot stand," he decided. "I believe this government cannot endure permanently, half slave and half free. . . . It will become all one thing, or all the other." To southerners, Lincoln was making the threat that he would never compromise with them. If Lincoln won the election, they feared, he would do everything to eliminate slavery, everywhere.[23]

* * *

FOR SEVERAL MONTHS in Washington, Sumner observed the advice of doctors to take it slow, by sitting quietly in the Senate, rarely raising his voice to speak. To avoid any stress, he had not even attended the Republican National Convention and had expressed no opinion about who ought to have been the nominee.

By the summer of 1860, Sumner was ready to get back to the action by giving another dramatic antislavery speech, a kind of follow-up to "The Crime Against Kansas." As Sumner confided in his friends and allies about his plans, they were alarmed at his confidence and audacity. "He calls himself well . . . but there is a change in him which strikes me unpleasantly," Senator William Fessenden wrote. The caning had intensified "the Puritanical sternness and intolerance of his nature," according to the young Black abolitionist Archibald Grimke, who wrote a biography of Sumner after the senator's death. "He was then in personal appearance the incarnation of iron will and iron convictions," Grimke recalled.[24]

When Howe visited Washington, he was startled by the sheer level of Sumner's resentment at his southern colleagues. In retrospect, Howe shouldn't have been surprised. For several years, Sumner had endured daily agony and pain while southerners celebrated the caning, laughed at his injuries, and mocked him for being a sham artist. "He is bent upon making an onslaught upon the Southern cohorts," Howe warned a friend. "I regret to say that too much of the impulse comes from combativeness and destructiveness." Howe pleaded with Sumner not to deliver an abrasive antislavery speech that could endanger his life. "We had an argument about it, and he was driven to Scripture and quoted the 'Scribes and Pharisees and Hypocrites,'" Howe recalled.[25]

* * *

ON JUNE 4, 1860, Sumner wrought his revenge against the South by delivering the most stinging, controversial, and passionately abolitionist speech that had been delivered in the Senate in several years. He called it "The Barbarism of Slavery." He gave these remarks in a newly built Senate Chamber, far larger than the intimate, antiquated, red-carpeted room where he had been bloodied. Being in a new room may have helped alleviate his PTSD, for he had regained the confidence that he had lost in the preceding years and did not feel the same pangs of trauma.[26]

After thanking "the Supreme Being" and apologizing for his truancy, Sumner began his remarks. "When last I entered into this debate, it became my duty to expose the Crime against Kansas. . . . Time has passed; but the question remains," he declared. Purporting to resume "the discussion precisely where I left it," he said he had "no personal griefs to utter" and "no personal wrongs to avenge" regarding his caning from four years earlier. There was only "the question before us" to discuss. "Slavery must be resisted not only on political grounds; but on all other grounds, whether social, economical, or moral," he continued. "Ours is no holiday contest . . . but it is a solemn battle between Right and Wrong; between Good and Evil."[27]

Sumner then set out to identify the origin of American slavery. "It is not derived from the Common Law, that fountain of liberty," he said, because even during English feudalism, serfs could marry and their children could seek freedom. Neither was it "derived from the Roman Law, that fountain of Tyranny," since the Romans kept enslaved families together. Nor was it from "the Mohammedan Law," because "the mild injunctions of the Koran" incentivized emancipation, regulated abuses by slaveholders, and freed their offspring. So where did American slavery come from? "It comes from Africa, ancient nurse of monsters,—from Guinea, Dahomey, and Congo," he said. Ever since the first slave ship "in 1620 landed its cruel cargo at Jamestown" (it was actually 1619), enslavers had been acting like "barbarous half-naked African chiefs" who sanctioned mayhem, robbery, the lash, and lechery.

Sumner tried to get under the skin of enslavers by associating them with the alleged barbarism of the people they most despised. He then took it a step farther, claiming that enslavers were uncivilized. He compared them to native New Zealanders, with their tattoos; Native American savages of the Northwest Coast, with flat heads; the "Carib of the Gulf," with their cannibalism; and Brigham Young of the Mormons with his polygamy. He then rattled off litanies of statistics that purported to show the backwardness of the South by illustrating that slave states were far behind in education, manufacturing, population, land values, and other metrics compared to the North.

There was a touch of racism and Western supremacism in Sumner's speech, despite his generally egalitarian impulses. On the one hand, Sumner never suggested that Blacks, Native Americans, Mormons, or foreigners were somehow inherently different or inferior to whites. He insisted that everyone of any race or background was entitled to equal rights in a democratic society. But when an abolitionist wrote to him after his speech to challenge his claim that Africans were barbarians, Sumner replied by insisting that the African coast was indeed an uncivilized place, full of unspeakable cruelty and animalistic horrors. That said, he conceded that there was "in the interior of Africa a considerable degree of civilization."

Sumner genuinely believed that the African coast had exhibited barbarism that was wrongly imported into America. He also thought that he came from a superior civilization, New England, which he believed was superior to both the South and the African Coast. To him, New England had reached the heights of human achievement, with its high literacy rates, religiosity, democratic norms, and greater racial tolerance. By associating the South with peoples who were conventionally considered barbaric and savage, and *more* barbaric than people in past civilizations like the Romans or the Muslims, Sumner implied that white southerners were a degenerate people compared to New Englanders.[28]

Anger raged through the room as Sumner continued speaking. Most proslavery senators either stormed out or babbled to one another to prove they were not paying attention. As he was ignored, Sumner went on to associate them with the characteristics of barbarism. "The passions and habits of Slave-masters are naturally represented in Congress." He described many violent acts that proslavery politicians had perpetrated there, most of which received little press coverage, unlike his caning. He also decried dueling, saying it was "part of that System of Violence which has its origin in Slavery."

Deploring the character of proslavery politicians, Sumner extolled the virtues of their polar opposites, men like John Quincy Adams, Joshua Giddings, William Lloyd Garrison, and Samuel Hoar. At the end of his speech, he restated his view that the Constitution banned slavery in territories and required "impartial Freedom, without distinction of color or race." Freedom would soon triumph over slavery, Sumner warned, thanks to the "charge of an awakened people, instructing a new President."[29]

When Sumner finished, South Carolina's James Chestnut Jr. rose to respond. "After ranging over Europe, crawling through the back doors to whine at the feet of British aristocracy, craving pity, and reaping a rich harvest of contempt," Chestnut growled, "the slanderer of States and men reappears in the Senate." Purporting to speak on behalf of all proslavery senators, Chestnut said they would not attack Sumner because it would only "increase the devotees at the shrine of this new idol"—the idol being Sumner. "We are not inclined again to send forth the recipient of punishment howling through the world, yelping fresh cries of slander and malice," Chestnut said. Sumner, for his part, simply replied that he would include Chestnut's vulgar comments in the appendix of his publication as another illustration of the barbarism of slavery.

Southerners were enraged by Sumner's speech. For the next several weeks, he received death threats in the mail. Fearing that somebody might try to take Sumner's life, Congressman Anson Burlingame and Senator John Sherman slept outside Sumner's room to keep him safe. Without telling Sumner, a few abolitionists in the city armed themselves with revolvers and followed the senator around, acting as self-appointed incognito bodyguards for Sumner, unbeknownst to him or to any of his potential assailants.[30]

* * *

EVERYONE UNDERSTOOD THAT if Lincoln were elected, Sumner would become one of the most powerful men in America. The public saw him as the moral spokesman of the Republican Party and effectively one of its founders. For this reason, Republican strategists were outraged and worried by Sumner's polarizing and vituperative speech. They had urged rhetorical caution, hoping not to lose vital support from hesitant moderates who were voting for an antislavery candidate for the first time. In their view, Sumner had impulsively let loose the radical strain of his party, putting their chances in an uncertain election at risk.

Sumner disagreed with these centrists. He thought Republicans should unabashedly stick to principles. He surmised that voters would have greater respect for a political party that had the courage to break from past political norms. That was the recipe he believed the Free-Soil Party had followed successfully to upend the two-party system that had existed before it. He believed that conviction, not concession, was the key to political success. Quoting Jonathan Swift, Sumner put it this way: "And know that to be brave is to be wise."[31]

The novelist Lydia Maria Child concurred with Sumner's calculus. "The Republican party don't know how to appreciate his honesty and moral courage," she said of Sumner. "They think he makes a mistake in speaking the truth and does it because he don't know any better. They do not perceive how immeasurably superior his straightforwardness is to their crookedness." Reflecting on Sumner's career years later, Republican senator Carl Schurz believed that Sumner was right to think voters were ahead of party leaders. "As it often happens," he noted, "the politicians trembled, but the people received the moral inspiration of a bold utterance with joy. They were in their sentiments and their courage far in advance of the party managers."[32]

Radicals widely distributed Sumner's speech to voters, to the consternation of party centrists. Frederick Douglass printed every word of it in his paper. Howe—who now saw the speech's value—solicited paid subscriptions in Boston to finance a wider distribution for free. Sumner's political manager Francis Bird mailed copies to every voter in his district. Members of the Massachusetts State House forced a vote on a resolution to praise the speech, which passed by overwhelming majorities. Then, allies sent the speech to editors at newspapers around the country, which promptly reprinted large swaths. Bundles of the speech were also sent to Republicans to distribute to people. The goal was to illustrate that the Republican Party meant what it said. Radicals also wanted to force centrists in the party to stick to principles.

"Behind you, stand a million of your fellow citizens in whose hearts your speech finds an echo," one admirer told Sumner. "The civilized world will hear you, and rejoice at the tremendous exposure of the meanness, brutality, blood-guiltiness, hell-black iniquity, and barbarism of American Slavery," wrote Frederick Douglass. "The gratitude of the colored people of this Country towards you is incalculable," said one Black businessman. "There is no man in the world in whom we have more confidence." Feeling the rush of his success, Sumner continued to speak into the late fall, painting the election in maximally existential terms.[33]

Sumner remained physically safe through the fall, and his party achieved a magnificent victory in November. In a stunning upheaval, Abraham Lincoln swept the electoral votes of every single northern state. Though he lacked the nationwide popular vote, claiming only 40 percent in a four-way race, he had a clear mandate for his antislavery agenda from the majority of northern voters. Radicals in Lincoln's party fared well, too. In Sumner's home state, his friend and protégé John Andrew earned the spot of governor. At last, after more than a decade of toil, antislavery men had won a stirring political victory that handed them the halls of power.

✳ ✳ ✳

WHEN THE ELECTION was over, South Carolina organized a statewide convention to decide whether to secede from the union. Delegates came together in Charleston. There was a rush of excitement in the atmosphere, a feeling that now was the opportunity to create the proslavery confederacy that many of South Carolina's leaders had long dreamed of. They drafted a Declaration of Secession. In their declaration, they cited Lincoln's claim that a "government cannot endure permanently half slave, half free" as a provocation. In their eyes, President-elect Lincoln was trying to tell the public that slavery deserved "ultimate extinction." Denouncing Lincoln and the North for being "hostile to slavery," South Carolina declared itself independent.

The lame-duck president Buchanan was attending a wedding when South Carolina had reached its decision. During the wedding, Congressman Laurence Keitt—the man who had advised Brooks on caning Sumner—barged into the hall. Jumping up and down, waving a telegram from his home state in his hand, Keitt began hollering, "Thank God! Oh, thank God! . . . South Carolina has seceded! . . . I feel like a boy let out from school!" When President Buchanan grasped the gravity of Keitt's news, he was stunned. He fell back, grasped the arms of his chair, and asked someone to take him home. He was in no mood to celebrate anymore. As another wedding guest recalled, "this was the tremendous event which was to change all our lives."[34]

PART III

THE WAR POWER

CHAPTER 14

THIS IS THE TIME
THAT TRIES MEN'S SOULS

On January 25, 1861, Charles Sumner went to the Treasury Building to meet Edwin Stanton, the attorney general, to discuss the dangerous situation. Over the past few weeks, four states in the Deep South had joined South Carolina's rebellion. Several more states seemed to be on the precipice of secession, carrying out the threat that many northerners had mistakenly believed was overblown. Several influential northern leaders were now desperately trying to hash a deal with southern leaders to avoid disunion. If powerful Upper South states like Virginia seceded, all hope for compromise would be doomed. If Maryland joined Virginia in seceding, the nation's capital would be compromised, too. The city would be surrounded by rebels on both sides.

Washington was abuzz with rumors about a southern plot to invade the nation's capital. "Many of the residents here are preparing to remove their families," a D.C. resident wrote in a letter. "Almost everyone has talked of certain civil war; of streets drowned in blood, and of the city a prey to the flames." By late January, Stanton was convinced that the rumors were true. He feared that his docile boss, the lame-duck president Buchanan, was not up to the task of protecting the capital. A lifelong Democrat, Stanton turned to Republicans for help. He warned Sumner about the conspiracy to take the city.

"We must be alone," Stanton whispered, explaining that he was "surrounded by Secessionists." He feared that anything he said would get leaked: the Washington bureaucracy was dominated by southerners. Seeing clerks in his office, Stanton took Sumner into another room. There were secretaries in that room, too. Passing through five more rooms, all occupied by clerks, Stanton gave up. In the corridor, he quietly told Sumner that he must see him "at some other time and place" and that "everything was as bad as could be . . . Virginia would certainly secede . . . Kentucky would surely follow, and Maryland, too." Snapping his fingers, Stanton told Sumner that Washington would fall after those states. "Stop, Mr. Attorney, not so fast," Sumner replied. He arranged to meet Stanton to learn more.

Around an hour past midnight, Stanton showed up at Sumner's lodgings so they could talk freely. He spent an hour trying to convince Sumner that a coup attempt in Washington was on the horizon. He was certain that southern leaders would attack the capital, seize it by force, and install a new government. While Sumner was unconvinced, he was incredibly anxious. The men met again two days later to talk until long past midnight. "I know from him what I cannot communicate," Sumner wrote in a letter. "Suffice it to say, *he does not think it probable, hardly possible*, that we shall be here on the 4th March [the date of Lincoln's inauguration]. . . , *It is feared that the Departments will be seized & occupied as forts.*"[1]

The rumored attack on Washington never materialized, but America was headed for dark days. Years ago, Sumner had feared their coming. In "The Crime Against Kansas," he had warned that the violent skirmishes in Kansas "foreshadow[ed] a strife which, unless happily averted by the triumph of Freedom, will become war—fratricidal, parricidal war—with an accumulated wickedness beyond the wickedness of any war in human annals; justly provoking the avenging judgment of Providence and the avenging pen of history."[2]

* * *

IT WASN'T OBVIOUS that war would come. After Lincoln's election, terrible suspense hung over the North during a period now known as secession winter. During these cold, dark months, northern politicians wondered whether the South really meant to secede. Perhaps it was a paranoid ploy to frighten antislavery Republicans into backing off their plan to ban slavery in the territories. Perhaps it would be just a small rebellion by a handful of Deep South states, one that would fizzle out quickly. Even if more slave states joined them, perhaps war could be avoided. "Let the South go if it wants to; we can get along without it," some said. Others hoped to craft a compromise to avert secession or at least to retain some of the slave states.[3]

The terror of possible war dramatically reshaped the fault lines of the political antislavery movement, beginning with its new leader, Lincoln. "This is the time that tries men's souls," one Republican remarked. Most

antislavery politicians who campaigned for Lincoln never wanted secession, much less bloodshed. They had regarded the threat of civil war as "a
mere bugaboo to frighten children," as one Republican recalled. Now that
bloodshed seemed possible, Lincoln was caught in a bind. He told some
Republicans that the North should stand firm regardless of what slave
states threatened. But to William Seward, whom he picked for secretary of
state, Lincoln privately advised overtures to the South, like cracking down
on fugitive slaves and sanctioning the domestic slave trade and slavery
in D.C. It was Lincoln's last-ditch effort to hold the country together. To
preserve the safety of white America, he was willing to make sacrifices to
Black liberty.[4]

Not Sumner. At first, the abolitionist senator wanted the few seceding
states to go peacefully. "If the secession can be restrained to the 'Cotton
States,' I shall be willing to let them go," he wrote, thinking that a small
confederacy would be weak, domestically and internationally isolated, and
vulnerable to slave rebellions. Their departure would strengthen his hand
in the Senate, too. "But can it be stopped there?" he wondered. As more
states joined the rebellion, Sumner came to welcome war. "Much as I desire
the extinction of Slavery, I do not wish to see it go down in blood," he confessed. "And yet the existing hallucination of the slave-masters is such that
I doubt if this calamity can be avoided. They seem to rush upon their destiny." In time, Sumner seemed to look "forward to the violence and slaughter of civil war . . . with a grim satisfaction," according to one of his friends.
"Detesting war . . . he yet more detested slavery," said another friend.[5]

Sumner had the same violent antislavery impulse as his mentor John
Quincy Adams. While serving as a congressman after being president,
Adams promised a Black audience that "the day of your redemption must
come. . . . It may come in peace or it may come in blood." Either way,
he thundered, "LET IT COME." A mortified Southern congressman confronted him about this strong rhetoric on the House floor. Without rising, the aging statesman defended himself from his seat. "I now say, *let
it come* . . . though it comes in the blood of millions of white men, let it
come." Adams's militancy stunned every peace-loving white man in the
room. "Let justice be done," he continued, "though the heavens fall."

Adams believed that a war to end slavery would not only be just; it
would also be legally sound under the right circumstances. If the South
ever fell into a state of "servile, civil, or foreign" war, Adams foretold, Congress could declare war to restore control over the region. Then, he said,

"all the powers incident to war are by necessary implication conferred" by the Constitution to both Congress and the executive branch. He observed that powers incidental to war had historically included seizing rebel property, such as slaves. "Not only the President of the United States, but the Commander of the Army, has power to order the universal emancipation of the slaves," he proclaimed. While the government had to honor the so-called property right to slaves in times of peace, Adams believed war annulled those obligations. He argued that his view was consistent with the manner in which many nations and empires had historically interpreted the laws of war.[6]

Sumner thought often about his mentor's wartime emancipation theory in early 1861. He also probably recalled the views of his teacher Joseph Story. Back in law school, Story had asked Sumner to proofread and index his treatise *The Conflict of Laws*. In the treatise, Story had raised the hypothetical of an American slave who arrived in England, where slavery was outlawed. The slave would "become ipso facto a freeman," Story decreed, because England was under no obligation to recognize a foreign property interest it believed to be immoral. This fact implied that slaves might be emancipated in the South, too, if rebel land were treated as enemy territory governed by national or martial law rather than state or municipal law.

Story had inadvertently laid the seeds for the wartime emancipation theory in other places as well. The judge had once said in an appellate ruling that the American government could legally seize timber privately owned by British merchants during the War of 1812. When the case was appealed to the Supreme Court, Chief Justice Marshall affirmed this issue in *Brown v. United States* (1814). "War gives to the sovereign full right," he decreed, "to take the persons and confiscate the property of the enemy."[7]

Drawing from Adams and Story, Sumner believed that when America fought a war, enemy property—including the so-called property in human beings—could be confiscated. His argument was bolstered by the fact that war permitted all kinds of things that were illegal in times of peace. "If it be constitutional to make war, to set armies in the field, to launch navies, to occupy fields and houses, to bombard cities, to kill in battle,—all without trial by jury, or any process of law, or judicial proceeding of any kind," he later explained, "it is equally constitutional, as a war measure, to confiscate the property of the enemy and to liberate his slaves."[8]

There was even more support for wartime emancipation as a military necessity. In one of the *Federalist Papers*, Alexander Hamilton said "no constitutional shackles" should be imposed on Congress to provide for the common defense. He believed that the power to defend "ought to exist without limitation, because it is impossible to foresee or define the extent and variety of national exigencies." In another Paper, James Madison said that "it is in vain to oppose constitutional barriers to the impulse of self-preservation." He argued that Congress could use any means necessary to win an existential war. Even Chief Justice Roger Taney—author of the *Dred Scott* decision—had upheld the Rhode Island state government's choice to trespass on a local insurrectionist's property after a dispute about the election results in the early 1840s. Taney said the property of rebels could be seized so long as it was a "necessary" measure during martial law.[9]

These ideas were circulating among abolitionists in the years leading up to the Civil War. And they were certainly familiar to Sumner, who swam in abolitionist circles and personally knew some of the jurists and thinkers who had propounded on wartime confiscation. According to the abolitionist Wendell Phillips, Sumner "was among the very first to insist that we should seize the opportunity the rebellion gave not only to fortify the Union, but to abolish slavery, and that abolition was inevitable." With hope for abolition, Sumner concluded that war should be accepted, not avoided. "I fear nothing now but compromise," he said.[10]

* * *

Two of Sumner's closest friends vehemently disagreed. As early as December, Charles Francis Adams had been toying with compromise. Although Sumner believed his friend was "as great a man as his father or his grandfather," the younger Adams had failed to make a name for himself in politics so far. Other antislavery men in Massachusetts, including Sumner, had been picked to run for positions Adams craved. Part of his failure was his lack of charisma and his fear of public speaking. It wasn't until 1860, at the age of fifty-one, that Adams won his first election and was sent to Congress.[11]

With the secession crisis impending, Adams decided to set himself apart. Unlike other antislavery men, he promised to help negotiate a compromise to save the Union that his grandfather had helped create. In December, he joined the House Committee of Thirty-Three, a group composed of one member from each state, to draft a compromise proposal.

The committee settled on the infamous Corwin Amendment, a proposal to change the Constitution to permanently stop Congress from interfering with slavery in any state. In late January, Adams also pitched the admission of New Mexico as a slave state and stronger fugitive slave laws.

While busy negotiating this peace deal, Adams moved his family to Washington. At their new home, as was their custom in Boston, they often invited Sumner to join family dinners. These must have been jovial occasions at first. The son Henry Adams said he "worshipped" Sumner as a boy. Sumner was his hero, a man "far closer than any relation of blood." Charles Francis Adams Jr. said that Sumner was once "the most intimate personal friend my father had." They were all close to him until the secession crisis tore them apart.[12]

Fights between the statesmen started at the dinner table in January 1861. They argued viciously about how to deal with the impending crisis. Adams was astonished to find Sumner unwilling to compromise in the least. When he accused Sumner of "stiff-necked obstinacy," Sumner refused to respond. A few days later, Adams drafted a letter to Massachusetts governor John Andrew requesting that he send delegates to a peace conference that Virginia had organized in a hopeful attempt to avert war. As if to provoke him, Adams asked Sumner to join other Massachusetts members of Congress as a cosigner. Sumner categorically refused, and the two argued bitterly. Sumner then boycotted dinner at the Adams home until Adams's wife, Abigail, begged him to come a few times more, if only to dispel rumors about their fighting. Even the sons got involved. Henry Adams was startled to see his quasi-uncle shouting so angrily at his father. "To bring him round is impossible," Henry complained. "God Almighty couldn't do it. . . . He will stand on his damned dignity."[13]

Sumner's anger was exacerbated by the feeling of betrayal from another longtime friend, William Seward. For decades, Seward had labored fiercely against slavery. He even used his property as one of the last stops on the Underground Railroad before Canada, and he had recently sold seven acres of his property to Harriet Tubman at a cheap rate for her family's use. But Seward was always temperamentally different from most abolitionists. In the Senate, he had friendly relations with many slaveholders, including Jefferson Davis, until the start of the war. He was usually moderate with his rhetoric, and he carefully directed his political machine in New York to appeal to many factions of his constituency apart from abolitionists. As the secession crisis unfolded, Seward joined the Senate's Committee of Thirteen, a group that drafted a series of compromise proposals offered by Kentucky senator John Crittenden. Though Seward ultimately voted against the deal, reaching a compromise with the slave states was still on his mind.

Seward invited Sumner to his home in early January to recite a draft speech to him. "I dread, as in my innermost soul I abhor, civil war," he read. "Congress, ought, if it can, to redress any real grievances of the offended States." Sumner listened intently until he heard Seward's concessions. To avert war, Seward said he would endorse the Corwin Amendment and new fugitive slave laws. Shocked, Sumner interrupted his friend and begged him not to deliver the speech. "I protested with my whole soul, for the sake of our cause, our country, and his own good name," he recalled. But Seward wouldn't relent. Evidently, he hated war and disunion even more than he hated slavery.[14]

Sumner was outraged when Seward delivered his speech in the Senate Chamber. Some weeks after, Sumner ran into Charles Francis Adams Jr. in the Senate cloakroom. "Seward had been demented all the session," Sumner growled. "[I] had pleaded with him, [I] had prayed him, besought him, implored him." He fumed to the twenty-six-year-old about the compromisers. As Adams Junior tried to squirm out of the conversation, Sumner insisted that the youngster stay put and listen up. "He talked like a crazy man, orating, gesticulating, rolling out deep periods in theatrical, whispered tones—repeating himself, and doing everything but reason," Adams Junior recalled. The half-hour tirade ended only when Seward awkwardly stepped into the cloakroom.[15]

"His vanity, or modesty, or what you will, is sensitive as a woman's," Henry Adams said of Sumner. From here on, Sumner looked upon his own allies with mistrust and often aggressively accused them of lacking backbones. He became known for being vain and obstinate not only to opponents, but also to friends. Though he once admitted to Abigail that her husband, Charles Francis Sr., was "honest" in his mistaken course, he held a grudge against the entire Adams family for the rest of his life. The feeling was mutual; the Adamses no longer wanted anything to do with him. Seward, by contrast, kept a working relationship with Sumner. But from now on, Sumner dealt with him at arm's length with a degree of coldness and animosity.[16]

Notably, Seward's wife, Frances, took Sumner's side. She warned her husband about "taking the path which led Daniel Webster to an unhonored grave ten years ago," for his role in the Compromise of 1850. "Compromises based on the idea that the preservation of the Union is more important than the liberty of nearly 4,000,000 human beings cannot be right," she said. Writing to Sumner, she blasted Adams's choice to favor slavery in New Mexico, noting that "three hundred thousand square miles of God's earth is a high price for the questionable advantage of a union with the slave States." A true abolitionist, she deplored compromisers—even those she loved. Though her marriage with Seward stayed solid, she often took Sumner's side in the years ahead. "She was nothing of a politician," Sumner said years later. "I have always admired her."[17]

Frances and Sumner arguably failed to appreciate that both Adams and Seward still wanted to end slavery. They simply felt that the price of war wasn't worth the chance of emancipation. With a deep faith that slavery could end slowly and peacefully, Adams and Seward scrambled to make compromises with the South. In so doing, they permanently tarnished their reputations among abolitionists. They also deluded themselves into thinking it was possible to avert secession. In the heat of the crisis, Seward forgot what he himself had once famously said: the fight between slave states and free states was "an irrepressible conflict."[18]

That said, there was strategic value in attempting compromise, even if it could not avert war. Four slave states straddled the border between North and South. These states—Missouri, Kentucky, Maryland, and Delaware—were torn on secession. Clear-eyed conciliators made overtures to the South to retain the states. Without these border states, it would be nearly impossible for the North to wage a successful war. For example, if Maryland seceded, Washington would be threatened at its northern front. And if Kentucky seceded, the North would lose control over the crucial Ohio and Mississippi Rivers. "I hope to have God on my side, but I must have Kentucky," Lincoln once reportedly said. Sumner, for his part, cared little about the border states. His goal was to keep the North galvanized and committed to the antislavery program no matter what.[19]

* * *

FURIOUS AT THE conciliators in Washington, Sumner focused his attention at home. Desperate to avert war, centrist Republicans and Unionists in the Bay State were considering a bill to repeal the personal liberty laws that granted fugitive slaves a modicum of protection from recapture. They wanted to voluntarily mass arrest and deport fugitive slaves as a gesture of goodwill to the South. Sumner signaled his vicious opposition. "If Massachusetts yields anything now to the outcry of the traitors, other States will yield everything," he warned one state lawmaker, who relayed Sumner's views to his colleagues. Sumner's goal was to make lawmakers too nervous to oppose him. "Pray, keep Massachusetts sound," he told Governor Andrew, "and *firm*—FIRM—FIRM—against every word or step of concession." Those who might sacrifice their principles, he declared to another Bay Stater, would be deemed guilty of "the treason of Judas" and "the cowardice of Peter."[20]

Andrew was caught in a bind between Sumner, his closest political mentor, and Adams, whom he considered a friend. Adams begged the governor to send delegates to the Washington Peace Conference while Sumner demanded that he not bend. "In God's name stand firm! . . . Don't cave, Andrew!" he wrote in one letter. Displeasing both men, Andrew sent delegates to the conference but opposed the repeal of fugitive slave protections. At the same time, he started preparing for war. After dispatching an aide to the capital to confer with Adams, Sumner, and Union general Winfield Scott, he started recruiting volunteers for nightly drills in the Bay State. They were gradually sorted into four regiments that would be among the first President Lincoln called to fight.[21]

While white people in Massachusetts hesitated and debated, Black Bay Staters stood ready to go to war. Two civil leaders of Boston's small but influential African American community, Robert Morris and Lewis Hayden, started recruiting soldiers in the spring. They hoped that by fighting valiantly for the flag, Black soldiers could open the eyes of prejudiced white northerners about the possibility of equal rights. They also believed that the North needed Black men to win and that winning would lead to emancipation. "[We] will show even to our enemies that we have the best wishes for our country's prosperity," declared John Rock, another Black Bostonian. By April, more than one hundred Black men had joined a drill company in Boston. But at the time, almost no white statesmen, not even Andrew or Sumner, seemed to be taking Morris, Hayden, and Rock seriously, and they did not make any effort to recruit Black soldiers until much later in the war.[22]

In February, Andrew came to Washington to attend an unsurprisingly fruitless meeting with Sumner and the lame-duck president Buchanan. Buchanan had been blaming the North's "intemperate interference" with slavery for South Carolina's secession. Hoping to craft a political solution with the rebels, he wanted Andrew to crack down on fugitive slaves with mass deportation and Sumner to support it. Sumner angrily retorted that the Bay State would rather "sink below the sea & become a sandbank." A few days later, several ex-Whig Bostonians—including Robert Winthrop and Edward Everett—visited Sumner to beg him to help make peace. To stroke his ego, they implied that the whole North looked to him for guidance and needed his wise and careful statesmanship. "The moment I compromise, I, too, should be lost," Sumner rebuffed them. Andrew also chose to join Sumner in opposing reconciliation. With their vocal opposition, compromisers in the commonwealth of Massachusetts failed.[23]

* * *

As MARCH 1861 approached, prospects for compromise looked grim at the national level as well. The peace conference called by Virginia failed to conclude with a compelling plan, and no conciliatory measures had passed through Congress. When Lincoln arrived in Washington in late February, both Adams and Sumner rushed to meet him. It is unclear what either man discussed in their separate meetings, but Adams no doubt wanted to urge more compromise measures, and Sumner doubtless hoped Lincoln would stick to the Republican line.

At the same time, Adams and Sumner were being buoyed by their allies to receive a nomination for the prestigious ambassadorship to England. Sumner's brother George was leading the effort to convince the Lincoln administration to offer the role to Charles. "If you don't accept the appointment, [we still] want the offer to be made," one of Charles Sumner's political friends explained to him. Otherwise, "our enemies will say that nothing was offered to the great apostle of Republicanism." At the time, receiving an offer for a presidential appointment significantly raised a politician's profile. Ultimately, Lincoln—per Seward's advice—offered the post to Adams. While Adams knew less about England than Sumner did, his conciliatory politics aligned better with Seward's and his father and grandfather were former English ambassadors. Adams eagerly accepted the nomination. While Sumner would likely have declined any potential offer, he was surely disappointed at not getting one.[24]

Sumner's disappointment in Lincoln was short-lived. The president's speech at the inauguration on March 4 thrilled him. Lincoln denied the right of states to secede and threatened war. Although he reaffirmed the Republican promise not to interfere with slavery *inside* states, he committed himself to the nonextension of slavery and declared that "the central idea of secession is the essence of anarchy." Despite appealing to "the better angels of our nature" and desiring "no bloodshed or violence," Lincoln's message was unmistakable: If the slave states refused to relent, there would be war. "In your hands, my dissatisfied fellow-countrymen, and not in mine, is the momentous issue of civil war," he said. He asked them bluntly, "Will you risk the commission of so fearful a mistake?"[25]

Shortly after the inauguration, Senate leadership announced that Sumner would head the Senate Foreign Relations Committee. The powerful post was an excellent consolation prize. He was put in charge of the committee that approved all treaties and performed oversight over Secretary Seward and all foreign ministers, including Adams. "Sumner's influence is very potential—more than every body's else put together," a Bay State lawmaker observed. With this post, he could wield real power for the first time in his political career.

In his new role, Sumner counseled Lincoln on a wide range of diplomatic appointments and other patronage posts. Though he took full advantage of the privilege, he also felt frustrated by it. "From early morning till late at night I see nothing but the contests of politicians & the incapacity of men in power," he lamented to a friend. "I long for my old place in Opposition, free, open, unembarrassed." Sumner always had a distaste for the politicking and backroom deals that were necessary for any politician. Although he was occasionally successful on the inside, he thrived best when he could use his thundering voice on the outside.[26]

New to Senate leadership, Sumner wanted to prove he was a serious leader. "No senator had ever saturated himself more thoroughly with the spirit and temper of the body," observed Henry Adams. In his first act as chair, Sumner banned liquor and tobacco from the committee room. He also appointed Benjamin Poore, a Democrat, as his committee clerk. Stephen Douglas, who served on the committee, was pleasantly surprised by Sumner's apparent willingness to work across the aisle. "I feared Sumner would send to Boston for a damned free n——r for a clerk," he jested with a sigh of relief. Sumner didn't mind appeasing Douglas, as Democrats had become politically weak. (Also, Douglas would die in June.) "I do not tremble at anything from our opponents, whoever they may be, but from our friends," Sumner explained to Governor Andrew.[27]

Seward was the friend whom Sumner feared most. The new secretary of state clung to the hope that he could end the crisis quickly. "Secession will all be done and over in three months," he overconfidently assured one journalist. Unbeknownst to Sumner, Seward advised Lincoln in an April 1 memo "to change the question before the Public from one upon Slavery . . . to one of Patriotism or Union." To transmogrify the crisis into a question of patriotism, Seward wanted to demand that Spain, France, Britain, and other countries provide "explanations," presumably about whether they supported the North or were neutral. If the explanations were unsatisfactory, Lincoln should "convene Congress and declare war against them." After the European powers were goaded into war, Seward hoped southerners would immediately feel a rush of patriotism, forget about secession, hoist the American flag, and help the North stave off foreign attacks. Lincoln dismissed Seward's bizarre and neurotic plan, which, in the words of one historian, "has puzzled historians ever since."[28]

Eager to avert war, Seward didn't stop there. Going behind Lincoln's back, he told the South that the White House would surrender Fort Sumter, a garrison off the coast of Charleston. It was the last federal fort standing in South Carolina, and Seward wanted to avoid a potential battle over its control. While most of the Cabinet was advising Lincoln to let the fort go, the president hadn't decided yet. As war fever grew in the South, Seward frantically decided to leak to Confederate leaders that the fort would be surrendered. To keep his actions covert, Seward asked intermediaries, including the Russian ambassador, to pass discreet messages to the South. Though he agreed to help, the ambassador found Seward to be shady.[29]

"There is not a foreign minister here who does not distrust our Sec[retary]," Sumner wrote to a friend. Given his familiarity with Europe and fluency in other languages, Sumner had long been friendly with foreign dignitaries in Washington. He knew that the Russian minister was just one of many who distrusted Seward. Weeks earlier, for example, Seward had shouted at the English and French ambassadors during a dinner party argument over a proposed Union blockade of Confederate ports, threatening war against their countries. "I think that no greater service could be rendered to the cause of peace," Ambassador Richard Lyons wrote to London, "than to make Mr. Sumner aware of the real perils to which Mr. Seward and the cabinet are exposing the country." Sumner resented Seward's neurotic diplomacy. "We are now reaping the fruits of *Seward-ism*," he growled.[30]

Much to Sumner's relief, Lincoln did not take Seward's foreign policy advice very seriously in the early days of the war. He also decided that

Seward and other Cabinet members were wrong to advise the surrender of Fort Sumter. The president told Sumner that he planned to publicly send a ship with food and provisions to the sea fort. Let the South attack it, Lincoln reasoned. Sumner was doubtless thrilled. "Then the war-power will be in motion, and with it great consequences," he explained to Lincoln. Sumner walked Lincoln through the wartime emancipation theory, which, most likely, Lincoln had not heard of before.[31]

On April 12, a day or two after Sumner's remarks to Lincoln, South Carolina started bombarding Fort Sumter. Prevented from accessing Lincoln's food shipment, the fort surrendered after thirty-six hours of attack. When he heard the news, Sumner rushed to the White House and told Lincoln that "I was with him now, heart and soul, and that under the war power the right had come to him to emancipate the slaves."

Sumner also wrote giddily to the abolitionist Joshua Giddings. "This generous & mighty uprising of the North seems to menace defeat to the rebels & the extinction of Slavery in blood," Sumner told him. "Never were the political heavens more bright or auspicious," Giddings eagerly replied. Samuel Howe decided that the war was a gift from God. "We have entered upon a struggle which ought not to be allowed to end until the Slave power is completely subjugated, & *emancipation made certain*," Howe advised Sumner.[32]

The bombardment of Fort Sumter outraged and electrified the North. "It seemed a purifying hurricane which swept away all sordid aims," a respected Civil War historian observed. "The flame of devotion to the principles of Washington, Hamilton, and Marshall was burning brightly again. Even the most timid took courage, even the most partisan became firm nationalists." Within days, Lincoln called for 75,000 troops. Northerners volunteered in droves. In Massachusetts, Governor Andrew's regiments prepared to depart to fight. "The cry now is for war," Frederick Douglass declared, "vigorous war, war to the bitter end."[33]

CHAPTER 15

SLAVERY IS THE VERY GOLIATH OF THE REBELLION

A N AMERICAN NAVAL OFFICER PAID CHARLES SUMNER A VISIT. DIS-
turbed by the actions at Fort Sumter, he wanted to seek the senator's
advice on what he should do. South Carolinian by birth and education, the
officer couldn't make up his mind about which side to serve. He was loyal
to the American flag, which he had sworn to protect, but his friends and
family were in South Carolina, which he called home. "What shall I do,
if my ship is ordered to the South to coerce my own people?" the officer
sheepishly asked Sumner.

"Read your commission, sir," Sumner replied. He was referring to the
official U.S. government certificate that the officer had received when
becoming a soldier. "But suppose my ship is ordered to Charleston?" The
officer pushed back. "Read your commission, sir," Sumner repeated. The
officer kept offering hypotheticals: "But suppose she ranges her broadsides against the city of my birth? But Senator, what if I am ordered to
fire on my father's plantation?" Sumner didn't think any of it mattered.
Frustrated by the officer's uncertainty, he barked at him, "Read your
commission, sir." In Sumner's mind, loyalty to the American flag had
no ifs, buts, or maybes. Reluctant as he was, the officer heeded Sumner's
advice and kept his post in the Union Navy.[1]

Tens of thousands of white Americans faced similar dilemmas in a war
that ripped apart brothers, friends, and even fathers and sons. In both
North and South, white men enlisted at rapid speed, far quicker than anyone expected in Washington or Richmond, which became the Confederate capital. Northerners and southerners alike believed it was a battle for
the soul of America, or of their own home state and for what it stood for.
Few Americans in either North or South realized how heart-wrenching

and bloody the war would become. Nearly everyone expected their region to achieve a quick victory. They were sorely wrong.

* * *

ON THE WAY home to Massachusetts in late April 1861, Sumner passed through Maryland. The border state had been rife with turmoil as secessionists street brawled with unionists about whose side Maryland should join. In Baltimore, Sumner was spotted by proslavery men on the street. A mob then formed outside his hotel, demanding that Sumner come out and face them. Hiding in a nondescript room, he spent the night nervously watching from the window as the rioters shouted his name.

Sneaking out in the early morning, Sumner passed by one of Governor Andrew's regiments on his way toward New York. He briefly spoke to the soldiers who were traveling southward. When they reached Baltimore, a mob attacked them. The rookie troops panicked and opened fire on the rioters. Twelve civilians and five soldiers were killed, and more than a hundred people were wounded. It was the first civilian bloodshed of the Civil War. If Sumner had taken a later train, he may have been among them. Speaking to another traveling Massachusetts regiment upon his arrival in New York, he compared the fallen soldiers to those who had died at Lexington, the first battle of the American Revolution, where Massachusetts men were also first to die. This war was "a continuation of the other," he declared. This was a war to fulfill the vision enshrined in the Declaration: a country where all men are created equal.[2]

Soon after Sumner's arrival in Boston, tragedy struck his own family. Caught up in the same patriotic war fever as everyone else, his brother George had volunteered to help supervise the loading of soldiers onto the trains. In a freak accident, he was hit by a train car and injured in the leg. Although the injury did not seem serious at first, it gradually resulted in paralysis of his entire right leg. Over the next two years, he would slowly decline. Charles spent some days with George and the rest of his family. "I cannot think of any invalid without turning to my brother George, whose case is the worst of all," he wrote to Samuel Howe sometime later, after meeting someone else who had been badly injured. "I am sad enough."

When Sumner wasn't home with George, he was busy entertaining the First Lady, Mary Todd Lincoln. Along with her cousin, she had come to Boston to visit her son Robert Lincoln, who was a student at Harvard.

"Everything [was] arranged for a charming reception at the Revere House [by Senator Charles Sumner], dining and drives, and we met many of the most distinguished men of Boston and Harvard," Mary's cousin fondly recalled. By being so hospitable, Sumner sparked a friendship with the First Lady that would blossom in the years to come. Yet his time in Boston with George, Mrs. Lincoln, and others did not very last long.[3]

On May 13, Queen Victoria issued a proclamation of neutrality in the U.S. Civil War. She infuriated the North by declining to support the Union. Meanwhile, the Confederacy rejoiced and started to cobble together a plan to gradually earn British support for their revolution. A panicked Secretary Seward decided that the North needed to take drastic action to retaliate against Britain. Discovering that Seward was crafting plans, Sumner grew anxious: Seward might rashly steer the North into a major foreign policy blunder. "He cannot talk five minutes without bringing in Mr. Seward, and always in bitter terms of denunciation," one Bostonian complained of Sumner. The senator went back to Washington.[4]

* * *

ARRIVING IN LATE May 1861, Sumner went straight to the White House. President Lincoln informed him that Seward had drafted a dispatch for Ambassador Charles Francis Adams Sr. to share with Great Britain. The dispatch threatened war if Britain had any dealings with Confederate ships. Sumner probably stated the obvious to Lincoln: England, a country he loved, was "the greatest and most powerful oligarchy in the history of the world." It would be a deadly mistake to provoke the empire on which the sun never set. Per Sumner's request, Lincoln toned down the letter and asked Seward to keep his dispatch to Adams absolutely confidential. Sumner had successfully averted a potential crisis. "I can positively assure you that only for Sumner . . . Seward would have sent a dispatch of such a character that a breach of relations would have been inevitable," leading British journalist William Howard Russell wrote in a private note.[5]

Soon afterward, Sumner stormed into Seward's office. He lectured his friend-now-foe about the stupidity of his diplomacy. Believing Seward to "understand foreign nations as little as he understood our crisis," Sumner pilloried Seward's belligerence and demanded that he treat Great Britain with caution and deference. "God damn them, I'll give them hell," Seward shouted back, kicking his desk. "I'm no more afraid of them than I am of Robert Toombs [the Confederate secretary of state]." Sumner rushed back to Lincoln to warn the president that the stress of war was turning Seward into an unhinged man. "You must watch him and overrule him," Sumner explained. From here on, Lincoln sought Sumner's advice before approving any major foreign policy decisions by Seward. Seward, for his part, resented Sumner's influence on the president. "There are too many secretaries of State in Washington," he grumbled.[6]

Having earned the president's trust in foreign policy, Sumner deftly used every opportunity to pressure Lincoln on domestic policy, too. During a one-on-one evening carriage ride, he told Lincoln that he agreed with the president's current silence on the slavery question. But he predicted that a moment would come when it would be opportune for Lincoln to invoke the war power and emancipate the slaves of rebel states. When the time came, he advised, Lincoln must be ready to strike. In the meantime, he assured the president that he would avoid criticizing the administration for its silence regarding slavery.

For the next two months, the Union Army practiced dutifully under Gen. Winfield Scott's direction. But public pressure demanded action, not more preparation. In late July, Scott ordered an advance on Confederate troops stationed at Manassas Junction, Virginia. The first Battle of Bull Run started well but ended in disaster when Union troops panicked and started scrambling back toward Washington. The ferocity of the under-resourced Confederate soldiers stunned the North. Nearly three thousand Union soldiers died.

Sumner went to Lincoln after the battle. "I told the Presdt that our defeat was the worst event & the best event in our history," he excitedly told Wendell Phillips. "The best, as it made the extinction of Slavery inevitable." The moment had come, he believed. Urging Lincoln to now issue an executive order for emancipating the slaves, Sumner was firmly rebuffed. Lincoln was adamant that it would be foolish to outrage the border states by adopting a radical policy that lacked support from most of the public. Nevertheless, in a sign that he was warming up to the idea, Lincoln argued about it with Sumner until midnight. "I have spoken to the Presdt & *a majority of the Cabinet* on the new power to be invoked," Sumner continued in his letter to Phillips. "I assure you there are men who do not hesitate. . . . Be hopeful. I am."[7]

Trusting Lincoln and other Cabinet members, Sumner still had ongoing friction with Seward. That summer, Robert Morris—the lawyer who had been organizing Black militiamen in Boston, to no avail—asked

Sumner for a favor. He wanted his son, banned from most American colleges on account of his skin color, to pursue higher education in France. Sumner asked Seward if, as secretary of state, he might issue the younger Morris a passport. "This will never do," Seward responded at first. "It won't do to acknowledge colored men as citizens." The once-firm Seward was caught in a political bind. On the one hand, he felt legally obliged to obey *Dred Scott*—the court ruling that said Blacks were not citizens—and worried about public reaction. On the other, he was personally sympathetic to Black rights. Eventually, Seward granted Morris the passport. But to Sumner's consternation, he did so on the condition that Morris's physical description be omitted from the paperwork.[8]

During the summer, Congress held an emergency session at Lincoln's request. The legislature entertained several bills—including two from Sumner—to authorize the government to seize rebel property, including slaves. The bills were inspired by the actions of enslaved people in Virginia who had escaped from their plantations and made it to the Union-held garrison of Fort Monroe. Offering their knowledge of the area and their readiness to work for wages, these men and women convinced Gen. Benjamin Butler to hire them. A lifelong Democrat who cared little about slavery, Butler was so convinced of the fugitives' usefulness that he invoked abolitionist legal ideas by calling them "enemy contraband" who could be lawfully confiscated by the Union Army. By the end of the session in August, Congress codified a process for Butler-like actions by army officers to assume jurisdiction over any enslaved people who liberated themselves by sneaking into Union lines.[9]

To Sumner's disappointment, Lincoln was displeased with the new law, now known as the First Confiscation Act. Believing that border staters and many northerners weren't ready for the bill, he reluctantly signed it after concluding that a veto would only draw more attention. Discreetly, Sumner helped finance abolitionist petitions and lectures in the capital to shift public opinion in favor of military emancipation. He also sent Lincoln a new book, *The Rejected Stone*, by a Virginia-born abolitionist who laid out the argument for wartime powers. "I wish you would visit Washington at once to press upon the Presdt. the duty of Emancipation, *in order to save the country*. . . . I am pained inexpressibly at the delay," Sumner told a friend. "Our Presdt is now dictator, Imperator," he told another. "How vain to have the power of a God if not to use it God-like."[10]

By late fall, Sumner, losing patience with Lincoln, rescinded his commitment to avoid the slavery issue in public. Weary of backroom deals and scheming politics, he returned to his greatest strength: galvanizing the public with charismatic, compelling oratory. At the state Republican convention in Worcester, Massachusetts, in October, Sumner made an hour-long speech about John Quincy Adams's wartime emancipation theory. Calling on the president to emancipate slaves by executive order, he also suggested that slaves be considered automatically free under the national Constitution in the lands the North conquered. After all, Republicans had always argued that slavery was unconstitutional in national territories.

Sumner hoped to pressure Lincoln into emancipating slaves immediately, and he suggested that the president could even compensate enslavers later, if he so desired. "If you are wise, prudent, economical, conservative, practical, you will strike quick and hard," he declared publicly. "Strike at the main-spring of the rebellion. Strike in the name of the Union," he pleaded. Notably, Sumner avoided appeals to morality in the speech, a stratagem to appeal to conservatives. "Emancipation is to be presented strictly as a measure of military necessity, rather than on grounds of philanthropy," he instructed an ally.[11]

At the Cooper Union in New York in November, Sumner again lectured on Adams's theory, while a group of Republicans and radical abolitionists sat behind his podium on the stage. This time, Sumner elevated his speech to a higher level of abstraction to propound on the historical meaning and ontology of the Civil War. Considering that it was only 1861, he spoke with stunning prescience. He described the war as "the third great epoch in the history of this Western Hemisphere; the first being its discovery by Christopher Columbus, and the second being the American Revolution." If Lincoln ended slavery with an "act of godlike justice," Sumner said, his name would be etched into history alongside those of Columbus and Washington. The government's current course was approximating what he prophetically called a "Proclamation of Emancipation." All Lincoln needed to do was deliver the final blow by issuing the proposed proclamation, Sumner believed, to end the war and earn eternal glory.

As far as Sumner was concerned, the war's origin was slavery. The South committed treason against the Constitution to protect slavery. Slavery powered its economy and gave white men the free time to fight battles. Slavery "digs trenches and builds hostile forts" and "pitches its white tents and stations its sentries." In fact, he proclaimed that the rebellion "is Slavery itself, incarnate, living, acting, raging, robbing, murdering, according to the essential law of its being." By striking at slavery, what he called "the ruling idea of this rebellion," Lincoln would win, and so would the North, and so would justice. "Slavery is the very Goliath of the rebellion," he declared. "But a stone from a simple sling will make the giant fall upon his face to the earth."[12]

* * *

PART OF SUMNER'S motivation for his rousing Cooper Union address was to reframe the Civil War in the eyes of the international community. He believed that a war to emancipate slaves would be politically popular overseas. He was aware from his travels how repulsive American slavery was to Europeans. While European empires still had slavery in their colonies, the institution was declining. Nearly all European countries had also abolished domestic slavery. For example, Austria had ended slavery in 1811; Great Britain and Canada, in 1834; and France, in 1848. By contrast, slavery in the United States was not only legal but expanding rapidly.

Seward firmly instructed American diplomats to insist that the war had nothing to do with slavery: it was purely a domestic rebellion that Lincoln planned to stamp out. Seward wanted the war to be framed in this manner to alleviate the concerns of border states and to leave room for a peaceful reunion with the South. But to foreign audiences, who knew little of domestic concerns, Seward's message made Lincoln seem to be the aggressor—a terrible messaging strategy, in Sumner's view. If the war concerned solely territorial integrity, Europeans would sympathize with the Confederacy. They would see a small band of states fighting a war for independence and national self-determination. Indeed, many Europeans found the South inspiring, analogizing their cause to the wave of anti-monarchy revolutions that swept Europe in 1848.

Capitalists, aristocrats, and monarchists in Europe were also excited by the war. It was a sight to behold: the radical, dangerous democratic experiment of America falling apart at last. In France, Napoléon III hoped to see the United States split into two weak nations, which would make his plan to invade Mexico easier. In Great Britain, the home secretary couldn't fathom what the war was all about. "The South fight for independence," he noted. "What do the North fight for, except to gratify passion or pride?"[13]

Pro-Confederate views were especially dominant in Great Britain. British elites had long been furious at northern tariffs that protected northern manufacturers at Britain's expense. They preferred the South, which exported to Great Britain three-quarters of the island nation's cotton. When Lincoln announced a blockade of southern ports at Seward's advice (a policy Sumner opposed, favoring an embargo), British aristocrats grew even angrier. Textile production was a key industry of their empire. Hoping to curry their favor, the Confederacy emphasized to Great Britain their deep economic ties. "Cotton is the tremendous lever by which we can work our destiny," Confederate vice president Alexander Stephens noted.[14]

"The upper and ruling class have some satisfaction . . . in your troubles," British statesman John Bright explained to Sumner. "Two nations on your northern continent . . . [are] more easy to deal with than one." Bright was an English radical who had met Sumner on his most recent European trip. The two had developed a strong friendship and political affinity. "If the war was for liberating the slave, we could see something worth fighting for," Bright explained. Another radical statesman, Richard Cobden, also wrote to Sumner. "We observe a mighty quarrel: on one side protectionists, on the other the slave owners. The protectionists say they do not seek to put down slavery. The slave-owners say they want Free Trade." Unless the North pursued emancipation, Cobden said his countrymen would support the South. Three-fourths of the House of Commons would gladly "vote for the dismemberment of the great republic," he warned. "I hardly know anybody, except our courageous friend Bright . . . that thinks you can put down the rebellion," Cobden informed Sumner.[15]

Fearing potential British intervention in favor of the South, Sumner hoped his speeches would help redefine the war around emancipation. That was a hard sell without Seward and Lincoln's support. "It is a war to prevent the foundation of a slave-holding Confederacy," he tried to persuade British abolitionist Harriet Martineau. But Martineau wrote back to say that most British sources "insist, loudly & persistently, that the war is not for the abolition of slavery." Leading British journalist William Howard Russell also dismissed Sumner's claim that the war would end slavery. "The pretence that this is an anti slavery war cannot be sustained for a moment & is sedulously disavowed by the Govt. itself," he observed. Admitting that "there would perhaps be an overwhelming sentiment of popular sympathy with the North in this conflict if they were fighting for freedom," Russell doubted that the North even cared about abolition.[16]

In late 1861, anti-American sentiment in Britain nearly spiraled into international war. On November 8, a Union Army officer abducted two Confederate diplomats who were headed for London on board the RMS

Trent, a British steamer. Lord Palmerston, the British prime minister, was furious. He decided it was time "to read a lesson to the United States which will not soon be forgotten." Informing Queen Victoria that the American "government is not guided by reasonable men," Palmerston predicted that "war was the probable result." He was not overreacting: even the German socialist revolutionary Friedrich Engels expected war between Britain and the U.S. North. "Have these Yankees then gone completely crazy to carry out the mad coup with the Confederate Commissioners?" he asked Karl Marx. "To take political prisoners by force, on a foreign ship, is the clearest *casus belli* there can be. The fellows must be sheer fools to land themselves in for a war with England."[17]

Under Palmerston's direction, the British Empire prepared to intervene in the Civil War. Palmerston sent an ultimatum to Lincoln to either give up the prisoners or expect a conflict. "We in England have ready a fleet surpassing in destructive force any naval armament the world ever saw . . . we have plenty of people who would be content to see this fleet turned against you," Cobden sternly warned Sumner. Cobden may have known that Palmerston had assembled more than ten thousand redcoats to sail to the British colony of Canada (with more to come). "The cry of war rings throughout the land," the *Toronto Globe* declared. A Cabinet war committee drafted plans for the Royal Navy to simultaneously blockade Maine, Boston, New Bedford, Newport, Long Island, New York, and the Delaware River. The British Cabinet hoped quick, decisive action would force the North and South to make peace and reopen the cotton trade.[18]

The American public had no clue about the war fever sweeping Great Britain, because British ships carrying mail and newspapers took at least ten days to cross the Atlantic. In the meantime, the North was jubilant at the news of the arrests of the diplomats. "We do not believe the American heart ever thrilled with more genuine delight," said the *New York Times*. The two Confederate abductees were Sumner's old enemies: former senators James Mason of Virginia and John Slidell of Louisiana. Mason had sponsored the Fugitive Slave Act in the Senate and had previously occupied Sumner's chairmanship of the Foreign Relations Committee. Slidell had jeered Sumner's caning. The two infamous politicians were reviled in the North; their capture signified a great Union victory.[19]

Sumner learned about the capture of his old colleagues as he was stepping off the train in Boston in early November. "They will have to be given up," he reportedly muttered to friends that evening. While Charles Sumner

declined to speak publicly about the matter, his brother George impru-
dently sent to the press a legal argument for keeping the men imprisoned.
Sumner distanced himself from his half-paralyzed brother's work, claiming implausibly that he hadn't seen it before it was published. He also
privately confessed to the victorious naval officer who captured the diplomats, Capt. Charles Wilkes, that he believed the arrests had been unwise.

The senator grew increasingly tense as he began receiving frantic letters from British friends pleading with him to stop a potential war before
it was too late. After returning to Washington in December, Sumner met
with Lincoln almost daily at the White House to sort out the trouble. Fortunately, his foreign policy rival was also getting nervous. Seward's macho
attitude toward Great Britain soured into frightful anxiety when he finally
registered that the British Empire was plotting a massive coastal attack
against the United States.[20]

On Christmas morning, Lincoln hosted an emergency Cabinet meeting
at the White House with Sumner as a guest. Like most Americans, most
Cabinet members had not heard the news from overseas. They were exuberant about Mason and Slidell's capture and believed their surrender would be
a sign of weakness. Seward and Sumner tried to prove to the Cabinet that
the British were hell-bent on war. Seward sternly advised their immediate
release to Great Britain; Sumner suggested that they propose to Great Britain a third-party arbitration on the matter. Both leaders struggled to get
their message across until an aide interrupted the meeting to inform Lincoln that France had just joined Great Britain in denouncing the capture as
a violation of international law. With rising apprehension, the Cabinet kept
deliberating for a couple of days while Sumner did his best to shut down jin-
goistic rhetoric in the Senate from politicians who demanded that Lincoln
not be a coward in the face of Great Britain. Reluctantly, Lincoln decided
that Seward was right about giving up the prisoners. Though Sumner preferred arbitration to Seward's proposal, he was still relieved.[21]

When he learned that the North had wised up, Palmerston called off the
war plans. "The case of the Trent is settled," Sumner triumphantly wrote to
Bright. A few weeks later, he delivered a Senate address that laid out why
international law had dictated Lincoln's decision. His speech set him apart
from many others, who had underestimated the British threat and were
angry at another example of Lincoln's perceived weakness. "Let the Rebels
go," Sumner said in defense of the White House. "Two wicked men, ungrateful to their country, are let loose with the brand of Cain upon their foreheads."

The speech strengthened Sumner's political hand as he positioned himself, rather than Seward, as the nation's most astute foreign policy thinker. "I heard Sumner's speech. It is the best thing for his popularity," Richard Dana wrote to Charles Francis Adams Sr. "It was the first opportunity he has had to speak without offending half the nation." Lincoln no doubt appreciated Sumner's public support; Seward probably didn't. Centrists were impressed that Sumner could act so reasonably. "I have considered Mr. Sumner a doctrinaire," one foreign diplomat confessed. "Henceforth I recognize him as a statesman."[22]

* * *

THE RESOLUTION OF "the Trent Affair" opened a new period in the Civil War. The affair even played a role in Lincoln's ongoing evolution on emancipation. In one of Sumner's first meetings with the president on the diplomatic crisis, he took the opportunity to lecture Lincoln on the administration's foreign policy follies. He argued that Lincoln's public silence on emancipation was undermining the Union's reputation with foreign nations. Lincoln was starting to agree. Early in 1862, he confessed to his minister to Germany that there was a strong foreign policy rationale to fight slavery directly. "I cannot imagine that any European power would dare to recognize and aid the Southern Confederacy if it becomes clear that the Confederacy stands for slavery and the Union for freedom," Lincoln admitted. The problem was that he doubted "whether public opinion at home was yet sufficiently prepared for it."

Still, Lincoln was optimistic on the issue. During one of his Trent Affair meetings with Sumner in December, he stated that he was going to eventually call for legislation to pay states to abolish slavery. It would be the first of several abolitionist steps Lincoln suggested he would take. "The only difference between you and me on this subject is a difference of a month or six weeks in time," he assured Sumner. Elated, Sumner confidentially passed along the good news to Wendell Phillips, informing him jubilantly that "the great end approaches." Perhaps too willing to trust Lincoln, he naïvely underestimated how long the president would take to develop an antislavery policy. Despite Sumner's begging him "to make Congress a New Year's present of your plan," Lincoln would wait several more months before acting. But Sumner was right to think the president's heart and mind were in the right place. Slavery's doom was only a matter of time.[23]

CHAPTER 16

LINCOLN'S BISHOP

ONE MORNING EARLY IN LINCOLN'S TERM (THE EXACT DATE IS, sadly, unknown), Charles Sumner barged into the White House and interrupted one of the president's meetings. He was exhausted by Lincoln's indecisiveness on emancipation. He probably reminded Lincoln that the country had almost bumbled into a war with Great Britain partly because the British saw no moral impulse in the Union's effort to stop the rebellion. He demanded a proclamation order immediately. "If you had done your duty earlier in the slavery matter," Sumner once lectured Lincoln, "you would not have this trouble on you. Now you have no friends, or the country has none, because it has no policy on slavery."

Lincoln had been in the middle of a conversation with John Forney, the secretary of the Senate, when Sumner disturbed him. For several minutes, Forney watched an irate Sumner berate the president with a stream of accusations about his poor decision-making abilities. "It is a mistake to say that Sumner was not a ready debater," Forney later said about the senator. "His logic was irresistible; for his cause was mighty. . . . He literally overran with information, and delighted to communicate it."

Lincoln quietly listened at first . . . until his patience with Sumner's long-winded tirade ran dry. Stretching out a long arm, the president started shouting at the senator to shut him up. "MR. SUMNER, I WILL NOT ISSUE A PROCLAMATION FREEING THE SLAVES NOW," Lincoln exclaimed. Sumner sprang to his feet. Without uttering another word, he stormed out of the room and slammed the door behind him. "Forney, what shall we do with that man?" Lincoln heaved. "I really can't answer that question, but it is best not to quarrel with him," Forney cautiously advised the president. "Quarrel!" Lincoln sighed. "Oh, no, that is the last thing I should think of doing."

After allowing passions to cool for a few hours, Lincoln reportedly paid Sumner a visit and invited him to join him and Forney for dinner. When Sumner arrived, Forney was stunned. "It was the happiest dinner that three men ever enjoyed," he remembered. He had no idea what Lincoln had said to calm Sumner down, but he said he "never saw Sumner in such high good spirits as he was that evening at dinner."[1]

Although Forney found the whole episode bizarre, heated fights between Sumner and Lincoln were quite common. These fights generally ended in warm mutual understanding. Lincoln oscillated between annoyance and appreciation for the dogmatic but experienced statesman; Sumner vacillated between condescension and deep respect for the folksy but brilliant politician. Their bewildering relationship became one of Washington's most important and consequential friendships during the Civil War.

* * *

THE PAIR STARTED off on strange footing. Lincoln apparently told a visitor at the Willard Hotel, where he stayed before his inauguration, about his first encounter with Sumner in February 1861. He loved matching backs with people to see who was taller, particularly with men like Sumner who, like him, were well above six feet. "You never put backs with Sumner, did you?" he asked his guest. "When he was in here, I asked him to measure with me, and do you know he made a little speech about it?" Lincoln's face glimmered. Unsurprisingly, Sumner didn't find the idea of matching backs to be funny. "He told me he thought this was a time for uniting our fronts and not our backs before the enemies of our country, or something like that," Lincoln told his guest. "I reckon the truth was, he was afraid to measure!" The president chuckled to himself. Getting serious, Lincoln went on to say, "he is a good piece of a man, though—Sumner—and a good man. I have never had much to do with bishops down where we live; but, do you know, Sumner is just my idea of a bishop."[2]

The bishop of the Senate left that first encounter with Lincoln baffled. He was "greatly amazed and puzzled by what he saw and heard," recalled his friend Carl Schurz, a German American diplomat and later a U.S. senator. "Lincoln was utterly unlike to Sumner's ideal of a statesman." Sumner had met many of the world's great leaders during three European tours. Much like him, they tended to be classically educated, deadly serious, fluent in several languages, and dressed to the nines. Lincoln was none of those things. He was a lanky self-made man from Kentucky who had never traveled abroad. Apart from a habitual taste for wearing top hats in public, he cared little about his dress. He liked to make crude jokes and tell quaint stories, and he rarely exhibited the sort of gravitas Sumner would have expected of a president.

It didn't help that Lincoln's most congenial trait was humor. "Poor Sumner can't take a joke, of any kind," Richard Henry Dana once wrote in his diary. He never understood so-called Lincolnisms: witty stories that Lincoln would tell to make his points. Sometimes, he would ask friends like Schurz to explain Lincoln's parables to him. He was especially confused by Lincoln's sarcasm. "If one told Charles Sumner that the moon was made of green cheese, he would controvert the alleged fact in all sincerity, and give good reasons why it could not be so," Oliver Wendell Holmes Sr. once quipped. He couldn't fathom why a statesman would ever resort to sarcasm. "Did you ever see a joke in one of my speeches?" Sumner supposedly once asked a young man. "Of course you never did. You might as well look for a joke in the book of Revelations."

Despite his own lack of humor, Sumner came to admire Lincoln. "Now and then," according to Schurz, Sumner noticed in Lincoln "flashes of thought and bursts of illuminating expression" that struck him as extraordinary. He never doubted that Lincoln "was a deeply convinced and faithful anti-slavery man," despite what he saw as "the slow working of Mr. Lincoln's mind and his deplorable hesitancy." Skeptical of Seward, Adams, and other antislavery men, he had a strange faith in Lincoln: a man most other abolitionists distrusted. His private conversations with the president assured him he was on the right track, even if he was slow to walk it. "I know Mr. Lincoln," Schurz once said to Sumner, who concurred with his friend's analysis. "I am sure his administration will very favorably disappoint those who look upon him as a 'conservative' man. His impulses are in the right direction, and I think he has courage enough to follow them."[3]

Sumner saw greatness in Lincoln, greatness that Lincoln did not see in himself. As early as fall 1861, Sumner foretold that Lincoln would surpass "the fame of the Discoverer and the fame of the Liberator—of Columbus and of Washington," if he signed an emancipation order. Ironically, Lincoln never wanted to be seen as a hero for the millions of enchained people. "What I do about Slavery and the colored race, I do because I believe it helps to save this Union," he insisted. "If I could save the Union without freeing any slave, I would do it." Still, Sumner had faith. In letter after letter, he justified Lincoln's decisions by saying he was "honest and slow" or "honest but inexperienced." He knew Lincoln's hatred of slavery far exceeded that of the general northern public. It was Sumner's belief in Lincoln that made him pester the president so much.[4]

Lincoln admired Sumner's penchant for giving pedantic but honest advice. He also genuinely relished Sumner's fellowship. He invited him to the White House many times to discuss emancipation, debating with him occasionally until past midnight. "Their cast of mind was very different, but their alliance, founded on mutual respect, became finally true friendship," observed one French journalist who saw them interact. "While he believed the senator to be a somewhat impractical statesman," one Union Army officer wrote, Lincoln knew that Sumner was "patriotic, sincere, and true; faithful in his friendships, and unassailable by corruption." In the words of one Lincoln biographer, Sumner was "his warmest friendship among the senators. . . . Strange as it seems, these two very different men also enjoyed each other's company."

There was a strategic calculus to Lincoln's friendliness with Sumner, too. By keeping him close, Lincoln made a friend out of the Senate's most radical statesman. He avoided problems with Sumner that arose with many other Republicans—many of whom even tried to unseat Lincoln a few years later, when he ran for a second term. "Sumner thinks he runs me," Lincoln once said with a twinkle in his eye. That was exactly what he wanted Sumner to think. The president consulted with Sumner twice a week or more and sometimes would send for him twice in a single day—just to make him feel important. "Lincoln was the only man living who ever managed Charles Sumner or could use him for his purpose," one Illinois congressman cynically quipped. A different Illinois congressman believed Lincoln genuinely needed Sumner. "Mr. Sumner had become the most sincere and confidential adviser of Mr. Lincoln," he said.[5]

* * *

BY FEBRUARY 1862, Sumner had solidified his relationship with another White House occupant—Mary Todd Lincoln. The First Lady struggled with her position. Unlike the past several First Ladies, she tried to play an active part in Washington society. But northern politicians resented her, a Kentucky-born belle, and made fun of her southern mannerisms and way of speaking. It didn't help that her brothers in Kentucky had joined the

Confederate Army or that the northern press delighted in mocking her supposedly profligate spending habits.

Things grew worse for Mary when two of their sons contracted tuberculosis. While the youngest son recovered, eleven-year-old Willie did not. He died on February 20. The parents were devastated by the loss of Willie, who had lit up the White House with his rambunctious antics in its dark days of wartime stress. Mary spent weeks in bed so distraught that a nurse had to look after her. (Aside from this, she had long struggled with her mental health, possibly suffering from bipolar disorder.) Four days into his wife's grief, the president sent Sumner a note. "Mrs. L needs your help," he scribbled on a small, black-bordered card. "Can you come?"[6]

Sumner spent some weeks consoling Mary Lincoln. He may have shared his own griefs with her. His brother George had been gradually deteriorating from his railroad accident. A few months earlier, his best friend Henry Longfellow had lost his beloved wife, Fanny—whom Sumner also called a friend—when her dress caught fire and set her ablaze. Back in his twenties, Sumner fell into a depression after his favorite sister died. (Coincidentally, her name was Mary.) She died of tuberculosis, the same terrible affliction that hit Willie.

Mary Lincoln came to regard Sumner as her closest male confidant in Washington. "I have no finer friend than him, or one, I like any better," she once said. Frequently, Sumner joined Mary at the opera or theater. They would have a "very gay little time," often without Lincoln. "I was pleased, knowing he visited no other lady," Mary reflected. She felt that Sumner, unlike other men in Washington, took her seriously. "That cold & haughty-looking man to the world would insist upon my telling him all the news," she once beamed. "I learned to converse with him with more freedom and *confidence* than any of my other friends." They sent each other flowers, exchanged books, wrote each other notes in French, and talked about poetry. "For the last eight years, Sumner has been as a brother to me," she once wrote in an undated letter.[7]

Long after her husband's death, Mary recounted how she, her husband, and Sumner formed a trio. "We would have such frequent & delightful conversations & often late in the evening. My darling husband would join & they would laugh together, like two schoolboys," she remembered. She once claimed that "Mr. Sumner & Mr. Lincoln were great chums after they became acquainted with one and other." Mary's reports seem stretched; it is hard to see the uptight Sumner and the affable Lincoln frolicking like two schoolboys. But there must have been some truth to Mary's recollection. Sumner often described Lincoln as his "personal friend," and he genuinely enjoyed Mary's company. "This is the first administration in which I have ever felt disposed to visit the house," he once said. Mary said Sumner was a "habitue of the White House, both the rooms of the President and my own reception-room. He was always sure of a heartfelt welcome."[8]

Naturally, Sumner couldn't help but try to evangelize Mary for the abolitionist cause. Raised on a plantation, Mary was intimately familiar with slavery. She disliked it, but she did not think much about its end until after becoming First Lady. Sumner often discussed emancipation with her. She also learned more about the horrors of slavery from her Black dressmaker, Elizabeth Keckley. Keckley recalled that Sumner was a "a gentleman that Mrs. Lincoln very much admired." Probably with his encouragement, Mary befriended the abolitionist Jane Grey Swisshelm, who further influenced her. By 1864, Mary considered herself to be a fierce abolitionist and often pushed her husband to do more for the enslaved and the newly freed. "Sumner says he wishes my husband was as ardent an abolitionist as I am," she once boasted.[9]

* * *

WHILE LINCOLN WAS grieving over his son Willie's illness and death, Sumner refrained from pressing him on emancipation. In the meantime, he was reflecting on the next issue: when slavery finally ended, as he hoped it would, what would happen to Black freedpeople? How would they be integrated into the social, political, and economic landscape of a postwar South? "Assuming that our military success is complete, and that the rebel armies are scattered," he asked his friend Francis Lieber, "what next? Unless I am mistaken, the most difficult thing of all—namely, the re-organization."[10]

The first experiment in "re-organization" began in November 1861, when the U.S. Navy took control of the Sea Islands, a group of islands and tidal barriers off the coast of South Carolina. As soon as Union troops reached shore, white southerners fled to the mainland while nearly ten thousand enslaved people remained on the islands' vast cotton plantations. Salmon Chase, now the secretary of the treasury, took charge. He affirmed that these ten thousand enslaved men and women, "confiscated" by the Union Army, were free. At the same time, he wanted the new freedpeople to keep picking cotton, a lucrative crop that would raise badly needed revenue for the cash-strapped government. Chase thus sent an army officer to implement a program of educating the Black freedpeople and paying them to pick cotton.[11]

Chase asked an adviser to monitor the situation: Edward Pierce, a Sumner protégé. Pierce had first met Sumner when he was fifteen, sparking a lifelong admiration. Becoming a Harvard-trained attorney and loyal Republican, he had once served as Chase's private secretary, a job he landed with Sumner's help. (After Sumner's death, he would spend twenty years writing a famous four-volume biography of him.)[12]

Chase wanted Pierce's help in the Sea Islands because of his work during the earlier days of the war. Back in the summer of 1861, Pierce had served under General Butler at Fort Monroe and had supervised the provision of food, shelter, and work for the Black refugees who escaped there. Afterward, he made the public case for Black citizenship based on what he had seen at Fort Monroe. Writing for *The Atlantic Monthly*, he authored a widely read piece that argued that every Black man he met at the fort "had vindicated beyond all future question, for himself, his wife, and their issue, a title to American citizenship, and become heir to all the immunities of Magna Charta, the Declaration of Independence, and the Constitution of the United States."[13]

Arriving in the Sea Islands in mid-January 1862, Pierce sent reports back to Washington to try to influence public opinion about the possibility of Black freedpeople living dignified and independent lives. "These people are naturally religious and simplehearted," he explained. After visiting many plantations and interviewing ex-slaves, Pierce concluded that they had all "the knowledge and experience requisite" to plant their own cotton and food crops. While he advised that white superintendents be appointed to initially oversee the plantation lands, Pierce strongly rejected a proposal to lease the land to white speculators in the North. He suggested instead that Black freedpeople eventually become farmers of their own land. "Here was a chance to establish an agrarian democracy in the South," the historian W. E. B. Du Bois would later declare, referring to Pierce's work in the Sea Islands.

At the time, few white men in Washington believed that Black ex-slaves could work the land on their own. White southerners had claimed for decades that Black people were lazy, dull, and incapable of self-sufficiency. Although most northern whites were opposed to slavery, many harbored deep doubts about the ability of Black people to live independently. "It is a sad fact that most Northerners are afflicted by intense colorphobia," one abolitionist despaired. Pierce's reports were intended to dispel those prejudices. In the tone of a missionary, he urged northerners to embrace a humanitarian experiment to prepare ex-slaves for a life of freedom. They could become "partially in this generation, and fully in the next, a happy, industrious, law-abiding, free and Christian people," he assured, "if we have but the courage and patience to accept it."[14]

While preparing his report, Pierce wrote candid notes to Sumner about his experience. Though tinged with some racial prejudice before his trip, Pierce was astonished at the dignity and perseverance of the Black freedpeople in the Sea Islands. "If white men only did as well under such adverse circumstances, they could be regarded as prodigies," he told Sumner. Sumner responded to say he was "proud" of his mentee's "excellent work."

Pierce had discovered what Sumner knew all along: if given the opportunity, Black Americans would thrive. Growing up, Sumner had seen firsthand a vibrant, thriving African American community that flourished despite immense systemic disadvantages. He was convinced that Black freedpeople in the South could similarly thrive despite the legacy of slavery and the scourge of racism. After the war, he hoped, the Union would "strike down the leaders of the Rebellion and lift up the slaves." In doing so, it could make the southern states more just and equitable for Black freedpeople, empowering them to chart the future of the American South.[15]

* * *

To reorganize the South, the Union would need a legal justification. For most of the nineteenth century, American lawyers believed the national government had extremely limited powers. All other powers were reserved to the states. Sumner feared that Lincoln and other centrists were wedded to this prewar legal thinking. More than anything, he worried that Lincoln would stop Congress from imposing radical changes in the southern states after the war. Doing so would waste a watershed moment. "God in his beneficence offers to nations, as to individuals, opportunity, *opportunity*, OPPORTUNITY," Sumner believed. "Never before in history has he offered such as is ours here." To make his case, he needed to show that Congress had sweeping legal powers.[16]

On February 11, 1862, Sumner spelled out his legal theory in a series of

Senate resolutions that argued that state governments that claimed to have seceded had ceased to exist. He contrasted his position with that of centrists like Lincoln, who thought secession was illegal and therefore impossible. "In point of law, no man can commit suicide," he later explained, given that suicide was illegal. But "in point of fact, men do." Similarly, he noted that southern state governments had factually seceded, even if secession was theoretically illegal. According to Sumner, they were guilty of felo-de-se, a Latin legal term for the felony of suicide.[17]

Sumner argued that although state *governments* could commit suicide, state *land* still belonged to the United States. The South had no power under the Constitution to break America's indestructible union. Despite rebellious pretension, the South was still American land, populated by American people, subject to the American rule of law. In the absence of valid state governments, Sumner said, state land had effectively become national territory, subject to national jurisdiction. The upshot of Sumner's theory was that under the Constitution, territories are governed by Congress. Limited only by the Bill of Rights, Congress has plenary power to do nearly anything in the territories—including deciding if, when, and under what terms a territory became a state.

Sumner's territorialization theory, sometimes dubbed the "state suicide theory," was creative, elaborate, and metaphysical. The theory also had a clear, unspoken agenda. If his theory were adopted, Sumner reasoned, Congress would have legal authority to rewrite the state constitutions of the South. Although he didn't say it openly (yet), he wanted to create new states in the South, along the same lines as the old ones, with new constitutions premised on racial equality. Congress could then grant Black men the right to vote, require the permanent abolition of slavery, and guarantee civil and social rights, among other things.

When Sumner finished explaining his resolutions, he expected a warm reception. Although his proposal was more elaborate than any other congressional reconstruction plan to date, some House members—such as John Bingham and James Ashley—had already said that the South had reverted to territories. Treasury secretary Salmon Chase agreed with them, saying that the rebelling states had "lapsed into the condition of a Territory with which we could do what we pleased." One House member, Thaddeus Stevens, went even farther, claiming that the South was *enemy* territory that could be treated under military law as *conquered* land.[18]

Despite the views of the House, the wartime Senate wanted nothing to do with Sumner's theory. Aware that anything coming from him would get more public attention than the actions under way in the House, Republican senators blasted his plan as a bizarre, spun-up theory. Senators worried that his remarks would provoke outcries from loyal white southerners who might be critical allies in any potential peace process. Ironically, Republicans would more or less adopt Sumner's plan by 1866, during a period now known as Congressional (or Radical) Reconstruction. Some historians have even described Sumner's set of resolutions as the first comprehensive legal theory to justify that period. But when Sumner first proposed it, Republican senators thought his resolutions were ill-timed: it was early 1862, and the war appeared far from over.

Careful not to overplay his hand, Sumner avoided further discussion about "state suicide" for the time being. Nevertheless, he kept pushing for his vision of a free, multiracial democracy in the months ahead.[19]

* * *

EARLY IN THE morning on March 6, 1862, Lincoln's two secretaries, John Nicolay and John Hay, went to Sumner's house and woke him up. They asked him to come to the White House after breakfast. Lincoln had been mulling over emancipation ever since Willie's death. Having consulted his Cabinet one day earlier, he decided to tell Congress that "the United States ought to co-operate with any state which may adopt gradual abolishment of slavery." Any state that participated would get congressional money to compensate enslavers.

"I want to read you my message. I want to know how you like it," Lincoln told Sumner upon his arrival. Sumner was thrilled. While he believed enslavers should morally get no compensation, he still thought "an empty treasury" was better than "a single slave." When Lincoln asked for feedback, Sumner said he had none. With no awareness of how patronizing he sounded, he replied, "There is to every man an idiosyncrasy. This is so clearly an aboriginal, autochthonous style of its own that I will not suggest an alteration."

After looking at the message more closely, though, Sumner said he wanted Lincoln to change one troubling sentence. Lincoln had planned to say that southern states that surrendered could "revive loyal state governments and again send Senators and Representatives to Congress . . . with no institutions changed." Sumner balked, probably arguing that the states had reverted to territories that Congress could govern. While Lincoln disagreed, he offered to save that question for another day. "Don't trouble yourself, I will strike it all out," he promised. Sumner was overjoyed. He praised the president and pledged not to make any public remarks on the plan, presumably to shield Lincoln from criticism by anyone who would accuse the president of listening to extremists like Sumner.[20]

After dismissing Sumner, Lincoln sent the plan to Congress to be read on the floor. It was widely celebrated. Conservatives preferred it to immediate emancipation; Sumner's allies were stunned that Lincoln had bothered to do anything at all. Republican centrists saw the plan as a brilliant maneuver—a chance to strike at slavery without alarming white northerners and to strike a deal with proslavery border states that remained in the Union. It was "perhaps the most important document ever addressed to Congress," said the *New York Tribune*. "We could hardly believe the news," declared the *Weekly Anglo-African*. "Who could have prophesized this three months ago?" Sumner attributed Lincoln's change of heart to his own skills of persuasion. "I had been the only Senator consulted from the beginning to the end," he later boasted.

Though Sumner's private consultations with Lincoln played a role in his changing policy, the senator's strategic maneuvering of public opinion arguably had an even larger impact. For the past several months, Sumner had been assisting a network of controversial New England abolitionists in their influence campaign targeted at the Republican mainstream. He had also been speaking out on his own. By shifting public opinion toward abolition, he gave Lincoln the necessary political cover to make this consequential decision.

Widespread public approval of the plan confirmed to Republicans in Congress that the North was starting to embrace antislavery ideals. Less than two weeks after Lincoln's announcement, the abolitionist Wendell Phillips visited Congress on Sumner's invitation. Republican senators were eager to meet him. "They crowded around me still more numerous," Phillips told his wife with shock. "A year ago, Phillips would have been sacrificed to the Devil of Slavery anywhere on Pennsylvania Avenue," wrote an astonished reporter for the *New York Tribune*. "Never has there been a time when Abolitionists were as much respected," another writer observed. Phillips was hosted at a dinner party by the Speaker of the House, met the president, and was invited to give lectures at the

Smithsonian. "The golden hour of the clock of the century has struck," he cried out in one lecture to an audience that included many senior politicians. "Seize the golden moment!"[21]

* * *

BY THIS TIME, many Republicans started openly calling themselves "Radicals." Once a term of derision that referred to opponents of the Fugitive Slave Act, the term was slowly embraced by antislavery politicians over the course of the 1850s. Now a large, informal faction of the Republican Party had adopted the label. Contrasting themselves with their more centrist colleagues, the Radical Republicans wanted fierce legislation to do what Wendell Phillips expected them to do: seize the golden moment, abolish slavery, and reconstruct the republic.

By the summer of 1862, the Radicals were starting to get their way in Congress. They helped secure the passage of the Second Confiscation Act, which guaranteed permanent freedom for any Black runaways who found refuge within the lines of the Union Army. Another act opened the door for the enlisting of Black soldiers, authorizing Lincoln to decide if, and when, to start recruiting them. And under the stewardship of Sumner's Radical Senate colleague Henry Wilson, Congress abolished slavery in all national territories and in the nation's capital.

When the D.C. emancipation bill reached his desk, Lincoln hesitated over whether to sign it. Sumner stormed into the White House to demand his signature. "I cannot see how you dare trust yourself to sleep tonight," he told Lincoln. "Supposed you should die, tonight, do you think your spirit could look back upon this great act of justice unperformed, and feel that Abraham Lincoln had done his duty?" Reminding Lincoln of his humble origins and his duty to voters, Sumner warned the president that he was "the largest slave-holder in this country" until he freed "the three thousand slaves of the District." On the following morning, April 16, Lincoln signed the bill. The act liberated all enslaved people in the District of Columbia and compensated their enslavers for the loss of so-called property. It was the first national statute to free slaves in American history.[22]

"I trust I am not dreaming, but the events taking place seem like a dream," Frederick Douglass wrote to Sumner afterward. Douglass was jubilant and stunned at how quickly things were moving. Although Sumner had played little role in the passage of these antislavery bills, Douglass believed the credit belonged to him. "To you, more than to any other

American Statesman, belongs the honor of this great triumph," he wrote. He said he rejoiced not only for his "freed brothers" but for Sumner himself. "You have lived to strike down in Washington the power—that lifted the bludgeon against your own free voice," Douglass observed. "There is, or ought to be, a head to every body. Whether you will or not, the slaveholder and the slave look to you as the best embodiment of the Antislavery idea now in the counsels of the nation."[23]

Sumner's written reply to Douglass has not survived. But he expressed delight about the letter to C. Edwards Lester, an abolitionist who was in a meeting with Sumner when he received Douglass's note. (Lester later wrote a little-known biography of Sumner.) With his face beaming, "his eyes swam in the luxury of gratitude," Lester recalled, Sumner rose and exclaimed with triumph. "Thank God we have such opportunities to do good!" he cried out. "Where on earth will you find hearts that so readily melt with gratitude, as in the negro breast?"

For all his adult life, Sumner enjoyed words of praise. He relished receiving letters that flattered him, particularly from the marginalized, and he often showed off these letters to friends. His correspondents, for their part, took care to stroke his ego when they wrote to him. There was a dose of narcissism to his love for praise. But there was also something profound about Sumner, a powerful white senator, forging deep ties of mutual affection with and desiring the applause of radical Black reformers like Douglass.[24]

Egged on by his admirers, Sumner pressed Lincoln on emancipation, often while joining him on his daily rides to and from Soldiers' Home, a summer cottage the Lincoln family enjoyed in the northern part of Washington, D.C. Over the summer, Sumner grew increasingly frustrated with Lincoln and complained about having to constantly be "screwing Old Abe up to the sticking point." On the Fourth of July, Sumner visited the president twice to urge him to issue a forceful military emancipation order that would be a "reconsecration of the day."

Sumner then took his argument even farther. "You need more men, not only at the North, but at the South, in the rear of the Rebels: you need the slaves," he told Lincoln. He believed that if the North recruited ex-slaves as soldiers, the Civil War could be ended. Lincoln retorted that he would do it at once if he didn't fear that "half the officers would fling down their arms and three more States would rise." While Sumner kept pushing, Lincoln demurred. "It would do no good to go ahead any faster

than the country would follow," he once told a group of Sumner's abolitionist allies. "I think Sumner and the rest of you would upset our apple-
cart altogether, if you had your way. . . . We must wait until every other
means has been exhausted."[25]

The truth was that every other means *was* being exhausted. Lincoln's
voluntary compensation plan, which Sumner heartily welcomed, wasn't
working. Not one border state took up Lincoln's offer despite his repeated
pleadings—suggesting that southern states would decline gradual emancipation after the war, too. The First and Second Confiscation Acts, which
liberated enslaved people who escaped to Union Army camps, didn't reach
enough people, either. The Confederate economy and military were still
powered by slave labor. And the Union Army desperately needed more
troops. Aware of these problems, Lincoln privately weighed whether to
finally issue an emancipation order—but he wasn't ready to commit yet.

Tired of the president's indecision, several Union Army officers started
taking the matter into their own hands. Gen. David Hunter, for example,
announced a proclamation to emancipate all slaves in Florida, Georgia, and
South Carolina under martial law (even though he lacked de facto control
over most of the land). Hunter also began recruiting Black troops in the
Sea Islands. "The experiment of arming the blacks, so far as I have made
it, has been a complete and marvellous success," Hunter publicly declared.
"They are sober, docile, attentive, and enthusiastic; displaying great natural capacities for acquiring the duties of the soldier. They are eager, beyond
all things, to take the field and be led into action."[26]

When news hit the rest of the country about the activities of Hunter and
others, Lincoln was upset. He had not yet made up his own mind about
whether to enlist Black soldiers. He thought white northerners would be
terrified about the prospect of armed Black men. Even Sumner, recognizing this fear, declined to publicly call for Black enlistment until after
gaining public support for emancipation. Lincoln worried about Union
soldiers refusing to fight side by side with them. Most significantly, he saw
decisions like these as acts of direct insubordination. "No commanding
general shall do such a thing," Lincoln reprimanded, "upon *my* responsibility, without consulting me." The president overturned Hunter's order.[27]

Despite his doubts over enlistment, Lincoln was warming up to emancipation. In late July 1862, he told his Cabinet that he had finally decided to
issue a general order. Seward urged him to wait until a major Union Army

In his thirties, Charles Sumner was one of Boston's most eligible bachelors, known for his dashing looks and promising career. Yet he did not marry for many years. This drawing includes an autograph: "Ever yours, Charles Sumner." He was not known for good handwriting.

Samuel Howe, a charismatic social reformer, loved Sumner dearly. Even after marrying Julia Ward, he was so close to Sumner that she joked that "Sumner ought to have been a woman."

As a pioneering twenty-six-year-old Black attorney, Robert Morris joined Sumner on the first interracial legal team in U.S. history. Together, they tried to integrate Boston schools and crafted the legal arguments that Thurgood Marshall and the NAACP later reused in *Brown v. Board of Education* (1954).

Born into slavery, Mary Williams had a white complexion, unlike her brother, Oscar. Sumner arranged for daguerreotypes of the children to be exhibited across New England. They were among the first photographs to ever be used for a political cause.

A South Carolina congressman and enslaver, Preston Brooks was outraged by "The Crime Against Kansas," a provocative antislavery speech by Sumner. On May 22, 1856, he beat Sumner nearly to death with a gutta percha cane on the Senate floor. He then advocated for the South to secede and create a proslavery confederacy.

The caning—perhaps the most jarring act of congressional violence in history— left Sumner soaking in a pool of his own blood. This depiction accentuates the architectural features of the crime scene: the Old Senate Chamber, a majestic hall that can still be visited on tours to the United States Capitol.

At the start of the Civil War, Sumner told President Lincoln to emancipate southern slaves by executive proclamation. On January 1, 1863, Lincoln issued the proclamation, describing emancipation as "an act of justice" and invoking "the gracious favor of Almighty God"—two key phrases that Sumner advised him to write.

Emancipation Petition.

To the Senate and House of Representatives of the United States in Congress assembled :

The undersigned, citizens of Racine County, Wisconsin, believing Slavery the great cause of the present rebellion, and an institution fatal to the life of Republican government, earnestly pray your honorable bodies to immediately abolish it throughout the United States; and to adopt measures for so amending the Constitution as forever to prohibit its existence in any portion of our common country.

MEN'S NAMES.	WOMEN'S NAMES.
Samuel Baumann Sr	Elizabeth Baumann
Elizabeth	
Horace Knapp	Mrs. Lucretia Knapp.
George Bucher	Mrs. Mary Bucher.
Caspar Egli	Mrs. F. Egli
Robert Bertholz	Mrs. H. Bertholz
Ernest Albrecht	Mrs. C. Albrecht.
F. Hubacheck	Marion Zillmann
C. G. Riftmann	Luly Maury.
Fr. Frahm	Augatha Maier
Fr. Florine	A. C. Brackwait,
L. Wolke.	Mrs. A. E. Peterson.

The Women's National Loyal League, led by Susan B. Anthony and Elizabeth Cady Stanton, gathered more than 400,000 signatures in favor of abolition. The League encouraged men and women to compete for signatures and then submitted the petition rolls to Sumner, who introduced them on the Senate floor during the Thirteenth Amendment debates of 1864.

Even into his fifties and sixties, Sumner was one of the most visually striking figures in the Senate. He had an aristocratic sense of fashion, commonly wore an eyeglass, and sometimes carried a cane because he had difficulty walking ever since the caning in 1856.

Desperate for love and belonging, Sumner married Alice Mason Hooper, a beautiful young widow, sometime in 1866. Their marriage fell apart only months after it took place. This photograph of Alice, one of the few to exist, appears to have been taken much later in her life.

In 1868, Sumner moved into a house on Lafayette Square, which he cluttered with his vast collection of paintings, photographs, books, and papers. This illustration depicts Sumner in his second-floor study.

Excecution in the U.S. Senate.

Grant's Senate allies—known as "Stalwarts"—removed Sumner from the chairmanship of the Foreign Relations Committee in March 1871. After his ousting, his friend Senator Carl Schurz delivered a speech lambasting the Stalwarts. The Austrian American satirist Joseph Keppler published this political cartoon of Sumner, Grant, Schurz, and two Stalwart senators.

Sumner asked John Mercer Langston, a renowned Black lawyer, to write the first draft of the Civil Rights Bill, which called for integrating hotels, restaurants, schools, colleges, churches, buses, and railroads. Sadly, most historians have overlooked Langston's role in crafting this bill—the blueprint of modern civil rights law.

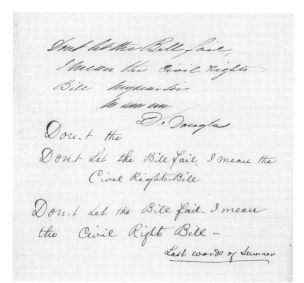

On his deathbed, Sumner pleaded with his visitors—including Frederick Douglass—to take care of the Civil Rights Bill. Douglass wrote these words, which he recalled Sumner saying, on this notecard: "Don't let the Bill fail. I mean the Civil Rights Bill."

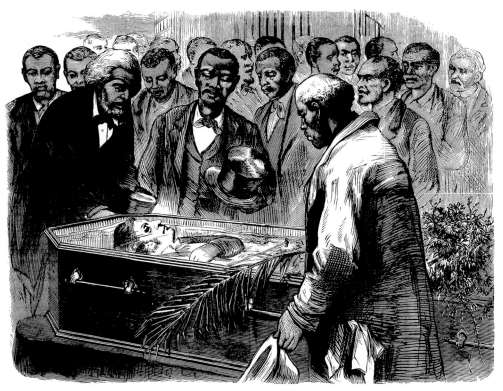

After Sumner's death on March 11, 1874, more than 50,000 people attended his memorial events. This drawing depicts Black men paying their last respects to Sumner as he lay in state at the United States Capitol. The two men above Sumner's head appear to be Frederick Douglass and Alexander Augusta.

The Black entrepreneur Peter Downing laid a floral shield on Sumner's casket as it lay in the Massachusetts State House. With blue violets, he inscribed Sumner's dying plea: "DO NOT LET THE CIVIL RIGHTS BILL FAIL." A drawing of the casket was published by *Harper's Weekly*.

The Republic of Haiti has long revered Sumner's memory. In 1999, the Haitian Embassy in Washington held an exhibition titled "Charles Sumner and the Struggle for Haiti's Diplomatic Recognition." The exhibit included this painting, by Haitian artist Garry Rochebrun, of Avenue Charles Sumner—a large boulevard in Port-au-Prince.

victory to make the announcement, so that it would appear to come from a position of strength rather than weakness. When Sumner found out about Seward's advice, he again pushed the president not to wait. "I protested against the delay, & wished it to be forth—the sooner the better—without any reference to our military condition," he recalled. Ignoring Sumner, Lincoln chose to draft an order and leave it in his desk until the right moment.[28]

* * *

LINCOLN HESITATED ABOUT emancipation partly because he didn't know what freedom should look like. At the time, he didn't share Sumner's vision for a multiracial democracy after the war. He found it impossible to imagine whites and Blacks living together as equals in the South. To solve this conundrum, he entertained the idea of getting rid of Black people. He sent multiple advisers to Central America to explore the feasibility of colonizing faraway lands to which Black freedpeople could voluntarily immigrate. As one of the few white abolitionists who had never once entertained colonization, Sumner opposed the plan fiercely.[29]

Sumner wanted Lincoln and the white public to imagine a world in which Black freedmen participated in political and economic life within America. During the summer of 1862, he introduced bills to permit Black men to testify in federal court, file patents with the U.S. Patent Office, and work as mail carriers. The last bill was intended to help Bostonian abolitionist William Cooper Nell be appointed as the first Black federal postal worker, a position he desired. Although Sumner's bills failed to pass in 1862, he used them as opportunities to advocate for Black civil equality. (The following year, his postal bill succeeded, and Nell earned the honor.) He also achieved one modest victory: Congress voted to permit Black men to testify in the D.C. courts. "This was the first step for the civil rights of colored persons," Sumner proudly proclaimed.[30]

Sumner also accomplished two major victories in foreign affairs that summer. First, working amiably with his foreign policy rival, Secretary of State William Seward, Sumner helped ratify a treaty with Great Britain to collaborate in stopping the transatlantic slave trade. Although the trade had been banned in the United States for decades, smugglers continued to kidnap men and women in Africa to bring to American shores forcibly. The new treaty permitted both parties to investigate any ships coming from either country that appeared to be transporting enslaved human beings. The treaty also established three international courts with both American and British judges to try those accused of participating in the abhorrent practice.[31]

Second, Sumner worked to secure diplomatic recognition of Haiti and Liberia. Ever since the Haitian Revolution at the turn of the nineteenth century, in which enslaved people liberated themselves and declared freedom from France, the United States had refused to recognize the island as its own country. It had also denied recognition to Liberia, a country on the West African coast founded in the 1820s by Black emigrants who had been sent by the American Colonization Society. Southern statesmen feared that the recognition of either country would bring Black ambassadors to the capital, a sight that none of them wanted to see. In a message to Congress, Lincoln suggested that both ought to be welcomed into diplomatic relations. Taking the hint, Sumner led the effort via the Foreign Relations Committee.[32]

Diplomatic recognition of Haiti was personal for Sumner. In 1798, his father, Charles Pinckney Sumner, had traveled to the island of San Domingo and personally met many of the Haitian revolutionaries, including the famous general Jean-Pierre Boyer. His father had regaled his children with stories of his trip to Haiti, and stood out among white antislavery men of his time in supporting its violent slave rebellion. At some point, Sumner acquired a cutout autograph of Toussaint Louverture, the leader of the Haitian Revolution, which he kept in a scrapbook along with the signatures of men like Jefferson and Washington. Haiti was proof that Black men could govern themselves.[33]

Sumner's bill authorized the White House to send paid diplomats to both countries and paved the way for the State Department to negotiate trade treaties with their governments. Speaking about his bill, Sumner avoided any references to the fact that both countries were run by Black men. Declaring Haiti to be a country that has "performed honorably all its duties in the family of nations" and Liberia to be a country that "may become the metropolitan Power on the whole African coast," Sumner talked about the vast economic potential of trading everything from bananas to iron ore with these independent republics. When multiple border state senators predictably denounced the possibility of "full-blooded negro" diplomats with "negro wives and negro daughters," Sumner responded that he "made no appeal for them on account of their color." Having met "citizens of these republics," he said the fact that they "had once been slaves" mattered not.

"The children of Africa all over the globe owe you the deepest gratefulness and last honor," the Liberian delegation wrote Sumner after the bill had passed. "Thanks to your friendship . . . the Republic of Liberia has been brought, through wise and cordial legislation, into brotherhood with the great Republic of America." When a young, flamboyant diplomat from Haiti arrived, he praised Sumner. "Signore CARLO IL SENATORE! Why, his picture is in every cottage in Hayti!" the diplomat waxed lyrical to Sumner's friend. "The name of no American is so dear to the Haytian people as Charles Sumner," he professed. A few years later, Haiti sent Sumner a gold medal that is now housed in the State Library of Massachusetts. "You have protected and defended," a letter that came with the medal read, "the dignity of a black people seeking to place itself, by its own efforts, at the banquet of the civilized world."[34]

* * *

WHILE THE ANTISLAVERY movement picked up momentum among Republicans in Washington, Democrats mobilized to stoke racist backlash among white voters across the North heading into the fall of 1862. The so-called Black Republicans planned to free "two or three million semi-savages," one Democratic newspaper declared. "Shall the Working Classes Be Equalized with Negroes?" another asked. Democrats warned that emancipation would lead to Blacks "overrunning the North and entering into competition with the white laboring masses." Some called for peace with the South, warning that Republicans were "carrying on a war that costs so much blood and treasure just to gratify a clique of Abolitionists."[35]

In Massachusetts, Republican centrists and Democrats hoped to oust Sumner in the upcoming election. They resented his take on racial issues and believed he was a radical agitator who was obstructing Lincoln's ability to maintain unity in the North. After November's election, the legislature would get to decide whether to reelect Sumner for his third term in the Senate. Painfully for him, one of his longtime friends, Richard Henry Dana, spearheaded the effort to replace him with a Republican centrist, such as his rival Charles Francis Adams. Sumner's friend turned rival William Seward also seemed to be yearning for Sumner's downfall. Seward's closest ally, the powerful newspaperman Thurlow Weed, publicly called on politicians in the Bay State to oust Sumner. "Massachusetts should choose as Senator, in this hour of peril, a man of practical sense," Weed wrote in an editorial. "In this quality, Mr. Sumner is eminently deficient."[36]

In response, Sumner's closest friends mobilized to protect him. His quasi-political manager, Frank Bird, cleverly asked some Republicans at the state party convention in October to introduce a resolution endorsing Sumner for the senate seat. The idea of preemptively endorsing a senate candidate prior to the election was unheard of in Massachusetts. In pulling the trick, Bird forced state Republicans to put their support for or antagonism toward Sumner on record. Surprised and disorganized, most Republican attendees—even many of Sumner's conservative critics—voted in favor of him, not knowing how to vote no.

Moreover, Samuel Gridley Howe revived the *Boston Commonwealth*, an antislavery newspaper that was started some years before but had fallen out of print. Howe printed widely distributed articles for months, praising Sumner and pushing his views on emancipation as the best weapon to win the Civil War. Another pro-Republican newspaper, the *Boston Traveler*, also heartily endorsed Sumner. "Mr. Sumner has been one of the powers 'behind the throne,'" the *Traveler* proclaimed. "He has had a strong influence over Mr. Lincoln."[37]

Unlike in his two past elections, Sumner positioned himself as a moderate in this campaign. Noting that he had been accused for years of using "no soft words" in criticizing southern slaveholders, Sumner asked the crowd, "Was I not right?" He explained that "while seeking to limit and constrain Slavery," he "never proposed anything except in strictest conformity with the Constitution." Declaring himself to be "by the side of the President," Sumner invoked the famous slogan of another moderate—his predecessor Daniel Webster. "Liberty and Union, now and forever, one and inseparable!" he cried out.[38]

In the end, Sumner's anxiety over his reelection was unfounded. While Democrats picked up many congressional seats in the upcoming election, Republicans preserved their majority in Congress and in the Massachusetts state legislature. They would reelect Sumner almost unanimously to the Senate in a few months. While the senator would extend grace to a few of those who schemed against him, like Dana (who was pleasantly surprised that his friend harbored no ill will), Sumner was deeply resentful of Seward. In December, he joined other Radicals in Congress to try to persuade Lincoln to remove the secretary of state. Personally friendly with

Seward and wanting to maintain diverse political views and interests in his Cabinet, Lincoln rebuffed the Radicals and kept Seward in his position.[39]

* * *

ONE REASON THAT Sumner kept his seat in Massachusetts was that the policy that was most closely associated with his name, emancipation, had at last been embraced by Lincoln. In mid-September 1862, the Union Army claimed a victory in one of the bloodiest battles of the Civil War. General McClellan's Army of the Potomac had met Robert E. Lee's Confederate forces at Antietam Creek in rural Maryland. The creek filled with blood as twenty-three thousand soldiers were killed or wounded in battle. In the aftermath of the carnage, Lee retreated into the South. A few days later, Lincoln convened his Cabinet, telling them he had a special announcement.

"I think the time has come now," the president revealed. "When the rebel army was at Frederick, I determined, as soon as it should be driven out of Maryland, to issue a Proclamation of Emancipation, such as I thought most likely to be useful. I said nothing to any one; but I made the promise to myself, and"—Lincoln paused, hesitating a little—"to my Maker. The rebel army is now driven out, and I am going to fulfill that promise." On September 22, 1862, the president announced his intention to emancipate all of the South's slaves on New Year's Day. (Sumner had advised him several times in the past to choose New Year's or the Fourth of July as the day to issue an order.) In a message to Congress now called the Preliminary Emancipation Proclamation, Lincoln made a pledge to his country:

"I, Abraham Lincoln, President of the United States of America, and Commander-in-Chief of the Army and Navy thereof, do hereby proclaim and declare . . . that on the first day of January . . . all persons held as slaves within any [rebel] State . . . shall be then, thenceforward, and forever free."[40]

CHAPTER 17

I FIND THE AFRICAN
READY TO BE OUR SAVIOUR

ABOLITIONISTS WERE ON PINS AND NEEDLES AS THE CALENDAR approached January 1, 1863. Abraham Lincoln had promised to sign the Emancipation Proclamation on New Year's Day, but Democrats, border state voters, and some Republican centrists were pressuring him to renege on his commitment. Rumors were spreading that out of an abundance of political caution, Lincoln might acquiesce. But in mid- to late December, he assured Charles Sumner that he intended to stay the course. "He says that he would not stop the Proclamation if he could, and he could not if he would," Sumner wrote.

When Sumner heard Lincoln say those words, he was so thrilled that he couldn't keep them to himself. Having spent more than a decade fighting for abolition, accustomed to losing much more than winning, Sumner was at last triumphant. He shared the fantastic news with many friends. "Let New Year's Day be a day of jubilee," he rejoiced to Samuel Howe. "Let the music sound, & the day be celebrated!" he told John Murray Forbes, the chair of the Republican National Committee. In an exultant Christmas Day letter to the novelist Harriet Beecher Stowe, Sumner disclosed that Lincoln planned to "stand by his Proclamation."

That Christmas may have been the happiest of Sumner's life. He could take righteous satisfaction in having succeeded after a year and a half of advocacy. Shortly after the attack on Fort Sumter in April 1861, he had told Lincoln that he was legally permitted to emancipate slaves during wartime in his capacity as commander in chief. "I believe that I am the first," he told Forbes, "who, in *our day*, called for this exercise of power." Despite his reputation for being stoic and stern, Sumner was absolutely giddy with boyish pride.[1]

He was even more gratified when Lincoln sought his input on the draft proclamation on December 27. The president wrote his revolutionary order in a stiff, logical, and legalistic tone to drive home that it was a military measure and not a moral one. But Sumner and Secretary Chase pleaded with Lincoln to add a little bit of pathos. "It should have something in it shewing that, though an act of military necessity & just self-defence, it was also an act of justice & humanity which must have the blessings of a benevolent God," Sumner urged. When Chase drafted a sentence a few days later that appears to have been modeled on Sumner's advice, Lincoln adopted it nearly in full. In his final proclamation, Lincoln closed by saying that the act was "sincerely believed to be an act of justice," and he invoked "the gracious favor of Almighty God."[2]

Sumner earned the honor of being gifted the pen that Lincoln used to sign the proclamation. "If nobody has yet spoken for it, let me," he had sheepishly written to Lincoln beforehand. He sought out the cedar-handled, steel-nibbed, ink-spattered pen at the request of the collector George Livermore. Believing the pen "will forever be associated with the greatest event of our country and our age," Livermore promised to ensure "its perpetual preservation." It is now a treasured item at the Massachusetts Historical Society.[3]

The Emancipation Proclamation expanded the meaning of the Civil War from a battle to save the Union to a moral crusade for freedom. Granted, Lincoln's order liberated only those slaves who lived on rebel land, leaving slavery in the border states untouched, and it left open the possibility of its being reintroduced in the South after the war. But its impact was still enormous: if the North won the war, more than three million enslaved people in the South would be free—a number greater than the total white population who had been liberated from King George in the Revolutionary War. Moreover, Lincoln wanted their help to win. To the surprise of many observers, his order invited suitable ex-slaves to be "received into the armed service of the United States."

* * *

WHEN THE GOOD news reached Boston by telegraph at nearly midnight on New Year's Eve, a crowd of Black churchgoers burst into loud cheers, singing, dancing, and tears of joy. They had waited all day to find out if Lincoln would keep his promise. People threw their hats and bonnets into the air, stomped their feet, cried, and prayed. "GLORY TO GOD!" somebody hooted. "GOD BLESS ABRAHAM LINCOLN!" Men and women broke into hymns, singing "Glory Hallelujah" and "Old John Brown." "Speeches of thrilling pathos were made," a newspaper reported, "augmented by Jubilee singing and shouts of thanksgiving." Frederick Douglass sang with the crowd. "I never saw enthusiasm before," he cried. "I never saw joy before."[4]

The midnight jubilee uplifted a long-suffering community. The past decade had been especially tough for Black Boston—a small, tightly integrated community that served as a sort of intellectual and cultural capital for Black Northerners. Ever since the passage of the Fugitive Slave Act of 1850, community members had lived under the constant threat of abduction. Work also became scarce after Irish refugees mass-migrated into the city during the 1850s and took jobs that were previously reserved for Blacks. Although schools and streetcars were integrated, racist whites continued to subjugate Blacks through housing and employment discrimination. Even when the war started and Black Bostonians offered to join the Union Army, they were refused the chance to enlist. As one angry white northerner explained, "This is a white man's war."

Sumner was one of the rare white antislavery men whom Black Bostonians trusted. After all, he had grown up in their community. With his mother's home still located on the North Slope of Beacon Hill, he comfortably walked the streets of the city's most important Black neighborhood. One of his favorite spots was a local barbershop. When he "could not be found at his home or office, he could usually be located at Smith's shop," an early twentieth-century historian reported. "Fond of Smith and the gossip [prevalent] . . . there," Sumner enjoyed his visits to the shop, which served as a social hub for Black locals and white abolitionists. He also liked the service: long before he was a senator, in 1844, he received an invoice for fifty-one shaves and one haircut from the owner, John J. Smith.[5]

Sumner also frequented the office of the American Anti-Slavery Society, located a few blocks east of Beacon Hill. Founded by William Lloyd Garrison, the radical multiracial society regularly accused Sumner of being too moderate. Despite his political differences, the senator kept good ties with Garrison and regularly visited the office. "I never allowed myself to have controversy with him in other days, when we differed on methods," Sumner later explained, "because, I knew he was earnest against slavery."[6]

Sumner visited Garrison's offices so frequently that local African Americans would go there to look for him. "This afternoon [I] went to the A[nti] S[lavery] [Society] hoping, I confess, to obtain a glimpse of Sumner," the Black abolitionist Charlotte Forten once wrote in her diary. Another time, she nervously wrote to Sumner, whom she had never met, to ask for his autograph. He sent back a signed speech and a set of autographs of *other* famous people, such as the Duchess of Sutherland, a celebrity abolitionist and friend of Queen Victoria's. "How very, very kind it was in Mr. Sumner! To an entire stranger, too," Forten wrote in her diary. She wondered why the busy senator had bothered to write back. "I suppose I have to thank my color for it," she decided.[7]

Thanks to his deep ties in the community, Sumner often received requests from Black constituents. One such request came shortly after the Emancipation Proclamation. Robert Morris, the local Black lawyer who had crafted the *Roberts v. Boston* case with Sumner, wanted to be commissioned as an officer in the Union Army. For years, Morris had been unsuccessfully lobbying the state legislature to allow Black men to enlist in the militia. He even organized a Black militia at the start of the Civil War that was denied permission to serve. Now that Lincoln had called for Black troops, Morris was doubtless excited to sign up. Sumner pressed the War Department on Morris's case, but the White House decreed that no Black man could serve as an officer (except chaplains). To add insult to injury, Black soldiers would be paid less than white ones. Enraged, Morris and other educated Black Bostonians announced a boycott: their self-respect wouldn't allow them to be enlisted as underpaid grunts. They wanted officer appointments for themselves and equal pay for all others.

Meanwhile, white Bostonians pleaded with Black leaders to be flexible about their rights. "True, all that could be desired was not yet granted," the abolitionist Wendell Phillips told Morris in a public meeting. "But if you cannot have a whole loaf, will you not take a slice?" Morris wouldn't budge. "Equality first, guns afterwards," one of Morris's allies insisted. Bypassing Black Bostonians, Gov. John Andrew formed an all-white group, ironically called the "Black Committee," to finance an advertising campaign across the North to convince Black men—especially those who lived in states that refused to recruit them—to come to Massachusetts to enlist. Breaking with Morris's principled boycott, some Black leaders like Lewis Hayden and Frederick Douglass offered to help with recruitment. "The wise thing for the colored man to do was to get into the army by any door open to him, no matter how narrow," Douglass argued, thinking Morris and others were being shortsighted. He hoped that equality would come in time after African American men proved themselves.[8]

* * *

DESPITE BEING SYMPATHETIC to friends like Morris, Sumner expected Black men to join the Union Army right away. "Enlist at once," he told attendees at a Black convention in Poughkeepsie. "This is not the time to hesitate or to haggle." It was ironic for Sumner, who notoriously hated compromise, to ask Black men to settle for less. But much like Douglass, he pragmatically reasoned that any chance for racial equality would require Black soldiers to exhibit enough courage and patriotism to move the hearts of white America. He also feared there was no way to win without more troops. "I find the African ready to be our saviour," he once declared. He told a friend that he wished to see "200,000 negroes with muskets in their hands."[9]

Sumner recognized an inextricable connection between military service and civil rights. Today, the connection between duties and rights is less obvious. But in mid-nineteenth-century America, it was a core part of the republican theory of citizenship. Government was *of* the people and *for* the people. That meant that only people who gave *to* the government would get benefits *from* the government. Citizenship was a reciprocal relationship. Although the Supreme Court had declared in *Dred Scott* that Blacks were incapable of citizenship, the Civil War offered a new chance to prove otherwise. If Blacks served the national government, the national government might serve them. It was cruel to ask the Black population to risk their lives for a mere chance at equality before the law. But in Sumner's eyes, it was the best political strategy to achieve racial equality.

Black Bostonians understood this better than almost anyone. A few years before the Civil War, one local Black abolitionist, William Cooper Nell, wrote a book about Black service during the American Revolution, documenting stories of some of the five thousand Black men who fought for the Continental Army. After the war, in 1780, Massachusetts's white voters extended voting rights to Black men as a meaningful but insufficient token of gratitude. Nell hoped that fighting in this Second American Revolution would render even more progress for his people. In the words of another Black Bostonian, John Rock, enlistment would "leave no excuse for these who would deprive us of our rights." Sumner heartily agreed.[10]

What postwar rights did Black Americans dream of? Sumner had been laying out some of those rights over the past year, through his bills to allow Black people to testify in court, file for patents, and work for the national bureaucracy without discrimination. It was clear to those who knew Massachusetts history that Black service in the army should also lead to the right to vote. In addition to civil and political rights, Black Americans expected economic independence. In the Sea Islands, for example, formerly enslaved people repeatedly told Edward Pierce that what they really wanted was access to land: land to own, land to grow food, land to live permanently free from having to work for white masters.

In February 1863, Sumner responded to the call of freedpeople for land ownership by proposing what was probably the first bill in Congress to redistribute land to Black Americans. The bill would impose a draft on three hundred thousand able-bodied men of age who were formerly enslaved. (At the time, Congress was debating a bill, which eventually passed, to conscript all eligible whites.) As a reward for their involuntary service, after the war, Black privates would receive ten acres of land and officers would get twenty-five acres. Had the bill passed, land plots would have been allotted from confiscated rebel land. While the plan was unrealistic, given the procedural hurdles to confiscating land under the Second Confiscation Act, Sumner's bill marked the starting point of a broader conversation about what freedmen would be owed in return for military service.[11]

* * *

DURING THE WAR, abolitionists had been forming freedmen's aid commissions to gather food, supplies, and clothing to send southward with missionaries who taught schools and ran churches in newly free communities. However, they wanted a government body to propel the private philanthropy. As Samuel Howe put it, "I have revolved much in mind the matter of an emancipation bureau." By March 1863, in response to requests from Governor Andrew and the abolitionist James McKim, Sumner persuaded the secretary of war, Edwin Stanton, to send three men to Union-occupied parts of the South to investigate the state of freedpeople. Sumner hoped the investigation would pave the way for creating some kind of emancipation bureau.

When Stanton assembled the American Freedmen's Inquiry Commission (AFIC), he chose Howe as one of the commissioners—likely on Sumner's recommendation. Howe, along with social reformers Robert Dale Owen and James McKaye, traveled across the South to interview freedpeople. Howe was excited about the adventure and the prospect of using his findings to push for the creation of a bureau. "We must collect facts and use them as ammunition," he explained. After Howe and the others embarked, Sumner championed their efforts in Washington and secured them additional funding, access to restricted areas, and other privileges.[12]

After a few months, the AFIC sent a preliminary report to Washington. Much like Pierce's report from the Sea Islands, the AFIC's report proposed a total reimagining of the South premised on Black autonomy. Some historians have characterized this report—coupled with the AFIC's final report in May 1864—as the "blueprint" for the project of Radical Reconstruction that Congress would undertake in a few years.[13]

The crux of the proposal was for the United States to confiscate the land of white rebels and redistribute it to Black southerners. "The chief object of ambition among the refugees is to own property, especially to possess land, if it be only a few acres, in their own State," the report noted. "The desirable result is that freedmen should become owners in fee of the farms or gardens they occupy." In addition, before land plots were allotted, the AFIC recommended that formerly enslaved people—who "placed a high value both on education for their children and religious instruction for themselves"—should be supplied with schools, health care, churches, and wage work to prepare them for their lives as freedpeople.

The AFIC argued that aid should be temporary. Many Republicans believed in self-reliance as a core virtue. They feared that long-term aid would lead to dependence. With a tinge of racial prejudice, the AFIC commissioners feared that Black freedpeople would turn into a "burden" and wouldn't work if they got too much aid. But to their credit, the commissioners were also convinced of the ability of African Americans to secure their own independence. To this end, they urged the North to prioritize the enlistment of Black soldiers. "The history of the world furnishes no example of an enslaved race which won its freedom without exertion of its own," the report noted. "A people, to be emancipated, must draw the sword in their own cause." The report argued that the Union should be giving "the negro an opportunity of working out, on those battle-fields that are to decide our own national destiny, *his* destiny." In so doing, "the African race can seek its own social salvation."

By May 1863, Massachusetts had successfully raised its first Black regiment: the Fifty-Fourth Massachusetts. Departing for South Carolina under the leadership of a young white colonel named Robert Gould Shaw, whose abolitionist parents were close friends with Sumner, the regiment bravely fought and lost a deadly battle at Fort Wagner in July. The northern press heralded Shaw for a heroic charge against the Confederate troops that led to his own martyred death.

The press was stunned by the courage of the colored troops who served under Shaw. At the time, most white northerners assumed Black men were weak, docile, and unable to show courage. This was one of the primary racist justifications white southerners used to explain slavery to northerners. "If slaves will make good soldiers," a southern politician once admitted, "our whole theory of slavery is wrong." The heroism of the Fifty-Fourth Massachusetts upended racial prejudices, transformed many whites into abolitionists, and inspired additional Black and white men to enlist in the Union Army with growing momentum.[14]

Sumner learned about the battle from his protégé Edward Pierce, who was an eyewitness. Unlike many abolitionists, who were heartbroken by the deaths of Shaw and his men, Sumner saw in their deaths the silver lining of martyrdom that animates any social revolution. "I cannot be consoled for the loss of Shaw," he wrote. "That death will be sacred in history and in art." (Sure enough, after the war, Shaw and his regiment were memorialized in a monument across from the Massachusetts State House—a monument that Sumner helped to create. More recently, a 1989 Hollywood film, *Glory*, paid homage to the heroes.) "Tell all of that regiment that you see that I honor them much," he wrote to Pierce. He said to tell them, "*Sic iter ad— Libertatem!*", the Latin phrase for "So it goes to freedom."

Optimistic that suffering would lead to liberation, Sumner hoped for more of it. "I fear our victories more than our defeats," he confided in Pierce. "There must be more delay and more suffering, yet another plague before all will agree to 'let my people go.'" While some in Washington scrambled to change tack, Sumner was content to let the war trudge along and allow more people to die. "We must lose other battles, and bury more children," he thought. Believing recent defeats were a "chastisement and expiation imposed by Providence for our crime towards a long-suffering race," he accepted that the price of victory would be high.[15]

* * *

BY THIS TIME, Sumner was at the height of his power in Washington. First seen by even his friends and mentors as a foolish youth wasting his brilliance on a hopeless cause, for more than a decade he had been one of the lone voices in Washington agitating for a unified antislavery North to fight the slave oligarchy of the South. Now he emerged a battle-scarred political veteran, proven to have been right all along.

In retrospect, the blows that had struck his head were the first blows of the Civil War. Though Sumner hadn't predicted the war, he did predict that the war would lead to emancipation. "He was among the first to proclaim that the war for slavery could only be put down by the annihilation of slavery," Congressman Aaron Augustus Sargent recalled. "Where others of his party timidly followed or resisted, he boldly led."

Once considered an unhinged radical, Sumner now seemed like a prophet. Most of his colleagues treated him as a martyr-like hero whose opinions deserved the utmost respect, if not agreement. "When he entered the Senate, there were but two others there of his political opinions," recalled the jurist and future attorney general Ebenezer Hoar. With a touch of exaggeration, Hoar said that Sumner had become "the leader of a majority of more than two-thirds of the body."

When Lincoln signed the Emancipation Proclamation, Sumner had been vindicated. To nearly anyone, he could justly say, *I told you so.* By this time, he and Lincoln had become "the two most influential men in public life," according to one eminent early twentieth-century historian. Sumner had more access to the president's Cabinet than nearly any other member of Congress. He controlled the powerful Senate Foreign Relations Committee. And he enjoyed friendships with both the president and the First Lady.[16]

Mary Lincoln grew increasingly fond of Sumner in the spring of 1863. With her husband always busy, she often insisted upon having Sumner's company and sometimes made Lincoln do the asking. "Mrs. L. is embarrassed a little," President Lincoln once wrote to Sumner. "She would be pleased to have your company again this evening, at the Opera, but she fears she may be taxing you. I have undertaken to clear up the little difficulty. If, for any reason, it will tax you, decline, without any hesitation; but if it will not, consider yourself already invited and drop me a note." Whenever Mrs. Lincoln called, Sumner happily obliged.[17]

Despite his power and influence, Sumner still had serious rivals in shaping public policy. First among them was William Seward. As secretary of state, Seward enjoyed an even closer working relationship and friendship with Lincoln than Sumner. In the spring of 1863, another spat between him and Sumner began.

* * *

HOPING TO "PROSECUTE the war with vigor," Secretary Seward asked Congress in February 1863 to authorize Lincoln to issue "letters of marque," licenses that essentially turned private ships into hired mercenaries. Under Seward's plan, Lincoln would offer cash money or salvage prizes to private northern vessels that successfully attacked private southern ships. All the high seas would turn into a civilian war zone. One of Seward's Senate allies, who introduced a bill to authorize these letters, said it was time "to let slip the dogs of war." The goal was to squeeze the Confederate economy by crushing any commercial southern vessels that escaped the Union's naval blockade. Seward was especially concerned about southern ships that were covertly trading with Great Britain; he also, contrary to Sumner, wanted to accelerate the pace of the war.

Sumner opposed the plan on moral and strategic grounds. In a speech on the Senate floor, he decried the idea that the Union should encourage "privateers" to attack "the commerce of an enemy" with "booty" as the incentive. Even though letters of marque were popular in the past, Sumner noted that European countries increasingly viewed the practice as a barbaric and uncivilized way to conduct naval warfare. He also warned it might provoke Britain's fearsome navy. Winning a score over Seward, Sumner persuaded Lincoln not to issue any letters after the bill was signed.[18]

Despite their disagreements, Sumner and Seward were equally frustrated by the Confederate success at sea. One newly built southern naval vessel, the CSS *Alabama*, penetrated the Union blockade at Galveston Bay, in southeast Texas. Another brand-new ship, the CSS *Florida*, escaped a blockade at Mobile Bay, Alabama, and captured a northern cargo vessel headed for New York. Northerners were alarmed by these Confederate victories at sea—a frontier the Union was supposed to be winning. Over the next two years, the *Alabama* single-handedly captured, sank, or burned more than sixty northern ships.

The culprit of new Confederate sea power was the world's greatest naval empire, Great Britain. Although British law forbade the sale of warships to foreign countries, a rich shipbuilder and member of Parliament named John Laird exploited a loophole in the law to sell vessels to the Confederacy.

Concealing his work by claiming the ships were being sold to fake buyers like the Pasha of Egypt, Laird collaborated with southern diplomats to orchestrate the scheme that led to the construction of the *Alabama* and the *Florida*. When news broke that Laird and other shipbuilders planned to sell more pristine warships to the South, the prime minister, Lord Palmerston, said he was legally powerless to stop them. American newspapers exploded in anger, and the northern public demanded a confrontation with Great Britain.

Fuming, Sumner sent off letters to British friends. "Yr Govt. recklessly & heartlessly seems bent on war," he screeched to John Bright. "England helping a Govt, whose inspiration, life & whole *raison d'etre* is Slavery! Bah!" Sumner feared that many Americans—including Seward, who had a notorious reputation for hating England—might plunge the country into a war with Great Britain in a foolish attempt to stop the empire's tacit support for the Confederacy. Warning Richard Cobden that many Americans "insist upon war," Sumner urged the British to stop tolerating the ship sales. In a letter to the Duchess of Argyll, he portended that "the best educated, the best-principled, and the wealthiest" Americans would join hands with "five hundred thousand Irish-Americans" to fight Great Britain if they kept helping the Confederate Navy. "All the signs are of war, more surely than in the time of the Trent," he warned, referring to the 1861 diplomatic crisis in which the North arrested two Confederate diplomats en route to Britain.[19]

Eager to stop a potential war but intent on halting the sale of warships, Sumner prepared a speech to lambaste Great Britain for its complicity with southern slavery. Perhaps wanting to set himself apart from Seward, Sumner didn't even bother to consult with the secretary of state before drafting his address. Regarding himself as one of the country's leading Anglophiles, he dubiously seemed to think he could single-handedly stop the warship sales by delivering an aggressive Sumner-style abolitionist speech. It was a bit of a contorted plan: although a harsh speech might coax the British into submission, it could just as easily poke the British lion and make the tense situation even worse. Having wisely prevented Seward and others from upsetting the British with letters of marque, Sumner now let his own anger, and ego, get the better of him.

* * *

SUMNER DELIVERED HIS address "Our Foreign Relations" at the Cooper Union on September 10, 1863. He started off by chastising France. Despite declaring itself to be formally neutral, France was partial to the South. Around the time that the Civil War began, Napoléon III had invaded Mexico to expand the French Empire. Because the Confederacy was more sympathetic to France's imperial scheme than the Union, Napoléon quietly rooted for the South, and independent French capitalists extended generous loans to the rebels to help them. Sumner—like all northerners—was outraged by France's behavior. But with only a few paragraphs dedicated to scolding France, his real target of ire quickly became apparent: Great Britain.[20]

The senator's verbal attack on the British was pointed, inflammatory, and *personal*. Blasting Britain's early decision to stay neutral in the Civil War as "a betrayal of civilization itself," Sumner declared that the country was at risk of "unpardonable apostasy" if it decided to help the Confederates outright. That was because the "corner-stone" of the South was slavery, and Britain had abolished slavery three decades before. Sumner pointedly criticized many of his British counterparts who had professed to being antislavery. Accusing them by name of being "false prophets," he warned that they would forever be hypocrites if they continued tacitly permitting the sale of warships—what he later called "floating slave castles"—to the South. Not sparing even Queen Victoria, he said that she had been "seduced . . . into unseemly dalliance with the scourgers of women and the auctioneers of children."

Sumner was eager to prevent the British Empire from ever extending diplomatic recognition to the Confederacy. Although the prospect was slim, given that British abolitionists supported the North, Sumner worried about what Britain would do if it ever started to look like the South might actually win. At the time, leading international law jurists said that nations should recognize rebellious states if and when they achieved de facto independence. But Sumner—who used to teach the law of nations at Harvard—broke with the prevailing doctrine and argued that de facto independence should not suffice for the Confederacy's international recognition because it was battling "against Human Rights."[21]

This was a novel idea. No international law jurist had ever argued for the rule that Sumner proposed. He asserted that nations should recognize revolutions and support them with arms only when that recognition was "sincerely made for the protection of Human Rights." As a corollary, he said nations should never recognize rebellions that, even if successful, make "*an open profession* of trampling justice under foot."

Claiming "there can be no peace founded on injustice," Sumner argued that a "Rule of Morality" ought to govern side by side with the "Rule of Law" among the "Family of Nations" who decide what new nations to recognize. His idea, entirely unfamiliar to his era, is closely akin to the modern practice of requiring new states that join the United Nations to adopt the morality and human rights–centric framework of the United Nations Charter.[22]

Although Sumner did not define what a justice- or human rights–based revolution would look like, he did provide one illustrative example that he knew would really sting in the hearts of Britons. "If Ireland were in triumphant rebellion against the British Queen, complaining of rights denied," he warned, "it would be our duty to recognize her as an Independent Power." At the time, the Irish were living under a centuries-long British subjugation and had tried many times to revolt. The British feared another uprising after a seven-year-long potato famine, caused in part by British control over the food supply, that had killed more than a million Irishmen (and prompted more than a million to flee to the United States). Sumner implied that any potential Irish revolution would be justified so long as the Irish were not bent on creating "a *new* Power" to presumably subjugate other people. In contrast to the Irish, Sumner suggested, the South was seeking white freedom at the expense of Black. Thus, he argued, its rebellion was illegitimate.

Ironically, half the point of Sumner's speech was moot by the time he delivered it. Although the news hadn't yet reached American shores, the British government had banned the departure of the new southern warships and redoubled its stated promise to stay neutral. When Sumner's inflammatory and superfluous speech crossed the pond, it shocked the British press. "Instead of using his influence, as the friend of many Englishmen," the London *Daily News* said, Sumner "has nourished and propagated a delusion" because he was "blinded by panic and perplexed by jealousy." His speech was "based neither on law nor on fact," exploded the London *Times*. The Edinburgh *Scotsman* remarked that Sumner's speech was "full of a strange injustice towards ourselves" that "no non-American man" could comprehend.[23]

Britons were baffled that Sumner expected them to choose a side in a domestic conflict they had little to do with. They felt betrayed that a leading Anglophile would use such incendiary language for a problem their government had just resolved. "The zeal of his cause ate him up," said one

British historian of Sumner. Even Sumner's closest English friends were taken aback. Richard Cobden and the Duchess of Argyll were upset that Sumner had focused on Britain rather than balance his comments with France. Lord Lyons, the British ambassador to the United States, stopped meeting with Sumner after reading the speech. "His usual fault—not to measure the weight of words," said Sumner's friend Carl Schurz. "But it had its effect in opening English eyes to the gravity of the situation."[24]

When Sumner found out that half the point of his speech was moot and that Britons resented his remarks, he became defensive. "Of course, I am abused. I expected it. I expected a sheaf of spears in my own bosom," he dubiously claimed to the Duchess of Argyll. For years, Sumner had used provocative speeches to engage his base and to force others to rethink their positions. But he had underestimated how badly an inflammatory speech would be received by a British audience. Though he insisted that he was "a friend who meant peace and not war," as a leading member of the governing party, he had neglected his diplomatic obligation to keep his rhetoric calm. Ironically, Seward came out ahead: British statesmen started to see *him* as their friend and *Sumner* as their foe.[25]

* * *

WHEN SUMNER RETURNED to Boston shortly after his speech, his family took another blow. He had spent much of the summer, and now the fall, at home supporting his ailing brother George. The paralysis from the railway accident was now spreading across George's body. "My poor brother still lingers; it seems as if each day must be his last," Sumner wrote. "For more than twenty days he has taken no food." Sumner spent nearly every day attending to his younger brother's every need at Massachusetts General Hospital. He likely felt indebted because when he had been caned, it was George who stayed with him for several weeks.

Charles and George Sumner weren't close in their youth. An adventurous, energetic, and gregarious fellow, George was in some ways the opposite of Charles. He didn't care much for books, and as a Democrat for much of his life, he often disagreed with Charles on politics. But as George grew older, he grew closer to Charles, as evidenced by the many letters they started to write each other. Both brothers loved to travel: Charles had finished three tours of Europe; George had spent fifteen years traversing Europe, Russia, and the Middle East. They also had many mutual friends: after returning to Boston, George had been swept into the same social circle as Samuel Gridley Howe and Henry Longfellow. And most important for the quality of any relationship in Sumner's orbit, the brothers shared a core value: they both hated slavery.

George died on October 6, 1863. "This change afflicts me more than I had anticipated," Sumner confessed. He was buried in a private family funeral attended by a few close friends, including Longfellow and the Howes, at Mount Auburn Cemetery. "It reminds me again of my loneliness in the world," Sumner mourned. Aside from his sister Julia, who moved to California after marriage and was now bedridden from an injury, Sumner was the lone survivor among his siblings. His mother, Relief, suffered from failing health. With no spouse, Sumner felt alone in Washington when he wasn't with her in Boston. "Life is weary and dark, full of pain and enmity," he later confided in Longfellow. "I am ready to go at once. And still I am left." He must have suffered from depression. "All my sunshine is little more than moon-shine," he once told Longfellow.[26]

George Sumner was one of many casualties of the war. By the end of the conflict, more than seven hundred thousand soldiers had lost their lives—not counting civilians like George who were fatally injured off the battlefield. Millions of families had been afflicted with gut-wrenching tragedies as the war mercilessly tore into their homes. Yet, for much of the war, civilians in the North had been spared the worst of the catastrophe. This changed when Confederate general Robert E. Lee invaded Pennsylvania in the summer of 1863 on the theory that a sea of blood gushing in the North might intimidate northerners into seeking a peace deal. Lee's incursion culminated in the Battle of Gettysburg in early July, which took more than fifty thousand men on both sides combined.

The morbid calamity at Gettysburg shook northern statesmen to their core, even though it was technically a victory that forced Lee's army back into the South. Yet Sumner took little interest in the battle. In fact, aside from policies related to slavery and naval affairs, he almost never had opinions about how the war was being waged. He generally deferred to the best judgment of his colleague Henry Wilson, who chaired the Military Affairs Committee, and of members of the Cabinet. "It sometimes seemed as if Sumner thought the Rebellion itself was put down by speeches in the Senate," his friend George Hoar once quipped, "and that the war was an unfortunate and most annoying, though trifling disturbance, as if a fire-engine had passed by."

Sumner took an interest in Gettysburg only after Lincoln traveled to its cemetery for a somber dedication ceremony. "Four score and seven years ago," Lincoln famously began, referring to the signing of the Declaration of Independence in 1776, "our fathers brought forth on this continent, a new nation, conceived in Liberty, and dedicated to the proposition that all men are created equal." Swearing that "these dead shall not have died in vain," Lincoln predicted that "this nation, under God, shall have a new birth of freedom."

Later describing Lincoln's Gettysburg Address as a "decisive precedent," Sumner would come to treat it as a quasi-legal text that guaranteed liberty and equality for everyone. "The battle itself was less important than the speech," he argued. "Ideas are more than battles." He believed that Lincoln's speech articulated the key significance of the Civil War. Before the war, America was principally governed by the Constitution. After the war, Sumner believed, the Declaration of Independence was rendered coextensive with that later document. A symbol of the natural equality of men, the Declaration had been the one thing upon which all antislavery men and women could agree. By nodding to the Declaration, Sumner believed, Lincoln was confirming the truly revolutionary implications of the current war. America wasn't just being restored. It was being remade altogether.[27]

* * *

WHEN SUMNER RETURNED to Washington, he tried to impress upon Lincoln the need to develop a reconstruction policy that would secure the promises of liberty and equality made at Gettysburg. Although the war was far from over, politicians were now debating ideas about how best to govern the South if the North won. To this end, Sumner published a lengthy and widely read piece that built on the ideas he had first presented in his series of resolutions from the previous year.

In the October 1863 volume of *The Atlantic Monthly*, Sumner anonymously laid out his legal theory for reconstruction. Celebrating that the war had defeated "the dogma and delusion of State Rights," he said that America was governed by We the People rather than We the States. Giving readers a history lesson on how different American actors conceived of sovereignty, Sumner pushed the theory that the Constitution vested sovereignty in the people, whose will was best expressed by their representatives in Congress. To secure liberty and equality for freedpeople, he called for temporary congressional rule over the rebel states, which he said had reverted to territorial status.[28]

Sumner also previewed a legal argument he would make more forcefully in later years. He argued that a little-known constitutional provision, which required the United States to "guarantee . . . a Republican Form of Government" in every state, granted Congress the power to secure liberty and equality for freedpeople, including protecting and expanding their legal rights. For Sumner, the so-called Republican Guarantee Clause was the "key-stone clause" that would form the bedrock of his postwar constitutional philosophy. "There is no clause like it," he believed. Later, he would go so far as to say the Clause was "the sleeping giant of the Constitution, never until this recent war awakened," a giant that now "comes forward with a giant's power."[29]

In December 1863, Lincoln invoked the sleeping giant. Announcing his first proposed political framework for Reconstruction, Lincoln said that any rebel state could be readmitted after 10 percent of its voting population took an oath to the Constitution and the Union. Residents in readmitted states would regain all property rights, "except as to slaves." States would be encouraged to educate former slaves and to make any other "temporary arrangements" to help this "laboring, landless, and homeless class." While his policy seemed overly lenient to traitors and made no concrete promises to freedpeople, Lincoln included the caveat that every newly admitted state was expected to have a "republican form of government."[30]

Radicals latched on to the wiggly phrase. A few weeks later, Sumner's ally in the House, Ohio's Radical congressman James Ashley, drafted a bill that purported to give some substance to the constitutional requirement for republican government. His bill would have eviscerated anti-Black state laws and required readmitted states to permit Black men to vote, among other things. Although Ashley's plan differed from Lincoln's, it was designed to be similar enough to serve as a starting point for a political compromise between Lincoln and the Radicals.[31]

Sumner believed that Lincoln would accept a Radical plan like Ashley's in time. Even though Lincoln rejected the state suicide theory, Sumner saw his insistence on the Republican Guarantee Clause as leaving the door open for Radical policies. He hoped that Lincoln's message signified the president's openness to rethinking federalism, the Constitution, and the country's duties toward Black Americans after the war. "Sumner speaks of the Message with great gratification," Lincoln's secretary John Hay wrote in his diary. "It satisfies his idea of proper reconstruction without insisting on the adoption of his peculiar theories."[32]

*   *   *

BUT THE WAR had a way to go. "We have more to suffer; we have deserved it," Sumner believed. As 1863 drew to a close, he mourned George's death and the state of his tattered country. The year had started in jubilee, with the signing of the Emancipation Proclamation, but ended in quagmire, with endless suffering on the battlefields and endless bickering in Washington. There was room for hope, but not for joy.

The war had hardened Sumner. Recently, he had received a letter from Joshua Giddings, one of the few true abolitionists ever to have served in Congress. Almost seventy years old, Giddings was just a few months away from his death. He told Sumner that many years before, when John Quincy Adams thought he was dying after a terrible stroke, Adams imparted some final words to Giddings. Believing his own time was coming to an end, Giddings relayed those same last words to Sumner: "I have more hope from you than from any other man."[33]

Sumner felt the burden of his role, as successor to Adams and Giddings, acutely. When the war began, he had stopped attending evening parties in Washington. He didn't understand how others could find moments for levity during a situation of such gravity. While he still socialized, his social life revolved around relationships that were not just enjoyable but politically valuable, such as his friendship with Mary Lincoln. Even his letters to Samuel Howe, which used to gush with emotion, were now stark and matter-of-fact. All he wanted to discuss with Howe were the war-related projects they had both been working on. No longer a private man, Sumner had no private life. The man who had once doubted public service now couldn't imagine life without it.

Spending a lonely Christmas Day in the capital at the end of 1863, Sumner visited some military hospitals. Walking past the rows of injured bodies, he was amazed at the state of "our poor soldiers" and the misery inside. While he was impressed with the dignity of the injured Union troops, he was repelled by the character of the Confederate soldiers being held as prisoners in the Washington hospitals. They "seemed in a different scale of existence. They were mostly rough, ignorant, brutal, scowling."

Sumner talked with several captured rebels, wishing them a blessed Christmas and inquiring after their health in an attempt to "[soften] them into a smile." To his surprise, many Confederates recognized him. "He is a man whom you would notice amongst other men, and whom, not knowing, you would turn round and look at as he passed by you," a writer once said of him. "He was a tall man of commanding appearance, rendered doubly conspicuous by the garments he wore," recalled General Grant's son Jesse. "He always wore the most glaring clothes I have ever seen on a civilized man; heavy plaids in vividly contrasting colors, looming above a foundation of white spats. . . . Sumner was as conspicuous as an Indian in blanket and feathers would have been."

Every educated southerner had a mental image of Sumner that was not entirely wrong: a pompous, overeducated, holier-than-thou New Englander who dressed flamboyantly, instigated war with the South, and never ceased to rant about Black rights. "When they knew who I was," Sumner recounted in a letter, as if chuckling to himself, "they seemed uncertain whether to scowl *extra* or to be civil." Walking through the ward of sickly prisoners, he was convinced that his antislavery crusade would eventually triumph over these rebels. "God has taken this business into his hands," he believed. He decided the war's "result is certain, sooner or later."[34]

CHAPTER 18

THE PRAYER OF
ONE HUNDRED THOUSAND

SOMETIME IN LATE 1863, CHARLES SUMNER TOLD FRANCIS LIEBER that he wanted to draft a constitutional amendment to abolish slavery permanently. One of Sumner's best friends, Lieber had known him for nearly thirty years and would exchange more than six hundred letters with him in his lifetime. Their friendship fell apart after Lieber purchased enslaved people while working as a professor in South Carolina in the early 1850s. But it was rekindled after he accepted a professorship at Columbia University, absolved himself of slavery, and professed his loyalty to the Union. A renowned legal scholar from Prussia, Lieber had drafted the Union Army's code of warfare—which would later form the framework for the Geneva Convention—and was one of Sumner's (and Lincoln's) most trusted legal advisers during the Civil War.

Sumner's idea was not new. His friend Wendell Phillips, a leading abolitionist, had proposed such a constitutional amendment in a public oration in mid-November. The abolitionist William Lloyd Garrison privately wrote to Sumner seeking much the same thing. Some newspapers had leaked that "a distinguished Western member of the House" planned to introduce a draft amendment as well. But the House contained many proslavery and racist Democrats, who constituted a sizable minority. If an amendment were to pass, it was likely to gain more traction in the Republican-dominated Senate. That's where Sumner could play a key role; he decided to introduce a draft during the next session.[1]

Lieber was skeptical of Sumner's plan. He recognized the need for constitutional change—and would later pitch some amendment proposals of his own to friends in Congress—but he worried that Sumner was misjudging public sentiment among white Americans about what emancipation and freedom should look like for Black freedpeople. "You will not find the people prepared," he warned. Although abolition was gaining momentum in the North, and the Emancipation Proclamation had already declared free most of the nation's enslaved people, slavery was still ingrained in the white American mind as a fact of life. Fearing that Sumner might "weaken our case or at least materially thin our numbers" by moving too fast, Lieber urged him to slow down. "Be, my dear friend, very cautious indeed in this matter," he warned.[2]

Lieber had every reason to be concerned. Amending the Constitution seemed to be beyond reach in the early 1860s, much as it is today. To ratify an amendment, two-thirds of both chambers of Congress and three-fourths of all state legislatures have to agree. This was a nearly impossible bar in antebellum America to meet, given the sharp political divides between the states. Not a single amendment had been made in roughly sixty years. Beyond that, the Constitution was considered a nearly sacred document; it was regarded as untouchable.

Sumner long shared the public's reverence for the Constitution. In his mid-twenties, he had delivered his first set of public lectures on constitutional law. His favorite book was *Commentaries on the Constitution*, a monumental treatise by his teacher, Supreme Court justice Joseph Story. "They make an invaluable work to every statesman and lawyer; in fact, to every citizen," Sumner believed. At the sprightly age of twenty-one, he even tried to persuade a friend that Story's dense fifteen-hundred-page work was an "entertaining and informing . . . light law-book." To anyone who would listen, Sumner professed how much he loved constitutional law.[3]

Sumner's affection for the Constitution had grown alongside his embrace of radical politics. When he began calling himself an abolitionist, he had defended the Constitution against the Garrisonians, who denounced the text as proslavery. When he was elected to the Senate, he had argued that the Constitution enshrined liberty on a national basis and that his proslavery colleagues were corrupting it. When the South seceded, he had insisted upon a war to uphold the Union and the Constitution. Among abolitionists, Sumner was a constitutional zealot. "If Daniel Webster merited the title of the great expounder of the constitution," the famous antislavery novelist Harriet Beecher Stowe wrote, "Sumner at this crisis merited that of the great defender of the constitution."[4]

There was a tension between Sumner's obedience to the Constitution and his visionary, idealistic politics. One of the great contradictions of his political career was that he defended a document that obstructed his two paramount goals: liberty and equality for Black America. While Sumner firmly held that the Constitution "was the work of Freedom-loving men," he reluctantly admitted that it shielded slavery in the states. While the Constitution and its amendments supposedly promoted liberty, he knew the text lacked a single word about equality. For all its virtues, the Constitution failed to meet basic egalitarian values.

To reconcile this tension, Sumner turned to the other sacrosanct text of the American Founding, the Declaration of Independence. The Declaration promoted several natural liberties and was premised on the belief "that all men are created equal." Those words were not empty platitudes in Sumner's mind. He learned from his mentor, John Quincy Adams, that the Declaration made a promise—what Sumner called a "baptismal vow." Unlike nations premised on race or religion, America had vowed to make liberty and equality its central ideals. That vow, however, remained unfulfilled in the Constitution. Years ago, Adams had proposed to amend the Constitution to abolish slavery slowly, in order to bring the text gradually into alignment with the Declaration. Sumner had publicly endorsed the idea as early as 1846. But not one member of Congress had drafted an abolition amendment since the release of Adams's proposal. Not until now. Sumner decided to pitch an amendment to erase the scourge of slavery, to make good on the promises of the American Founding by engaging in a re-founding of the nation.[5]

* * *

IN EARLY DECEMBER 1863, Charles Sumner bumped into abolitionist Henry Wright aboard a ferry on the Long Island Sound. Sumner was off to Washington for the next congressional session; Wright was going to Philadelphia for the thirtieth convention of the American Anti-Slavery Society, the abolitionist group founded by William Lloyd Garrison. In their brief encounter, Sumner told Wright about his plan to propose a constitutional amendment. Keeping Lieber's concerns in mind, he sought Wright's help in drumming up public support before the amendment's introduction. Jotting down a note, he asked Wright to read it out at the Anti-Slavery Society's meeting.

The convention began on December 3. Garrisonian abolitionists from across the country packed Philadelphia's Concert Hall to mark thirty years of activism and strategize the organization's future. Reviled for decades as radical agitators on the fringe of society, Garrisonians were now praised by the mainstream Republican Party as prophetic humanitarians. When the North solidified behind the antislavery cause, Garrisonians altered their relationship with the nation and the Constitution, which they had long reviled. A large flag stood behind the speaker's platform at the hall, bedecked by an eagle, a national shield, and a banner with the words "UNION AND LIBERTY." Abolitionists, once the fiercest critics of America, had arguably become the nation's most sincere patriots.

"I have spoken to one of the leading members of the United States Senate," Wright told the jubilant crowd of organizers, preachers, and theorists who had once scorned politics. He said an anonymous senator planned to propose an amendment to the Constitution to abolish slavery. Before the senator did so, Wright explained, he would need help from the Garrisonians. While the senator worked on the inside, abolitionists needed to mobilize on the outside. Pulling out Sumner's note, Wright read a resolution that asked attendees to organize a mass petition drive to rally thousands of ordinary Americans behind a movement to liberate the Constitution from slavery and bring it in line with the Declaration. Wright's resolution passed unanimously.

The next day, Susan B. Anthony spoke to the convention. A women's activist and abolitionist, she declared that petition campaigns were *her* forte, something she and other women were better equipped to organize than men. "Women can neither take the ballot nor the bullet," she explained. "To us, the right to petition is the one sacred right." For decades, white women had leveraged petitions to express their voices, which American democracy otherwise excluded. It was customary at the time for state legislatures and Congress to read petitions on the floor and to channel them into committees, where they occasionally morphed into bills that had the potential to become law. Petitions were a politically active white woman's best friend.

Anthony explained that she and her colleague Elizabeth Cady Stanton had been working on an antislavery petition for months—long before Sumner or anyone else had the idea. While their petition asked Congress to pass a law, not an amendment, it offered the same potential to mobilize the nation behind the cause of permanently ending slavery. Anthony called on the women in the room—not the men—to join her and Stanton in spreading petitions to all their friends and neighbors. She proposed that they amass the largest, most impactful petition in the history of the United States at the time. She envisioned "the signatures of a million of the men and women of the North, poured in upon Congress." That, she argued, would make Congress "feel" enough pressure from constituencies to hold "the strictest faithfulness to freedom."

After the convention, the Women's National Loyal League took charge of the petition movement with Anthony and Stanton at the helm. "TO THE WOMEN OF THE REPUBLIC," one of the league's public letters began. "Go to the rich, the poor, the high, the low, the soldier, the civilian, the white, the black—gather up the names of all who *hate* slavery—all who love LIBERTY." By early 1864, the League had recruited hundreds of women around the country as grassroots campaigners with letters like these. In time, the league decided to enlist the help of men and children, too. Ultimately recruiting around two thousand volunteers, it used clever gimmicks to make the petition drive fun and effective. For example, many petitions created friendly competition between the genders by tallying men's and women' signatures in separate columns, and children who collected at least fifty signatures on their own earned honorary badges to wear on their chests.[6]

The League called their work "the Mammoth Petition." Anthony and Stanton often wrote to Sumner to update him on their progress and to seek his help on some tasks, such as securing free postage stamps from the Senate. When the first hundred thousand petitions were signed, the league rolled up the pages and glued them together by state. Stanton sent them to Sumner, in a box with a key, on February 1. "Please note the petitions come from the Women's National League," she urged. She asked Sumner to present the petitions to the Senate and afterward deposit them in the National Archives (where they remain today). "Voices have spoken in the Senate that have never been heard before," Stanton proudly proclaimed. "The great hearts of the people are beating for freedom."[7]

* * *

AS THE WOMEN'S League agitated on Sumner's behalf, Sumner strategized about how to shuttle his amendment through Congress. The problem was that despite his access to the White House and his command over the Radical wing of the electorate, he had a relatively weak legislative position. Centrist Republicans resented his proximity to Lincoln. Moreover, Radicals begrudged his popularity with the public, as he often received credit for the antislavery efforts of others. Sumner's haughty and moralizing attitude further complicated his position. Although his erudition and vast personal network were valued on foreign affairs matters, he had few allies willing to work with him on domestic policy.

While alienated in the Senate, Sumner had a close relationship with one House member. James Ashley, a handsome, burly six-foot-tall Ohioan, had looked up to Sumner long before joining Congress on the eve of the Civil War. He venerated Sumner's erudition and soaring oratory. Sumner, in turn, was impressed with Ashley's sharp legal mind and his commitment to abolition and racial justice. Sumner frequently backed the younger man's Radical proposals with Senate resolutions, and breaking with his personal rule of staying out of electioneering, he publicly endorsed Ashley during his tough reelection in 1862. Sometime in 1864, Ashley's wife gave birth to the couple's third son; they named him Charles Sumner Ashley.[8]

On December 14, 1863, in the House, Ashley proposed a constitutional amendment to abolish slavery. He likely assumed that Sumner would introduce a similar draft in the Senate. Along with a proposal from Iowa representative James Wilson, Ashley's amendment was referred to the Judiciary Committee. As a member of the committee, he reasonably felt he was well positioned to shepherd the amendment through the House. Although Republicans fell shy of the two-thirds majority needed to pass an amendment, Ashley had proven to be a skilled legislator who could work with disagreeable colleagues despite his inexperience.[9]

Sumner, meanwhile, had all the experience to pass major laws, but far less skill. In mid-January, he successfully persuaded the Senate to create a Select Committee on Slavery and Freedom and to appoint him as chair. "The appointment of the Slavery Slavery Comttee. marks an epoch of history," Sumner boasted to a friend. After this initial success, he assumed the Senate would direct all antislavery petitions and bills, including any proposed abolition amendments, to his committee. He was wrong.[10]

Sumner received the first batch of the Mammoth Petition from Elizabeth Cady Stanton in early February. However, he pitched his proposed constitutional amendment *before* introducing the fat stack of one hundred thousand signatures that demanded the abolition of slavery. (Stanton's letter with the petition box was postmarked February 1; perhaps Sumner didn't receive it until after releasing his draft.) On February 8, he presented his draft to the Senate: "Everywhere within the limits of the United States, and of each State or Territory thereof, all persons are equal before the law, so that no person can hold another as a slave."

When Sumner asked the Senate to refer the draft to his select committee, he was instantly rebuffed by the cool, lawyerly chair of the Senate Judiciary Committee, Lyman Trumbull. A talented Illinois politician who had bested Abraham Lincoln to win a spot in the Senate in 1855, Trumbull was a force to reckon with. A centrist whose main motivation for abolishing slavery was to preserve the Union, he had often tussled with the abolitionist Sumner due to their different perspectives—albeit collaborating with him on many bills. "The relationship of Trumbull to Sumner was analogous to the leaders of two absolutely independent guerrilla bands," Trumbull's biographer wrote. "They fought a common enemy, but each in his own way."

Trumbull demanded that Sumner's draft constitutional amendment be referred to *his* committee, not Sumner's. From the moment he started to speak, Trumbull had the upper hand. He was better liked and more effective at passing laws than Sumner. Plus, it was understood that constitutional amendments generally belonged in the Judiciary Committee. Just a few weeks earlier, another draft abolition amendment, by Senator John Henderson of Missouri, had been sent to the Judiciary Committee. Despite Sumner's fruitless protests, the Senate sent his draft to Trumbull's committee—where, Sumner may have feared, it would be watered down.[11]

On the next day, Sumner did what he should have done *before* announcing his draft. In a dramatic show, he asked two tall Black men to march into the Senate and plop the hefty Mammoth Petition on his desk. "I offer a petition which is now lying on the desk before me. It is too bulky for me to take up," he declared. Senators were no doubt stupefied: no petition in American history had ever received so many signatures. Sumner then gave a short speech, later published as a famous pamphlet, *The Prayer of One Hundred Thousand*. "The prayer speaks for itself," he insisted. "Here they are, a mighty army, one hundred thousand strong."[12]

Sumner's impressive show of people power stirred the Senate into action. The next day, Trumbull promised that he and his colleagues on the Judiciary Committee would draft an amendment right away. One week later, Trumbull said his committee's draft amendment was ready and would soon be introduced. In the meantime, Sumner ratcheted up his pressure campaign. Every time the Women's National Loyal League sent him a new batch of signatures, he would present them to the Senate. On more than twenty separate occasions over a few months, he waved petitions on the Senate floor. In total, four hundred thousand signatures were amassed.[13]

* * *

A MASTER AT public engagement, Sumner nonetheless lacked the skills to navigate the inner halls of Congress to help draft and pass what became the Thirteenth Amendment. But that didn't stop him from having some other legislative successes. In spring 1864, he pushed for bills to repeal the Fugitive Slave Act of 1850; to hire Black federal postal workers; and to open federal courts to Black testimony. The passage of all three bills (which Sumner introduced) indicated Republican openness to some forms of racial egalitarianism. Still, most Republicans were willing to go only so far: the Senate voted down a fourth bill, which Sumner vocally supported but had not introduced, that would have granted suffrage to Black men in the Montana Territory.

One of Sumner's legislative efforts deserves particular attention. The same week that he pitched his abolition amendment, he received an impassioned letter from Alexander Augusta, a Black solider in the Union Army. Augusta had always stood up for himself. He had left his hometown of Norfolk, Virginia, where he was born free, to study medicine in Canada after being refused entrance to the University of Pennsylvania. Returning to the United States on the eve of the war, he offered his services to the Union Army as a surgeon. After being refused because of his race, Augusta successfully demanded his way into becoming the army's first Black physician. Stationed at a Washington hospital near present-day Logan Circle, he proudly served injured colored troops.[14]

In early February 1864, Augusta was thrown out of a streetcar on the grounds that the car was reserved for whites. Adamant about enforcing his rights, he filed a complaint in court and wrote to the best senator he could think of: Charles Sumner. The doctor explained to Sumner that he had been "compelled to walk the distance in the mud and rain" due to the streetcar company's racist policy. Augusta may have known that in 1863, Sumner had persuaded Congress to amend some streetcar charters to hold "that no person shall be excluded from the cars on account of color." To circumvent the spirit of Sumner's provision, however, some streetcar companies offered separate cars to Black passengers.

The corporate evasion of Sumner's provision was effectively a form of proto–Jim Crow. By limiting Black Washingtonians to inferior streetcars that came along less frequently than those for whites, streetcar companies were effectively imposing a badge of inferiority that hearkened back to the days of slavery, which had only recently been abolished in the capital. After receiving Augusta's letter, Sumner angrily read it out loud on the Senate floor, demanding that the Senate clarify that his provision required *all* streetcars to be open to *all* residents irrespective of color.[15]

Senator Trumbull, among others, admitted that Augusta had been wronged, but he thought his recourse was in the courts—and he criticized Sumner for drawing attention to racial mixing in streetcars when slavery still needed to be abolished. Any public demand for *equality*, Trumbull worried, undermined the Republican effort to secure *freedom*. "If a single negro is expelled from the cars in the District of Columbia the voice of the Senator of Massachusetts is heard in this hall," Trumbull later complained. He wasn't alone. Even William Lloyd Garrison, one of the most firebrand white abolitionists in the country, urged Sumner to put "concentrated effort upon the proposition to abolish slavery, instead of looking after its details."[16]

But African Americans demanded no less from Sumner. Ever since the army started recruiting colored troops under unequal terms, Black civil leaders, particularly in Boston, had pressed Sumner on equal pay. In the capital, Black freedpeople openly hosted parades, marches, and conventions in the call for equal rights. They demanded funding for public schools and government jobs. They were so steadfast that Sumner was confronted daily by locals who expected him to do more to integrate streetcars. "Protest in my name, in the name of every intelligent colored person," the D.C. restaurateur George Downing later wrote him, "against each and every proposition that makes any invidious proscribing distinction based on color or race."[17]

For several months, Sumner relayed local concerns and repeatedly asked the Senate to vote on his bill to integrate streetcars. Threatening to "take every proper occasion to call the bill up," he planned simply to annoy his colleagues into submission. Eventually, it worked. The Senate approved one of Sumner's proposed changes to a streetcar company charter to specify that "there shall be no regulation excluding any person from any car on account of color." The change was especially significant because streetcars were used by all Washingtonians, including many members of Congress, as a mode of transportation. By voting for Sumner's bill, congressmen were effectively agreeing to sit side by side with Black Washingtonians on their daily commutes as they were debating an amendment to abolish slavery. The bill passed the House and became law in 1865.[18]

* * *

SUMNER ARGUED THAT the integration of streetcars achieved three objectives: "to sustain the principles of humanity, to uphold human rights, and to vindicate human equality." These three phrases shed enormous light on Sumner's political philosophy, which informed his outlook on the constitutional transformation the Thirteenth Amendment presaged.[19]

First, Sumner wished "to sustain the principles of humanity." He was referring to the Founding-era belief, best articulated by John Adams in the Massachusetts Constitution, that "all men are born free and equal." Freedom and equality, for Sumner, were inalienable gifts from God that the law ought to respect. A student of the Enlightenment and the natural law tradition, which his teacher Joseph Story had imparted to him, Sumner believed that a lawmaker's duty was to strip statute books of anything that violated natural egalitarian principles.[20]

Second, he wished "to uphold human rights." Having used the nascent term "human rights" in the international context in 1863, he began invoking it in nearly every speech he gave about Black rights in 1864. In so doing, he may have been implying that rights afforded to Black men should also be afforded to women, who were textually excluded from similar phrases like "the rights of man." Although Sumner never engaged in the women's suffrage movement directly, he knew those who did, having worked with them on antislavery petitions. Activists like Theodore Parker, Angelina Grimke, and Ernestine Rose occasionally used "human rights" precisely to include women. In the years ahead, Elizabeth Cady Stanton and Susan B. Anthony would quote from the human rights language in Sumner's speeches to draw attention to women's rights, too.[21]

Remarkably, historians generally attribute the birth of "human rights" as a concept to the period after World War II. Although some historians have noted that antislavery figures like Sumner's mentors William Channing and John Quincy Adams sporadically used the term, they have not picked up on Sumner's regular usage. One historian noted that Sumner used "human rights" once in "one of the very rare invocations of the phrase in English prior to the 1940s." In fact, Sumner used the term nearly *three hundred times* over the course of his speeches. He may have used the expression more than any other major figure of the nineteenth century.[22]

Sumner offered an expansive vision of the rights that Black Americans should possess. At the time, antebellum lawyers often subdivided rights onto civil, political, and social planes. By 1864, most Republicans agreed that Black men should have *civil* rights, like the right to property, contracts, and access to courts. But some didn't yet think they should have *political* rights, like the right to vote. Some also hesitated about whether Blacks should have *social* rights. Social rights involved intermingling, such as attending the same schools, sitting together at the theater, and marrying one another. In pushing for bills to open federal courts to Black testimony, permit Black men to vote in Montana, and integrate Washington's streetcars, Sumner exhibited a belief in all three planes of rights, which he united under the concept of human rights.[23]

Third, Sumner wished to vindicate human equality, a core value of the Republican Party. Secretary of State William Seward once said Republicans were "a party of one idea . . . equality, the equality of all men before human tribunals and human laws." But he didn't say *who* got to be equal. To some Republicans, "all men" meant "all *white* men." These Republicans hated slavery mainly because it enabled some whites to get richer than other whites by exploiting the labor of Blacks. To other Republicans, equality was to apply to all people, but only in the civil realm. They would accept Black attendance in court, for example, but not on streetcars.[24]

Some Republicans, including Sumner, espoused a prescient, sweeping kind of egalitarianism that entailed the obliteration of status distinctions in nearly all aspects of public life. Merely tolerating Blacks in some civil spaces would not do. Repeatedly, Sumner denounced the "oligarchy of the skin," seeing hierarchies based on skin color as a relic of the tyrannical slave oligarchy. To him, racial discrimination was not just an individual prejudice but a structured system of caste that was repugnant to American founding principles. It was his belief that the Republican Party should be steadfastly committed—above all else—to the equal rights of Black Americans.[25]

* * *

WHEN SENATOR TRUMBULL announced the Judiciary Committee's draft constitutional amendment to abolish slavery, there was a glaring omission. Although the proposed amendment would render all enslaved people free, it didn't include the key phrase that was embedded in Sumner's draft: "equality before the law." Even though Trumbull and his colleague Senator Jacob Howard insisted that "free" and "equal" were the same "in a legal and technical sense," Sumner believed that equality should be made explicit in the text.[26]

More than anyone, Sumner knew the instrumental value of a constitutional provision that referred to equality. Back in 1849, in the *Roberts v. City of Boston* case, he, along with Black lawyer Robert Morris, had pointed to the statement "all men are born free and equal" in the Massachusetts Constitution to argue to the state supreme court that Boston's white-only public schools were unconstitutional and should be open to Black students. Although they lost the case, their argument paved the path for Boston's Black community to lobby the state legislature successfully in 1855 to integrate the city's public schools. It also led to the state supreme court's acknowledging in dicta that "all persons without distinction of age or sex, birth or color, origin or condition, are equal before the law."[27]

Soon after Sumner and Morris presented their case in *Roberts*, Sumner published a pamphlet edition of his argument for school integration. That pamphlet popularized the expression "equality before the law," which Sumner had effectively introduced into the English language. Adopted by several French constitutions and the constitutions of at least eight other non-English-speaking countries, the principle of "equality before the law" was rarely invoked in America before his pamphlet's release.[28] For the next fifteen years, leading into the amendment debates of 1864, abolitionists regularly used his phrase "equality before the law"—and the phrase is still commonly used today. Contemporaries, such as the Black law professor John Mercer Langston and the abolitionist Wendell Phillips, have attributed the slogan's genesis in American legal thought to Sumner.[29]

In an April 8, 1864, speech, Sumner advocated for the inclusion of "equality before the law" in what became the Thirteenth Amendment. Admitting that "the language may be new in our country," he argued that it "gives precision to that idea of human rights which is enunciated in our Declaration of Independence." But Sumner's speech was in vain. He delivered it on the same day the amendment was to be voted upon. With the amendment's passage imminent, Trumbull and other senators had no interest in changing its language to please Sumner. Neither were they impressed with his references to Europe. "I would not go to the French Revolution to find the proper words for a constitution," Trumbull scoffed after Sumner had finished.[30]

The Senate passed the Judiciary Committee's two-section draft of the amendment verbatim. "Neither slavery nor involuntary servitude, except as a punishment for crime, whereof the party shall have been duly convicted, shall exist within the United States, or any place subject to their jurisdiction," the first section read. The second section said, "Congress shall have power to enforce this article by appropriate legislation."

Section 1 hearkened to language from the 1787 Northwest Ordinance, one of the earliest statutes of Congress, which prohibited slavery in all the American territories adjacent to the Great Lakes. At the time, the ordinance had deep sentimental resonance with westerners, as it basically served as the founding charter for their region. Many states that banned slavery used the ordinance's language in doing so. Reasoning that the familiar language would help get the amendment ratified, Trumbull insisted upon using similar verbiage.[31]

In his speech, Sumner objected to the ordinance's language, in particular its "punishment for crime" clause. "I venture to doubt the expediency of perpetuating in the Constitution language which," he argued, "seems to imply that 'slavery or involuntary servitude' may be provided 'for the punishment of crime.'" Even if there were some "reason for that language when it was first employed," he said, "that reason no longer exists." He asked his colleague to "put aside" this clause in favor of his own equality-based draft.

Sumner's concern over the "punishment for crime" clause may have been rooted in his familiarity with the criminal justice system. Back in the 1840s, he was loosely involved in the prison reform movement. That movement criticized corporal punishments as barbaric and offered prison as a liberal alternative. Sumner particularly liked the Pennsylvania system, which used solitary confinement and other methods that would supposedly help prisoners engage in self-reflection and become prepared for their reemergence in society.[32]

But by the 1860s, Sumner had become disillusioned with prisons. He often visited the overcrowded Washington jail, a decrepit stone building on Judiciary Square. Local law enforcement routinely threw Black Washingtonians into jail with wanton disregard for due process, typically for petty crimes or the mere suspicion that they were fugitives from slavery. City officials were enforcing so-called Black Codes, laws administered solely against Black residents that were intended to maintain their subordination and inferiority. By 1864, Republicans had eliminated the city's

Black Codes and released most of the jail's inmates. "To expunge that black code from the statute-book," Sumner had argued, "is to expunge slavery itself."[33]

Black Codes and the Washington jail were likely on Sumner's mind when he unsuccessfully urged colleagues to remove the "punishment for crime" clause from the amendment. He had seen firsthand how criminal law was ripe for exploitation to perpetuate slavery. Years later, he said he "regretted infinitely" that the clause wasn't removed. Despite his belief that the Senate intended it to be "simply applicable to ordinary imprisonment," former slave states exploited the clause to target Blacks for arrest and force them into slavery. After the fall of Reconstruction, the South used Black Codes and prisons to reimpose forms of slavery on large swaths of the region's African American population, prolonging a system of racial caste that some believe has continued to this day.[34]

While Sumner was frustrated with Section 1 of the draft Thirteenth Amendment, he appreciated Section 2, which is now commonly known as the Enforcement Clause. The clause represented the first time in U.S. history that an amendment expanded, rather than limited, the national government's power. Before the war, it was widely understood that states had exclusive authority over slavery and the treatment of Black residents. But the Enforcement Clause put much of that power into the hands of Congress over the states. In awarding Congress "power to enforce this article by appropriate legislation," the section alluded to the famous case *McCulloch v. Maryland*, in which Chief Justice John Marshall said Congress can use "all means which are appropriate" to make legislation that advances valid constitutional goals. If the ends were valid, Congress could employ any appropriate means—even without express authority.[35]

Sumner admired the jurisprudence of John Marshall and his right-hand man, Joseph Story, more than that of any other judges. When Sumner visited Washington in his twenties, Story had invited his star student to dine with Marshall many nights. Sumner would even walk with Marshall to the Court in the mornings. The two jurists imparted to Sumner a belief in constitutional nationalism, the idea that the national government reigns supreme over the states. Nationalists fiercely opposed the states' rights doctrine, which they associated with slavery and the South. Believing that the Enforcement Clause enshrined Marshall's nationalist jurisprudence, especially in the arena of human rights, Sumner would champion the clause so passionately in the years ahead that some historians have mistakenly assumed he wrote it. (It was originated by Representative James Wilson.)[36]

* * *

AFTER THE THIRTEENTH Amendment passed in the Senate, the job fell to Sumner's friend James Ashley to get it through the House. In the meantime, Sumner turned to other legislative business that illustrated his vision for a strong national government. With encouragement from Ralph Waldo Emerson and Oliver Wendell Holmes Sr., he unsuccessfully tried to create national academies for "literature and art" and "moral and political science" to complement the National Academy of Sciences, which had been authorized in 1863. The academies would have extended government resources to artists and intellectuals of Sumner's era, much as the National Endowment for the Humanities, founded in 1965, does today.

Sumner also introduced an innovative bill to transform the national bureaucracy—filled with political appointees at the time—into an independent, meritocratic system based on competitive exams. While Sumner didn't expect anything to come of it, his bill gained surprising favor in the press and among leading intellectuals. Two years later, a junior congressman picked up on his vision for civil service reform and, with Sumner's blessing, pushed for many years for what ultimately became the Pendleton Civil Service Reform Act of 1883—which, in the words of one historian, was "remarkably similar" to Sumner's original 1864 bill.[37]

Most important, Sumner advocated for a bill to create what became the Freedmen's Bureau, an administrative agency tasked with the most major question of Reconstruction: How to transition the South's millions of formerly enslaved people to live as free people? Democrats and others were stunned by the proposal, which contradicted their antebellum notions of a limited national government that had little role in the states. The bill delegated "overwhelming power," said one critic, to the executive branch without much legislative direction. As the attorney general later put it, "there are few statutes that are disfigured by loose and indefinite phraseology to a greater extent." Another critic derided the administrative delegation as "arbitrary power, without any limitation, without any rules or regulations to govern these masters and drivers in the exercise of their most extraordinary authority."[38]

To set the stage for a national bureau, Sumner had pushed for the creation of the American Freedmen's Inquiry Commission (AFIC) back in early 1863. The AFIC had traveled through the South to examine the state of freedpeople and had reported to Washington on the necessity of a bureau that could pursue policies like mass land redistribution, educational programs, and short-term financial assistance.[39]

The House narrowly passed the Freedmen's Bureau bill in March 1864. Drafted by Thomas Eliot, a Massachusetts representative, the bill called for a new bureau to control the cultivation of rebel land, organize and direct the labor of freedpeople, help them negotiate and collect wages, serve as arbitrators in their disputes, and "make all needful rules and regulations for the general superintendence" of freedpeople in the rebel states. With vague provisions and only five pages long, the bill granted incredible rulemaking and adjudicatory power to the Executive Branch. Since "there is not experience or knowledge enough of what is wanted to make a detailed system safe in the organic law," Eliot told Sumner, the bill "was made as small as possible and with as few details as possible and with general powers to organize the Bureau."[40]

When the House bill arrived in the Senate Committee on Slavery and Freedom, Sumner's colleagues wanted to amend it to place the bureau under the Treasury Department, instead of the War Department, where the House had put it. Sumner was persuaded by those colleagues. After all, his friend, Secretary of the Treasury Salmon Chase, commanded more than fifteen thousand Treasury workers and had control over all rebel lands. "Any plan that separates the care and disposition of the freedmen from the disposition of the abandoned lands at the south will be a great mistake," the AFIC commissioner James McKaye explained to him. If the land was in Chase's control at Treasury, Sumner decided the bureau should be under him, too.[41]

To Sumner, abolishing slavery and distributing land were inextricably connected. There was no true freedom without minimal entitlements to land. "Can emancipation be carried out without using the land of the slave-masters[?]" he rhetorically asked John Bright a few months later. "We must see that the freedmen are established on the soil, and that they may become proprietors." By putting the Freedmen's Bureau under the same agency that controlled the land, freedpeople, Sumner believed, would be more likely to attain ownership over land plots, which would help actualize their freedom. "The main interest for the moment in regard to the freedmen," he candidly explained to the Senate, "is how to bring them in connection with the lands."[42]

* * *

BECAUSE OF DISAGREEMENTS over where to put the bureau, under Treasury or War, more than a year transpired before the Freedmen's Bureau bill finally passed in the Senate. All the while, for the rest of 1864, debates over the rights of freedpeople, the treatment of rebels, the distribution of land, and the restoration of the southern states raged in the Senate and the country. The draft Thirteenth Amendment was also languishing in the House. Amid these weighty questions, Americans watched with horror as the Civil War continued to swallow the lives of tens of thousands of additional soldiers. Against this backdrop, the North debated whether to reward or punish the man most responsible for waging the war: Abraham Lincoln.

On the whole, northerners were dissatisfied with Lincoln by the summer of 1864. Abolitionists and Radicals saw him as too weak; Democrats and some Republicans were exhausted by his war. At both ends of the spectrum, voters lacked faith in Lincoln's ability to either win or make peace. "There is a distrust and fear that he is too undecided and inefficient ever to put down the rebellion," Lincoln's ally Lyman Trumbull admitted. Without a major Union victory before the election, Republicans feared, the president would be defeated. Sensing his vulnerability, Democrats campaigned on an end to the bloodshed with a peace deal. Adding to Lincoln's woes, former Union general John Frémont, a favorite of abolitionists, launched a third-party candidacy.[43]

Radical Republicans were especially furious with Lincoln. Despite having signed the Emancipation Proclamation, the president hesitated on how to treat freedpeople in the South. When Sumner and other Radicals in Congress pushed for Black rights in the spring, Lincoln stayed silent. He didn't take a public position on the proposed Freedmen's Bureau, and he was late to endorse the Thirteenth Amendment. On top of looking skittish, Lincoln seemed selfish. No incumbent had run for reelection since Martin Van Buren, in 1840 (and Van Buren lost). Radicals believed it wasn't proper custom or smart politics to run twice in a row.[44]

In August, Sumner attended a secret meeting with other Radicals to discuss whether Republicans should try to hold a new convention to oust

Lincoln, who had already been nominated at the convention in June, and to convince Frémont to stop his third-party campaign. Sumner declared that the country needed a "president with brains" and thought a new candidate might be able to unite the party. But after giving it a second thought, he pulled out from the group. He decided that he couldn't imagine a challenge against Lincoln leading to anything but disunity. He also felt personally obliged to Lincoln, with whom he shared a warm friendship and healthy partnership. "I see no way of meeting the difficulties from the candidacy of Mr Lincoln," Sumner admitted to John Andrew, "*unless he withdraws patriotically and kindly, so as to leave no breach in the party.*"[45]

Even when Salmon Chase was floated as Lincoln's potential replacement at a hypothetical new convention, Sumner stayed out. Despite their close friendship, he hadn't helped Chase when he entertained a primary contest against Lincoln at the original convention, and he wouldn't help him now. Although Sumner hoped Lincoln would voluntarily step out of the race, he insisted on supporting him if the president chose to stay in the running. It helped that Lincoln, feeling the heat from Radicals and abolitionists, increasingly embraced the Thirteenth Amendment.[46]

Sumner considered himself a statesman who stood for principles, not a politician who played with politics. Walking along a street in Boston, one of Sumner's friends passed a storefront window that displayed a cartoon. In it, a swarm of ambitious politicians at the foot of a towering cliff clamored for the Republican presidential nomination with catchphrases and self-aggrandizing placards. Above them, a long ladder stretched to the cliff's summit, where an eagle was perched. Next to the eagle, Sumner balanced precariously atop the ladder while painting, with composed determination, enormous words onto the rock face for all to see: "Amendment of the Constitution."

The cartoon aimed to illustrate Sumner's singular dedication to his paramount goal: abolishing slavery. The jockeying, the politicking, the who-should-be-president-ing, mattered comparatively little to him. Writing to Sumner to describe the cartoon he had seen, his friend remarked, "There was something in your quiet air up above all the tumult below which struck me as very true and very much to your honor."[47]

★ ★ ★

IN SEPTEMBER, THE Union Army captured Atlanta, a Confederate stronghold. Northerners celebrated in the streets. It was the first major victory in months. In a span of weeks, the Union Army won a series of new battles, and the Confederacy fell into rapid decline. Northerners were especially impressed by the fearless and talented leadership of Gen. Ulysses Grant, whom Lincoln had recently appointed to lead the army. Thanks to Grant's victories, Lincoln's reelection campaign gained steam. Moreover, the president's Democratic opponent, Gen. George McClellan, floundered on the campaign trail, oscillating between tepid support and opposition to the war effort. When the November election took place, Lincoln won in a landslide.

As soon as it was obvious that Lincoln would win, Sumner rushed to Faneuil Hall, in Boston, for an impromptu jamboree of relieved Republicans. "The trumpet of victory is now sounding through the land, GLORY, HALLELUJAH!" he shouted to the crowd, which erupted in hoots and cheers. "From this time forward, the Rebellion is subdued," he declared. "Patriot Unionists in the Rebel States, take courage! Freedmen, slaves no longer, be of good cheer!" There was a genuine excitement in the room, a belief that the war was about to end and the glory days of a renewed republic were now to come. Although Sumner believed that people had "voted *against* McClellan rather than *for* Lincoln," he couldn't help but be hopeful for Lincoln's second term.

Sumner happily assured the crowd, "The hour of deliverance has arrived."[48]

CHAPTER 19

I WAS ALWAYS HONEST WITH MR. LINCOLN

A SPECTACLE WAS WITNESSED IN THE SUPREME COURT TODAY," a correspondent reported on February 1, 1865. Lawyers and spectators were aghast to see Charles Sumner sitting in the front of the courtroom next to a suited Black man, whom one journalist derisively described as being "jet-black, with hair of an extra twist . . . of an aggravating 'kink.'" The man was John Rock, a polymath dentist turned doctor from Boston who had taken the bar exam and passed. After launching his third career as a lawyer, Rock visited Sumner's home and sought his help to get admitted to the Supreme Court Bar. Sumner warned him that it was impossible: racial prejudice and exclusion at the Court were all but guaranteed so long as Chief Justice Roger Taney presided.[1]

Taney had written the infamous *Dred Scott* decision, holding that Blacks could never be American citizens. When the justice fell into poor health in spring 1864, Sumner rejoiced. He pestered Abraham Lincoln into promising to nominate his friend (and Lincoln's rival) Salmon Chase as Taney's successor. After Taney passed away, Sumner led the effort to kill Senator Lyman Trumbull's bill to place a bust of Taney in the Court next to other former chief justices. "Let such a vacant space in our Court-Room testify to the justice of our Republic," Sumner declared. (Congress commissioned a Taney bust ten years later, and the Supreme Court also acquired its own Taney bust, which is still on display in the Court's Great Hall to this day.)[2]

After Chase became chief justice, Rock again asked Sumner to get him admitted, arguing that the "great and good man for our Chief Justice" would be willing to do it. Sumner wrote to Chase, asking if it was possible. It stood to reason that allowing a Black man to practice law at the Court implicitly overturned *Dred Scott*. If Blacks could argue cases, then surely they could be citizens. Remarkably, Chase's colleagues, including those who had participated in *Dred Scott*, unanimously agreed to admit Rock, albeit with reluctance and after some prodding from Chase. Chase gave Sumner the green light to bring Rock to the Court.[3]

At eleven o'clock sharp, Chase and six other black-gowned justices marched into the courtroom to begin the day's session. Those in the gallery stood up respectfully. Chase bowed to them, giving them the go-ahead to sit down, but Sumner remained standing. "May it please the Court," he said. "I move that John S. Rock, a member of the Supreme Court of Massachusetts, be admitted to practice as a member of this Court." Chase nodded and directed the clerk to administer to Rock the customary oath. Shocked white-shoe lawyers in the courtroom sat quietly as a proud and brilliant Black Bostonian joined their ranks.

"The grave to bury the Dred Scott decision was in that one sentence dug," declared the *New York Tribune*. The correspondent wrote that it was extraordinary to witness Sumner's presence in the room: at the time, the Court was holding sessions in the Old Senate Chamber, the very place where Sumner had been beaten nearly to death nine years before. After healing from his injuries and from the lingering trauma of the attack, he was now vindicating the rights of those for whom he had nearly died. "Thus it will be seen," said the *Adams Sentinel*, "that the black man has rights which the white man . . . is bound to respect."

* * *

THE DAY BEFORE Rock's admission to the Supreme Court Bar, the House of Representatives passed the Thirteenth Amendment and sent it to the state legislatures for ratification. This incredible victory was due partly to President Lincoln, who proclaimed his reelection a mandate from the people to abolish slavery. However, the bulk of the credit belonged to Sumner's friend Representative James Ashley. Deftly working with the White House and other allies, Ashley had wrangled enough Democrats in the House to vote in favor of the amendment. It was arguably the biggest legislative achievement by a Radical Republican during the war.

Aside from Ashley, Sumner had few friends among his fellow Radicals in Washington. Fiercely independent and hard to work with, he brushed up against his allies several times in early 1865. One conflict emerged when Senators Jacob Howard and Benjamin Wade wanted to restrict the food, clothing, and medicine of captured Confederate officers in retaliation for how the South had treated Union soldiers. Sumner was appalled. "With pain I differ from valued friends whose friendship is among the treasures of my life," he admitted to the Senate. "But I cannot help it. I cannot do otherwise." He then unleashed a moral tirade against his allies. "My friends from Ohio and Michigan called for retaliation in kind—an eye for an eye, tooth for tooth, death for death, starvation for starvation, freezing for freezing, cruelty for cruelty," he declared.

Howard and Wade were stunned to hear Sumner disparage them so uncharitably. Neither professed to cruel motives. Their goal was to temporarily punish Confederate prisoners to pressure the South into agreeing to a deal to treat all prisoners more humanely. Even so, Sumner was repulsed that his allies were suggesting starvation as a bargaining chip "in this age of Christian light." Signifying his moral displeasure, he opted to embarrass them. When they claimed that the Union Army's code of war permitted retaliation, Sumner wrote to the code's author, Francis Lieber, who happened to be one of his best friends. When Lieber wrote a letter in reply to state that the "sickening" plan didn't meet his code's bar for valid retaliation, Sumner recited the letter on the Senate floor to shame fellow Radicals into backing down.

Needless to say, it would have been more diplomatic of Sumner to have shown Lieber's letter to his Radical colleagues privately first. But this was not Sumner's way. He had often scorned the backroom dealings of politics. He never took a bribe and almost never formed gentlemen's agreements with other senators on particular bills. He wasn't even happy about the fact that the minutes of committee hearings, at the time, were not reported to the press. He preferred to negotiate and argue with his colleagues in public, on the Senate floor, rather than anywhere else more discreet. "He was one of those, who, when they attack, attack always in front, and in broad daylight," his friend and later Senate colleague Carl Schurz explained.[4]

In addition to attacking Howard and Wade publicly, Sumner openly collaborated with Democrats, his sworn enemies, to oppose this bill that had been introduced by his allies. Radical as he was, Sumner was willing to work with Democrats at times and had a nuanced attitude toward Confederates as human beings. While he wanted to deprive rebels of property and voting rights, for example, he disliked punishing for punishment's sake. He didn't want wartime sanctions against rebels to go beyond that which was necessary for uplifting freedpeople. Later that same year, he told a friend that he "desired two measures,—universal suffrage and universal amnesty." When freedmen effectively had the vote—and presumably some property—Sumner believed that rebels wouldn't need to be deprived of their rights anymore.

Sumner also didn't want the Union to gloat about battles the rebels had lost. Back in 1862, he had opposed putting the names of Union victories on regimental flags. In February 1865, he tried to stop Congress from commissioning a mural in the U.S. Capitol to glorify the Union Army. "I doubt if it be desirable to keep before us any picture of war with our own fellow-countrymen," he argued. "There are moral triumphs which are more worthy of commemoration by art. I need only refer to the proclamation of emancipation." For Sumner, the Civil War was a moral cause intended to stop sin, not to shame sinners.[5]

If Sumner's charitable attitude toward rebels irked some Radicals, his belief in charity for freedpeople upset others. Also in February, he introduced a bill to create an independent agency for freedpeople that wasn't tied to either the Treasury or War Departments; the bill arose from negotiations in a joint House-Senate committee he chaired. To Sumner's surprise, several Republicans—including Radicals—opposed his bill because they believed the government shouldn't get involved in the lives of Black freedpeople. "The better policy is to regard them as free," argued Missouri's John Henderson, "have it understood that we ourselves regard them as freemen, and that they are to be treated as such upon every occasion; and that they need no guardians, no superintendents, no overseers."

Some Radicals were stunned that Sumner wanted Black Americans to receive special benefits not afforded to whites. "When he asks me to neglect my own kith and kin to legislate for the exclusive protection and benefit of colored men he goes a little further than I am willing to go," New Hampshire's John Hale declared. "I have an old-fashioned way of thinking," the antislavery Indiana senator Henry Lane explained, "which induces me to believe that a white man is as good as a negro if he behaves himself."

Sumner was baffled by their myopia. His reasons for backing governmental charity for freedpeople followed a logic similar to that for many modern arguments for reparations. "Whose sweat is it that has fertilized these lands?" he once angrily implored. "Whose rights lie at the very foundation of the war in which we are now engaged? Whose rights have for generations been assailed?" Believing "the curse of slavery is still upon them," Sumner urged the passage of a Freedmen's Bureau bill to help Black Southerners. "The freedmen should enjoy the first-fruits of returning justice."[6]

Sumner's bill for the bureau was voted down by the Senate. Afterward, Massachusetts senator Henry Wilson pitched a new committee with himself, rather than Sumner, as chair, to take Sumner's draft and improve it. The Senate agreed. Calmer in temperament, Wilson shared Sumner's radicalism but was better at negotiating with opponents. Fifteen years earlier, he had served as Sumner's quasi-political manager and negotiated a backroom deal with Democrats to get Sumner into office. After being elected to the Senate himself, Wilson became Sumner's colleague rather than his lieutenant. While the two were not personally close, they saw eye to eye on most issues and had an effective working relationship. "I do not believe any man in the Senate in his time, not even Sumner, had more influence over his colleagues than [Wilson]," said future Massachusetts senator George Hoar.

Wilson quickly negotiated the draft bill, which put the Freedmen's Bureau under the aegis of the War Department. He then successfully rammed the bill through both chambers in early March, right before the session ended. Although Sumner shepherded the bill for more than a year, it was Wilson who took it across the finish line.[7]

* * *

ALTHOUGH RADICALS DISAGREED on war policies and the Freedmen's Bureau bill, they stood united to oppose Lincoln's plan to readmit the first southern state since the start of the war: Louisiana. After the Union Army seized the New Orleans region, Lincoln established a provisional government under the leadership of former House speaker Nathaniel Banks. While Banks enforced the abolition of slavery, he also forced freedpeople to work effectively as low-paid serfs on sugar plantations. He approved a new state constitution that restored nearly all property and voting rights to whites but didn't grant Black men the right to vote. Hoping to placate southern loyalists, Lincoln said he was pleased with Banks's repressive policies and asked Congress to readmit Louisiana on these terms. He also suggested that Louisiana might be a model for future states.

Desperate to stop Lincoln's plan, Radicals like Sumner, James Ashley, and others tried to make a deal with him in December 1864. In exchange for admitting Louisiana without Black suffrage, Lincoln assented to sign a

Reconstruction bill that would award suffrage to either all Black men, or at least all Black veterans, in every other southern state—so long as Radicals could get it passed through Congress. "I will hold my peace, *if I can secure a rule for the other States,*" Sumner wrote to a friend. When Ashley drafted the bill, Representative Henry Davis noted in his diary that "Sumner & Ashley say Lincoln will sign it!!" However, the Radicals couldn't muster the votes for their deal; most centrists were horrified by the idea of requiring readmitted states to let Black men vote.[8]

By February, Lincoln's ally Senator Lyman Trumbull planned to pass a Louisiana readmission bill through Congress in the last few days of session without any voting rights for Blacks. Lincoln passionately supported Trumbull's bill, which newspapers described as his "pet project," out of a desire to begin Reconstruction. Having lost once to Trumbull in the drafting of the Thirteenth Amendment, Sumner was determined not to lose again. Moreover, he understood the stakes; if Louisiana were admitted without Black suffrage, it could set a standard that would undermine Sumner's dreams of an egalitarian, multiracial South. He had refused to stoop to political maneuvering for the sake of the presidential election, but for suffrage, he would enter the ring. If he had to fight Lincoln and rupture the Republican Party to kill Trumbull's bill, so be it.

* * *

WHEN TRUMBULL MADE a motion on February 23, 1865, for the Senate to proceed to consider his bill, Sumner interrupted him to say, "I hope not." Soon after Trumbull insisted upon discussing his bill, Sumner ominously explained that "there are two ways of killing a measure; one is by voting it down; the other is by postponing it until you lose an opportunity of voting upon it." There were fewer than ten days left in the session. If debate continued until the very end of session, the bill—and every other bill that hadn't yet been voted upon—would die. At the time, the Senate rules contained no mechanism for cutting off debate.

For the rest of that day and the next, Sumner repeatedly encouraged the Senate to delay debate on Trumbull's bill and kept pointing out other pressing matters that should be voted upon. He threatened a "dance of debate" if the bill were discussed, a "dance which is to last through the remainder of this session." After humoring him for some time by allowing delays, Trumbull insisted upon discussing his bill.[9]

Sumner implied, again, that he would debate Trumbull's bill long enough to kill it, even if he stood alone. "Give up!" a few senators exclaimed when Sumner started speaking. "That is not my habit," he retorted. When one senator cheekily replied, "We know that," the Senate burst into nervous laughter. There was a massive pile of documents, books, and papers on Sumner's desk, suggesting he was prepared to make the last few days of session miserable for everybody. "Do you intend by parliamentary tactics, to stop all the business of the Chamber?" one senator pleaded with him. "I do," Sumner retorted. "I shall employ every parliamentary device which is allowable. I shall propose amendments. I shall talk and talk, till you are glad to surrender."[10]

Debate began at noon on Saturday, February 25. Sumner proffered amendments, introduced dilatory motions, and argued with others on countless topics related to the bill. To move things along, the Senate resumed session at seven o'clock. That evening, Sumner kept railing against Trumbull for trying to "cram his measure down the throats of the Senate" and demanded more time to negotiate a bill that granted the vote to Black Louisianans. Otherwise, the bill was "a mere seven-months' abortion, begotten by the bayonet in criminal conjunction with the spirit of caste, and born before its time, rickety, unformed, unfinished."[11]

At one point, Sumner got personal. "There was a Senator from Illinois once in this Chamber. His name was Douglas," he hissed, referring to the late senator who had once been Trumbull's hated rival. "I had the honor of a seat here," Sumner continued, when Douglas tried to force through the Kansas-Nebraska Act "proudly, confidently, almost menacingly . . . as my friend from Illinois now brings this in." Sumner had famously exposed Douglas's bill and fought a legendary debate with him. Benjamin Wade, another Radical who was involved in those debates, backed up Sumner's stinging remarks. They breathlessly maligned Trumbull's character.[12]

"Look at the clock," Sumner taunted Trumbull after nearly five hours of speaking. "It is approaching Sunday morning." He sneered that it would be fruitless to try to pass the bill, like "sowing salt in the sand by the seashore." Exhausted and resigned by Sumner's gall and tenacity, Trumbull agreed to let the Senate adjourn until Monday. On Monday morning, he tried to resume debate on his bill, but Sumner started speaking again, warning that he had plenty to say and would make it "utterly impossible to take the vote." Soon enough, Senator John Sherman persuaded Trumbull to give up: there were many other bills on the docket.[13]

Many antislavery whites were appalled by Sumner's incivility. He was "a madman in the Louisiana question," according to his Boston-based friend Richard Dana. Comparing Sumner to haughty slave-owning senators, Dana thought he was even more "insolent and overbearing" and wished he could attribute Sumner's actions to being "out of his head from opium or . . . rum." Dana wasn't alone; one of many critical newspapers called it "disgraceful" that Sumner had resorted "to the trickery of a pot-house politician." But Samuel Howe sympathized with his best friend's struggles against his fellow Republicans. "Your task is herculean & Sisyphean, for you have to boost up those who are continually shrinking backward," he noted.[14]

Meanwhile, African Americans celebrated Sumner's cutting filibuster. *"The white people of this country have been so accustomed to regard and treat us as their natural inferiors,"* wrote Joshua Smith from Boston. "I know of no words of any language adequate to convey to you the gratitude I feel in my inmost soul," Smith said. Frederick Douglass was elated: "God grant you strength equal to your day and your duties! is my prayer and that of millions." Although Radicals like Wade had helped, it was Sumner who led the effort to stop the bill. As one historian put it, Sumner was "the central figure of the Senate, gazed at by all." Without him, Louisiana might have had a white-only government.

When Lincoln learned about Sumner's filibuster, he was furious. "Sumner had kicked the pet scheme of the President down the marble steps of the Senate Chamber," joked one editorial. The president tried to work with Radicals like Sumner and Ashley on his first Reconstruction plan. When their deal fell apart, he wrongly calculated that Trumbull could get his bill passed in spite of them. "These humanitarians break down all state rights and constitutional rights," Lincoln fumed at a Cabinet meeting. The president indignantly adverted to Sumner's filibuster "over and over again in the presence of strangers," according to one correspondent. "Still," the journalist surmised, "he respects Mr. Sumner, confers with him, and perhaps fears him."[15]

⋆ ⋆ ⋆

ONLY A FEW days after the session ended, Lincoln extended an olive branch to Sumner. He knew he needed Sumner, valued their friendship, and was perhaps, upon reflection, grateful that the habitually caustic senator had not personally criticized the president during the debates. (Sumner only attacked Trumbull.) For days, Sumner wondered whether

Lincoln would uphold their friendship given the nasty fight. "I was always honest and very plain with Mr. Lincoln, so much so that sometimes he was almost angry with me," Sumner later confessed. "But he never allowed difference of opinion or frankness to interrupt our familiar and confidential intercourse."[16]

On March 5, 1865, Sumner received a note from the president. "My dear Sir, I should be pleased for you to accompany us to-morrow evening, at ten o'clock, on a visit of half an hour to the Inaugural Ball." For four years, ever since the start of the Civil War, Sumner had almost always abstained from evening parties. But he agreed to attend this party, celebrating Lincoln's inauguration on the previous day, in a show of goodwill. Mr. and Mrs. Lincoln, joined by House Speaker Schuyler Colfax, picked up Sumner by carriage from his doorstep.

When Lincoln's entourage reached the Patent Office (now the National Portrait Gallery), the party promenaded across the long marble floor under the auspices of army shields and the flags of foreign nations. A band played "Hail to the Chief" as hundreds of attendees, in two long rows on both sides of the party, cheered. Lincoln and Colfax strolled first; behind them sauntered Mrs. Lincoln and Charles Sumner, arm in arm, with other notables following. Coming up on a grand dais at the front, Mrs. Lincoln joined her husband on one of the richly gilded armchairs that presided over the dance hall. Lincoln asked Sumner, who tried to squirm his way out, to sit behind the couple, alongside Colfax, William Seward, Robert Todd Lincoln, and others. There he stayed, ogled by admirers like everyone else in the presidential suite, until he escorted Mrs. Lincoln to dinner.

Reporters naturally speculated that Sumner's prominence at the inaugural ball signified that Lincoln had had a change of heart on his Reconstruction policy. That wasn't quite true: Lincoln stood his ground, even as he continued to make overtures toward Sumner that caused many to believe he was open to persuasion.[17]

One indication that Lincoln's views were not changing was the fact that his inaugural ball was limited to whites. While Sumner sat on the splendid dais with the Lincolns, John Rock—the attorney whom Sumner had admitted to the Supreme Court—was standing outside with his wife. Despite having already purchased the ten-dollar tickets, Rock and his wife were being denied entrance. Only a few days earlier, the organizing committee had declared that only white people would be permitted to attend. If "coloured people were allowed to be present," explained the (London) *Times*, ". . . [it]

would lead to unpleasantness, and cause the white *belles* of Washington to absent themselves *en masse*." To the *Times*, this proved that "Congress may pass what laws it pleases about the negro race, but fashion and the ladies are more powerful than the Legislature."

In the weeks ahead, Sumner conspicuously appeared in public with the Lincolns at the theater and the opera, places that were often limited to whites. The remnants of caste were everywhere. Despite this, and despite the fiery Reconstruction debates, Lincoln seemed very happy, and Sumner was relieved, too. No matter what problems remained, at least the war was winding down. Paying Lincoln many personal and business calls at the White House, Sumner chatted with him hopefully about the future of the country.[18]

In early April, the Union Army took over the rebel capital of Richmond. Mary Lincoln dashed off in a note to Sumner: "This is almost too much happiness to be realized!" In it, she invited him to accompany her on a trip to the conquered Virginia city, where Lincoln had already arrived. The two embarked on April 5 with Cabinet members James Harlan, James Speed, and their wives, among others. Venturing into Richmond with a cavalry escort the next day, they toured the State Capitol Building. Sumner inquired after the well-being of various southerners whom he hadn't heard from since the war. Like any former Harvard professor would have, he also went to the Confederate archives and reminded the vanquished bureaucrats to preserve their records for the sake of history.

After Richmond, Mary Lincoln's party met the president at City Point, an army encampment outside the city. "We had a gay time," she recalled. Lincoln shook hands with thousands of wounded soldiers, telling an amazed Sumner that his long arms never got tired. After boarding a riverboat, the group slowly sailed back to Washington. "Breakfasting, lunching, and dining in one small family party," as Sumner fondly recalled, the party listened to Lincoln regale them with stories and poems, including one by Sumner's friend Henry Longfellow. "Even our stately, dignified Mr. Sumner acknowledged himself transformed, into a lad of sixteen," Mary Lincoln remembered about "that pleasant Sabbath morning on the boat." At some point, Lincoln turned to Sumner. Quietly, he said, "they say I have been under Seward's influence." Sumner's ears pricked up. "I have counselled with you twice as much as I ever did with him," the president assured him. This left Sumner wondering whether Lincoln might soon ask him to replace Seward as secretary of state.[19]

On April 10, Mary Lincoln sent Sumner a bouquet of flowers. She was celebrating the long-awaited news: on the previous day, Confederate general Robert E. Lee had surrendered to Union general Ulysses Grant at Appomattox Court House in central Virginia. Few statesmen could take more pride than Sumner in defeating Lee's army. "Grant won with the sword at Appomattox what Charles Sumner contended for half a century—an idea," an abolitionist later celebrated. "That idea is the liberty of all, limited by the like liberty of each."[20]

The First Lady asked Sumner to come to the White House to watch Washington's city lights be illuminated in honor of the final victory, but Sumner demurred. He knew that Lincoln planned to deliver a short speech at the celebration. Afraid that the president would double down on a postwar policy that deprived Blacks of the vote, Sumner didn't want to be seen on the platform when Lincoln spoke, implying an assent to the president's policy, especially after weeks of their having appeared together in public. Sure enough, Lincoln again urged that Louisiana be readmitted into the union under its proposed white-only government.

Although the South had officially surrendered, there was still the risk of danger. During their trip, Sumner had feared violence from spiteful southerners. "On the way to Richmond, he said that there might well be a bullet waiting for him but that he was prepared for it," wrote a French aristocrat whom Sumner had invited to accompany the entourage. As he walked through the city, though, Sumner was amazed at how safe it was. "The Presdt . . . saw with his own eyes at Richmond & Petersburg, that the only people *who showed themselves were negroes*," he later wrote to Chief Justice Chase. "All others had fled or were retired in their houses. Never was I more convinced of the utter impossibility of any organization which is not founded on the votes of the negroes." Black southerners were patriotic loyalists, Sumner believed: it was white southerners whom the president needed to fear.[21]

* * *

ON APRIL 14, Abraham Lincoln attended a performance at Ford's Theatre with his wife. Sumner, who had joined the couple on their most recent trip to a theater to see *Faust* a few weeks earlier, wasn't there this time. At around 10:20 p.m., John Wilkes Booth took advantage of the crowd's laughter after a joke onstage, quietly entered the presidential box, aimed his pistol behind Lincoln's left ear, and fired a clean shot through the president's skull. Mary Lincoln shrieked while Booth knifed another attendee, leaped from the box, stumbled awkwardly onto the stage, and roared a sentence that sounded like "SIC SEMPER TYRANNIS, THE SOUTH IS AVENGED!" before he scrambled out a side door. Booth, a famous Maryland actor who had been dubbed "the handsomest man in America," vocally supported the Confederacy and hated Lincoln for unilaterally emancipating the South's slaves.

Around the same time, ex–Confederate soldier Lewis Powell entered the home of Secretary of State William Seward under the pretense of delivering medication. (Seward was sound asleep, recovering from a carriage accident.) Running into Seward's son Frederick upstairs, Powell beat Frederick with his revolver before storming into Seward's room and repeatedly stabbing the secretary in the neck and face. An army nurse jumped Powell from behind, and the two grappled on the floor until Powell broke free, stabbed the nurse, scrambled down the stairs, gashed Seward's other son and one of Seward's guests, and fled. The assassin mounted his horse and rode off while the household raced to find out if Seward had survived.[22]

Sumner was enjoying wine with Senator William Stewart at the home of Senator John Conness when a Treasury Department clerk rushed into the house exclaiming that Lincoln and Seward had been murdered. Sumner didn't believe it. "Young man, be moderate in your statements," he replied sternly. "What has happened?" When the clerk insisted it was true, the three senators bolted to Seward's home; Sumner lagged behind, panting. Stewart forced his way into the house. After confirming that Seward was hurt but had survived, the trio ran across the street to the White House. Discovering that Lincoln wasn't home, Sumner frantically told a porter, "They say that the President has been assassinated." The porter located Robert Todd Lincoln, who jumped into a carriage with Sumner and the others; the carriage then sped toward Ford's Theatre. Learning that President Lincoln had indeed been shot, they crossed the street to the house where the president was said to be resting.

At the door, Sumner met Mary Lincoln, who begged him to tell her whether her husband still lived. He said he didn't know, and after escorting Robert to his mother, he rushed to Lincoln's sickroom. At the doorstep, Sumner ran into Surgeon General Joseph Barnes. Barnes said nobody else should go inside. "But you can go in if you insist, as you are a Senator," he huffed. "I WILL GO IN!" Sumner howled, rushing past the surgeon while the other two senators obediently stayed outside. Lincoln lay diagonally across the bed, breathing heavily, unconscious, with his eyes half open. Grabbing the president's right hand, Sumner hysterically started talking to him while a doctor said it wasn't of any use, because he was dead. "No, he isn't dead—look at his face—he is breathing," Sumner panted. "It will never be anything more than this," the doctor replied.[23]

For more than seven hours, Sumner sat at the head of Lincoln's bed, clutching the president's right hand as it sometimes quivered feebly. "Sumner was sobbing like a woman," a visitor noted, "with his head bowed down almost on the pillow." Many mourners stepped in and out of the sickroom as Sumner stayed there motionless, tears streaming down his cheeks while he listened intently to Lincoln's slow breathing. At times, Robert left his mother and joined Sumner, leaning on Sumner's shoulder while crying his heart out. When the final struggle with death began, Mary Lincoln joined Robert and Sumner to pay her final visit to her husband. There, they grieved together, along with twenty or so other visitors, until Lincoln drew his last breath at 7:22 a.m.[24]

Once Lincoln had passed, Sumner left the late president's side and stepped out into the morning sun. There, he saw a multiracial crowd of Washingtonians who had kept vigil all night long. "How is Mr. Lincoln? Is he alive?" somebody asked. Shaking his head, Sumner left the crowd of mourners to board a carriage with Gen. Henry Halleck to visit Seward. On the way, they briefly stopped at the home of Andrew Johnson, Lincoln's vice president, where Halleck warned the president-to-be not to leave his house without a guard.

When they reached Seward's house, soldiers denied them entrance; they were allowing no visitors. "Send my card to Mrs. Seward or Miss Fannie, they will wish to see me," Sumner told the guards. Despite his quarrels with Seward, Sumner was very friendly with Seward's wife, Frances. Frances came down in her nightgown. "Charles, they have murdered my husband, they have murdered my son," she cried. (In fact, both men were alive, albeit grievously injured.) She clutched Sumner with both her hands and sat with him for a few minutes, before rushing back to her loved ones upstairs. Sumner never saw her again; though Seward and his son survived, Frances died of a heart attack a few weeks later.

At nearly 8 a.m., Sumner made it home, scurrying past a guard that Secretary of War Edwin Stanton had sent to his doorstep. He slumped over an untasted plate of breakfast, looking stern and haggard. Several of Sumner's friends, after hearing rumors about the horrible overnight news, visited the house to confirm that Sumner himself had not been assassinated. Sumner reassured one caller, who worried that the war would restart, that there was "no fear of a second rebellion" because southerners would be ashamed by the cowardly killings. "Our leaders are gone," the guest exclaimed. Sumner responded, "But the republic remains."[25]

*　*　*

TWO DAYS AFTER Lincoln's demise, Sumner and other members of Congress who were still in Washington put together an ad hoc session. They selected a committee of five, with Sumner as chair, to draft an initial plan for the state funeral. They decided that Lincoln's body should be sent back to Illinois, and they appointed a group of congressional pallbearers. In a statement that Sumner undoubtedly penned, the group commemorated Lincoln as "a martyr whose memory will become more precious as men learn to prize those principles of constitutional order, and those rights, civil, political, and human, for which he was made a sacrifice." They instructed the new president, Andrew Johnson, to pick a day for national commemoration.[26]

Johnson, a Tennessee slaveowner, had surprised his peers in the Senate when he denounced his home state's decision to join the Confederacy in 1861. Believing firmly in the Union, Johnson resented wealthy slave oligarchs and said he represented the interests of poor white farmers who had never wanted war. Impressed, Lincoln had appointed Johnson military governor of Tennessee. In 1864, he added Johnson, a Democrat, to his ticket in a show of political unity and to garner support in the border states. Few knew what to expect from the handsome southern man who suddenly held the reins of power in the wake of a crisis.

On the evening after Lincoln's death, Sumner paid Johnson a visit. He hadn't liked Johnson before. During Lincoln's inauguration in March, Johnson had shamelessly showed up drunk in the Senate. Sumner was so appalled by this boorish behavior that he openly suggested Johnson resign or be impeached. But now, with Johnson as the new president and the country reeling from the assassination, Sumner decided to give him a second chance. Ostensibly meeting to tell him about the new British ambassador to the United States, Sumner raised the issue of how to treat rebels, hoping that Johnson wouldn't adopt Lincoln's leniency. "I found him careful in what he said, but very determined," Sumner recalled.[27]

For the next few weeks, Sumner met with Johnson multiple times at a hotel where he resided while Mary Lincoln and her family grieved in the White House. He also called on Mary several times to pay his respects. She gifted Sumner one of the late president's canes. "Your unwavering kindness to my idolized husband, and the great regard he entertained for you," she wrote, "prompts me to offer for your acceptance this simple relic." Calling him a "cherished friend of my husband and myself," she bade him goodbye before departing for Illinois in late May. "I go hence, broken hearted, with every hope almost in life—crushed."[28]

By May, Sumner said he had "seen a good deal of the new President." The two met regularly to discuss Reconstruction. Chief Justice Chase joined them in at least one conversation to discuss Black suffrage in the South. "Without their votes we cannot establish stable governments in the rebel States. Their votes are as necessary as their muskets," Sumner believed. "Unless the black man is given the right to vote his freedom is a mockery." To his pleasant surprise, Johnson seemed to agree. "In the question of colored suffrage the President is with us," Sumner told a friend with relief. To get things going, Johnson allowed Chase to travel through the South on a lecture tour encouraging Black suffrage, and he sent Union Army general Carl Schurz to study the conditions in the South and report back. "The objects he aims at are all the most progressive friends of human liberty can desire," Schurz happily told Sumner about the new president.[29]

Johnson's apparent clear-sightedness on Black suffrage enabled Sumner to cope with Lincoln's death by assigning it higher meaning. In a eulogy delivered over the summer, Sumner said "the work left undone by Washington was continued by Lincoln." By ending slavery, Lincoln "consummate[d] all the original promises of the Declaration." But in the last months of his life, Lincoln was hesitating again. Initially heartbroken, Sumner decided that Lincoln had died on time. "Family and friends may mourn," he told a friend, "but his death will do more for the cause than any human life." Now whites would be inspired by Lincoln's martyrdom to do more for Black America. And with Lincoln's obstinacy on Louisiana out of the way, Johnson might enact the vision the martyred president had so eloquently articulated but couldn't bring himself to endorse: a government of the people, by the people, for the people, where the word *people* included those of all races, not just whites.[30]

Sumner explained what he understood to be Johnson's Reconstruction plan to friends like John Bright, Francis Lieber, and Wendell Phillips. "He deprecates haste; is unwilling that States should be precipitated back;

thinks there must be a period of probation, but that meanwhile all loyal people, without distinction of color, must be treated as citizens." Thinking that "none of the old traitors should be allowed to take part in establishing new govts," Johnson apparently agreed with Sumner on exiling rebel leaders. "A considerable number of the leading rebels, say 100, or better still, 500," Sumner believed, should be deported. That way, they couldn't be "centers of influence" in the postwar South who might try to roll back the racial progress made by the Civil War.

Sumner couldn't have been more relieved: with Johnson's support, everything he had fought for seemed likely to transpire. "The end is coming & just as you & I desire. . . . Never so grand & fair & beautiful," he reassured Phillips. "I said during this winter that the rebel States could not come back, except on the footing of the Decltn of Indep. & the complete recognition of Human Rights," he told Lieber. "I feel more than ever confident that all this will be fulfilled. And then what a regenerated land!" Content to trust Johnson until the Senate resumed session, Sumner reiterated the need for equal rights in the South at his final meeting with the new president on May 12 before departing for Boston for the summer. When he apologized to Johnson for incessantly bringing up the theme of racial justice in every meeting, he was reassured warmly.

"Have I not always listened to you?" Johnson replied, smiling.[31]

PART IV

THE REPUBLICAN GUARANTEE

CHAPTER 20

A MAGNA CARTA
OF DEMOCRACY IN AMERICA

PRESIDENT JOHNSON LIED ABOUT SUPPORTING BLACK SUFFRAGE.
When he released a batch of Reconstruction policies in late May 1865,
they were nothing like what he had told Sumner to expect. "I had every
reason to believe that Presdt. Johnson would incline to the side of Equal
Rights," Sumner wrote. "This is madness," he fumed. "It is also inconsistent with his sayings to the Chief Justice & myself." Believing that Johnson
had been influenced by conservatives in his Cabinet like William Seward
and Montgomery Blair, Sumner was horrified by the change, which he
described as being "like a somersault or an apostasy."[1]

First, Johnson recognized the Lincoln-created governments in Arkansas, Louisiana, Tennessee, and Virginia, none of which had enfranchised
Blacks. Second, he formed a provisional government in North Carolina
that restricted the suffrage to those who had possessed it prior to the Civil
War—effectively limiting voting rights to white men. Finally, he issued a
blanket amnesty to all who had supported the Confederacy except high-
ranking officials and the wealthiest rebels. After taking a simple oath of
allegiance, Confederates would see restored "all rights of property," except
as to slaves and some military confiscation.

In one fell swoop, Johnson reaffirmed Lincoln's policy of disenfran-
chising African Americans, extended that exclusion to North Carolina,
and obliterated any chance of mass land reform for freedpeople across
the South. Evidently, Sumner had misjudged him. For years, Johnson had
publicly blamed wealthy slaveholders for precipitating the war. While
Sumner took this as a promising sign, he had failed to discern that Johnson equally blamed abolitionists and Blacks. Willing to abolish slavery to
punish big slaveholders, he had no interest in helping freedpeople. "The
radicals . . . are wild upon negro franchise," Johnson vented to one of his

appointed governors. "White men alone must manage the South," he told Senator John Conness.[2]

Johnson's goal was to preserve white supremacy even while enforcing the abolition of slavery. He required rebel states to ban slavery but ordered the Freedmen's Bureau to relinquish land titles that had been awarded to Black freedpeople. He permitted some states to organize militias with Confederate veterans and ordered the recall of Black Union soldiers. While refusing to let top Confederates hold office, he allowed hundreds of ordinary former rebels to be hired as revenue assessors, tax collectors, postmasters, and other lower federal posts across the national bureaucracy. Johnson's appointed governor in Florida explained the president's policies by telling an audience of African Americans that "you must not think because you are as *free* as white people, that you are their *equal*."

With Johnson's tacit permission, newly organized Southern states imposed Black Codes to keep freedpeople in subjugation. South Carolina required all Black residents to work as farmers or servants. Mississippi forced involuntary plantation work on any Black person who didn't have a job. Louisiana and Texas made all Black families, including women and children, enter annual labor contracts with white masters. Johnson believed it was a state's constitutional prerogative to subjugate their Black populations so long as slavery was gone in name. "Every political right which the State possessed under the Federal Constitution, is hers to-day, with the single exception relating to slavery," bragged Alabama's Johnson-appointed governor.[3]

Sumner was horrified, but he felt powerless: Congress wouldn't meet until December 1865. Until then, he frantically delivered speeches to stir public opinion against Johnson's policies. While he didn't want "to break with the Presdt. unless it becomes absolutely necessary," he hoped that Johnson, like Lincoln, would willingly change his policies if public opinion changed. Praying that Johnson was open to advice, he begged members of the Cabinet to talk to their boss. But most Republicans were exhausted by years of war and relentless activism. Even John Andrew, the stalwart abolitionist governor of Massachusetts, split from Sumner. Governor Andrew thought that Johnson, and white southerners, needed time to adjust to life with Black freedpeople. If more aggressive action were needed, he figured, Congress could act later.[4]

While Johnson led Reconstruction through the summer and fall of 1865, Sumner corresponded with like-minded Radicals who nervously awaited the start of the next session. "Is there any hope that Congress will over-rule the Presdt? I fear we are ruined, for I have little faith in Congress," the pessimistic House Radical Thaddeus Stevens wrote to Sumner. But Sumner had high hopes that Congress would make its own Reconstruction policies. When a Black community leader in Washington complained to him, he wrote back with a promise: "Work on. Fight on. When Congress meets, we shall insist upon JUSTICE."[5]

* * *

ON DECEMBER 2, 1865, Sumner arrived in Washington for the new con-gressional session and went straight to the White House. For two and a half hours, he told Johnson about the horrible conditions in the South. He probably described some letters he had obtained from people travel-ing through the region. One letter decried that "former masters exhibit a most cruel, remorseless, and vindictive spirit toward the colored peo-ple." There were "murders, shootings, whippings, robbing, and brutal treatment . . . inflicted upon them." Another letter said that Black child orphans were being seized by judges as virtual slaves. Yet another horrified traveler said he saw colored women being "treated in the most outrageous manner," with "no rights that are respected," to the extent that some were "mutilated by having ears and noses cut off."[6]

Johnson could hardly bother to listen to Sumner's stories. "The Senator was shedding his crocodile tears over the poor freedmen," said a Johnson ally who attended the meeting with a shrug. The president paid so little attention that at one point, he mistakenly spat tobacco into Sumner's hat, thinking it was a spittoon, given that it was lying on the floor. Running out of patience, Sumner exploded. He accused Johnson of throwing away the fruits of Union victory and threatened war against him in Congress. He stormed out of the White House and never met the president one-on-one again after Johnson angrily defended himself. "Much that he said was pain-ful, from its prejudice, ignorance & perversity," Sumner seethed.[7]

Two weeks later, Johnson reluctantly released the *Report on the Condi-tion of the South*, a document he commissioned by the German American former general Carl Schurz. Traveling through five former Confederate states, Schurz observed widespread disloyalty and violence. "Not only the former slaveholders, but the non-slaveholding whites," he observed, "are possessed by a singularly bitter and vindictive feeling against the col-ored race since the negro has ceased to be property." Johnson had tried to bury the report because it contradicted his own views. "The only great mistake I have yet made was to send Schurz to the South," he had muttered to a senator. Johnson was defeated by Sumner, who passed a congressional motion instructing the White House to release the report and later ensured that more than one hundred thousand copies of it were printed.

Unbeknownst to Johnson, Sumner had helped Schurz in the report's production. Before the general went on his expedition, he secured for Schurz a stenographer and a life insurance policy. Schurz wrote to Sumner regularly to discuss his travels and the report's potential contents. Government reports were Sumner's forte. During the war, he had played a similar role in assisting Edward Pierce in the drafting of *The Negroes at Port Royal*, which called for education and land distribution to freedpeople on the Sea Islands, and the three men who proffered similar recommendations for the entire South in the *Report of the American Freedmen's Inquiry Commission*. Sumner knew how to use these reports to put pressure on the government.[8]

While Schurz's report was being distributed to politicians and the press, Sumner introduced a barrage of bills and resolutions to undo the damage of Johnson's white supremacist policies. He wanted Congress to refuse to honor rebel debts, establish multiracial public schools in the South, and forbid those who had served in the rebellion from participating in southern conventions to draft new constitutions. To protect African Americans from violence, he wanted Congress to remove all cases concerning Black people from state court to federal court, make all grand juries consist of one-half Black people, and recognize the Black man's constitutional right to vote. "The power that gave freedom must see that freedom is maintained," he argued.[9]

While Sumner unfurled his Reconstruction program immediately at the start of the congressional session, most Republicans preferred a more strategic approach. Thaddeus Stevens led the charge. A rugged Pennsylvania man with a clubfoot and a wry wit, Stevens was the leading Radical in the House. A tactical backroom legislator, he asked Congress to form a Joint Committee on Reconstruction. This committee would hear testimony from southerners, review the repugnant Black Codes, and—when the time was right—release bills and potential constitutional amendments.

After Stevens was chosen as the House chair of the committee, Sumner tried to chair it in the Senate. But the Senate chose William Fessenden, a Republican centrist from Maine. A skinny, sickly senator with a surprisingly hot head, Fessenden detested Sumner's moralizing attitude. "My constituents did not send me here to philosophize," he once snorted while Sumner was speaking. Considered to be the most influential New England senator apart from Sumner, Fessenden was proud to have been picked over his rival, who was considered too ideological for the job. "Mr. Sumner was very anxious for the place," Fessenden boasted, "but, standing as he does before the country, and committed to the most ultra views, even his friends declined to support him, and almost to a man fixed upon me."[10]

Over the next few weeks, the Joint Committee debated a variety of Reconstruction proposals. Top of mind was Black suffrage. Worried that rebel states would gain political power after ex-slaves were counted as whole persons (rather than three-fifths of a person) in the next census, many Radicals wanted the committee to propose a constitutional amendment to grant Black men the suffrage. That, they believed, would flip southern elections to favor pro–civil rights Republicans. But Stevens feared it wasn't politically feasible to get a Black suffrage amendment ratified. After all, even many northern states denied Black men the right to vote.

Stevens convinced Fessenden and the committee to draft a more politically viable amendment, which actually originated with Sumner. Back in February and again in December 1865, Sumner had pitched an amendment at the urging of one of his best friends, the legal theorist Francis Lieber, to apportion House seats "according to the number of male citizens of age" who could vote. If a state allowed more men to vote, it would be allotted more seats in the House. But if a state excluded eligible men—such as Blacks or those without property—it would get fewer seats. This clever scheme, Stevens hoped, created a strong incentive for states to voluntarily enfranchise all men.[11]

Sumner was irate when the House passed the Joint Committee's so-called Apportionment Amendment. Even though apportionment was his own idea, Sumner now said it was too complicated and a cop-out from recognizing Black suffrage full stop. Believing "a moral principle cannot be compromised," he warned Fessenden that when the proposal came to the Senate, he would "put his foot on it and crush it." Sumner probably held a grudge against Fessenden for taking his spot on the Joint Committee. But he was also right to think the proposal was unworkable. In fact, the Apportionment Amendment—which turned into Section 2 of the Fourteenth Amendment—has never been put into practice. Not once.[12]

* * *

INSTEAD OF AN amendment, Sumner wanted a national law banning states from restricting the vote to whites. He believed the Constitution already banned racial discrimination. While the text allowed states to make "qualifications" for voting, Sumner said these qualifications had to be reasonable—an argument that would have been familiar to lawyers who engaged in statutory interpretation. Qualifications like age, residence, crime, or education were reasonable, he conceded. Those based on "permanent and insurmountable" traits like skin color were not.[13]

Few Republicans agreed with Sumner's constitutional argument even if they were receptive to Black suffrage. In antebellum America, voting was a privilege, not a right. Women, for example, were citizens who couldn't vote, ostensibly because they were under the authority of their fathers or husbands. In some places, men without property couldn't vote, either, ostensibly because they didn't pay taxes. Sumner pointed out that Black freedmen were now citizens—no longer under the authority of enslavers—who could own property and be taxed. Plus, nearly 180,000 Black men had fought for the Union Army, proving their capacity for loyal citizenship. "If he was willing to die for the Republic, he is surely good enough to vote," Sumner argued.[14]

As a young lawyer, Sumner had shared the view that voting was a privilege that should perhaps be restricted to those who could read or write. But he gradually came around to thinking that suffrage should be a birthright of citizenship. "For a long time I was perplexed by the subtlety, so often presented, that the suffrage is a 'privilege' & not a 'right,'" he confessed. "The more I think of it, the more it seems to me, an essential right, which govt. can only regulate & guard, but cannot abridge. All *just* govt. stands on 'the consent of the governed.'"[15]

Sumner's change of heart can be credited largely to Black leaders who were vigorously campaigning for the right to vote. They held conventions in at least ten states in 1865 and 1866 to mobilize for the suffrage. Believing "slavery is not abolished until the black man has the ballot," Frederick Douglass and others told a large convention of Black leaders in Washington to urge that their "one thought" be "the immediate, complete, and universal enfranchisement of the colored people of the whole country." Not long after, Black organizers across the country launched the National Equal Rights League, a group dedicated to secure "equal political rights without distinction of race or color" as "the birth-right of American citizens." Around this time, Sumner adopted the same language about birth-rights, a concept African Americans had popularized.[16]

While reflecting on the relationship between birthright suffrage and democracy, Sumner prepared to advocate for a national law on Black suffrage instead of the Joint Committee's draft Apportionment Amendment. He was one of the few Senate Republicans to vocally oppose the draft, which House Republicans had already passed. To make his case, Sumner needed to show that Congress had authority to pass a suffrage law. Prior to the Civil War, states had had full control in deciding who could vote in elections. Claiming that Congress could play no part, Johnson had declared that former rebel states could disenfranchise Blacks if they so chose. "Here again we have State Rights in the way of Equality, as they were in the way of Liberty," Sumner complained.[17]

Sumner believed that Congress had plenary (absolute) power to protect voting rights in rebel states. He grounded his claim in the Constitution's Republican Guarantee Clause. The clause, which states that "the United States shall guarantee to every State in this Union a Republican Form of Government," has never received much attention by constitutional law-yers—not in Sumner's time, and not today. To Sumner, it was the "key-stone clause" of the Constitution, among the most important set of words in the entire document. Many years after Sumner's death, the Supreme Court coolly dismissed the Republican Guarantee Clause's relevance to voting rights cases. Even when Congress passed the Voting Rights Act of 1965, and when the Executive Branch has defended the act's legality in court, the clause has rarely been invoked.

Sumner argued that the Republican Guarantee Clause, overlooked in his time and long after his death, gave Congress "supreme power" over the states whenever republicanism needed saving. He said that "next after the Dcltn. of Indep. & the Preamble of the Constitution, this is the most important clause of the Constitution." But when, according to Sumner, did a state constitutionally lack a republican form of government?[18]

"The time has come to fix a meaning upon these words," Sumner told Francis Lieber. To figure out the best legal meaning of the word *republic*, Sumner "read everything on the subject from Plato to the last French pamphlet," according to one of Johnson's Cabinet members. He also pondered what the Founding Fathers might have meant by a republic. "Did they simply mean a guarantee against a king?" he asked Lieber. "Something more, I believe." Recognizing that words might "receive expansion & elevation with time," Sumner figured that "our fathers builded wiser than they knew" by using such a loaded term as *republican*.

Sumner predicted that the debate on the "meaning of a 'Republican govt.' will be the greatest in our history." To this end, in early 1866, he decided to make American republicanism the theme of a major speech opposing the Apportionment Amendment, which he delivered on the first day it was up for debate. His speech was one of the most thorough expositions on the Republican Guarantee Clause in American constitutional history. Years later, the Black intellectual W. E. B. Du Bois would say the speech "laid down a Magna Carta of democracy in America."[19]

* * *

SUMNER DELIVERED HIS highly anticipated speech, "The Equal Rights of All," on February 5 and 6, 1866. "Emancipation itself will fail without Enfranchisement," he said on the first day. Senators were at their desks listening intently; two Cabinet secretaries, several foreign diplomats, and scores of House members sat on the sofas and stood in groups on the Senate floor. From the galleries, Frederick Douglass, joined by many Black soldiers and other members of the public, watched Sumner with high expectations. "The galleries were literally packed with earnest men and women, who drank in every word as the gifted orator proceeded," said one newspaper.[20]

"By Enfranchisement I mean the establishment of the Equal Rights of All, so that there shall be no exclusion of any kind, civil or political, founded on color, and the promises of the Fathers shall be fulfilled," Sumner continued. Without this, he warned, violence might transpire. Bringing up the case of Haiti, where enslaved people had liberated themselves in a bloody revolution, Sumner said "it was the denial of rights to colored people, upon successive promises, which caused that fearful insurrection." It was in white people's own interests to enfranchise Black southerners. Otherwise, America's democratic experiment could collapse.

Sumner said that the country also needed Black voters to protect democracy in the South from being undermined by disloyal whites. If former Confederates retook power, he warned, they would force the North to inherit rebel debts, leading to financial ruin, and reimpose racial caste hierarchy, bringing moral ruin to the country. "All this is inevitable," he argued, "if you give them the power; it is madness to tempt them." Believing apportionment could be subverted by what he later called "tricks and evasion,"

Sumner said it was "a delusion and a snare" to think white Southerners would willingly give Blacks the vote, even if they were incentivized to do so.

Sumner called on Congress to protect democracy by passing legislation to directly enfranchise Black southerners. Although such a law would impinge on states' rights, he believed the Guarantee Clause provided Congress with the authority. All Congress needed to do was invoke it and define it. Helpfully, in a case brought before the war, the Supreme Court had said that Congress could define a republican form of government without the Court's intervention. "In affixing the proper meaning to the text," Sumner said to his colleagues, "you act as a court in the last resort . . . rarely in history has such an opportunity been offered to the statesman." With all that said, he devoted the next few hours, and some hours the following day, to an exposition on the Guarantee Clause.

To find the meaning of a republic, Sumner first looked to European intellects. After subjecting his audience to the myriad contradictory definitions he had found from Plato, Aristotle, Cicero, Marcus Aurelius, Montesquieu, Kant, Locke, and others, he said all their ideas were unhelpful. He explained that John Adams, having tried a similarly exhausting exercise, was left to admit that "the word republic, as it is used, may signify anything, everything or nothing." The solution, Sumner argued, was to stop searching abroad. "It is in vain that you cite philosophers or publicists, or the examples of former history," he declared. To define a republic for constitutional purposes, Americans should study "the history and example of their own country."

Sumner began at the Founding. "By 'a republican form of government' our fathers plainly intended that government which embodied the principles for which they had struggled." After examining what the Founders claimed before the Revolution, as asserted in the Declaration, enshrined in the Constitution, and embodied during the earliest years of the Republic, he argued that the "American idea of a Republic, which must be adopted in the interpretation of the National Constitution," rested on two principles: "First, that all men are Equal in rights; and secondly, that Governments derive their just powers from the consent of the governed."

Sumner believed that the idea of equal rights had seeped into the Founders' vision of government by consent. For example, the Founder who coined "taxation without representation," James Otis, had openly believed that his principles applied to both whites and Blacks. "The Colonists are by the law of nature free born, as indeed all men are, white and black," Otis observed. Similarly, Benjamin Franklin, who grew to hate slavery, said that "to be enslaved is to . . . be subject to laws *made by the representatives of others*, without having had representatives of our own to give consent in *our* behalf." Founders guilty of the crime of slavery also testified to the centrality of equal rights in a republic built on consent. For example, Jefferson said that "the first principle of republicanism is, that the *lex majoris partis* [majority rule] is the fundamental law of every society of individuals of *equal rights*."

The horrific irony of the American Founding was that a nation born on the principles of equality and consent sanctioned a system of slavery. "While confessing sorrowfully their inconsistency in recognizing slavery," Sumner argued that the Founders never accepted inequality and lack of representation for *free* Black citizens. In his speech, he surveyed the constitutions of all thirteen colonies. By the time the Constitution was ratified in 1789, only one of the thirteen (South Carolina) restricted suffrage to whites in its constitution. In the twelve other colonies turned states, free Blacks, especially those who owned property, could vote. Remarkably, Black colonists even participated in some of the ratifying conventions for the Constitution.

In Sumner's view, whatever unrepublican features the Founders hypocritically tolerated with regard to slavery did not apply to free Blacks. The crowning jewel of his argument was an excerpt from *Federalist Paper* No. 54. Attributed to both James Madison and Alexander Hamilton, the essay states that "if the laws were to restore the rights which have been taken away, the negroes could no longer be refused an equal share of representation with the other inhabitants." In other words: all ex-slaves should be able to vote.

Having established his interpretation of republicanism at the American Founding, Sumner applied it to the problem of Reconstruction. Millions of enslaved people in the South were now free American taxpayers. Yet they were being denied the vote by Johnson's provisional governments, "even though they surpassed in numbers, by at least a million, the whole population of the Colonies at the time our fathers raised the cry." While being denied suffrage as *slaves* was potentially compatible with how the Founders understood the idea of a republic, being denied the vote as *taxpaying free people* was not. "Call it an Oligarchy, call it an Aristocracy, call it a Caste, call it a Monopoly," Sumner said, referring to the reconstructed South. "But do not call it a Republic."

With slavery now eliminated, Sumner argued, there was a moral and constitutional imperative to guarantee equality for all recently emancipated people in the former Confederacy. That was the only way to make the region a republic. Believing "Equality in rights is the first of rights," and in "Liberty and Equality as the God-given birthright of all men," Sumner said both values were central to the American experiment. "What is Liberty without Equality? What is Equality without Liberty?" he asked. "One is the complement of the other. The two are necessary to round and complete the circle of American citizenship."

Thus, Sumner called on Congress to ditch the Apportionment Amendment and immediately interpret the Republican Guarantee Clause as granting it constitutional authority to force southern states to let Black freedmen vote. "Even if the text were doubtful," he conceded, "the war makes it clear. The victory which overthrew slavery carried away all those glosses and constructions by which this wrong was originally fastened upon the Constitution." Proclaiming that "one of the great victories— perhaps the greatest" was "the Emancipation of the Constitution itself," Sumner said it was time for a new rule of constitutional interpretation that would fulfill "the promises of the Fathers." The postwar Constitution, he argued, "must be interpreted, in harmony with the Declaration of Independence, so that Human Rights shall always prevail."

* * *

WHEN SUMNER FINISHED speaking, the Senate galleries burst into applause. The presiding officer tried to quell the exuberance from above while several senators went up to Sumner to congratulate him. "As an exposition of the American theory of Republicanism, this speech is unsurpassed in the history of American oratory," the *Dayton Journal* celebrated. "It is the most powerful oration of his life," pronounced the Boston *Commonwealth*. "The crowning glory of his scholarship and statesmanship." Many papers described Sumner's speech as his greatest work. One paper went even farther: "It is not only *the* great speech of Charles Sumner's life, but it is the great speech of the age," declared the *Portland Daily Press*.

Commentators noted that Sumner's speech would not persuade Congress. To extend voting rights to Blacks was politically untenable; to breach states' rights via a little-known constitutional provision was legally questionable. But even though he did not fully prove that the Constitution *required* Black suffrage, said the *New York Tribune*, "he has very clearly demonstrated that it *ought* to be so extended."

Other critics of the speech's substance praised its oratory. It was "by far the most elaborate and comprehensive speech made in Congress for many years," reported the *New York Times*. The *Richmond Republic*, a Virginia paper launched after the fall of the Confederacy, criticized Sumner's belief in human equality. But even the *Republic* conceded that his speech was "a monument of laborious research and good English" that hearkened back to "the best days of Clay and Webster."

It was probably Sumner's most widely circulated address since "The Crime Against Kansas" nearly ten years before. "Sumner's argument for the Rights of Men ought to be printed by the hundred thousand," praised the *New York Independent*. "Standing in some respects almost alone in the Senate, his position is all the more morally grand for his isolation, and his plea all the more eloquent for his moral heroism." Dozens of papers printed large parts of the speech while Sumner characteristically published his own pamphlet edition. Soon, the speech even reached Europe. "All the news from the United States show that the effect produced by the speech of Mr. Sumner has been immense," reported *Revue des Deux Mondes*.[21]

While the press lavished Sumner with praise, his Republican colleagues were far less impressed. Though Congressman (and, later, Speaker of the House) James Blaine thought the speech "an exhaustive and masterly essay unfolding and illuminating the doctrine of human rights," he thought it was "singularly inapt." The Radical senator Zachariah Chandler believed the oration was another one of those overly theoretical addresses. "Sumner is one of them literary fellows," he once croaked. Many Republican colleagues felt that Sumner had wasted six hours of their time, and they were concerned that his moral aggrandizing would tank the Apportionment Amendment, which they sincerely believed was the best that could be done at the time.

"I earnestly hope that it may not be defeated and especially that it may not be defeated by your vote," Salmon Chase wrote Sumner soon after his speech. Thaddeus Stevens also wrote Sumner, pleading with him to back down and let the party get behind the compromise. "If we are to be slain, it will not be by our friends," he hoped. Stevens deeply resented Sumner's speech, which he called a "puerile and pedantic criticism, by a perversion of philological definition." Most of all, William Fessenden was furious. "Mr. Sumner, with his impracticable notions, his vanity, his hatred of the President . . . is doing infinite harm," he fumed.[22]

Naturally, Andrew Johnson grew to hate Sumner, too. The day after Sumner's speech, Johnson met with Frederick Douglass, abolitionist George

Downing, and a few other Black activists. They urged him to force rebel states to allow Black men to vote—a political position more closely associated with Sumner than any other politician. "I do not like to be arraigned by some who can get up handsomely rounded periods, and deal in rhetoric, and talk about abstract ideas of liberty, who never perilled life, liberty, or property," Johnson growled, likely referring to Sumner. Dubiously claiming to the activists that he personally supported universal suffrage, Johnson barked that "it would be tyrannical" to force it upon states and might "commence a race war."

On another occasion, Johnson met with a delegation of Black civic leaders from North Carolina who tried to impress upon him the need for Black suffrage. "I suppose Sumner is your God," Johnson scoffed. He ranted about Radicals like Sumner, claiming that if it weren't for them, he would get more credit as the "Moses of the colored race." Johnson insisted that Blacks should treat him with gratitude. "I have owned slaves and bought slaves, but I never sold one," he had told Douglass and his allies in an effort to prove he was a good man. "So far as my connection with slaves has gone, I have been their slave instead of their being mine."[23]

Reports about Johnson's encounters with Black civic leaders infuriated Sumner. "The president is neither crazy or drunk," Sumner believed. "He is simply himself;—as he has been for months—essentially perverse, pigheaded, bad." While other Republicans still tried to see the best in Johnson, Sumner found him to be repulsive. "I despair of the Presdt. He is no Moses, but a Pharoah to the colored race, & they now regard him so." In Sumner's view, Johnson "looked upon the colored race as out of the pale of Humanity," regardless of whatever grandiose claims he made about being a humanitarian.[24]

✳ ✳ ✳

WHILE JOHNSON WAS fiercely opposed to Congress recognizing the political rights of Black freedpeople, Republicans who met with the president believed he was open to recognizing Black civil rights. At the time, civil rights were generally understood to be the kinds of rights that involved a free person's engagement with the state and the economy, like the right to buy and sell property, form contracts, and access the courts. Those rights were less threatening to white southerners than political rights. As one racist Mississippi newspaper put it, "negro equality in the courts is not as nauseating a dose as negro equality in all political privileges."[25]

To bring together Radicals like Sumner and conservatives like Johnson, Senator Lyman Trumbull drafted a civil rights bill that he thought Republicans would endorse and white southerners would swallow. The bill said that everyone born in the United States was a citizen (except Native people and those subject to foreign powers). As citizens, they were to possess the same civil rights that were "enjoyed by white citizens." Openly defying the Supreme Court's precedent in *Dred Scott*, Congress proclaimed citizenship a birthright.

The Civil Rights Act of 1866 was the first law of its kind in the history of the United States. Before the war, nobody could have imagined Congress passing laws that delineated the rights of citizens. That was a state's duty. But the Thirteenth Amendment, Trumbull argued, had expanded congressional power over the states. Now any "appropriate legislation" to enforce the abolition of slavery could be imposed by Congress.[26]

Sumner assented to the bill even though it was a compromise that brushed aside political rights. Perhaps he was pleased that Trumbull had privately consulted with him on the draft before introducing it, unlike Fessenden, who probably didn't talk to Sumner about the Apportionment Amendment beforehand. As the bill headed toward passage, Sumner reiterated the constitutionality of a potential future statute recognizing Black suffrage. "If Congress can decree equality in civil rights, by the same reason, if not *a fortiori*, it can decree equality in political rights," he argued. Both were necessary "to enforce the abolition of slavery."[27]

Quietly, Sumner assented to another bill from Trumbull. Congress had created the Freedmen's Bureau in 1866 after enacting a Sumner-sponsored bill. The Second Freedmen's Bureau Act delegated greater powers and extended the lifetime of the bureau. The bill directed the president to divide the South into several districts and to appoint bureau agents who would help assemble schools, protect freedpeople whose rights were being denied, and, in some parts of the South, rent land to freedpeople at discounted rates. Pleased with the bill, Sumner refrained from speaking publicly on it, probably to avoid tainting it with Radicalism. After all, the First Freedmen's Bureau Act had passed only after he was removed from the process.[28]

Staying silent didn't work. When the Second Freedmen's Bureau Act reached the White House for signature, President Johnson vetoed it. When the Civil Rights Act went to his desk weeks later, he vetoed that, too. Both vetoes caught centrists like Trumbull off guard. They had been led to believe Johnson supported their efforts, much like Sumner had been deceived a few months earlier. Flabbergasted, Trumbull and others scrambled to persuade Johnson to be cooperative. He wouldn't budge. "He is endeavoring to ignore all the good that has been accomplished and returning the slave into his bondage," scoffed Mary Lincoln.

Because Congress never built schools for "our own people" nor spent money to provide homes for the "thousands, not to say millions, of the white race who are honestly toiling," Johnson denounced Congress for now trying to help Black freedpeople. Believing Black freedpeople needed to learn to be "a self-sustaining population," Johnson implied that a larger Freedmen's Bureau would make them lazy. Turning his attention to the Civil Rights Act a few weeks later, he blamed Congress for acting in favor of "the colored and against the white race," which would "foment discord between the two races." States had a right to discriminate, he contended.[29]

On February 22, Johnson escalated his attack on Congress into a frontal assault. He delivered an aggressive speech to White House guests on George Washington's birthday—what should have been a happy apolitical occasion. Praising himself as a southerner who had successfully "fought traitors and treason in the South," Johnson declared that he was now at war with northerners who were similarly "laboring to destroy" the Union. "Name them— who are they?" somebody shouted in the crowd. Thus encouraged, Johnson decided to name some names. "You ask me who they are?" he asked. "I say, Thaddeus Stevens of Pennsylvania . . . Mr. Sumner of the Senate . . . and Wendell Phillips is another."

Some speculated that Johnson was drunk. Implying that Stevens, Sumner, and Phillips might try to behead him someday, Johnson portrayed himself as a hero who would champion states' rights no matter what Radicals might try to do. "Pardon me for being a little egoistical," he smirked. "Sometimes it has been said . . . that that Johnson is a lucky man. They can never defeat him." Declaring that he had always had "good luck," Johnson said the American people—that is, white people—would rise up to resist Radicals and support him.[30]

* * *

HORRIFIED AND ASHAMED by President Johnson's vetoes and obnoxious conduct, Republican centrists felt a new kinship with their Radical colleagues. A congressional pariah at the time, Sumner was now being vindicated thanks to Johnson's intemperance. Sumner had been telling other senators for months that Johnson was an arrogant buffoon. Hitherto trying to moderate their politics to placate Johnson, Republican centrists now openly collaborated with the Radicals to oppose him.[31]

To override a presidential veto, Republicans needed to get two-thirds of both chambers of Congress to agree on the Freedmen's Bureau and Civil Rights Acts. This was an extremely high bar, and overrides were exceedingly rare in antebellum America. Yet thanks to the exclusion of southern representatives, Republicans had a large majority in the House. In the Senate, they had close to two-thirds of the seats—but not quite. To get to the two-thirds threshold, they needed to eliminate one Democrat.

In a series of devious maneuvers in late March 1866, Sumner helped remove his Democratic colleague John Stockton by pointing out irregularities in his New Jersey election. While there had indeed been irregularities, Sumner's actions were nakedly partisan. When it was time to certify Stockton's seat, he told Republicans to vote no. Seeing that the vote was close, he loudly whispered to one Republican, who promised to abstain, to break his promise. When that Republican did so, Stockton, who had also promised to abstain, voted in favor of certifying himself in order to save his own seat. A few days later, Sumner successfully convinced the Senate to conduct a revote to punish Stockton for voting for himself. When that succeeded, Stockton was sent home jobless. "I have for him nothing but kindness and respect," Sumner claimed afterward.[32]

Sumner's wildly unparliamentary scheme prompted respect from his rival William Fessenden. The two had collaborated to oust Stockton to secure Republican power. Only a few weeks earlier, they had been at odds with each other due to the Apportionment Amendment. Now they knew they needed one another to stop Andrew Johnson. "Andy's conduct has rendered this course a necessity," Fessenden believed.

Shortly thereafter, Sumner and Fessenden both attended the funeral of a mutual friend. Saddened by their animosity, Sumner approached Fessenden later and offered his hand. The two shook, as if to declare a new alliance. "If we only went together, we might rule the Senate," Sumner believed. "I don't love him and never can, but the hatchet is buried, and I shall not dig it up again," Fessenden wrote.[33]

With Fessenden and Sumner on speaking terms, centrist and Radical Republicans were able to unite in the spring of 1866. Now holding two-thirds control over both chambers of Congress, Republicans overrode Johnson's vetoes to successfully pass both the Freedmen's Bureau Act and the Civil Rights Act. Yet there was another major Reconstruction policy that still had to be debated: the Fourteenth Amendment. After Sumner had helped kill the Apportionment Amendment, the Joint Committee went back to the drawing board. The committee decided to put together a hodgepodge of amendments into one gargantuan proposal in which every Republican in Congress could find something to like. On April 30, Thaddeus Stevens introduced this five-section constitutional amendment on the House floor. On May 23, Senator Jacob Howard introduced a similar five-section proposal to the Senate on behalf of Fessenden, who was sick. That proposal, with some additional editing, ultimately became what is now known as the Fourteenth Amendment.

Section 1 of the Fourteenth Amendment stood out. Drafted by Congressman John Bingham of Ohio, the section was largely intended to graft the principles of the already passed Civil Rights Act of 1866 into the Constitution. It enshrined the idea of equality, declaring that no state shall "deny to any person within its jurisdiction the equal protection of the laws." It also affirmed the idea of birthright citizenship, which came with "privileges or immunities" that no state could abridge. And it said no state shall "deprive any person of life, liberty, or property without due process of law." Coupled with Section 5, which gave Congress enforcement power, Section 1 dramatically contracted state power to strengthen Congress.

Quoting Sumner's famous phrase, Senator Howard captured Bingham's Section 1 by saying "it establishes equality before the law." Sumner was no doubt pleased. As the first member of Congress to introduce an equality amendment, which he had done in his proposal for the Thirteenth Amendment in early 1865, he could take significant credit for the equality theme in Section 1 of the Fourteenth. There were also traces of his influence in Section 1's principle of birthright citizenship, which was a core theme of his February 1866 speech, "The Equal Rights of All," opposing the Apportionment Amendment.[34]

Sumner's approval of Section 1 was overshadowed by his anger over the final draft of Section 2. After the first draft was rejected, Thaddeus Stevens tried a second draft that he received from the antislavery reformer (and past member of the American Freedmen's Inquiry Commission) Robert Dale Owen. Owen advised that apportionment be given a ten-year time span, after which all Black men would have the right to vote. But that wasn't satisfying to Sumner, either. "It is a question of abstract principle, not of expediency," he told Owen, who was his friend. "I must do my whole duty" he explained, "without looking to consequences." Stevens, for his part, couldn't get the committee to agree on Owen's plan, either.

Then Stevens earned approval from the committee for a final version of what became Section 2. This draft simply said that "the basis of representation" in a state would be "reduced in proportion" to "the whole number of [voting] male citizens twenty-one years of age in such State." Stevens found this draft's language clever because it didn't explicitly say anything about discrimination on the basis of "race" or "color." But Sumner was again unsatisfied, believing, correctly, that the text still allowed states to restrict male suffrage to only whites.[35]

Women's rights activists were also upset with the committee's final draft. Unlike in the second version put together by Owen, a feminist, the committee decided to include the word *male*, foreclosing any chance that the amendment might incentivize enfranchising women. When Elizabeth Cady Stanton and Susan B. Anthony learned about the insertion, they protested fiercely, sending heaps of petitions upon petitions to Congress. It was to no avail. They were especially upset that Sumner, hell-bent on enfranchising Black men, had said nothing about the suffrage rights of women. "What sadness of heart we *women* have written and spoken in words of criticism of your assent," Anthony wrote him, feeling betrayed. Sumner's response, if any, does not survive.[36]

When the final draft, after being passed in the House, came up for debate in the Senate in late May, Sumner urged more delay. Noting that the draft had improved greatly over the past few months, he wanted more time. "If we adopted the advice of the Senator from Massachusetts," Fessenden replied, "we should wait until the next century." Recovering from a mild form of smallpox, he croaked that the amendment should get its vote immediately. "We are late in the session," he pleaded. By now, almost every Republican was on board.

In reply, Sumner *apologized* to Fessenden—something he rarely did to anyone. "I may be in error," he admitted. "It is probable that I am in error, since I find that most of those about me have a different opinion." Conceding that others "have substantially at heart the same objects as myself," Sumner said for the third time, "most probably I am in error." Implying that he was still uncomfortable with apportionment and would have preferred suffrage, he wanted further delay. But he realized that "others do not agree with me." Urging delay, knowing he wouldn't get it, he meekly said that all he wanted to do was "to file a *caveat*" before the debate began.[37]

Sure enough, the debate did begin. While occasionally proposing supplementary bills for Black suffrage and equality before the law, Sumner sheepishly stayed silent during the final amendment debates and made no effort to slow things down further. With reluctance, he accepted that for the sake of practicality, the Fourteenth Amendment should get passed as is. When it came for a vote on June 8, Sumner voted yes. But he had already diminished his credibility with centrists by being so critical of the compromise measure. Republican centrists "disliked Sumner because he kept himself always on that upper level of principle," Unitarian theologian James Freeman Clarke once observed. "The air was too thin for them to breathe."[38]

* * *

WHILE THE FOURTEENTH Amendment debates were unfolding, a spasm tore at Sumner's heart. He felt a tight, merciless squeeze in his chest. It was as if a cold, invisible hand were trying to crush the life out of him from the inside. "I . . . have fallen into the doctor's hands," Sumner wrote a friend. "He finds my brain and nervous system overtasked; and [that I am] suffering from my original injuries." While recovering from the caning that occurred nearly ten years before, Sumner had suffered his first bout of angina pectoris, a heart disease that arises when the heart does not get enough blood and oxygen. Angina brings about debilitating chest pains that can come and go through life. Years might pass between attacks. In some cases, angina episodes can lead to fatal heart attacks.

"I long for rest & yet every day I grind in my mill," Sumner mourned. For the past several years, the senator had worked so vigorously, it was as if he had never been brutally caned. While critics claimed that the caning changed his personality by hardening his moral attitudes and bloating his ego with a martyr complex, in truth, the effects of the caning upon him were mostly physical. He often used a walking stick to get around, and he lost some of the natural athleticism that had defined his young adult life. Getting exhausted quickly from walking, he rarely went out to parties in Washington and expected people to visit him at his home.

Once, Samuel Howe visited his best friend in Washington and was horrified to see how little he socialized and how hard he worked. "You cannot revert to the Ch. Sumner of 35 years old," Howe told him. Although he pleaded with him to "exercise in the open air" and "sleep eight hours every night," Sumner wouldn't listen. "He goes to the Senate at noon and only gets back at midnight or one o'clock in the morning," reported one of Sumner's friends. "If there is any person in the Senate who works more hours on public business than I do, with less relaxation or vacation," Sumner once told a friend, "I do not know him."[39]

Reluctantly taking a doctor's advice, Sumner spoke infrequently in the late spring and early summer, which may partly explain why he was somewhat withdrawn at the last stage of the Fourteenth Amendment debates. But he couldn't hold himself back for long. By midsummer, claiming to feel better, he was hard at work again. Friends were concerned. "The health of no man in the land is a matter of deeper solicitude than yours," Frederick Douglass wrote him, sternly demanding that he take rest. "What confidence Sumner has in Sumner!" Henry Longfellow bemoaned. "This relapse is a warning that he can no longer work day and night."[40]

Reflecting on his health, Sumner wondered whether it might be time to retire. The upcoming 1866 election offered a potentially ideal time for him to step down and allow someone else, perhaps his protégé Gov. John Andrew, to run for the seat. "Should I quit the national service, I should find employment with my pen or as a lecturer, after a visit to Europe," Sumner wrote Frank Bird. After fancifully entertaining the idea, he decided against it: "There are two objects which I should like to see accomplished before I quit. One is the establishment of our govt. on the principles of the Declaration of Independence & the other is the revision of international maritime law."[41]

While he never had the chance to revise international maritime law, Sumner achieved a fabulous legal success in June 1866. For fourteen years, he had been pushing Congress to authorize a commission to codify American law. At the time, congressional statutes were never organized, categorized, or sectionalized in ways accessible to lawyers or ordinary citizens alike, but were only compiled in the United States Statutes at Large, a gargantuan set of volumes of laws stacked one atop the other.

Sumner's interest in codification began in his early days as a law student, when his teacher Joseph Story worked to partially codify Massachusetts statutes. A talkative young student, Sumner repeatedly urged his teacher to pursue even more codification than Story was willing to undertake. As an elder senator, he continued to believe in the promise of codification. The law "ought to be in every public library, and also in the offices of lawyers throughout the country," Sumner believed. "That can be only by reducing them in size so that they will form a single volume, which is entirely practicable."

After Congressman George Boutwell listened to Sumner's pleadings to get his codification bill out of the House Judiciary Committee, it passed both chambers without any opposition. Sumner was delighted. While generally ineffective at passing legislation, he had precipitated a codification project for the entire body of U.S. law. He even persuaded Andrew Johnson to appoint his friend Caleb Cushing as one of the three commissioners in this apolitical project. The commission's work led to the publication of the First Revised Statutes of the United States in 1874. Those volumes were the predecessors to what lawyers rely upon today: the United States Code. In many ways, Sumner deserves the credit for the code.[42]

* * *

In early June 1866, Sumner received a telegram from his mother's doctor that said she was ailing. She had been sick since March. "Tell him his country needs him more than his mother does now," she whispered to a friend who visited her to pay last respects. Sumner instantly boarded a train for Boston. He would make it in time to spend a couple of days with his eighty-one-year-old mother before her death on June 15. "There are none who can ever love us with a mother's love. No, not one," he later said solemnly. Simple, reclusive, and not much of a letter writer, Relief Sumner left behind few traces in the historical record. But "she was an excellent and remarkable person," according to Sumner, "whose death leaves me more than ever alone."

Within eighteen months of her death, Sumner would sell the Hancock Street house on the North Slope of Beacon Hill, which had served as his home base in Boston ever since childhood. No longer would he have a domicile in the heart of Black Boston. "I have buried from this house my father, my mother, a brother and sister; and now I am leaving it, the deadest of them," he muttered to Henry Longfellow when the house was given up.

All the while, Sumner's own health was declining with the return of his angina. While only fifty-five, he knew that his body was losing its vigor. Yet there was so much more work to be done, for the human rights revolution precipitated by Reconstruction remained unfinished. "You are the keystone of our arch," the abolitionist Gerrit Smith reminded him. "If you fail, all falls."[43]

CHAPTER 21

READING, WRITING, AND SNORING

WHENEVER CHARLES SUMNER WANTED TO RELAX DURING THE turbulent years of the Johnson administration, he went to Samuel Hooper's house in Washington. A wealthy Boston merchant who was elected to Congress during the war, Hooper had more money and more space in his luxury mansion than he knew what to do with. He had happily extended loans to the treasury secretary, Salmon Chase, when the North was in dire need of funds. He had opened his home to George McClellan when the general lacked army headquarters. He had even converted his mansion into a temporary White House when Johnson needed an office while the Lincolns were in bereavement.

Generous, jovial, and politically moderate, Hooper enjoyed the company of nearly everyone in Washington. But he took a special liking to Sumner. He invited him to his house almost daily to dine, wrote to him often about work matters, served as a kind of mentor figure who helped mend Sumner's relationships with colleagues like Senator William Fessenden, and introduced Sumner to his daughter-in-law Alice.[1]

Alice Mason Hooper was only twenty-six years old when she met Sumner. A vivacious widow who everyone said was beautiful beyond compare, Alice had lost her husband—Hooper's son—when he died while serving in the Union Army in mid-1863. Feeling terrible for her and heartbroken for himself, Hooper had invited Alice and her six-year-old daughter to leave Boston and live with him and his wife in 1865. A graceful daughter of a wealthy Brahmin family, she rapidly picked up admirers. Fessenden would frequent the Hooper house to play cards with her, until he decided she "looked prettier than ever" and that it was unwise to keep visiting. "She looks like a young lady of 16," reported one admirer. "She was a most comfortable creature," said another.[2]

Alice was intelligent, sociable, and passionate about the North's anti-slavery efforts. When the war was ongoing, she had volunteered at various Union Army hospitals in the city. Afterward, she had continued to follow the political scene closely and mingled with the most senior politicians and foreign dignitaries in the country.

Almost daily, Alice came to the Senate to watch Sumner speak, often at the senator's invitation. Nosy people noticed. "I begin to think Mr. Sumner is looking in that direction," Fessenden wrote in his diary in early 1866. "He is always in attendance at the Senate, finding seats, and on hand to wait on them out—a most unusual thing for him." Sometimes, Sumner even took her to exclusive events in the city. On one occasion, he introduced her to Mary Lincoln, who told Sumner she was struck by Alice's "attractiveness" and "pleasant impression."[3]

Nothing about Sumner's consorting with Alice was out of sync with his character or the social norms of the times. A bachelor in his early fifties, Sumner had time to socialize when other men did not. Women took him up on it. Mary Lincoln used to take him as her date to the opera house and the theater, especially when the president wasn't available. Salmon Chase's daughter Kate adored Sumner's company. And he was the favorite politician of many politicians' wives, including Frances Seward and Julia Fish, who enjoyed innocently flirting with him. "His good looks had caused many a feminine heart to flutter," a young socialite once remarked.

When Sumner's mother passed in June 1866, he started to reflect on his relationship to Hooper's family and his friendship with Alice. Taking a carriage ride with the young lawyer Edward Pierce, he disclosed that for the first time in his life, he had the means to support a family. In addition to the money he had made selling his late mother's house, Sumner had inherited a larger sum than he expected from her, much of which he invested in securities that would earn him income. "I have come to an epoch in life. My mother is dead," he wrote to his best friend Henry Longfellow. "I have a moderate competency. What next?"[4]

* * *

IN EARLY SEPTEMBER 1866, Sumner scrawled many curt notes to friends and acquaintances and put them in the mail. "My dear Governor, you are my neighbor in the Senate," he wrote in one such note to New York senator Edwin Morgan. "Therefore, I prefer that you should hear of my engagement directly from myself. After much that has been said, you may be surprised even to incredulity. But you may regard this note as my affidavit of the fact."

In announcing his shocking, out-of-nowhere decision to get engaged, Sumner didn't even mention his fiancée's name in most courtesy letters. "A name will not tell you so much as the enclosed photograph," he told the Duchess of Argyll. "The lady is a near neighbor of yours," he told Morgan. "She is the daughter of one of your classmates, you may divine the rest," he told the minister John Palfrey. "Charles Sumner the hitherto invincible is engaged," exclaimed Lincoln's former secretary John Hay. "The most characteristic point of the matter is that he wrote a long letter full of joy and happiness to Mrs. Adams, announcing his engagement without even mentioning the lady. He will forget he is married more than half the time."[5]

Sumner seemed to care more about the idea of getting married than about the woman he was marrying. There are hardly any traces in his letters of affection or interest in Alice, apart from the fact that she was beautiful. By this time, Sumner had a dizzying array of friendships and relationships. He apparently didn't care to make more. Once, Julia Ward Howe invited him to tea to meet a friend. "I don't know that I should care to meet him," Sumner responded. "I have outlived my interest in individuals." This disinterest seemed to have extended to his own future wife. While he brought Alice along to interesting events to meet fashionable people, he likely didn't take much interest in her as a human being and expected her to go along with his lifestyle and habits.[6]

It is not hard to see why. Living in a patriarchal world where women were generally expected to fawn over male interests and curb their own desires, Sumner doubtless subscribed to contemporary norms about a woman's place in her social environment and the relationship between man and wife. Men of his age and stature were typically married or widowed homeowners whose wives or daughters stayed home and sustained family lives that were supposed to make these men happy. Women who cared about Sumner's well-being seemed to know that this is what he wanted. Wishing the heartiest congratulations to Sumner and "the nameless One," Julia Ward Howe expressed hope that Sumner's marriage would make "the house of Sumner flourish."[7]

There was also probably a lack of heterosexual attraction. All his adult life, Sumner had felt despair over his lonely bachelor condition and wondered why he couldn't find a woman to love. "Some persons seem to find it very easy to become engaged—all of which is contrary to my experience," he once wrote. Whenever a prospect was interested in him in his younger days, he would back out. At Samuel Howe's urging, for example, Sumner courted Julia's younger sister Louisa in the 1840s. But when Louisa bought Sumner a birthday gift, he stopped visiting her for months. "I wish I could find somebody to love," he once confided in her older brother. Eventually, he gave up hope.[8]

After resigning himself to bachelorhood, Sumner realized his loneliness would never subside. He suffered from lifelong depression, which only made things worse. When Henry Longfellow told him about the death of novelist Nathaniel Hawthorne, a mutual friend, Sumner replied with deep sadness for his own spouseless and family-less condition. "We shall be alone soon," he said. "I forget. I shall be alone. You have your children. Life is weary and dark—full of pain and enmity. I am ready to go at once. And still I am left."[9]

On top of this, Sumner was a bit of a social outcast in Washington as one of the only bachelors in the Senate. The fact that he was controversial didn't help. While loved and revered in abolitionist circles around the country, he wanted to be popular and respectable in elite Washington society. He believed marriage was the key to belonging in his own political community and to happiness in his own heart. Otherwise, he would remain, as one Frenchman called him, "a sort of monk, who remains apart from worldly things."

A woman in her late twenties with a young daughter, Alice was perhaps being foolish in choosing to marry a man twice her age who had never raised a family, had such high expectations, and took comparatively little interest in her. But she probably came to believe, prodded by her doting father-in-law, Sam Hooper, that Sumner was still a catch. After all, a young widow who delighted in the social atmosphere of Washington couldn't do much better than marry a leading senator who was close to her late husband's family.

Although his hair was graying, his belly had grown portly, and he walked slowly with a cane, Sumner remained a barrel-chested six-foot-four senator with striking brows, a handsome face, and a foppish taste in fashion. Plus, he was powerful. Rumors circulated that Alice expected him to someday become president, making her First Lady of the United States. Whatever she hoped for from their marriage, she could reasonably expect that the two of them would make an attractive and influential couple in postwar Washington. "The marriage which he contracted late in life was not based on enduring principles," claimed one contemporary. "It was more like the marriages that princes make than a true republican courtship."[10]

* * *

"I AM AN idealist, and I now hope to live my idea," Sumner incredulously told Francis Lieber shortly before his wedding, which took place only a few weeks after his surprise engagement. For a man who always consulted like-minded friends for advice, Sumner didn't bother to ask anyone, at least not by letter, whether his marriage with Alice Hooper was wise. It even remains unclear who first proposed the marriage or when that proposal took place. Sumner barreled forward, as if he were trying to get married before he started having any doubts. "I hope to be very happy," he explained to a friend. "Tardily, I begin."[11]

Years later, Samuel Hooper's daughter said she feared for Alice and Sumner with "an increasing fear all through that summer of 1866." Alice's friends warned her about marrying a man who was old and who may have wanted her money. Sumner, for his part, knew he was taking a gamble by marrying a pretty aristocrat. "I tremble sometimes at the responsibility I assume. I am to make another happy; for unless I do this there can be no happiness *for me* and my idea will be quenched in darkness," he admitted to George Bancroft. "Now, Alice," Sumner said more than once to his fiancée, "unless we are both satisfied that this union is to be a happy one, we had better separate now." But Alice wanted to move forward; Sumner refused to slow down.[12]

On October 17, 1866, Sumner and Alice married in a small ceremony at Alice's brother's home in Boston. "To-day at 3 o'clock I shall be married, and at the age of 55, begin to live," Sumner told the poet John Whittier. The same day, he departed with Alice for Newport, where he used to visit his brother Albert's vacation home. For three weeks, Sumner and his wife relaxed in the breezy weather and presumably enjoyed the beach. Sumner's friends could hardly believe it. "Just think of it," exclaimed Whittier. "Instead of taking his carpet-bag and starting off for the Washington [railroad] cars, as aforetime, he went this winter, filling a coach with his family:—Mr. Sumner and Mrs. Sumner, and Mrs. Sumner's child, and Mrs. Sumner's child's nurse, and . . . little dog!" The honeymoon, according to Sumner, was "enchantment."[13]

Returning to Washington in late 1866 after packing up his mother's house in Boston, Sumner began leasing a home that was previously occupied by Senator Samuel Pomeroy with Sam Hooper's help. He instantly discovered the challenges of domesticity. "I am still in the trials of a young house-keeper," he giddily told a friend. "This question of furniture is one of the most difficult I have ever encountered." Apparently, Sumner had never thought about furniture before, having always lived with his mother or in Washington boardinghouses. He was so proud to be designing his own home with Alice's help. "Let me show you my little kingdom," he said to one friend, urging her to visit. "I hope that my subjects will be content & happy."

Alice and Sumner started hosting popular evening events. "Sumner apparently wanted a handsome wife to preside at his dinner parties in Washington," somebody observed. Alice, for her part, enjoyed entertaining fashionable people, according to her brother. "Mr. and Mrs. Senator Sumner are leaders of the most intellectual and *distingue* society," reported the *Boston Transcript*. "The gentlemen and ladies who frequent Mrs. Sumner's *salons* are men of ideas and women of the highest culture."[14]

Guests were impressed to see Charles and Alice Sumner together. "It was quite startling to see Sumner in the bosom of his family," John Hay wrote in his diary. "It was so strange," Representative Henry Dawes reported with excitement, "to find him instead of a recluse, as he has always been before, up to his chin in documents and dust . . . now neatly attired and nicely seated in a very comfortable easy chair by the side of a sofa, on which was reclining his wife, happy as he himself, opening his vast mail for him, and enjoying with him its contents." Representative James Ashley's wife was gleeful. "Sumner and his beautiful wife are themselves history and romance," she wrote. "They ought to be handsomely bound and opened a page at a time."[15]

* * *

BY THE NOVEMBER 1866 midterm election, Sumner had even more to reason to be happy. He had recently delivered a well-publicized Republican campaign speech, "The One Man Power vs. Congress," which framed the election as a referendum on the president. By unilaterally "giving present power to ex-Rebels, at the expense of constant Unionists, white or black," Sumner argued, Johnson had betrayed the martyred Lincoln. He recounted his private meetings with Johnson where the president had lied and exposed his racism. Calling on the public to empower Congress to counteract Johnson, Sumner said it was time to adopt the four *E*s of reconstruction: "Emancipation, Enfranchisement, Equality, and Education."[16]

To Sumner's delight and Johnson's fury, the northern public over-whelmingly voted in favor of congressional Republicans. "This is the most decisive and emphatic victory ever seen in American politics," declared *The Nation*. Adamant to ensure that the war was not fought in vain and could never happen again, a large majority of northerners wanted Congress to remake the South. Northern states also eagerly ratified the Fourteenth Amendment, which the *New York Times* said was the "single issue" of the election, infuriating Johnson to no end.[17]

Northerners empowered Republicans in Congress because Johnson's preliminary state governments in the South largely operated as if they were neo-Confederate states. Even though slavery had been abolished, southern states enforced harsh Black Codes to protect the racial hierarchy despite congressional passage of the Civil Rights Act of 1866. Further, they refused to ratify the Fourteenth Amendment, which would guarantee equal protection to all Black people and create incentives for states to enfranchise Black men. On top of this, former rebels were holding major public offices and permitting wanton vigilante violence against Blacks and loyal whites.

When session resumed in December 1866, congressional Republicans realized that Black political rights were necessary to secure the gains of abolition, protect Republican power, and counteract the influence of ex-rebels. Responding to years of local Black organizing, Congress passed a bill to grant suffrage to Black men in Washington, D.C. At Sumner's insistence, Congress also banned "exclusion from the suffrage on account of color" in the new states of Nebraska and Colorado and in any future territories. "And thus ends a long contest, where at first I was alone," Sumner wrote to Frank Bird in blissful triumph.[18]

"Congress is doing pretty well; every step is forward," Sumner believed. In January 1867, Thaddeus Stevens led the House in passing a bill to dissolve Johnson's state governments and impose military rule over the South. By putting Black and white troops in charge, Republicans hoped to remake the South's social and political order. When the bill reached the Senate, the Republican Caucus formed an informal committee to decide what criteria states needed to achieve to be relieved of military rule. In a testament to how quickly his views were becoming mainstream, Sumner was tapped for the seven-person group, which met on February 16.

Led by the powerful centrists Lyman Trumbull and William Fessenden, the committee decided that civilian governments should be restored as soon as rebel states adopted new constitutions and ratified the Fourteenth

Amendment. This decision upset Radicals, who wanted more stringent protections for freedpeople before restoring civilian governments. "The whole social & political system must be remodelled," Sumner thought. Desiring funding for public schools, land redistribution, and other reconstruction measures, he focused especially on universal suffrage. But after pushing hard for suffrage as a precondition for readmission, he won the support of only one colleague on the committee.

When the committee presented its plan to the Republican Caucus, Sumner demanded that the entire caucus vote on whether to require universal suffrage in the rebel states. It was an extraordinary proposal, a proposal that would have been mocked and reviled in the antebellum era. In front of the entire caucus, Sumner called on Republicans to embark on a nationwide project of multiracial democracy, in which every Black man could vote, at least in the South. As far as Sumner was concerned, freedom to former slaves required giving them power, responsibilities, and the ability to practice self-governance. There was no other path to true emancipation except through the immediate, universal enfranchisement of freedmen.

Probably to everyone's shock, the caucus approved Sumner's motion for Black male suffrage in the South in a hurried vote before dinnertime. Stunned, Fessenden asked for a revote. A slight majority of Republican senators, many of whom had never supported Black suffrage before, boldly rose to endorse universal suffrage. They had come to believe, like Sumner, that "*Union govts. cannot be organized with out the blacks.*" In order to protect the victories of the Civil War, Republicans decided to give the vote to people who had been slaves just a few years ago.

Previously, Republicans had derided Sumner for being impractical in demanding Black suffrage in the South. Many had dismissed his constitutional arguments about Congress having the power to directly impose suffrage. But Johnson's obstinance and the open defiance of white-only southern state governments had radicalized Congress. "If I was ever Conservative," one Republican confessed, "I am Radical now." Republicans came to realize, as Sumner had warned, that suffrage would not expand voluntarily. He now seemed prophetic and right all along. He effectively functioned, as the eminent Black historian W. E. B. Du Bois would later describe him, as America's "seer of democracy."

And so, the Republican Senate Caucus decided to include suffrage in the bill that became the First Reconstruction Act. The act said that for southern states to be relieved of military rule and readmitted into the

Union, they needed to form new constitutions with universal suffrage for Blacks and whites alike, with no property limitations whatsoever, for everyone except those who had joined the rebellion or committed felonies. In so doing, Republicans brought about a democratic revolution in the South, a transformation so extraordinary and egalitarian that it was perhaps rivaled only by the ratification of the Constitution itself in 1788. "Then and there, in that small room, in that caucus," Senator Henry Wilson recalled, "was decided the greatest pending question on the North American continent."[19]

* * *

WHILE SUMNER WAS occupied with founding America's first experiment in multiracial democracy, his wife, Alice, started getting bored. "I am always left alone," she complained to a friend. "Mr. Sumner is always reading, writing, and snoring." After the excitement of the honeymoon phase had waned, the couple started fighting. Half his age and largely unoccupied, Alice wanted to stay out at parties when Sumner wanted to come home. She wanted to invite her friends to dinner when Sumner wanted to keep the house quiet. She expected attention; Sumner wasn't willing or able to give it.

Sumner discovered Alice's anger issues. "I should like to see Sumner the first time Alice says to him," one of Alice's friends mused, "Go to hell; God damn you—it is none of your business." She used to have "outbreaks," according to Sumner. Hooper's daughter Anne said Alice had a "hothead temper." Alice also seemed resentful of Sumner's proximity to her first husband's family. Once, when Sumner tried to invite Samuel Hooper for dinner, she lashed out, screaming that "she could not bear him and would not have him near, that he was stupid and a nuisance."[20]

There is no doubt that Sumner gave her reasons to be upset. A longtime bachelor, he was used to having things go his way and rarely had to make sacrifices for his family. A U.S. senator, he was accustomed to being doted upon by his friends. And as a man who had until now lived mostly alone, he had never learned how to share a room or a bed with somebody else, much less with a woman. Alice, for her part, couldn't remain patient for very long with the man she had chosen to marry. "She was a gay, fashionable creature, fond of admiration," Washington gossip went, "while he is a settled old bachelor, fond of himself."

Alice started openly flirting with Friedrich von Holstein, a strapping

young man closer to her age and full of great stories. A dashing, adventurous, worldly diplomat in his late twenties, Holstein had been dubbed "the
lion at Saratoga" while traveling through New York in the summer of 1866.
In December, he came to Washington. Already one of Bismarck's favorite
foreign officers, Holstein had been allowed to travel freely to gain experience before being assigned more formal diplomatic roles. (He later led
the German Foreign Office.) "There is not too much to say about society
here," Holstein wrote home. "The ladies are very elegant, some of them
too elegant, and quite entertaining." Although he didn't like big parties
or dances, Holstein loved spending his work hours mingling with society
women simply for the fun of it. "There are a few houses where I can go
during the day or in the evening whenever I like," he bragged a few weeks
into his stay.[21]

Nobody enjoyed Holstein's company more than Alice Sumner. She met
Holstein at a dinner party at her house, which he attended on Sumner's
invitation. She took her new Prussian friend everywhere in public, from
ho-hum receptions to the most elegant society balls. They quickly became
inseparable. As if to embarrass Sumner, Alice even started to watch her
husband from the Senate gallery with Holstein by her side. When Mary
Lincoln learned about the affair, she was mortified. "[Sumner is] the most
agreeable and delightful of men. How could his wife have acted as she has
done?" she asked herself. Mrs. Lincoln chalked it up to Sumner's older age:
"It was a great mistake he made in marrying so late in life!!"[22]

Alice's flirtation with Holstein probably did not amount to anything
sexual—she likely would have been more discreet if there was an actual
sexual affair, and Holstein ended up a lifelong bachelor who, according
to his biographer, probably remained chaste. Believing she had nothing
to be ashamed of, Alice dismissed Sumner's entreaties to stop seeing Holstein so often and so publicly. "Instead of a helpmeet and a companion,"
Sumner's friend Kate Chase noted, his wife was "a flutterfly." Once, Alice
was whisked away with Holstein and another diplomatic couple in a carriage in front of Sumner's home, crying, "I am going to enjoy myself," as
Sumner stood helplessly outside. Another time, she went off alone with
Holstein to a cemetery outside the city, returning only after midnight. "All
the time, day and late in the night," Sumner later bemoaned, "she was off
with her paramour!"[23]

A stickler for decorum and his own stately reputation, Sumner was
furious that Alice was humiliating him. She may have expected her

husband to feel jealous and for him to try to win her back. But the senator seemed more concerned with how things *looked* than how either of them *felt*. Rumor had it that when Alice wore an extravagant amber necklace that had been gifted to her by Holstein, Sumner didn't angrily destroy it or send it back. Mindful of unwritten ethical norms that forbade senators from accepting gifts from foreign officers, he instead supposedly asked Holstein to send him the bill to pay for Alice's necklace himself.

Alice probably discovered that Sumner was unable to please her, emotionally or sexually. Rumors spread in Washington that she spent time with Holstein because her husband was impotent. During the mid-nineteenth century, it was widely believed that bachelors grew impotent if they were chaste for too many years. Perhaps a better explanation was that Sumner was gay and uninterested or incapable of sexually pleasing his wife. Eventually, so many childhood friends were gossiping about his inability to find love during his younger years that even the American minister to France learned about Sumner's marital troubles and speculated that they arose from "his apparent insensibility to the charms of the fair sex during that period of life when they usually exert most influence."[24]

* * *

WHILE SUMNER'S MARITAL problems arose, his hopes in Congress dwindled. He was initially excited about the prospect of Congress making democratic reforms in the South despite Johnson's obstructions. He had even convinced his colleagues to agree to require southern states to grant Black men the suffrage as a precondition of readmission. But by March 1867, when the Reconstruction Act had passed and a small supplementary bill was being considered, Sumner found no such interest in two other core tenets of his democratic program: land reform and public education.

On March 7, he introduced a resolution that called on Congress to issue "the homestead, which must be secured to the freedmen, so that at least every head of a family may have a piece of land." During the Civil War, Congress had passed the Homestead Act, which offered nearly free land plots to anyone who wished to become independent farmers on free soil in the West. While theoretically applicable to Black settlers, almost all land plots under the act were given to white men. Sumner wanted to extend the Homestead Act's vision of agrarian democracy to Black freedpeople in the South by granting land to them on the soil they tilled, even if this meant seizing the land of white enslavers. "The great plantations ... must be broken up," Sumner once said, "and the freedmen must have the pieces."

Land reform was a revolutionary Reconstruction proposal that could be described today as a form of reparations. Repeatedly, Sumner insisted that land that belonged to white plantation masters should be specifically and solely redistributed to Black freedpeople, and not to poor propertyless whites. "White men have never been in slavery," he pointed out. "There is no emancipation and no enfranchisement of white men to be consummated." To be truly free, Sumner believed, ex-slaves needed and deserved their own property and financial independence apart from the masters who had exploited them for so long.

Sumner's proposal in the Senate—similar to a proposal by Thaddeus Stevens in the House—went nowhere. During the Lincoln years, many Republicans had endorsed the confiscation of rebel land and its redistribution to formerly enslaved people, citing military necessity as the legal justification for doing so. This ended when Andrew Johnson revoked military land orders, some of which had already given land to freedpeople, and gave the land back to large plantation owners. Many Republicans now believed land reform couldn't be constitutional anymore, given that Johnson had "restored" property rights and the war had ended. Sumner tried to argue that land reform was still justified by military necessity and the Thirteenth Amendment's Enforcement Clause. Though some Republicans privately agreed, there was no longer any political will to embark on a major national project to confiscate white men's land.[25]

On March 15, Sumner tried to amend the Reconstruction supplement bill to require new state constitutions to include a provision "to establish and sustain a system of public schools open to all, without distinction of race or color," a program that was being similarly pursued by his friend James Ashley in the House. At the time, public education was nearly nonexistent in the South, and there was almost no concept of guaranteeing public education as a matter of state constitutional law. Sumner wanted public schools for everyone, white or Black, believing that education was a vital component of America's new experiment in multiracial democracy.

Sumner first articulated his vision for free and open public schools when he represented a young girl seeking access to a white-only school in *Roberts v. City of Boston* (1849). He had interpreted the Declaration of Independence and the Massachusetts Constitution, which said "all men are born free and equal," to mean that everyone was entitled to "equality before the law." To him, this meant that "no person can be *born*, with civil or political privileges not enjoyed equally by all his fellow-citizens; nor can any institution be established, recognizing distinction of birth." In Sumner's eyes, every child in his state had a constitutional right of access to nondiscriminatory public schools. "He may be poor, weak, humble, black—he may be of Caucasian, Jewish, Indian, or Ethiopian race—he may be of French, German, English, or Irish extraction," Sumner had said.

Section 1 of the Fourteenth Amendment offered crisp language that arguably codified Sumner's principle of equality before the law. Thinking this principle was already enshrined in the Declaration, on top of the not-yet-ratified amendment, Sumner called for a system of nondiscriminatory public schools across the South. He had long believed that the best way to preserve multiracial democracy was through schooling, developing pre-scient arguments that were echoed by civil rights activists who called for integrated public schools around one hundred years later. "The school is the little world in which the child is trained for the larger world of life," he had declared. If children learn "those relations of Equality which our Con-stitution and Laws promise to all" by being "taught *all together*," Sumner believed, they would grow up to treat everybody "without distinction of color . . . in the performance of civil duties."[26]

Sumner's amendment for free and open public schools failed by a tie vote of 20–20. While most Republicans favored his measure, Democrats combined with some conservative Republicans to kill it. Sumner tried to use other parliamentary means to force a revote on his education pro-posal, but he was thwarted by his colleagues, who were exhausted and wanted to adjourn the session. Despite his protests, Congress passed the Reconstruction Act without his education measures and adjourned. Feel-ing defeated by the tie vote, he cried that night at home.

* * *

SUMNER WAS OFTEN criticized for being an impractical lawmaker, as he advocated for radical reforms that seemed impossibly idealistic to cen-trists. He was "so much occupied with thoughts of how the world is to be made better," his conservative friend George Hillard once rued, "that he does not pause to consider and observe what the world really is." In the words of Senator William Stewart, Sumner was "a theorist, a grand, gorgeous, extensive theorist, but he is not a practical man." While being so visionary, Stewart believed, Sumner was blind to political realities and failed to draft legislation that was passable and workable in practice. "My experience," Stewart claimed, "is that he has failed utterly to help us get practical measures."[27]

Sumner wasn't just being ambitious in proposing radical reforms. He was being naïve, arguably, for he failed to spend time spelling out the details of his ideas in precise bills and amendments that would be more likely to actually get passed. He also rarely attempted to engage in the compromises and backroom dealmaking necessary to turn bills into law.

In Sumner's defense, he didn't believe the craft of legislation was his main role in public life. He was so blasé about lawmaking that he was often content to introduce nonbinding resolutions on the floor, which expressed the general contours of policy proposals, rather than pitch actual bills. One of his secretaries, Arnold Johnson, asked Sumner about the merits of this theoretical approach.

In response, Sumner explained that his legislative strategy mirrored the habits of a mother cuckoo bird. Beginning with Aristotle, bird-watchers have noticed that a cuckoo mother never raises her own eggs or hatchlings. A bright, plump, colorful bird with a fearsome face and piercing eyes, the cuckoo lays her many eggs in other birds' nests. Wagtails, pigeons, sparrows, and other species take care of these cuckoo eggs, often confusing them for their own, until they hatch. Then, these birds raise the cuckoo hatchlings as if they were theirs, bringing most of them sucessfully into adulthood. Their cuckoo mother, meanwhile, neglects her young while prowling the forest looking for more nests to drop more eggs, benefiting from the free time she enjoys by not being tied down. In being so crafty, cuckoos have more offspring than the birds of other species, who are stuck raising eggs and hatchlings in their own nests.

Like the cuckoo mother, Sumner did not think it worth his time to personally raise his theoretical eggs and hatchlings to maturity. Instead, he deposited his ideas in the nests of other senators, letting them figure out how to bring those ideas to fruition. In so doing, Sumner was able to implant ideas into the minds of his colleagues and let them germinate, until they were convinced that his ideas were actually theirs. Not all his ideas—like land reform and public schools—would end up hatching as a result of his political strategy. But by offering so many ideas over time, through resolutions and other proposals, Sumner was still able to shape the overall legislative agenda of Reconstruction. He considered that to be his chief success, and he was proud of his approach to politics. "The cuckoo is a practical bird," Sumner explained to his secretary. "She leaves the hatching of her eggs to other birds; she is content to produce them."[28]

* * *

DESPITE LACKING PROVISIONS on education and land reform, the Reconstruction Act of 1867 marked a major turning point in American democracy. Thanks largely to Sumner's idealistic proposals, the act required southern states to launch new constitutional conventions based on universal suffrage for every loyal citizen, without distinction of race or property. In giving birth to a new political system premised on loyalty and equal rights, Congress invalidated Johnson's state governments and imposed military rule on the South until new constitutions were approved. To be readmitted on their new charters, states had to ratify the Fourteenth Amendment.

While displeased with the final product, Sumner knew Congress was doing something truly revolutionary that embodied many of the ideas he had been advocating for so long, years before his colleagues deemed them practical. That revolution was effectively re-founding the American republic. "Do not forget the grandeur of the work in which you are engaged. You are forming States," Sumner told the Senate shortly before the act's passage. "The Old must give way to the New, and the New must be worthy of a Republic, which, ransomed from Slavery has become an example to mankind," he said. "Farewell to the Old!" he declared. "All hail to the New!"[29]

CHAPTER 22

THE IMPERIALISM OF
THE DECLARATION OF INDEPENDENCE

O N MARCH 29, 1867, THE VERY EVENING BEFORE CONGRESS WAS SET to adjourn, Secretary Seward asked Sumner, "Can you come to my house this evening?" After narrowly surviving his assassination on the night Lincoln was killed, Seward dutifully continued his role as secretary of state under Johnson. Much to Sumner's consternation, he was loyal to Johnson despite the president's opposition to Black civil rights. Disliking Seward's political views fiercely, Sumner, who chaired the Foreign Relations Committee, still had no choice but to work with him regularly on foreign affairs matters. He went to Seward's house that night.

On arrival, Sumner was surprised to see the Russian ambassador sitting with Seward's son Frederick, who was assistant secretary of state. The two men told Sumner they had secretly drafted a treaty for Russia to sell to the United States an expanse of land west of British Canada near the Arctic Circle. It was an icy land that practically no American knew anything about, known at the time as Sitka. Chatting until midnight, Sumner promised to consider the treaty, which, per the Constitution, had to be approved by the Senate.

Sumner was intrigued by the plan. Before the war, he had hoped America would one day expand northward, believing northern land could counteract the power of the enslaving South. Disliking the ominous presence of the British Empire on the continent, Sumner had also hoped to one day take British Canada. "I wish to have that whole zone from Newfoundland to Vancouver," he once told Samuel Howe. Here was a chance to expand American territory and make the case for Canadian annexation someday stronger.[1]

On the following morning, the Senate discovered that their long-awaited vacation would need to wait a bit longer for them to review and decide on the treaty to buy the land. Sumner stopped an immediate floor vote on the treaty, which was almost certain to fail, and had the matter referred to the Foreign Relations Committee. When the committee began discussing it, senators voiced opposition to the expensive land deal, priced at $7.2 million (equivalent to more than $100 million today). It was dubbed years later as "Seward's Folly." Even prominent journalists such as Horace Greeley wondered why Seward wanted taxpayers to pay money for a wasteland of "ice, snow, and rock." But after some difficulty, Sumner managed to persuade the committee to recommend the adoption of the Russian treaty. He and others were all too tempted by the prospect of expanding America's reach.[2]

Controversial on issues of race and Reconstruction, Sumner was treated by Capitol Hill as an astute and balanced foreign policy thinker. Addressing the full Senate, he spoke for hours in the treaty's defense. People were surprised to see Sumner, one of the White House's fiercest opponents, endorsing a deal made by Andrew Johnson's administration. But he persuasively argued that Seward and Johnson were right this time. Russia was an important ally to American interests, and there were many economic benefits, from fur trading to whaling, in the new land. Deferring to Sumner's judgment, the Senate ratified Seward's agreement.

Inspired by the nationalism of Alexander Hamilton, John Quincy Adams, Joseph Story, and others, Sumner hoped the entire North American continent would someday be under the American flag. Believing the Civil War had eviscerated the idea of states' rights, he equally hoped the national government would start to treat all Americans as citizens of a single unified nation. Passing laws like the First Reconstruction Act and signing treaties to buy Russian land were just a start to fulfilling Sumner's postwar vision for his country.

* * *

A FEW WEEKS after the treaty's passage, Sumner went to the Library of Congress. Likely looking for a distraction from his tumultuous marriage, he decided to bury himself in piles of books and papers about the Russian territory that America was about to purchase. As he read deeper into the materials, he realized that there was no good book about the new territory in the English language. So, he decided to write it. "I am living with seals, and walruses, and black foxes and martins in Russian America," he mused to a friend, as he pored through zoological reports in Russian and French about the region. With the help of clerks from the State Department who translated sources for him, Sumner wrote a lengthy treatise on the history, economy, geography, and fauna of the region. His book became the definitive English-language work on the subject.

In his book, Sumner called the newly acquired land "Alaska," a term derived from a word used by some Native people to describe the region in which they lived. "Following these natives, whose places are now ours," Sumner said in his manuscript, "we, too, should call this 'great land' Alaska." While Seward formally chose the name, Sumner may have been the first to suggest it to him, and he became very publicly associated with the term. He effectively popularized the term "Alaska," giving a name to the region. One historian of the U.S. Senate put it this way: "It's been called 'Seward's Folly,' but it could just as well be known as 'Sumner's Project.'"

With a hint of dismay, Sumner acknowledged the legacy of enslavement, slaughter, and exploitation that Native people had endured at the hands of the Russians who had taken Alaska. But apart from a gentle nod to past sin, which he perhaps thought could be atoned for by a land acknowledgment, Sumner expressed no concern over the fact that America was buying land that, at the time, more than fifty thousand Native Alaskans called their own. While he admitted that some Native people were intelligent, Sumner generally described Natives as savages, cannibals, and superstitious people, who, he implied, should be educated in missionary schools.[3]

In a long career fighting for racial justice, Sumner raised the plight of Native people only a couple times. At the tail end of the Civil War, for example, he spoke in favor of a resolution condemning an infamous massacre at Sand Creek, Colorado, where hundreds of Cheyenne and Arapaho women and children were slaughtered by a sadistic Union Army regiment. And after the war, he asked the Judiciary Committee to investigate whether New Mexico had violated the Thirteenth Amendment by permitting debt peonage, a practice that effectively forced Native people who couldn't pay back financial loans in the region into slavery.

Other than that, Sumner almost never voiced opposition to his country's ongoing colonization and genocide of people indigenous to the Americas. Practically speaking, he was indifferent to it. Even during his heroic fight against the admission of Kansas and Nebraska in 1854, for example, he expressed no concern over the fact that many Americans wanted Native tribes in those territories to be ethnically cleansed. He was solely focused on stopping the spread of slavery, and, unlike his Texas col-league Senator Sam Houston, he did not raise the plight of both Blacks *and* Natives as reasons to oppose the Kansas-Nebraska Act.[4]

Sumner was decidedly an American expansionist. He hoped the nation, now that it was free of the stain of slavery, would gradually expand from sea to shining sea and from the top of Canada to the south of Mexico. He believed the nation, as it expanded, should recognize and protect the rights of all its national citizens on an equal basis in a vibrant multiracial democracy. It never seemed to dawn on him that there was terrible hypoc-risy in his views, given that American expansion was premised on the occupation and taking of Native land. "Mr. Sumner was thoroughly and truly an American," said the jurist and future attorney general Ebenezer Hoar. "He believed in his country, in her unity, her grandeur, her ideas, and her destiny."

Sumner believed that America had a duty to become a shining bea-con of democracy and human rights to the world, which he hoped would stand in stark contrast to monarchical European powers like England. In Hoar's colorful words, Sumner "saw in the future of America a noble and pursuant nation, its grand Constitution conformed to and construed by the grander Declaration of 1776, purged of every stain and inconsistency, the home of the homeless, the refuge of the oppressed, the paradise of the poor, the example of honor, justice, peace, and freedom to the nations of the earth." With America expanding and Reconstruction well under way, Sumner's dream seemed—at least to him—to be coming true.[5]

* * *

SADLY, HIS DREAMING for the future could not distract him from his mar-ital woes. He was so proud of his role as a leading foreign policy figure in Washington. So, it was especially humiliating for him to continue to watch his wife, Alice, gallivant around the capital with a German diplomat, a dalliance that some speculated was an extramarital affair. Sumner was get-ting desperate to stop the relationship that was "bringing scandal upon my name." Trying to be "forbearing, gentle & kind" with Alice, which he claimed he always was, he patiently pleaded with her not to see Holstein anymore. But Alice wouldn't budge.[6]

On April 26, 1867, Holstein was issued orders from Otto von Bismarck to return to Prussia "as soon as circumstances will allow." Though Alice left behind almost no letters or diaries that have survived, she must have been saddened, or perhaps heartbroken, when Holstein departed. For the next few weeks, her pain smoldered into anger, which she directed toward Sumner. She blamed him for Holstein's abrupt exit.

Holstein's biographer found nothing in German archives to suggest that Sumner ever asked Bismarck to transfer Holstein, and Sumner resolutely denied it. "I had nothing to do in any way directly or indirectly with the recall . . . never made any suggestion or gave any hint on the subject to a human being," he wrote. Chances are, Bismarck recalled Holstein as a routine matter. After all, he had been in America for quite some time without clear instructions. But it remains plausible that Bismarck brought Holstein home after catching wind of the scandal. No smart foreign leader would think it wise to let a diplomat enrage a senator who co-led American foreign policy by flirting with that senator's wife.[7]

After Holstein's departure, Alice made Sumner's life hell. Every time they were in a carriage together, according to Sumner's recollection, she would barrage him with insults and hot words. "I was obliged to find myself in tears," he recalled. "She has said things that made me hang my head with shame." Alice's verbal abuse tore at Sumner's soul. "You cannot enter into the depths of my sorrows," he confided in a friend. He told another that "life is a burden hard to bear in such a desolation as mine."[8]

Sometime in May, Sumner decided to make a last-ditch effort to reform his wife. While the couple was on their way to Boston for a summer break before Congress resumed in late July, he handed her a French novel to read. The novel was about a shameless woman who had betrayed her spouse. Once Alice realized what the book was about, she was inflamed. Her husband wasn't being subtle with his passive aggression. When they reached his house on Hancock Street, which had not yet sold, she exploded. "GOD DAMN YOU," she shouted, sweeping ahead of him to their bedroom and slamming the door in his face.[9]

After the post-train fight, Alice insisted on separate sleeping quarters from her husband. That arrangement lasted a few weeks before she decided to take her daughter and travel to Lenox, Massachusetts, to stay with family. For a while, she kept up the pretense that Sumner was going to join her shortly in Lenox, but she would in fact never deign to meet Sumner again. Later in the summer, she went to Europe to spend time with her sister, who was traveling through the Continent at the time. While she would visit New England from time to time, Alice Sumner would spend the rest of her life living in Europe, leaving her husband forever.

* * *

WHEN CONGRESS BRIEFLY reconvened in early July 1867, Sumner came back broken, beaten, alone, and exhausted. Things only got worse for him when the Senate decided in a resolution that it was "not expedient" to consider "further legislation, at this session, on the subject of Reconstruction." Hoping to keep the session brief and focused on a few implementation issues with the Reconstruction Act, the Senate prevented Sumner and others from proposing land reform or public education measures.

Sumner was livid. During Reconstruction, Congress would never guarantee integrated public education in the South, and only a minority of Black southerners would ever become owners of the land they lived on. No matter how passionately he complained that the resolution to stop Congress from considering any additional Reconstruction proposals was "so open to criticism, so doubtful in point of order, so plainly contrary to the spirit of the Constitution," his protest fell on deaf ears. In particular, William Fessenden berated him for trying to slow down the legislative process. Sumner in reply declared that Fessenden was trying to gag him and other Radicals, comparing the resolution to when the House of Representatives infamously banned John Quincy Adams and others from presenting antislavery petitions on the floor. But Sumner was unable to stop it.[10]

The July congressional session went by smoothly while Sumner and some other Radicals sat mostly quiet, brimming with rage and anxiety about the future of the South. He feared that Republicans, having reached the peak of their power, might inadvertently doom Reconstruction by failing to build schools and restructure southern land.

In September, Sumner exacted his revenge on his timid Republican colleagues. "I do not like to speak of any of my associates . . . except most kindly," he said dubiously to the reporter James Redpath, who interviewed him for a prominent feature piece. He then launched a barrage of invectives at his associates, accusing them of being prodigies of "obstructiveness and technicality" on Reconstruction.

Directing his ire especially at Fessenden, Sumner accused him, with no introspection, of being "nothing if not personal" and "very unkind to me." He imputed so many negative personality traits on his centrist colleague, while conceding some of his good work, that he permanently ruptured the uneasy truce the two had enjoyed since mid-1866. Aside from exasperating Fessenden, Sumner's interview served virtually no purpose. Lost and hurt, Sumner channeled his resentment and frustration into a mean-spirited and vengeful interview.[11]

In October 1867, Sumner tried to escape his emotional exhaustion by leaving the East Coast for a paid western lecture circuit to boost his finances. He figured that he would use the opportunity to make the public case for the Radical Reconstruction program being pursued by Congress. Northern Democrats and some centrists believed that Congress had effectively imposed a dictatorship over the South, in total disrespect for the rights of states and southern whites. Sumner believed these critics were missing the point. "Call it imperialism, if you please," he declared. "It is simply the imperialism of the Declaration of Independence, with all its promises fulfilled."

As he traveled through more than ten states, Sumner spoke several dozen times about the postwar constitutional philosophy that justified Radical Reconstruction. Invoking Joseph Story, Alexander Hamilton, and John Quincy Adams as his primary intellectual influences, he declared that "State Rights, in all their denationalizing pretensions, must be trampled out forever." He said that "the whole case must be settled now. The constant duel between the Nation and the States must cease."[12]

To make his argument, Sumner distinguished between two words: *federal* and *national*. *Federal* implied that America was a compact among sovereign states, an idea that many constitutional scholars—who are proponents of a theory called "federalism"—argue to this day. *National*, by contrast, implied that America was a single unity in which states have little or no sovereignty. "To my mind, our government is not Federal, but National," Sumner argued. "Our Constitution is not Federal, but National; our courts under the Constitution are not Federal, but National."

What did the nation stand for? "The equal rights of all," Sumner declared—as first promised in the Declaration, then in the Constitution, then affirmed by the victory of the Civil War, and finally enshrined in several constitutional amendments. Sumner said that equality was now a coextensive value with liberty. "No local claim of self-government can for a moment interfere with the supremacy of the Nation, in the maintenance of Human Rights," he insisted. Now "every person, no matter what his birth, condition, or color . . . has a right to require at the hands of the Nation, that it shall do its utmost, by all its central powers, to uphold the

National Unity, to protect the citizen in the rights of citizenship, and to perform the original promises of the Nation."

Pithy, precise, and eloquent, Sumner's "Are We a Nation?" address laid out his legal defense of Congressional Reconstruction. He believed America was no longer, if it ever was, a confederation of states. Now, it was a single nation tasked with protecting the individual rights of every citizen. No pretension of states' rights could be allowed to get in the way. Under the banner of constitutional nationalism, Congress had charged every southern state to rewrite its constitution to guarantee Black suffrage and pass the Fourteenth Amendment. In Sumner's view, Congress had effectively gifted to the nation, as Lincoln once put it, "a new birth of freedom."

* * *

LEGAL SCHOLARS TODAY describe this new birth of freedom as America's Second Founding. Even the Supreme Court has lately used the term in a decision. But scholars, including perhaps Supreme Court justices, disagree about what the Second Founding signified. Was it a rejection of the First Founding to create something new, or a reaffirmation of the old?[13]

From Sumner's perspective, the Second Founding radically transformed American law. He believed that the country had *repudiated* its prewar constitutional order by abolishing slavery, upending states' rights, and expanding congressional power to advance human rights. At the same time, he believed the Union had simply *redeemed* the original Founding vision. "Sumner had drunk deep from the sources of American institutions, in the writings and lives of our Revolutionary fathers," observed Ebenezer Hoar. In his mind, the Founders had always been nationalistic, antislavery, and believers in equality. According to the abolitionist Gilbert Haven, he treated the Constitution—as written by the Founders, even before it was amended—as "an object of love, not fear."[14]

The prominent Republican Carl Schurz was skeptical of Sumner's ideas. He believed that Reconstruction required necessary, but temporary, congressional actions that infringed on states' rights. As soon as Black suffrage and other measures were secured, Schurz thought the prewar constitutional order between states and the national government should resume. In his view, the Second Founding did not eliminate states' rights or create some unlimited congressional power to advance human rights.

Many years later, Schurz reflected on Sumner's constitutional ideas in "Are We a Nation?" and other speeches. He acknowledged that Sumner

sincerely "believed himself to be faithful to the Constitution" as understood by the Founding Fathers. At the same time, he was convinced that
Sumner was radically transforming constitutional law by breaking from
the Founders to create something entirely new. "Sumner may well be
classed among revolutionary characters," Schurz argued. "He was, uncon-
sciously, seeking to revolutionize the Constitution in its own name."[15]

* * *

IT WAS A shame for Sumner's supporters that his constitutional speeches
in the fall of 1867, eloquently written and argued, came at such a difficult moment in his life. Audiences noted how feeble and exhausted he
appeared when delivering his remarks. He wasn't as young or capable of
traveling far distances to speak anymore. He had caught a bad cold while
on the trip, making his voice rough and hoarse for many speaking events.
He ended up canceling several speeches in Iowa as he recovered from the
illness. On the way to Indiana, he bumped into Mary Lincoln on a train. "I
never saw his manner so gentle and sad," Mrs. Lincoln noted. Soon after,
he stepped off a moving train, accidentally fell over, and badly bruised his
nose. Though the injury could've been much worse, Sumner felt dejected,
weak, and fragile. All in all, his visionary constitutional philosophy was
being overshadowed by the personal travails that affected him so deeply.

While traveling solo, Sumner hoped to stay tight-lipped about his
estrangement from his wife. It was hard for him to confess to himself,
much less to anyone else, how badly his marriage had been going. Sumner
rarely admitted to mistakes, and this marriage was arguably the biggest
mistake of his life. Feeling a deep sense of shame, he had already been pro-
crastinating for months in telling his friends that he and Alice had separated. "I vowed myself to silence—kept my sorrow to myself," he confessed
later. Shame aside, Sumner also felt protective. He probably never loved
Alice in the romantic sense of the term, but he genuinely believed that his
manly role of husband involved guarding her and her daughter's reputations. "I was full of the idea of protecting her & her child & I was unwilling
to have her over to public controversy," he later explained.[16]

Despite Sumner's attempt to keep things quiet, the media eventually
found out about his failed marriage. "The great prophet of the 'higher law'
is not so married as he once was," mocked one tabloid. The tabloid blamed
the separation on "the Senator's narrow and selfish character," which
"began to manifest itself after marriage." An unidentified Boston socialite

in another paper claimed that the couple's estrangement was due to class differences. "Miss Hooper was a fashionable lady, of the *creme de la creme*," she observed. But Sumner had grown up in a poor household, a little-known fact that only select Bostonians would have known. "His family never was much, and the best people look down on him," she jeered.[17]

Several reports of dubious veracity claimed that Alice had left Sumner after the latter sent Holstein out of the country. Papers presented Sumner as an overbearing and hysterical man who had overreacted to his wife's mere "acquaintanceship,—it cannot be properly called an intimacy,—" with Holstein. After Sumner insinuated that a dishonorable affair had taken place, according to one tabloid, Holstein challenged him to a duel. Rather than accept, Sumner took the coward's way out: he abused his senatorial office by writing to Bismarck to get Holstein sent back to Berlin. "The Senator made a complete ass of himself," exclaimed one paper.[18]

Sumner was appalled to see these stories coming out. It was the first scandal of his career, and he blamed it on his wife's allegedly loud mouth. "She & her friends have been trying to throw blame upon me," he wrote to a friend in horror. "This is a terrible blow under which I stagger; & the reports & calumnies to which I have been exposed increase my trials." He didn't know how to cope with being dragged through the mud. Accustomed to bad press for his controversial views, he had never been vilified this badly for his private life or personal conduct. "Would that I have divine power to see how this terrible calamity could be best borne. It is hard."[19]

Sumner had married to improve his social standing; now he felt his reputation was being destroyed. He felt the urge to speak up and tell his side of the story, about how Alice had treated him miserably, with relentless verbal abuse and malicious antics designed to embarrass him. "My house was made a hell & my life a torment," he recalled. Alice's behavior was apparently so bad that Sumner was haunted by the thought of leaving Washington just to escape her. "So complete was her misconduct & so impossible seemed to her any chance—such was my despair—that I proposed last spring to resign my public trust & hide my sorrow & shame in some cheap valley of Switzerland."[20]

Over the next year, friends repeatedly reminded Sumner not to defend himself in the press. "Sumner's silence is heroic, but he must keep it & will gain in the end by it," Henry Longfellow told Sumner's friend Anna Cabot Lodge. "Pray be at rest & never breathe your convictions, for you would then lose the sympathy," Lodge instructed him. Sumner's friends tried to assure him that people didn't believe the stories coming out. But it was hard for him to accept this. He felt like the respectability he craved was being pulled out from under him.[21]

To cope with the pain, Sumner absolved himself completely. In a series of letters to Samuel Howe, he explained that he didn't believe he had made any mistake in marrying Alice. Rather, she was a fine person as far as he was concerned, until "her whole nature was poisoned by her intimacy with a foreigner." Calling himself "an innocent person," he said Alice had become "utterly wicked & false, lawless, reckless, heartless, setting at naught every vow, shameless." He was "filled of tenderness," while "she was essentially a bad woman." He was happy "to shield her—for her own sake" by letting their marriage "smolder in darkness," but she had insisted on being "shamelessly untruthful" by inventing stories about him. "There are not two sides," he tried to convince Howe. "I know that in this terrible trial I have been careful, considerate, kind & gentle."[22]

Worst of all for Sumner was Alice's apparent disclosure that he couldn't sexually please her. His sense of betrayal reached new heights when Howe heard a rumor that Alice had told folks that she separated from Sumner because of his inability to satisfy, in Howe's words, "what coarse natured women consider a just desire." Sure enough, rumors about Sumner's lack of potency, which he had always insisted were untrue, hit the press. Alice was tired of "Mr. Sumner's inability to obey the command given to Adam and Eve in the garden of Eden," the *New York Express* charged, referring to God's order to the couple in Genesis to "be fruitful and multiply."[23]

✳ ✳ ✳

THERE IS ANOTHER factor in Sumner's marriage with Alice that bears attention, though the evidence is sparse. One year after his separation, Sumner dined with his friend the young lawyer Edward Pierce. When asked about his marital woes, Sumner spoke in generalities about Alice being a bad woman. When Pierce pressed him for more details, Sumner said reluctantly, "She has gone to the verge of the criminal law, if she has not passed it." He wouldn't elaborate.

In the late 1880s, long after Sumner's death and two decades after his marriage, Pierce was writing a biography of Sumner and commissioned a set of interviews with Sumner's friends about his separation from Alice. The claims made in those interviews shocked him. Several people testified that Alice, in the spring of 1867, appeared to be "enceinte," a French word for "pregnant" that was in vogue at the time. That June, according to the publisher James Fields, Sumner believed he was going to become a father. But then, according to Senator Pomeroy and his wife, Sumner discovered from a doctor's confession that Alice had an abortion without his knowledge. He confronted Alice in her bed, shouting at her, "You are a murderer."

Despite his best efforts, Pierce never found evidence to corroborate these major after-the-fact allegations against Alice. He couldn't even find solid evidence to support the claim that Sumner had genuinely believed Alice had an abortion. To respect the Hooper family's privacy, Pierce never published these interview notes, which were stored at Harvard University after his death. He was never able to figure out the truth. Perhaps Sumner's friends, who despised Alice, invented this scandalous story about her to make her look bad, in the hopes Pierce would publish it. Perhaps Alice staged an abortion to irk Sumner even more. Perhaps Alice did have an abortion, leaving open the question of whether the unborn child belonged to Sumner or to Holstein. Whatever it was, the truth may never be known. Not one contemporary letter has been found, from Sumner or anyone else, that makes any claims about Alice's pregnancy or abortion. The hefty claim was only made in these secret notes from interviews that were held two decades after the alleged act.

If the story of Alice's abortion were true, then Sumner had successfully kept it secret, so secret that he never put it down in writing to anyone. Women who had abortions at the time were extremely stigmatized. If the allegation became public, Alice's reputation would have been ruined, and her young daughter would have grown up with the shame of having a sinful mother. Sumner may have reflected on the hard life endured by his own father, a bastard who suffered the disgrace of being born to sinful parents. No matter how much he resented Alice or despised her alleged decision to terminate the unborn child, assuming this story is true, Sumner resisted the temptation of slandering his estranged wife. If these interview notes are to be trusted, to protect Alice and her daughter, Sumner took any knowledge of this alleged sin to his grave.[24]

* * *

NOBODY WAS MORE troubled by the Sumners' marital breakdown than Samuel Hooper, whose dead son was Alice's first husband. Having helped bring the couple together, Hooper felt deep pain and regret over the turmoil happening between them. A good-humored politician who prided himself in bridging divides in Washington, Hooper—along with his wife, Anne—set to work to try to heal the marriage despite the animosity brooding between the couple.

It wasn't easy to try to mend the gap. Ashamed and mortified to be called impotent, Sumner started to wonder if Alice had really cheated on him. He wrote tactless letters to Hooper to complain about Alice's potentially lecherous behavior, as if he had completely forgotten that Alice was Hooper's daughter-in-law. Notably, he never gave a hint of a potential pregnancy or abortion. All he said was that Alice may have been party to "an illicit intimacy, which demoralized her nature." He explained that his wife "had seen others since her marriage that she likes better than me," a thinly veiled reference to Holstein.[25]

Hooper was mortified by Sumner's vulgar allegations against Alice and found them to be excessive. While he didn't think Alice was blameless, he wanted Sumner to stop indulging in speculations. So, he wrote Sumner a firm but tactful reply. "This way of exciting yourself by piling on strong expressions and overstating your troubles can have no other effect than to produce an unfavorable impression towards you and create sympathy for Mrs. Sumner," he told him frankly. "It presents to me a view of your difficulties which had never occurred to me before."

While inviting Sumner to dinner, which he would do repeatedly over the next few months, Hooper proposed to him that they never speak about Alice. She would be off limits. "Consider it hereafter a forbidden subject between us," he said. Hooper didn't think it productive to let Sumner continue to defame Alice. He explained to Sumner that his own wife, Anne, similarly spent time in public with other men, but that wasn't a cause for concern for him. The older couple had a strong relationship and were determined not to let the younger couple undermine the family. While Hooper would stay close to Sumner, his wife, Anne, cultivated her relationship with Alice, traveling with her to Europe.

In the year ahead, Samuel and Anne Hooper made an effort to learn more about the marital woes of Charles and Alice Sumner, respectively, and bring them back together. While they wouldn't succeed, they were at least able to maintain ties to both parties individually. For the rest of Sumner's life, the Hoopers effectively acted as his loving parents-in-law, who helped keep him, a grown man, emotionally grounded.

To this end, Samuel Hooper urged Sumner to move forward with building his own house in Washington. Earlier in the year, he and Alice had acquired a house that was currently being constructed next to the Hooper home. Given Alice's exit, Sumner wanted to abandon the project. "I took this house for another. I have no heart about it or any thing else. I am afflicted & unhappy. What can I do?" he asked Longfellow. Longfellow agreed that it would be better for Sumner to live in a boardinghouse instead. "Why go into an empty haunted house? You would only feel your loneliness the more," he advised. But Hooper insisted it would be good for Sumner.

"At last I have yielded to Mr. Hooper," Sumner wrote to a friend in mid-December 1867. "If Mr. H were not so positive & pressing, I should not think of the house." A doting father-in-law, Hooper took it on himself to oversee the final construction of the house. He once wrote a long and detailed letter updating Sumner on its progress while he was on his western tour and in Boston. He was confident that a big house would help Sumner heal. Thanks to Hooper's caring and meticulous help, construction was finished in mid-December. Just in time for Christmas, Sumner moved into the first, and last, home he could truly call his own.[26]

CHAPTER 23

SUMNER'S HOSPITALITY
WAS PERFECT

I N JANUARY 1868, MOORFIELD STOREY ARRIVED AT THE DOORSTEP
of Charles Sumner's brand-new house. The *Chicago Tribune* called it
"the Sumner Mansion." A stately three-story brick house with a mansard
roof, the home was located on the corner of H Street and Vermont Avenue,
across from the Dolley Madison House and adjoining the then-famous
Arlington Hotel (now home to the Department of Veterans Affairs).

Sumner's mansion was in the best spot in town, across the street from
Lafayette Square, a lively park encircled by the luxurious homes of prominent statesmen and much of the foreign legation. "There is the perpetual
cheerfulness around it of carriages coming and going, ladies and children
walking," marveled the *Tribune*. Even better, "the street is paved with
asphalte, so that no loud reverberations shake the house." From Sumner's
home, a visitor was "within hallooing distance of the White House."

Storey opened the green iron gate, stepped into Sumner's small yard,
and walked up the broad brownstone steps to the double front doors handsomely carved of black walnut. He was excited to meet Sumner. A bright
but bored student looking to quit his studies at Harvard Law School, Storey had landed a clerkship with the Senate Foreign Relations Committee,
which effectively made him Sumner's private secretary.

Storey had met the aging senator only once before, when Sumner was
recovering from his brutal caning in 1856. More than ten years had passed
since that fateful day, but in many ways, the worn-out Sumner was experiencing emotions in 1868 similar to those he experienced after the assault.
He was demoralized nearly beyond repair, believing his best days were
behind him. He was buried in books and art, trying to distract himself
from the political situation that seemed so dire. And most of all, he again

felt like a martyr recovering from iniquities—this time, by a wife who was fond of verbal abuse and who had humiliated him to the world.

Determined not to be alone, Sumner decided that his young secretary would live with him in his new house. Welcoming Storey inside, he walked him through the foyer, where he later placed a bust of Minerva. He may have shown him the rooms on the ground floor: a parlor, a dining room, and a library too small for all of Sumner's books. Probably skipping the basement, which had a kitchen and small rooms for servants, he took Storey upstairs. Along the wall next to the steps, he later placed photographs of famous stairwells. "As you go up my poor stairs, you can imagine you are on any of these grand stairways!" he would cheerfully tell guests.

"I am trying to make it pretty inside," Sumner explained. Over time, he chaotically adorned every inch of every wall of every room with more than a hundred engravings, lithographs, photographs, and autographs. There were pictures of historic places, ranging from the Alhambra Palace to Notre Dame. There was Christian iconography of Jesus and other biblical figures. Most of all, there were depictions of the eclectic set of people he respected most, such as Demosthenes, Louis XIV, Napoléon, Edmund Burke, Joseph Story, Horace Mann, the Duchess of Sutherland, Abraham Lincoln, and his late brother George. "Do not laugh if I tell you I am buying pictures—originals!" Sumner said. "It is full of books and pictures, and many rare old engravings," one lady who later toured the house observed. "But it looks like the home of a lonely man."

At the head of his staircase, Sumner later placed photographs of Giotto's Bell Tower, the façade of the Louvre, and the grand staircase at Versailles. "See, here are three perfect things," he once explained. "When I come home from the Senate tired and cross, I like to look at these; it comforts one to think there is something perfect, something that has never been criticised." Upstairs, there were three rooms. At one end was Sumner's bedroom, which had a grand view of the White House. On the other end was a guest room, where Storey would stay. Between the two was Sumner's study, a magnificent sun-filled office with three large windows, two desks, and a long, flat table. "His study was heaped with books and papers thrown down in promiscuous piles until at some times it was difficult to move about among them," recalled somebody who visited the house. "If his house was in some ways a gallery, in others it was a workshop."[1]

To Storey's relief, his own room was clean and neat. When they stepped inside it, Sumner's eyes carefully traced the room, inspecting it to ensure that every provision was made for Storey's comfort. "Chancellor Kent had rendered [me] the same service," Sumner told Storey. As a young lawyer, Sumner had resided often at the New York home of Chancellor Kent, a great early-1800s jurist who has been called the American Blackstone. "Alexander Hamilton had done it for him," Sumner continued. When Kent was a young lawyer, he had stayed often at the Poughkeepsie home of *his* mentor, a visionary and energetic lawyer who became a Founding Father.

Sumner believed he would be remembered as a significant figure in the history of American law, like Hamilton and Kent. He felt a great burden, a deep sense that he was a man who could make or break a nation. He knew posterity would judge him, as it had judged the many dead figures on his walls. He expected Storey to carry his legacy and that of his mentors. Long after Sumner's death, Storey would become the nation's leading civil rights lawyer and the founding president of the National Association for the Advancement of Colored People (NAACP). "In the universe of God," Sumner once said, "there are no accidents."[2]

* * *

ALMOST IMMEDIATELY, STOREY noticed Sumner's peculiarities. "He was a good listener and a good talker, but not both in the same conversation," he wrote. "Mr. Sumner liked praise and doubtless felt that he deserved it," and he had a total "lack of humor." He never smoked and drank little. He also seemed to be arrogant and snobbish to his colleagues. Indeed, Senator William Stewart once said that Sumner's "egotism was such as to make it impossible for him to admit that he had an equal in either House of Congress." But Storey believed that Sumner didn't intentionally affect "any air of superiority" to others. He said Sumner came across this way "because he was in fact superior in taste, in purpose, in his whole atmosphere."

Secretaries who preceded Storey had made similar observations about Sumner. "His familiarity with history, with letters, with society, with art, was to me simply astonishing," recalled Francis Balch. Given his boss's learning, Balch said, "Mr. Sumner was a man not ready to yield to his equals. 'Domineering' is a strong word; but he felt a superiority which really existed, and his manner asserted it." Another secretary, Arnold Johnson, seemed to think Sumner's alleged superiority complex was merited. "It has been said that no man can be a hero to his valet," Johnson noted. "Truly, he is a hero. I have been accused of hero worship, and I do not deny the accusation."

Sumner trusted his secretaries, rarely overworked them, and always sought their advice, even when he didn't expect to take it. "To his subordinates no one could be more considerate, more generous," Balch recalled. "He showed me a side of his character that few except his intimate friends saw," Storey said. "A paternal, personal kindliness, of which I have a very grateful remembrance." Johnson claimed that Sumner never really needed a secretary, given that he conducted most of his own research and wrote almost all his own letters. He didn't even want help in organizing the heaps of papers that filled up his living space, which had to be dumped elsewhere to make space for guests. "He was systematic in his disorder, and could always find the paper or book he wanted, provided it had not been misplaced by another person," Johnson reported.

Sumner entertained constantly, which his father-in-law, Samuel Hooper, advised him to do to distract himself from the otherwise inevitable loneliness. He often invited his former secretary, the journalist Benjamin Perley Poore, to dinner. "He knew how to order a good dinner, and when it was before him he enjoyed it, with a temperate use of good wines," Poore recalled. At dinner, Sumner was famous for being a talker, regaling guests with stories from his travels and his readings. He also became famous for serving mandarin tea, which he acquired from his friend Anna Cabot Lodge, who would send him packets of it frequently.

Storey was surprised at how gracious Sumner was with his guests, despite lacking a housewife to help him host. "In essence a gentleman," Sumner welcomed "the society of ladies" and "men of every rank, race, and color," according to Storey. The range of daily visitors was staggering, from ordinary strangers seeking the senator's help to the most powerful men of the era. "Reporters, clients, & visiters come in & consult him at breakfast, etc. & seem never to be excluded," marveled the poet Ralph Waldo Emerson while staying with him for a few days. "Sumner's hospitality was perfect," Emerson recalled. Even Senator Justin Morrill, who viciously debated Sumner many times in the Senate, recalled that Sumner often invited him to dinner with a "cordial greeting, and genial smile," being hospitable despite any political disagreements.[3]

Sumner rarely dined alone, sometimes inviting as many as ten guests to dinner. Storey was occasionally invited as well, including, to Storey's great excitement, when Charles Dickens visited in February 1868. The novelist refused every dinner while in Washington except at the home of his "old friend" Charles Sumner. Roughly the same age, the two had first met in 1842, when Dickens visited Boston on his first tour of America. Sumner and his friend Longfellow had taken Dickens through the city at night on an oyster crawl. Regaling guests with such memories at dinner, Dickens asked Sumner and Secretary Stanton about the night of Lincoln's assassination. Storey eagerly wrote down what Sumner and Stanton recalled, publishing it years later.[4]

Not regularly invited to Sumner's table, Storey often dined at Wormley's, an establishment located only a block away from Sumner's house. Wormley's was owned by James Wormley, a friend of Sumner's who would play an important role in his life as a homeowner.

* * *

A WASHINGTON NATIVE, James Wormley grew up giving carriage rides to the city's prominent white men on behalf of his father's livery stable. Friendly, ambitious, and always dressed to the nines, he persuaded some whites to let him take charge of a popular local club. After cultivating a reputation as a famous Black steward, he launched his own restaurant in the 1850s near his father's old stables. He also built a catering service that boasted a clientele of wealthy white men, such as Sumner's father-in-law, Samuel Hooper.

At Hooper's request, Wormley had received a pair of keys to Sumner's new home and helped oversee its final construction. He offered to help manage it. "I can get you a good Steward, Cook & Maid," he told Sumner shortly before he moved in. Taking a liking to Wormley, Sumner paid the caterer to hire his servants, buy his furniture, and acquire other supplies for the house. He often relied on Wormley to host his events, too. Wormley was eager to help: he delighted in Sumner's company and named his grandson after the senator.[5]

Grateful for Wormley's reliable service, Sumner and Hooper championed their friend's business. In 1871, Hooper agreed to be Wormley's mortgagor so the latter could build a five-story hotel atop the land where his father had his stables. Wormley transformed the space into one of the nation's most fashionable hotels, a watering hole for politicians and a destination spot for European travelers that boasted fifty-seven bedrooms, a reception parlor, smoking and wine rooms, and a high-end restaurant. "Wormley is very successful. He is sure that his is the best house in the country," Sumner proudly boasted of his friend and neighbor. "How can you look after my small affairs!" he teased Wormley. "The great hotel will demand all your energies."[6]

Whenever Wormley was busy, Sumner catered his house events from George Downing. A college-educated member of the Black middle class, Downing expanded his father's New York restaurant business by launching an upscale oyster bar and catering service in Newport, Rhode Island, Sumner's favorite vacation spot and probably where the two men had first met. "He is intelligent, experienced, and honest," Sumner said of Downing in 1863, when recommending him for an officer position in the Union Army. In 1865, Downing's career reached new heights when he was hired to move to Washington to run the mess hall, known as the Refectory, at the U.S. House of Representatives. There, he interacted daily with leading politicians.[7]

Downing and Wormley were members of an emerging Black middle class in the North that experienced astonishing upward mobility during Reconstruction. America, once defined by a rigid caste hierarchy, was now in a state of flux where Blacks were envisioning new possibilities for themselves and challenging the antebellum racial order. Downing and Wormley weren't content simply to make money by keeping quiet and pleasing whites under the precarious prosperity they were now enjoying. Unlike some Black restaurateurs, they insisted on opening their establishments to Black customers, too, even if it displeased some of their wealthier white patrons. While grateful for their success, they were frustrated that hospitality seemed to be one of the few industries where free Blacks were able to thrive. They leveraged their social network and status to lobby for their community. For example, Downing pushed to integrate the public schools of Newport, and Wormley financed the building of several Black schools in Washington, D.C.

Sumner enjoyed the company of these two Washington caterers, who reminded him of one of his best friends, Joshua Smith, whom he had met when Smith was in his youth. Smith had come to Boston as a fugitive from slavery and worked as a house servant for the abolitionists Francis and Sarah Shaw (parents of the famous Civil War officer Robert Gould Shaw). One day in the early 1840s, an argument exploded at the dinner table when a guest screeched at the Shaws that "Abolitionists, with their negro friends, ought to be hanged." The guest then turned to Sumner, who was also a guest that evening, and asked him bitterly what he thought of "the negro question." Sumner was in his early thirties then, a promising young lawyer beloved by Boston's elite. He had never expressed public opinions on racial issues before. Pointing to Smith, who stood as a butler behind his chair, he responded by indignantly asking the older gentleman, "Would you have that man a slave?" Impressed by Sumner's reply, Smith struck up a friendship with him. Sometime later, they chatted at Boston Common about the racism that Smith experienced daily. "Smith, some day I'll fight for you," Sumner promised.

By that time, Smith had started his own restaurant business. Clever and entrepreneurial, he hustled for some years before earning the massive opportunity to cater the formal dinner after Boston's 1845 Fourth of July celebration, where Sumner made his first major public oration. Delighted by the scrumptious feast, Boston elite hired Smith for countless events over the next several years, which earned him the nickname "Prince of Caterers." Not content to merely cater to the elite, he joined Sumner at the Boston Vigilance Committee, where they and others protected fugitives from slavery. After the war, he worked with Sumner to build a memorial in honor of Robert Gould Shaw and his colored regiment; it now stands across from the Massachusetts State House.

When Sumner sold his mother's Hancock Street house, he sought Smith's help in packing it up. Whenever he came to Boston afterward, he asked Smith to arrange his quarters at a local hotel. Utterly inept at home chores and reliant on men like Smith, Sumner was keen to ensure that his Black helpers knew they were his *friends*, not just his hired labor. "Come to Washington & inspect my new quarters," he wrote to Smith after moving into his new house. "I have a friend's chamber where you will be welcome."

When Smith spent a few nights at Sumner's house, he was struck by the kindness of his host and how warmly they got along; their friendship truly blossomed around this time. Smith said to Sumner afterward that it was "the only visit of my life where I felt at home." As periodic tokens of their comradery, Smith would send to Sumner by first-class mail leftover treats from his catering inventory—fresh grapes, peaches, strawberries, pears, and even salmon, trout, and turkey. Naturally, Sumner returned the favor by sending the best gifts he could think of: rare and expensive books.[8]

* * *

SUMNER'S FRIENDSHIPS WITH Wormley, Downing, and Smith were well known at the time. "All Sumner now needs is a divorce from his wife, who has abandoned him," mocked one Democratic newspaper. "He will then be able to . . . [marry] the daughter, or the widow of some colored barber or restaurateur." The senator made it a point to often meet these three Black entrepreneurs to solicit their advice on various political issues. Another Black leader, the nation's first Black congressman, Joseph Rainey, was impressed at how easy it was to talk to Sumner despite the wide education gap between them. "He possessed, in an astonishing degree, the faculty of adapting himself to social intercourse with those whose attainments were not commensurate with his own," Rainey recalled. "Never did I call but I found him glad to see me."

Sumner's regular consultations with these African American leaders kept him alert to the interests of the urban Black middle class, who held him accountable to their cause. A lesser-known Black individual who influenced Sumner's views on race and Reconstruction came from the rural South. His name was Edwin Belcher.

Unlike most of Sumner's Black friends, Belcher grew up in slavery and lived in Georgia. "I am a colored man, was born the slave of my father in South Carolina in 1845," Belcher once explained to William Lloyd Garrison. "At an early age through the exertions of my mother I was sent to the North where I was attending school when the war commenced in 1861." When Lincoln called for troops, "I ran away from school and volunteered as a soldier." The son of a slaveholder who impregnated his mother, Belcher looked so white that no one questioned his race when he was made a Union Army captain at the age of nineteen, becoming one of the first commissioned Black officers in combat. Captured by Confederates during Sherman's March to the Sea, he was released from a Georgia prison after the war and settled in the state.[9]

At the start of Reconstruction, Belcher taught at a freedmen's school in Augusta—one of more than a thousand free public schools the Freedmen's Bureau had built for Black children across the South. In March 1867, he was made a bureau agent. Agents helped freedpeople negotiate wage contracts; access food, medicine, and financial aid; reunite displaced families; and more. Everywhere bureau agents went, they were harassed by angry ex-rebels. President Johnson made things worse by undermining the Freedmen Bureau's military courts and openly calling for resistance. Worried for his safety, Belcher wrote a solemn plea to Sumner asking for his help in being reappointed an army officer.

Sumner failed to convince Gen. Ulysses Grant, who served under President Johnson, to offer Belcher an army position. Having never met Belcher before, Sumner couldn't vouch for him much. But the young man became his pen pal of sorts for several years before they finally met in real life in Washington in 1872. Every few weeks, Belcher wrote long, emotional pleas to Sumner about the instability of Reconstruction in Georgia. While Sumner's replies do not survive, Belcher's letters shed light on what Sumner knew was happening in the South as a response to Washington's policies.[10]

Following the Reconstruction Act of 1867, Georgia and other states held constitutional conventions. Thanks to Sumner's work, loyal men of any color were eligible to run to be convention delegates. In March 1868, nearly 40 elected Blacks joined 120 white delegates in Atlanta to rewrite the state's constitution. "The social status of the citizen shall never be the subject of legislation," the new constitution said. It guaranteed equal protection to every person, a homestead to every family, free schools open to all children, the property rights of married women, and freedom from imprisonment for debtors. Other southern states crafted similarly progressive constitutions in 1867–69, which, in the words of one British visitor to the South, mirrored "the mighty revolution that had taken place in America" in the late 1700s; in other words, a Second Founding.[11]

Inspired by Georgia's new constitution, Belcher ran for a seat in the State House. Even though most whites were fiercely opposed to the idea of Black officeholders, Belcher won. His base was surely Black voters, who now constituted nearly half the state's voting population. Some southern white loyalists, mostly ex-Whigs (derisively called scalawags), likely voted for him, too. There were also northern whites (derisively known as carpetbaggers) who moved to the South after the war in search of opportunity. Across the South, precarious coalitions of so-called scalawags, carpetbaggers, and Blacks elected Republican majorities to state legislatures. These coalitions were unstable: whites couldn't fathom allying in the long run with Blacks.

In the spring of 1868, Belcher and other African American officeholders in the South were full of hope, planning to rebuild their states as multiracial democracies with equal rights for everyone. But white ex-rebels were seething. Mortified by what they called "Negro rule," they were hell-bent on restoring the prewar racial hierarchy. Emboldened by the fiery and racist rhetoric of Andrew Johnson, ex-rebels formed secret militias, including chapters of the new Ku Klux Klan, to terrorize ex-slaves who dared assert their freedom. Sometimes violence was spurred out into the open, such as when angry white mobs carried out lynchings and pogroms. Groups like the Klan promised mass violence if Blacks were allowed to participate in politics; they pledged so-called peace if their fellow whites agreed to exclude Blacks from the process.

In some states, African American lawmakers overcame threats of violence in 1867–69. For example, they ably governed in South Carolina, which elected a majority Black legislature under its new constitution, and in Mississippi and Louisiana, where Blacks were large pluralities. Lawmakers charted a revolutionary agenda to tax former enslavers, redistribute land, create jobs for Black citizens, and arm them for their safety. But in states like Georgia, white ex-rebels subverted the movement and retook power.

On the pretense of restoring peace, white lawmakers in Georgia expelled their Black colleagues from the state legislature. With his light complexion and half-white blood, Belcher was spared from the purge; it was unclear if he was legally considered Black. But the Klan was onto him. In his home county, Klan members harassed white officials who agreed to work with him, and local boys would ominously sneer at them, saying, "I smell Belcher!" In nearby counties, white militiamen drove a Freedmen's Bureau teacher out of town, tortured a white man who gave lodgings to the teacher, and shot and killed a Black lawmaker who was Belcher's colleague. All this occurred while federal troops were leaving Georgia, as Congress had readmitted it into the Union.[12]

"We have no adequate protection," Belcher informed Sumner. "We are not free from murderous attack on the Rail Roads," he warned. Referring to Black lawmakers, he decried that these "poor men who staked their all upon the completion of reconstruction in this state . . . have had their businesses destroyed and had to flee from home to save their lives—and those that . . . were allowed to remain at home, were under constant fears of assassination." He begged Sumner to stop the withdrawal of Union troops from the South. "Do not place us into the hands of the white men in this country (South)," Belcher pleaded. He was scared, helpless, and—a young man in his twenties—worried about his future in post-Reconstruction America. "To the colored man, this is a life & death struggle. We must win. For God's sake, aid us."[13]

* * *

PANICKED LETTERS FROM Belcher and other Black southerners kept Sumner in a state of dread. Their experience of unmitigated terror contrasted sharply with the experiences of men like Smith, Wormley, and Downing, whose lives seemed more promising than ever. White ex-rebels were threatening to unravel America's Second Founding and its multiracial democratic experiment. He wanted the nation to guarantee equal protection to Black southerners, as stated in Section 1 of the Fourteenth Amendment. He also wanted to eliminate the man most responsible for enabling white terror: President Andrew Johnson.

There was a chance the previous year when his friend James Ashley pushed through a House resolution that launched an impeachment inquiry against Johnson. But in what Sumner called a "great calamity," a majority of the House did not agree that Johnson had committed "Treason, Bribery, or other high Crimes and Misdemeanors," as the Constitution required. Most Republicans were waiting for him to make a big enough overstep that would fit these criteria.[14]

That overstep took place on February 21, 1868, when Johnson unilaterally fired his secretary of war, Edwin Stanton. This violated the Tenure of Office Act of 1867, which generally required Johnson to get the Senate's consent before removing civil officers. Johnson lacked Lincoln's tolerance for Cabinet members who disagreed with him on policy. Because Stanton openly denounced Johnson's views at Cabinet meetings and somewhat obstructed his military policies, Johnson wanted him gone. But Stanton wouldn't resign despite Johnson's repeated pleas and creative attempts to remove him. A close friend of Sumner's and an ally of the Radicals, he stayed in office to be a spy and a bulwark against the White House.

When Stanton learned that he had been fired, he sent a message to Congress asking if the legislature believed Johnson had breached the Tenure of Office Act. The news struck Congress "like a thunderbolt," according to a reporter. "The gauntlet was flung into its very chamber, and there it lay on the floor," Sumner colorfully recalled. In a mixed eruption of anger, shock, and excitement, Congress launched into a debate on whether Johnson should be impeached. Several Republicans wrote Stanton asking him to stay at his post. Grabbing a pencil, Sumner jotted down a famous single-word message for him: "Stick."

Stanton took the advice and stuck, declaring that he was still the lawful secretary and barricading himself within his War Department office. That night, House members drafted an impeachment resolution against Johnson, and the Senate passed a resolution stating that he had acted unconstitutionally. In just three days, the House impeached Johnson. It was the first presidential impeachment in U.S. history. An impeachment trial would now occur in the Senate, where two-thirds of the chamber needed to convict Johnson for him to be removed.[15]

* * *

IN A SHOW of fairness, the Senate gave Johnson's defense lawyers two months to prepare for an impeachment trial. By the time the trial took place, Sumner was furious at the long delay. "This is one of the last great battles with Slavery," he said in a filed opinion. He believed no more time should be wasted. "Andrew Johnson is the impersonation of the tyrannical slave power. In him it lives again. He is the lineal successor of John C. Calhoun and Jefferson Davis," Sumner declared.[16]

Sumner had also been upset at the *nature* of the trial. Afraid of being called partisan and overly zealous, Republicans kept the proceeding narrowly focused on the president's alleged breach of the Tenure of Office Act. Centrist Republicans didn't want to be seen as pursuing a political vendetta against the president. But Sumner and other Radicals openly denounced this façade. "The formal accusation is founded on certain recent transgressions," Sumner conceded, ". . . but it is wrong to suppose that this is the whole case."

In Sumner's view, impeachment was "a political proceeding before a political body, with political purposes." With help from his private secretary Moorfield Storey, he compiled evidence that the British Parliament historically viewed impeachment as such. He then ascribed to Johnson a long list of political offenses: despoiling Freedmen's Bureau land intended for freedpeople; prostituting the pardoning power to forgive rebels; weaponizing the veto power to stop laws passed to benefit colored people; excusing massacres and granting license to the Ku Klux Klan; and much more. These offenses, he declared, were enough to expel Johnson from office.[17]

Going a step farther, Sumner maligned those who obscured the political stakes of impeachment. Given Johnson's many transgressions, it was "utterly unworthy of this historic occasion" to make the legality of Stanton's removal the key theme of the impeachment trial. Sumner believed that Senate Republicans had missed the forest for the trees, spending too much time, in his words, picking the "vermin gendered in a lion's mane." He seethed over the fact that "technicalities, devices, quirks, and quibbles . . . have infested this great proceeding."

As the trial focused on the Tenure of Office Act, senators debated whether Johnson could ignore it. Democrats argued that Congress couldn't legally restrain a president's removal power. Because the law was unconstitutional, Johnson didn't have to follow it. Lincoln, for example, had ignored Supreme Court decisions (like *Dred Scott*) that he said were unconstitutional.

Sumner believed the entire debate was misguided because he thought the president (and the Supreme Court, for that matter) should obey statutes that Congress deemed to be constitutionally valid. Today, legal scholars tend to promote the doctrine of "judicial supremacy," wherein the Court has the final word on the constitutionality of legislation. In contrast, Sumner believed in something akin to *congressional supremacy*.

"Whether the statute is constitutional or not is immaterial," he argued. "The President, after the statute has become a law, is not the person to decide." Neither could the Court decide. "The Supreme Court is not the arbiter of acts of Congress," he believed. "If this pretension ever found favor, it was from the partisans of slavery and State rights." The Court's business was "to decide 'cases;' not to sit in judgment on acts of Congress and issue its tribunitial veto." What did Sumner think the Court should do if it viewed a law as unconstitutional? "If a 'case' arises where a statute is said to clash with the Constitution," Sumner explained, "it must be decided as any other case of conflict of laws . . . and then its judgment is binding only on the parties." Unless a statute was "*on its face unconstitutional*," which Sumner reserved for the most extreme and obvious circumstances, both the Court and the president were obligated in his view to defer to its legality, as determined by Congress.

The idea of congressional supremacy may seem surprising today. But in Sumner's era, Congress was considered the most legitimate branch of government. President Johnson had reached the White House by virtue of Lincoln's assassination, not by the electoral will of the people. Supreme Court appointments were usually political favors to the president's friends, and abhorrent antidemocratic decisions, like *Dred Scott*, were still recent in public memory. Among the three branches, Congress was seen as the most democratic, the best expression of "We the People." It was widely believed the Framers saw it that way, too. After all, they had put Congress in the first article of the Constitution; the executive branch and the judiciary came afterward.

By 1868, Congress was in one of the most powerful positions it had ever been in. A veto-proof Republican majority had passed scores of bills over Johnson's vetoes. Those bills included military control over southern states, which were denied representation in Congress until they drafted constitutions that Congress approved of. With new enforcement powers from two far-reaching constitutional amendments, Congress had also passed civil rights laws that would have been unthinkable prior to the war. Now, at last, Sumner hoped, Congress would reach its zenith by removing the president of the United States.

* * *

THE REMOVAL VOTES took place on May 16 and May 26, 1868, for different articles of impeachment. On both days, shortly after noon, Chief Justice Salmon Chase, who presided over the trial, started with the roll call. "How say you?" he asked each senator alphabetically. The "guilty" and "not guilty" replies came one by one and as people anxiously watched. They "progressed in perfect stillness," reported the *New York Herald*, while "the most intense anxiety" was "manifested when the name was called on any of those republican Senators who had voted 'not guilty.'" To survive removal, Johnson needed seven Republicans to break ranks on all counts. When it was all done, Chase tallied the votes. In a tone of voice showing considerable emotion, he declared, "Two-thirds of the Senators not having pronounced him guilty, he stands acquitted." With exactly seven Republicans choosing to acquit, Johnson survived by a hair's breadth.[18]

"Give me a lawyer to betray a great cause," Sumner bitterly lamented. "He can always find an excuse." The seven dissenting Republicans argued that they disliked Johnson as much as anyone, but that his impeachment lacked a strong legal basis. This reasoning irked Sumner to no end. Ever since law school, he had resented judges and politicians who hid behind the law to avert just outcomes. "I had rather be a toad and live upon a dungeon's vapor," he had written a friend while in his early twenties, "than one of those lumps of flesh that are christened lawyers, and who know only how to wring from quibbles and obscurities that justice which else they never could reach."[19]

Sumner was especially upset that conservative Republicans had cited legal reasons to acquit Johnson when some had more cynical motives. While they disliked Johnson, these conservatives were arguably even more afraid of his potential successor, Benjamin Wade, the president of the Senate. Because there was no vice president, Wade would have assumed the White House if Johnson had been removed. Nearly as radical as Sumner,

Wade was reviled for being too outspoken on Black civil rights and other progressive causes, including a woman's right to vote. He also favored printing fiat paper dollars, which would make it easier for debtors to pay off loans, rather than resuming the gold and silver standards that had been suspended at the start of the Civil War. "At the very mention of impeachment," Frederick Douglass keenly observed, "Wall Street turns pale."

Conservatives worried that Wade planned to bring other Radicals into the Cabinet. That was indeed Wade's plan. He had even quietly suggested to Sumner that he would ask him to serve as Secretary of State. "Mr. Wade would have relied upon me, & wished me to leave the Senate," Sumner told a friend. He and other Radicals were dismayed by the loss of a potential Wade presidency.[20]

Radicals faced another blow when, in early August 1868, Thaddeus Stevens died. A political giant, Stevens had been the unofficial leader of the Republican House caucus, which was more radical than the Senate caucus. While not personally close to Stevens, Sumner believed him "a great leader" and served as a pallbearer at his Washington funeral ceremony. Soon thereafter, Wade, James Ashley, and other Radicals lost their reelection campaigns. It looked as if Radicals were now falling into decline.[21]

* * *

RETURNING TO BOSTON in September 1868, Sumner was depressed, dejected, and defeated. Because his house had already been sold and Longfellow and Howe were traveling at the time, he had nowhere to stay. "There is no roof for me in the city of my birth," he wrote to Howe, complaining about how "entirely homeless" he was. Joshua Smith arranged Sumner's stay at a hotel. "Here I am in the third story looking from the back of this house over a stable & a machine shop, where I hear constantly the tread of horses & the hisses of steam," he said to Longfellow. "For the time this is my home—all that I have here."

By losing his home, Sumner was no longer as deeply in touch with the Black Bostonian community in which he had grown up. When he was invited to attend a Republican political rally in his old neighborhood, Ward Six on the North Slope of Beacon Hill, he spoke about his attachment to the neighborhood and his nostalgia for having lost his connection with it. "I find a special motive for being here to-night, in the circumstance that this is the ward where I was born and have always voted," he said to the predominantly Black audience. "According to familiar phrase—this is my ward." No longer having an address there, he wondered out loud about where he might vote in November, saying he just "expects" to vote in this ward in the future.

When the poet John Whittier inquired after his health, Sumner replied, "I am reasonably well; but there is very little happiness for me." Feeling bad for the man, Smith hosted Sumner for dinner. Whittier invited Sumner to stay with him, but the proud senator declined. "This is my lot, and I try to bear it." While he mourned his loneliness, he didn't miss his estranged wife, Alice, who was living in Europe. "It is an infinite solace that she is outside of my house never more to disturb me by her presence or to degrade the house."[22]

In Boston, Sumner felt more isolated than before and faced a bout of depression. He was fifty-seven years old. Many of his friends, even some his age or younger, were dying or dead. This included many old friends in Europe, where Sumner hadn't been for nearly ten years. Abolitionists like William Lloyd Garrison had also dialed down their activism now that slavery had been abolished. A new generation of political aspirants was rising: men who didn't share the same idealistic moral vision that had animated reformers of Sumner's generation. Even older white northerners were exhausted by the many years of wartime sacrifice and were losing faith in Reconstruction.

As an orator and politician, Sumner had lost much of his spunk. By the late 1860s, his style of soaring oratory had fallen out of favor. Most people preferred crisp, cogent speaking styles like Lincoln's. It didn't help that Sumner was now perpetually exhausted, often reading from his remarks rather than memorizing them, and frequently sick, his voice coarse and less captivating. Having served for seventeen years, Sumner was no longer the fresh figure he had once been. He was instead perceived by critics as a relic of the antebellum years, clinging to power because of incumbency. While his support from African Americans and Radicals was strong and even growing, it was fading with everyone else.

Accordingly, Boston conservatives invited William Fessenden for a public dinner soon after he voted for Johnson's acquittal. The move was seen as a slight to Sumner and a signal that conservatives might plot, with Fessenden's blessing, to persuade the Massachusetts Legislature to put another Republican in Sumner's seat when his term expired after the November 1868 election. The most popular name being floated was

Sumner's rival Charles Francis Adams, who, having returned from his ambassadorship to England, was looking for a job.

Aware of his difficulties, Sumner wanted to shore up his support from conservative Republicans. He broke with radicals like Wade by strongly favoring the gold and silver standards that had been suspended during the war. This pleased Boston's merchant class, which hoped a return to the gold standard would stop inflation. Inflation was arguably destabilizing the market, and it cut into the profits of rich creditors who had extended wartime loans. Sumner also vigorously supported additional tariffs to help Boston manufacturers, who no longer offended him now that their profits didn't rely on raw materials like slave-produced cotton.

The strategy worked. Impressed by their senator's rigid fiscal conservatism, Boston elites gratefully thanked Sumner for supporting gold-backed money and tariffs. Moreover, Adams refused to campaign for himself, expecting conservatives to come to him first. Other potential candidates, like Benjamin Butler and Nathaniel Banks, couldn't rally enough support for themselves. By November, it was clear that Sumner was going to be reappointed.[23]

* * *

THE NOVEMBER 1868 election was marred by violence, as white ex-rebels desperately tried to stop Republicans from winning in southern states, retaining Congress, and retaking the White House. Many Blacks were harassed and forced to vote Democratic or stay home. In some places, white mobs beat or killed those who voted Republican. "The fall campaign has opened with a bitterness never before employed in this Country," Edwin Belcher wrote to Sumner from Georgia. "We have no adequate protection," he explained. "How are we to prevent our people from being driven to the polls and forced to vote against all they hold dear on Earth?"[24]

Despite the white terrorism, Republicans won thanks to the bravery of Black voters. The party nominee, Ulysses Grant, narrowly beat Democrat Horatio Seymour. Grant probably lost the majority of white votes, but he earned nearly all of the Black vote. Expecting Grant to be grateful, George Downing asked him to appoint "numbers of our race to important positions," a striking demand that would have been unimaginable under Lincoln or Johnson. Black voters had high hopes for Grant, a respected Union general, even though the career soldier had no known political views before running for office. Sumner was more circumspect. "Who can say that, as President, he would give to the freedmen ... that kindly and sympathetic support which they need?" he wondered. Sumner barely knew Grant, even though both lived in Washington.[25]

Grant recognized his indebtedness to Black voters and believed he had a moral duty to advance Black suffrage. After the election, he endorsed a congressional effort to draft what became the Fifteenth Amendment, which banned racial discrimination in voting, at the start of the new session in December 1868. Republicans realized that Black voters in the South needed firmer protection than the First Reconstruction Act, which could be over-turned if Democrats retook control of Congress. They also discovered that northern states couldn't be trusted to enfranchise Black voters themselves; several state referenda on the issue had failed in recent years. An amend-ment was necessary to secure multiracial democracy and Republican polit-ical power.[26]

In January 1869, Downing and two hundred Black officeholders and civic leaders converged on Washington to advocate for universal suffrage. In the words of one historian, "it was the biggest and most widely noticed black convention ever." Unanimously approving a resolution endorsing the amendment, the conventioneers appointed Downing and others to testify to congressional committees and to Grant on the need to pass it. Tirelessly, Downing and his allies pushed Republicans to enfranchise all Black American men.[27]

To advance his cause, Downing also attended the Universal Franchise Convention, which was organized by white feminists, including Elizabeth Cady Stanton and Susan B. Anthony. The convention ostensibly con-cerned suffrage for *everyone*, but some feminists were furious that Black men might get voting rights before women. To Downing's shock, Stanton unleashed an angry, racist screed against Black male suffrage, even though she had been an abolitionist and longtime friend of Frederick Douglass. White women were "nobler types of American womanhood" compared to "lower orders of foreigners now crowding our shores," she seethed. "Pat-rick and Sambo and Hans and Yung Tung," she decried, should not get to vote before she did.[28]

Stanton had been harboring racist resentment against Black people for years. After leading a petition drive for abolition on Sumner's behalf, she had expected Sumner and other Republicans to endorse women's suf-frage in gratitude. That didn't happen. While some were open to it, none treated it like a priority. Sumner had gone as far as to say that women's suffrage was "not judicious for them at this moment" because freedmen's suffrage mattered more. It was "obviously the great question of the future," he noted, saying he wanted to leave it "untouched." He predicted it "will be easily settled, whenever the women in any considerable proportion" insist on it, a tepid response at best and one that contrasted sharply with his passionate advocacy for Black suffrage.

Feeling betrayed, Stanton, joined by Anthony, courted racist Democrats who were willing to promote white women's suffrage. They ridiculed people like Sumner for arguing that Blacks deserved to vote because they were taxed without representation. After all, property-owning women were taxed but couldn't vote, either. In reply, Sumner insisted that disenfranchised women could be represented by the men in their families, while Blacks had no one to represent them. That argument wouldn't satisfy Democrats, Anthony, and Stanton.[29]

As the cause for Black male suffrage gained traction, the feminist duo formed a white-only women's group to fight it. They demanded that white women get suffrage before Black men. When they invited Sumner to attend their first convention, unsurprisingly, he declined. Undeterred, they repeatedly asked him to support white women's suffrage in the years ahead. He wouldn't do it. Realizing that anti-Black racism hurt her case, Anthony even tried once to appeal for the rights of Black women. "Grateful for all your service for black men, I now ask them equally for black women & white," she wrote Sumner. His reply, if any, does not survive.[30]

Uncomfortable with their racism, Sumner was also uncomfortable with women's suffrage. He never gave a speech in support of it, even when fellow Radicals like Benjamin Wade did. He was silent about it despite privately admitting to its logic. "Take my speeches and when I say 'color' or 'race,' put 'sex' and you will have the strongest argument I can make for women's enfranchisement," he once told Anthony. While pleased with his admission, she never forgave Sumner for failing to publicly advocate for it. "He was true to the negro," Anthony once wrote scornfully, "but never uttered a public word for Equal rights to women."[31]

Sumner might have made a justifiable strategic choice not to prioritize women's rights. If Radicals commingled women's suffrage with Black suffrage, they probably would have failed to achieve either. At the same time, Sumner surely imbibed some of the misogynistic prejudices of his era. He had almost no female friends apart from those related to his male friends.

He never attended a women's convention and rarely corresponded with women's rights activists, except perhaps the novelist Lydia Maria Child. And some critics took the debacle of his marriage to mean he had no empathy for the other sex.

Julia Ward Howe, basking in the fame she had received from authoring the Union song "Battle Hymn of the Republic," once came to Washington without her husband Samuel Howe's permission to publicly read her poetry. Samuel never approved of his wife's participating in public events like these, believing that respectable women of society did not do such things. Sumner told Julia—in a letter she described in her diary as "very kind"—that he agreed with his best friend Samuel that she shouldn't speak. She was crushed. "He disapproved of women's speaking in public," her daughters later complained about their father's closest friend.

That said, Sumner did help women participate in politics. He cosigned an invitation to Anna Dickinson, a female abolitionist, to give a political speech on the House floor; she was the first woman to do so. He routinely brought Stanton and Anthony's petitions to the Senate floor, even when he criticized them. And when Stanton testified before the Senate District Committee about enfranchising women in the capital city, Sumner listened attentively to every word she spoke. After Stanton was done, Sumner approached her and her allies, who all resented him. "I have been in this place, ladies, for twenty years," he confessed to the activists, his voice full of emotion. "I have followed or led in every movement toward liberty and enfranchisement; but I have it to say to you now, that I never attended such a committee meeting as this in my life, it exceeds all that I have ever witnessed."[32]

Impressed by women's steady advocacy for suffrage, Sumner believed they would someday earn the constitutional right to vote—without any help from him. A friend once asked him whether the Supreme Court could plausibly interpret the Fourteenth and Fifteenth Amendments to include women. "I suppose I know more about judges than any man in America," Sumner replied. Referring to his relationships with John Marshall and Joseph Story, he went on to explain that "there were two ways in which almost any judge could regard almost any question—according to the letter or to the spirit." Then, he predicted, "Whenever any man on the Supreme Bench was heartily of the opinion that women ought to vote, he would probably have little difficulty in seeing authority for woman suffrage in these constitutional amendments."[33]

* * *

SUMNER FAILED TO see the point of the Fifteenth Amendment. Ratifying an amendment was a cumbersome process that could easily fail. He and a few other Radicals believed the better path to enfranchising Black men was simply to pass a statute. But centrists argued that the Constitution, as it currently stood, left the question of suffrage to the states. In response, Sumner denied the existence of states' rights and asserted that several clauses, including the Republican Guarantee Clause and the Enforcement Clauses of the new amendments, authorized Congress to pass a law. "Already Congress, in the exercise of this power, has passed a *civil rights act*," he explained. "It only remains that it should now pass a *political rights act*, which, like the former, shall help consummate the abolition of slavery."[34]

To those who said a suffrage law would infringe on states' rights, Sumner had no patience. "In the name of State Rights . . . Slavery, with all its brood of wrong, was upheld. Now, in the name of State Rights . . . Caste, fruitful also in wrong, is upheld," he decried. Conceding that a state could exercise most government functions within its jurisdiction, he argued that "a State transcends its proper function, when it interferes with those equal rights, whether civil or political, which . . . are under the safeguard of the nation."

Sumner believed human rights were at the center of the postwar Constitution that had been forged during the period now called the Second Founding. "Beyond all question the true rule under the National Constitution, especially since its additional amendments," he argued, "is that *anything for Human Rights is constitutional.*" Under his rule, Congress could easily interpret the Constitution to give it power to pass a suffrage law. In fact, Congress could legally do almost anything to advance human rights. "There can be no State Rights against Human Rights," he insisted. "This is the supreme law of the land, anything in the Constitution or laws of any State to the contrary notwithstanding."

Sumner's human rights–centered constitutional philosophy put him at odds with prewar constitutional thinking, which focused on the principles of limited government, states' rights, and positivism (the idea that rules should be obeyed regardless of their underlying morality). Many contemporary lawyers were still guided by antebellum thought. "I am surrounded by lawyers," he acknowledged. But that didn't deter him. "Men ordinarily find in the Constitution what is in themselves, so that the Constitution in its meaning is little more than a reflection of their own inner nature," he noted. Advocacy for human rights was in his nature, even if it wasn't in that of other lawyers. "No learning in books, no skill acquired in courts, no sharpness of forensic dialectics, no cunning in splitting hairs, can impair the vigor of the constitutional principle which I announce," he declared. "Whatever you enact for Human Rights is constitutional."[35]

When the Senate passed the Fifteenth Amendment in late February 1869, Sumner left the room to avoid having to vote on it. He couldn't bring himself to pass an amendment when he thought a law could do the trick. He also believed that by passing an amendment, Congress was implicitly acknowledging that political discrimination based on race had been constitutionally allowed beforehand. This offended his sensibilities about human rights constitutionalism. And he worried about the amendment's implementation. The final text, which said that "the right of citizens of the United States to vote shall not be denied or abridged . . . on account of race, color, or previous condition of servitude," said nothing about other practices to disenfranchise African Americans, such as imposing educational tests or poll taxes on the right to vote.

Still, Sumner was pleased that steps were being taken to enfranchise Black men. The prospect of true multiracial democracy in America never before seemed so close as it did at this moment, during the apex of the Second Founding. "The rule of Equal Rights, once applied by Congress under the National Constitution, will be a permanent institution as long as the Republic endures," Sumner believed. "It will be a vital part of that Republican Government to which the nation is pledged."[36]

PART V

EQUALITY BEFORE THE LAW

CHAPTER 24

GRAWNT

SUMNER WASN'T PARTICULARLY EXCITED ABOUT PRESIDENT ULYSSES S Grant. He barely knew the general, an austere Ohio-born West Point graduate who started as a simple officer and rose to national fame while leading the Union Army during the final phase of the Civil War. "Personally, I like him," Sumner said before the election. After the election, he told a newspaper that Grant was "a good soldier, and nothing more." The best public compliment he could muster was to say that "in conversation, he is neat and precise, with clean cut ideas and words."[1]

Lurking behind the tepidness for Grant was Sumner's suspicion of military officers. Sumner's first public address, on July 4, 1845, had decried war as a pagan ritual that glorified false gods and led to needless slaughter. He implied that soldiers were bloodthirsty, and he mocked West Point for being "a seminary of idleness and vice." Sumner *had* proudly supported the Union Army during the Civil War, due to his patriotism and his hatred of slavery. But now, with the war behind him, he had reverted to his instinctive pacifism and distaste for soldiers.[2]

Because Grant lacked a political track record, Sumner wished Republicans had picked somebody else at the convention. With plenty of worthy candidates, he apparently thought that choosing Grant was like the Christian Church "casting aside of the Holy Bible . . . in search of some new experiment." But Grant, who was a popular leader with the public for having defeated the Confederacy, felt like the safest nominee to Republicans. After he won, Sumner was uncertain about how the new president would approach foreign policy. He was also anxious about Grant's Cabinet choices. When Grant revealed his political inexperience by nominating a Cabinet member who wasn't eligible for the office, Sumner grew even more skeptical of the man.

"I hope General Grant will make no more mistakes," he nervously wrote a friend.[3]

* * *

WHEN GRANT FIRST won the election, Sumner told Francis Lieber that he expected to be offered the office of secretary of state. He felt so entitled to the position, and so confident Grant would nominate him, that he was already wondering whether to accept or decline it. After all, "the headship of the first committee of the Senate," Sumner believed, "is equal in position to any thing in our govt. under the Presdt."[4]

While Sumner may have come across as self-aggrandizing, he wasn't exaggerating his importance. As chair of the Senate Foreign Relations Committee, he had been co-leading American diplomacy with Secretary of State William Seward for the past eight years. As one of the most powerful Republicans in Washington, he reasonably expected Grant—even though he didn't know him well and hadn't campaigned for him much—either to offer him the secretary of state position, or, at the very least, consult with him before choosing someone else for it.

Grant did neither. Inundated by greedy office seekers, he consulted no one on Cabinet choices. He wouldn't even tell his wife, Julia, whom he planned to nominate, leading her to sheepishly ask Sumner once if he had any idea. Sumner was as clueless as anybody else. An adroit military leader who always kept his plans secret, Grant believed a similar approach would work well in Washington. He failed, at first, to realize that politics required dialogue, consultation, and negotiation with other leaders—men like Sumner. "Sumner does not, when with friends, conceal his wrath and indignation at Grant's course," former navy secretary Gideon Welles was told by his secretary.[5]

When Grant announced his initial Cabinet appointments, the city of Washington was appalled. Many nominees were personal friends with no serious qualifications. The worst choice was Elihu Washburne, a sickly congressman with no background in foreign affairs, to lead the Department of State. He resigned after only eleven days. Grant had apparently appointed Washburne, one of his closest allies, to give him the prestige of being a *former* secretary of state. "Who ever heard before of a Cabinet officer being appointed as a *compliment*?" Senator William Fessenden indignantly muttered to Sumner after learning of the nomination.[6]

Grant then offered secretary of state to a senator from Oregon who, also lacking foreign policy experience, declined. He finally turned to Hamilton Fish, a retired New York politician. Sumner, who was one of the most logical choices, clearly wasn't one of Grant's top three choices for the prestigious position. Adding insult to injury, Grant didn't even consult Sumner on who *would* make a good secretary.

A wealthy former New York governor and senator, Fish was not the worst choice. While he knew no international law and lacked foreign policy experience, he at least spoke four languages. Fish, who enjoyed being retired, was stunned at being nominated, as he barely knew Grant and had expressed no interest in the position. Once, he had hosted Grant's family for a few nights, and his hospitality left a deep impression on Grant. Based almost solely on this impression, Grant appointed him to one of the most important positions in government.

While Sumner was offended that Grant had overlooked him, he was content with Fish's nomination. He and Fish had been friends ever since they started serving in the Senate together in 1851. While Fish lacked Sumner's antislavery zeal, the two shared a love for literature, and Sumner had always enjoyed the company of Fish's wife and daughters.[7]

Fish felt awkward for one-upping Sumner. "Very much against my own wishes, & after a very positive refusal, I am going to Washington to undertake duties for which I have little taste and less fitness," he wrote to Sumner in a conciliatory note. "In yielding, I hoped that I could rely upon your friendship & your experience & ability."[8]

At the time, senators were accustomed to asking the president to dole out prestigious overseas posts to their friends. Sumner immediately recommended several qualified men, who happened to be close allies, for diplomatic appointments. For minister to Greece, he suggested his best friend Samuel Howe, who had spent time in his youth fighting in the Greek Revolution as an army doctor. For consul to Naples, he pushed for George Greene, a Brown University historian who had previously been consul to Rome. And for consul to Sicily, he pitched James Russell Lowell, a Harvard professor who studied European languages and Dante.[9]

Grant rebuffed every Sumner recommendation. Fish provided Sumner various reasons for Grant's denials, including his not wanting too many appointees from Massachusetts. "Mr. Sumner . . . was among the first senators to ask offices for his friends," Grant grumbled. "He expected offices as a right." Meanwhile, Sumner was stunned that Grant had denied his every request, dismissing his role on Senate Foreign Relations. "Our foreign list is poor enough to fill the patriot with despair," he lamented.[10]

Catching Grant in the White House stairwell one day, Sumner asked him to consider John Lothrop Motley. Motley and Sumner were lifelong friends, having attended the Boston Latin School together as children. Sumner recommended Motley, a wealthy merchant, scholar of Dutch history, and former diplomat to Russia and Austria, for the nation's most important foreign post: minister to England. To placate Sumner, Grant agreed. Sumner was ecstatic. Motley "had been originally nominated by the Presdt on my recommendation," he boasted, "&, as the Secy of State informs me 'as a compliment' to me." In time, Grant was glad to have appointed him. "I have no doubt he will prove the very best man that could have been selected for the English mission," he said a few months later.[11]

*　*　*

MOTLEY WAS SET to sail for England in late spring 1869, when British-American relations were at a delicate state. Ever since the conclusion of the Civil War, the United States had been demanding that Great Britain pay reparations for allowing shipbuilders to sell warships to the Confederacy—most famously the CSS *Alabama*. Americans were also furious that Queen Victoria had issued a proclamation of neutrality in the early days of the war, rather than side with the Union. To repair relations, the Johnson administration had signed a treaty with Britain to resolve the so-called Alabama Claims.

Sumner and Motley believed that the Johnson-Clarendon Treaty was a bad deal for the United States. The treaty created a neutral arbitration process to adjudicate the Alabama Claims. However, it limited claims to those brought by American *citizens* rather than those brought by the American *government*. By reducing Britain's liability to actions that harmed individuals, rather than the state, the treaty failed to redress much of the American grievance against Great Britain.

Sumner wanted to kill the weak treaty in the Senate during the ratification process. Meanwhile, Motley planned to negotiate a new treaty. The Americans had some leverage: At the time, the British were fighting off Irish rebels, and they reasonably feared the United States might issue a proclamation of neutrality and permit the sale of rebel warships. For the time being, Sumner was staving off House bills to aid the Irish. But if

Britain didn't agree to a deal that pleased him, he could easily advance the bill in the Senate.

On April 13, Sumner addressed the treaty in "Claims on England—Individual and National." Putting on his law professor hat, as a man who used to teach the law of nations at Harvard, Sumner carefully noted the defects in the Johnson-Clarendon Treaty and reiterated "the massive grievance" the United States had with Britain. Then he said Britain owed the United States $15 million for its damage to Union ships and $110 million for the economic loss, based on estimates he collected from government statisticians and his own calculations. Finally, he accused Britain of prolonging the American Civil War by two years—a claim that was widely believed at the time but is generally discredited by military historians today—for having been neutral from the start. For the damages caused by two additional years of war, Sumner estimated that Great Britain owed the United States at least $2 billion.

Sumner's speech was lawyerly and convincing to most senators, up until the whopping cost he tacked onto the end. The Senate almost unanimously voted against the treaty. Even Sumner's exorbitant cost estimate helped the American cause by shocking English statesmen, who had underestimated the depth of American anger. Soon thereafter, Ambassador Motley and Secretary Fish started negotiating a new treaty that would allow all American claims, from citizens *and* the government, to be raised against the British.

The final deal became known as the Treaty of Washington. Commissioners selected by Britain, the United States, and three neutral parties—Italy, Brazil, and Switzerland—met to arbitrate all claims and decide the total amount of British liability. Ultimately, Great Britain was ordered to pay $15 million, consistent with Sumner's estimate, for its actual damages to American ships. Thanks to the dogged persistence of Sumner, Fish, Motley, and others, the powerful British Empire had agreed to submit a national issue to a tribunal. The case became a key precedent in public international law; the treaty was, in the words of one early twentieth-century scholar, "the greatest treaty of actual and immediate arbitration the world has ever seen."[12]

* * *

FOREIGN AFFAIRS DOMINATED Sumner's attention during the early months of the Grant administration. But he was still committed to racial justice and wanted to strengthen the feeble multiracial democracy that was emerging in the South. Sumner's focus on foreign relations may have even inspired him to reflect more on the global dimensions of racial hegemony.

In the fall of 1869, Sumner embarked on a paid lecture circuit across a dozen cities in the Northeast to deliver "The Question of Caste." He needed the income to pay for his house. "Let me carry you to that ancient India," he said near the start of his speech. He explained the Indian caste system, wherein people are divided for life into impenetrable hereditary social class strata. At the top were Brahmins, who Sumner said absorbed the wealth of the lower castes and expected deference from the rest of Indian society. At the bottom were Pariahs (today known as Dalits), who were considered so defiling that other castes treated them as untouchable.[13]

Sumner analogized the Indian caste system to the American racial hierarchy. Pariahs have "no rights which a Brahmin is bound to respect," he said, much like *Dred Scott* said Blacks "had no rights which the white man was bound to respect." In America, "the Caste claiming hereditary rank and privilege is white; the caste doomed to hereditary degradation and disability is black or yellow." By separating races into castes, Sumner argued, America was guilty of the same crime as India: "idolatry and all heathen abomination." To be saved from idolatry, one must turn to the Christianity that professed "the Unity of the Human Family."

In professing human unity, Sumner was responding to European and American white intellectuals who undermined human equality by claiming people belonged to distinct racial groups. Developing various racial pseudosciences, these intellectuals tried to prove that a person's alleged race could be identified by their skin color, language, skull shape, and other features. They believed these traits indicated different mental and physical abilities and suitable geographies. They tended to think that the white man's features were superior and attuned to northern climates, while the traits of other races were better suited to the rest of the world.

It would have been hard for Sumner to outright contradict these beliefs, because they were widely espoused by the scientific community at the time, including by his friends Louis Agassiz and Samuel Howe. "It is obvious to the most superficial observer that there are divisions or varieties in the Human Family, commonly called races," he conceded. But he cast doubt on the importance of these superficial divisions by noting that even "the most careful exploration of science leave[s] the number of races uncertain."

How many so-called races were there? Some said four: European, Asiatic, American, and African. Others said five: Caucasian, Mongolian, Ethiopian, Malay, and American. Still others claimed sixty-three.[14]

Sumner observed that any attempt to classify races by the study of skulls or skin colors would be in vain. Similarly, languages proved nothing about race: most languages had common origins, like Greek or Sanskrit, indicating that all human beings had a common origin and that their differences came about over time. "The variance, whether of complexion, configuration or language, is external and superficial only, like the dress we wear," he argued. "Look at Man on the dissecting table," he continued. "He is always the same, no matter in what color he is clad—same limbs, same bones, same proportions, same structure, same upright stature."

To prove his point, Sumner offered a parable. "There is a lesson in the dog, is there not?" he asked his audiences. To the dog, it does not matter who the master is, "whether the child of wealth or the rough shepherd tending his flocks; nor does it matter of what complexion, whether Caucasian white, or Ethiopian black or Mongolian yellow." For the dog, "it is enough that the master is Man." Therefore, "even through the instincts of a brute, does Nature testify to that Unity of the Human Family, by virtue of which all are alike in rights." Dogs did not notice race—thus, neither should humans.

Driving it home, Sumner condemned all forms of racial bigotry. "There is no human being, black or yellow," he declared, "who may not apply to himself the language of Shakespeare's Jew." Borrowing from Shakespeare's famous passage in *The Merchant of Venice*, Sumner asked his crowds, "Hath not a Jew eyes? Hath not a Jew hands, organs, dimensions, senses, affections, passions . . . ?" Given the truth of human unity, Sumner argued that a true republic required the treatment of everyone as equal, regardless of race. He especially dwelled on the need to integrate Chinese immigrants, who had been coming to the American West in search of work on railroads and mines. "If they come for citizenship," Sumner said, "then do they offer the pledge of incorporation in our Republic, filling it with increase."

Soon thereafter, Sumner pushed to strike out the word *white* from a naturalization law that allowed only "free white" immigrants to become citizens. Western Republicans were furious. Willing to amend the law to permit Black immigrants to get naturalized, they resisted the integration of the Chinese, who were "pagans in religion, monarchists in theory," according to one senator. Demanding "racial justice" for the Chinese,

Sumner called on Republicans to recognize that the Founding Fathers envisioned a nation where anyone, from any nation, could become a citizen so long as they were willing to pledge allegiance. But his proposal failed: Congress wouldn't allow Chinese-born immigrants to become citizens until 1952. "As usual, you are in the van[guard]," Frederick Douglass wrote Sumner afterward. "The country is in the rear."[15]

* * *

BY THE TIME Sumner had returned to Washington in December 1869, he was working on compiling all his great speeches, including "The Question of Caste," into a collected set. "I hope it is not unpardonable in me to desire to see them together, especially as I have nothing else," he confided in Samuel Howe. From the start of his public career until his very death, Sumner prized his speeches more than anything. He poured all his research and reflections into them. Never taking a speech for granted, he practiced incessantly before delivering any address. He believed in the power of oratory—the unique ability of the spoken word to shake the foundations of society and remake the world. "These speeches are my life," he told Howe. "As a connected series they will illustrate the progress of the great battle with Slavery, & what I have done in it."

Sumner's speeches were notable in several ways. First, they were infamously verbose, full of literary references and flowery language. Plenty of contemporaries found his grandiloquence over the top. "He works his adjectives so hard that if they ever catch him alone, they will murder him," one literary critic joked. But despite their ostentatiousness, Sumner's speeches were accessible. Even now, an average reader would find them easy to follow. A master at conveying complicated ideas clearly, Sumner wrote speeches that resonated with common people. Simultaneously, he treated his speeches as serious scholarly productions. Unlike other politicians who believed oratory was a *means*, Sumner almost always published his orations because they were *ends in themselves*, important contributions to the intellectual milieu.

Nearly every day for the rest of his life, Sumner spent hours reviewing old speeches for his collection. He made revisions, created footnotes, added explanatory context, and compiled critical and favorable letters, newspaper records, and responses to every speech. "Do not smile at my audacity," he wrote to Henry Longfellow. "I am to fill 8 or 10 vols." Hoping to put together something akin to the annotated volumes of the works of

British statesman Edmund Burke, Sumner decided to include not only his speeches but all his published texts. It turned into his late-life obsession. "I think he loves the author," one publisher quipped.

The final product, *The Works of Charles Sumner*, was fifteen volumes long and covered more than five hundred of Sumner's speeches and other works. It was a magisterial but exhausting production, and Sumner struggled and failed to finish it in his lifetime. He completed the first ten volumes; Longfellow and other executors compiled the remaining five. While mostly faithful to the originals, Sumner and the other editors sometimes altered his speeches and other works to reflect changes in his views and to make him look more favorable. They also filled the appendixes with praise he had received in the press or from letter writers, though occasionally including critical remarks. "They say that he indulged in overweening self-appreciation," Carl Schurz once said of Sumner, his friend and colleague. "Ay; he did have a magnificent pride, a lofty self-esteem."[16]

* * *

FEW MEN FOUND Sumner's ego more intolerable than President Ulysses Grant. A soldier at heart, Grant measured men by their results and resented attention seekers. In judging character, he looked for grit. Arguably, Sumner should have earned Grant's respect. Sumner had proved his courage fighting the Slave Power in the 1850s, and his tenacity fighting centrists in the 1860s. But Grant found him foppish and self-indulgent. He didn't know Sumner when the senator was an underdog. He worked with Sumner only after becoming president, and even then, mostly on foreign affairs, where Sumner was imperious and tended to boast about his international connections. When asked if he had ever conversed with Sumner, Grant wryly replied, "No, but I have heard him lecture."[17]

Grant was worlds apart from Sumner. He was raised on a family farm in the Midwest; Sumner spent his entire life in Boston, Washington, and Europe. He was a notoriously bad student at West Point; Sumner was a Harvard man who could read Greek and Latin. He was a military man who knew how to kill; Sumner sparred with words and didn't know how to use a gun. He was quiet and plainspoken; Sumner spoke in full sentences, never cursed, and insisted on pronouncing the president's name like an Englishman—he called him *Grawnt*.[18]

Grant was accustomed to being in charge. He expected deference from party members, but Sumner refused to give it. "Mr. Sumner was an extremely intolerant man; a species of Sir Anthony Absolute in politics," a Washington clerk once said. As the clerk put it, Sumner was "very easy to get along with if you always humbly agreed with him." Sumner was not alone: many senior senators saw themselves as nearly equal in stature to the president. Before the war, the Senate was generally considered the most important body in Washington, more so than the White House. While Lincoln had expanded the presidency's powers, he did so while cajoling men like Sumner. Grant, for his part, disliked the idea of flattering the big egos of others.

During his first year, Grant tried currying Sumner's favor. But the socially awkward general couldn't adapt to Sumner's difficult personality. "Although fond of conversation, Sumner did not possess the facile art of small talk," recalled his friend Carl Schurz. "Nobody would ever have felt himself tempted to slap him on the back or to call him 'Charley.' He relished friendly social intercourse but lacked that spirit of boon companionship which easily enters into other people's tastes."

It didn't help that Grant was a short man with poor posture who was easy to underestimate, especially when he wore clothes that reeked of tobacco. Moreover, Sumner was always dressed to the nines. Ten years older and more than six inches taller, Sumner towered over the president and treated him like he was insignificant. Understandably, Grant was exasperated. "Sumner is the only man I was ever anything but my real self to; the only man I ever tried to conciliate by artificial means," he once complained.[19]

* * *

PERHAPS FOR THESE reasons, Grant dragged his feet for months before telling the Senate's leading foreign policymaker about his chief foreign policy initiative. In the summer of 1869, Grant started exploring the idea of expanding American presence in the Caribbean. He had his eye on the Dominican Republic, which was then called Santo Domingo. Twice the size of Massachusetts but with only 150,000 people, Santo Domingo was a beautiful tropical nation with vast, lush land that was mostly underutilized.

Santo Domingo was a Spanish-speaking former colony. It shared an island with French-speaking Haiti, a much larger and richer nation. For the past few decades, Santo Domingo had been embroiled in civil wars, European occupations, and invasions from Haiti. Recently, Santo Domingo had been under the loose control of President Buenaventura Báez, a brutal dictator who had been seeking American help to keep his regime afloat as it faced challenges from General José Cabral, a Dominican opposition leader who had the backing of Haiti.[20]

To build his power against Cabral, Báez had traveled to Washington in 1866. In exchange for American weapons, he promised to give American investors almost unlimited access to his nation's untouched plantation lands, ripe for extracting mineral wealth and for the planting of sugar, tobacco, timber, coffee, and other cash crops. Báez had even met Sumner, who was disturbed by the attempt to entangle the United States in a foreign war and not in the least impressed with the general's salesmanship. "I listened to his bad French by the hour," Sumner had grumbled.[21]

Deeply in debt and nervous about his tenuous grip on power by 1869, Báez offered to sell to the United States his country's most prized possession: its magnificent harbor at Samaná Bay. With the help of several corrupt American military officers who owned large plots of land in Santo Domingo, Báez proposed that the United States convert the bay into a fueling station for American steamships and a Carribean military base for the American navy. He also entertained the idea of giving up his country to the United States in exchange for his own personal security.

A military man in postwar America, Grant was excited about acquiring Samaná Bay. The United States could then assert its influence over the Caribbean, facilitate cross-ocean trade through the isthmus of Panama, and better protect itself from European naval powers. Inspired by the Monroe Doctrine, a foreign policy vision first articulated in 1823 by President Monroe that called for American dominance in the Western Hemisphere, Grant sent his secretary Orville Babcock to Santo Domingo to negotiate a purchase of the bay.

When Babcock arrived in Santo Domingo, Báez proposed selling both the bay and the entire nation to the United States. Babcock was eager about the prospect. A military officer who became notorious for corruption, Babcock bought some land in Santo Domingo while negotiating with Báez so that he might personally profit from the diplomatic transaction. Collaborating with Báez, he drafted a treaty for the United States to annex Santo Domingo and Samaná Bay. When Babcock returned home with a draft treaty in hand, Grant ordered Secretary Fish to formalize it. He also asked his Cabinet to keep the annexation secret. While he permitted them to discuss the purchase of Samaná Bay openly, he wanted to keep the bigger project under wraps until Fish was ready to deliver the final treaty to the Senate in January 1870.[22]

* * *

ON JANUARY 2, 1870, Grant walked over to Sumner's house to break the news about the annexation treaty. It was an incredible act of deference for a president to visit a senator's home for an official meeting. He was hoping to assuage Sumner, for he was nervous about how Sumner would react: the White House didn't usually hide major monthslong diplomatic endeavors of such complexity and importance from the Senate Foreign Relations chairman.

Grant's visit started off inauspiciously. Sumner's servant, seeing a small, stern, bearded man he didn't recognize, tried to shoo him away, assuming he was a random petitioner like so many who habitually came to Sumner's door. Overhearing a voice that sounded like Grant's, Sumner rushed to his foyer and was startled to see his servant talking down to the president of the United States. A bit flustered, he hurriedly beckoned Grant inside and offered him a glass of sherry, which Grant refused.

Grant was interrupting Sumner's dinner with the newspaper publisher John Forney (the former secretary of the Senate) and journalist Benjamin Perley Poore (Sumner's former secretary). "Don't leave," Grant told Poore, who offered to excuse himself. "I recognize you and Colonel Forney as friends." Then Forney jumped at the opportunity to ask Grant to reinstate his friend James Ashley to the governorship of the Montana Territory. This was Grant's pet peeve: he hated being pestered by Washington insiders about whom to appoint to various civil offices.[23]

Grant's irritation must have grown only worse when Sumner seconded this request. Ashley, a former congressman, was one of Sumner's close friends. Acting on the advice of General Tecumseh Sherman, Grant had fired Ashley—a rival of Sherman's brother. Losing his cool in front of Sumner and his guests, Grant lambasted Ashley "in no measured terms, denouncing him as a mischief-maker and a worthless fellow."[24]

Changing the subject, Grant broke the news that the United States planned not only to buy Samaná Bay but to annex all of Santo Domingo. Sumner was stunned. Not too long ago, Secretary Fish had assured Sumner that any rumors about annexation were idle gossip. Sumner listened politely as Grant spoke about the project in general terms, having brought none of the actual treaty papers with him. Grant also informed Sumner that the deal had been negotiated by his secretary, Orville Babcock. Explaining Babcock's trips to Santo Domingo, Grant confessed that his secretary had been accused of misusing funds for the trip. He asked Sumner to help him refute the charge of Babcock's corruption, which he did not believe because he considered Babcock to be a close personal friend. Asking Sumner to advocate for Babcock was a tactical mistake: having never taken a bribe in his life, Sumner never had any patience or tolerance for people credibly accused of corruption.[25]

Grant's tense meeting with Sumner was interrupted when Secretary of the Treasury George Boutwell stopped by Sumner's house on unrelated business. The president promptly finished up. "I will send the papers over to you in the morning by Gen. Babcock," he told Sumner. Sumner expressed his wish to study the papers and again brought up Ashley's removal, asking Grant to reinstate him. Annoyed, Grant made no response. Getting up, he walked toward the door. Sumner bade him goodbye with words that would turn into a political controversy.

"Mr. President," Sumner recalled telling Grant as he left, "I am an Administration man, and whatever you do will always find in me the most careful and candid consideration." Grant walked back to the White House pleased; he had heard Sumner make a promise to support the treaty. Sumner's guests were unsure about what Sumner had actually said, recalling different variations between a solemn promise to approve the treaty to a polite goodbye that offered nothing more than Sumner's consideration.

On the next day, Babcock paid Sumner a visit with the treaty in hand. He explained that Santo Domingo would become a U.S. territory eligible for future statehood. In exchange, the United States would assume the Báez regime's hefty debts. If the Senate failed to ratify the treaty by early May 1870, the United States would still retain the right to purchase Samaná Bay for $2 million at any point over the next fifty years.

Here again, dispute arose over the tenor of the meeting. Babcock, who had once mockingly called Sumner "a poor sexless fool," rosily informed Grant that Sumner was happy to support the treaty. But Poore, who was briefed by Sumner, recalled that Sumner informed Babcock that he was skeptical of the treaty because it was negotiated under a fraught, secret process. According to Poore, Sumner was especially upset at one clause that said Grant would personally influence the U.S. Senate to ratify the document. "He did not believe that the President of the United States should be made lobbyist to bring about annexation by Congress," Poore remembered.[26]

In all likelihood, Sumner was unclear to Grant, Grant heard what he wanted to hear, and Babcock deceived Grant into thinking that he had Sumner's support because of his own financial interests in getting the treaty ratified. There was no chance Sumner had supported annexation off the bat, given that he had resisted previous attempted American interventions in Mexico, Cuba, and the Danish West Indies. The confusion between him and Grant would cause a terrible rift between the two men—between the nation's leading abolitionist and the military hero of the Civil War.[27]

* * *

At first, Sumner tried to kill the treaty as gently as possible. When the Foreign Relations Committee began deliberations, he presented himself as neutral and surmised that other senators would bash the treaty without his influence. "I am anxious that this interesting question should be considered on its merits," he reassured Secretary Fish. Just as Sumner expected, almost no senator believed annexation was worth the costs.

While the Senate deliberated on the treaty, Báez feared being toppled by his adversary, General Cabral, who openly denounced Báez as a threat to the country's independence. Afraid of losing power, Báez asked the American navy to send ships to patrol Dominican waters and intimidate dissidents. Shocked to learn this, Sumner promptly visited the Navy Department to review its dispatches. He discovered that the navy had consented to Báez's request and had even sent warships to Port-au-Prince, Haiti's capital, to deter men who were believed to be undermining Báez's regime.

Sumner was horrified that Grant was apparently willing to use military force, without congressional authority, to protect a foreign dictator. "I had not imagined any such indefensible transgressions," he confessed. Sumner concluded that the annexation treaty "was obtained through a ruler owing power to our war-ships," and he doubted Grant's claim that the vast majority of Dominicans wanted annexation. "Evidently they desire peace, security & a stable govt.; but it is very questionable whether they would consent without a pang to the loss of national life," he thought. He feared the United States was "engaged in forcing upon a weak people the sacrifice of their country."

To make matters worse, Báez held a plebiscite in late February 1870 to prove that his countrymen supported annexation. The referendum was announced only four days in advance. On that day, Báez and his soldiers threatened exile or the firing squad for people in the capital city who voted against annexation. In some other cities, ballots were fraudulently recorded, and employers ordered their workers to vote yes. In the end, more than 15,000 Dominicans voted in favor of annexation—and only 11 against.[28]

Despite his horror about Báez's regime, Sumner held his tongue on annexation, praying that if he stalled long enough, Grant would give up and let the treaty die in committee without a vote. He didn't wish to fight with the president of his own party. He also couldn't figure out how to go public about Grant's naval activities because the dispatches he read were highly confidential.

While Sumner stalled, Grant grew agitated. "Mr. Sumner did not oppose the treaty in the Senate, but tried to smother it," he angrily recalled. In a private handwritten memo, which he never shared, he explained why he was so passionate about annexation. He wrote that Santo Domingo would make for a great island base for shipping activity. He also noted that Dominican land could be culled by American investors to generate profits from lucrative cash crops. Finally, and most important, Grant wrote that annexation would help Dominican Blacks and American Blacks alike.

Grant dreamed of incorporating a state where the "citizens would be almost wholly colored." That state, he thought, could help Black people learn the art of democratic self-governance. As an added benefit, African Americans, Grant hoped, could escape to Santo Domingo if white terrorism escalated in the Reconstruction South. The island nation was "capable of supporting the entire colored population of the United States, should it choose to emigrate," he believed. Santo Domingo was Grant's solution to America's race problem.

Even though most Dominicans traced their ancestry to Spain and viewed themselves as white, Grant viewed the islanders as colored people. White Americans also derogatorily described the nation of mixed-race people as a "Black Republic." Knowing this, Grant feared any public talk of race could jeopardize his treaty. Accordingly, he kept his vision of racial justice and multiracial democracy in Santo Domingo to himself, not even sharing it with Sumner. Meanwhile, plenty of senators opposed annexation due to Dominican demographics. "*We don't want any* of those islands just yet, with their mongrel, cut-throat races & foreign languages &

religion," screeched Connecticut Republican Joseph Hawley in a letter to Sumner.[29]

* * *

GRANT'S ASPIRATIONS FOR Santo Domingo were naïve, but they were well intentioned. He was far more egalitarian than any of his predecessors, and he appointed a record number of African Americans to civil posts. He was deeply committed to protecting the safety of Black voters in the South. As general, he had won the Civil War by relentlessly pursuing far-fetched, nigh-impossible missions with dogged perseverance. He now planned to win the fight for racial justice by pursuing another audacious project: annexing Santo Domingo.

In mid-March 1870, Grant decided to stop relying on Sumner and take matters into his own hands. He marched into the Capitol Building to occupy the President's Room, an event hall that was ceremoniously used for signing bills. "Somewhat in the style of Oliver Cromwell," reported one paper, Grant ordered Republican senators to come to the room to hear his pitch for the treaty. It was an unprecedented move for a president to personally lobby the Senate in this manner. Most senators weren't persuaded, but each left with a clear impression that if they voted yes, Grant would be very much pleased with them.[30]

Meanwhile, Col. Joseph Fabens, a corrupt military officer who, like Babcock, had purchased land for himself in Santo Domingo, directly lobbied Sumner for the treaty. Over a four-hour home visit, Fabens laid out the economic bounties America could exploit from Dominican land. Feigning ambivalence, Sumner asked Fabens what else America should take. "You must have Hayti too," Fabens eagerly replied. "And is that all?" Sumner inquired. After thinking about it, Fabens said the United States should take the whole Caribbean.

Sumner was disturbed by Fabens's thirst for land. It reminded him of the conquering spirit of his proslavery colleagues of the 1850s, who had dreamed of a pan-American empire fueled by slave labor. "They do not seem to be aware of it, but they talk like pirates. They speak of getting Cuba, & getting the Amason, & this & that, in disregard of all principles of the law of nations, & of common faith," Sumner had written back then. Now he feared that Babcock, Fabens, and, most worrisomely, Grant, aspired to take Santo Domingo to profit from its plantation economy. It was a harrowing prospect. What would happen to small, weak countries like Haiti if America started pursuing Caribbean annexations? "We are to them as a hawk to chickens," he feared.[31]

Fortunately for Sumner, a five-man majority on the Foreign Relations Committee agreed with him. On March 24, 1870, he spoke on behalf of his committee against the treaty. He argued that the Dominican masses would likely revolt if the United States purchased their country, no matter what the Dominican regime claimed. "Annexation would only bring us a fresh crop of rebellions," he warned. He compared Dominican annexation to America's acquisition of Spanish Florida in 1821, which had prompted rebellions by the Seminole tribes who lived there. Sumner argued that the Caribbean islands "should remain independent powers, and should try for themselves to make the experiment of self-government."[32]

* * *

SUMNER'S SPEECH INFURIATED Grant. Believing Sumner had promised to support the treaty at the outset, the president had failed to notice the hints and rumors that he opposed the deal. Sumner, for his part, didn't think to personally alert Grant of his opposition beforehand. He badly underestimated how deeply Grant cared about annexing Santo Domingo. Deluding himself into thinking that he could placate Grant by letting the treaty die slowly, thus allowing Grant to save face, Sumner stalled the vote for the treaty until the summer of 1870.

Sumner's ally Senator Carl Schurz went to Grant to urge him to give up on annexation. "Drop it now," Schurz advised, "and if you do, the hearts of all those Senators who have opposed it will warm toward you." Schurz warned Grant that if he persisted, his relationship with many senators— especially Sumner—could fall apart and split the party. "The success of your Administration does not depend upon the success of the San Domingo scheme," he said. "But if you make it dependent upon the success of that scheme, Heaven knows where we shall land."[33]

Absolutely determined to get his way, Grant wouldn't listen to Schurz. Fearing the coming storm, Secretary Fish went to Sumner to make a similar plea. In the interest of party unity, he begged Sumner to let this go and willingly lose to Grant. Fish confessed his own qualms with Grant's annexation plan but explained that Republicans had a duty to obey the president. That was a poor argument to make: Sumner had always scoffed at the idea of party loyalty. "You should resign rather than do this thing," he coolly replied.

During one visit in mid-June, Fish made a last-ditch effort to press Sumner on the treaty. "Mr. Sumner, you are wronging yourself to let things trouble you as you do," he insisted. But Sumner, caught in a dreary mood, was uninterested in another long argument. He diverted the conversation to his own troubles. "You can't understand my situation. Your family relations are all pleasant," he replied. "Why, many and many a night when I go to bed I almost wish that I may never awake." Perturbed by Sumner's depression, Fish had an idea. "Why not go to London?" he proposed. "I offer you the English mission; it is yours."

By offering the diplomatic post, Fish was implying that Grant would be willing to fire Ambassador Motley—Sumner's friend—to replace him with Sumner. Fish later claimed that this suggestion was a foolish, off-the-cuff remark, which he regretted. Sumner wouldn't hear any of it. "We have a Minister there who cannot be bettered," he sternly replied. Leaving the conversation of Motley's role at that, he and Fish continued to discuss Santo Domingo until midnight. Sumner wouldn't be moved. He was determined to kill the treaty.[34]

When the Senate finally voted on the Santo Domingo treaty on June 30, 1870, it failed with an even vote of 28 to 28. The treaty needed two-thirds to pass. Many senators simply deferred to Sumner, the most widely respected foreign policy thinker on Capitol Hill. Others were motivated by racist distaste at the idea of annexing a Black-majority nation. Still others believed the treaty had come about by corruption, given that so many of its chief advocates owned land on the island, and knew about the American threats of military violence.

Just as Fish had warned, Grant was enraged by the Senate's failure to ratify his treaty. He instantly blamed Sumner, taking it as an act of betrayal. According to Fish's diary, a few days before the treaty vote, Grant warned members of his Cabinet that whoever failed to support his policies was not "entitled to influence in obtaining positions" and that he would "not let those who oppose him name Ministers to London, etc., etc."

Grant followed through on his threat. Because he couldn't retaliate directly against Sumner, he fired Ambassador Motley, who he had already believed was doing a poor job negotiating the Alabama Claims and had been acting as Sumner's stooge. "I will not allow Mr. Sumner to ride over me," Grant growled. When Fish urged him to extend grace to Motley, who had nothing to do with Santo Domingo, the president wouldn't budge. "But it is not Mr. Sumner, but Mr. Motley, whom you are striking," Fish pointed out. "It is the same thing," Grant retorted.

Grant's advisers warned him against his decision. "I fear you will make a sad mistake if you remove [Motley]," Senator Henry Wilson told him. "His removal will be regarded by the Republicans of Massachusetts as a blow not only at him, but at Mr. Sumner." Secretary of the Interior Jacob Cox accused Grant of being vengeful, which Grant denied. When the removal was announced, Grant was roundly criticized. Fish's son-in-law said Grant was "a vulgar bull dog" who "turned Motley out because he is a snob & the friend of Sumner." Mary Lincoln noted that Grant had "lessen[ed] himself very much in public estimation."[35]

By wrecking Motley's career, Grant struck Sumner where it hurt most. The senator loved his friends and took pride in advancing their careers. Sumner boiled with rage. "The removal of Motley is simply *brutal*. This is the only word to describe it; add also heartless and cruel," he wrote. Even worse in Sumner's eyes, Fish decided to cover up for the president by claiming that Motley had been removed for being a poor diplomat. Sumner had hitherto considered Fish a personal friend; now he felt betrayed.

Grant had no regrets about retaliating against Sumner. He wanted to make an example out of Sumner so that other Republicans in Congress toed the line. He also may have hoped to crush Sumner's self-conceit. A humble man who rarely boasted about his own plentiful accomplishments, he couldn't stand Sumner's haughty braggadocio. It was about time, Grant seemed to believe, that somebody checked Sumner's ego and curbed his political power.

Somebody had once told Grant that Sumner had no faith in the Bible. It wasn't true—Sumner kept two Bibles by his bedside and believed in his bones that God played an active role in shaping the events of human history. But Grant, an agnostic himself who knew how much Sumner obsessed over his own speeches and writings, joked that he wasn't surprised the senator lacked faith in the holy book. "Well," Grant replied sardonically. "He didn't write it."[36]

CHAPTER 25

LAW-GIVERS ARE AMONG
THE MOST GOD-LIKE CHARACTERS

ON APRIL 1, 1870, A PROCESSION OF BLACK WASHINGTONIANS HELD a late-night serenade in the dark on the White House Lawn. After they sang hymns like "John Brown's Body," President Grant gave remarks to celebrate the ratification of the Fifteenth Amendment, which had just been approved by three-fourths of state legislatures. Roughly 250 years after the first Black people were forcibly brought to American shores, African American men could now vote in every state and territory in the country.

There was so much to celebrate. Earlier in the year, the Mississippi Legislature had chosen Hiram Revels, a freeborn Black minister, to serve as a senator in the seat that had once belonged to Jefferson Davis. When Democrats claimed that Revels lacked the requisite nine years of citizenship to be a senator, Republicans unanimously ignored them. They also ignored the judgment of the Supreme Court, which said in *Dred Scott* that Black Americans were not citizens, such that Revels was not a citizen until the Fourteenth Amendment's adoption. "I take it that each branch of the Government can interpret the Constitution for itself. I think that Congress is as good an authority in its interpretation as the Supreme Court," Sumner had once declared. Soon after being admitted on a party line vote, Revels—the nation's first Black senator—asked Sumner to coach him as he prepared to deliver his first speech, which was widely acclaimed.

After rejoicing at the White House for their new political freedoms, exemplified by Senator Revels, the Black celebrants crossed Lafayette Square and spontaneously went to Sumner's house. They chanted his name, calling him to come out. His friend and neighbor James Wormley, who had a pair of spare keys, went inside and up the stairs to find Sumner in his bedroom. Sumner came down, presumably in his nightgown, and spoke impromptu from his front door.

He was in no celebratory mood. "It is my nature, fellow-citizens, to think more of what remains to be done than what has been done," he grunted. He must have been upset that the American Anti-Slavery Society, William Lloyd Garrison's abolitionist group, had recently disbanded on the belief that their work was done. "You all go together to vote, and any person may find a seat in the Senate of the United States," he conceded, "but the child is shut out of the common school on account of color." On top of this, immigrants were being denied citizenship due to their race, and Blacks were being denied equal access to public places.

"You have advanced step by step until you have reached your present position," Sumner noted. He thought they should stay focused, not celebrate. "Now it only remains that you should continue to the end earnest, faithful, and determined; then will the whole work be done." After offering half-hearted felicitations, he bade them good night. The group went on to party on the lawns of other prominent Republicans in town.[1]

* * *

AROUND THIS TIME, Sumner penned a fateful letter to John Mercer Langston, a Black attorney. "I wish a bill carefully drawn, supplementary to the existing Civil Rights Law," he wrote. In Sumner's view, Republicans— and some Black leaders—were wrong to think the civil rights work was done. While the Civil Rights Act of 1866 protected the right to buy and sell property, enter contracts, and testify in court, African Americans were still excluded from many aspects of public life. Sumner wanted Langston to draft for him a new bill to add on to the 1866 law. "Can you do this?" he asked.[2]

Langston accepted. A freeborn lawyer who had studied theology at Oberlin College and who taught himself law when no law school would take him, Langston became one of the nation's first elected Black officials in 1855 (town clerk of Brownhelm, Ohio). During the war, he cofounded America's first national civil rights group, the National Equal Rights League, a network of Black leaders who advocated for universal suffrage. In 1868, he became the first law dean of Howard University, a new institution in Washington, D.C., chartered by Congress to teach women and Black Americans, who were excluded from most other colleges.[3]

A slender, debonair law professor with a well-trimmed beard, Langston resented those who pitied Blacks. "Nothing would make me spit in a man's face and knock him down, if it were on the floor of the Senate, quicker than to have a man pat me on the back because of the color of my face and the curl of my hair," he once declared. Sharp-tonged and extremely well read, Langston impressed Sumner from the start. The senator had often invited Langston to his house to benefit from his political and legal advice and even gifted Langston a few trees that the professor proudly planted in the front yard of his new Washington home.[4]

Like Sumner, Langston didn't think the problems faced by Black Americans could be remedied solely by the passage of time, moral persuasion, and simple acts of charity. There had to be changes in *law*. Once, Langston instructed a client (his half brother) to plead for lenient sentencing by telling the judge "that the courts of this country, that the laws of this country, that the governmental machinery of this country, are so constituted as to oppress and outrage colored men, men of my complexion." He was referring to what is now commonly called "institutional racism," a system of racial dominance that Langston believed was created by law and could only be dismantled by law. "Law-givers are among the greatest and most God-like characters," Langston once recalled Sumner saying. "They are reformers of nations; they are builders of human society."[5]

In a remarkable act of interracial collaboration, Langston and Sumner designed the Civil Rights Bill—a bill so astonishing for its prescience that, nearly a century later, it became the template for the Civil Rights Act of 1964. Introduced on May 13, 1870, the four-page bill declared that "all citizens of the United States, without distinction of race, color, or previous condition of servitude" were "entitled to the equal and impartial enjoyment" of buses, trains, hotels, "theaters or other places of public amusement," schools, churches, cemeteries, and other "benevolent institutions." The bill specified criminal and civil penalties for those who denied equal access. Federal courts would have jurisdiction over civil rights cases; federal officers were made personally liable if they failed to prosecute cases; racial discrimination in jury selection was prohibited; any corporation convicted under the act would have its charter revoked; and any discriminatory law that used the word "white" was repealed.[6]

Langston and Sumner thought their bill would sail through the Republican-dominated Congress. This belief was tragically naïve. Many of the bill's provisions would not become enduring law until the civil rights movement of the 1950s and 1960s. Even then, some of the bill's provisions have never become law, not even today. For example, most civil rights violations have never been subject to criminal penalties. Corporations do not face dire repercussions for breaking civil rights laws, usually facing fines at most. Congress has never acted on jury discrimination, which continues to be practiced in many forms, even though the 1986 Supreme Court ruling in *Batson v. Kentucky* formally outlawed it. And federal officials generally cannot be sued or prosecuted for failing to enforce civil rights laws. Most of these laws, if federal officials so wished, could be turned into dead letters at any moment without any consequences.

Despite their naïveté, Sumner and Langston were being farsighted in at least four ways. First, as one historian has noted, the term *civil rights* is today "commonly associated with claims for equal access to public spaces." But during the mid-nineteenth century, civil rights were generally limited to claims around the right to own property, sign contracts, and access courts. By invoking a whole other set of rights under the banner of *civil rights*, Langston and Sumner expanded the meaning of the term, giving rise to its modern definition.[7]

Second, Sumner and Langston may have been the first to propose an individual, statutory right to equal public access. They were building on the work of Black state lawmakers who, across the reconstructed South, had been writing and passing state laws to integrate public spaces. But as one scholar put it, those laws "regulated places rather than entitling persons." They created no "positive grant of rights," instead requiring state officials to enforce the law on their own (which state officials rarely did). The Civil Rights Bill, on the other hand, put the power to enforce in the people themselves, entitling them to go to court to demand their rights. The bill also enabled people to ask state officials to prosecute violators and penalized officials who failed to do so.[8]

Third, Sumner and Langston were able to articulate a modern vision of racial egalitarianism that was grounded in a series of legal concepts drawn from the ancient English common law. Ever since the fifteenth century or earlier, English courts had banned innkeepers from denying rooms to travelers for reasons other than affordability or decorum. That was because an inn was a public space, ostensibly open to any paying traveler. Travelers who were arbitrarily denied could sue innkeepers and collect damages. Over time, English and American courts had expanded this time-old right of access to other common carriers, like streetcars and railroads. In their Civil Rights Bill, Sumner and Langston leveraged these court-made doctrines and proposed to codify them into statute, expand them to schools, and clarify that common law access could not be denied on the basis of race.[9]

Finally, Sumner and Langston came up with an unheard-of right to

seek amusement in public places. Until then, common law courts and legislative statutes had restricted the right-of-access doctrine to places that
seemed to be public goods. Theaters were often deemed at the time to be
places of no good at all, bastions of immorality and indolence. Sumner
turned this notion on its head. "Here are institutions whose peculiar
object is the 'pursuit of happiness,'" he argued. Invoking the Declaration of
Independence's famous words, he articulated a vision of human rights that
encompassed pleasure seeking as being fundamental, a remarkable break
from all past conceptions of civil and human rights in American history.[10]

* * *

THE CIVIL RIGHTS Bill was sent to the Judiciary Committee, which would
get to decide whether to report the bill to the floor of the Senate. In the
meantime, Sumner spent the summer of 1870 advocating for racial justice
in Washington, D.C. Believing "millions, will be encouraged or depressed
by what is done here," he had joined the Senate District Committee in 1865
to legislate over the capital's affairs. He had successfully pushed for laws to
permit Blacks to testify and serve on juries in local courts, integrate city
streetcars, and work in city government.

Now Sumner pushed to integrate District of Columbia schools—at
the urging of his friend James Wormley, who was on the Colored School
Board. In his honor, two years later, the Colored School Board built the
Charles Sumner School—a gorgeous three-story redbrick building near
Dupont Circle that was considered an architectural feat in its day and is
now a museum for the D.C. public school system. As a first step to integrate D.C. schools, Sumner republished his argument in *Roberts v. City of
Boston*, the 1849 case he co-argued with Robert Morris, in a new pamphlet
edition to be widely distributed to the public. Then, he introduced a bill to
desegregate the school system. On May 6, 1870, the bill was reported out
of committee.[11]

Sumner's school integration bill allowed Black schoolteachers—not
just schoolchildren—to sue schools for damages if they were excluded
due to their race. Washington mayor Sayles Bowen originally opposed the
idea, fearing it was "impracticable" because white parents would pull their
children out of school rather than see them mix with Black ones. But he
had recently confessed to Sumner his desire "to try the experiment" to see if
it could "remove that prejudice and place all on an equality." Believing segregated schools were, in the words of local Black pastor John Sella Martin,

"the last 'ditch' of oppression," Sumner worked with Bowen, Wormley, and others to get the Senate to vote on the integration bill. Unfortunately, the Senate declined to take it up.[12]

By May 1870, Sumner was also pushing to integrate Washington's local medical community. At the time, doctors conducted referrals and consultations in societies. In 1869, the Medical Society of the District of Columbia refused to admit three Black doctors—including Alexander Augusta, the Howard medical professor who once sought Sumner's help after being expelled from a white-only streetcar. After a few white doctors voiced their solidarity with Augusta and his colleagues, they were expelled, too. When these doctors formed an interracial medical group, the American Medical Association denied them recognition.

Outraged, Sumner drafted a bill to revoke the Washington medical society's congressional charter. "This principle of proscription and caste driven away from the ballot-box here in the District, driven away from the cars and public conveyances, finds its citadel among the medical fraternity," he decried. So long as the group had a public charter, he maintained, it was obliged to be open to all. He believed that Black men, as a privilege of citizenship, had a right to be part of any and all state-sanctioned associations. Otherwise, "the society is transmitted into a social club," which "becomes a nuisance and a sham" not deserving of legal recognition. Although his bill made it out of committee, the Senate passed over the bill without a vote on June 10.[13]

* * *

BY THE SUMMER of 1870, Republicans had little interest in Sumner's pathbreaking bills to integrate schools, medical societies, and common carriers. They were only willing to enforce preexisting Reconstruction laws. To this end, Congress passed the Enforcement Act, which criminalized blocking a person's right to vote and gave national courts the power to enforce the law. It also created the Department of Justice, a new government agency overseen by the attorney general and stacked with lawyers, to enforce national laws, particularly in the South. Sumner supported these bills but said little during their debates. He—like many African American leaders—was focused on the pursuit of racial integration.

For many Republicans, integration was a bridge too far. Most of the leading Radicals of the 1860s were dead or out of office. Responding to the changing political winds, Radicals still in Congress had moderated their stances. The party was getting hammered by Democrats, who conceded ground on civil and politics rights for Black Americans but objected to so-called social rights: rights that involved intermixing in public or private spaces. While claiming to support Black men owning property, appearing in court, and voting, they were outraged at the idea of sharing hotels or schoolhouses with them. "We give the colored man equal political and legal rights, but social equality?" asked one Democratic congressman. "Never! Never! Never!"[14]

Democratic papers mercilessly blasted Sumner over school integration and what one paper called "Sumner's Social Equality bill." Their rhetoric hearkened to the prewar days. "CHAWLES SUMNER," sneered the *Hancock Courier*, was "the New England Senator who represents Africa in the United States." He was leader of the "Radical Amalgamation Party," which stood for the "social and political fusion of Chinese, Africans, Piegans and Digger Indians," said the *Southern Home*. "Hear the drawling Nastychusetts eunuch, Sumner, whimper in the upper house of the Washington Cabal," wrote the *Weekly Caucasian*. "Eunuch Sumner" became a favorite epithet for several papers, which, rather than respond to Sumner's arguments on the merits, mocked his manhood. "Massachusetts eunuchs like Sumner are called 'statesmen,'" jeered the *Argus and Patriot*.[15]

One Ohio Democrat, Rep. William Mungen, capitalized on Sumner's vulnerability with a speech so lurid that he published it without delivery on the floor (to avoid being called out of order). Mungen said "unsexed creatures" like Sumner were so "envious of all virility" that they would devote their lives to making life worse for other men. Out of "misanthropic spite," Sumner wanted to promote "miscegenation." If racial intermarriage were pursued, Mungen warned, it would lead to an "emasculated nation." While Mungen was nearly censured for his speech, many southern papers loved it. "Mr. Sumner is dragged from his pedestal, as false gods should be, and stripped of his outward garb of manhood," the *Georgia Telegraph* said. Informed readers knew the subtext: Sumner's wife, Alice, was rumored to have left him over his supposed impotence.[16]

In part because racial integration looked like a losing issue, many Republican senators distanced themselves from Sumner. This took place at a notable time in his career. Recently, he had become Dean of the Senate, a symbolic title for the body's longest-serving member. The honorific position carried enormous prestige and entitled him to respect from colleagues. Yet it also signified to his counterparts that his best days were behind him. Sumner was an antiquated relic, a statesman to be respected but not listened to.

The Republican Party was also changing. When the party was born in 1854, its unifying cause was preventing the expansion of slavery. After abolition, however, the party no longer had an ideological core. By 1870, Republicans were beholden to all sorts of interest groups who advocated for conflicting causes, such as laissez-faire limited government, subsidies for big business, land for white farmers, specie money, greenbacks, high tariffs, low tariffs, nativism, and civil rights. There were more than fifty Republican senators now. Unlike a decade or two earlier, no salient cause united them. Losing its single-issue moral idealism, the party had stopped lionizing moral lodestars like Sumner, one of its symbolic founders.[17]

* * *

SUMNER BECAME PAINFULLY aware of the party's sorry state and his own waning influence when he kept trying and failing to convince the Senate to award a pension to Mary Lincoln. When former secretary of war Edwin Stanton died, Republicans privately fundraised $110,000 for his bereaved widow. Mrs. Lincoln did not get a similar benefit, despite her repeated claims in the press and letters to congressmen that she was destitute. Having been stigmatized for being a spendthrift while First Lady, she was now being portrayed in the media as an ungrateful and sinful widow. To avoid paparazzi and the shady merchants who had been tricking her out of money, she fled to Germany and lived alone in a hotel. "Shame on my countrymen," Mary's friend wrote to Sumner about her state. "She lives *alone*. I never knew what the word *Alone* meant before."[18]

Nearly ten times in two years, Sumner had raised the issue of Mary's pension. Although the House had already passed a pension bill, the Senate sneered at the prospect. "Select a proper object, select a Martha Washington," one senator jeered. "Why should she be an absentee from America? Did not Mrs. Madison win fame by staying here at home?" another inquired. Believing all the accusations the media had spun about Mary Lincoln, only some of which were true, the Senate rejected the pension bill several times. The worst smear of all was that Mary hadn't loved Lincoln: "A woman should be true to her husband," one senator snickered.

Appalled at the misogyny and disrespect for Lincoln's family, Sumner could hardly contain himself. During the war, Mary was his closest female friend. He knew what it was like to be alone, ostracized, and partnerless. On July 14, 1870, with only one day left in session, Sumner desperately tried to get a pension for her. Apparently on the verge of tears, he begged the Senate. "Surely the honorable members of the Senate must be weary of casting mud on the garments of the wife of Lincoln," he implored. "She was the chosen companion of his heart," he swore. "She loved him. I speak of that which I know. He had all her love."[19]

Later that day, the Senate finally passed a pension bill that annually awarded three thousand dollars to Mary Lincoln. It would be one of Sumner's last legislative achievements. Shortly thereafter, in need of money, he ventured off on a lecture tour through the Northeast and Midwest, delivering speeches on the Franco-Prussian War and the life of the Marquis de Lafayette, the French hero of the American Revolution. Delivering thirty-eight lectures in over a dozen cities exhausted the aging senator, who now routinely fell ill. "The travel is very fatiguing," he told someone who inquired after him. "I shall be glad indeed when I get back to my bed in Washington."[20]

* * *

When Sumner returned to Washington, he didn't get the rest he wanted. He was instead embroiled in a minor scandal. In late November 1870, the *Chicago Republican* released an exclusive interview that he had reportedly agreed to. Sumner had allegedly said that "Grant is honest, but he don't know everything, and, unfortunately, he don't know that he don't know it." Sumner had then supposedly portrayed Grant as a gullible man duped by corrupt advisers into pursuing annexation. "Oh, it was a bad business, that St. Domingo scheme," he was quoted as saying.

Sumner claimed that none of his words were supposed to have been published; he had apparently been tricked by a reporter who met him for an off-the-record social visit. "It was a stolen thing, with a mixture of truth, of falsehood, and of exaggeration," he said defensively. But the damage was done. Grant decided that Sumner was publicly smearing him. "Mr Sumner has spoken of me in harsh terms in the streetcars, at dinner tables, in the executive sessions of the Senate, in Boston and at the West," the president ranted to a friend. "If I was not President of the United States," he declared, "I should hold him personally responsible."[21]

Tensions grew even worse when Grant released his annual message to Congress on December 5. Top of mind for Sumner was passing the Civil Rights Bill and advancing school integration in the capital city. But Grant mentioned neither proposal. Focusing instead on what would be appealing to white voters, Grant celebrated in his message that all but one former Confederate state had been readmitted into the Union. The last state, Georgia, was to be restored shortly, upon which, he hoped, "will be completed the work of reconstruction." Aside from reiterating his commitment to protecting Black voters in the South, which was sincere, Grant had nothing to say about racial integration.

Once again, Grant brought up annexation. "San Domingo was his pet topic," groaned Ohio governor and future president Rutherford B. Hayes. The issue divided the Republican Caucus so much that even some of Grant's allies hoped he would give it up. But Grant was indomitable. He asked Congress to authorize a three-man commission to study the island nation and the prospect of annexation.

Grant's message referred to "the island of San Domingo," as if he were interested in acquiring the entire island of Hispaniola, including Haiti. Alarmed, the Haitian ambassador to Washington, Stephen Preston, asked Secretary Fish to clarify whether Grant planned to "destroy the autonomy of my country." Rather than relieve Ambassador Preston's anxieties, Fish sent a rude note to the Haitian minister, scolding him for asking for clarification. Grant's message was a "strictly and exclusively domestic document," Fish said, "to which, it is conceived, no foreign Power can take just exception."

Preston panicked after receiving Fish's response, which implied that Haitian annexation was on the table. While there is no evidence that Grant ever made plans to annex Haiti, the Haitians were understandably concerned given that Grant easily could if he wanted to. The White House had already sent warships to Hispaniola without congressional authorization, to protect President Báez's regime and menace the Haitians. Even if the United States annexed Santo Domingo and left Haiti alone, a future president might be tempted to swallow the whole island.

Preston was the grandson of a British officer who had died in Haiti. An educated mixed-race man with unwieldy muttonchops, he was committed to Haitian freedom above anything else. Rushing letters back to Haiti about the possibility that Grant planned to one day attack his nation, Preston sought Sumner's help. Though he lived in New York, he routinely visited Washington, where he stayed at the Arlington Hotel, which was on the same block as Sumner's home. He conferred with Sumner—the rare senator who fluently spoke his native language, French—and urged him to resist annexation with all his might.

"You'll notice that the powerful republic of the United States never avoids, and invents when necessary, the opportunity to apply the rod to the poor black republic of Hayti," Preston had once told Sumner. "We want to remain a people, free, independent, under the republican institutions that you put so well in motion in the United States," he explained. "The Haytian government appeals to me for protection," Sumner relayed to Samuel Howe. "I am in the midst of a struggle as in the olden time for the down-trodden."[22]

Sumner believed passionately in protecting the independence of Haiti, the first nation in world history to fully abolish slavery. Born after a revolution against France, Haiti was a powerful model for Black self-governance and republicanism. "The freedom that has come to the colored race the world over," Frederick Douglass once explained, "is largely due to the brave stand taken by the black sons of Haiti."

Solidarity with Haiti was personal for Sumner. His father, Charles Pinckney Sumner, had visited the island amid its revolution and had dined with its leading revolutionary, Jean-Pierre Boyer. "You must pardon my sympathy with the Haytians, which dates to my childhood," Sumner once explained to Samuel Howe. "My father was in Hayti shortly after leaving college, & his stories of the people there are among my earliest memories."[23] He also argued that Haiti "represents the Slave" in a letter to the abolitionist Gerrit Smith. He told Smith that he had been taught as a child "to cherish Hayti & her struggling people" and "from that time I watched its fortunes & tried to serve it."

* * *

To SUMNER, THE question of Dominican annexation cut to the *soul* of the Republican Party. It wasn't a fringe political issue or a minor controversy that could easily be brushed aside. He feared the Republican Party was about to sanction large-scale Europe-style imperialism in Caribbean plantation societies, not unlike how southern slaveholders had treated their enslaved people. "Nothing has aroused me more since the Fug. Sl. Bill & the outrages in Kansas," Sumner explained to Gerrit Smith. "The same old spirit is revived in the treatment of the Haytian Republic."[24]

On December 21, 1870, Sumner spoke out on the Senate floor against Grant's proposed three-man commission to the island in a major speech. At the start, he declared that Grant's commission would cause a "dance of blood" in Santo Domingo and Haiti. Sumner then went personal, viciously blasting Grant.

Sumner compared Grant's behavior to the British Empire's undertakings in what is now Nicaragua. In the 1600s, the British installed a puppet dynasty to rule over the Miskito tribal people. For two centuries, that Anglophilic dynasty permitted the British to plunder the region's resources and gave the British cover to claim they were acting at the local people's request. Similarly, Grant kept Báez "in power by the naval force of the United States, and, that being in power, we seek to negotiate with him that he may sell his country."

Many Republicans were shocked by the sheer vitriol in Sumner's speech. "The Senator began his speech by saying that this resolution inaugurated a 'dance of blood,'" Indiana senator Oliver Morton decried. "I might inquire whether blood can dance, if that was ever heard of before." Nevada senator James Nye scolded Sumner for his over-the-top rhetoric. "Blood, blood, blood!" Nye mocked. "My friend overlooked all the good things in that message. He was looking for what seems to be the nightmare of his mind."[25]

Doubling down, Sumner released his remarks in a pamphlet titled *Naboth's Vineyard*. He included on the front page a few verses from the Book of Kings that referenced a famous biblical parable. The story went like this: The Israelite king Ahab desired a vineyard owned by Naboth. But Naboth refused to sell it because he had inherited the land from his ancestors. To please her greedy husband, Ahab's wife, Jezebel, asked nobles in the city to recruit two men to spread lies about Naboth being an idolater. A mob then stoned Naboth to death, and King Ahab stole his land. He was pleased until the prophet Elijah warned him that God could ruin his kingdom for what he had done.

Sumner seemed to be implying that Grant was like King Ahab, listening to corrupt Jezebel-like advisers who had devised a scheme to defame the character and reputation of Dominicans. That scheme was a three-man commission, which would spread disinformation that Grant could use to persuade the public to let him loot the vineyards of Santo Domingo. In so doing, Grant would forever tarnish the reputation of the Republicans and risk invoking God's punishment upon the United States. Sumner apparently believed he was the modern prophet Elijah: the only way to avert God's punishment was to listen to his dire clarion call.

* * *

THE SENATE DIDN'T heed Sumner's call and passed the president's resolution. Grant then released the names of the commissioners and staff members of the Commission of Inquiry to Santo Domingo in January 1871.

Sumner was mortified to find the names of people whose political views and character he sincerely admired. For one, Frederick Douglass had agreed to serve as one of the assistant secretaries to the project. "If that country honestly wishes to come to us, I now see no reason against the policy of receiving her," Douglass explained to Sumner. Believing that Dominican locals wanted to be annexed, Douglass thought they could benefit and learn from American republicanism. He pictured Santo Domingo as a future U.S. state, composed largely of Black and mixed-race people, that could become an example of multiracial democracy in practice.

Douglass had desired a public office for some time. Once an activist who disavowed politics, he was now seeking to enmesh himself in the Republican Party, believing it was the best vehicle for Black progress. He had hoped for a prestigious political appointment to an ambassadorship or the like. But this was the best Grant was willing to do for the nation's top Black leader. Douglass felt he couldn't decline. Plus, according to a friend, he was "enchanted at the prospect of visiting a tropical island."[26]

Sumner's closest Black allies were outraged at Douglass. His neighbor, the hotel operator James Wormley, thought Douglass had "compromised his dignity" by agreeing to be an *assistant* to a *secretary*. He seemed to think Douglass, a de facto representative of Black America, had humiliated his people by groveling before Grant and lending their collective sanction to a spurious project. "He said, if he had been in Mr. Douglass' place, . . . he would have spit in General Grant's face," somebody recalled Wormley saying. Moreover, the caterer George Downing discovered that Douglass had spoken ill of Sumner's attempt to stop annexation. "I have in conversations with his friends taken exception to his language touching Charles Sumner in the Dominican controversy," Downing wrote in a newspaper about Douglass. "In fact, I felt indignant."[27]

Sumner refrained from criticizing Douglass in public. He also avoided attacking his only African American colleague, Hiram Revels. The Mississippi senator decided to support annexation as well. A devout Methodist minister, Revels asked Sumner "whether it is not the duty of our powerful, wealthy, and Christian nation" to offer "enlightenment and intellectual, moral, and religious elevation" to the country. Sumner was disappointed. No matter what missionary language was being used by annexation's proponents, he was confident the scheme would enrich capitalists by military force at the expense of the poor and oppressed.[28]

In private, Sumner was far more perturbed over a different appointment. Out of all people, his best friend, Samuel Howe, had accepted a position as a commissioner. "You & I, usually in such accord, are so far asunder," Sumner lamented to Howe. Like Douglass, Howe considered it a "sort of national duty to extend the benefit of our political institutions by peaceful means over the [West Indies] islands." Over the years, he had often pleaded with Sumner to support American intervention overseas—to help revolutions in Hungary and Cuba, for example. Sumner never agreed, preferring to avoid entanglement in foreign actions.

While waiting for a train in early January, a friend had spotted Howe and suggested he volunteer for the commission. When Howe laughed it off, the friend offered to send an application on his behalf. He nonchalantly agreed. Without ever meeting Howe before, Grant accepted the application upon its receipt. He knew Howe and Sumner were best friends. That was all he needed to know. By choosing Howe, Grant looked magnanimous and nonbiased. If Howe recommended against annexation, the president surely surmised, the press would say he had yielded to Sumner's interference. And if he favored it, all the better: Sumner would be absolutely cornered.

Howe had been unhappy with his life for some time. He spent almost all of it in Boston, operating the school for the blind he had so famously founded. While the work was fulfilling, he had always felt his true destiny lay elsewhere. "The Lord did not make me for a philanthropist," he once sighed. An adventurer at heart, Howe much preferred to be traveling, such as when he explored the Union-occupied South during the war to study the status of freedmen for the commission to which Sumner had helped appoint him. In his younger days, Howe had spent considerable time in Greece, fighting in the Greek War of Independence against the Ottomans. For the past several years, he had been begging Sumner to get him nominated to serve as ambassador to Greece. But despite Sumner's best efforts at lobbying Johnson and Grant, Howe never got an offer. When he received Grant's offer, he felt that he couldn't refuse it despite his friendship with

Sumner. Here was a chance to return to the thick of travel, public service, and adventure—in this case, without Sumner's help at all.[29]

On January 17, 1871, the commission embarked for Santo Domingo. Two other commissioners went with Howe: former Ohio senator Benjamin Wade and the president of Cornell University, Andrew White. Along with them, Grant sent 10 news correspondents, 14 assistants (including Douglass), and 9 scientists—including a botanist, a geologist, a zoologist, and a paleontologist. As Sumner feared, the information gatherers were to be perceived by Haitians and Dominicans as members of a military action. To ostensibly protect the civilian team, Grant sent them on a man-of-war equipped with 500 crew members and 100 marines. All in all, his 3-man commission ended up being a roughly 635-man expedition.[30]

∗ ∗ ∗

THAT SAME WEEK, Sumner's friend Carl Schurz escalated the fight against Grant's annexation scheme even further. A German American general who had fought at Gettysburg and Chancellorsville, Schurz had befriended Sumner after the war and, with his help, had written an 1865 report that demanded Congress take jurisdiction over the South away from Andrew Johnson. Soon thereafter, he was elected to the Senate from Missouri. Having helped Sumner combat Johnson's Reconstruction policies, he was ready to join Sumner in fighting Grant's imperialism.

"The Anglo-Saxon race is somewhat notorious for its land hunger, and such appetites are always morbidly stimulated by eating," Schurz observed in a speech against Grant's commission, which had been approved by the Senate in December but was up for a revote after an amendment had been made to the resolution by the House. If America were to annex Santo Domingo, Schurz feared, Haiti, Cuba, Puerto Rico, and the rest of Central America were next. Worse, Schurz warned, "if you incorporate those tropical countries with the Republic of the United States, you will have to incorporate their people too."

Schurz then presented a bizarre argument against annexation that intertwined racism, pseudoscience, and anti-imperialism. For one, "people of the Latin race mixed with Indian and African blood" might one day be senators or representatives from annexed lands. "Does not your imagination recoil?" he asked, warning that it would be impossible to absorb "people who . . . have neither language nor traditions nor habits nor political institutions nor morals in common with us." Alternatively, if the United States were not so generous as to award them citizenship, they might be reduced into slavery or face "rapid extermination" by American colonizers. A better solution would be to leave them alone where nature had put them so that they could self-govern. "The tropics should belong to the colored race," he implored. "Let that region belong to them; let them cultivate that soil in freedom; let them be happy there."

Schurz's messaging was outrageous but effective. He offered distinct reasons for African Americans, abolitionists, Democrats, and racist Republicans to oppose annexation. His racist reasons were especially politically potent, so much so that even Sumner indulged in them, insisting the island was "theirs by right of possession, by their sweat and blood mingling with the soil, by tropical position, by its burning sun, and by unalterable laws of climate." The idea that Hispaniola *inherently* belonged to people based on skin color and climate contradicted Sumner's professed views in past speeches. But he used the argument anyway: he was willing to say it to help kill public support for an imperial project.[31]

In deploying racist language, Schurz had a broader agenda than Sumner. Even though he had urged a radical Reconstruction program in the wake of the war, his tune had changed when he ran for office in 1867. Eyeing a vacant Senate seat, Schurz moved to Missouri, where he could appeal to a large German American population. In an opportunistic bid to grab votes from Democrats and disgruntled Republicans, he argued that Reconstruction had gone too far. While still committed to Black suffrage, he claimed that the Missouri Constitution treated ex-rebels unfairly by preventing them from voting and working in many ordinary jobs. Calling for an end to all Reconstruction policies except Black suffrage, Schurz managed to swing enough state lawmakers in his direction. After proving the electoral success of his platform, he proffered an alternative vision for the Republican Party to the nation.[32]

The premise of Schurz's ideology was that Republicans had finished their mission. "The Republican Party fought against slavery and that sort of State sovereignty which formed the protection of slavery, and they have disappeared," Schurz noted. "Thus the great issues which originally formed the line of division exist no longer." Because the party had "virtually accomplished those things" it stood for—such as abolition, Black suffrage, and national unity—it was time to move on. To do so, former rebels should regain the vote. That way—all men, white or Black, loyal or not— could enjoy "the largest possible liberty." There was no need to fear, Schurz seemed to genuinely think, that anyone would try to roll back Reconstruction's progress.[33]

What next? Schurz said voters should abandon Grant and embrace what he called "Liberal Republicanism." Grounded in the classical liberal tradition, Schurz wanted to end cronyism, militarism, protective tariffs, railroad monopolies, and business subsidies, all of which Grant had endorsed or tolerated. The Republican Party had been corrupted by special interest groups, he argued. Pointing out corruption in projects like Dominican annexation, Schurz especially called for civil service reform. At the time, parties relied on patronage networks for power: elected officials appointed friends to civil servant positions. Decrying Grant's seeming inability to choose good people for office, Schurz proposed that all civil servants be hired on merit-based exams, as was done in Europe. His platform appealed to disquieted Republicans and Democrats alike.

Sumner was particularly drawn to Schurz's platform. Even though he had met him only a few years before, Schurz was one of the only senators whom he currently called a friend. Both having spent time in Europe, they got along well. They had warred against the Johnson administration hand in glove, and now they were warring together against Grant. Schurz's ideas resonated with Sumner, who was the first statesman in the country to advocate for civil service reform, angered by corruption, and sympathetic to classical liberal economics. It was a natural fit.

But there was one sticking point: Reconstruction. No matter how often Schurz appealed to Sumner to join his nascent movement, given his alienation from the Republican Party, Sumner demurred. He could not understand how Liberal Republicans thought Reconstruction was complete. "The Rebellion is said to be suppressed. This is a mistake," Sumner wrote in a magazine article, noting "painful reports from States lately in rebellion, showing that life is unsafe and society disorganized." Fearing what might happen if former rebels regained the vote and Union troops left the South, he was troubled that Schurz had voted against the Enforcement Act. "Too late it may be for the piece of land for every adult freedman," he lamented, "but it is not too late for the vigorous enforcement of Reconstruction." While Schurz insisted that white southerners would honor Black civil and political rights if their own rights were restored, Sumner was skeptical.[34]

And yet, he was tempted. While Grant was vigorously enforcing preexisting Reconstruction policies, including Black suffrage, he wasn't endorsing the Civil Rights Bill that Sumner believed was vital to multiracial democracy. "Grant and his faction carry at present everything before them by *force majeure*. The organization of the Republican party is almost entirely in the hands of the officeholders and ruled by selfish interest," Schurz told Sumner. Sumner agreed with Schurz that Grant was driving the party toward corruption. "Thieves and money-changers, whether Democrats or Republicans, must be driven out of our Temple," Sumner declared. "There is a *dementia* in the Republican party," he wrote to Schurz. "We must save it."[35]

CHAPTER 26

THE DIGNITY OF A BLACK PEOPLE

On February 3, 1871, Charles Sumner went to the First Congregational Church on the corner of Tenth and G Streets, next to the modern-day Martin Luther King Jr. Memorial Library. It was an auspicious day: the day of the inaugural graduation ceremony for the law students at Howard University. Founded a few years earlier, Howard was the first university to open its doors to all law students, men and women, Black and white. To be inclusive of students who would not otherwise have been able to afford fees, classes were taught in the evenings. For students who lacked day jobs, the dean helped find them employment in the public sector or at the university.

Dean John Mercer Langston invited Sumner, his collaborator on the draft Civil Rights Bill, to deliver the commencement address, but Sumner had already accepted an invitation to speak at the Columbia Law School graduation for a large honorarium. Langston pleaded with him, noting that "this was the first class of young colored lawyers ever graduating in the world." Swayed, Sumner canceled on Columbia to speak at Howard. He was joined onstage by Gen. Oliver Howard, Gen. Tecumseh Sherman, Senator John Sherman, and Attorney General Amos Akerman, all of whom came to mark this moment of triumph for abolitionist ideals.

Sumner listened to eight graduating students deliver orations on legal topics of their choice before he stepped onstage to deliver the main address. "I was a student at the law school of Harvard University, as you are students in the law school of Howard University," he told the students. "I cannot think of those days without fondness. They were the happiest days of my life."

He had two pieces of advice. First, "you must not cease your studies, now that you leave the law school. You must be students always," he explained.

"But your studies must not be confined to the law," he continued. He recommended that they study literature, science, and character, and that they especially read the works of Dante and Cicero.

Second, Sumner added, "the good lawyer should always be on the side of human rights." Noting that "lawyers have too often lent their learning and subtle tongues to sustain wrong," he called on the graduating students to pursue a kind of lawyering that was so uncommon at the time: lawyering for a cause. "You are still shut out from rights which are justly yours," he explained. He urged students, "not by violence, but by every mode known to the Constitution and law," to fight for integration in "the school-room, the jury-box, in the public hotel, in the steamboat, and in public conveyances." This was an "allegiance" that he expected of the students by virtue of their race and their profession. "See to it that this is done," he instructed.

Unfortunately, no law student in Howard's first class rose to prominence, as they struggled to practice in a profession dominated by white men with clients who rarely hired anyone else. Yet the idea of civil rights lawyering seeped into the ether of Howard Law, which eventually became the home of many famous attorneys who fought for racial integration—including Charles Hamilton Houston and Thurgood Marshall. Sumner had no patience for lawyers who would settle for anything less than full racial equality, thereby choosing to be complicit in the system. "Cicero, in his work describing the orator, says that he must be a good man; that otherwise he cannot be a true orator," Sumner explained. The same rule applied to lawyers. "Remember well, do not forget, you cannot be a good lawyer unless you are a good man. Nothing is more certain."[1]

* * *

FIVE DAYS AFTER his commencement address, Sumner renewed his call for school integration in the capital. On the Senate floor, he read from a report newly issued by the Trustees of the Colored Schools for Washington and Georgetown. "The laws creating the present system of separate schools for colored children in this District were enacted as a temporary expedient," the report read, referring to when schools were established right after the abolition of slavery. Now it was time to integrate them. Otherwise, separate schools would "beget and intensify" prejudice in children "so to perpetuate it to future generations."

Anticipating the claim that separate schools could be equal, Sumner contrasted "equivalency" with what he called "equality." He insisted that a Black child "will not have the same kind of education" in an *equivalent* system, because he would bear a mark of "degradation," while a white child would be affected by "prejudice," which "is a burden to him who has it." For a child to be in an *equal* system, he said, he would need "the same teachers, in the same school-room, without any discrimination founded on his color." That, he argued, was "the promise of the Declaration of the Independence" when it said that "all men are created equal."[2]

Sumner's impassioned speech for school integration led to little success. He was growing increasingly angry with his Republican colleagues, who were distracted with issues like Dominican annexation, for their failure to fulfill what he saw as the party's final duty. That anger was exacerbating his already bad health. "During much of the session he suffered from some difficulty in his throat or lungs, which gradually weakened him," recalled his secretary Moorfield Storey. In mid-February, as he listened to colleagues drone on during another frustrating day in the Senate, his stress reached new heights: he felt his heart squeezing and twisting violently.

Rushing out of the chamber and charging toward home, Sumner went straight to bed and collapsed in debilitating pain. Two doctors quickly arrived and administered bromide. But it wasn't enough to dull the pain. A footbath didn't help, either. As a last resort, doctors injected morphine. Sumner was suffering from possibly his worst angina pectoris attack in at least a decade. Luckily, he survived. "The doctor says it is not probable that Mr. Sumner will ever be himself again, either mentally or physically," said a correspondent of the *Boston Post*. Startled by the news, Congressman James Garfield rushed to Sumner's house. The future president had grown fond of the elder senator. Relieved to hear he had survived, Garfield left a note on the door. "*Serus in coelum redeas*," he wrote in Latin—which meant, "May it be long before you return to heaven."

Aware of his falling health, Sumner still couldn't take his focus away from his fight with the party. "I am weary and old, and much disheartened by the course of our President, who is not the man we supposed," he had complained to his old doctor Brown-Séquard, who was visiting the United States, shortly before the attack. The abolitionist Wendell Phillips came to Washington to stay with Sumner for two days during his recovery. At the urging of the Russian ambassador to the United States, who deeply admired Sumner and wanted to keep him healthy, Phillips begged him to take a break. Despite his praying and pleading, though, Sumner refused to spend any time away from the Senate. "I have had enough of combat & am very weary," he admitted to a friend. "And yet combat is before me."[3]

* * *

By 1871, THE Republican Party was fracturing over Dominican annexation and other polarizing issues. While Sumner and other leading party members broke with Grant, most Republicans stood with the president. These loyalists became known as "Stalwarts," who stood by Grant despite dissent in the ranks.

The loudest Stalwart was Roscoe Conkling, an ambitious young senator in his first term. A sleazy New York lawyer with a sharp intellect and smug demeanor, Conkling sought to control his state by appeasing the Grant White House into offering as many contracts and patronage posts to his local allies as possible. Sumner believed that Conkling and his young allies were mere opportunists, professing to be sincere Republicans but lacking the ideological convictions of the old guard who had battled the slave oligarchy.

For the past few years, Conkling had jumped at opportunities to taunt Sumner in Senate debate, hoping to goad him into saying regrettable things that Grant could use to weaken him. Calling himself one of "the humbler members of the body," Conkling often mocked Sumner for being so old. Sarcastically, he would say Sumner was a "fountain of light," with "almost forbidden insight into the secret springs and dark solitudes of human nature," and "the great orb of the State Department, who rises periodically in his effulgence and sends his rays down the steep places here to cast a good many dollars into the sea." During one Santo Domingo debate, Conkling declared that "no sane man, no man of common sense, not maddened by passion or blinded by bigotry or hate," could defame Grant as Sumner had been doing.

To punish Sumner for his disloyalty to Grant, Conkling suggested that the Senate remove Sumner from his chairmanship. "The time has come when the Republican majority here owes to itself to see that the Committee on Foreign Relations is reorganized," he declared.[4] When Sumner caught wind of the effort to oust him, which had already been attempted once before by Senator Zachariah Chandler, he was stressed. This time, he feared that Conkling, Chandler, and other Stalwarts would be successful in stripping him from power. According to a British diplomat, Sumner "looked ill" and had "a touch of wildness in his eye" around this time.[5]

In March 1871, the Senate Republican Caucus Committee met to decide committee positions for the new term. The elder two committee members, Senators Sherman and Morill, had no love for Sumner but opposed his removal out of respect for their long service together. The younger two, Senators Pool and Nye, were fiercely loyal to Grant. They were ready to oust Sumner and break with tradition, which prescribed that committees be chaired by the longest-serving senator of the majority party. The last, Senator Howe, was torn. Under intense pressure from Conkling and other Stalwarts, Howe decided to proceed with removal.

When the decision was announced within the Republican Caucus, Sumner rose to defend himself. "I began as chairman with Mr. Lincoln's Administration in 1861," he pleaded. "I would summon the dead to testify if I have ever failed in any duty of labor or patriotism." Invoking Jacob Collamer, Stephen Douglas, and William Pitt Fessenden—none of whom was his friend or ally, but all of whom had approved of his leadership over the committee—Sumner implied that they would never have approved of a politically motivated ouster. The problem was that they were all dead. After a test vote of 26 to 21, the caucus met again the next morning for a final vote, which decided narrowly, at 23 to 21 (3 abstained), to dethrone Sumner.

Despite their victory, Grant's allies were embarrassed that so many senators had stood by Sumner. Nearly every New England senator and senior senator resisted pressure from Grant and the Stalwarts. And many senators who voted to remove Sumner "were compelled . . . to commit an act against their conceptions of right," according to future House Speaker James Blaine. Sumner also remained the recognized foreign affairs leader despite his removal. "No man in Washington can fill his place,—*no man,* NO MAN. We foreigners all know he is honest. We do not think that of many," the Russian minister had recently said. Even the English commissioners who had come to Washington to settle the Alabama Claims would still dine at Sumner's home.

The close vote indicated that Dominican annexation was probably doomed. A treaty required two-thirds approval from the Senate. Most senators who voted against Sumner's removal would likely vote against the annexation deal, now or in the future. In removing Sumner, caucus leadership had undermined Grant's annexation efforts and made the president look even more vindictive. Yet the deed was already done.

To save face, the caucus committee offered Sumner a conciliation prize: chairmanship over a new Committee on Privileges and Elections. Sumner wanted no part of it. After the Republicans left the caucus room and went to the Senate Chamber, he publicly urged the Senate not to give him the new post. "After twenty years in this service, I have a right to expect that my associates in this Chamber will not impose upon me a new class of duties when I expressly say they are not welcome to me." At his urging, his name was cut.[6]

* * *

CAUCUS LEADERS TRIED to keep the internal debate over Sumner's removal from spilling onto the Senate floor. But they couldn't hold back some senators from bewailing what pro-Grant Stalwarts were doing to the party. "I am not the special friend of the Senator of Massachusetts," said Lyman Trumbull, a conservative Republican who was one of Sumner's fiercest opponents on Reconstruction issues. Trumbull noted that he, Henry Wilson, and Sumner had been serving as committee chairs for ten years. Once upon a time, they were the only three Republicans in the Senate. Trumbull affirmed his solidarity with Sumner. "I stood by him when he was stricken down in his seat by a hostile party, by the powers of slavery. I stand by him to-day," he declared. Sumner later went up to Trumbull and embraced him, his eyes brimming with tears of gratitude.

Even more indignant, Henry Wilson denounced the idea that loyalty to Grant should be expected from Republican senators. "Senators are nobody's servants," Wilson shouted, hearkening to the Lincoln era, when senators routinely sparred with the president. "You cannot discipline the Republican party," he argued. "The Republican party came into being against discipline." Wilson feared that the younger Republican Stalwarts were pulling the party apart, so much so that party veterans like Sumner might abandon it. "There are hundreds of thousands of men that will see neither justice nor wisdom nor political sagacity in this act," Wilson warned.

Nebraska's Thomas Tipton pointed out that Sumner was the "most revered, oldest, and long-tried standard-bearer" of the Republican Party. "I have always believed," Tipton said, "that the war was to be consummated, was to culminate, and it was to be ascertained," whenever the "Senator from Massachusetts or those connected with the executive department should triumph before the country." Even if Sumner was not a practical senator, Tipton admitted, he was the moral prophet who got to decide when the work of the Civil War and Reconstruction was complete. If he was being ostracized, the Republican Party was going astray.[7]

Loudest of all in Sumner's defense was Carl Schurz. He capitalized on the party's internal strife to repeat his call for a movement against Grant's domineering approach to politics. That movement, Liberal Republicanism, was increasingly becoming attractive to Sumner. "There are rumors afloat, and there is but too much ground to believe them," Schurz noted, that Grant had desired Sumner's removal. Because the president "has taken a propelling part which was rather stronger than in the better days of this Republic," Schurz suggested that Grant had run amok with power. "It is perhaps time for the Republican party of this country to consider whether they are quite ready to sacrifice their cause to the whims of one single man."[8]

Sure enough, the rumors were true. The day after Sumner's official removal, several senators found a jubilant Grant at the White House. He was gleeful over Sumner's removal. Although his Senate allies had tried to shield the president's name from being involved in their political trickery, Grant seemed "perfectly willing to assume" responsibility for the ousting, according to a correspondent of the *Boston Evening Transcript* who reported on the meeting. "He says it was necessary to make an example of Sumner in order to teach these men that they cannot assail the Administration with impunity," the *Transcript* related.[9]

Democrats delighted in the intraparty fighting. "Senator Sumner is a dangerous man full of political guile," said one Democratic editorial. "Can Grant afford to insult him?" Certainly not, the writer thought. Soon enough, Sumner would attack Grant so viciously that the Republican Party would unravel, allowing Democrats to win the presidential contest in 1872. "There are too many Republicans who heartily despise their incompetent pig-headed President for this quarrel to blow over," the writer predicted. "Before Sumner gets through roasting him, Grant will wish the Island of Santo Domingo sunk in the Caribbean Sea."

Some Republicans were also wary of what might happen next. "No act of either branch of Congress, since I have been a member, equals this in folly," James Garfield groaned. "It is a step fraught with mischief to the dominant party," noted one editorial. "Senator Sumner, with all his peculiarities, represents a vast body of the Republican voters in all parts of the Union." The "Grant-Sumner trouble will be taken as a text for the argument prophesying the death of Republicanism and the resurrection of the

Democracy," speculated another. "It is a fall in which we all fall down," lamented Republican editorialist George William Curtis.[10]

Stalwarts believed fears of party disunity were overblown. As if to mock those anxieties, Senator Howe sent a flippant note to the press, which some feared would prove dangerously prophetic. "When the Republican party is killed and entombed," Howe wrote sarcastically, "let this epitaph be inscribed upon its grave stone: Here lies the Republican party. . . . It took a monster Rebellion by the throat and strangled it. It found four millions of human beings in bondage and emancipated them. . . . But in an evil hour, it tried to transfer Mr. Sumner from the Committee on Foreign Relations to that of Privileges and Elections, and perished in the attempt."[11]

* * *

DESPITE HIS REMOVAL, Sumner planned to keep fighting Dominican annexation. Aware that Grant's commission to Santo Domingo was planning to return soon, Sumner decided to deliver another speech against annexation shortly before their arrival in order to take control of the public narrative beforehand.

As the delivery day of Sumner's speech approached, it was expected that he would drop a vengeful screed against Grant over his removal. His allies in Washington spread the word to get the public to come watch the drama. For good measure, Sumner hosted a dinner for news correspondents ahead of the speech. He also sent advanced copies to the press. "He told me yesterday that the address would be in the hands of thousands of readers in New York, Philadelphia, Boston, Chicago," reported a correspondent of the London *Daily Telegraph*.

The upper galleries thundered with applause when Sumner entered the Senate Chamber on March 27, 1871. A master at spectacle, he had organized over a thousand loyal audience members to clap at his words. Carrying a mountain of books and papers, he sat in front of Senator Schurz, who sorted his materials for him. "The galleries, doorways, cloak rooms and even the floor of the Senate was crowded with spectators. There must have been two thousand persons turned away from the doors," noted one paper. "I was struck by his increased resemblance to the well-known mezzotint engraving of Edmund Burke," said the *Daily Telegraph* writer.[12]

Not once did Sumner bring up his removal. Acting as if he were still chairman of Foreign Relations, he spent three and a half hours pillorying Grant's annexation scheme. Months ago, he had pushed through a congressional resolution demanding that the State Department turn over all papers related to the scheme. Thanks to that, he had at his disposal all the private documents to prove the points he had been making for so long. Methodically, as if he were a prosecutor, he laid out his case. Robbed of his power, he would use his voice.

Relying on these previously secret documents, Sumner revealed that the U.S. Navy admiral sent by Grant to Santo Domingo was prepared to go to war with Haiti. "If the Haytians attack the Dominicans with their ships, *destroy or capture them,*" the admiral had been instructed by the U.S. Navy. After docking his ships in Haiti's capital, the admiral met with the Haitian president to inform him that if anything were to happen to the Báez regime during its annexation treaty negotiations, it would be regarded "as an act of hostility to the United States flag, and would provoke hostility in return." In addition to menacing Haiti with violence, the admiral ordered his ships to patrol Dominican waters and ensure there were no protests in coastal cities against the Dominican regime or the annexation program. In a note to Washington, the admiral explained that the regime needed to be propped up by the United States military in order to stay in power.

After reading through these papers, Sumner denounced Grant as an imperialist, warmonger, and bully who disrespected the sovereignty of poorer nations. "Violence begets violence, and that in St. Domingo naturally extended," he explained. He warned that the United States, beginning with these breaches, might force more countries to negotiate treaties against their own interests, at the threat of military destruction. That wouldn't happen to "populous, large, strong, or white" nations, of course. It would happen to "thinly-peopled, small, weak, or black" ones, whom the United States could bully into submission. In making these arguments, Sumner was foreshadowing multiple generations of American imperialism in the Caribbean, including military incursions into Haiti and neighboring nations, that took place in the decades after his death.

In his speech, Sumner expanded his idea of legal equality beyond the domestic sphere into the international domain. He argued that an axiom of international law was that "all nations are equal, without distinction of population, size, or power." That was indeed what great jurists like Emer de Vattel and Sumner's mentor Chancellor Kent had basically said. But in practice, no Western nation treated nonwhite countries with any respect under international law. At the time, European empires collectively controlled most of the land in the world, subjecting nonwhite (and some white) people to routine genocides, forced starvation, slavery, apartheid, military occupation, and other unlawful obscenities.

Sumner never discussed the reality of global colonialism in any depth, but he did seem to think the United States ought to respect rules, irrespective of what other Western nations did. He pointed out, as an example, that Americans would be rightly outraged if Queen Victoria or Napoléon sent warships to threaten the United States into agreeing to a treaty to sell Texas. Similarly, it was wrong for America to menace Santo Domingo and Haiti into selling land. "We did not treat Hayti as our peer. The great principle of the Equality of Nations was openly set at nought," he insisted. If land were to be bought, the transaction had to take place peacefully, democratically, and in accordance with international law. Otherwise, it was void, wrong, and illegal.

For hours, Sumner enraptured his audience. In a show of disrespect, Senator Conkling and some other Stalwarts loudly talked and acted disinterested during the speech. But they couldn't distract the thunderous crowd of spectators, who clapped loudly at many moments in Sumner's speech while the presiding officer tried in vain to keep order. With the force of the crowd and his voice, Sumner had sent a powerful signal to the Senate: there would never be annexation on his watch, whether he was chairman or not. "It may be urged that Sumner is egotistical and impracticable, and that the politicians hate him," noted one editorial. "Granted, if you please; but the people believe he can't be corrupted and will do what he thinks is right."[13]

* * *

ON THE VERY day that Sumner spoke, Samuel Howe and the rest of Grant's commission and its staff returned to Washington. Sure enough, Howe and the others had loved the trip and now doggedly favored annexation. "Verily, whose eyes have not seen the tropics, they have not seen the earthly glory of the Lord," Howe swore. He had marveled "at the gorgeous panorama of hills and mountains, of diversified shape, and covered by the richest verdure," and he had loved the fruits, which were "so plentiful, so varied, so fresh." Enraptured by the Caribbean's wonders, he dreamed of buying a home there to enjoy his summers with his wife, Julia. How wondrous it would be, he felt, if Santo Domingo were a part of the United States.[14]

Benjamin Wade had found the island to be equally breathtaking. Everywhere he went, locals told him they wanted to become part of the United States. Oblivious to the fact that no sensible local would tell him otherwise, given that he often traveled with President Báez's troops and a cadre of American forces, Wade was convinced that annexation was universally popular on the island nation. "There is no more fruitful Country on Earth, and they are so far all without exception crazy to be annexed—All that Grant said about it is true—all that Sumner said is false," he avowed.[15]

Frederick Douglass excitedly wanted the United States to annex the country and teach its people about American democracy. "It may, indeed, be important to know what Santo Domingo can do for us, but it is vastly more important to know what we can do for Santo Domingo," he declared, in language evocative of the famous phrase used much later by President John F. Kennedy. "To Mr. Sumner, annexation was a measure to extinguish a colored nation, and to do so by dishonorable means and for selfish motives," Douglass explained. "To me it meant the alliance of a weak and defenseless people, having few or none of the attributes of a nation . . . to a government which would give it peace, stability, prosperity, and civilization."[16]

Eager to civilize the nation, Howe and Douglass financially entangled themselves in its annexation. Sometime after returning, Howe made a deal with Colonel Joseph Fabens—the financial speculator who owned land in Santo Domingo and was among the first to pitch its annexation to Grant. He joined a corporate syndicate that was co-led by Fabens that planned to lease Samaná Bay, the largest port on the island, and develop it on behalf of President Báez. Moreover, Báez reportedly gifted Douglass three hundred acres of land. "Thus Mr Douglass had received three hundred reasons for changing his opinions," alleged the Black abolitionist Henry Garnet in a letter to Sumner, based on news he had supposedly learned from Douglass's son Charles.[17]

Howe, Wade, and Douglass were furious with Sumner for tearing down Grant's annexation project on the very day they had returned to promote it. As if the situation weren't awkward enough, Howe stayed at Sumner's home for a few days after his return. And as if to add fuel to the fire, Douglass divulged bits of Howe's private talks with Sumner in his newspaper. "It is understood that the question of annexation was discussed by them in all its aspects," Douglass reported in the *National Era*.

He claimed that Sumner had "not only failed to convert his friend to his policy of opposition, but was forced to admit that there were arguments in favor of annexation which were unanswerable." While he was probably momentarily furious at Douglass and Howe for the leak, Sumner kept his friendships with both men intact.

Douglass eventually lost interest in the project, but Howe would spend the rest of his life focused on Santo Domingo. He continued to travel there to work on his development scheme for Samaná Bay and to enjoy the island's natural warmth and beauty. His family would spend months on the island, too, and his wife, Julia, would preach to a local church congregation composed of African Americans who had fled the United States and resettled there many years earlier. To his dying day, Howe worked with President Báez to continue the annexation talks. "You send a sword," Sumner accused Howe, "when I would send peace."

For the rest of their lives, Howe and Sumner would write to and visit each other far less frequently than they had in all their previous decades. "I hesitate to write to you of any thing where you & I, usually in such accord, are so far asunder," Sumner later confessed to his closest friend. The strain in their relationship became a permanent ache. "So do I feel this difference, that, when this question began, could I have foreseen that you were to rush into it, so intensely, I should have been tempted to resign my seat in the Senate," Sumner explained. Once, Howe sent him a fond note that has, sadly, been lost. "My dear Howe, I was glad to hear from you," Sumner wrote back. "That you were in the camp of my personal enemies was a great sorrow to me. I did not deserve it," he insisted. "But," he confessed at the end, "I cannot here think of you without a gush of affection & devotion." He closed, "*Ever yours, Charles Sumner.*"[18]

* * *

CLINGING TO HOWE and Douglass, whose friendships he could never fully let go, Sumner spared no grace for other people in his social circle. When a distinguished gentleman from Massachusetts visited him in Washington, Sumner reportedly declared to his guest that Grant was "a Colossus of ignorance and incapacity." When the gentleman sheepishly confessed that he was planning to go see Grant while staying in the city, Sumner "broke out in a raging manner, denouncing the President for almost every possible wrong." Grant was "worse than Tiberius," Sumner

proclaimed. To a different acquaintance from Boston who said he supported Grant's annexation plan, Sumner apparently shouted, "Be no more
friend of mine."[19]

Speaking to the *New York Herald*, Sumner unleashed a tirade against
Grant. When asked whether Grant had knowingly broken international
and constitutional law in pursuing annexation, Sumner screeched, "What
does Grant know? He doesn't know anything, sir. I do not accuse him of
any knowledge whatever." He had never appreciated Grant's ingenuity for
winning the war. "All he knows is how to execute. Put him on a horse,
and he will blunder along somehow in the field," Sumner scoffed. "There's
where his vocation ends."[20]

Sumner was so angry in part because he felt like Grant had wasted
everyone's time. In early April 1871, the president sent Congress the final
commission report, but it didn't include a request to make steps toward
annexation. Coming to terms with the fact that he lacked the votes, Grant
had chosen to suspend the scheme indefinitely. While Howe and others
continued to travel to the island and tried to rehabilitate the project, Grant
had more or less given up. Eventually, Báez was overthrown and replaced
by a government that stood for Dominican nationalism and independence. "We should have made of St. Domingo a new Texas or a new California," Grant lamented afterward. "If St. Domingo had come we should
have had Hayti," he added.[21]

In May 1871, the Haitian president gifted Sumner (through Ambassador Preston) a gold medal. "You have protected and defended something
more august even than the liberty of the blacks in America," read the letter
accompanying the medal. "It is the dignity of a black people seeking to
place itself, by its own efforts, at the banquet of the civilized world. Hayti
thanks you." In reply, Sumner said it was improper for a senator to receive
gifts from foreign nations. Still, he said he was grateful. "Your successful
independence will be the triumph of the black man everywhere, in all the
isles of the sea," he responded. Haiti then had the medal sent to the Commonwealth of Massachusetts, which installed it in the State Library, where
it remains today.[22]

For fifteen months, Sumner had fought tooth and nail against annexation. In the end, he won. But in the process, he had decimated his reputation, ruined friendships, and lost his chairmanship. "They only asked
him to be silent," the Unitarian theologian James Freeman Clarke later
explained. "If he had consented to that, he might have continued the most

powerful statesman in the country. But he could not be silent in the face of any question of right and wrong. So it was decided that he should be crushed." As his young secretary Moorfield Storey—who would go on to be one of America's leading anti-imperialist activists, alongside W. E. B. Du Bois—put it, "Sumner had helped to keep the country right, though at terrible cost to himself."

Sumner wished he could have spent his efforts on something good rather than stopping something bad. The same could be said of Grant. If Grant had spent "one half, nay, Sir, one quarter, of the time, money, zeal, will, personal attention, personal effort, and personal intercession, which he has bestowed on his attempt to obtain half an island in the Caribbean Sea," Sumner argued, "our Southern Ku-Klux would have existed in name only, while tranquility reigned everywhere within our borders."[23]

* * *

Ku Klux Klan violence was raging in the South, terrorizing freedmen and threatening to overthrow the Reconstruction governments Sumner and other Radicals had worked so hard to form. All the while, Republicans were engaged in infighting in Washington. Even worse, white northerners were growing exhausted by the national government's efforts to protect Black southerners. They wondered when the last Union troops would finally come home. While Republicans did pass additional enforcement legislation to try to muzzle the Klan, they failed to reinvigorate the political will for Reconstruction among the white public. Meanwhile, Black voters were demanding far more protection and rights from the Republican Party than the party was willing to give.

By the summer of 1871, Black civic leader George Downing was especially furious. He saw Sumner's removal as a sign that the party was losing its moral core. "History informs us that yours is too commonly the fate of the good on earth; the good, the disinterested seem to suffer to bear the cross," he wrote Sumner. Sumner's political ostracism, Downing feared, jeopardized the fate of the integration bills that Black Americans so strongly desired. While conceding that the Republican Party deserved some credit, he denounced "it for falling short of its mission and duty in not passing Senator Sumner's bill supplementary to the Civil Rights Bill, intended to effect the caste in question."

As the operator of the House of Representatives mess hall, Downing fed the mouths of Republican politicians every day. He was losing patience. "I see discriminations made daily by the party that are odious, unfair, ungenerous, depressing; that feed a lack of respect for colored men."[24] For the upcoming presidential race in 1872, he wondered whom to vote for. "If your bill supplementary to the Civil Rights Act shall not pass, and the colored man be not molested in the South from the outrages to which he is constantly subjected, would it be strange if he should not vote the Republican ticket?" he asked Sumner. "It would require consideration on my part before I should be at liberty to condemn him, unmeasurably, for not doing so."[25]

Among Sumner's Black correspondents, Downing was not alone in feeling this way. "Congressmen who worked earnestly for the success of republican principles are now listening to the syren song of a class of men that would sink the republican party if necessary to attain the zenith of their ambitious schemes," Edwin Belcher told Sumner. Ku Klux Klan terrorism had grown so much that Belcher, a Black politician in Georgia who thought Republicans were not doing enough to protect men like him, fled his home to study law at Howard.[26]

While Sumner continued to lobby for his integration bills, it was in vain. He was now powerless, and Congress wouldn't touch any bills that would increase any degree of social mixing between Blacks and whites. He tried and failed to get a vote on his Civil Rights Bill in the spring of 1871. "Senators may vote it down," he said meekly. "They may take that responsibility; but I shall take mine, God willing."[27]

In October 1871, Sumner publicly declared that Black civic leaders should rethink their relationship to the Republican Party. "You must at all times insist upon your rights," he wrote in an open letter to the National Convention of Colored Citizens, held in South Carolina. He noted that Republicans had yet to vote on his Civil Rights Bill. "Will not colored fellow citizens see that those in power no longer postpone this essential safeguard?" he asked. "Surely here is an object worthy of effort. Nor has the Republican party done its work until this is accomplished." If current Republicans were unwilling to do the work, then new politicians were needed. "Let . . . Republican self-seekers be overthrown," Sumner advised.

Whereas some Black leaders shared his hesitation in supporting the Republicans, Frederick Douglass argued fiercely that Black voters should stick with the party. While tepid on integration, Republicans were still trying to protect Blacks in the South, even if some, like Belcher, believed they weren't doing enough. "Whatsoever may be the faults of the Republican party," Douglass said publicly to Downing, "it has within it the only element of friendship for the colored man's rights, which is found anywhere in this country."[28]

* * *

BY THE FALL of 1871, all three major political groups—Republicans, Democrats, and the so-called Liberal Republicans—claimed to support "the colored man's rights." But Douglass was rightly skeptical that Democrats and Liberals, who seemed untroubled by the scale of the racial violence taking place in the South, were telling the truth. Led by Carl Schurz, the Liberals were a loose body of disgruntled Republicans who were planning to incorporate as a political party and seeking to make inroads with Democrats and white southerners to unite against Grant.

Sumner agreed with Democrats and Liberals that Grant was too corrupt, militant, and powerful. The Liberals hoped either to contest his renomination at the next Republican convention or to run their own contender, possibly in coalition with Democrats. The Liberals wanted civil service reform and to stop Grant's imperial adventures in the Caribbean. Sumner agreed with both those goals. But the Liberals' third goal disturbed him: ending Grant's allegedly heavy-handed approach to Reconstruction.

Liberals affirmed that Blacks were citizens who were equal under the law. Some leading Liberals, like Schurz and Trumbull, had even supported Radical Reconstruction. But they thought the days of Radicalism were over. Grant had gone too far, supposedly trampling on the freedom of white southerners to overly protect Black rights. "In protecting the rights of some," Schurz bewailed, Grant had broken "down the bulwarks of the citizen against arbitrary authority, and by transgressing all Constitutional limitations of power, endanger[ed] the rights of all." Liberals decried that Grant had sent federal troops to monitor polling stations, suspended habeas corpus to arrest suspected Klansmen without due process, and enlarged the bureaucracy by forming the Department of Justice. They deplored a big national government that was at Grant's fingertips.[29]

Grant was a smarter politician than Schurz, Trumbull, or Sumner ever gave him credit for. Expecting a Liberal challenger in his reelection race, he unexpectedly preempted a core Liberal policy issue. "More than six years [have] elapsed since the last hostile gun was fired between the armies then arrayed against each other," Grant noted in his December 1871 message to Congress. He said it was time to offer amnesty to former Confederate officeholders. The Fourteenth Amendment barred federal and state office-holders who had participated in an insurrection from holding public office again. It required a two-thirds vote by both houses of Congress to remove the disability on officeholding. Liberals said that Congress needed to remove this disability by granting collective amnesty to former Confederate officeholders in order to heal the wounds of the Civil War. Grant now agreed and asked the Senate to pass a sweeping congressional law, already passed by the House, to provide blanket amnesty. Now he could deflect criticism that he was being too harsh on the South.[30]

Schurz encouraged Sumner to also endorse amnesty. While sympathetic, Sumner balked. He suspected that many of Schurz's allies, who included former rebels, were lying about their newfound commitment to respecting Black rights. Schurz tried to reassure him. "They are sincerely willing to uphold the new order of things *in every direction*, if they are generously treated," he claimed. If Republicans like Sumner offered amnesty to former rebels, Schurz promised, they would be so emotionally moved that they would reciprocate by respecting Black rights. Racial tension in the South couldn't be resolved by more military force. That would only harden white hearts, he argued. The solution was grace.

Sumner didn't think Democrats could be trusted with protecting Black rights, even if Republicans offered clemency to former rebels. "I also tremble when I think of reconstruction, with Liberty & Equality, committed for four years to the tender mercies of the Democrats," he wrote Schurz. At the same time, he didn't think that Grant Republicans should be in power, either. "I tremble for my country when I contemplate the possibility of this man being fastened upon us for another four years. Which way is daylight?"

Schurz responded by saying the daylight pointed to the Liberals. All Sumner had to do was believe him. Schurz promised that Liberals wouldn't be corrupt or militaristic like Grant. He swore that with generosity and moral persuasion, they would bring former rebels back into politics and coax them into respecting Black rights. "We shall have a third movement," Schurz said enthusiastically to Sumner. "*You* ought to be the great leader of this movement, which will create the party of the future."[31]

CHAPTER 27

THE CONSTITUTION IS NOT MEAN, STINGY, AND PETTIFOGGING

SOMETIME IN 1871, A GROUP OF WHITE SOUTHERNERS FROM GEORgia visited Sumner at his home. For the past two decades, proslavery southerners had considered him their "bitter and avowed enemy." But after he was effectively exiled from the Republican Party, some southerners hoped he could be turned into an ally. "The South insisted that I was revengeful," Sumner had once said. "Never."[1]

He was a humanitarian, after all. During the Civil War, he had broken with his party to demand that Confederate prisoners of war be treated humanely. He had also opposed battle murals in the U.S. Capitol commemorating Union victories, deeming them needlessly offensive to the South. When the war concluded, he asked Lincoln not to seek the death penalty for the captured Confederate leader Jefferson Davis. Southerners now hoped his generosity would extend to granting amnesty to former rebel officeholders. Back in 1865, Sumner was open to the idea. He had privately told a friend that he was willing to offer universal amnesty to all rebels. There was only one condition: he wanted to couple universal amnesty to universal suffrage.[2]

Sumner welcomed the Georgians inside and allowed them to plead their case. No doubt, they told him they had accepted their defeat after the war. They likely confessed that they had been wrong about slavery. Singing the new tune of the Democratic Party, they probably acknowledged that African American men should have the right to vote and the rights of citizenship. Now that they accepted these things, it was time for the North to extend an olive branch to the South by withdrawing federal troops, offering amnesty, and turning a new leaf.

Sumner had been hearing a different story from Black Georgians. For years, he had been receiving letters from Black lawmakers in Georgia, especially his friend Edwin Belcher, describing their terror. At night, Klansmen were attacking Black churches, burning down homes, raping women, and lynching whole families to spread fear and undermine hopes of racial equality. All the while, white lawmakers in Georgia were doing little to quell the terrorism. If former Confederate officeholders were allowed to return to power and if federal troops withdrew from the state, several of Sumner's Black correspondents warned, Black Georgians were likely to be completely resubjugated.

According to one of Belcher's letters to Sumner, former rebels were "civilized savages." While they put on respectable faces when they spoke to white northerners, back in Georgia they were "more barbarous than the Comanche Indians." Knowing this, Sumner was skeptical of his guests. After listening to them for some time, he raised his finger and pointed at Joshua Smith, a Black Bostonian caterer who happened to be staying with him for a few days. "There is my friend; my equal at home and your equal anywhere," Sumner declared. "When you are ready to make eternal justice law, then call upon me and I will help you, and not before."[3]

* * *

ON DECEMBER 20, 1871, Sumner threw down a gauntlet to southerners and their allies. The universal amnesty bill, which Grant had recently endorsed and the House had passed months before, had just reached the Senate. Almost as soon as it did, Sumner stood up to link amnesty to civil rights. "Now that it is proposed that we should be generous to those who were engaged in the rebellion," he declared, "I insist upon justice to the colored race." He made a motion to attach to the bottom of the amnesty bill the entirety of his Civil Rights Bill—which required the integration of all juries, schools, churches, cemeteries, theaters, restaurants, and common carriers like trains and streetcars. Let rebels and Blacks earn their rights "side by side," he said, so they learn "they are linked together in the community of a common citizenship." Amnesty and civil rights hand in hand, generosity and justice at the same time.[4]

Sumner's proposal was extraordinary in its prescience and moral clarity. Unlike many abolitionists and former Radicals, he was willing to extend forgiveness to ex-Confederates and let go of the deep wounds that had been cut during the Civil War. But unlike northern centrists and conservatives, Sumner wanted forgiveness to come alongside justice. He wouldn't accept it any other way. Before welcoming Confederate officeholders back into democratic society, Sumner wanted African Americans in the South to have their full civil rights awarded and protected.

Sumner forced a debate that Republicans, Democrats, and Liberals alike were hoping to avoid before the 1872 election. To speak against integration could cost support from many Black voters. To speak in favor of integration could cost support from many white voters. Accordingly, the Judiciary Committee had been holding his bill for two years without any action. But by offering it as an amendment, Sumner could bypass the committee. Even better, Senate rules required all valid amendments to get a debate and a vote on the floor. There was no escaping it. Some colleagues tried to make procedural objections to attaching civil rights issues to the amnesty bill, but the presiding officer held the amendment to be in order.

In forcing the debate, Sumner was testing whether Democrats and Liberals genuinely supported Black rights. If they truly did, they would vote in favor of his civil rights amendment. "I entreat senators over the way who really seek reconciliation now to unite in this honest effort," he declared. If they agreed to attach civil rights to amnesty, Sumner would willingly support both. "Give me an opportunity to vote for their bill; I long to do it. Gladly would I reach out the olive branch," he said. "But I know no way in which that can be done unless you begin by justice to the colored race."[5]

Stalwart Republicans were also being tested by Sumner for the strength of their commitment to Black voters. It was widely believed that their leader, Grant, had narrowly *lost* the majority of white voters in his 1868 election. Grant won because of Black voters, who voted for him almost unanimously. Would Grant and the Stalwarts show their gratitude by ensuring that Congress passed Sumner's Civil Rights Bill as an amendment to the amnesty bill? If not, Sumner could potentially drive Black voters out of the Republican Party—as he had been threatening to do.

Sumner urged George William Curtis, the *Harper's Weekly* editorialist, to call on President Grant to support his effort. "The colored people are stirring, &, I think, will show force at the opening of Congress," he warned. "Pass this,—& let me drop," he proposed. "Willingly will I go. Give me up; but save the Bill." In effect, Sumner was offering to resign or not run for reelection if Grant secured passage of his Civil Rights Bill to benefit Black Americans. "I hope Mr. Douglass will help secure this victory. He may then dismiss me to private life," Sumner wrote to a friend, asking him to relay the offer to Douglass, who had lately been furious with him over the Santo Domingo issue. "It will be the capstone of my work," Sumner assured Henry Longfellow. "Then, perhaps, I had better withdraw, and leave to others this laborious life."[6]

* * *

ON JANUARY 2, 1872, Sumner held a planning meeting at his house with local African American civic leaders. At the head of the group was John Mercer Langston, the Howard Law dean and professor who had helped him draft the original bill. The group told Sumner they had used their networks to call on Black freedpeople across the South to organize petitions and letter-writing campaigns targeted at Congress. "Besides petitions & letters there must be a strong committee to visit every Republican Senator," Sumner advised. "Not a vote must be lost." By the end of the meeting, according to a report in the *Boston Journal*, "it was evidently felt that the colored persons of all sections of the country must make the recognition of their rights the condition of political support."

One week later, Professor Langston and the other civic leaders went to the White House to talk to President Grant. When they demanded that he send a message to Congress in support of Sumner's Civil Rights Bill, Grant equivocated. "Not being a lawyer, it was not possible for him to advise as to what was the best course to pursue," said an unofficial readout in the *National Era*. "Not having read it attentively, he was unable to speak as to the specific provisions contained therein." Nevertheless, he said there was "sufficient merit and justice" in the bill "to commend itself to the thoughtful consideration" of members of Congress. "If the President hopes to have the vote of the colored people," threatened an anonymous letter in the *New York Tribune* afterward, he would have to do better than this "unfortunate reply to the colored delegation."

On January 13, Langston went to a school-wide meeting at Howard University for all students, staff, faculty, and officers. Even the school's white president, Gen. Oliver Otis Howard, attended. Together, they drafted a statement on behalf of the university and organized committees mixed with students and adults to lobby for Sumner's Civil Rights Bill. "Representing as we do a university that knows no distinction on account of color," the statement read, "we feel that we would not be true to ourselves, to the principles which we have again and again asserted, did we not on this occasion raise our united voices against what we believe to be the most flagrant injustice ever committed against any people." Asking "the Republican party, as our friends," to support Sumner's effort, the university demanded that the party "be not timid in this manner."

Langston and others from Howard went straight to Sumner's house afterward. Welcoming them inside, Sumner took them up to his study. "I am glad now that *you* visit me, young men," he said. "It is the day that I long wished to see, when the colored people would take their cause into their own hands." He got emotional as he spoke. "Before I die I hope to do all I can to remedy your wrongs. I wish I could do more. I wish I was stronger. I wish I had more influence," he said. "I hope for success. Your efforts will do much to secure it. But I am not entirely confident," he confessed. "Meanwhile, let me say, I hope that you will spare no effort."[7]

Across the country in the winter and spring of 1871–72, African Americans flooded Sumner with letters supporting his Civil Rights Bill. Those letters made his heart soar. For most of his career, he had acted as the de facto voice in Congress for Black Americans. Seeing Blacks organize and push their own arguments helped him realize his own insignificance: African Americans did not need him to explain their case. "Sir, are not these excellent words?" he said about one letter he received. "Who among us can speak better than they speak in the passages I am about to read?" he asked rhetorically about another.[8]

On the Senate floor, Sumner started reading letters from Black Americans who advocated for his bill. A father from Rhode Island wanted to bury his beloved four-year-old child in a nice cemetery but had been denied by every private cemetery in town. A widow from West Virginia said her mentally ill son lived in a prison because the asylum had refused to take him. A lawmaker from North Carolina helped enact a charter for a steamboat company that afterward refused to let him ride in the first-class rooms. A traveler had to sleep in a hotel lobby in Massachusetts; the hotel clerk would not give him a bed. "We keenly feel all efforts made to keep us down & degrade us," said a petition from Black women in D.C. "We are subjected to mortifications, insults & injuries such as no free women can endure . . . our grievances contain the essence of Slavery."[9]

Over a few months, Sumner read aloud from more than sixty letters and petitions like these. "I feel that in justice to our colored fellow-citizens I ought to see that they have a hearing on this floor," he declared. "They have a title to be heard themselves. They are able; they can speak for themselves." In so speaking, Black correspondents were not just trying to tug at heartstrings: they were demonstrating agency and flexing muscle as new political actors. "The colored voter demands from all for whom he casts a vote, from President of the United States down, that they give of whatever influence or power that they may have," said Langston in a letter Sumner read on the floor. "There is a new power in our country," Sumner observed. "It is the colored people of the United States counted by the million; a new power with votes, and they now insist upon their rights."[10]

* * *

SURE ENOUGH, DEMOCRATS and Liberals denounced Sumner's attempt to combine the Civil Rights Bill with the amnesty bill despite their pretensions of supporting Black rights. The Kentucky Democrat Garrett Davis said he was stunned that Sumner would introduce something "as offensive, as oppressive, and as annoying as his amendment would be in all the old slave States." Lyman Trumbull, a leading Liberal from Illinois, decried it as "a monstrosity." Even the Missouri Liberal Carl Schurz didn't want civil rights attached to amnesty. Out of respect for his close friend, Schurz stayed quiet during the debate. But he wouldn't give Sumner his vote.[11]

The loudest opponents of Sumner's bill decided to claim it was unconstitutional rather than to criticize integration on the merits. In so doing, they inspired a rich debate on the meaning of civil rights, the scope of congressional power, and the significance of the postwar Constitution. That debate offered Sumner another opportunity to persuade others of his human rights–oriented vision of constitutional law.[12]

Among Democrats and Liberals, two constitutional arguments stood out. First, they argued that the Fourteenth Amendment authorized Congress to enforce civil rights laws only against state governments. For example, Senator Davis admitted that ex–slave states were now required to treat people equally, but he said it was unconstitutional to force *private* associations to do the same. After all, the amendment said that "No State" shall deny privileges and immunities, due process, and equal protection. The text said nothing about nonstate actors. "The State of Kentucky, if you please, has citizens that organize hotel companies, theatrical companies, schools, &c.," he noted. Discrimination by them was "acts of citizens, not of the Legislature."[13]

Davis's argument presaged what courts now call the "state action doctrine," a concept that Sumner thought was nonsensical. He believed these organizations were never truly private: states gave out licenses, recognized charters, and otherwise regulated places like restaurants and hotels all the time. Because of this, those associations were creatures of state law. To this end, Sumner's bill applied only to associations that were "licensed," "incorporated," or "supported or authorized by law." If an unincorporated group wished to discriminate, that would be fine under his bill. Only those *recognized* by law could not do so.[14]

Second, Trumbull said the Fourteenth Amendment authorized Congress to enforce only *civil* rights, not *social* rights. As author of the Civil Rights Act of 1866, he wanted Blacks to be able to own property, sign contracts, and sue in court. But he drew the line at the right to intermingle, which he called "a social right" that only states could legislate. Under Sumner's bill, whites would lose the right "to associate with those whom, by inclination, they prefer," one editorial warned. "To deprive white people of the right of choosing their own company would be to introduce another kind of slavery," Joseph Bradley, an associate justice of the Supreme Court, privately decried.[15]

In Sumner's view, Trumbull's argument boiled down to a tautology. While some lawyers of his era grouped rights into three categories—civil, social, and political—Sumner never recognized a "social" category. Neither did many other abolitionists or Radical Republicans. Back in 1849, when Sumner argued *Roberts v. City of Boston*, he repeatedly called for "equality in civil and political rights" with reference to a young Black girl's attempt to attend a white-only public school. He gave no recognition then, or any time in the future, to any kind of social rights that were not civil rights. Over time, he stopped recognizing a distinction between civil rights and political rights, too. "I cannot bring myself to make any question whether it is a civil right or a political right," he replied when asked whether jury participation was a civil or a political right. "It is a right."[16]

Sumner also quoted from his Black correspondents to reply to men like Trumbull and Davis. "We do not wish to force ourselves into American society unwelcomed," explained Douglass Griffing from Oberlin, Ohio. "What we ask now, is simply equal public privileges." Griffing was arguing that white people were free to choose their company in their private lives. But in public, they must admit Black people as equal participants. "In a few sentences, in a very clear handwriting, he has answered the Senator better than I could do it," Sumner said of Griffing. "We do not ask for legislation to regulate social intercourse," explained some Black petitioners from Newport, Rhode Island. "We petition legislation in our behalf only where the civil law may control."[17]

* * *

REPUBLICAN REACTION TO Sumner's Civil Rights Bill was far more mixed than that of Democrats and Liberals. Some Republicans proudly favored integration. Others wanted to see the amnesty bill fall apart and were happy to attach integration to the bill as a poison pill. Still others wanted to modify Sumner's amendment, and a few viciously opposed it. Among Republicans, two men stand out for their strong and surprising views on the bill: Lot Morrill and Matthew Carpenter. Both men battled with Sumner over competing visions of civil rights, congressional power, and the postwar Constitution.

To date, Morrill had enjoyed a good working relationship with Sumner; he was one of the first men whom Sumner told about his engagement and marriage. A generally soft-spoken and amiable senator from Maine, Morrill had been so disturbed by the South's conduct during the Civil War and early Reconstruction that he became an earnest Radical. By now, though, he had mellowed. While claiming to share Sumner's goal of racial integration, Morrill argued that Sumner's bill wasn't authorized by the Fourteenth Amendment.

On January 25, 1872, Morrill embarked on an argument that Sumner described as "most extraordinary, almost eccentric." The former Radical who had worked so tirelessly on Reconstruction now argued that all four clauses of the amendment's first section were virtually meaningless. The Citizenship Clause "was always so." It added "nothing in the way of legislative authority or legislative power to the Congress." The Privileges and Immunities Clause meant "very little comparatively of the rights of man." It was "a political truism" that only reaffirmed the rights already enshrined in the Civil Rights Act of 1866. The Due Process Clause just restated the "ordinary privileges" that had existed "ever since the Constitution had an existence." And while he admitted that the Equal Protection Clause banned states from treating citizens unequally because of race, he said the clause gave Congress no "substantive power" whatsoever to enforce this ban on the states.[18]

Morrill seemed to be suffering from amnesia over what Republicans had believed. Back in 1866, a Kentucky senator had accused the Republicans of acting like revolutionaries. "I accept what the Senator from Kentucky thinks so obnoxious," Morrill had boasted. "We are in the midst of revolution. We have revolutionized this Constitution of ours." He said the war "had changed the fundamental principles of our Government in some respects." And he hailed the Civil Rights Act of 1866 for being wildly unprecedented. "There is no parallel for it in the history of any country, because no nation hitherto has ever cherished a liberty so universal."[19]

To Morrill, Reconstruction's constitutional revolution seemed to be over and was perhaps never revolutionary at all. To Sumner, Reconstruction was—as one eminent modern historian has described it—"an unfinished revolution." In his rebuttal on January 31, Sumner pulled out and read from a letter from his friend Edwin Belcher, who had become president of the new Georgia Civil Rights Association. "Now is the opportunity to give to the colored race the Magna Charta of our liberties," Belcher wrote. "When that becomes a law, the freedom of my race will then be complete," he continued. "Such, sir, is the statement of one once a slave, and who knows whereof he speaks," Sumner explained. He said the letter was evidence that Congress needed to pass his bill to enforce the abolition of slavery, per the Thirteenth Amendment. He argued that "not till the passage of the supplemental civil rights bill" will slavery cease to exist. "When I voted for that article, I meant what it said, that slavery should cease absolutely, entirely, and completely," he avowed.

Soon after reading Belcher's words, Sumner pulled out a letter from his friend George Downing, the congressional caterer. Putting Downing "face to face" with Morrill, Sumner said he wanted "to show that he understands the question, even constitutionally," better than Morrill. "I . . . invoke the letter of the Constitution in behalf of congressional action to protect me in the rights of an American citizen," Downing wrote. Citing the Judicial Vesting Clause, the Supremacy Clause, the Republican Guarantee Clause, the Privileges and Immunities Clause, and others, Downing concluded by saying Congress could do anything "necessary and proper" to protect the rights of Black citizens like him when their rights were being disregarded by a state.

"Mr. Downing placed himself on the texts of the Constitution and interpreted them liberally, justly, for the rights of his race," Sumner explained to the Senate. That was the correct way to do constitutional law. Meanwhile, Morrill had engaged in "malignant interpretation." In dealing with ambiguous clauses, he chose to interpret them against the enforcement of rights because his *default* assumption was against granting power to the government. "He makes that system of interpretation, born of slavery, his guide," Sumner accused. He was referring to what is now called "strict construction," a legal philosophy still shared by many lawyers today that calls for narrowly interpreting the Constitution to limit the government's powers to what is expressly written. "He questions everything; denies everything," Sumner complained. "He finds no power for anything unless it be distinctly written in positive and precise words. He cannot read between the lines."

As he had been saying for years, Sumner argued that the postwar Constitution should be interpreted generously toward human rights—just as Downing had done in his letter. "The Constitution is not mean, stingy, and pettifogging, but open-handed, liberal, and just, inclining always in favor of Freedom," he had argued back in 1862. He believed the Constitution was far more expansive than strict constructionists had construed it.

Sumner believed the Civil War—the war *itself*—had inaugurated this liberal mode of constitutionalism, during an era that scholars now call the Second Founding. "Before the rebellion, the Constitution was interpreted always, in every clause and line and word, for human slavery," Sumner explained. But a "great rule of interpretation" was "conquered at Appomattox," he argued. "I say a new rule of interpretation for the Constitution, according to which, in every clause and every line and every word, it is to be interpreted uniformly for human rights."[20]

Sumner believed the constitutional transformation of the Second Founding redeemed the First Founding rather than repudiated it. All the war did was vindicate the principles of the Declaration of Independence, which Sumner believed best embodied the principles of human rights that should bind constitutional law. That text was "the pledge which our fathers took upon their lips," Sumner said to Morrill. "Every word in the Constitution is subordinate to the Declaration," he argued. "Show me any words in the Constitution applicable to human rights, and I invoke at once the great truths of the Declaration as the absolute guide in determining their meaning," he proclaimed. "The grandest victory of the war was the establishment of the new rule by which the Declaration became supreme as interpreter of the Constitution."[21]

* * *

ON THE FOLLOWING day, the nation's top constitutional litigator, Wisconsin senator Matthew Carpenter, replied to Morrill and Sumner. A protégé of the great attorney Rufus Choate, Carpenter ran a thriving law practice while serving as senator. Notably, he had argued (and won) three of the biggest Supreme Court cases of his generation, all of which are still cited and taught in law schools today: *Ex parte Garland* (1866), *Ex parte McCardle* (1869), and the *Slaughter-House Cases* (1873). A short, muscular man with a shaggy mustache and stumpy neck, Carpenter seemed built to wrestle. A friend once warned him against debating Sumner on the law. "If I am to lock horns with anyone," he replied, "it might as well be with the biggest ox in the pen."[22]

Carpenter had long resented Sumner for his supposedly "loose method of construction." All the "loose thought and wild talk inspired by a civil war . . . all this extravagance and absolute wildness," he once groaned, "are sanctioned, sanctified, and canonized by the endorsement of the Senator from Massachusetts." He had once tried to get Sumner to stop using soaring rhetoric and stinging insults to answer a basic constitutional question. "I ask the Senator to descend from his tripod, to emerge from his oracular and profane mysteries," Carpenter pleaded. Naturally, Sumner wouldn't do it. "Instead of treating it like a lawyer, with reason and argument, he flies at his opponent with denunciation and malediction," Carpenter grumbled.[23]

Carpenter rejected the idea that the Declaration had a unique interpretative role in constitutional law. "In doubtful cases it is the duty of a court or the duty of the Senate or the duty of any public officer to consider the Declaration of Independence," he admitted. But legal interpreters should consider it just like "the writings of Washington and of Jefferson and of Madison, the writings in the Federalist—everything that pertained to that day and gives color and tone to the Constitution." The goal was to understand what the Founding Fathers actually intended in the Constitution, not to privilege their lofty human rights aspirations in the Declaration. "If you find a provision of the Constitution not in harmony with the Declaration of Independence, you must follow the Constitution," Carpenter said. "You have sworn to support the Constitution and not sworn to support the Declaration," he reminded Sumner.

At the same time, Carpenter disagreed with Morrill's narrow reading of the postwar Constitution. "Here, I adopt the principle which I understand the Senator from Massachusetts at last to lay down," he said. According to Carpenter, strict construction was proper when interpreting the "old Constitution." That was because Americans had "sensitiveness" over "State sovereignty and State rights" in the Founding era. But he thought Sumner was correct that during the mid-1860s, the so-called Second Founding, those sensitivities around states' rights "had been drowned in blood." Carpenter said that because states had been "faithless to their constitutional obligations," Americans had ratified three new amendments to empower Congress to regulate the states. Those powers were "totally and substantially different" from what came before. Thus, in Carpenter's view, it was proper to use strict construction to interpret the original constitutional provisions, but it was utterly inapt to use strict construction to interpret the Reconstruction amendments.

Carpenter agreed with Sumner that Congress had nearly plenary (absolute) power over the states to pass "affirmative legislation" to enforce "the objects intended to be secured" by the Fourteenth Amendment. To this end, he announced that he largely supported Sumner's Civil Rights Bill. But first, he wanted to make a few changes to the draft. After talking privately to Sumner, who declined to voluntarily make his requested changes, Carpenter made a motion on the floor to substitute Sumner's bill with his own version. He removed or changed Sumner's provisions on churches, juries, cemeteries, and enforcement to correct what he thought were constitutional defects in the original bill. The rest of his bill was substantially the same.

Out of everything in Sumner's bill, Carpenter especially wanted to recognize a right of nondiscriminatory access to public schools. "I never will countenance or give the slightest support," he promised, to the idea "that the children of one class of citizens shall not have the benefit of a common school supported at the public expense by general taxation." When it came to integrating schools, Carpenter thought the party should not cave to public pressure. "Upon that subject I do hope this Republican party will never back one inch."[24]

* * *

IF SUMNER HAD been a more tactical statesman, he would have tried to work with Carpenter, despite their many personal spats over the years. Widely known as one of the ablest lawyers in the nation, Carpenter had given him a godsend by heartily endorsing the bulk of his controversial bill. All Sumner had to do was compromise on some details to win Carpenter over. But Sumner brimmed with anger instead. He couldn't get over Carpenter's criticism of the Declaration of Independence as a source of legal meaning. To Sumner, the Declaration was *everything*. "His political creed, his political Bible, his Ten Commandments, his Golden Rule, were the Declaration of Independence and the Constitution of the United States penetrated, illuminated, interpreted by the Declaration of Independence," recalled his friend George Hoar.[25] Sumner was determined to respond to Carpenter's remarks.

Carpenter discovered that Sumner planned to disparage him on February 5, 1872. He found it unfortunate, but expected. To him, Sumner was a vain, sensitive man who couldn't emotionally handle intellectual disagreement. "You had better come down to the Senate chamber this afternoon; there is going to be some fun and music by the band," Carpenter said cheerfully to a friend on the appointed date. "Sumner has the floor to-day and is going to reply to some comments which I made the other day on the unconstitutionality of his Civil Rights Bill," he went on to say, lighting a fresh cigar. "I suppose he will chew me up very fine."[26]

Sure enough, Sumner unleashed a stream of insults at Carpenter. He denounced him as "a representative of caste" for stripping some parts of the bill. He took it personally that Carpenter cited a passage from Story's writings on the First Amendment. Story was "the much venerated friend of my early life, and my master," Sumner declared, dubiously accusing Carpenter of misrepresenting his teacher. In another needless potshot, he noted that Carpenter's mentor Rufus Choate was also "a much valued friend of my own." He said he could not think of Choate's views on the Declaration, which were imparted to Carpenter, "without a pang of regret."

On the merits, Sumner defended his view of the Declaration. He clarified that the Declaration did not create "substantive powers" for the national government; powers came from the Constitution. That said, the *scope* of any constitutional powers should be interpreted by the Declaration's principles of liberty and equality. "When you come to those several specific powers abolishing slavery, defining citizenship, securing citizens in their privileges and immunities, guarding them against any denial of the equal protection of the laws, and then again securing them in the right to vote, every one of those safeguards must be interpreted so as best to maintain equal rights," he argued. "Such I assert to be constitutional law," he declared.[27]

Sumner then cited his seniority in the Senate, as if that were persuasive. "I have served the Constitution longer than he has," Sumner snarled. "I have served it at moments of peril, when the great principles of liberty to which I have been devoted were in jeopardy; I have served it when there were few to stand by me," he pronounced. Then he made a claim that seemed to embody his entire legal philosophy: "In upholding that Constitution, never did I fail at the same time to uphold human rights."[28]

* * *

SUMNER'S UNCOMPROMISING STANCE was arguably admirable. But it was also self-defeating. While he was victorious in blocking Carpenter's amendment, he had lost a potentially valuable ally in the process. "Why, sir, he comes into this Chamber and elects me as his principal opponent. I, who agree with him as to what is desirable," Carpenter bitterly regretted. On February 9, 1872, Sumner's own amendment came up for a vote. The Senate deadlocked at 28–28.[29]

Per the Constitution, the vice president has the power to break ties in the Senate, and Vice President Schuyler Colfax broke the tie in Sumner's favor. In so doing, the administration doomed the now-joint Amnesty and Civil Rights Bill. The bill needed support from two-thirds of the House and the Senate per the Fourteenth Amendment due to the amnesty provisions, a nearly impossible bar now that civil rights were attached to it. Predictably, the bill failed because Democrats, Liberals, and some others refused to vote for integration. Politically, Grant struck gold: most Republicans were now on record voting in favor of both civil rights and amnesty, which made Grant look generous to all. As a bonus, they could blame Democrats for voting against both. And because civil rights didn't pass, Grant didn't have to fear much backlash from angry whites.[30]

Sumner wasn't too upset. Soon enough, somebody would reintroduce an amnesty bill, at which point, he would reintroduce his civil rights amendment. The next time it came around, Congress would act, he thought. With political conventions coming up in the early summer and the presidential election in the fall, he figured politicians would gradually warm to civil rights in order to attract support from Black voters, now a powerful constituency. "I have been gratified by the success of the Civil Rights Bill," he wrote Longfellow shortly after his initial defeat. "I begin to believe it will become a law. Then will there be joy."[31]

Three months later, Sumner got a second chance to push for his Civil Rights Bill on the floor. In the meantime, he had another terrible angina pectoris attack. Suffering from debilitating pain, he was forced to spend nearly two weeks at home. His friends sent him stern letters. "Consent to play sick for our sakes, who want to lean on you, and so need a strong man," Wendell Phillips begged him. "Take care of your health," Francis Lieber demanded. "Remember that it was in 1828 or 1829 that I became acquainted with you. We are not young."[32]

Sumner was now sixty-one years old. But he didn't prioritize his health. While abstaining from some duties, he fell into another ugly spat with Carpenter in the spring. After hearing a rumor that some White House officials had unlawfully sold leftover Union Army weapons to France, Sumner and his friend the Liberal senator Carl Schurz asked the Senate to form an investigative committee. The Senate obliged him, but appointed only Grant's allies and named Carpenter as chairman. As one of the first steps in the investigation, Carpenter demanded that Sumner testify before the committee on who had told him about the possible crimes. Sumner was stunned—it seemed that Carpenter, a Stalwart who was loyal to Grant, planned to run a sham investigation to protect Grant's reputation and expose the whistleblowers. Rather than testify, Sumner showed up, denounced Carpenter's investigation by reading a prewritten statement, and stormed out.[33]

Carpenter believed that Sumner had insulted his integrity and had disrespected the committee's time. Not one to avoid battles, he escalated the situation. He sent the sergeant at arms to deliver Sumner a subpoena and threaten to arrest him if he didn't testify. "People are already laughing over the probable incarceration," reported a correspondent. Begrudgingly, Sumner appeared on the following day to give his testimony. He started by arguing that the committee was illegitimate, and he repeatedly mocked Carpenter by calling him "Acting Chairman" rather than "Chairman." The situation became petty on all sides.

When the investigation was complete, Carpenter's committee absolved the Grant administration of any wrongdoing in the sale of the Union Army weapons. Sumner was skeptical, but having found no solid proof of wrongdoing himself, he let the issue go. The only real outcome of the investigation was that Sumner and Carpenter became even more bitter rivals. All the while, the stress from the fight worsened Sumner's heart problems.[34]

* * *

By mid-April, 1872, Sumner was so dismayed by Grant and Grant's Senate allies that he was nearly ready to leave the Republican Party. He went on record denouncing Grant as "unfit to be President of the United States." Grant was "venal, ambitious, vulgar in his habits, and possesses a cunning which is low and dogged." If Grant were renominated at the Republican National Convention in early June, Sumner would make his exit. "I cannot honorably support a party that will sustain such a man," he swore. At the same time, he struggled with the idea of joining the Liberals. He was nervous about what would happen to Black Americans in the South under the Liberal plan of grace to ex-rebels. It didn't help that leading Senate Liberals Lyman Trumbull and Carl Schurz voted against his Civil Rights Bill despite claiming to be allies of the Black community.[35]

To coax Sumner into joining his movement, the leading Liberal economist David Ames Wells visited Sumner at his home. He explained to Sumner that he shouldn't wait until June to decide whether to leave the Republicans and join the Liberals. That was because the Liberals were holding their convention in early May. If Sumner joined the Liberals before the convention, Wells explained, he could help shape the party's platform and influence its choice of a nominee. To win him over, Wells offered to try to secure a plank on the platform in support of Sumner's Civil Rights Bill. Thinking it over, Sumner agreed to endorse the Liberals. He promised to write a letter of endorsement later in the day for Wells to pick up in the evening.

Soon after Wells left, Professor Langston stopped by Sumner's home. Sumner told his friend about his meeting with Wells. Langston was appalled. For months, Langston—much like Sumner—had been publicly threatening to leave the Republican Party if it failed to pass their Civil Rights Bill. But he couldn't go through with the threat. As much as he was frustrated with the Republicans, he was even more troubled by the Liberals. He urged Sumner to reconsider.

When Wells returned that evening, Sumner explained that Langston had convinced him not to write the letter of support. "The Grant leaders are using the colored people to prevent your endorsement," Wells argued. But Sumner wouldn't budge. Holding out hope that Grant wouldn't win renomination, Sumner said he would wait until after the Republican convention took place in Philadelphia to make his decision. Meanwhile, he wanted Wells to still ensure that his bill would be included on the Liberal platform at their convention in Cincinnati. "I think I understand Sumner's position now," Wells reported to Senator Trumbull. "He is for the negro first & last. He means to make Cincinnati come out for equality irrespective of caste or color before the law, & then force Philadelphia to bid higher."[36]

Frank Bird also tried to recruit Sumner to the Liberals. Bird, the Republican lobbyist and wealthy businessman who had informally managed each of Sumner's Senate campaigns since 1850, was more loyal to Sumner than any other man. He was so outraged by Grant's maneuvering to remove Sumner from the chairmanship of the Foreign Relations Committee that he opposed Grant's reelection. Feeling encouraged by Sumner, Bird started organizing a Liberal movement in Massachusetts. That movement was naturally more committed to Black civil rights than were Liberal factions in the South and West.

With Sumner's public endorsement, Bird felt confident he could steer the Liberal platform toward their principles at the convention in Cincinnati. He also believed a majority of Liberal delegates might be willing to nominate Sumner for president. All he needed was Sumner's approval to launch the campaign. "I believe that no public man in this country ever had such an opportunity to bring about great results as you now have," Bird wrote him. If Sumner were the nominee, Bird believed, "the reformers would carry the country."[37]

Sumner resolutely declined. If he had any interest in the White House, he didn't show it. Perhaps he knew that his health was in no state for him to run for president or be president. More likely, he just wasn't interested. He was content with being in the Senate. He took pride in not being an office seeker. And Bird's aspirations for him were nearly fantastical: Democrats, whom many Liberals were trying to court, had long hated Sumner.

While Bird and two other lifelong political associates (Salmon Chase and James Ashley) begged Sumner to join the Liberals, three of his closest friends decided to stick with the Republicans. Edward Pierce, Samuel Hooper, and Henry Wilson detested Grant's actions and were disturbed by the direction of the Republican Party, but the Liberals disturbed them even more. The three men thought Sumner was being terribly naïve in considering an alliance with those who wanted to end Reconstruction.

Wilson felt special sorrow. "I have not felt a moment for more than twenty years that I would not do anything in my power for you," he told Sumner after a home visit. "When you said that we must part in the future but hoped that we should be personal friends, I deeply regretted the one but clung to the other with hope." Back in the fall of 1850, Wilson had worked with Bird to run Sumner's first Senate campaign. Together, the three men had built their state's Free-Soil and Republican Parties in the 1840s and 1850s. Now they were all breaking apart.[38]

Torn between his friends, Sumner failed to decide before the Liberal convention whether he would support them. Perhaps he hoped his silence would further motivate Liberals to covet his endorsement. On May 1, the first day of the convention, Bird wrote an anguished letter to Sumner: "I am pained that we get no word of encouragement from you. Urged by you to the perilous ridge, we are left to fight the battle alone."[39]

* * *

SUMNER SEEMED TO genuinely believe that Republicans and Liberals would vie for the support of Black voters in the election of 1872. After all, there were roughly two million Black men in the South. That was surely a powerful enough voting bloc to force politicians in Washington to listen, he reasoned. In so thinking, Sumner was being extremely naïve. Blacks constituted less than 15 percent of the American population. Liberals were far more concerned with courting white voters than Black ones. This left Black voters with little choice but to vote for Republicans, and Republicans seemed to think those voters could be taken for granted as a result.

Senator Carpenter had outright explained the Republican position when Sumner's civil rights amendment was first debated on the Senate floor. "I do not believe that the colored people of this country are so lacking in intelligence as to be at all disposed, even if this amendment should not pass in the precise form in which it is proposed, to entertain any unkind feeling toward the President of the United States," he observed. He said African Americans would be ignorant, foolish, and ungrateful to "turn their backs upon the only party in the country that has given them a single right." Thus, Carpenter thought Republicans *should* pass a Civil Rights Bill but certainly did not *need* to.[40]

Most Liberal leaders didn't think much of Sumner's Civil Rights Bill, either. Although some men, like Frank Bird, hoped the party could be used as a vehicle for advancing Sumner's bill, the most prominent Liberals, such as Senators Carl Schurz and Lyman Trumbull, had actively opposed it. Sure enough, when Bird arrived at the Liberal convention, he found himself greatly outnumbered by Liberals who opposed civil rights. While wanting Sumner's endorsement, most party delegates did not want to endorse Sumner's policies. Ultimately, Liberal delegates decided to include an ambiguous plank on their platform that recognized "the equality of all men before the law" and the need for government "to mete out equal and exact justice to all, of whatever nativity, race, color, or persuasion, religious or political." Those were nice enough words, but there was no explicit position on Sumner's bill. Effectively, it was a bone thrown at Sumner without much meat.[41]

The Liberals ended up choosing Horace Greeley, editor of the *New York Tribune*, as their presidential nominee. Greeley, a wealthy newspaper mogul, had never been satisfied with his life as a journalist and businessman. He wanted political power. Undeterred by several failed attempts at running for office in his home state of New York, he had sent a cadre of his supporters to the convention. With backroom deals and sheer dumb luck, Greeley's men secured his nomination. In the process, Greeley marginalized key figures like Schurz, Trumbull, and Bird, who would have preferred a politician with principles over a sleazy mogul.[42]

For the past thirty years, Greeley had used the *Tribune* to advocate for all sorts of causes. In the 1840s and '50s, he was a staunch Whig who built a readership of over two hundred thousand, making his paper the dominant voice of the Whig Party. When abolitionism gained traction, Greeley became an abolitionist, making the *Tribune* a crucial antislavery newspaper. During the war, he oscillated between support for and antagonism toward Lincoln. Afterward, he personally paid for Confederate president Jefferson Davis's bail and blasted Reconstruction policies. When the Radicals became popular, though, Greeley endorsed Radical Reconstruction. As Frederick Douglass put it, Greeley was "an uncertain man; an inconsistent man." A crafty writer always in search of more readers, he was "one whom you do not know today and can give no guess what he will do to-morrow."[43]

Greeley somewhat co-opted the Liberal movement by minimizing its call for economic and political reforms and centering the party's entire focus on bringing an end to Reconstruction. His goal was to appeal to Democrats—to bring them into his fold, with an eye toward convincing them not to run a third candidate in the race. That way, it would be just him against Grant. Since he owned the *Tribune*, one of the nation's leading news outlets, Greeley hoped to run a massive media campaign to delegitimize Grant's Reconstruction policies and win the presidency that way. At first, Greeley was perceived to be a dangerous threat to Grant.

Sumner predicted that the upcoming election would be "between Greeley & Grant—between the two G's—the *great* G & the little g." One *G* was a military man; the other *G* was a journalist. "Is not the pen mightier than the sword?" he asked one of his friends rhetorically. "The two are about to meet."[44]

∗ ∗ ∗

ON MAY 8, 1872, five days after the conclusion of the Liberal convention, the Senate considered a new amnesty bill that was identical to the old one. Republicans were deeply unnerved by the Liberal threat and Greeley's nomination. Taking a lead from Grant, the party hoped to pass amnesty quickly so that the Liberals couldn't make it an issue in the general election. But Sumner was ready to intercept them to make civil rights an issue, too. Almost as soon as the amnesty bill was read, Sumner stood up and offered his Civil Rights Bill as an amendment. Like clockwork, senators argued that Sumner's amendment was out of order, and the presiding officer overruled those objections. And thus, once again, just as Sumner had hoped, another debate commenced.

One day later, Grant refused yet again to explicitly endorse Sumner's bill. Replying to a request to meet with Black civic leaders, including Frederick Douglass and George Downing, the president claimed he was not available. He cryptically explained to them in a letter that he supported "any effort to secure . . . the exercise of those rights to which every citizen should be entitled." He left out *what* rights a citizen was entitled to. With an eye toward reelection, Grant calculated that amnesty was a winning issue, while racial integration was not.[45]

Over and over, several senators tried to kill Sumner's bill. The closest they got was a 28–28 vote, where Vice President Colfax broke the tie by voting to save it. All the while, Sumner tried to pass his bill. Once, he offered it as a substitute to *replace* the amnesty bill. This failed by 27–28. Then he tried again to amend the amnesty bill by *adding* civil rights to it. This tied at 28–28, with Vice President Colfax ruling for him. But the dual Amnesty–Civil Rights Bill lacked the votes to reach the necessary two-thirds support to pass. The Senate was thus stuck in a quandary. It lacked two-thirds support to *pass* civil rights coupled with amnesty. It also lacked a majority to *kill* civil rights or just to separate it from amnesty.[46]

The heated debate on amnesty and civil rights kept delaying other business as the clock slowly approached the end of the session. Accordingly, on May 20, the Senate opted for a marathon day-and-night session to debate and vote on the myriad of unrelated bills that needed their attention. As evening approached, Sumner went home on instructions from his doctor. He had been trying to follow advice from Phillips, Lieber, and other friends who were urging him to take it easy. Seeing that amnesty was not on the schedule, he felt it was safe to leave.

This was when Senator Carpenter struck. Tired of Sumner's obstinacy on amnesty and his unwillingness to accept amendments to his Civil Rights Bill, Carpenter decided to destroy Sumner's bill and replace it with his own. Shortly before 6 a.m., he asked the Senate to take up Sumner's bill. Almost half the room was empty.

Some half-awake senators protested. "It is unfair and unjust to take a vote upon this bill during the absence of the Senator from Massachusetts," Alabama's Republican senator George Spencer groaned. Ohio senator Allen Thurman thought it wrong to vote on this bill "at this hour, when Senators did not expect that it would be done, when the Senate did not expect it would be taken up." Somebody sent a messenger to Sumner's home to warn him about Carpenter's trick, but he lived two miles away. If the messenger went by foot, he would have taken at least forty-five minutes to reach Sumner.[47]

Barely acknowledging his critics in the meantime, Carpenter sped along. Reneging on his promise in February to push for school integration, he moved to replace Sumner's bill with a new version that had weaker enforcement measures and did not mention schooling, churches, or juries. "I consider it emasculating the bill entirely," Spencer protested. "I understand that this substitute strikes out public schools, and thereby very much impairs the effect of the bill," grumbled New Jersey's Frederick Frelinghuysen. Sumner's Bay State colleague Henry Wilson declared he would vote against it. But they were in the minority. Not bothering to explain or defend himself or his amendment, Carpenter asked to move to a vote on the motion to replace Sumner's bill with his own text. That motion passed 22–20. Then he asked the Senate to pass his bill, without attaching it to amnesty. It passed with a large majority.

A livid Sumner stormed into the chamber too late. "I understand that in my absence and without any notice to me from any quarter the Senate have adopted an emasculated civil rights bill," he shouted. "I insist that the Senate shall not lose this great opportunity," he continued. "I cannot, I will not cease." Attempting to subvert the amnesty vote again, he moved to attach his Civil Rights Bill to the amnesty bill. But this time, the Senate turned against him. The sun was already rising. The senators were exhausted, and the fight seemed not worth having anymore. Sumner's motion failed 13–29. The Senate then voted on the stand-alone amnesty bill. The bill passed almost unanimously; Sumner was one of only two dissenters.[48]

All the while, Carpenter stayed almost completely silent. In the dead of night, he was able to secure three victories. First, the Senate had now passed the House's stand-alone amnesty bill, which would go straight to Grant's desk for his signature. That was a political win for the Republicans, who had wanted to stifle the Liberal insurgency. Second, the Senate had passed Carpenter's watered-down Civil Rights Bill. That was a political win for Carpenter, who could claim to be a more practical statesman than Sumner, who had failed to pass any Civil Rights Bill at all. Third, Carpenter could wreak his personal vengeance upon Sumner by killing his beloved bill. Ultimately, Carpenter's bill would fail to get a vote in the House; no Civil Rights Bill passed in 1872.

"Sir, I sound the cry," Sumner whimpered after losing his motion to reattach his original Civil Rights Bill to the amnesty bill. "The rights of the colored race have been sacrificed in this Chamber where the Republican party has a large majority—that party by its history, its traditions, and all its professions bound to their vindication. Sir, I sound the cry. Let it go forth that the sacrifice has been perpetrated."[49]

CHAPTER 28

YOU ARE THE JESUS
OF THE NEGRO RACE

CHARLES SUMNER OCCASIONALLY RECEIVED LETTERS FROM NEW parents who had named their baby son after him. These letters never pleased him, despite his love for flattery. "Don't make a mistake," he once wrote to a father who named his son Charles Sumner. "Never name a child after a living man." He urged the father to "simply un-name" his son and pick something else. "Who knows that I may not fail? I, too, may grow faint, or may turn aside to false gods."[1]

By the summer of 1872, many Republicans feared that Sumner was turning aside to false gods. After the Civil Rights Bill failed, Sumner blamed "Republican lukewarmness and the want of support in the President" instead of opposition by Democrats and Liberals. He was so angry at President Grant, Senator Carpenter, and the entire Republican Party, that he was ready to punish them by any means necessary. And so, he began openly exploring the idea of asking Black voters to support a known racist, Horace Greeley, for president of the United States.

To many of Sumner's closest Republican friends, his plan seemed horrific—a sign that he, in his old age, was so broken, sick, lonely, and resentful that he was losing his mind. They tried to talk some sense into him. William Lloyd Garrison bluntly told Sumner to swallow his pride and endorse Grant. "I know how extremely distasteful he is to you for various reasons," Garrison acknowledged. But this was "no time for the indulgence of personal dislikes." While Sumner responded kindly to Garrison, he grew indignant at others who questioned his motives. "I know the integrity of my conduct and the motives of my life. Never were they more clear or absolutely blameless than now," he insisted to Edward Pierce. "I utterly deny that I am controlled by personal motives," he swore to someone else. "Possibly my own personal experience has enabled me to see the absolute unfitness of Grant in a clearer light than [I] should otherwise have seen it."

Samuel Howe feared that Sumner was becoming delusional. Decades earlier, he had told his best friend that if he ever lost faith in him, it "would indeed shiver, for a time, my faith in God." Howe had now lost faith. "I have been slowly & painfully led to the sad conclusion that Charles Sumner has become morally insane," he wrote. "The great moral influence over the public which he has gained by a noble & brilliant career, he is now wielding to gratify personal hate & envy." Howe made a prayer: "God help him; for he knows not what he does."[2]

* * *

ON MAY 31, 1872, just one week before the Republican National Convention, Sumner delivered his most stinging remarks against President Grant to date. While Grant had no challenger and was almost certain to be renominated, Sumner held out hope that his speech might induce Republicans to pick someone else. "Any thing else," he kept telling his friend George William Curtis, the editor of *Harper's Weekly*. "Any other candidacy I can support, and it would save the party and the country."[3]

In his speech "Republicanism vs. Grantism," Sumner accused Grant of turning a party that was "dedicated to Human Rights and to the guardianship of the African Race" into "the instrument of one man and his personal will." Charging Grant with breaking international and constitutional law in pursuing Dominican annexation, he said that Grant should be impeached. He also called the president a criminal, accusing him of corruption and nepotism. And he declared that no president was above the law, arguing that everyone must be "a foremost servant of the law, bound to obey its slightest mandate."

Sumner's speech had some strong points. But overall, it was a meandering, factually weak screed that indulged in bizarre digressions, such as a three-thousand-word history lesson on how nepotism had been practiced by the Holy See. Even worse, Sumner's speech dwelled on the argument that a "successful soldier is rarely changed to a successful civilian." He blasted Grant for being a military man, as if patriotic Americans would consider that a downside. And, as usual, he gave no credit to Grant for winning the Civil War. After his three-hour tirade, Sumner exultantly told Henry Wilson that "there will not be 3 states to vote for Grant." He seemed to have forgotten that Wilson, Sumner's lifelong political ally, supported Grant.

Sure enough, on June 5, the Republican convention nominated Grant. Surprisingly, delegates also selected Wilson as Grant's running mate. Because Wilson was a devoted Radical and fellow Massachusetts senator, Republicans thought he could counteract Sumner's influence among New Englanders, abolitionists, and Black Americans. Eager to be vice president, Wilson accepted. On top of this, Republicans welcomed Joshua Smith, Sumner's closest Black friend, as a delegate to the convention. Smith was also permitted to run on the Republican ticket for a State House seat in Cambridge, Massachusetts. Once again, Republicans had isolated Sumner from his friends.[4]

Sumner was heartbroken that so many of his friends were siding with Grant. He met with Curtis, the *Harper's Weekly* editor, to ask him if he would join him in the Liberal Party. For years, Curtis had dined at Sumner's house nearly daily, benefiting from his hospitality and using him to get media scoops. A leading advocate of civil service reform who criticized the White House for several corruption scandals, Curtis seemed to be a natural ally of the Liberals. But Curtis told Sumner he would stick with Grant and the Republicans. With his eyes filled with tears, Sumner charged Curtis with betrayal. "When Brooks struck me down, Douglas stood by. Now when Grant strikes, you stand by."

Curtis feared that Sumner was going to sacrifice Black Americans to satisfy his own personal grudge against Grant. He tried to get Sumner to see this. "The slave of yesterday in Alabama, in Carolina, in Mississippi," Curtis asked, "will his heart leap with joy or droop dismayed when he knows that Charles Sumner has given his great name as a club to smite the party that gave him and his children their liberty?"

Sumner grew quiet. Lowering his big mane of gray hair, he stared helplessly at the ground. Curtis realized that Sumner was crying. In between his sobs, with his voice quivering, he replied, "I must do my duty."[5]

* * *

THE 1872 ELECTION between Greeley and Grant was extremely divisive for the Republican Party. Those who had become Liberals and voted for Greeley were branded as racists and traitors; those who had stuck with Grant were considered raw partisans willing to overlook past militarism and corruption. Many voters felt stuck between two bad choices. Either choice risked social exclusion, anger, and lasting animosity from friends on the other side. As Sumner put it, "it is not pleasant to differ from friends."

Months earlier, Sumner had sworn to the press that he would exit the Republican Party if Grant were renominated. He had repeatedly told the Senate that he would call on Black voters to punish Republicans if they failed to pass integration bills. The time had now come to execute his threat. Otherwise, if his threats were seen as empty, he feared Republicans would continue to take Black voters for granted. After all, back in 1868, Grant had won his election despite having likely lost the majority of white voters: he owed his victory to Black voters. If Republicans were not staying true to African Americans, they ought to pay a political price.

The problem was that Sumner's only anti-Grant choice was Horace Greeley, who was arguably a huckster with rotten policies and few principles. "I was, in the days of slavery, an enemy of slavery," Greeley said at one rally, referring to his prewar abolitionism. "That might have been a mistake." Pioneering some of the racist messaging that generations of politicians after him would use, Greeley told white voters that their hard-earned taxpayer dollars were being spent on welfare to lazy Black people, who wasted their money on "drink, tobacco, balls, gambling, and other dissipations." Even worse, Greeley tried to delegitimize Reconstruction by spreading false and exaggerated news about corruption among Black officeholders in southern state governments. He pledged that, if elected, he would terminate aid programs to freedpeople, remove Union troops protecting Black voters, and stop so-called "Negro Rule" in the South.[6]

On July 9, Democrats decided to join forces with Liberals by also nominating Greeley. While paying lip service to equal civil and political rights, the Democrats' convention president let it slip that he hoped Greeley would end "negro supremacy" in the South. "The Ku Klux Klan are only sleeping," a North Carolina Republican warned Sumner. If Greeley became president, he feared "the beginning of new Slavery."

The day after the Democrats nominated Greeley, Howard medical professor Alexander Augusta and other Black leaders wrote a public letter to Sumner asking him whether African Americans should vote for Grant or Greeley. While Sumner hemmed and hawed about how to reply, Black civic leaders started lobbying him.

Frederick Douglass told Sumner that if he picked Greeley, African Americans would lose their trust in him. "You cannot give up your relation to those who have looked to you as their political Redeemer. You cannot give up the almost dumb millions to whom you have been mind and voice during a quarter of a century."

Joshua Smith feared the opposite: that Black voters would trust Sumner and would thus be led by him to their graves. "You are the Jesus of the Negro Race—they will take up the cross and follow when ever you start and command—but be sure you do not land them in the Hands of the Enemy," he told Sumner. Smith freely admitted the Republican Party's weaknesses. "You protected [the Republican Party] when it was young and pure—you have a right to destroy it when it becomes old & evil," he noted. He just didn't want Sumner to destroy the party in *this* election, with *these* opponents. "I cannot trust the Democrats. I cannot trust Horace Greeley."[7]

At least one Black leader encouraged Sumner to punish Republicans: Robert Morris. As the second Black man in the nation to pass the bar exam, Morris had spent the past twenty years fighting for Black civil rights, including for school integration with Sumner in 1849. He was tired of waiting, tired of hoping Republicans would incrementally advance equal rights. And he was afraid it would take a very long time to get integration if Blacks continued to vote for a single party. "Ever since the negro came upon the political stage, the Republicans have never ceased to flatter him and make great promises. But there they have stopped," Morris declared. "The colored people everywhere are anxiously waiting for Senator Sumner to speak out."[8]

* * *

ON JULY 29, Sumner finally spoke out and said that Black voters should choose Greeley. "I cannot forget the civil rights bill," he declared. "President Grant, who could lobby so assiduously for his San Domingo scheme, full of wrong to the colored race, could do nothing for this beneficent measure," he said. "Grant, except as a soldier summoned by the terrible accident of war, never did anything against Slavery, nor has he at any time shown any sympathy with the colored race, but rather indifference, if not aversion."

Ignoring Greeley's awful rhetoric, Sumner offered a fanciful defense of Greeley, Liberals, and Democrats. Greeley "is a person of large heart and large understanding, trained to the support of human rights," he claimed. The Liberals stood for reconciliation, which should be accepted by all. And Democrats—an explicitly racist party just four years ago—had converted into a party of equal rights, according to Sumner. As one Republican paper put it, "Mr. Sumner's faith in Horace and the Democracy would be sublime, if it was not ridiculous."[9]

Published on the front page of Greeley's *New York Tribune*, along with at least five hundred thousand printed copies in Liberal campaign pamphlets, Sumner's letter stirred panic among Republicans.[10] They hoped to convince Black voters to ignore him and stick with the party. "The colored men of this country are not as a class enlightened; but they have wonderful instincts," House Speaker James Blaine wrote in an open letter to Sumner. "When they read your letter, they will know that at a great crisis in their fate you deserted them." Some Black leaders went farther: "Colored citizens . . . ought to be branded as traitors to their race, should they follow Sumner's advice and vote for Horace Greeley," declared Robert Harlan, whose white half brother later served on the Supreme Court.[11]

Republicans nationwide sent Sumner angry notes for his betrayal. "What evil spirit has possessed thee? Friend Wendell Phillips truly says . . . that thee 'has made the greatest mistake in thy life,'" said a Philadelphia abolitionist. "The alliance you have made, with the haters and persecutors of our race, has struck the colored population of this city with astonishment," said a Black man from New York. "I never had anything in my life to annoy me so much as the possibility of my having to be placed in an attitude of hostility to you, the best friend I ever had," wrote Edwin Belcher from Georgia. Robert Morris, for his part, told Sumner that he endorsed his letter "entirely."

Sumner was undeterred. In early August, he spoke to an audience of African Americans that held a serenade in front of his house. He warned these Black voters not to stick to a single party. "Never vote for any man who is not true to you," he advised. "Make allegiance to you the measure of your support. So doing, all parties will seek your vote."[12]

* * *

WHEN SUMNER RETURNED to Boston in mid-August, he hoped to campaign for Horace Greeley. But his health had been terrible. Perpetually exhausted, short of breath, barely able to climb a staircase or walk a quarter mile, Sumner consulted Samuel Howe. A doctor by training, Howe checked his pulse and found it weak and irregular. He and another physician, both Republicans, warned Sumner against participating in the Liberal campaign because the stress might compromise his frail health. After he was hit by another angina pectoris attack while staying with Longfellow, Sumner uncharacteristically agreed to suspend political work.[13]

Sumner probably didn't need much convincing to avoid the campaign. His favored candidate now openly embraced white supremacy, inviting an ex–Confederate general (and Klansman) to come to the North to campaign for him on behalf of the white "superior race." Naturally, the press ridiculed Sumner for asking Black voters to support Greeley. In August, the *Harper's Weekly* cartoonist Thomas Nast depicted Sumner helping Greeley send a Black man to the Ku Klux Klan to be lynched. Nast drew a card in the cartoon Sumner's pocket that said, "I AM AGAINST THE POLICY OF HATE, EXCEPT TO BEAT GRANT."[14]

To escape the campaign and improve his health, Sumner decided to go to Europe. Before leaving, he wrote a speech that emphasized Greeley's prewar abolitionism. He asked his Liberal friend Frank Bird to publish it in the papers on the day of his departure. Then he asked Joshua Smith, Edward Pierce, and George Hillard to help him go to Europe as discreetly as possible. He didn't want it known that he was leaving during an ugly high-stakes election he had partly instigated—in other words, he didn't want to look like a coward.[15]

On September 3, 1872, Smith drove Sumner in his carriage to a quiet spot in Boston Harbor. There, Pierce, Hillard, and others dropped Sumner in a service boat that took him out to the *Malta*, an undocked ship already in the water. After Smith handed him a bouquet of flowers and his ticket, which was under a fake name, Sumner boarded the ship from the service boat. For ten days in the Atlantic, he felt some peace.

The peace didn't last when he made it to shore and found an article in the London *Times* that said he was running for governor of Massachusetts. Without Sumner's consent, Bird, his informal political manager, had told Bay State Liberals and Democrats to nominate him. He hoped Sumner's name on the ticket would increase turnout on their side, leading to more seats in the state legislature. Expecting Sumner to lose the governor's race, Bird figured Sumner wouldn't have to worry about actually becoming governor.

Sumner was livid. The campaign manager he had trusted for decades had decided to make him look like a self-seeking opportunist. After sending a cordial note to party officials declining the nomination, Sumner sent angry, rageful letters to Bird. "I came abroad for rest & repose, & you put me in a position, which makes these impossible," he accused Bird, charging him with "total disregard of my feelings & sentiments." Saying that "few things in my political life have troubled me more," Sumner said it cost him "a night without sleep."[16]

Upon landing, Sumner may also have discovered that a close friend—it is not clear who—had leaked his European itinerary to the Republican press only hours after his secret departure. The friend's leak enabled Republicans to mock Sumner for running away like a coward. "Gone to Europe—Charles Sumner, in search of *his* lost cause," jeered one Republican paper. "The belief generally is that he has deserted a politically sinking ship," another paper said. "I feel grateful to his physician for sending him over the ocean," Republican senator Matthew Carpenter snorted. "I pray God that its cool breezes may allay the 'fever of his brain.'"

Sumner was now in the political wilderness, with reasons to feel betrayed by both Liberals and Republicans. "He stands on a bridge," Francis Lieber said of him, "and has set fire to both ends."[17]

* * *

IN LONDON, SUMNER had dinner with the London correspondent of Greeley's *Tribune*, the evolutionist Herbert Spencer, and the American diplomat John Bigelow. "I did not discuss the presidential question with him, that being as I supposed what he left his country mainly to avoid discussing," Bigelow said. Without even discussing politics, Sumner came across as self-absorbed and quite sick. Bigelow said "his illness has not improved his manners, but rather brought out his worst points. He is more than ever the center of the system in which he lives. He did not ask a question which indicated the least interest in any mortal or thing but himself."

To his credit, Sumner knew he was ill. Just a week after reaching England, he ventured to Paris in the hope of seeing his old doctor Charles Brown-Séquard. A quixotic physician who loved trying new experiments, Brown-Séquard had treated Sumner in 1858 after the caning. Opting for an ancient Chinese technique, he had put pieces of fungi or cottonwood on Sumner's bare back and lit them on fire. Sumner had screamed in agony, but Brown-Séquard told him to forgo painkillers and undergo the treatment seven times. Soon after, Sumner faced his first angina pectoris attack. Ever since, he had been suffering from heart issues.

None of Sumner's medical friends had liked the experiment, but Sumner believed Brown-Séquard was the best doctor he ever had. He took to heart an aphorism that the doctor had once told him: "The greater is the pain you have suffered . . . the greater also is your chance of being cured." In coming to France, he seemed to have hoped Brown-Séquard could cook up a new painful experiment to fix his ailing heart. But just by chance, Brown-Séquard had left for a trip to America only days before Sumner came to Paris to see him. "We passed each other on the ocean," Sumner said bitterly.[18]

Dismayed, Sumner spent his month in Paris ransacking bookshops and art galleries, loading up on books and art he couldn't afford. Piling on debt, as if to distract himself from his woes, he also vigilantly avoided reading American newspapers, believing they might stress him out. This may have worked well at first, but then he learned that one of his best friends, Francis Lieber, had died. "I have learned the great grief you have been called to bear—which is to me a grief also," he wrote to Lieber's widow. Heartbroken, Sumner looked for solace in the Parisian gardens. But even short walks left him out of breath and exhausted. "The garden of the Tuileries looked once very short compared with now," he wrote mournfully to Longfellow.[19]

Sumner couldn't find quiet anywhere in Paris. Wherever he went, to his surprise, he was recognized. On his arrival in France, the customs officers had grown excited at meeting the great American abolitionist and eagerly let him pass without checking his bags. When he dined with the father-in-law of an old friend, the man used Sumner as an excuse to invite two French ministers to come to his house, who were all eager to meet him. Sure enough, French president Adolphe Thiers soon learned about Sumner's presence and invited him to dine at the Élysée Palace.

Soon after, the Queen of Holland discovered that Sumner was in Europe and asked to see him. But as it happened, she left for England a few hours before Sumner's arrival in Holland. So, instead, Sumner spent a few days with the former ambassador John Motley, who had chosen to live in Holland after being fired by Grant. The two men commiserated about the tragedies that had befallen their careers and the Republican Party. After a few days, Sumner went to Belgium before returning to England, where Motley later came and introduced him to the queen.[20]

Sumner was excited to return to a country he loved. For thirteen years—ever since 1859—he had wanted to come back to England, but the Civil War and Reconstruction had occupied him so much that he never found the time. No longer in power in the Senate, Sumner finally had some free time. But upon arrival, it hit him that most of his British friends were already dead. People that he had sorely missed and hoped to see again—like Charles Dickens, the Duchess of Sutherland, and Lord Macaulay—had passed years ago. "Constantly I think of the dead whom I have known and honored here," he wrote sadly. "I feel like one who has no longer available funds in [the] bank against which to draw."[21]

* * *

BEFORE SUMNER HAD embarked for Europe, he had promised himself he would return by November. When the Black lawyer Augustus Straker told him not to be in such a rush, Sumner said he had to come back to reintroduce the Civil Rights Bill at the start of the December congressional session. Straker explained that the Civil Rights Bill could wait until Sumner was healthy. African Americans needed him alive. "When a man cannot do his duty to his fellow-man, and thus to his God," Sumner replied, "it were well that he die."[22]

While in Europe, though, Sumner felt increasingly hesitant about going back to reintroduce the Civil Rights Bill. He recognized that he was clearly unwell and that returning to the muck of Washington politics would aggravate his heart problems. "The thought of the return voyage in November haunts me," he confessed to Edward Pierce. In Europe, while avoiding American news, he felt so much healthier.

Even worse for Sumner, President Grant was resoundingly reelected in the presidential election. By co-opting Liberal issues like amnesty and softening his messaging on Reconstruction, Grant had persuaded white voters to stick with his party. Meanwhile, few Black voters followed Sumner's advice to turn on the Republicans. And Greeley's race baiting was too little to persuade many Democrats who disliked his prewar abolitionism, but too much for many principled Liberals motivated by liberal economics. As luck would have it, Greeley died of a heart attack after losing the election. When Sumner came home, as one editorial put it, he would have to face "the ridiculosity of his own connection with the defunct Greeley-Democratic Confederacy."[23]

Until midnight, Sumner vented to English statesman John Bright about how terrible Grant and the Republicans had become. "There was a great gentleness in all he said, with a sadness and a melancholy," Bright recalled. Bright was left with the impression that Sumner believed "himself seriously ill, and that his life of work was nearly ended." Staying at Bright's house, Sumner confessed the next morning that he barely slept due to his heart pain. When Bright's puppy ran up to him to play, Sumner ignored the little dog. Reflecting on his long, difficult life, he confessed sadly, to Bright's wife, that he "had never had time to play with dogs."[24]

Sumner admitted how much he dreaded going home to William Story, a Rome-based artist who was visiting London at the time. Back in the 1840s, Story had worked as a legal apprentice to Sumner. His father, Judge Joseph Story, had asked Sumner to train his son to become a great lawyer. But without the judge's knowledge, Sumner kindled William's childhood love for the arts. He encouraged him to abandon his legal career, move to Europe, and become a sculptor. When William did so, Sumner was thrilled, delighted that he was "enjoying fresh breezes, and the beautiful lake, with books and pencil, with pleasant friends." Sumner always advised William to "avoid public life." He wanted him to be happy— something *he* never was. "How often I think with envy of you," Sumner once said. "No such days for me."

William was startled to see Sumner, whom he considered an older brother, so depressed. It reminded him of Sumner's condition after the caning. He invited Sumner to stay with him in Rome for a while, as he had done after the caning. Sumner responded that he "should like nothing better." He was tempted to briefly leave behind "the toils of politics and the anxieties of public life," as William advised. When William suggested that an extended stay in Europe would strengthen Sumner's heart and prolong his life, Sumner agreed that he was probably right. But Sumner was uncertain about whether to take up William's offer.

Ultimately, he had made a promise to himself to return to the United States. "It is useless; I must go. My duty requires it," he told William. William pleaded with him to stay, but Sumner did not budge. "I cannot; I ought not; tempt me no further," he ordered. Soon thereafter, William had his last breakfast with Sumner before he left. He never forgot the expression on Sumner's face when he said goodbye:

"He tried to smile, but the tears were in his eyes."[25]

* * *

SUMNER'S RETURN VOYAGE began well. He booked his return through the White Star Line, a British shipping company that operated many cross-Atlantic vessels (including, some years later, the RMS *Titanic*). When the company learned that one of the world's most distinguished statesmen was to be on board, it offered him free passage, but he politely declined and paid for a first-class ticket on the *Baltic*, a recently built ocean liner. Typically prone to seasickness, he was astonished at how easily the new iron ship managed the waters: "I was quite in a fever of joy."

The joy didn't last long. Five days into the journey, a severe gale began to blow against the *Baltic*. Sumner immediately took to his bed. Getting queasy and growing nervous, he struggled to hold himself together as the ship rocked back and forth. He "could hear the hammering of the heavy waves" upon the ship as it was "pounded without mercy."

When ocean water began gushing through the air vents in his luxury suite, Sumner started to panic. He rushed out of his room to find a new one and discovered that other parts of the ship were also flooding. An officer grabbed him and, given Sumner's status, took him down a distant recess in the ship to put him in a safer room while the ship braved the storm.

In this small, dark room, as the steamship swayed with increasing velocity, Sumner clung to his bed. For more than twenty-four hours, he did not dare leave his bed even once. His heart must have been racing: He had lost two brothers, Horace and Albert, to shipwrecks while they were crossing from Europe to the United States. Albert's whole family had been killed. For a man who supposedly knew no fear, Sumner was petrified. He wasn't ready to die.

When the waves slightly let up the next day, he finally left his room to find some lunch. That was when he and other passengers learned that a sinking boat had been spotted on the horizon. Rushing to the deck, Sumner saw in the distance a huddle of men holding onto the rigging of a boat almost entirely submerged.

Even though the gale was still strong, the *Baltic*'s captain directed his ship toward the wreck. Sumner watched anxiously as volunteers—some sailors, some passengers—jumped into lifeboats and attempted rescues. The waters were so tempestuous that one lifeboat nearly capsized. Some men were plunged into the ocean, as sailors on deck threw them ropes. Ultimately, everybody was saved. "Had it not been for them and Divine providence," recalled a sailor rescued from the sinking boat, "we all would have met a watery grave."

Sumner was emotionally moved by what he saw: tenacity, selflessness, and courage in the face of death, all the things that had been on his mind in recent days. When the eighty first-class passengers gathered for dinner that night, Sumner gave a speech. He proclaimed the volunteers heroes and proposed a collection of money in gratitude to the rescuers and the shipwreck's survivors. Sumner ended up chairing a committee of passengers that, in a few hours, raised an astounding £84—roughly $13,000 today.

The next day, Sumner brought together the committee. For three or four hours, the senator led a discussion with these strangers on how to disburse the money. They settled on £2 to each sailor and £4 to each passenger who volunteered for the rescue operation, along with £1 to each shipwreck victim. Sumner then convened everybody on the *Baltic* for an all-ship meeting, presented his committee's plan, and put it up for a vote of all the passengers. The plan passed unanimously, and the funds were disbursed accordingly. Sumner was so proud of what they did together. "We conducted the business in true Congressional style," he fondly remembered.[26]

* * *

SUMNER FELT REFRESHED when the *Baltic* arrived in New York Harbor. His near-death experience and the sight of sheer heroism seemed to give him new resolve on how to conduct the remainder of his life.

He first went to Dr. Brown-Séquard, who just happened to be in New York, and explained his health issues. He had his heart problems: angina attacks and shortness of breath. But he also confided in Brown-Séquard about something he shared with almost no one: he was struggling to hold his bladder. This kept him perpetually sleep deprived, as he had to get up so often to urinate.

This time, Brown-Séquard advised pain*killers*, not pain. Though he never let it be known to Sumner, Brown-Séquard seemed to have felt guilty about burning his patient's bare back in 1858. While he would always insist that his experiment worked, he confessed after Sumner's death that he never attempted the treatment on any other patient, knowing that Sumner had "passed through that terrible suffering, the greatest that I have ever inflicted upon any being, man or animal."

Brown-Séquard told Sumner that instead of resorting to "more powerful remedies" like "fire," he would first attempt "more rational treatments." Sticking to the common medical wisdom of the time, he advised Sumner to take bromide, morphine, atropine, and other drugs to ease the heart pain and get more sleep without having to urinate. He also sternly advised him to avoid stress as much as possible, and as if to deny that his fire treatment ever had something to do with his heart issues, he told Sumner with complete confidence that the caning had damaged his spine, which somehow had caused his angina. To his dying day, Sumner blamed "the network of nerves indirectly connecting the spinal cord with the heart," insisting he did not have heart disease.[27]

Sumner promised to follow the pain regimen, rather than arguing with Brown-Séquard to request another outlandish treatment. He was determined to get healthy, saying shortly after that "health itself is valuable only as it enables us to perform the duties of life." He also took solace in the belief that the caning had caused his heart problems, for that meant his challenges had a higher meaning. Dutifully, he arranged for a young Washington physician, Dr. Joseph Tabor Johnson, the brother of one of his former secretaries, to administer the regimen and keep Brown-Séquard in touch. "I take medicine enough to cure a family," Sumner later joked. "Poison by phial, poison by pill, poison by powder and poison by injection."[28]

After seeing Brown-Séquard, Sumner received a New York *Sun* reporter at his hotel room. Only hours after finishing a long, tumultuous journey, he was already dressed in "a black coat and vest, and a pair of coarse, checkered English pants." The *Sun* reporter marveled at this "powerfully built man with a massive head, and eyes which seemed to pierce whatever they rested upon." As he half reclined on his hotel suite sofa, "he was the very picture of an American nobleman."

Rising from the sofa, Sumner shook the *Sun* correspondent's hand. "I am happy to see you," he said. He beckoned the reporter to sit down and informed him that he wouldn't discuss Grant's reelection. When the reporter protested, Sumner "dismissed the suggestion with a wave of the hand." Stretching himself on the sofa, he said he wished to discuss his ocean journey instead. Relying on what may have been a photographic memory, Sumner then recounted in exceptional detail what had taken place. "Mr. Sumner tells a story as he makes a speech in Congress," the *Sun* relayed. "He is fertile in illustration, and talks in a slow, deliberate style."

After finishing his story, Sumner stood up and signaled that the interview was over. The reporter asked him if he planned to go to Boston next. "Oh, no," Sumner replied, smiling. "To Washington."[29]

* * *

ON DECEMBER 2, 1872, just days after Sumner returned to Washington, a correspondent of the *New York Herald* visited his house for an interview. Sumner was chatting with a handful of members of Congress who were paying him a social visit to see how he was doing after his European trip. While the reporter sat there, Sumner regaled his guests with stories of the

European celebrities he had met—the French president Adolphe Thiers, the Queen of Holland, and the renowned English statesman John Bright, among others. But whenever anyone brought up some issue in American politics, he evaded the topic.

After the members of Congress left, the *Herald* reporter interviewed Sumner. Over and over, Sumner avoided discussing the latest presidential election, explaining that he planned to "have only sentiments of moderation toward all." He shared that he had recently consulted Dr. Brown-Séquard, who warned him of the dangers to his heart if he engaged in any "excessive labor." Accordingly, Sumner said, "I do not propose to do any more at the Capitol than I can avoid without any neglect of duty." Believing his health was bad and time was running out, he had only three goals in mind for the session. First, he planned to reintroduce his Civil Rights Bill, having already met a group of Black Washingtonians to discuss the measure.[30]

Then Sumner discussed two other priorities that reflected his anxieties over the future of American democracy, having dealt with two presidents (Johnson and Grant) who he thought had dangerously acted like kings. Ever since February 1867, Sumner had tried to get the Senate to vote on two constitutional amendments to address what he called "the One Man Power," whereby a single man in the White House acts as a threat to the republic. But he never had the chance to prioritize them. Now feeling like his time was running out, he told the *Herald* that he was committed to getting the Senate to vote on these amendments.[31]

Sumner's first amendment would limit the presidency to a single term. At the time, the Constitution had no formal term limits for presidents (the Twenty-Second Amendment, ratified in 1951, would later set it at two). Despite this, during a long span of Sumner's adult years, from the age of thirty to fifty (1841 to 1861), no sitting president had run for reelection. It was widely considered bad form to run for reelection. It was even worse for presidents to *expect* their parties to renominate them. In Sumner's view, President Grant had governed so badly in part because he was so focused on enforcing party discipline to win renomination and reelection.[32]

Sumner also feared that the desire to cling to power increased over time. Quoting President Andrew Jackson, he warned that "the agent most likely to contravene this design of the Constitution is the Chief Magistrate." To limit a president's temptation to become a dictator over time, Jackson had argued that the presidency should be reduced to a single term. (Ironically, as if to prove his point, he served two.) Even Jackson's sworn enemy Henry Clay endorsed the idea. But their proposed amendment never came to fruition—and so, Sumner pitched it again.

Sumner had written his second amendment proposal in 1867, modeling it on an 1866 proposal from his friend the former congressman James Ashley. It seemed presciently designed to address the problems he had struggled with in the recent presidential election between Grant and Greeley.

He called for a national popular vote to choose the president. At the time, as Sumner explained, a political party chose its nominee at a convention prone to "intrigue." That nominee then became "the exclusive representative of a political party," such that party dissenters were reduced "to conformity." The nominees then targeted their campaigns in states with large numbers of delegates who were sent to the Electoral College, which picked the president. That denied "minorities in distant States an opportunity of being heard." All in all, Sumner believed that this convoluted system of choosing presidents was "highly artificial . . . cumbersome . . . radically defective, and unrepublican."[33]

Sumner proposed that, every four years, Americans should go to the polls to vote for their candidate under rules that Congress prescribed. States and political parties would play almost no role. A candidate who earned a majority of the votes would become president. But if no candidate earned a majority, there would be a runoff election a few months later—among the leading three.

In Sumner's lifetime, some presidential elections had several major candidates. Abraham Lincoln, for example, was one of four major candidates in 1860. But most elections had only two genuine choices. This troubled Sumner, who struggled with the idea of being forced to choose, especially in the election between Grant and Greeley. "This is a painful experience," he had confessed to poet John Whittier when deciding whom to endorse. "But we are not choosers in this world. Certainly, I did not choose this."[34]

Over the course of his career, Sumner had been part of three different political parties: the Free Soilers, the Republicans, and the Liberals. All three parties had begun as challengers to prevailing two-party systems that left voters with no alternatives. In drafting his amendment, Sumner was offering a pathway for future movements to unsettle prevailing partisan gridlock, by proposing that Americans would always get to choose from among three options in a presidential race, so long as no option had majority support.

* * *

AS SUMNER EAGERLY explained his hopes for more constitutional change, and his plan to get the Civil Rights Bill passed, the *New York Herald* reporter pressed him on how any of his aspirations were realistic. After all, he was no longer living in the climate of Radicalism that had defined the mid-1860s, when he first developed these ideas. There was no more appetite for constitutional transformation or for civil rights.

Sumner was also no longer the leading figure of the Senate. Removed from his committees, he had been declared an enemy by the White House. Then he had abandoned the Republican Party and endorsed a losing candidate. Despite being the longest-serving member in the Senate, he was arguably its loneliest.

"I have only sentiments of moderation toward all," he claimed, as if he never partook in any vicious fights this year. Repeatedly, he declined to comment on the recent election. From here on out, he seemed to be saying, he wanted to play nice. "On the whole," the *New York Herald* correspondent concluded, "his attitude is that of attention, ready to strike back if assailed, but not anxious to provoke a contest."

CHAPTER 29

I HAVE A TOOTHACHE
IN MY HEART

ON THE VERY NIGHT OF HIS DREAMY INTERVIEW WITH THE *NEW York Herald*, Charles Sumner suffered a violent episode of angina, proving that his short trip to Europe didn't give him the recovery he sought. He tried to ignore his chest pain and dragged himself into the Senate Chamber for the next few days, desperate not to let heartache prevent him from advocating for the Civil Rights Bill and for Electoral College reforms. But then he became embroiled in more political controversy at the very moment he was hoping to avoid it.

On December 12, 1872, a small band of pro-Grant Republican state lawmakers raised hell in the Massachusetts State House over an obscure Sumner bill that would have prohibited the military from wearing regimental colors celebrating Union victories in Civil War battles. The bill, which Sumner had first pitched in 1862, reflected his long-held belief that civilized militaries shouldn't enthusiastically commemorate victories over "fellow citizens," no matter how just those civil wars were. It was an innocuous bill—a bill so low on Sumner's priority list that he didn't even mention it to the *New York Herald*.

These lawmakers jumped at the opportunity to paint Sumner as a traitorous anti-veteran senator. They knew his reelection was only two years away; it was the perfect moment to damage his reputation and make it easier for a Republican challenger to defeat him. They called on the state legislature to censure Sumner for having insulted the "loyal soldiery." While technically symbolic, a censure is a formal reprimand and one of the strongest expressions of disapproval a legislative body can make.[1]

Here was a chance to deal Sumner a finishing blow, to finally vanquish the great statesman for being an apostate to the Republican Party. "If Mr. Sumner had any object," Representative George Hoyt declared, "it was to secure the oblivion of the deeds and heroism of the Union soldiers." Sumner was against "the soldier and his widow and orphans," accused Representative Ezra Winslow. Representative Thomas Porter denounced Sumner's record as a pacifist prior to the Civil War, charging him with "undermining and opposing the military ever since." He said it was high time to punish Sumner for the crime of having "married Mr. Greeley and attacking the 'great figger-head' of the military organization, Gen. Grant."

Democrats, Liberals, and even several Republicans in the State House urged caution. While not wishing to defend Sumner's bill and appear anti-veteran, they suggested that Sumner at least be given a chance to explain himself. Representative Charles Thompson pointed to Sumner's health, warning that a censure might add to his stress. Those who demanded a censure didn't care about any of that: "Mr. Sumner has been feeding a kind of meat that has made a Caesar of him," Representative Winslow sneered. He avowed that he would vote for the censure even if he "knew it would bring Charles Sumner to a premature grave."[2]

* * *

ON DECEMBER 18, 1872, the Massachusetts House of Representatives narrowly voted to censure Sumner after a tie-breaking vote by Speaker John Sanford. Two days later, the Senate censured him, too. In so doing, both chambers had trampled many norms and broken several proce-dural rules. For one, the censure was rushed through the final days of a lame-duck session before a new legislature convened in January. For another, the House voted on the censure during dinnertime, while many lawmakers were absent from their seats. During the rush to get it passed, the House presiding officer also failed to notice that the censure wasn't supported by a majority of the Committee of Federal Relations, which had reported it. Instead, there was a tie within the committee, which meant the censure should never have received a floor vote according to House rules.[3]

Lawmakers paid the price for their overconfidence. Across Massa-chusetts, voters expressed outrage at the censure and reacted with an outpouring of love for Sumner. Nearly overnight, John Whittier gath-ered five thousand signatures demanding that the State House walk back the censure. While elected officials were still smarting over Sumner's endorsement of Greeley, ordinary Bay Staters had already forgotten about it. After all, Sumner was at the time the longest-serving senator in

Massachusetts history, an abolitionist hero, and certainly not worthy of censure by an irregular, possibly unlawful process.

After the next legislative session began, the Committee of Federal Relations convened public hearings in March 1873 to discuss the matter. Both the current and former governors showed up to testify. "The state owes it to her history to take back what she has said in a hasty, unguarded manner," declared Governor William Washburn. Former governor William Claflin said the censure clearly "did not express the feelings of the people of the State," regardless of how people felt about Sumner's underlying bill.

The abolitionist minister James Freeman Clarke, now in his mid-sixties, testified and charged lawmakers with being ungrateful. These lawmakers, many of whom were young, did not remember the days when Sumner was one of the most hated men in Boston, when he gave up his legal career to advocate for abolition and civil rights. In Reverend Clarke's view, these lawmakers were opportunistic and ignorant men who were young children "playing marbles" when Sumner "was fighting their battles" for the sake of God.

Reverend Clarke grew emotional as he thought about how besmirched Sumner's reputation had become among elected Republicans. "He is the Abdiel of our day," Clarke swore. He was referring to Abdiel in Milton's *Paradise Lost*, a character whose Hebrew name meant "servant of God." In the story, Abdiel was one of Satan's rebel angels who loved God too much to stay silent about Satan's evil. Denouncing Satan in front of all the rebels, Abdiel found himself expelled from his community and lost all the power that Satan had promised him. He had sacrificed everything to stand up for God. God honored Abdiel for his courage, sacrifice, and conviction, and his story was taught to Adam and Eve as a lesson for humankind.

Sitting in the audience, Julia Ward Howe listened uneasily as Reverend Clarke compared Sumner to one of God's beloved angels. Nearly two decades earlier, after Sumner's caning, Julia wrote a poem describing Sumner as a friend of heaven who wore "the crown of the martyr" and belonged in "the record of heroes." But she had seen too much of his petulance, need for praise, questionable political instincts, and clinginess to her husband Samuel to still think he was God's chosen servant. To her, Sumner was just an ordinary person, like anyone else. "He never seemed to me exactly a great man," she later wrote in her diary.

Having signed the petition to rescind the censure, Julia had come to watch the first day of hearings out of curiosity. She was so troubled by Reverend Clarke's "idolatrous man worship" that she contemplated switching sides to speak against Sumner. She walked up to William Lloyd Garrison, who had also come to watch, and discovered that Garrison was thinking about criticizing Sumner, too. For months, Garrison had seethed over Sumner's endorsement of Greeley and the fact that people still revered Sumner. "To make any man oracular in utterance, or infallible in judgment," Garrison thought, "is a sure symptom of popular degeneracy."

Garrison and Julia Howe testified the next day. Both claimed to be neutral about the censure, but they devoted their remarks to chastising Sumner. Garrison's words were especially biting; he claimed that Sumner had never possessed "moral courage" and was too "sensitive" to be a true reformer. When Garrison was done, two Black lawmakers called him out. State representative John J. Smith, a former barbershop owner who used to cut Sumner's hair, angrily confronted Garrison. And state representative Joshua Smith, one of Sumner's closest friends, nearly shouted at him, declaring that "the colored people . . . are for Mr. Sumner."

Garrison stood back up, visibly shaken and offended that Smith would challenge him, the nation's foremost white abolitionist. He declared that "it was not true that the colored people were with Mr Sumner," insisting that "they were with him" instead.[4]

* * *

GIVEN THE RAUCOUS hearing, state lawmakers decided to leave the subject alone and let the censure stay on the books for the time being. Meanwhile, newspaper editorialists lamented how contentious and awful the hearing had become. One editorial writer reflected on Garrison's legacy and noted that he, like Sumner, was now an old man. Garrison seemed to be driven by a "feeling of rivalry" on whom history would judge as having been more influential to slavery's abolition: him or Sumner. "It has always seemed to me stupid business, this apportioning out of the relative measure of fame to the various prominent abolitionists, now living," the writer noted. And yet, this was exactly what some abolitionists were doing.[5]

Sumner was heartbroken to read the censure debates that were ongoing in Boston, which he followed from his home in Washington. Tired, sick, and resigned, he didn't want to fight anyone anymore. "I am now, where I have always been, in the breach," he said with a sigh. He felt exhausted at being enmeshed in constant conflict, especially with friends. He was baffled at how young people in his beloved home state of Massachusetts could forget everything he had done during the Civil War, which had ended less than ten years before. "I am at a loss how after all my work through the war . . . any body can charge me with insulting the soldier," he wrote to a friend. "There seems to be a dementia against me," he confided in Henry Longfellow. As if he felt worse for *them* than for himself, he wrote, "I think that there are men who will regret their rage."[6]

Sumner felt unappreciated, lonely, and like a failure. His health had again collapsed. "He was sensitive in his back, shoulders, and neck, so that he was uneasy in sitting," recalled Edward Pierce. Sumner walked with great difficulty, using a cane even to get around his house. He also had to get up regularly each night to urinate. Once a week or so, his heart would be squeezed again, causing searing pain in his chest and left arm, sometimes for several hours. Sumner told Longfellow he felt comfortable only when "sitting in an easy chair, wrapped in a dressing gown." He spent almost the entire spring at home, in his chair or on his bed.

In April, Sumner was heartened to receive a short, awkward visit from his estranged best friend, Samuel Howe. Despite still being mad with him, Howe couldn't bear the thought of Sumner being in such pain. While passing through Washington, he stopped by Sumner's house for what he seemed to have treated as a strictly medical visit. He looked at Sumner's medications, which Sumner fondly called "my poisons." Sumner especially craved the morphine injections he received at ten thirty each night, for they instantly halted his pain. The injection "works upon me like magic," Sumner said. "It is like a commander-in-chief who cries, 'halt.'"

A trained medical doctor, Howe had never trusted Dr. Brown-Séquard and hated that Sumner put all his faith in him. Already believing that Sumner had become delusional during the past election, Howe seemed to regard his friend's drug taking as another example of his descent into madness. He demanded that Sumner stop his pain medications immediately. Ten years older than Sumner, he had often adopted a fatherly tone with his best friend. For years, he had told him that his health would improve if he read less, exercised more, and traveled to a southern climate. But it was of no use. While Sumner appreciated Howe's visit, he ignored his advice, stuck to the painkillers, and kept to his bed.[7]

* * *

WHILE SUFFERING THROUGH the spring of 1873, Sumner spent any energy he could muster reviewing proofs from his copyeditor for *The Works of*

Charles Sumner, a compilation of his past works that he had begun some years earlier. While he lacked Garrison's sense of envy, he equally cared about his legacy and reflected on how he might be remembered after his death, given how controversial he had been during his life.

Sumner believed history would redeem him, Garrison, and other abolitionists who, over the course of their lives, had been reviled, condemned, assaulted, and persecuted. He considered himself to be an American hero, even if many Americans didn't know it yet. He was already a hero to Black America. "Your devotion to our cause has been the main cause of the nation's coldness toward you," Frederick Douglass had reassured him at one of his low moments in 1869. "The nation will cease to hate us, as it learns to love you."[8]

Despite being emotionally sensitive and hungry for praise, Sumner never shied away from following his conscience, no matter whom he offended in the process. To him, duty to his conscience was his duty to God and to man. Whenever that meant being scorned in life, he willingly suffered it. For he believed fervently that he would be redeemed by God and mankind after death. He was convinced this redemption would take place here, on earth, notwithstanding whatever he may have thought about the afterlife.

In one of the earliest speeches in the *Works*, Sumner explained this piece of his theological outlook. Speaking at Amherst College in 1847, four years before he entered the U.S. Senate, Sumner told the students that the heroes of the present age wouldn't be venerated in the future. At the time, Alexander the Great, Julius Caesar, and Cortés the Conquistador were glorious historical figures. Sumner predicted that humanity would one day condemn these "golden calves" and "*false gods*," for they were "grovelling, selfish, and inhuman in their aims, with little of love to God and less to man." For "they were not poor in spirit, or meek, or merciful, or pure in heart. They did not hunger and thirst after Justice. They were not peacemakers. They did not suffer persecution for Justice's sake."

Sumner believed that humanity would soon choose to honor a "new order of heroes and of great men." These great men would be people who embodied God's attributes. Two of His attributes were "Knowledge and Power." But intelligence and strength were not enough to earn theological and historical favor. One also needed to embody "Justice and Benevolence." In the Book of Exodus, Sumner noted, Moses asked the Lord, "show me thy Glory." The Lord replied, "I will make all my Goodness pass before thee." To Sumner, the verse proved that goodness was the ultimate source of true glory in the long run. He decided that "*no true and permanent Fame can be founded except in labors which promote the happiness of mankind.*"

Sumner seldom discussed his personal faith in his public or private writings. While he often quoted from two Bibles he kept by his bedside and had images of Jesus, Mary, and other biblical figures in his home, he rarely attended King's Chapel, a Unitarian church of which his mother had been a member. Raised a Unitarian by his parents, Sumner did not believe in the Trinity or the divinity of Jesus. Neither did he believe in miracles. The afterlife seems to have crossed his mind rarely, if ever. But he did believe in God, in the goodness of God, and in the duty to follow what he called "those two suns of Christian truth, love to God and love to man"—no matter how difficult, self-sacrificing, or painful it might be to follow that duty. He often reminded himself, quoting a favorite saying of his father, that "the duties of life are more than life."[9]

Around this time, while Sumner was sick and reflecting on his faith, duty, and legacy, Vice President Henry Wilson paid him a visit at his Washington home. A key architect of the antislavery movement, Wilson was also wondering whether America would turn him into a hero. At the time, he was writing *The History of the Rise and Fall of the Slave Power in America*, a three-volume saga on the antebellum era, the Civil War, and Reconstruction. He hoped his treatise would become the decisive history on these eras, so that his role would not be forgotten. Afraid of dying before finishing his work, he was writing as furiously as he could.

Wilson and Sumner conversed for a while. Given both their reflective states, it is safe to assume they discussed their long pasts, having spent nearly thirty years together fighting the Slave Power and now seeking racial justice. They also likely chatted about their health, for both men were keenly aware that they were approaching their ends. At the close of their chat, Sumner raised his finger and pointed at the door to his study. "If my *Works* were completed, and my civil-rights bill passed," he confessed, "no visitor could enter that door that would be more welcome than Death."[10]

* * *

BY MAY 1873, Sumner began to feel a bit better, and he made a conscious decision to pursue things he hoped would cheer him up. Every so often, he would venture outside for short walks. His neighbor, and father-in-law, Samuel Hooper, lent him a carriage, which Sumner drove to visit friends in Washington's northern suburbs. He also occasionally consulted a doctor who practiced cupping, an East Asian and Middle Eastern technique of using suction cups to pull the skin, with the aim of removing toxins from the blood.

Sumner was also pleased that his attorney finally settled his divorce with Alice. She had now been in Europe for five years, the legal period of separation required to pursue a divorce on the grounds of desertion. Alice was happy to get divorced, for she never wanted to see Sumner again. Sumner, for his part, never used her name, preferring to call her "that woman," and he never talked about his marriage. "I rejoice that you are free at last," Edward Pierce wrote him.

As the summer progressed, Sumner regained enough energy to spend nearly all hours of the day compiling, editing, and annotating his *Works*. When a friend tried to convince him to come stay with her family in Boston, he declined because he needed to be near his research materials. "That large airy room in the large house is most tempting," he wrote. "But you know not the size of the elephant you invite. Beyond his own natural proportions and ordinary trunk are other trunks larger still, with supplementary boxes packed with books, papers, and documents, various, vast, extensive; you have no idea of the mass."

In the fall, Sumner felt healthy enough to go to Boston, where he stayed in the homes of friends whose houses were big enough for his books and papers. He was surprised to discover that people in Boston society wanted to fawn over him now. Probably because he was so ill and because they felt bad about the censure, many Boston Brahmins invited Sumner to dinners and events. The irony wasn't lost on him that many of these same men had been neutral at best when he was waging his fight against slavery. Even now, these aristocrats who were treating the great abolitionist as a moral hero took no interest in his Civil Rights Bill.

Nevertheless, Sumner was easygoing with everyone in high society who wished to mingle with him. Every so often, he attended the Saturday Club, a literary society hosted by Ralph Waldo Emerson. He was finally accepted as a member of the Massachusetts Historical Society, which had been led for decades by the wealthy Robert Winthrop. Winthrop, a former Whig politician, held a lasting grudge against Sumner after losing the Senate race to him in 1851. Too tired to conflict with anyone anymore, Sumner was pleased to now be reacquainted with Winthrop, and he enjoyed the fellowship with other Brahmins.[11]

In late November, Sumner received an invitation from Reverend Clarke to visit his Unitarian church. He wasn't sure whether to go. On the one hand, he was grateful to the reverend for having defended him so passionately at the public hearing on his censure. On the other, he rarely went to church. In what was probably a spur-of-the-moment decision, Sumner hopped on a streetcar one evening and traveled from Cambridge to the South End of Boston. Stepping out of the car, he asked a stranger for directions to Reverend Clarke's Church of the Disciples. After entering the vestry unannounced, he began shaking hands with the worshipers, who were shocked to meet somebody so revered. They begged him to give some remarks to the congregation.

Sumner didn't know what to say until he spotted some youths in the audience. With a beaming smile, he spoke straight to the church youths, predicting that America would have a "magnificent future," far better than what he had lived through. "I wish I was born later," he confessed. When he finished speaking, an older lady walked up to him. In a gentle tone of reverence, she reminded Sumner that he didn't get to decide when he could be useful to society. "The Lord knew better than you did when you ought to have been born," she said. All the while, Reverend Clarke felt that there was some kind of spiritual presence in his church, for he thought Sumner was one of the sweetest characters he had ever known. Years later, Clarke told his congregants that when Sumner came, he was thinking to himself, "Old experience did attain, to something of prophetic strain."[12]

*　*　*

IN LATE NOVEMBER 1873, Sumner returned to Washington, feeling healthy enough to resume his Senate work and push for his Civil Rights Bill. During one of his first evenings back home, he was greeted by the sound of music and loud chatter from a crowd of happy Black churchgoers. These roughly four hundred men, women, and children had come to his front lawn to play him some songs, welcome him home, and thank him for his past work and his commitment to integration. They seemed to believe, as the nation's first Black congressman Joseph Rainey put it, that Sumner was "God's chosen advocate of freedom."

Sumner felt unworthy as he stood before the multitude of adoring Black churchgoers at his doorstep. "I am touched by this manifestation of regard and sympathy," Sumner admitted. "But allow me to say most sincerely that I cannot claim any special merit. I have acted always at the prompting of conscience, and could not have done otherwise." He credited his voters in the Bay State: "Had I at any time hesitated," he said, "I should have been rebuked . . . by the liberty-loving people of Massachusetts."[13]

Sumner's faith in predominantly white Massachusetts was misplaced. In the 1850s and '60s, abolitionism and radicalism were so fervent in the Bay State that some voters would have punished Sumner if he had failed to support human rights. By the 1870s, however, white voters had generally lost faith in Reconstruction. Advocating for integration was especially unpopular, but Sumner did it anyway, even though so many other white abolitionists had already decided that the work for racial justice had gone far enough.

Frederick Douglass recognized Sumner's moral majesty more than anyone. For his entire active life, Douglass had fought viciously with Sumner on various issues and strategies. He was so mad about Sumner's stance on Dominican annexation that he once reportedly called him the "worst foe that the colored race has on this continent." Despite this, Sumner was the only prominent Republican who wrote to Douglass regularly. Although he occasionally cut off correspondence with white friends during heated disagreements, he had never done so with any Black civic leader, including Douglass. While arguing fiercely over Grant's reelection, the two had stayed friends. According to one report, they dined weekly and were often seen walking arm in arm in the Senate Chamber.[14]

At the National Colored Convention in New Orleans in April of the previous year, Douglass had grown upset listening to delegates accuse Sumner of being a traitor to their race for exiting the Republican Party. No matter how harshly he disagreed with Sumner at times, he believed Sumner acted from a place of sincerity and complete devotion to their shared cause of advancing the rights of African Americans.

Douglass spoke at that convention, initially devoting his address to extolling Grant and endorsing him for reelection. But then he made a pivot: "There is now a man at Washington who represents the future and is a majority in himself . . . a man at whose feet Grant learns wisdom— Charles Sumner," Douglass said. "I know them both, and they are great men, but Sumner is as steady as the north star—he is no flickering light," Douglass confessed. "Not all the Grants in Christendom will rob him of his well-earned character." He ended his speech by invoking Psalm 137, swearing an oath in the Lord's name:

"May my right hand lose its cunning," Douglass pledged. "May my tongue cleave to the roof of my mouth, and may the day I was born grow dark and be cursed when I say one word that reflects on Charles Sumner."[15]

* * *

IN DECEMBER 1873, Frederick Douglass, George Downing, John Mercer Langston, and other Black civic leaders in Washington launched a new lobbying campaign to build support for Sumner's bill. To do so, they invited hundreds of Black leaders around the nation to attend the National Civil Rights Convention in the city. Dressed in elegant tuxedos and top hats, these 330 delegates from 29 states debated strategies for how to support Sumner, put pressure on Grant, and lobby members of Congress to pass the bill.

The civil rights convention was an astonishing feat, a remarkable indication of how much change had been wrought during Reconstruction. Here were hundreds of African American civic leaders around the nation mobilizing for a national integration bill. Roughly ninety years before Freedom Riders and the March on Washington, these Black activists participated in what historians have dubbed "America's First Civil Rights Movement." It was a tragedy for the nation that white Americans refused to heed the calls of these prescient civil rights activists.

While the conventioneers carried out their advocacy, Sumner did his part in the Senate. On the first day of the new congressional session, he introduced his bill so quickly that it became "Senate Bill No. 1." He asked the Senate to pass it by Christmas. Sumner felt optimistic this time, partly because he had been gone for so long, avoiding all political controversies, and partly because Grant had finally endorsed the bill in his Second Inaugural Address.

Sumner's hope dissipated after several Republicans balked at the bill's potential unconstitutionality. In a recent Supreme Court decision, the *Slaughter-House Cases*, five of the Court's nine justices suggested that many rights—for example, the right to integrated schools or restaurants— were state citizenship rights that the federal government couldn't legislate on. Citing the case, Republican senator Orris Ferry, from Norwalk, Connecticut, said Black voters should stop seeking an unconstitutional bill if they had "intelligence."[16]

Ferry's remarks outraged Black leaders. Downing penned an open letter to Congress—signed by all the convention delegates—that declared that the delegates wouldn't kowtow to the legal ideas of narrow-minded white lawyers in Congress or in the courts. "We do not feel bound, in a manner involving rights, to be circumscribed," they declared. Echoing many of Sumner's constitutional arguments, the delegates argued that the Court's decision had "no imperative binding force" on Congress. They called on Congress to use its independent constitutional authority to validate Sumner's bill no matter what the Court said. They further contended that the Civil War had sent the "State-rights theory" into the "grave-yard" such that no lawyer should follow its precepts anymore.[17]

Looking for support from whomever they could get, Douglass and Downing dared to meet with the unlikeliest of potential allies, former Confederate vice president Alexander Stephens. Thanks to the amnesty law, Stephens had become eligible for public office and had won a seat in the House. Once a slaveholder who believed in "the great truth that the negro is not equal to the white man," Stephens now told people in Washington that he was reformed. Speaking to General Tecumseh Sherman, he even claimed that he "would go further than Charles Sumner in securing every right to the negro."

On December 23, Stephens received Douglass, Downing, and four other delegates. The former traitor reaffirmed that his views had changed since he helped lead a rebellion that had caused more than seven hundred thousand deaths. He claimed that he now believed "the colored men, as citizens, were entitled to full protection in their civil rights." He explained that he had some concerns only that the House version of Sumner's bill possibly interfered with states' rights, which he would elaborate on the floor.[18]

Stephens spoke on the floor on January 5. He reiterated that he had no prejudice anymore and believed "all men have an equal right to justice." But he argued that Congress must follow *Slaughter-House* and respect the "seminal principle of American constitutional liberty": the right of states to decide their "purely internal municipal affairs." The Civil Rights Bill was a nice idea, Stephens argued, but it had to be implemented at the state level. Otherwise, the ultimate value of American constitutional law—states' rights—would be infringed.[19]

Black leaders quickly caught on to Stephens's cynical game. By pretending to be morally reformed, he had hoped to soothe white northerners into believing it was time for reconciliation. By professing to support equal rights on the state level, Stephens had hoped to convince white northerners to leave civil rights to the South—unguarded, unmonitored, and unregulated by the national government—such that the South could bring back white supremacy.

Black congressmen denounced Stephens in impassioned speeches. But it was not enough. Even though most Republicans resented his role in the Confederacy, many Republicans were desperate to stymie integration efforts and adopted Stephens's convenient rationale that civil rights should be handled at the state level. Rather than deal with the racial question head-on, many Republicans said they opposed Sumner's bill out of respect for *Slaughter-House* and respect for states' rights. In doing so, they revived the prewar constitutional regime that men like Sumner and many Black civic leaders believed the war had eviscerated.[20]

Sumner was heartbroken to watch Republicans regress into prewar form. He may have also known that one of the nation's largest philanthropies, the Peabody Education Fund, was lobbying against his bill. Founded by George Peabody, a Republican financier who cocreated J.P. Morgan Bank, the fund spent its wealth on improving public schools in the South that weren't getting enough state money. The fund's director Barnas Sears, a former president of Brown University, thought *white* children deserved comprehensive public schools, while *Black* children only needed a brief rudimentary education. Sears also worried that integration would undermine public support for public schools, a relatively novel idea in the country. Avoiding "Sumner and his trained negroes" on Capitol Hill, Sears visited many senators, congressmen, and President Grant, who was on the board of trustees of his philanthropy. He warned that if Congress dared to integrate schools, the philanthropy would build white-only private schools across the South and not give money to mixed schools.[21]

In a desperate plea on January 27, Sumner asked the Senate to pass the Civil Rights Bill on the floor. He was afraid of the bill being sent into the Judiciary Committee, where it was more likely that a colleague might try to eviscerate it—such as by removing the schools provision—or kill the bill altogether. For several minutes, Sumner rehashed the tangled procedural history of the bill since he had first introduced it in May 1870. "Until this great question is completely settled the results of the war are not all secured," he said.

By this time, Sumner was suffering from illness again, due to a severe cold through much of the winter and the constant waking up at night to urinate. He frequently skipped Senate sessions and probably looked exhausted as he spoke. He no longer stooped to personal attacks against senators who disagreed with him. All he did was plead, beg, and plead again.

When he was in the Senate, Sumner pronounced to his fellow senators, "Sir, my desire—the darling desire, if I may say so, of my soul at this moment is to close forever this question, so that it shall never again intrude into these Chambers, so that hereafter in all our legislation there shall be no such word as 'black' or 'white,' but that we shall speak only of citizens and of men." He longed to see the day that race would cease to be the defining feature of American life, believing that day would not come until racial injustices were addressed.

"Is that not an aspiration worthy of a Senator?" he asked. "I have been laborious for years," he pleaded. As his despair grew, Sumner finally realized the Senate wouldn't give him his wish. Reluctantly, he agreed to let the bill go to the Judiciary Committee rather than demand a floor vote. While one senator reassured Sumner that the committee would review his bill within "a fortnight" and then return it to the floor, Sumner didn't seem to believe him. He had been in the Senate too long to believe such promises. "I put too much faith in this body, which I ought to know well. I did, sir, have generous trust," he confessed. "I have been disappointed."[22]

* * *

DISPIRITED BY THE Senate's attitude toward his Civil Rights Bill and the lobbying against it, Sumner was also despondent that the Massachusetts Legislature still had a resolution of censure against him for being supposedly anti-veteran. "Mr. Sumner felt keenly the injustice of the censure, and far more than he would have felt it at an earlier stage of his career," Edward Pierce recalled. Pierce said that while Sumner always had "a nature finely sensitive to the blame of associates and friends," he was now "at a period of life when one craves the general gratitude and esteem."[23]

When Joshua Smith was first elected to the legislature, he pledged to do everything in his power to get the censure rescinded. "I will look after your interests at the State House, your name *shall* be *protected*," he told Sumner. "Believe me I will stop and fight it to the end." Smith may have played a role in getting several national figures—including Vice President Henry Wilson, Chief Justice Salmon Chase, and Frederick Douglass—to write open letters to the Massachusetts Legislature explaining that it reflected poorly on the Bay State to censure a man like Charles Sumner.[24]

On January 29, 1874, Smith finally convinced a committee of his colleagues to report a resolution to rescind the censure. By mid-February, the State House and Senate both voted by large majorities to do so. Governor Washburn suggested that Smith personally deliver the official censure rescission to the U.S. Senate, so that it could be read on the floor, and to give the documents to Sumner to cheer him up. Having wanted to visit Sumner all winter, Smith eagerly agreed to do so.

While Smith was on his way, Sumner's chest tightened into another attack. Frightened by his condition, George Downing and Wendell Phillips paid him a social visit. Sumner told his two friends that he had recently spoken to Congressman Ebenezer Hoar, a longtime friend and the first head of the U.S. Department of Justice. Looking glum, Sumner shared that Hoar, who was widely respected by his colleagues for his legal mind, had told him he thought the Civil Rights Bill was "unconstitutional and an infringement on state rights."

On Saturday, March 7, Smith arrived to find a barely recovered Sumner. Eager to help him feel better, he handed Sumner the rescission resolutions. Sumner began to shake and cry uncontrollably as he read them. Turning his face away, he sobbed so strongly that Smith said he "wept as I never saw man weep before." With his voice caught in his throat, Sumner wailed, "I knew Massachusetts would do me justice."

Smith could only stand and watch Sumner weep. "I could not but think of that passage of Scripture which says, 'Jesus wept.' Not for himself, but for a poor, unbelieving world," Smith recalled. "Sumner wept; not for himself, but for the State he loved and served so well." On the following evening, Sumner bade Smith farewell. Shaking his hand, he asked Smith to relay his gratitude to the Massachusetts legislature. "Tell those that voted against me that I forgive them all," Sumner requested, "for I know that if they knew my heart they would not have done it."[25]

A few hours later, Sumner's heart was afflicted by one of the worst episodes of angina it had ever endured. He writhed in bed until four in the morning, tortured by what he called "a clasp of steel crushing my heart into atoms." His physician frantically tried morphine and other narcotics to numb the pain. "Life, at the price I have to pay, is not worth the having," he cried to his doctor.

By Tuesday, he was feeling much better. After a pleasant breakfast with his secretary Arnold Johnson, he went to Capitol Hill. He had asked George Boutwell, who had replaced Henry Wilson as Massachusetts's other senator, to read the censure rescission into the Senate record. Although Boutwell was quite sick as well, Sumner pleaded with him to come read it. Once Boutwell read the resolution on the floor as Sumner eagerly listened, Sumner threw his arm around him and escorted him out of the building, thanking him graciously for coming.

Sumner then went back into the Senate. He chatted for a while with a handful of senators and congressmen who were floating around the chamber during an afternoon recess. Walking up to Senator Ferry, who had so fiercely denounced his Civil Rights Bill as unconstitutional, Sumner sympathetically inquired after Ferry's health. Ferry suffered from a spinal affliction, and the two commiserated over their shared chronic pain. All the while, Sumner felt tingles of pain in his left arm. He had already arranged a carriage ride back to his house with Samuel Hooper. Shortly before it was time to go, he said to the Connecticut senator, "Ferry, I have a toothache in my heart. I think I shall go home."[26]

EPILOGUE

LATER THAT NIGHT, SUMNER HAD A HEART ATTACK. HE CRASHED onto the floor in his study. Startled by the loud thump, a few servants ran upstairs to find Sumner on the ground, groaning in pain, struggling to get back onto the sofa. They immediately sent for his local doctor Joseph Johnson, his secretary Arnold Johnson, and his neighbor James Wormley. By the time these men arrived at Sumner's house, he was in bed, clearly in agony, with his limbs already cold and pale. But his face was warm, pleasant, and welcoming. Cheerfully, he asked for morphine.[1]

As Dr. Johnson prepared a morphine injection, Wormley and Mr. Johnson laid bottles of hot water mixed with mustard powder along Sumner's feet and sides. They gave him brandy and champagne to relieve his pain while he kept apologizing for the late-night trouble. After consuming enough alcohol and narcotics, he fell asleep. Twenty minutes later, he woke up in searing pain. He cried for another injection of morphine. The doctor obliged him. When the morphine kicked in, he grew cheerful again. "There, now I have turned the corner; the pain is decreasing," he said. "I shall sleep." He asked everyone to go home.

They didn't go anywhere. Frightened by Sumner's clammy skin and faint pulse, the men told Samuel Hooper and some other friends who lived nearby to join them at the house. All night long, they took shifts to keep vigil over Sumner, who kept waking up, groaning about his chest pain, gurgling in his throat, and coughing up bloody mucus. He complained about being "tired" and "weary" between short bouts of sleep. In his drowsy stupor, he occasionally moaned, "My book! my book!" referring to the *Works of Charles Sumner*. "If it were not for my unfinished book," he said to himself at one point, "I should not regret this."

Around 5 a.m., Sumner's worried caregivers sent a telegram to

Dr. Brown-Séquard, then in New York, asking him to take the first train to Washington. Before boarding his train, the eccentric doctor sent a telegram explaining that Sumner should be given an electric bath, a medical treatment that involved putting a patient in a tub and shocking him with lightly electrified water. Before anyone could try this strange form of electrotherapy, the surgeon general of the United States arrived at the house. In consultation with other doctors, he decided Sumner's heart was beyond saving. To keep him comfortable, they wrapped his limbs in plasters of mustard powder and fed him iced champagne.[2]

Word spread in Washington in the early hours of the morning that Sumner was on the brink of death. By 9 a.m., several hundred people had gathered in front of his house. "Colored men and women mingled with white in knots about his home," reported the *New York Tribune*. Ordinary bureaucrats, merchants, shopmen, waiters, and even "old colored women with baskets and bundles on their arms" stood together, many of them crying and begging to be let inside. One of Sumner's friends stood guard with two policemen to stop these mourners from entering the home.

The policemen couldn't stop Sumner's closest friends or the many senators, congressmen, military generals, foreign dignitaries, and their wives who came to the house from going inside. While the men went upstairs to the library, the women gathered in the parlor downstairs. Some women offered to tend to Sumner in his sickbed. But the doctors insisted on limiting his visitors to the men he already knew and trusted. At one side sat Wormley, who kept helping him shift his position on the pillows. At the other side sat George Downing, who tenderly held his hand and listened to his soft, raspy, slowing breaths.

By 10 a.m., Sumner was awake but high on morphine and only half in his senses. He tried to pull himself together and get out of bed, insisting that he must get dressed and go to the Senate right away. While attempting to roll over, he plopped his hulking head on the arm of Arnold Johnson, his secretary. He nestled his head comfortably into Johnson's elbow, no longer trying to get up. When Johnson knelt at the bedside so that he could straighten out his arm, he locked eyes with Sumner's foggy gaze. "Don't let the bill be lost," Sumner whispered. Johnson promised his boss that he would find any missing household bills and get them paid in full. "You mistake," Sumner groaned. He waved in the opposite direction, where Congressman Ebenezer Hoar was standing. "Judge!" Sumner moaned, referring to Hoar. "My bill!—don't let it fail!" He then clarified his words. "The Civil Rights Bill," he said. "Don't let it fail!"

Around this time, Hoar had sent a message to Speaker of the House James Blaine to inform him of Sumner's deadly illness. When Blaine made an announcement on the House floor, members of Congress began to walk out of the Capitol in droves before they even formally voted to adjourn. As if in pilgrimage, dozens of members boarded buggies or marched nearly two miles on foot to Sumner's house on Lafayette Square. On arrival, they went straight to Sumner's library, where the Senate chaplain was reading tearfully from the fourteenth chapter of John. "Do not let your hearts be troubled," Jesus said in the chapter. "If you love me, keep my commands."[3]

Frederick Douglass went to the house. Trembling with shock and heavy grief in the upstairs hallway, he could hear Sumner whimper, "the bill, the bill, the bill," over and over in his morphine-induced haze. More than once, Sumner tried to get up so that he could go to the Senate. Wormley and Downing held him down. While doing so, perhaps Downing recalled what Sumner had told him during a previous angina attack: "All prostrate as I am, could I crawl to the Capitol and have the Civil Rights Bill pass, I would be reconciled to death."

By the early afternoon, the library was packed with members of Congress, including Representative Hoar. A leading Massachusetts congressman and the first attorney general of the Department of Justice, Hoar was a likely contender to be Sumner's replacement in the Senate. He had told Sumner only days earlier that he didn't think the Civil Rights Bill was constitutional. After standing in the library for a while, Hoar returned to the sickroom to check Sumner's status. He sat on a low chair next to the bed and stroked Sumner's hand. "I am trying to warm it," Hoar explained. "You never will," Sumner replied. He fixed his eyes on Hoar's face with a deep intensity. He spoke slowly, struggling to put his words together. In a voice full of desperation, pleading to his potential successor, he repeated his request from earlier in the day. "Don't let the Bill fail. I mean the Civil Rights Bill," Sumner begged Hoar. "Take care of the Civil Rights Bill."

Hoar broke down as he listened to Sumner's pleading, sobbing like a child while kissing Sumner's hand. Somebody in the room went to the library to tell the men that Sumner, the longest-serving senator in the United States at the time, was spending his final moments advocating for civil rights. Speaker Blaine was moved to tears. Senator Schurz and Congressman Hooper also cried. "There were no dry eyes in that room,"

Arnold Johnson recalled. "The room seemed to be hallowed ground," Downing said. "Its air was sacred."

Sumner fell asleep after pleading with Hoar. Every so often, he woke up again, moaning phrases like, "I am so tired" and "I can't last much longer." Around 2 p.m., he asked for more morphine, which Dr. Johnson declined to give. Then his health briefly improved, so much so that people wondered if he was going to recover. When Hooper entered the bedroom, Sumner looked pleased and cheerily motioned for him to sit down. Seconds later, his body convulsed. He threw himself back, vomited, gripped Downing's hand so hard he nearly crushed it, and began gasping for air. By 2:47 p.m., he was gone. Downing shut Sumner's eyelids.

Just minutes before, Sumner had spoken his final words to Hoar. His voice choking as he struggled to speak, he instructed Hoar out of the blue to "tell Emerson that I love him and revere him." Remembering what the famous poet had said about Sumner after the brutal caning, Hoar replied, "I will tell Emerson that you love him and revere him, for he said to me that you have the largest soul of any man alive."[4]

* * *

TWO DAYS AFTER Sumner's death, on Friday, March 13, Frederick Douglass, James Wormley, and three hundred other Black men marched five abreast of a congressional delegation that escorted Sumner's casket in a carriage down Pennsylvania Avenue toward the U.S. Capitol. Some locals said it was the coldest March day in memory, as the temperature was below freezing. There were "dull, leaden clouds in the skies," according to the *New York Tribune*, and strong gales that "whistled around the corners and carried great clouds of sand along the broad avenues of the city." In the *Tribune's* words, "even nature seemed to mourn to-day."

The procession reached the Capitol around 10 a.m. "A shade of gloom" pervaded the building, which had been draped in black bombazine, according to the *Washington Evening Star*. Even the murals in the Capitol Rotunda were covered in heavy black curtains. In the Rotunda, Sumner's casket was hoisted on the same catafalque that had been used for Abraham Lincoln. No one had lain in state on Lincoln's catafalque before. "No event since the assassination of President LINCOLN," reported *Harper's Weekly* and other newspapers, "has more deeply touched the hearts of the American people than the death of CHARLES SUMNER."[5]

As many as ten thousand people walked through the Capitol Rotunda to catch a final glimpse of Sumner's body. By some estimates, nearly half the mourners were African American, and many were children. All colored schools in Washington had closed for the day to pay homage to Sumner. These thousands of Black mourners packed the corridors, stairwells, porticoes, and hallways of the Capitol to the very brim, as if to claim Sumner and America's temple of democracy as their own.

Around noon, members of the House of Representatives gathered in two straight lines behind Speaker Blaine. With black crapes over their left arms, the congressmen marched into the Senate Chamber for a short ceremony. President Grant, General Sherman, the presidential cabinet, the justices of the Supreme Court, numerous foreign diplomats, their families, and roughly five thousand spectators attended. Every chair was occupied except Sumner's, which stayed vacant, as it had been for three years after his caning. Grant's daughter Nellie adorned the chair with flowers.

After the solemn service, Sumner's casket was escorted in a hearse to a nearby train depot with a procession of several hundred African Americans led by Douglass walking behind it. Loaded onto a train draped in black curtains, Sumner's casket and a few members of Congress passed by Baltimore, Wilmington, and Philadelphia without stopping. Arriving in Jersey City around 11 p.m., the casket was transported by ferry to New York. After staying there overnight, it was sent on a new train to the Bay State.[6]

Beginning in Springfield, throngs gathered at every Massachusetts station to watch Sumner's special train pass by on its way to Boston. When Sumner's casket finally arrived on the afternoon of Saturday, March 14, in a train depot not far from today's South Station, around ten thousand Bostonians were waiting there. The crowd of mourners was so large that police struggled to keep order as the casket was escorted up Beacon Hill to the gold-domed Massachusetts State House. During the Boston procession, every church in the city tolled its bells in Sumner's honor.

On Sunday, Sumner's sealed coffin lay in state in the State House, guarded by the Black veterans of the Shaw Guard, the famed Civil War regiment Sumner had helped put in place. Before his burial in Mount Auburn Cemetery on Monday, around forty thousand people filed through the State House to pay their respects. They left behind generous tributes, including an anchor, a harp, a six-foot cross, and many bouquets of flowers. The most impactful tribute, seen by thousands of mourners and featured in a famous drawing in *Harper's Weekly*, was an immense floral shield laid near the casket by George Downing's brother, Peter. On top of a disk of white carnations, he carefully placed a series of blue violets to spell out eight mighty words:

DO NOT

LET THE

CIVIL RIGHTS

BILL FAIL[7]

* * *

SUMNER HAD SPENT four years advocating for the Civil Rights Bill in vain. Less than three months after his death, a majority of his Senate colleagues granted him his dying wish by passing the bill. They voted to integrate every train, bus, hotel, and restaurant in the United States. They voted to integrate every single public school and college in the nation. They voted to bring about the fruition of the multiracial democracy that Sumner had believed in. But their vote was largely symbolic. In many ways, the posthumous passage of Sumner's bill in the Senate signified the high-water mark of Reconstruction; it was the peak before the fall.

The House of Representatives never passed the comprehensive Civil Rights Bill, even though the Senate did. Instead, in February 1875, the House passed the Civil Rights Act of 1875—a stripped-down version of Sumner's bill that lacked key enforcement measures and said nothing about integrating schools. The Senate approved it, President Grant signed it, and almost no government official bothered to enforce it. For the next eighty years, Congress didn't pass any additional civil rights legislation. "The progress of the cause of the negro in this country," said George Hoar, whose older brother had sat at Sumner's bedside when he lay dying, "stopped when he died."[8]

In September 1875, Republicans organized an opulent cookout with music, ice cream, and barbecue in Clinton, Mississippi, inviting more than two thousand African American freedpeople to celebrate their political rights and encourage them to vote in the upcoming election. Shortly after a Black state senator gave his remarks, a band of white attendees pulled out weapons by surprise and opened fire on the crowd. Black people screamed and ran for their lives amid a flurry of bullets. For the next few days, white people hunted African Americans in the streets and killed more than fifty residents in one of the worst civilian massacres of its time.

Democrats orchestrated this bloodbath to intimidate Black Mississippians from participating in politics. In the wake of the massacre, President

Grant debated how to respond. On the one hand, he wanted to send Union troops to Mississippi to protect Black voters. On the other hand, he felt enormous political pressure to let the matter go. White northerners were exhausted by the unending violence in the South and wanted to keep the troops at home. Some of Grant's legal advisers also argued that Reconstruction was infringing on the right of southern states to self-govern. Ultimately, Grant decided not to send any troops—a decision he later described as one of his biggest regrets.

In the absence of Union troops, Mississippi Democrats organized Confederate veterans into paramilitary groups called White Leagues. They attacked Republican political meetings, forced African Americans to vote for Democrats, and seized polling locations to stuff ballots. After retaking the state legislature, they impeached the Black lieutenant governor, destroyed Black businesses, and allowed Black politicians to be lynched. Emboldened by the success of the so-called Mississippi Plan, southern Democrats replicated this violent strategy in other states, while most northern voters looked on.[9]

By November 1876, Democrats had fostered political lawlessness across the South, leading to a disputed presidential election. When several southern states sent different slates of electors to the Electoral College after widespread voter fraud on both sides, lawmakers had to decide who would take the presidency after Grant. Many historians believe, although there is no definitive proof, that the election was secretly settled by a group of Republican and Democratic lawmakers who formed a gentlemen's agreement at a meeting in the Wormley Hotel, right next door to Sumner's former home.

Here, within the nation's leading Black-owned hotel, Republicans allegedly pledged to withdraw Union troops from the South (among other promises) in exchange for Democrats letting them win the presidency. The location of the rumored deal was a profound poetic injustice. It may have even taken place in the Sumner Parlor, an elegant room in the lobby that James Wormley had outfitted with Sumner's furniture after his friend's death. Even if the rumored meeting did not happen, the outcome of the 1876 election was clear: it spelled the doom of Reconstruction and reversed the achievements of the Civil War. After being allowed to enter the White House, Republican president Rutherford B. Hayes withdrew every Union troop that remained in the former Confederacy. Then, southern Democrats unleashed a bloody wave of violence to destroy all semblances of racial equality and disenfranchise more than two million freedmen.[10]

By 1883, Republicans had fully abandoned freedpeople and Democrats fully controlled the South. That year, the Supreme Court overturned the Civil Rights Act, invoking the doctrine of states' rights and other legal ideas that Sumner had decried. Around the same time, former senator Roscoe Conkling—the last surviving Republican who had helped draft the Fourteenth Amendment—claimed that his party wrote the amendment such that corporations were legal "persons" entitled to rights. By 1886, the Court had adopted Conkling's specious claim. For the next few decades, nearly every Fourteenth Amendment case concerned corporate law, not civil rights. It was almost as if Sumner's constitutional revolution had never happened.[11]

By 1896, southern Democrats had reinstituted "Black Codes," special laws that enforced racial apartheid by blocking the physical and economic mobility of freedpeople. In *Plessy v. Ferguson*, the Supreme Court upheld a Black code in Louisiana that banned African Americans from sitting on the same trains as white people so long as Blacks were offered "separate but equal" railway options. The Court claimed that the Fourteenth Amendment permitted this sort of nakedly racist legislation. "If one race be inferior to the other socially," the Court declared, "the Constitution of the United States cannot put them upon the same plane."

Thus began a new stage of white supremacy, one that contradicted everything that Sumner had lived and died for. His dream—of a racially egalitarian America that fulfilled the promises of the Declaration of Independence—was replaced by the nightmare called Jim Crow. As the great Black historian W. E. B. Du Bois put it, "the slave went free; stood a brief moment in the sun; then moved back again toward slavery."[12]

* * *

SUMNER'S STORY CUTS against the conventional narrative of American racial progress, a narrative that claims that America's treatment of racial minorities has consistently become better over time. In fact, life for most African Americans became worse in the decades after Reconstruction with the rise of Jim Crow, much like it became worse in the decades after the Founding with the rise of the Slave Power. This is a frightening fact that should force readers of history to recognize that racial oppression can deepen and worsen even after significant steps forward are taken. Without ongoing vigilance, racial progress can be turned back at any moment.[13]

At the same time, Sumner's story counsels hope rather than despair. Long before the Civil Rights Movement of the 1950s and 1960s, he envisioned a future in which every American had a fair shot at life, liberty, and the pursuit of happiness regardless of race. He pursued this prescient vision at great personal cost and despite his own personal flaws, navigating countless roundabout, morally gray, and complex questions along the way. In so doing, he helped to abolish chattel slavery, transform the Constitution, enfranchise millions of people, and, ever so briefly, reconstruct the republic. Sumner's life demonstrates that individuals like him, with enough courage and drive, can alter the trajectory of American racial history, even if they are not able to succeed fully.

Success may come long after one's death. In 1907, Moorfield Storey—Sumner's protégé and former secretary—published a pamphlet lambasting the United States government for having annexed the Philippines, echoing the work of his former boss in denouncing the attempt to annex the modern-day Dominican Republic. After releasing his pamphlet, Storey received a letter of praise from W. E. B. Du Bois. In reply, he suggested that the two of them get together to discuss American imperialism. When the pair met, a friendship was sprung.

Three years later, Storey and Du Bois collaborated on a project to address domestic human rights issues rather than foreign ones. Alongside a larger group of Black and white leaders, they established a new civil rights organization that Storey would lead as its founding president for nearly two decades. The organization was called the National Association for the Advancement of Colored People: the NAACP. On January 6, 1911, Storey and Du Bois hosted "Sumner Centennial" events on behalf of the NAACP to commemorate the birth anniversary of their mutual hero.

Storey, a former president of the American Bar Association, crafted a legal strategy for the NAACP that Sumner would have admired—a strategy to dismantle Jim Crow by emphasizing the true meaning of the post–Civil War Constitution. Storey believed, like Sumner, that constitutional law could be effectively leveraged to advance racial justice in America. Ever since, the NAACP has carried out the work he pioneered, leading to victories such as *Brown v. Board of Education*. Tragically, while these victories have reset the trajectory of American racial history, the country has not yet ended racial segregation, inequality, and discrimination.[14]

* * *

THE MARCH FOR equality must go on. Roughly one year before Sumner was buried, on April 16, 1873, Frederick Douglass led a parade to celebrate the anniversary of emancipation in the District of Columbia. As usual, Sumner wasn't in a celebratory mood and did not take part in the procession. Instead, he wrote a letter that was read aloud to the crowd. The letter reminded people not to take their rights for granted, not to declare victory too soon. "Much has been done, but more remains to be done," Sumner explained. "The great work is not yet accomplished."

In the letter, Sumner compared the state of American race relations to the structure of the Washington Monument, which was only half completed at the time. "Until your equality in civil rights is assured, the pillar of your citizenship is like the column in honor of Washington, unfinished and imperfect," he said. He could have also noted that the first half of the obelisk had been built with slave labor prior to the Civil War. As Douglass once observed, the monument was a contradiction. A symbol of freedom, it was "built up by the price of human blood."

The second half of the Washington Monument was built during Reconstruction with free labor. The finished obelisk signified the Second Founding of America, a nation now dedicated to liberty and equality for all. It was completed more than a century ago. Yet in 2011, it almost broke. An earthquake ruptured major cracks in the monument that nearly caused it to collapse. These fissures, perhaps, represent the painful aspects of American life, fissures from the past that have never closed. They will take a long time to heal. Yet the wounds of the past can heal, will heal, if the human rights work of those who came before is remembered, honored, and continued. "Liberty has been won," Sumner once said. "The battle for Equality is still pending."[15]

NOTES

I have attributed most of Sumner's correspondence to two sources. The first source, the Papers of Charles Sumner (abbreviated in these notes as PCS), is a microfilm collection of more than 25,000 original letters that is available at several libraries, including the Houghton Library and the Library of Congress, and digitally available at the Princeton University Library. For the archival location of each letter in the microfilm, see Beverly Wilson Palmer, *Guide and Index to the Papers of Charles Sumner* (Chadwyck-Healy, 1988). For a curated selection of these letters, see both volumes of Beverly Wilson Palmer, *The Selected Letters of Charles Sumner* (Boston: Northeastern University Press, 1990).

The second source, *Memoir and Letters of Charles Sumner (MLCS)*, is a four-volume biography by Edward Pierce, published by Roberts Brothers between 1877 and 1893. Pierce transcribed hundreds of letters but made minor changes to the text; generally, I only cited Pierce if the original source could not be found.

I cited most of Sumner's speeches and other works using the earliest available pamphlet edition, the *Congressional Globe*, or a contemporary newspaper. If I was unable to find an early printed source, I cited the edition that was republished in *The Works of Charles Sumner (WCS)*, a compilation of Sumner's works that was heavily revised by Sumner and his executors. I used the fifteen-volume edition of the *Works*, published by Lee & Shepard between 1870 and 1883, not the twenty-volume edition published by the same in 1900. The two editions are identical but have different pagination.

Readers should bear in mind that I have used the 1970 Knopf edition of David Donald's *Charles Sumner and the Rights of Man* and the 2009 Sourcebooks edition of Donald's *Charles Sumner and the Coming of the Civil War*, which has a different pagination than the original 1960 Knopf edition.

With the help of diligent fact-checkers, I made every effort to match the spelling and style of the original sources, with two exceptions. First, I wrote "n——r" whenever the "N-word" was used in the original source. Second, I used italics whenever the original source underlined a word or phrase. Since Sumner and some of his correspondents underlined a great deal, this book has many italics.

Finally, the abbreviation "CS" in the endnotes stands for "Charles Sumner."

Introduction

1. Andrew Hilen, ed., *The Letters of Henry Wadsworth Longfellow*, vol. 2 (Cambridge, Mass.: Harvard University Press, 1966), 93.
2. CS, *Argument of Charles Sumner, Esq. Against the Constitutionality of Separate Colored Schools* (Boston: B. F. Roberts, 1849), 10, 16; J. Clay Smith, *Emancipation: The Making of the Black Lawyer, 1844–1944* (Philadelphia: University of Pennsylvania Press, 1993), 96–97.
3. CS, *The Slave Oligarchy and Its Usurpations* (Washington: Buell & Blanchard, 1855); George William Curtis, "Charles Sumner: A Eulogy," *Harper's Weekly*, June 20, 1874.
4. "Patriotism," *The Weekly Caucasian*, February 12, 1870, 2; "From Washington: Mungen's Speech," *Georgia Weekly Telegraph, Journal and Messenger*, March 8, 1870; "Senator Sumner—Young Negroes and Daguerreotypes," *The Washington Sentinel*, March 2, 1855; Cong. Globe, 33rd Cong., 1st. Sess. App., 1854, 233–34 (remarks of Sen. Butler).
5. CS, "The Crime Against Kansas" (Speech, U.S. Senate, May 19, 1856), 4:125, *WCS*; Robert L. Meriwether, "Preston S. Brooks on the Caning of Charles Sumner," *South Carolina Historical and Genealogical Magazine* 52, no. 1 (1951): 2–3.
6. Cong. Globe, 34th Cong., 1st. Sess. App., 1856, 633 (remarks of Sen. Butler); Manisha Sinha, "The

Caning of Charles Sumner: Slavery, Race, and Ideology in the Age of the Civil War," *Journal of the Early Republic* 23, no. 2 (2003): 256; Ralph Waldo Emerson, *The Complete Works of Ralph Waldo Emerson*, ed. Edward W. Emerson, vol. 11 (Boston: Houghton Mifflin, 1913), 251–52.

7. John G. Whittier and Wendell Phillips, eds., *Letters of Lydia Maria Child* (Boston: Houghton Mifflin, 1883), 88; Carl Schurz, "Eulogy Before City Authorities of Boston (Music Hall, April 29, 1874)," in *Charles Sumner: Memoir and Eulogies*, ed. William M. Cornell (Boston: James H. Earle, 1874), 125.

8. Anonymous, "The Diary of a Public Man: Unpublished Passages of the Secret History of the American Civil War, Part II," ed. Allen Thorndike Rice, *North American Review* 129, no. 279 (1879): 266–67; Benjamin Perley Poore, *Perley's Reminiscences of Sixty Years in the National Metropolis*, vol. 2 (Philadelphia: Hubbard's Bros., 1886), 62–63.

9. "Mr. Douglass Interviewed," *Washington Post*, January 26, 1884.

10. Peter Randolph, *From Slave Cabin to the Pulpit* (Boston: James H. Earle, 1893), 137.

11. Edward Pierce, *Memoir and Letters of Charles Sumner*, vol. 2 (Boston: Roberts Bros., 1877), 287; Julia Ward Howe, "Reminiscences of Julia Ward Howe," *The Atlantic*, March 1899, 341.

12. CS, "Retrospect and Promise: Address at a Serenade" (Speech, Sumner's House in Washington, August 9, 1872), 15:202–204, WCS.

13. J. C. Levenson et al., eds., *The Letters of Henry Adams*, vol. 1 (Cambridge, Mass.: Belknap Press, 1982), 222; David Donald, *Charles Sumner and the Coming of the Civil War* (Naperville, Ill.: Sourcebooks, 2009), 203.

14. "Delegation of Colored Men," *New National Era*, January 18, 1872.

15. Wendell Phillips, "Sumner (Charles)," in *Johnson's Universal Cyclopaedia: A Scientific and Popular Treasury of Useful Knowledge*, ed. Frederick A. P. Barnard and Arnold Guyot (New York: A. J. Johnson, 1886), 622.

16. Louis Ruchames, "Charles Sumner and American Historiography," *The Journal of Negro History* 38, no. 2 (1953); William E. Woodward, *A New American History* (New York: Garden City Publishing, 1938), 479; Avery Craven, "Review of Charles Sumner and the Coming of the Civil War," *The Mississippi Valley Historical Review* 47, no. 4 (1961): 699; J. T. Adams, *The Epic of America* (Boston: Little, Brown, 1931), 285. For critiques of this Sumner historiography, see the aforementioned Ruchames article and Ronald N. Stromberg, "Sumner's Tragedy," *The Negro History Bulletin* 11, no. 6 (1948): 131–32, 141–43.

17. Brotherhood of Liberty, *Justice and Jurisprudence: An Inquiry Concerning the Constitutional Limitations of the Thirteenth, Fourteenth, and Fifteenth Amendments* (Philadelphia: J.B. Lippincott, 1889); Carl M. Frasure, "Charles Sumner and the Rights of the Negro," *Journal of Negro History* 13, no. 2 (1928): 149; W. E. Burghardt Du Bois, *Black Reconstruction* (New York: Harcourt, Brace, 1935), 197, 723.

18. Donald, *Charles Sumner and the Coming of the Civil War*, 31.

19. Louis Ruchames, "The Pulitzer Prize Treatment of Charles Sumner," *The Massachusetts Review* 2, no. 4 (1961): 749. For more critical reviews of Donald's biography, see Paul Goodman, "David Donald's Charles Sumner Reconsidered," *New England Quarterly* 37, no. 3 (1964): 373–87; Gilbert Osofsky, "Cardboard Yankee: How Not to Study the Mind of Charles Sumner," *Reviews in American History* 1, no. 4 (1973): 595–606.

20. For a study on Sumner historiography in American textbooks, see Tom Donnelly, "Our Forgotten Founders: Reconstruction, Public Education, and Constitutional Heroism," *Cleveland State Law Review* 115 (2010): 175–78.

21. "Hon. Preston S. Brooks at Home," *Charleston Courier*, October 7, 1856; CS, *The Works of Charles Sumner*, vol. 2 (Boston: Lee & Shepard, 1875), 331.

22. Cong. Globe, 42nd Cong., 2nd Sess., 1872, 727 (remarks of Sen. Sumner).

23. Cong. Globe, 39th Cong., 1st. Sess., 1866, 680 (remarks of Sen. Sumner).

24. CS, *Argument of Charles Sumner, Esq. Against the Constitutionality of Separate Colored Schools*, 10; Cong. Globe, 40th Cong., 3rd Sess., 1869, 902 (remarks of Sen. Sumner).

25. Arthur Reed Hogue, ed., *Charles Sumner: An Essay by Carl Schurz* (Urbana: University of Illinois Press, 1951), 42–43.

26. See many references to the "Second Founding" by the Supreme Court in *Students for Fair Admissions, Inc. v. President & Fellows of Harvard Coll.*, 600 U.S. 181 (2023). There are many recent books and papers on the Second Founding. To begin, see Eric Foner, *The Second Founding: How the Civil War and Reconstruction Remade the Constitution* (New York: W. W. Norton, 2019).

27. CS, *The Works of Charles Sumner*, vol. 7 (Boston: Lee & Shepard, 1875), 216; Cong. Globe, 40th

Cong., 2nd Sess., 1868, 3025 (remarks of Sen. Sumner); William M. Cornell, ed., *Charles Sumner: Memoir and Eulogies* (Boston: James H. Earle, 1874), 280–81.

28. Curtis, "Charles Sumner: A Eulogy," 230; CS, *The Works of Charles Sumner*, vol. 12 (Boston: Lee & Shepard, 1875), 380, 384, 400; CS, *Works of Charles Sumner*, vol. 14 (Boston: Lee & Shepard, 1875), 148.

29. Harriet Beecher Stowe, *The Lives and Deeds of Our Self-Made Men* (Hartford: Worthington, Dustin, 1872), 229; Cornell, *Charles Sumner: Memoir and Eulogies*, 59–61.

30. "Linda Brown on Her Involvement in *Brown v. Board of Education* Supreme Court Case (University of Michigan Event)," C-SPAN, April 3, 2004, https://www.c-span.org/video/?c4720634/linda-brown-involvement-brown-v-board-education-supreme-court-case; Brief for Appellants in Nos. 1, 2, and 4 and for Respondents in No. 10 on Reargument, *Brown v. Board of Education of Topeka*, 347 U.S. 483, 1954, 70.

Chapter 1: A Blemished Family

1. Robert M. Spector, "The Quock Walker Cases (1781–1783): Slavery, Its Abolition, and Negro Citizenship in Early Massachusetts," *Journal of Negro History* 53, no. 1 (n.d.): 12–32; Lemuel Shattuck, *Report to the Committee of the City Council Appointed to Obtain the Census of Boston for the Year 1845* (Boston: J. H. Eastburn, 1846), 43; John Daniels, *In Freedom's Birthplace: A Study of the Boston Negroes* (Boston: Houghton Mifflin, 1914), 17–19, 21–23; James Oliver Horton and Lois E. Horton, *Black Bostonians: Family Life and Community Struggle in the Antebellum North* (New York: Holmes and Meier, 1979), 28–33; Adelaide M. Cromwell, *The Other Brahmins: Boston's Black Upper Class, 1750–1950* (Fayetteville: University of Arkansas Press, 1994), 33–35; Kathryn Grover and Janine V. da Silva, *Historic Resource Study: Boston African American National Historic Site* (Washington, D.C.: National Park Service, 2002), 29–32, 73–76; Stephen Kendrick and Paul Kendrick, *Sarah's Long Walk: The Free Blacks of Boston and How Their Struggle for Equality Changed America* (Boston: Beacon Press, 2004), 21–25.

2. Shattuck, *Report to the Committee of the City Council Appointed to Obtain the Census of Boston for the Year 1845*, 43; Peter P. Hinks, *To Awaken My Afflicted Brethren: David Walker and the Problem of Antebellum Slave Resistance* (University Park: Pennsylvania State University Press, 1997), 79–82; Horton and Horton, *Black Bostonians*, 7.

3. Edward Pierce, *Memoir and Letters of Charles Sumner*, vol. 1 (London: Sampson Low, Marston, Searle and Rivington, 1878) (hereafter cited as *MLCS*), 1:1–4.

4. Pierce, *MLCS*, 1:4; William Sumner Appleton, *Record of the Descendants of William Sumner* (Boston: David Clapp and Son, 1879), 176; E. F. Vose and E. P. Martin, "Daniel Vose and His Inn," Milton Historical Society, October 1912, http://www.miltonhistoricalsociety.org/DigitalArchives/1912%20Oct%20Daniel%20Vose%20and%20His%20Inn.pdf; Ralph Waldo Emerson, "Concord Hymn," Poetry Foundation (Poetry Foundation, 1837), https://www.poetryfoundation.org/poems/45870/concord-hymn. For more on the Suffolk Resolves, see Mary Phillips Webster and Charles R. Morris, "The Story of the Suffolk Resolves," Milton Historical Society, 1973, http://www.miltonhistoricalsociety.org/DigitalArchives/1973%20The%20Story%20of%20the%20Suffolk%20Resolves.pdf; Ray Raphael, *The First American Revolution: Before Lexington and Concord* (New York: The New Press, 2002).

5. Josiah Quincy, *The History of Harvard University* (Cambridge, Mass.: John Owen, 1840), 164; J. L. Bell, *George Washington's Headquarters and Home: Cambridge, Massachusetts* (Washington, D.C.: National Park Service, 2012), 560–61.

6. Massachusetts Society of the Cincinnati and Francis Samuel Drake, *Memorials of the Society of the Cincinnati of Massachusetts* (Boston: Society, 1873); Pierce, *MLCS*, 1:5–6; Duane Hamilton Hurd, *History of Norfolk County, Massachusetts: With Biographical Sketches of Many of Its Pioneers and Prominent Men* (Philadelphia: J. W. Lewis, 1884), 742–43; James Spear Loring, *The Hundred Boston Orators Appointed by the Municipal Authorities and Other Public Bodies from 1770 to 1852* (Boston: John P. Jewett, 1853), 325; Henry Knox, "Certificate of Service for Major Job Sumner," July 29, 1784, Collection Reference No. GLC02437.03026, Henry Knox Papers, Gilder Lehrman Institute of American History, http://www.americanhistory.amdigital.co.uk/Documents/Details/Certificate-of-service-for-Major-Job-Sumner/GLC02437.03026; John C. Fitzpatrick, *The Writings of George Washington from the Original Manuscript Sources, 1745–1799*, vol. 21 (Washington, D.C.: U.S. Government Printing Office, 1937), 36; John C. Fitzpatrick, *The Writings of George Washington from the Original Manuscript Sources, 1745–1799*, vol. 26 (Washington, D.C.: U.S. Government Printing Office, 1937), 37–38. One report indicates that Job Sumner served for Col. John Robinson's

regiment at the Battle of Concord in April 1775. This seems unlikely given that Robinson's regiment came from Westford, Massachusetts. Westford was more than twenty miles away from Cambridge, where Job Sumner was studying, and fifty miles from Milton, which was his home. All other extant reports state that Job Sumner was in Cambridge during the Battle of Concord. See Samuel F. Batchelder, "The Students in Arms—Old Style," *The Harvard Graduates' Magazine* 29, no. 116 (June 1921): 564.

7. Maria Campbell and James Freeman Clarke, *Revolutionary Services and Civil Life of General William Hull* (New York: D. Appleton, 1848), 207–10; Loring, *The Hundred Boston Orators*, 325–26; Pierce, *MLCS*, 1:7; Ron Chernow, *Washington: A Life* (New York: Penguin, 2011), 449–50.

8. Charles Pinckney Sumner, *Eulogy on the Illustrious George Washington* (Dedham, Mass.: H. Mann, 1800), 11; Campbell and Clarke, *Revolutionary Services and Civil Life of General William Hull*, 209–10; Chernow, *Washington*, 451–52.

9. *New York Daily Advertiser*, September 17, 1789, 2; Loring, *The Hundred Boston Orators*, 326; Pierce, *MLCS*, 1:8–9.

10. *New York Weekly Museum*, September 19, 1789, 3; "Maj Job Sumner (1754–1789)," Find a Grave, n.d., https://www.findagrave.com/memorial/18084966/job-sumner.

11. Pierce, *MLCS*, 1:11; Appleton, *Record of the Descendants of William Sumner*, 176; Wendell Phillips, "Sumner (Charles)," in *Johnson's Universal Cyclopaedia: A Scientific and Popular Treasury of Useful Knowledge*, ed. Frederick A. P. Barnard and Arnold Guyot (New York: A. J. Johnson, 1886), 620–21. While Phillips's encyclopedia entry on Sumner was anonymous, Edward Pierce noted his authorship. See Pierce, *MLCS*, 3:32.

12. Pierce, *MLCS*, 1:9–14; John Phelps Taylor, "Melville C. Day as a Student in Phillips Academy," *The Phillips Bulletin* 8, no. 3 (1914): 13; Sumner, *Eulogy on the Illustrious George Washington*, 11.

13. CS, "Charles Sumner's Autobiographical Notes," n.d., Palfrey Papers, Houghton Library, Harvard University.

14. Theodore Parsons and Eliphalet Pearson, "A Forensic Dispute on the Legality of Enslaving the Africans," in *Blacks at Harvard: A Documentary History of African-American Experience at Harvard and Radcliffe*, ed. Werner Sollors, Caldwell Titcomb, and Thomas A. Underwood (New York: New York University Press, 1993), 16; Barbara L. Packer, *The Transcendentalists* (Athens: University of Georgia Press, 2007), 3–4; Pierce, *MLCS*, 1:12, 45; John Stauffer, "Charles Sumner's Political Culture and the Foundation of Civil Rights; Or, the Education of Charles Sumner," *New England Quarterly* 156, no. 4 (December 2023): 330.

15. Pierce, *MLCS*, 1:16; Joseph Story to Charles Pinckney Sumner, April 1797, Charles Pinckney Sumner Papers, Massachusetts Historical Society, Boston; Charles Pinckney Sumner to Joseph Story, April 13, 1797, Charles Pinckney Sumner Papers, Massachusetts Historical Society, Boston.

16. Charles P. Sumner, "The Compass," *The Magazine of History with Notes and Queries* 24 (1923): 163–67.

17. Loring, *The Hundred Boston Orators*, 328; Charles Pinckney Sumner, "Miscellaneous Notebook," n.d., 180, Charles Pickney Sumner Papers, Massachusetts Historical Society, Boston; CS to Samuel Howe, August 3, 1871, 64/705, PCS.

18. Sumner, *Eulogy on the Illustrious George Washington*.

19. Loring, *The Hundred Boston Orators*, 328–29; Pierce, *MLCS*, 1:16–17, 19–20.

20. Pierce, *MLCS*, 1:29–30; Walter G. Shotwell, *Life of Charles Sumner* (New York: Thomas Y. Crowell, 1910), 4.

21. Jedediah Dwelley and John F. Simmons, *History of the Town of Hanover, Massachusetts, with Family Genealogies* (Hanover, Mass.: Town of Hanover, 1910), 239; Anne-Marie Taylor, *Young Charles Sumner and the Legacy of the American Enlightenment, 1811–1851* (Amherst: University of Massachusetts Press, 2001), 12–13.

22. Pierce, *MLCS*, 1:3; Frank Preston Stearns, *Cambridge Sketches* (Philadelphia: J. B. Lippincott, 1905), 180; Dwelley and Simmons, *History of the Town of Hanover, Massachusetts, with Family Genealogies*, 193, 239; John Stetson Barry, *A Historical Sketch of the Town of Hanover, Mass., with Family Genealogies* (Boston: Samuel G. Drake, 1853), 176.

23. "David Jacobs Jr. (1763–1799)," FamilySearch, n.d., https://ancestors.familysearch.org/en/LCVJ-4G4/david-jacobs-jr.-1763-1799; Taylor, *Young Charles Sumner*, 12–13; Stauffer, "Charles Sumner's Political Culture and the Foundation of Civil Rights," 325–26.

24. Taylor, *Young Charles Sumner*, 17–18.

Chapter 2: Gawky Sumner

1. Jeremiah Chaplin and J. D. Chaplin, *Life of Charles Sumner* (Boston: D. Lothrop, 1874), 18, 28–30; Elias Nason, *The Life and Times of Charles Sumner* (Boston: B. B. Russell, 1874), 18–21; Pierce, *MLCS*, 1:40–42.

2. For more on the Sumner siblings, see Pierce, *MLCS*, 1:31–34. For more specifically on George Sumner, see Robert C. Waterston, "Memoir of George Sumner," *Proceedings of the Massachusetts Historical Society, 1880–1881* 18 (1880): 189–223; Charles S. Hamlin, "Letters of George Sumner," *Proceedings of the Massachusetts Historical Society, Oct. 1912–June 1913* 46 (1914): 341–70.

3. Robert Francis Lucid, ed., *The Journal of Richard Henry Dana Jr.*, vol. 2 (Cambridge, Mass.: Harvard University Press, 1968), 662; CS, "Charles Sumner's Autobiographical Notes," n.d., Palfrey Papers, Houghton Library, Harvard University, 8; Pierce, *MLCS*, 1:42–43.

4. For more on the role that the Latin schools and Harvard played in serving Boston's social elite, see Pauline Holmes, *A Tercentenary History of the Boston Public Latin School, 1635–1935* (Cambridge, Mass.: Harvard University Press, 1935); Ronald Story, *The Forging of an Aristocracy: Harvard and the Boston Upper Class, 1800–1870* (Middletown, Conn.: Wesleyan University Press, 1980).

5. *Yankee*, June 11, 1818, 1; *Yankee*, May 15, 1818, 3. Charles Pinckney Sumner wrote several other letters regarding the public school system, all of which were published in the Boston *Yankee* between May 15 and July 31, 1818.

6. Frank Preston Stearns, *Cambridge Sketches* (Philadelphia: J. B. Lippincott, 1905), 181; David Donald, *Charles Sumner and the Coming of the Civil War* (Naperville, Ill.: Sourcebooks, 2009), 4; Irving H. Bartlett, *Wendell Phillips: Brahmin Radical* (Boston: Beacon Press, 1961), 11.

7. Oliver Wendell Holmes, *Elsie Venner: A Romance of Destiny*, vol. 1 (Boston: Ticknor and Fields, 1861), 16–17.

8. Donald, *Charles Sumner and the Coming of the Civil War*, 6; Edward Everett Hale, ed., *James Freeman Clarke: Autobiography, Diary and Correspondence* (Boston: Houghton, Mifflin, 1891), 26; Pierce, *MLCS*, 1:37–40.

9. Stephen Puleo, *The Great Abolitionist: Charles Sumner and the Fight for a More Perfect Union* (New York: St. Martin's Press, 2024), 26; CS, "A Chronological Compendium of English History by Charles Sumner" (1825), Charles Sumner Papers, Houghton Library, Harvard University.

10. Mary S. Withington, "From the Boston Beacon: The Home of Charles Sumner," *Dorchester News-Gatherer*, January 26, 1878.

11. Pierce, *MLCS*, 1:42–44, 106; "How Sumner Escaped the Army," *Springfield Daily Republican*, March 19, 1900; Anne-Marie Taylor, *Young Charles Sumner and the Legacy of the American Enlightenment, 1811–1851* (Amherst: University of Massachusetts Press, 2001), 29; Richard A. Pratt, "The Essence of Military Education: Contributions of Captain Alden Partridge to the United States Military Academy, 1806–1817," November 14, 1997, https://usmalibrary.contentdm.oclc.org/digital /collection/p16919coll1/id/16/. Pinckney Sumner described his position as a "more humble sphere" than that of "a young lawyer in this country" (C. P. Sumner, "Sheriff Sumner's Discourse," *American Jurist and Law Magazine* 2, no. 1 [1829]: 17).

12. Donald, *Charles Sumner and the Coming of the Civil War*, 8–12; Pierce, *MLCS*, 1:57–60.

13. Julia Ward Howe, "Reminiscences of Julia Ward Howe," *The Atlantic*, March 1899, 341; Hal Bridges, *Iron Millionaire: Life of Charlemagne Tower* (Philadelphia: University of Pennsylvania Press, 1952), 13; Hale, *James Freeman Clarke*, 40–41; Donald, *Charles Sumner and the Coming of the Civil War*, 9.

14. CS to Joseph Story, September 24, 1839, PCS; Pierce, *MLCS*, 1:51. Many contemporaries observed that Sumner had an astonishing memory. Wendell Phillips, for example, declared that Sumner's "memory never lost a phrase or a fact he had once heard, and could always recall it at the right moment." Wendell Phillips, "Sumner (Charles)," in *Johnson's Universal Cyclopaedia: A Scientific and Popular Treasury of Useful Knowledge*, ed. Frederick A. P. Barnard and Arnold Guyot (New York: A. J. Johnson, 1886) 622.

15. Chaplin and Chaplin, *Life of Charles Sumner*, 18–19; *A Memorial of Charles Sumner* (Boston: Wright and Porter, Printers to the Commonwealth of Massachusetts, 1874), 47; Pierce, *MLCS*, 1:71; Kathryn Grover and Janine V. da Silva, *Historic Resource Study: Boston African American National Historic Site* (Washington, D.C.: National Park Service, 2002), 251.

16. Stephen Kendrick and Paul Kendrick, *Sarah's Long Walk: The Free Blacks of Boston and How Their Struggle for Equality Changed America* (Boston: Beacon Press, 2004), 30; Peter P. Hinks, *To Awaken My Afflicted Brethren: David Walker and the Problem of Antebellum Slave Resistance* (University Park: Pennsylvania State University Press, 1997), 84.

17. Hinks, *To Awaken My Afflicted Brethren*, 74; Terry Alford, *Prince Among Slaves* (New York: Oxford

University Press, 1986), 136–41; "From the Boston Centinel," *Freedom's Journal*, September 5, 1828, 2; "Public Dinner in Boston," *Freedom's Journal*, October 24, 1828, 3. See also *Prince Among Slaves*, directed by Andrea Kalin and Bill Duke (Unity Productions Foundation, 2008).

18. David Walker, *Walker's Appeal, in Four Articulates; Together with a Preamble, to the Coloured Citizens of the World* (David Walker, 1830), 73, 86, 85, 49; Pierce, *MLCS*, 1:24; Taylor, *Young Charles Sumner*, 17–18.

Chapter 3: I Am Enamored of the Law

1. CS to Jonathan F. Stearns, September 28, 1830, 62/008, PCS; CS to Jonathan F. Stearns, August 7, 1831, 62/016, PCS; Pierce, *MLCS*, 1:84.

2. William W. Story, ed., *Life and Letters of Joseph Story*, vol. 1 (Boston: Charles C. Little and James Brown, 1851), 273–74; *Proceedings of the Massachusetts Historical Society, 1901–1902*, vol. 15 [vol. 35 of continuous numbering] (Boston: Massachusetts Historical Society, n.d.), 202–4. For more letters between Charles Pinckney Sumner and Joseph Story, see "Story, Joseph, 1779–1845: 7 Letters to Charles Pinckney Sumner, 1808–1833 and Undated," n.d., Documents Relating to Charles Sumner, Houghton Library, Harvard University.

3. Anne-Marie Taylor, *Young Charles Sumner and the Legacy of the American Enlightenment, 1811–1851* (Amherst: University of Massachusetts Press, 2001), 50; James Spear Loring, *The Hundred Boston Orators Appointed by the Municipal Authorities and Other Public Bodies from 1770 to 1852* (Boston: John P. Jewett, 1853), 330; Pierce, *MLCS*, 1:30.

4. Morgan D. Dowd, "Justice Joseph Story and the Politics of Appointment," *The American Journal of Legal History* 9, no. 4 (1965): 265–85; R. Kent Newmyer, *Supreme Court Justice Joseph Story: Statesman of the Old Republic* (Chapel Hill: University of North Carolina Press, 1985); Martin v. Hunter's Lessee, 14 U.S. 304 (1816); CS, "Tribute of Friendship: The Late Joseph Story," *Boston Daily Advertiser*, September 16, 1845, 137; CS to Charlemagne Tower, January 31, 1832, 65/029, PCS.

5. Pierce, *MLCS*, 1:111; CS, "Tribute of Friendship;" CS to Charlemagne Tower, September 29, 1831, 65/027, PCS.

6. For more on the teaching methods used by Story and his colleagues, see Simon Greenleaf, "Sketch of the Law School at Cambridge," in *The American Jurist and Law Magazine for January and April, 1835*, ed. Charles Sumner, vol. 13 (Boston: Samuel Coleman, 1835), 122–25; CS, "Tribute of Friendship," 141; Jeffrey L. Amestoy, *Slavish Shore: The Odyssey of Richard Henry Dana Jr.* (Cambridge, Mass.: Harvard University Press, 2015), 51–54.

7. CS, "Charles Sumner's Autobiographical Notes," n.d., Palfrey Papers, Houghton Library, Harvard University, 1; Pierce, *MLCS*, 1:102–4.

8. Pierce, *MLCS*, 1:108–11; CS to Charlemagne Tower, May 27, 1831, 65/015, PCS.

9. David Donald, *Charles Sumner and the Coming of the Civil War* (Naperville, Ill.: Sourcebooks, 2009), 21–22; CS to Joseph Story, July 13, 1837, 65/256, PCS; CS, *WCS*, vol. 1 (Boston: Lee and Shepard, 1875), 46; Story, *Life and Letters of Joseph Story*, 2:119–20; Pierce, *MLCS*, 1:105.

10. Joseph Story to CS, February 4, 1834, 01/061, PCS; Pierce, *MLCS*, 1:104; CS to Jonathan F. Stearns, May 14, 1832, 65/034, PCS.

11. Pierce, *MLCS*, 1:102–3, 107.

12. Greenleaf, "Sketch of the Law School at Cambridge," 122, 125; Donald, *Charles Sumner and the Coming of the Civil War*, 21–22; CS, *A Catalogue of the Law Library of Harvard University* (Cambridge, Mass.: Charles Folsom, 1834); Archibald H. Grimke, *Charles Sumner: The Scholar in Politics* (New York: Funk and Wagnalls, 1892), 36. While the quote about the law library is attributed to Simon Greenleaf, it is possible that it was created by Charles Sumner. Greenleaf's remarks were published in *The American Jurist and Law Magazine*, where Sumner served as an editor. He may have potentially expanded on Greenleaf's remarks to some degree to make them more thorough. See Pierce, *MLCS*, 1:151. There was also a previous library catalogue put together by two students in 1826, but this was an informal catalogue circulated among students and not a serious published work. See *The Centennial History of the Harvard Law School, 1817–1917* (Boston: Harvard Law School Association, 1918), 345–46.

13. Donald, *Charles Sumner and the Coming of the Civil War*, 22.

14. Jeremiah Chaplin and J. D. Chaplin, *Life of Charles Sumner* (Boston: D. Lothrop, 1874), 25; Donald, *Charles Sumner and the Coming of the Civil War*, 7; *Columbian Centinel*, August 25, 1827, 2.

15. Frank Preston Stearns, *Cambridge Sketches* (Philadelphia: J. B. Lippincott, 1905), 180; Howe, "Reminiscences of Julia Ward Howe," 339; "Public Execution," *Gazette (Gazette of Maine)*, March 7, 1826;

"Border Gossip," *Daily Albany Argus*, October 16, 1866; *Boston Daily American Statesman*, April 3, 1826, 2. Unlike his father, Charles Sumner would end up being morally opposed to capital punishment. See CS to Committee of the Massachusetts Legislature, "Against Capital Punishment," February 12, 1855, 3:527–28.

16. Charles Pinckney Sumner was, for a time, a clerk for King's Chapel. Relief Sumner was a lifelong congregant and close to the pastor Henry W. Foote. Their son Charles Sumner was not a regular churchgoer, but he would attend King's Chapel occasionally and kept two Bibles by his bed in Washington, one of which was a gift from his mother when he first became a senator. His depth of biblical literacy surprised clergymen, and in the words of Pastor Foote, "the clarion call of the Gospel wrought within him more than he was himself aware." Henry W. Foote, *In Memory of Charles Sumner: Sermon Preached at King's Chapel* (Boston: Alfred Mudge and Sons, 1874), 6, 37; Arnold B. Johnson, "Recollections of Charles Sumner," *Scribner's Monthly* 8 (1874), 477–78; George Sewall Boutwell, *Reminiscences of Sixty Years in Public Affairs: Governor of Massachusetts, 1851–1852*, vol. 2 (New York: McClure, Phillips, 1902), 216; Henry G. Spaulding, *Charles Sumner: An Address* (Boston: Geo. H. Ellis, 1910), 20–21.

17. Winthrop S. Hudson and John Corrigan, *Religion in America: A Historical Account of the Development of American Religious Life*, 6th ed. (Upper Saddle River, N.J.: Prentice Hall, 1999), 167; William E. Channing, "Unitarian Christianity: Discourse at the Ordination of the Rev. Jared Sparks. Baltimore, 1819" (Boston: American Unitarian Association, 1878), 367–68; James Freeman Clarke, *Vexed Questions in Theology: A Series of Essays* (Boston: Geo. H. Ellis, 1886), 15–16; John R. McKivigan, "Garrisonianism, the Churches, and the Division of the Abolitionist Movement," in *The War Against Proslavery Religion* (Ithaca, N.Y.: Cornell University Press, 2018), 56–73; Pierce, *MLCS*, 1:27. For more on Unitarianism in Boston's social reform culture, see generally Stephen Budiansky, *Oliver Wendell Holmes: A Life in War, Law, and Ideas* (New York: W. W. Norton, 2019), chap. 1.

18. Pierce, *MLCS*, 1:24–26; *Liberator*, August 6, 1836; Sumner, "Miscellaneous Notebook," August 1835.

19. Taylor, *Young Charles Sumner*, 41; Charles Pinckney Sumner, *A Letter on Speculative Masonry* (Boston: John Marsh, 1829), 19. For more on the Anti-Masonic Party, see Preston Vaughn, *The Anti-Masonic Party in the United States: 1826–1843* (Lexington: University Press of Kentucky, 2009).

20. Pierce, *MLCS*, 1:30; CS to Samuel Howe, August 16, 1844, 67/190, PCS; Henry R. Cleveland to CS, May 2, 1839, 65/642, PCS.

21. CS to Jonathan F. Stearns, September 25, 1831, 62/017, PCS.

22. CS to Simon Greenleaf, June 29, 1836, 65/174, PCS. Charles Sumner published several articles for the *Jurist*. See generally *The American Jurist* 12–14 (1834–1835).

23. CS to Henry R. Cleveland, August 27, 1839, 65/674–75, PCS; CS to Henry R. Cleveland, January 1, 1839, 65/560, PCS; Walter G. Shotwell, *Life of Charles Sumner* (New York: Thomas Y. Crowell, 1910), 27; Pierce, *MLCS*, 1:146; Browne to CS, July 24, 1834, *MLCS*, 1:124.

24. CS to Simon Greenleaf, August 30, 1836, 65/194, PCS; CS to Francis Lieber, October 21, 1837, 62/135–36, PCS; CS to William F. Frick, December 7, 1837, 62/141–42, PCS.

25. Story, *Life and Letters of Joseph Story*, 2:189–90; Simon Greenleaf to CS, September 7, 1838, 01/564, PCS; Pierce, *MLCS*, 2:283–84; Donald, *Charles Sumner and the Coming of the Civil War*, 25–26. The law publisher's remark about Sumner's legal acumen was made in 1844, but it was equally applicable in the 1830s.

Chapter 4: Mad Democratic Tendencies

1. One politician who impressed Sumner was Henry Clay, whose "eloquence was spending and thrilling." Sumner admired Clay's ability to show emotions and use strong language in his speeches. Other notables whom Sumner met include Daniel Webster and Supreme Court reporters Henry Wheaton and Richard Peters. Of these, Sumner was closest to Peters. See CS to Charles Pinckney Sumner, March 21, 1834, 62/048, PCS; CS to Simon Greenleaf, March 8, 1834, 01/069, PCS; CS to Charles Pinckney Sumner, March 19, 1834, 62/046, PCS; CS to Mary Sumner, March 18, 1834, 62/044, PCS; CS to Jane Sumner, March 4, 1834, 62/042, PCS; CS to Simon Greenleaf, February 19, 1834, 65/076, PCS.

2. Arthur Reed Hogue, ed., *Charles Sumner: An Essay by Carl Schurz* (Urbana: University of Illinois Press, 1951), 15; CS to Simon Greenleaf, March 8, 1834.

3. Pierce, *MLCS*, 1:136; Craig Joyce, "'A Curious Chapter in the History of Judicature': Wheaton v. Peters and the Rest of the Story (of Copyright in the New Republic)," *Houston Law Review* 42, no. 2 (2005): 376–78.

4. "Residences of the Court: Past and Present, Part II: The Capitol Years," *The Supreme Court Historical Society Quarterly* 3 (Winter 1981): 2–6; Joseph Story and CS, May 28, 1844, 04/050, PCS; CS, *WCS*, 8:238–39; CS to Relief Sumner and Charles Pinckney Sumner, March 3, 1834, 62/038, PCS; Carl Schurz, "Eulogy Before City Authorities of Boston (Music Hall, April 29, 1874)," in *Charles Sumner: Memoir and Eulogies*, ed. William M. Cornell (Boston: James H. Earle, 1874), 107; CS, "Charles Sumner's Autobiographical Notes," n.d., Palfrey Papers, Houghton Library, Harvard University, 2.

5. Joseph Story, *Commentaries on the Constitution of the United States*, vol. 1 (Boston: Charles C. Little and James Brown, 1851); Newmyer, *Supreme Court Justice Joseph Story*, 181; Story, *Life and Letters of Joseph Story*, 2:578. For more on John Marshall and Joseph Story's role in preserving the vision of constitutional nationalism, see Akhil Reed Amar, *The Words That Made Us: America's Constitutional Conversation, 1760–1840* (New York: Basic Books, 2021), 525–83. For more on Marshall and Story's relationship, see Charles Warren, "The Story-Marshall Correspondence (1819–1831)," *William and Mary College Quarterly Historical Magazine* 21, no. 1 (1941).

6. James Spear Loring, *The Hundred Boston Orators Appointed by the Municipal Authorities and Other Public Bodies from 1770 to 1852* (Boston: John P. Jewett, 1853), 624. For Sumner's attitude toward *Prigg v. Pennsylvania*, see CS to Charles Francis Adams, March 1, 1843, 66/442, PCS.

7. Charles Warren, "The Story-Marshall Correspondence (1819–1831)"; Adolph Moses, "The Friendship Between Marshall and Story," *American Law Review* 35 (1901): 321–42; CS to Charlemagne Tower, July 15, 1833, 65/051, PCS; CS, "Adelphi Union Lecture Notes" (1837), Charles Sumner Papers, Houghton Library, Harvard University.

8. CS, "Lawyer's Common-Place Book" (1831), 60–61, Charles Sumner Papers, Houghton Library, https://curiosity.lib.harvard.edu/reading/catalog/42-990069824080203941.

9. Francis Vesey, *Reports of Cases Argued and Determined in the High Court of Chancery: From the Year MDCCLXXXIX to DCCCXVII: With a Digested Index*, ed. Charles Sumner, vol. 1 (Boston: C. C. Little and J. Brown, 1844), vi; CS to Joseph Story, May 28, 1844, 4/050, PCS; CS to Relief Jacobs Sumner and Charles Pinckney Sumner, February 21, 1834, 62/034, PCS. For Kent and Story as leading equity jurists, see John H. Langbein, Renee Lettow Lerner, and Bruce P. Smith, *History of the Common Law: The Development of Anglo-American Legal Institutions* (New York: Aspen Publishing, 2009), 381.

10. Loring, *The Hundred Boston Orators*, 624; M. A. De Wolfe Howe, *Portrait of an Independent: Moorfield Storey, 1845–1929* (Boston: Houghton Mifflin, 1932), 52. For Kent's relationship to Hamilton, see John H. Langbein, "Chancellor Kent and the History of Legal Literature," *Columbia Law Review* 93, no. 3 (1993): 556–57.

11. Pierce, *MLCS*, 1:154; Pierce, *MLCS*, 3:69; William Lloyd Garrison, *Liberator*, January 1, 1831, 1; Donald M. Jacobs, "William Lloyd Garrison's Liberator and Boston's Blacks," *New England Quarterly* 44, no. 2 (June 1971): 259–77; Wendell Phillips Garrison and Francis Jackson Garrison, *William Lloyd Garrison: The Story of His Life Told by His Children*, vol. 1 (New York: The Century Company, 1885), 432; Wendell Phillips, *Speeches, Lectures, and Letters*, ed. Theodore C. Pease (Boston: Lee and Shepard, 1905), 466.

12. David Donald incorrectly claimed that Sumner's relationship with Channing began after the former's trip to Europe. In fact, they grew close in the early to mid-1830s. See Pierce, *MLCS*, 1:157; CS to Charles Francis Adams, April 9, 1850, 63/340–41, PCS; William E. Channing, *Slavery* (Boston: James Munroe, 1835); William Hague, *Life Notes or Fifty Years' Outlook* (Boston: Lee and Shepard, 1888), 163; David Donald, *Charles Sumner and the Coming of the Civil War* (Naperville, Ill.: Sourcebooks, 2009), 84–85; Anne-Marie Taylor, *Young Charles Sumner and the Legacy of the American Enlightenment, 1811–1851* (Amherst: University of Massachusetts Press, 2001), 139–45.

13. C. C. Burleigh, "Response to 'Another Argument for Sir Robert Peel,'" *Liberator*, October 24, 1835; Garrison and Garrison, *William Lloyd Garrison*, 29. Charles Sumner reportedly watched the mob attack Garrison from his law office. Arnold B. Johnson, "Recollections of Charles Sumner: The Senator's Home and Pictures," *Scribner's Monthly* 7 (1875), 109.

14. Carlos Martyn, *Wendell Phillips: The Agitator* (New York: Funk and Wagnalls, 1890), 78–82.

15. William Lloyd Garrison, *Liberator*, December 29, 1832; Gilbert Haven, "The Very Chiefest of Our Statesmen," in *Charles Sumner: Memoir and Eulogies*, ed. William M. Cornell (Boston: James H. Earle, 1874), 49; CS, "Adelphi Union Lecture Notes"; Pierce, *MLCS*, 2:196; Pierce, *MLCS*, 3:141.

16. Lydia Maria Child, *An Appeal in Favor of That Class of Americans Called Africans* (New York: John S. Taylor, 1836), 57, 98–99, 201; Lydia Moland, *Lydia Maria Child: A Radical American Life* (Chicago: University of Chicago Press, 2022), 89–90; CS to Lydia Maria Child, January 14, 1853, 70/646, PCS;

Lydia Maria Child, *Letters of Lydia Maria Child* (Boston: Houghton Mifflin, 1883), 77; CS to Francis Lieber, January 9, 1836, 62/088, PCS.

17. Donald, *Charles Sumner and the Coming of the Civil War*, 34; CS to Francis Lieber, June 17, 1837, 65/253, PCS; Pierce, *MLCS*, 1:199; Robert Francis Lucid, ed., *The Journal of Richard Henry Dana Jr.*, vol. 2 (Cambridge, Mass.: Harvard University Press, 1968), 662.

18. CS to Charles S. Daveis, August 4, 1837, 65/261, PCS; CS to Joseph Story, December 7, 1837, 65/346, PCS; Pierce, *MLCS*, 1:213–14; CS to Joseph Story, July 13, 1837, 65/256, PCS. It is unclear who, if anyone, was the recipient of Henry Clay's letter; Sumner preserved the letter in his autograph collection. See CS, "Charles Sumner Autograph Collection, 1624–1846," n.d., 1:74, Houghton Library, Harvard University.

19. CS to Joseph Story, February 14, 1838, 65/377, PCS; CS to Simon Greenleaf, April 13, 1838, 65/407, PCS; CS to Henry R. Cleveland, January 6, 1838, 65/358–60, PCS; Pierce, *MLCS*, 1:228.

20. Pierce, *MLCS*, 1:241–42.

21. Shelby T. McCloy, *The Negro in France* (Lexington: University of Kentucky Press, 1961), 204–8; Taylor, *Young Charles Sumner*, 251.

22. Alexis de Tocqueville to CS, May 18, 1838, 65/441, PCS; CS to Alexis de Tocqueville, September 15, 1847, 63/191, PCS; Pierce, *MLCS*, 1:226–97; CS to Henry R. Cleveland, March 21, 1838, 65/394, PCS; CS to Simon Greenleaf, January 6, 1838, 65/362, PCS.

23. Augustin Cochin, *The Results of Emancipation*, trans. Mary L. Booth (Boston: Walker, Wise, 1864), 37–38; CS to George S. Hillard, May 11, 1838, 62/180, PCS; Pierce, *MLCS*, 1:243, 255–56, 265, and 296.

24. Pierce, *MLCS*, 1:305–7.

25. CS to Benjamin Rand, February 20, 1839, 65/580, PCS; CS to Joseph Story, April 21, 1838, 65/416, PCS; CS to George Hillard, March 1, 1839, 62/341, PCS; CS to George Sumner, December 8, 1837, 62/153, PCS.

26. Simon Greenleaf to CS, September 7, 1838, 01/564, PCS; Joseph Story to CS, August 11, 1838, 01/546, PCS; Francis Lieber to CS, October 9, 1838, *MLCS*, 2:7.

27. Donald, *Charles Sumner and the Coming of the Civil War*, 45; CS to Joseph Story, March 18, 1839, 62/376, PCS. For more on radicalism, see Isaac Kramnick, *Republicanism and Bourgeois Radicalism: Political Ideology in Late Eighteenth-Century England and America* (Ithaca, N.Y.: Cornell University Press, 1990); Paul McLaughlin, *Radicalism: A Philosophical Study* (London: Palgrave Macmillan, 2012). See also Manisha Sinha, *The Slave's Cause: A History of Abolition* (New Haven: Yale University Press, 2016), 363–71.

28. CS to Simon Greenleaf, January 25, 1837, 62/112, PCS; CS to Joseph Story, March 18, 1839, 62/363, PCS.

29. CS to John Gorham Palfrey, August 12, 1838, 65/484, PCS; Pierce, *MLCS*, 1:307; Donald, *Charles Sumner and the Coming of the Civil War*, 60.

30. CS to George Hillard, September 29, 1839, 62/423, PCS; CS to John Jay, May 25, 1843, 66/484, PCS.

31. Pierce, *MLCS*, 2:94–95. For more on Sumner's study of the arts in Italy, see Taylor, *Young Charles Sumner*, 116–21.

32. CS to William Story, July 6, 1839, 65/661, PCS. For a focused study on the friendship between Crawford and Sumner, see Katya Miller, "Behold the Statue of Freedom: Sculptor Thomas Crawford and Senator Charles Sumner," *The Capitol Dome* 50, no. 3 (2013): 16–23.

33. Henry R. Cleveland to CS, May 2, 1839, 65/642, PCS; Pierce, *MLCS*, 2:96; CS to George Hillard, July 13, 1839, 62/401, PCS.

Chapter 5: Sumner Ought to Have Been a Woman

1. CS and Joseph Story, March 24, 1840, 62/444, PCS; Pierce, *MLCS*, 2:122.

2. Mary Caroline Crawford, *Romantic Days in Old Boston: The Story of the City and of Its People During the Nineteenth Century* (Boston: Little, Brown, 1910), 317–18; Pierce, *MLCS*, 2:148. For more on Ticknor's Park Street mansion, see Robert Means Lawrence, *Old Park Street and Its Vicinity* (Boston: Houghton Mifflin, 1922), 81–91. For Ticknor's biography, see generally Charles Henry Hart, *Memoir of George Ticknor, Etc.* (Philadelphia: Collins, 1871); David B. Tyack, *George Ticknor and the Boston Brahmins* (Cambridge, Mass.: Harvard University Press, 1967). Anna Eliot Ticknor inherited roughly $84,000 in 1821. See Tyack, *George Ticknor and the Boston Brahmins*, 90. The Massachusetts State House dome did not become gold until much later. See Amy Sokolow, "Secrets of the Golden Dome at the Massachusetts State House," n.d., https://www.bostonherald.com/2022/04/16/secrets-of-the-golden-dome-at-the-massachusetts-state-house/.

3. Leo Damrosch, *Tocqueville's Discovery of America* (New York: Macmillan, 2010), 96–99; Anonymous,

Our First Men: A Calendar of Wealth, Fashion and Gentility; Containing a List of Those Persons Taxed in the City of Boston with Biographical Notices of the Principal Persons (Boston: The Booksellers, 1846), 5–6; Pierce, *MLCS*, 2:122; Tyack, *George Ticknor and the Boston Brahmins*, 90. For more on Boston elites, see Tyack, *George Ticknor and the Boston Brahmins*, 173–87; Jeffrey L. Amestoy, *Slavish Shore: The Odyssey of Richard Henry Dana Jr.* (Cambridge, Mass.: Harvard University Press, 2015), 70–78.

4. Pierce, *MLCS*, 2:156; Crawford, *Romantic Days in Old Boston*, 317–18; Charles Dickens, *American Notes* (New York: St. Martin's Press, 1985), 26.

5. U.S. District Court, Docket Book, December 1841, Nos. 32–36, 38–40, 42 (Federal Records Center, Waltham); U.S. Circuit Court, Docket Book, Term beginning October 1841, Nos. 25–26, 31–32, 43, 93, 99–103 (Federal Records Center, Waltham); CS to Francis Lieber, September 23, 1840, *MLCS*, 2:166; CS and Francis Lieber, December 10, 1841, *MLCS*, 2:188–89; David Donald, *Charles Sumner and the Coming of the Civil War* (Naperville, Ill.: Sourcebooks, 2009), 61.

6. Pierce, *MLCS*, 2:122, 147; Samuel Longfellow, ed., *Life of Henry Wadsworth Longfellow: With Extracts from His Journals and Correspondence*, vol. 1 (Boston: Houghton Mifflin, 1891), 365; *Boston Post*, May 6, 1840.

7. Longfellow, *Life of Henry Wadsworth Longfellow*, 1:367; Donald, *Charles Sumner and the Coming of the Civil War*, 63–64; Samuel Howe to CS, March 5, 1843, 66/444, PCS.

8. CS to Francis Lieber, June 27, 1842, *MLCS*, 2:212–13; CS to George Sumner, May 9, 1841, *MLCS*, 2:179; Donald, *Charles Sumner and the Coming of the Civil War*, 146. For Longfellow's life, see generally Nicholas A. Basbanes, *Cross of Snow: A Life of Henry Wadsworth Longfellow* (New York: Alfred A. Knopf/Doubleday, 2020).

9. Pierce, *MLCS*, 2:151; Edwin Percy Whipple, "Recollections of Charles Sumner," *Harper's Monthly Magazine*, July 1879, 270.

10. Edwin Percy Whipple, "Dickens's American Notes," *The Atlantic Monthly*, April 1877; CS to Joseph Story, January 31, 1842, 66/232, PCS.

11. William M. Cornell, ed., *Charles Sumner: Memoir and Eulogies* (Boston: James H. Earle, 1874), 302; Donald, *Charles Sumner and the Coming of the Civil War*, 70–71.

12. Donald, *Charles Sumner and the Coming of the Civil War*, 70–71; Edwin Percy Whipple, "Recollections of Charles Sumner," 275; Henry F. Kletzing and Elmer L. Kletzing, *Traits of Character Illustrated in Bible Light* (Kletzing Bros., 1898), 227; Pierce, *MLCS*, 1:125–27, 199; Phillips, "Sumner (Charles)," 620; Charles Francis Adams, *Richard Henry Dana: A Biography*, vol. 1 (Boston: Houghton Mifflin, 1890), 29–30.

13. Franklin Benjamin Sanborn, *Dr. S. G. Howe, the Philanthropist* (New York: Funk and Wagnalls, 1891), 349; Elaine Showalter, *The Civil Wars of Julia Ward Howe: A Biography* (New York: Simon and Schuster, 2017), 53. For more on Samuel Howe's life, see generally Sanborn, *Dr. S. G. Howe, the Philanthropist*; Harold Schwartz, *Samuel Gridley Howe, Social Reformer* (Cambridge, Mass.: Harvard University Press, 1956); James W. Trent Jr., *The Manliest Man: Samuel G. Howe and the Contours of Nineteenth-Century American Reform* (Amherst: University of Massachusetts Press, 2012).

14. Pierce, *MLCS*, 1:162; Frank Preston Stearns, *Cambridge Sketches* (Philadelphia: J. B. Lippincott, 1905), 188.

15. Pierce, *MLCS*, 1:165; CS to George Washington Greene, August 17, 1843, 66/560, PCS; Samuel Howe to CS, February 1, 1842, 66/234, PCS.

16. Gary Williams, *Hungry Heart: The Literary Emergence of Julia Ward Howe* (Amherst: University of Massachusetts Press, 1999), 45.

17. Showalter, *The Civil Wars of Julia Ward Howe*, 50; Valarie H. Ziegler, *Diva Julia: The Public Romance and Private Agony of Julia Ward Howe* (New York: Bloomsbury Academic, 2003), 29.

18. CS to Julia Ward Howe, February 1843, 66/440, PCS; CS to Samuel Ward, February 21, 1843, 66/426, PCS; CS to Henry Longfellow, June 6, 1842, 66/300, PCS; CS to Henry Longfellow, July 22, 1842, 66/319, PCS.

19. Williams, *Hungry Heart*, 49; Samuel Howe to CS, February 22, 1843, 62/582, PCS; Samuel Howe to CS, May 13, 1843, 66/480, PCS.

20. Longfellow, *Life of Henry Wadsworth Longfellow*, 1:279; Williams, *Hungry Heart*, 59; Samuel Howe to CS, April 20, 1852, Howe Family Papers, 1819–1910, HL; Basbanes, *Cross of Snow*, 238.

21. CS to Samuel Howe, August 31, 1843, 62/593, PCS; Samuel Howe to CS, February 2, 1844, 67/094, PCS; Williams, *Hungry Heart*, 59; Longfellow, *Life of Henry Wadsworth Longfellow*, 1:279.

22. On romantic friendships and homosexuality in New England in the early to mid-1800s, see Karen V. Hansen, "'Our Eyes Behold Each Other': Masculinity and Intimate Friendship in Antebel-

lum New England," in *Men's Friendships*, ed. Peter M. Nardi (Newbury Park, Calif.: Sage Publications, 1992); E. Anthony Rotundo, "Romantic Friendship: Male Intimacy and Middle-Class Youth in the Northern United States, 1800–1900," *Journal of Social History* 23, no. 1 (1989): 1–25; David S. Reynolds, *Walt Whitman's America: A Cultural Biography* (New York: Alfred A. Knopf/ Doubleday, 1996), 390–403; William E. Benemann, *Male-Male Intimacy in Early America: Beyond Romantic Friendships* (New York: Routledge, 2014), preface.

23. For focused studies on Longfellow and Sumner's romantic friendship, see Frederick J. Blue, "The Poet and the Reformer: Longfellow, Sumner, and the Bonds of Male Friendship, 1837–1874," *Journal of the Early Republic* 15, no. 2 (1995); Edward M. Cifelli, *Longfellow in Love: Passion and Tragedy in the Life of the Poet* (Jefferson, N.C.: McFarland, 2018), 121–23; "An Era of Romantic Friendships: Sumner, Longfellow, and Howe," National Park Service, n.d., https://www.nps.gov /articles/an-era-of-romantic-friendships-sumner-longfellow-and-howe.htm; "Charles Sumner and Romantic Friendships," National Park Service, n.d., https://www.nps.gov/articles/000 /charles-sumner-and-romantic-friendships.htm.

24. Schwartz, *Samuel Gridley Howe, Social Reformer*, 108. For focused studies on Samuel Howe and Sumner's sexuality, see Williams, *Hungry Heart*, chap. 2; Michael Bronski, *A Queer History of the United States* (Boston: Beacon Press, 2011), 55–56; "'Let Me Be All Yours': The Romantic Friendship of Charles Sumner and Samuel Gridley Howe," Meaghan Michel, King's Chapel History Program, 2021, YouTube video, n.d., https://www.youtube.com/watch?v=jJayFkj66cw; "An Era of Romantic Friendships: Sumner, Longfellow, and Howe"; "Charles Sumner and Romantic Friendships."

25. Pierce, *MLCS*, 1:107; Schwartz, *Samuel Gridley Howe, Social Reformer*, 108.

26. Samuel Howe to CS, February 2, 1844, 67/094, PCS; Samuel Howe to CS, July 23, 1848, 63/262, PCS; Samuel Howe to CS, July 1848, 63/264, PCS.

27. Samuel Howe to CS, June 18, 1843, 66/502, PCS; Samuel Howe to CS, May 13, 1843, 66/480, PCS.

28. Samuel Howe to CS, September 11, 1844, 67/199, PCS. For more on Julia Ward and Samuel Howe's complicated marriage, see generally Ziegler, *Diva Julia*; and Showalter, *The Civil Wars of Julia Ward Howe*.

29. Williams, *Hungry Heart*, 80–105; Julia Ward Howe, *The Hermaphrodite*, ed. Gary Williams (Lincoln: University of Nebraska Press, 2004); Showalter, *The Civil Wars of Julia Ward Howe*, 87–92.

30. Samuel Howe to CS, April 20, 1852, 70/337, PCS; Showalter, *The Civil Wars of Julia Ward Howe*, 204.

31. Howe to CS, May 13, 1843.

32. CS to Francis Lieber, June 27, 1842, *MLCS*, 2:212; CS to Francis Lieber, July 13, 1848, *MLCS*, 2:263.

33. Pierce, *MLCS*, 2:282–87.

34. Pierce, *MLCS*, 2:287, 289; CS to George Sumner, July 31, 1844, 63/027, PCS; CS to Samuel Howe, August 16, 1844, 67/190, PCS.

35. Williams, *Hungry Heart*, 59; Howe, "Reminiscences of Julia Ward Howe," *The Atlantic*, March 1899, 338–42; Pierce, *MLCS*, 2:287–88; Pierce, *MLCS*, 3:31.

36. Williams, *Hungry Heart*, 59; CS to George Sumner, May 15, 1844, 63/012, PCS; CS to George Sumner, July 31, 1844, 63/027, PCS; CS to Howe, August 16, 1844, 67/190, PCS.

37. Pierce, *MLCS*, 2:287, 289; CS to George Sumner, July 31, 1844, 63/027, PCS; CS to Howe, August 16, 1844, 67/190, PCS.

38. Pierce, *MLCS*, 2:324–29; "Massachusetts Legislature," *Greenfield Recorder*, March 11, 1845; "A Munificent Donation," *Pittsfield Sun*, January 30, 1845; Julia Ward Howe, *Reminiscences of Julia Ward Howe, 1819–1899* (Boston: Houghton, Mifflin, 1899), 172.

39. For more on Sumner's involvement in prison reform, the peace movement, and the Boston Athenaeum, see Donald, *Charles Sumner and the Coming of the Civil War*, 98–108; and Anne-Marie Taylor, *Young Charles Sumner and the Legacy of the American Enlightenment, 1811–1851* (Amherst: University of Massachusetts Press, 2001), 168–71.

40. Jeremiah Chaplin and J. D. Chaplin, *Life of Charles Sumner* (Boston: D. Lothrop, 1874), 96–97; Pierce, *MLCS*, 2:340.

41. James Spear Loring, *The Hundred Boston Orators Appointed by the Municipal Authorities and Other Public Bodies from 1770 to 1852* (Boston: John P. Jewett, 1853), 156; Charles Francis Adams, *The Works of John Adams*, vol. 10 (Boston: Little, Brown, 1856), 201–4. For a full list of Fourth of July orators from 1783 to 1908, see *Index to the City Documents: 1834 to 1909* (City of Boston Printing Department, 1910), 133–42, 164–67.

42. Pierce, *MLCS*, 2:341–42; William M. Cornell, "Memoir of Charles Sumner," in *Cornell, Charles Sumner: Memoir and Eulogies*, 13; Edward Pierce, "Mr. Pierce's Address," in *Dinner Commemorative*

of Charles Sumner and Complimentary to Edward L. Pierce (Cambridge, Mass.: John Wilson and Son, 1895), 53; "Boston: Celebration of the Fourth by the City Authorities," *Boston Post*, July 7, 1845.

43. All quotes of Sumner's speech for the next few paragraphs were obtained from CS, *The True Grandeur of Nations: An Oration Delivered Before the Authorities of the City of Boston* (Boston: William D. Ticknor, 1845).

44. "Boston: Celebration of the Fourth by the City Authorities."

45. Sumner elaborated on his idea of a Congress of Nations in the appendix to the published pamphlet edition of his speech. CS, *The True Grandeur of Nations*, 94–97.

46. Cornell, "Memoir of Charles Sumner," 15–16; Whipple, "Recollections of Charles Sumner," 272; Pierce, *MLCS*, 2:355–58; "Boston: Celebration of the Fourth by the City Authorities."

47. CS, *The True Grandeur of Nations*, 1; Pierce, *MLCS*, 2:357–58, 364–65, 374–78. For a compilation of letters that Sumner received after the speech, see "Sumner's Oration on the 'True Grandeur of Nations,' July 4, 1845," *Proceedings of the Massachusetts Historical Society, Oct. 1916–June 1917* 50 (1917): 249–307.

48. CS to James Miller McKim, November 17, 1845, 67/360, PCS. For many decades after Sumner first delivered the speech, *The True Grandeur of Nations* continued to be annually published and distributed by peace societies in England and the United States. When Henry Longfellow visited England in the summer of 1846, he wrote in his diary that Sumner's "oration on Peace is hawked about the streets in England" (Longfellow, *Life of Henry Wadsworth Longfellow*, 1:46).

49. Whipple, "Recollections of Charles Sumner," 272–73; Thomas Sergeant Perry, ed., *The Life and Letters of Francis Lieber* (Boston: James R. Osgood, 1882), 198; Charles Eliot Norton, ed., *Letters of James Russell Lowell*, vol. 1 (New York: Harper and Bros., 1894), 97.

50. Joseph Story to CS, August 11, 1845, 04/386, PCS.

Chapter 6: He Is Outside the Pale of Society

1. CS to Committee of the New Bedford Lyceum, November 29, 1845, *WCS*, 1:160–62. Ralph Waldo Emerson, Theodore Parker, and Horace Mann also protested the New Bedford Lyceum's white-only policy in the main seats. The Lyceum eventually relented and integrated its events. See *Liberator*, January 16, 1846; Frederick Douglass, *Life and Times of Frederick Douglass* (Hartford: Park Publishing, 1882), 261.

2. A Citizen of Boston, *Remarks upon an Oration Delivered by Charles Sumner Before the Authorities of the City of Boston* (Boston: W. M. Crosby and H. P. Nichols, 1845), 5; *Boston Post*, August 21, 1845; Allan Nevins, *Ordeal of the Union*, vol. 1 (New York: Charles Scribner's Sons, 1947), 393.

3. Charles Warren, *History of the Harvard Law School and of Early Legal Conditions in America* (New York: Lewis, 1908), 98; D. A. Harsha, *The Life of Charles Sumner* (New York: H. Dayton, 1858), 40; Daniel R. Coquillette and Bruce A. Kimball, *On the Battlefield of Merit: Harvard Law School, the First Century* (Cambridge, Mass.: Harvard University Press, 2015), 192–94.

4. Pierce, *MLCS*, 3:11–12, 60–61; David Donald, *Charles Sumner and the Coming of the Civil War* (Naperville, Ill.: Sourcebooks, 2009), 108. Many decades later, Sumner's acquaintance Peleg Chandler recalled that he "was deeply disappointed that he was not offered a position in the Law School on the death of Judge Story" (Pierce, *MLCS*, 2:252). In a short write-up about his life, Sumner spent considerable time emphasizing that after being implicitly promised the position, it was "never offered to me" (CS, "Charles Sumner's Autobiographical Notes," n.d., Palfrey Papers, Houghton Library, Harvard University, 3–4).

5. Anne-Marie Taylor, *Young Charles Sumner and the Legacy of the American Enlightenment, 1811–1851* (Amherst: University of Massachusetts Press, 2001), 201. For more on the Constitution burning affair, see Larry J. Reynolds, *Righteous Violence: Revolution, Slavery, and the American Renaissance* (Athens: University of Georgia Press, 2011), 24–25. For the list of members of the Anti-Texas Committee, see "State Anti-Texas Committee," *The Liberator*, November 7, 1845.

6. Taylor, *Young Charles Sumner*, 198–200; CS to John Bigelow, January 21, 1851, 69/490, PCS.

7. CS, "The Wrong of Slavery" (Speech, Faneuil Hall, Boston, November 4, 1845), 1:85, *WCS*.

8. Edward Pierce, *Memoir and Letters of Charles Sumner*, vol. 3 (London: Sampson Low, Marston, Searle & Rivington, 1893), 114–19; "Mr. Winthrop's Vote on the War Bill," *Boston Courier*, July 31, 1845; "Mr. Winthrop's Vote on the War Bill," *Boston Courier*, August 13, 1845; Donald, *Charles Sumner and the Coming of the Civil War*, 121–22. For more on the Three-Fifths Clause, see Akhil Reed Amar, *America's Constitution: A Biography* (New York: Random House, 2005), 87–98.

9. Donald, *Charles Sumner and the Coming of the Civil War*, 130.

10. Donald, *Charles Sumner and the Coming of the Civil War*, 130–31, 144–45; Edward L. Pierce, *Enfranchisement and Citizenship: Addresses and Papers*, ed. A. W. Stevens (Boston: Roberts Bros., 1896), 188.

11. Cornelius Felton to CS, April 1846, 05/027, PCS; CS to Cornelius Felton, April 9, 1850, 63/340, PCS; CS to Cornelius Felton, April 10, 1850, 63/343, PCS; Taylor, *Young Charles Sumner*, 233–35, 301–4; Pierce, *MLCS*, 3:50–51.

12. Harold Schwartz, *Samuel Gridley Howe, Social Reformer* (Cambridge, Mass.: Harvard University Press, 1956), 190; Pierce, *MLCS*, 3:119–20, 181; Taylor, *Young Charles Sumner*, 226–28; Charles Francis Adams, *Richard Henry Dana: A Biography*, vol. 1 (Boston: Houghton Mifflin, 1890), 128; Nicholas A. Basbanes, *Cross of Snow: A Life of Henry Wadsworth Longfellow* (New York: Knopf/Doubleday, 2020), 259.

13. Schwartz, *Samuel Gridley Howe, Social Reformer*, 190; Taylor, *Young Charles Sumner*, 303; Henry G. Spaulding, *Charles Sumner: An Address* (Boston: Geo. H. Ellis, 1910), 15.

14. Kent P. Ljungquist, "Lectures and the Lyceum Movement," in *The Oxford Handbook of Transcendentalism*, ed. Sandra Harbert Petrulionis et al. (London: Oxford University Press, 2010), 330–47.

15. Sumner's yearly earnings were reportedly less than one to two thousand dollars at this time. He was boarding in his family home. Walter G. Shotwell, *Life of Charles Sumner* (New York: Thomas Y. Crowell, 1910), 179.

16. CS, "White Slavery in the Barbary States" (Speech, Boston Mercantile Library Association, February 17, 1847), *WCS*, 2:383. The speech was later sold as a popular book with forty illustrations. See CS, *White Slavery in the Barbary States* (Boston: John Jewett, 1853); CS, "White Slavery in the Barbary States," *Daily National Era*, February 23, 1852. See also Precious Rasheeda Muhammad, *Muslims and the Making of America* (Muslim Public Affairs Council, 2013), 53–54.

17. Pierce, *MLCS*, 3:18. In an encyclopedia article he wrote about his friend, Wendell Phillips claimed that by the late 1840s, Sumner "was recognized as the leader of the young men of the Commonwealth, and hidden in their hearts. . . . He always had, to the day of his death, the hearty, entire, steadfast, and loving confidence of the young men of Massachusetts," Wendell Phillips, "Sumner (Charles)," in *Johnson's Universal Cyclopaedia: A Scientific and Popular Treasury of Useful Knowledge*, ed. Frederick A. P. Barnard and Arnold Guyot (New York: A. J. Johnson, 1886), 621.

18. CS, *The Works of Charles Sumner*, vol. 1 (Boston: Lee & Shepard, 1875), 243.

19. William Hague, *Life Notes or Fifty Years' Outlook* (Boston: Lee and Shepard, 1888), 163–65; Donald, *Charles Sumner and the Coming of the Civil War*, 128–29; Taylor, *Young Charles Sumner*, 128–29; Pierce, *MLCS*, 3:185.

20. Joshua R. Giddings, *History of the Rebellion: Its Authors and Causes* (New York: Follet, Foster, 1864), 217–18; John Quincy Adams, *Speech of the Hon. John Quincy Adams, in the House of Representatives, on the State of the Nation: Delivered May 25, 1836* (New York: H.R. Piercy, 1836); Cong. Globe, 27th Cong., 2nd Sess., 429 (1842) (remarks of Rep. Adams); CS, *The Works of Charles Sumner*, vol. 2 (Boston: Lee & Shepard, 1875), 184.

21. For more on Adams's constitutionalism, see generally Gary V. Wood, *Heir to the Fathers: John Quincy Adams and the Spirit of Constitutional Government* (Lanham, Md.: Lexington Books, 2004).

22. Taylor, *Young Charles Sumner*, 278; Pierce, *MLCS*, 3:19.

23. Pierce, *MLCS*, 1:123; "Thomas Clarkson," *Anti-Slavery Bugle*, January 16, 1846; Stuart Weems Bruchey, *Cotton and the Growth of the American Economy, 1790–1860* (New York: Random House, 1967), 7–43; Alexis de Tocqueville, *Democracy in America*, trans. Henry Reeve, vol. 1 (University Park: Pennsylvania State University Press, 2002), 409; Thomas H. O'Connor, *Lords of the Loom: The Cotton Whigs and the Coming of the Civil War* (New York: Charles Scribner's Sons, 1968), 1–42; William Moran, *The Belles of New England: The Women of the Textile Mills and the Families Whose Wealth They Wove* (New York: St. Martin's Press, 2002), 47–52; J. David Hacker, "From '20. and Odd' to 10 Million: The Growth of the Slave Population in the United States," *Slavery and Abolition* 41, no. 4 (2020): 840–55, https://doi.org/10.1080/0144039x.2020.1755502; Frederic Cople Jaher, *The Urban Establishment: Upper Strata in Boston, New York, Charleston, Chicago, and Los Angeles* (Champaign: University of Illinois Press, 1982), 54–57.

24. CS, *WCS*, 1875, 2:81; Donald, *Charles Sumner and the Coming of the Civil War*, 119.

25. CS, "Antislavery Duties of the Whig Party" (Speech, Faneuil Hall, Boston, September 23, 1846), 1:303–16, *WCS*. For more on Adams's amendment, see Michael Vorenberg, *Final Freedom* (London: Cambridge University Press, 2001), 12, 51; Randall Woods, *John Quincy Adams* (New York: Dutton, 2024), 647–51.

26. Samuel Tilden, "Supplement: The First Gun for Free Soil," in *The Writings and Speeches of Samuel J. Tilden*, ed. John Bigelow (New York: Harper and Bros., 1885), 2:535–36. For more on Martin Van Buren's relationship with political antislavery, see Donald B. Cole, *Martin Van Buren and the American Political System* (Princeton: Princeton University Press, 2014), chap. 14.

27. Walter Stahr, *Salmon Chase: Lincoln's Vital Rival* (New York: Simon and Schuster, 2021), 123–26; Eric Foner, *Free Soil, Free Labor, Free Men: The Ideology of the Republican Party Before the Civil War* (New York: Oxford University Press, 1995), chaps. 3–4; "Free Soil Party Platform of 1848 | The American Presidency Project," accessed September 1, 2024, https://www.presidency.ucsb.edu/documents/free-soil-party-platform-1848.

28. CS to John Whittier, July 12, 1848, *MLCS*, 3:168; Pierce, *MLCS*, 3:174–75.

29. CS to George Sumner, November 15, 1848, *MLCS*, 3:185; CS to George Sumner, July 31, 1849, *MLCS*, 3:186; CS to John Jay, December 5, 1848, *MLCS*, 3:185.

30. Pierce, *MLCS*, 3:47.

Chapter 7: From Pisgah to the Promised Land

1. "Speech of Mr. Emery T. Morris," *The Boston Guardian*, January 14, 1911; Edwin G. Walker, "Eulogy" (Speech, Robert Morris Memorial Meeting, March 5, 1882), BL; J. Clay Smith, *Emancipation: The Making of the Black Lawyer, 1844–1944* (Philadelphia: University of Pennsylvania Press, 1993), 96–97; Stephen Kendrick and Paul Kendrick, *Sarah's Long Walk: The Free Blacks of Boston and How Their Struggle for Equality Changed America* (Boston: Beacon Press, 2004), 13–20; John Daniels, *In Freedom's Birthplace: A Study of the Boston Negroes* (Boston: Houghton Mifflin, 1914), 450–51.

2. Boston School Committee, *Report to the Primary School Committee, June 15, 1846, on the Petition of Sundry Colored Persons, for the Abolition of the Schools for Colored Children: With the City Solicitor's Opinion* (Boston: J. H. Eastburn, 1846), 13.

3. Frank Preston Stearns, *The Life and Public Services of George Luther Stearns* (Philadelphia: J. B. Lippincott, 1907), 58.

4. Benjamin F. Roberts to Amos Augustus Phelps, June 19, 1838, Anti-Slavery Collections, Boston Public Library, https://www.digitalcommonwealth.org/search/commonwealth:m900qj668.

5. James Oliver Horton and Lois E. Horton, *Black Bostonians: Family Life and Community Struggle in the Antebellum North* (New York: Holmes and Meier, 1979), 76–77; Kendrick and Kendrick, *Sarah's Long Walk*, 73–77.

6. Arthur O. White, "Blacks and Education in Antebellum Massachusetts" (Ph.D. diss., Buffalo, State University of New York, 1971), 208–9.

7. *Liberator*, September 4, 1846; Smith, *Emancipation*, 96–97.

8. Brown v. Kendall, 60 Mass. 292 (1850); Frederic Hathaway Chase, *Lemuel Shaw: Chief Justice of the Supreme Judicial Court of Massachusetts, 1830–1860* (Boston: Houghton Mifflin, 1918), 277.

9. All quotes of Sumner's argument in *Roberts* were obtained from the earliest published pamphlet edition of his remarks. See CS, *Argument of Charles Sumner, Esq. Against the Constitutionality of Separate Colored Schools* (Boston: B. F. Roberts, 1849).

10. The phrase "equality before the law" was in the 1814, 1815, and 1830 French constitutions and in the constitutions of Holland, the Grand Duchy of Warsaw, the Canton of Zug, Switzerland, Bavaria, Bolivia, Portugal, and Greece. See CS, *WCS*, 8:394–95. In searching the Library of Congress's Chronicling America database of American newspapers, I found fifty-nine articles that used "equality before the law" prior to Sumner's usage on December 14, 1849. Almost all these newspaper articles were describing the constitutions of the aforementioned countries. After Sumner's usage, the frequency of "equality before the law" in newspaper records skyrocketed. That leads me to conclude that Sumner effectively coined the expression. See National Endowment for the Humanities, "Chronicling America," Text, Library of Congress, n.d., https://chroniclingamerica.loc.gov/.

11. Roberts v. City of Boston, 59 Mass. 198 (1850); Plessy v. Ferguson, 163 U.S. 537, 544 (1896).

12. Kendrick and Kendrick, *Sarah's Long Walk*, 180; *Liberator*, April 26, 1850; Robert Morris to CS, June 11, 1860, 19/567, PCS.

13. "A Voice from Faneuil Hall," *Bangor Daily Whig*, October 1, 1846; Edward Pierce, *Memoir and Letters of Charles Sumner*, vol. 3 (London: Sampson Low, Marston, Searle & Rivington, 1893), 130–33.

14. Lance Newman, "Thoreau and Violence," *The Concord Saunterer* 23 (2015): 110–14; Gary Grieve-Carlson, "Extremism in the Defense of Liberty: Henry David Thoreau & John Brown," *Amerika-*

studien / American Studies 63, no. 3 (2018): 321–35; Jack Doyle, "Thoreau's Advocacy of Violent Resistance," *The Thoreau Society Bulletin*, no. 269 (2010): 5–7.

15. CS, *The Works of Charles Sumner*, vol. 10 (Boston: Lee & Shepard, 1875), 343.

16. R. J. M. Blackett, *The Captive's Quest for Freedom: Fugitive Slaves, the 1850 Fugitive Slave Law, and the Politics of Slavery* (New York: Cambridge University Press, 2018), 52–53; CS, *The Works of Charles Sumner*, vol. 2 (Boston: Lee & Shepard, 1875), 403.

17. R. J. M. Blackett, "Fugitive Slaves in Britain: The Odyssey of William and Ellen Craft," *Journal of American Studies* 12, no. 1 (1978): 42; Wilbur H. Seibert, "The Vigilance Committee of Boston," in *The Proceedings of the Bostonian Society: Annual Meeting of January 27, 1953* (Boston: The Bostonian Society, 1951), 26.

18. For more on the Crafts' escape, see William Craft and Ellen Craft, *Running a Thousand Miles for Freedom* (Athens: University of Georgia Press, 1999).

19. Lawrence Lader, *The Bold Brahmins: New England's War Against Slavery, 1831–1863* (New York: Dutton, 1961), 140; Donald Martin Jacobs, "A History of the Boston Negro from the Revolution to the Civil War" (Ph.D. diss., Boston University, 1968), 271.

20. Jeremiah Chaplin and J. D. Chaplin, *Life of Charles Sumner* (Boston: D. Lothrop, 1874), 156–58; CS, *WCS*, 1875, 2:412. For more on Lewis Hayden, see Stanley J. Robboy and Anita W. Robboy, "Lewis Hayden: From Fugitive Slave to Statesman," *The New England Quarterly* 46, no. 4 (1973): 591–613; Joel Strangis, *Lewis Hayden and the War Against Slavery* (New Haven: Linnet Books, 1999); Harriet Beecher Stowe, *A Key to Uncle Tom's Cabin* (Boston: Jewett, Proctor & Worthington, 1853), 154–55.

21. "Boston Nullification," *The Weekly North Carolina Standard*, November 13, 1850; Seibert, "The Vigilance Committee of Boston," 26–28; Gary Collison, *Shadrach Minkins: From Fugitive Slave to Citizen* (Cambridge, Mass.: Harvard University Press, 1997), 92–99; Kendrick and Kendrick, *Sarah's Long Walk*, 190–92; Steven Lubet, *Fugitive Justice: Runaways, Rescuers, and Slavery on Trial* (Cambridge, Mass.: Harvard University Press, 2011), 133–35. For more on antislavery lawyering against the Fugitive Slave Act, see Daniel Farbman, "Resistance Lawyering," *California Law Review* 107 (2019): 1877–1954.

22. Andrew Delbanco, *The War Before the War: Fugitive Slaves and the Struggle for America's Soul from the Revolution to the Civil War* (New York: Penguin, 2018), 266.

23. Pierce, *MLCS*, 3:213–14, 218.

24. CS, *WCS*, 1875, 2:422.

25. Gamaliel Bailey to CS, November 27, 1850, 07/429, PCS.

26. Frederick J. Blue, *The Free Soilers: Third Party Politics, 1848–54* (Urbana: University of Illinois Press, 1973), 214.

27. No author, *Francis William Bird: A Biographical Sketch* (Priv. print., 1897), 44, https://www.google.com/books/edition/Francis_William_Bird/mNXNggJgxdIC?hl=en&gbpv=0.

28. CS to Henry Longfellow, January 24, 1850, 69/069, PCS; CS to Samuel Howe, July 30, 1850, 63/383, PCS. Henry Longfellow wrote in his diary that Sumner was "really not wanting to be Senator; though few, if any, will believe that." Samuel Longfellow, ed., *Life of Henry Wadsworth Longfellow: With Extracts from His Journals and Correspondence*, vol. 2 (Boston: Houghton Mifflin, 1891), 187.

29. CS, *WCS*, 1875, 2:414–15.

30. CS to John G. Whittier, September 11, 1851, 70/011, PCS; CS to John G. Palfrey, October 15, 1850, 69/411, PCS; Anne-Marie Taylor, *Young Charles Sumner and the Legacy of the American Enlightenment, 1811–1851* (Amherst: University of Massachusetts Press, 2001), 317, 323.

31. David Donald, *Charles Sumner and the Coming of the Civil War* (Naperville, Ill.: Sourcebooks, 2009), 164.

32. Leonard W. Levy, "Sims' Case: The Fugitive Slave Law in Boston in 1851," *The Journal of Negro History* 35, no. 1 (1950): 41; "Proclamation 56—Calling on Citizens to Assist in the Recapture of a Fugitive Slave Arrested in Boston, Massachusetts," The American Presidency Project, accessed September 4, 2024, https://www.presidency.ucsb.edu/documents/proclamation-56-calling-citizens-assist-the-recapture-fugitive-slave-arrested-boston.

33. Chase, *Lemuel Shaw*, 171–72; Charles Francis Adams, *Richard Henry Dana: A Biography*, vol. 1 (Boston: Houghton Mifflin, 1890), 185–95; Levy, "Sims' Case: The Fugitive Slave Law in Boston in 1851," 39–74; Stephen Puleo, *The Great Abolitionist: Charles Sumner and the Fight for a More Perfect Union* (New York: St. Martin's Press, 2024), chap. 10.

34. Donald, *Charles Sumner and the Coming of the Civil War*, 169–70.

35. Chaplin and Chaplin, *Life of Charles Sumner*, 171–72; Taylor, *Young Charles Sumner*, 334; Samuel T. Pickard, *Life and Letters of John Greenleaf Whittier*, vol. 1 (Boston: Houghton Mifflin, 1894), 356.

36. Pierce, *MLCS*, 3:19; Longfellow, *Life of Henry Wadsworth Longfellow*, 2:194.

Chapter 8: The Senate Is a Dirty House

1. CS to Henry Longfellow, November 26, 1851, 70/057, PCS.
2. Chris Myers Asch and George Derek Musgrove, *Chocolate City: A History of Race and Democracy in the Nation's Capital* (Chapel Hill: University of North Carolina Press, 2017), 31, 94, 98, 99–105.
3. Arthur Reed Hogue, ed., *Charles Sumner: An Essay by Carl Schurz* (Urbana: University of Illinois Press, 1951), 25; Theodore Parker to CS, April 26, 1851, 007/686, PCS. The physical description of Charles Sumner and his style of speaking during his early days in the Senate was obtained from a variety of sources. See, e.g., D. A. Harsha, *The Life of Charles Sumner* (New York: H. Dayton, 1858), 152–55; Edward Dicey, *Six Months in the Federal States* (London: Macmillan, 1863), 236–37; Arnold B. Johnson, "Recollections of Charles Sumner," *Scribner's Monthly* 8 (1874), 475–76, 480; Pierce, *MLCS*, 4:85; Pierce, "Mr. Pierce's Address," 23–24; Walter G. Shotwell, *Life of Charles Sumner* (New York: Thomas Y. Crowell, 1910), 253; Marian Gouverneur, *As I Remember: Recollections of American Society During the Nineteenth Century* (New York: D. Appleton, 1911), 243–44; Charles Francis Adams, *Charles Francis Adams, 1835–1915, an Autobiography* (Boston: Houghton Mifflin, 1916), 60–61; David Donald, *Charles Sumner and the Coming of the Civil War* (Naperville, Ill.: Sourcebooks, 2009), 177, 180–81. I obtained the apt phrase "every inch a classical Roman senator" from Michael Les Benedict, *A Compromise of Principle: Congressional Republicans and Reconstruction, 1863–1869* (New York: W. W. Norton, 1974), 37.
4. Joseph M. Rogers, *Thomas H. Benton* (Philadelphia: George W. Jacobs, 1905), 279; Mary Tyler Peabody Mann, *Life of Horace Mann* (Boston: Walker, Fuller, 1865), 45. For alternative renditions of Benton's advice to Sumner, see Benjamin Perley Poore, *Perley's Reminiscences of Sixty Years in the National Metropolis*, vol. 1 (Philadelphia: Hubbard's Bros., 1886), 419.
5. George H. Haynes, *Charles Sumner* (Philadelphia: George W. Jacobs, 1909), 140; Elias Nason, *The Life and Times of Charles Sumner* (Boston: B. B. Russell, 1874), 180; Pierce, *MLCS*, 3:262; CS to Richard Henry Dana Jr., December 8, 1851, 70/076, PCS.
6. George H. Haynes, *The Senate of the United States: Its History and Practice*, vol. 2 (Boston: Houghton Mifflin, 1938), 1002.
7. Haynes, *The Senate of the United States*, 2:916; Margaret B. Klapthor, "Furniture in the Capitol: Desks and Chairs Used in the Chamber of the House of Representatives, 1819–1857," *Records of the Columbia Historical Society, Washington, D.C.* 69/70 (1969/1970): 192–93.
8. CS to Charles Francis Adams, December 28, 1851, 70/124, PCS; Joanne B. Freeman, *The Field of Blood: Violence in Congress and the Road to Civil War* (New York: Farrar, Straus and Giroux, 2018), 3–4, 33–34, 167–68; CS to Richard Henry Dana Jr., December 8, 1851; Charles Dickens, *American Notes* (New York: St. Martin's Press, 1985), 111–12; Haynes, *The Senate of the United States*, 2:942–43; Pierce, *MLCS*, 3:455; CS to Samuel Howe, December 30, 1851, 63/474, PCS; CS to Horace Greeley, July 21, 1854, 71/405, PCS. While Sumner called the Senate "a dirty house" in a letter to Greeley in 1854, the sentiment equally applied in 1851.
9. CS to Amasa Walker, December 19, 1851, 70/109, PCS.
10. Pierce, *MLCS*, 3:263; CS to Henry Longfellow, December 28, 1851, 70/134, PCS; Donald, *Charles Sumner and the Coming of the Civil War*, 176–77; Varina Davis, *Jefferson Davis, Ex-President of the Confederate States of America: A Memoir by His Wife*, vol. 1 (New York: Belford, 1890), 557–58.
11. Pierce, *MLCS*, 3:265–73; CS to Samuel Howe, December 1851, *MLCS*, 3:270.
12. CS to Henry Longfellow, December 28, 1851, 70/134, PCS; CS to William Story, August 2, 1853, 71/102, PCS.
13. Daniel Drayton, *Personal Memoir of Daniel Drayton* (Boston: Bela Marsh, 1854), 115–19. Sumner visited Drayton and Sayres frequently during their confinement. See Johnson, "Recollections of Charles Sumner," 1874, 8:480.
14. *Liberator*, February 19, 1852, 3; *Liberator*, April 23, 1852, 2; CS to Henry Wilson, April 29, 1845, *MLCS*, 3:278.
15. Pierce, *MLCS*, 3:277–78; Mann, *Life of Horace Mann*, 1:379; "The Liberation of Drayton and Sayres," *Boston Commonwealth*, August 24, 1852.
16. Jeremiah Chaplin and J. D. Chaplin, *Life of Charles Sumner* (Boston: D. Lothrop, 1874), 188; Theodore Parker to Samuel Howe, August 30, 1852, Documents Relating to Charles Sumner, Folder 95, Box 2, HL; John Weiss, *Life and Correspondence of Theodore Parker*, vol. 2 (New York: Appleton, 1864), 213; CS to Samuel Howe, April 5, 1852, 63/516, PCS; Harold Schwartz, *Samuel Gridley Howe, Social Reformer* (Cambridge, Mass.: Harvard University Press, 1956), 177–83; Carlisle to CS, February 28, 1851, 07/593, PCS.

17. Donald, *Charles Sumner and the Coming of the Civil War*, 199; Robert C. Winthrop, *Addresses and Speeches on Various Occasions* (Boston: Little, Brown, 1852), 770–71.

18. Haynes, *The Senate of the United States*, 2:893, 924; Salmon Chase to CS, April 28, 1851, 07/693, PCS; CS to Henry Wilson, June 29, 1852, 09/202, PCS; Richard H. Abbott, *Cobbler in Congress: The Life of Henry Wilson, 1812–1875* (Lexington: University Press of Kentucky, 1972), 48.

19. CS to Charles Francis Adams, June 21, 1852, 70/404, PCS; Salmon P. Chase, *An Argument for the Defendant Submitted to the Supreme Court of the United States, in the Case of Wharton Jones v. John Van Zandt* (Cincinnati: R. P. Donogh, 1847); Samuel Tilden, "Supplement: The First Gun for Free Soil," in *The Writings and Speeches of Samuel J. Tilden*, ed. John Bigelow (New York: Harper and Bros., 1885), 2:535–36.; Thomas Wentworth Higginson, *Contemporaries* (Boston: Houghton Mifflin, 1899), 285; Donald, *Charles Sumner and the Coming of the Civil War*, 196. For more on Salmon Chase's antislavery constitutionalism, see Randy E. Barnett, "From Antislavery Lawyer to Chief Justice: The Remarkable but Forgotten Career of Salmon P. Chase," *Case Western Reserve Law Review* 63, no. 3 (2013): 653–702. For more on the Barnburner Manifesto, see chapter 6.

20. Frederick W. Seward, *Seward at Washington* (New York: Derby and Miller, 1891), 190; Cong. Globe, 32nd Cong., 1st. Sess., 1952 (1852) (remarks of Senator Butler); Pierce, *MLCS*, 3:289–90; Elizabeth Fries Ellet, *The Court Circles of the Republic* (Hartford: Hartford Publishing Company, 1870), 471–72; Walter G. Shotwell, *Life of Charles Sumner* (New York: Thomas Y. Crowell, 1910), 271.

21. CS to Wendell Phillips, April 27, 1852, 09/058, PCS; Charles Francis Adams to CS, August 1, 1852, 70/466, PCS; CS to Edward Pierce, August 6, 1852, 63/562, PCS; Pierce, *MLCS*, 3:292–93.

22. All quotes to Sumner's speech "Freedom National" are obtained from the *Congressional Globe*. Cong. Globe, 32nd Cong., 1st. Sess., 1102–13 (1852). For a published version, see CS, "Freedom National, Slavery Sectional" (Speech, U.S. Senate, August 26, 1852), *WCS*, 3:87. The reader may wish to consult the published version, even though modest changes were made, because it is easier to read than the *Globe*'s.

23. Somerset v. Stewart, 98 ER 499 (1772).

24. For the original Sherman and Madison quotes, see Max Farrand, ed., *The Records of the Federal Convention of 1787*, vol. 2 (New Haven: Yale University Press, 1901), 416–17. For the Supreme Court case, see Groves v. Slaughter, 40 U.S. 449, 507 (1841) (McLean, J., concurring).

25. For the letter from Congress, see United States Congress to the States, April 25, 1783, Founders Online, National Archive, https://founders.archives.gov/documents/Madison/01-06-02-0180. The phrase "freedom national, slavery sectional" was effectively coined by Salmon Chase in 1850. But it did not pick up steam until after Sumner's address; he can be fairly credited with popularizing the slogan and turning it into a rallying cry for the antislavery movement. See Cong. Globe, 31st Cong., 1st. Sess., 474 (1850) (remarks of Senator Chase); Henry G. Spaulding, *Charles Sumner: An Address* (Boston: Geo. H. Ellis, 1910), 14; Eric Foner, *Free Soil, Free Labor, Free Men: The Ideology of the Republican Party Before the Civil War* (New York: Oxford University Press, 1995), 83; James Oakes, *Freedom National: The Destruction of Slavery in the United States, 1861–1865* (New York: W. W. Norton, 2012), ix; Manisha Sinha, *The Slave's Cause: A History of Abolition* (New Haven: Yale University Press, 2016), 477.

26. Joseph Story, *Commentaries on the Constitution of the United States*, vol. 1 (Boston: Charles C. Little and James Brown, 1851), sec. 318. For one modern view of what Story might have meant by general citizenship, see Jud Campbell, "General Citizenship Rights," *Yale Law Journal* 132, no. 3 (2023): 611–701.

27. CS, "Our Immediate Antislavery Duties" (Speech, Faneuil Hall, Boston, November 6, 1850), 403, *WCS*, 2:398.

28. The Madison quote is obtained from David Robertson, *Debates and Other Proceedings of the Convention of Virginia*, 2nd ed. (Richmond: Ritchie and Worsley and Augustine Davis, 1805), 322. For a concise and intelligent discussion of the Constitution's Fugitive Slave Clause and its debated parameters, see Akhil Reed Amar, *America's Constitution: A Biography* (New York: Random House, 2005), 256–64. One exchange of letters illustrates how Sumner may have understood the weakness of his argument about the clause. An individual who appears to have been a friend of his brother George wrote to the senator suggesting that his strict construction of the clause was implausible because it rendered the clause utterly superfluous. Charles Sumner wrote back arguing that it was the South that had insisted on strict construction in the first place and that his goal in using *their* method of interpretation "was to beat down the existing [Fugitive Slave] Act and assumption of power." He admitted that his approach may "have weakened in some minds the

force of the attack on the Act." See Isaac Ray to CS, September 16, 1852, 09/409, PCS; CS to Isaac Ray, September 21, 1852, 70/475, PCS.

29. The Washington letter is reprinted in full in Fritz Hirschfeld, *George Washington and Slavery: A Documentary Portrayal* (Columbia: University of Missouri Press, 1997), 115–16. One book from 1858 claims that Sumner was the first person to publish this letter (in the published version of his "Freedom National" speech), a claim that appears to be true. Daniel R. Goodloe, *The Southern Platform* (Boston: John P. Jewett, 1858), 8. That said, Sumner's retelling of the story of Ona Judge is misleading at best. George Washington relentlessly—and violently—sought Judge's recapture, and he subverted Pennsylvania laws that ought to have granted her freedom. It is unclear how much Sumner knew or could have known about the full story. For more on Ona Judge and Washington's pursuit of her, see Erica Armstrong Dunbar, *Never Caught: The Washingtons' Relentless Pursuit of Their Runaway Slave, Ona Judge* (New York: Simon and Schuster, 2017).

30. CS to John Bigelow, January 21, 1851, 69/490, PCS. The Garrisonian view of the Constitution is aptly captured in Wendell Phillips, *The Constitution: A Pro-Slavery Compact* (New York: American Anti-Slavery Society, 1856). For Spooner's view, see Lysander Spooner, *The Unconstitutionality of Slavery* (Boston: Bela Marsh, 1845). The relationship between Sumner and the Garrisonians—personally, politically, and intellectually—is complex, fascinating, and deserves its own study. Sumner was criticized by Wendell Phillips for his loyalty to the Constitution in a speech delivered in early 1853 (and later published as a pamphlet in 1860). Hurt, Sumner wrote to Phillips urging him to criticize without being personal. "Our system has differed," Sumner wrote, "but it is a source of real joy to me that we have ever been friends." Phillips wrote back kindly, but only after some time had passed. See Wendell Phillips, *The Philosophy of the Abolition Movement* (New York: The American Anti-Slavery Society, 1860); CS to Wendell Phillips, January 30, 1853, 70/679, PCS; Wendell Phillips to CS, March 7, 1853, 10/30, PCS; CS to Wendell Phillips, January 30, 1853. By contrast, the relationship between Sumner and Spooner was almost nonexistent. Spooner had once reportedly asked Samuel Howe what Sumner thought of his argument. Howe replied that "Sumner always said it was true, but somehow or other he could not think it was practical." Upon learning this, Spooner sent Sumner an eccentric and angry letter accusing the senator of treason against his oath to the Constitution. Sumner does not seem to have replied to Spooner's diatribe. Lysander Spooner, *Public Letters and Political Essays*, ed. Phillip W. Magness (Great Barrington, Mass.: American Institute for Economic Research, 2019), 17–18.

31. Thoreau's famous essay, now known as "Civil Disobedience," was originally called "Resistance to Civil Government." The edition that Sumner would have read is Henry David Thoreau, "Resistance to Civil Government; a Lecture Delivered in 1847," in *Aesthetic Papers*, ed. Elizabeth Palmer Peabody, 1849, 189–213. Though they were not close friends, Sumner and Thoreau were acquainted with each other by 1850 at the latest. See CS to Henry David Thoreau, July 2, 1850, 07/297, PCS; Henry David Thoreau to CS, July 31, 1850, 69/297, PCS. On Dr. Martin Luther King Jr.'s use of St. Augustine, see "Letter from a Birmingham Jail [King, Jr.]," African Studies Center—University of Pennsylvania, https://www.africa.upenn.edu/Articles_Gen/Letter_Birmingham.html.

32. Cong. Globe, 32nd Cong., 1st. Sess., app., 1113–19 (1852) (remarks of Senators Clemens, Dodge, and Badger). Congressman Horace Mann, who watched Sumner's speech from the Senate Chamber, observed that Clemens was drunk. Mann, *Life of Horace Mann*, 381. In one letter, Sumner went out of his way to mention that one congressman was sober—implying that most members were inebriated. CS to John Bigelow, August 30, 1852, *MLCS*, 3:309.

33. Cong. Globe, 32nd Cong., 1st. Sess., app., 1119–20 (1852) (remarks of Senators Weller and Douglas); Mann, *Life of Horace Mann*, 381; George William Curtis, "Eulogy Before Massachusetts State Government," in *Charles Sumner: Memoir and Eulogies*, ed. William M. Cornell (Boston: James H. Earle, 1874), 202–3.

34. Salmon Chase to CS, September 9, 1852, 09/391, PCS; Carl Schurz, "Eulogy Before City Authorities of Boston (Music Hall, April 29, 1874)," in Cornell, *Charles Sumner: Memoir and Eulogies*, 121; Wendell Phillips to CS, September 3, 1852, 09/369, PCS; CS, *WCS*, 3:94; George William Curtis, *Orations and Addresses of George William Curtis*, vol. 3 (New York: Harper and Bros., 1894), 230. Salmon Chase also told Sumner that Supreme Court justice John McLean had read the speech and "spoke of it with praise."

35. Frances Seward to CS, September 18, 1852, 09/414, PCS; Hamilton Fish to CS, September 1852, *MLCS*, 3:306; Theodore Parker to CS, September 6, 1852, 09/379, PCS; Nason, *The Life and Times of Charles Sumner*, 163.

36. Hermann Eduard von Holst, *The Constitutional and Political History of the United States*, trans. John J. Lalor (Chicago: Callaghan, 1885), 219; The Earl of Carlisle, "Preface," in *Uncle Tom's Cabin* (London: George Routledge and Sons, 1852); Pierce, *MLCS*, 3:57, 458; CS to Lord Wharncliffe, December 19, 1852, 70/602, PCS. Henry Wilson said the speech had "placed the new senator at once among the foremost of the forensic debaters of America." Henry Wilson, *History of the Rise and Fall of the Slave Power in America*, vol. 2 (Boston: Houghton Mifflin, 1874), 355.

37. "Thirty-Second Congress" (Washington, D.C.: U.S. Government Publishing Office), n.d., https://www.govinfo.gov/content/pkg/GPO-CDOC-108hdoc222/pdf/GPO-CDOC-108hdoc222-3-32.pdf; CS, "The Party of Freedom: Its Necessity and Practicability" (Speech, State Convention of the Free-Soil Party of Massachusetts, Held at Lowell, September 15, 1852), *WCS*, 3:199, 205.

38. Ernest McKay, *Henry Wilson: Practical Radical* (Port Washington, N.Y.: National University Publications, 1971), 80; Martin B. Duberman, *Charles Francis Adams: 1807–1886* (Boston: Houghton Mifflin, 1961), 183; Mann, *Life of Horace Mann*, 383; Donald, *Charles Sumner and the Coming of the Civil War*, 119–20. A journalist marveled at how one of the state's most powerful politicians, respected in Washington and internationally acclaimed, could be so isolated from the elites of his own hometown. The journalist quipped that it was a kind of "fashionable ostracism." Edwin Percy Whipple, "Recollections of Charles Sumner," *Harper's Monthly Magazine*, July 1879, 276.

39. CS to John Bigelow, August 30, 1852, *MLCS*, 3:309; Samuel Howe to CS, October 1852, 70/551, PCS.

40. Pierce, *MLCS*, 3:317–19; McKay, *Henry Wilson*, 80, 82. In fairness to Sumner, he also believed that avoiding local politics kept him out of entanglements and let him focus on the antislavery cause at the national stage. He once told Salmon Chase that John Quincy Adams remained aloof from local politics for this reason. CS to Salmon Chase, August 26, 1856, 72/278, PCS.

41. Francis Lieber to CS, May 20, 1851, 69/599, PCS; Frank Freidel, "Francis Lieber, Charles Sumner, and Slavery," *Journal of Southern History* 9, no. 1 (February 1943): 89; Donald, *Charles Sumner and the Coming of the Civil War*, 203.

42. Cong. Globe, 32nd Cong., 2nd. Sess., 40 (1852) (remarks of Senator Bright).

43. CS to Lydia Maria Child, January 14, 1853, 70/646, PCS.

44. CS to Henry Wilson, March 24, 1853, 71/042, PCS; Pierce, *MLCS*, 3:336; CS to Wharncliffe, June 5, 1852, 70/386, PCS. For more on the constitutional convention, see *Journal of the Constitutional Convention of the Commonwealth of Massachusetts* (Boston: White and Potter, 1853).

45. While copies of Sumner's stump speeches on the draft constitution do not survive, his rhetoric was gleaned from a few letters he wrote after the loss. See CS to Charles Francis Adams, November 21, 1853, 71/136, PCS; CS to William Seward, November 15, 1853, 71/129, PCS; CS to Edward Pierce, December 18, 1853, 63/622, PCS; CS to John Whittier, November 21, 1853, 71/133, PCS. After much ambivalence, Palfrey published his opposition to the reform. John Palfrey, *Remarks on the Proposed State Constitution by a Free-Soiler from the Start* (Boston: Crosby, Nichols, 1853).

46. Pierce, *MLCS*, 3:339–42; Samuel Shapiro, "The Conservative Dilemma: The Massachusetts Constitutional Convention of 1853," *New England Quarterly* 33, no. 2 (June 1960): 207–24; Claude Moore Fuess, *The Life of Caleb Cushing*, vol. 2 (New York: Harcourt, Brace, 1923), 139–40.

Chapter 9: Let the Pulpits Thunder Against Oppression

1. CS to Samuel Howe, December 8, 1853, 63/620, PCS; Pierce, *MLCS*, 3:345; Alice Elizabeth Malavasic, *The F Street Mess: How Southern Senators Rewrote the Kansas-Nebraska Act* (Chapel Hill: University of North Carolina Press, 2017), 154.

2. *Annual Report of the Commissioner of Indian Affairs* (Washington, D.C.: Department of the Interior, 1853), 35; James C. Malin, *The Nebraska Question: 1852–1854* (Ann Arbor: Edwards Bros., 1953), 16–19, 128–37; Roy F. Nichols, "The Kansas-Nebraska Act: A Century of Historiography," *Journal of American History* 43, no. 2 (November 1956): 187–212.

3. *New York Times*, May 30, 1854, 3.

4. For more on the F Street Mess, see generally Malavasic, *The F Street Mess*, 60–142.

5. Mrs. Archibald Dixon, *The True History of the Missouri Compromise and Its Repeal* (Cincinnati: Robert Clarke, 1899), 444–45. Douglas made this remark to Archibald Dixon, a proslavery Whig senator from Kentucky.

6. CS, *The Slave Oligarchy and Its Usurpations* (Washington, D.C.: Buell and Blanchard, 1855).

7. Akhil Reed Amar, *The Words That Made Us: America's Constitutional Conversation, 1760–1840* (New York: Basic Books, 2021), 595; Don Edward Fehrenbacher, *Constitutions and Constitutionalism in the Slaveholding South* (Athens: University of Georgia Press, 1989), 54; Malavasic, *The F*

Street Mess, 84–85; Thomas Wentworth Higginson, *Contemporaries* (Boston: Houghton Mifflin, 1899), 282. In the privacy of the home of his friend Richard Henry Dana, Sumner also claimed that senators had acted on thousands of nominations in executive session based solely on the test of the nominee's fidelity to the Fugitive Slave Act and the Kansas-Nebraska Act. "The most minute and gossiping evidence is gone into, on each side, pro and con, to prove or throw in doubt the position of the nominee" toward the "slave-power," he claimed. Charles Francis Adams, *Richard Henry Dana: A Biography*, vol. 1 (Boston: Houghton Mifflin, 1890), 289.

8. For more on the socioeconomic dimensions of political antislavery critique, from Sumner and other key figures, see generally Forrest A. Nabors, *From Oligarchy to Republicanism: The Great Task of Reconstruction* (Columbia: University of Missouri Press, 2017); Joseph Fishkin and William E. Forbath, *The Anti-Oligarchy Constitution: Reconstructing the Economic Foundations of American Democracy* (Cambridge, Mass.: Harvard University Press, 2022), chaps. 2–3.

9. "Hon. Preston S. Brooks at Home," *Charleston Courier*, October 7, 1856. See also James Redpath, *A Guide to Hayti* (Boston: Haytian Bureau of Emigration, 1861), 10. For more on the scorpion's sting theory, see James Oakes, Freedom National: *The Destruction of Slavery in the United States, 1861–1865* (New York: W. W. Norton, 2012), 256–300; James Oakes, *The Scorpion's Sting: Antislavery and the Coming of the Civil War* (New York: W. W. Norton, 2014), 13–21.

10. S. P. Chase et al., *Appeal of the Independent Democrats in Congress to the People of the United States* (Washington, D.C.: Towers, 1854); Samuel Howe to CS, January 18, 1854, 71/190, PCS; Samuel Howe to CS, January 25, 1854, 71/206, PCS. The signatories of the *Appeal* were Salmon Chase, Charles Sumner, Joshua Giddings, Edward Wade, Gerrit Smith, and Alex de Witt. Giddings wrote the first draft, which Chase significantly revised, and Sumner provided a final literary flourish. George W. Julian, *The Life of Joshua R. Giddings* (Chicago: A. C. McClurg, 1892), 311. For a list of the newspapers that reported leaks on the Nebraska issue prior to the *Appeal*, see Pierce, *MLCS*, 3:349.

11. *New National Era*, January 24, 1854.

12. David M. Potter, *The Impending Crisis: 1846–1861* (New York: Harper and Row, 1963), 162–65; "Latest Intelligence from Washington: The Debate on the Nebraska Bill," *New York Times*, February 1, 1854.

13. Cong. Globe, 33rd Cong., 1st. Sess., 275–82 (1854) (remarks of Senators Douglas, Chase, and Sumner); Robert W. Johannsen, *Stephen A. Douglas* (New York: Oxford University Press, 1973), 418–22; "The Nebraska Question," *Daily Pennsylvanian*, February 1, 1854. Douglas's abusive remark with the string of "isms" is reported in the *Daily Pennsylvanian* but not in the *Congressional Globe* or most news outlets. In the original text, Douglas used the N-word. Reporters frequently omitted comments that were deemed too abrasive. See Joanne B. Freeman, *The Field of Blood: Violence in Congress and the Road to Civil War* (New York: Farrar, Straus and Giroux, 2018), 6.

14. Eric Foner, *Free Soil, Free Labor, Free Men: The Ideology of the Republican Party Before the Civil War* (New York: Oxford University Press, 1995), 94; Allan Nevins, *Ordeal of the Union, vol. 1* (New York: Charles Scribner's Sons, 1947), 122–32. Even Stephen Douglas's authorized biographer, a sympathetic pro-Douglas newspaperman, lamented that Chase and Sumner's *Appeal* "was more successful, perhaps, than any like disreputable act had ever been." James W. Sheahan, *The Life of Stephen A. Douglas* (New York: Harper and Bros., 1860), 195–97.

15. Malavasic, *The F Street Mess*, 119; Michael F. Holt, *The Rise and Fall of the American Whig Party: Jacksonian Politics and the Onset of the Civil War* (Oxford: Oxford University Press, 2003), 804–35; Gaillard Hunt, *Israel, Elihu and Cadwallader Washburn: A Chapter in American Biography* (New York: Macmillan, 1925), 37; Frederick W. Seward, *Seward at Washington* (New York: Derby and Miller, 1891), 219.

16. Pierce, *MLCS*, 3:356. All quotes to Sumner's speech "The Landmark of Freedom" are obtained from the *Congressional Globe*. Cong. Globe, 33rd Cong., 1st. Sess., app., 262–70 (1854) (remarks of Senator Sumner). For a published version, see CS, "The Landmark of Freedom: No Repeal of the Missouri Compromise" (Speech, U.S. Senate, February 21, 1854), *WCS*, 3:277. Readers may wish to consult the published version, even though modest changes were made, because it is easier to read than the *Globe's*.

17. *Boston Evening Transcript*, February 28, 1854, 2; Pierce, *MLCS*, 3:364–66; George Livermore to CS, May 4, 1854, 11/035, PCS; George Hillard to CS, March 15, 1854, *MLCS*, 3:359–60. For more on the opposition to the Kansas-Nebraska Act by the previously proslavery merchant class, see Philip S. Foner, *Business and Slavery: The New York Merchants and the Irrepressible Conflict* (New York: Russell and Russell, 1968), 88–105.

18. Elizabeth Fries Ellet, *The Court Circles of the Republic* (Hartford: Hartford Publishing Company, 1870), 471–72; Benjamin Perley Poore, *Perley's Reminiscences of Sixty Years in the National Metropolis, vol. 1* (Philadelphia: Hubbard's Bros., 1886), 408–9; Cong. Globe, 33rd Cong., 1st. Sess., app., 233–34 (1854) (remarks of Senator Butler); Walter G. Shotwell, *Life of Charles Sumner* (New York: Thomas Y. Crowell, 1910), 271.

19. A Bachelor, "Disinterested Friendship," *Harper's Monthly Magazine*, December 1855, 41. With the help of my research assistant, Rachel Zhu, I looked into the background of every senator of the Thirty-Third Congress to determine that all were married or widowed except Charles Sumner and David Atchison. For more on bachelorhood in mid-nineteenth-century America, see Vincent J. Bertolini, "Fireside Chastity: The Erotics of Sentimental Bachelorhood in the 1850s," *American Literature* 68, no. 4 (1996): 707–37; Katherine Snyder, *Bachelors, Manhood, and the Novel, 1850–1925* (Cambridge: Cambridge University Press, 2004), chap. 1; John Gilbert McCurdy, *Citizen Bachelors: Manhood and the Creation of the United States* (Ithaca, N.Y.: Cornell University Press, 2011), epilogue.

20. McCurdy, *Citizen Bachelors*, 199; Walter Harding, "Thoreau's Sexuality," *Journal of Homosexuality* 21, no. 3 (1991): 27–28.

21. Bertolini, "Fireside Chastity," 711–15; J. S. Haller, "Bachelor's Disease. Etiology, Pathology, and Treatment of Spermatorrhea in the Nineteenth Century," *New York State Journal of Medicine* 73, no. 16 (August 15, 1973): 2076–82.

22. Donald, *Charles Sumner and the Coming of the Civil War*, 75; David Donald, *Charles Sumner and the Rights of Man* (New York: Knopf, 1970), 328.

23. See the interview of "Henry Ryan" on "Image 75 of Federal Writers' Project: Slave Narrative Project, Vol. 14, South Carolina, Part 2, Eddington-Hunter," Library of Congress, n.d., https://www.loc.gov /resource/mesn.144/?sp=75&st=image&r=-0.222,-0.107,1.524,0.706,0. Numerous sources state that Butler did not remarry after the death of his second wife. See, e.g., Theodore D. Jervey, "The Butlers of South Carolina," *The South Carolina Historical and Genealogical Magazine* 4, no. 4 (1903): 306; Paul Christopher Anderson, "Butler, Andrew Pickens," *South Carolina Encyclopedia—University of South Carolina Institute for Southern Studies* (blog), https://www.scencyclopedia.org/sce/entries /butler-andrew-pickens; "Andrew Pickens Butler (1796–1857), Find a Grave," n.d., https://www .findagrave.com/memorial/8063282/andrew_pickens-butler. There is some dispute about the number of people Andrew Butler enslaved because of ambiguities in the U.S. Federal Census Slave Schedule. Anderson counted sixty-four while Malavasic counted seventy-three. In truth, the number is probably higher than seventy-three because of difficulties in searching through slave schedule records. See Malavasic, *The F Street Mess*, 69 n. 12; Allen Johnson, ed., "Andrew Pickens Butler," in *Dictionary of American Biography* (New York: Charles Scribner's Sons, 1929), 355.

24. Orville Vernon Burton, *In My Father's House and Many Mansions: Family and Community in Edgefield, South Carolina* (Chapel Hill: University of North Carolina Press, 1985), 130, 186–87. See generally Annette Gordon-Reed, *Thomas Jefferson and Sally Hemings: An American Controversy* (Charlottesville: University of Virginia Press, 1998).

25. Andrew Butler recalled June 1854 to be when "the bridge had been cut down" between him and Sumner, after which he told Sumner that they "should have no communication" anymore. Although Butler perceived this June incident to be the unprompted cause of their broken relations, Sumner had likely been angry with Butler since February 1854, when the latter insulted his chastity. The June incident occurred when Sumner presented a petition calling for the abolition of the Fugitive Slave Act. See Cong. Globe, 34th Cong., 1st. Sess., 1403 (1856) (remarks of Senator Butler); Cong. Globe, 33rd Cong., 1st. Sess., 1517, 1554–59 (1854) (remarks of Senators Sumner and Butler); Cong. Globe, 33rd Cong., 1st. Sess., app., 1011–15 (1854) (remarks of Senators Sumner and Butler). Sumner's secretary claimed that Sumner enjoyed chummy friendships with many proslavery senators despite their political sparring in the Senate. The claim, made three decades later, is overstated. He was friendly with a good number of proslavery politicians at the start of his Senate career; these relationships dwindled to a handful by the mid-1850s. See Arnold Burges Johnson, "Charles Sumner—III, Recollections," *The Cosmopolitan: A Monthly Illustrated Magazine*, October 1887, 146–48.

26. Frederick Douglass to CS, February 27, 1854, 10/530, PCS; Seward, *Seward at Washington*, 226; CS to Earl of Carlisle, October 26, 1855, *MLCS*, 3:405–6. Sumner made a habit of showing off to his friends the flattering letters he received. But he also reveled in hearing friends share their accomplishments with him. Edwin Percy Whipple, "Recollections of Charles Sumner," *Harper's Monthly Magazine*, July 1879, 269.

27. Pierce, *MLCS*, 3:52, 366–67; Cong. Globe, 33rd Cong., 1st. Sess., 785 (1854) (remarks of Senator Sumner). For more on abolitionist jeremiads during the Civil War era, see Andrew R. Murphy, "Decline, Slavery, and War: The Jeremiad in Antebellum and Civil War America," in *Prodigal Nation: Moral Decline and Divine Punishment from New England to 9/11* (Oxford: Oxford University Press, 2008), 44–76.

28. Cong. Globe, 33rd Cong., 1st. Sess., app. 787 (1854) (remarks of Senator Douglas).

29. Albert J. Von Frank, *The Trials of Anthony Burns: Freedom and Slavery in Emerson's Boston* (Cambridge, Mass.: Harvard University Press, 1998), 54–68; CS, *WCS*, 3:350–51.

30. "Abolition Mob and Murder in Boston," *Washington Union*, May 28, 1854; "The Fugitive Slave Case in Boston," *Washington Evening Star*, May 30, 1854, 2; *New York Times*, May 31, 1854; *Washington Union*, May 30, 1854; CS, *WCS*, 3:347–52.

31. Pierce, *MLCS*, 3:375–77; CS, *WCS*, 3:347–52; CS to Theodore Parker, June 12, 1854, 71/356, PCS.

32. CS, *WCS*, 9:61; "From the Washington Union: Triumphant Capture of the Northern Whigs by the Abolitionists," *Liberator*, April 14, 1854; Marquis Adolphe de Chambrun, *Impressions of Lincoln and the Civil War: A Foreigner's Account*, trans. General Aldebert de Chambrun (New York: Random House, 1952), 28; J. W. Schuckers, *The Life and Public Services of Salmon Portland Chase* (New York: D. Appleton, 1874), 156.

Chapter 10: The Slave Oligarchy Is Mad

1. Schurz, "Eulogy Before City Authorities of Boston (Music Hall, April 29, 1874)," in *Charles Sumner: Memoir and Eulogies*, ed. William M. Cornell (Boston: James H. Earle, 1874), 123. It is not clear when Douglas made this remark.

2. Cong. Globe, 33rd Cong., 1st. Sess., 1517–18 (1854) (remarks of Senators Butler, Mason, and Pettit). Sumner's replies to the senators who belittled him illustrate how personal the dispute was becoming. He began by citing famous words from Thomas Jefferson, who once said that "the man must be a prodigy, who can retain his manners and morals undepraved" as a slave master. (Cong. Globe, 33rd Cong., 1st. Sess., app. 1011–12 [1854] [remarks of Senator Sumner]).

3. Curtis, "Eulogy Before Massachusetts State Government," in Cornell, *Charles Sumner: Memoir and Eulogies*, 198; Edwin Percy Whipple, "Recollections of Charles Sumner," *Harper's Monthly Magazine*, July 1879, 274–75.

4. Cong. Globe, 33rd Cong., 1st. Sess., app., 1012 (1854) (remarks of Senator Sumner); Andrew Jackson, "Bank Veto" (July 10, 1832), Presidential Speeches, UVA Miller Center, https://millercenter .org/the-presidency/presidential-speeches/july-10-1832-bank-veto; Thomas Jefferson to Abigail Adams, September 11, 1804, Founders Online, National Archive, https://founders.archives.gov /documents/Jefferson/01-44-02-0341; CS to Heman Lincoln, July 24, 1854, 71/408, PCS.

5. Gilbert Haven, "The Very Chiefest of Our Statesmen," in Cornell, *Charles Sumner: Memoir and Eulogies*, 59; Heman Lincoln to CS, July 22, 1854, 11/501, PCS.

6. Allan Nevins, *Ordeal of the Union, vol. 1* (New York: Charles Scribner's Sons, 1947), 316–23; David M. Potter, *The Impending Crisis: 1846–1861* (New York: Harper and Row, 1963), 225–66; James M. McPherson, *Battle Cry of Freedom: The Civil War Era* (New York: Oxford University Press, 1988), 120.

7. Pierce, *MLCS*, 3:395–403; Henry Watterson, *Marse Henry, Complete: An Autobiography* (DigiCat, 2022), chap. 13; Frank Preston Stearns, *The Life and Public Services of George Luther Stearns* (Philadelphia: J. B. Lippincott, 1907), 189.

8. Eric Foner, *Free Soil, Free Labor, Free Men: The Ideology of the Republican Party Before the Civil War* (New York: Oxford University Press, 1995), 226–60; Nevins, *Ordeal of the Union*, 1:323–28; Potter, *The Impending Crisis*, 225–66.

9. Ernest McKay, *Henry Wilson: Practical Radical* (Port Washington, N.Y.: National University Publications, 1971), 87–96; Frederick W. Seward, *Seward at Washington* (New York: Derby and Miller, 1891), 314; CS to Julius Rockwell, November 26, 1854, 71/482, PCS.

10. Cong. Globe, 33rd Cong., 2nd. Sess., app., 244–46 (1855) (remarks of Senators Sumner, Rusk, and Butler); "The Proceedings of Congress," *National Era*, March 8, 1855.

11. For more on Henry Williams and his daughter Mary "Ida May" Williams, see generally Jessie Morgan-Owens, *Girl in Black and White: The Story of Mary Mildred Williams and the Abolition Movement* (New York: W. W. Norton, 2019); Mary Niall Mitchell, "The Real Ida May: A Fugitive Tale in the Archives," *Massachusetts Historical Review* 15 (2013): 54–88. See also Pierce, *MLCS*, 3:131, 413–14.

12. Robert Ferguson, *America During and After the War* (London: Longmans, Green, 1866), 32; John-

son, "Recollections of Charles Sumner," 1874, 479; Laura E. Richards and Maud Howe Elliott, *Julia Ward Howe, 1819–1910*, vol. 1 (Boston: Houghton Mifflin, 1915), 152; CS to Samuel Howe, April 30, 1844, 67/144, PCS; John Andrew, *History of Ida May* (Boston: J. S. Potter, 1855). Andrew's pamphlet is reprinted in Morgan-Owens, *Girl in Black and White*, 136.

13. For more on the commercial success of *Uncle Tom's Cabin* and *Ida May*, see Donald E. Liedel, "The Puffing of Ida May: Publishers Exploit the Antislavery Novel," *Journal of Popular Culture* 3, no. 2 (1969): 287–306.

14. "Letter from Hon. Charles Sumner—Another Ida May," *New York Times*, March 1, 1855; "Another Ida May," *Liberator*, March 30, 1855, 2; "Rescue of a White Family from Slavery," *Albany Evening Journal*, February 28, 1855; "A White Slave from Virginia," *Pittsburgh Post-Gazette*, March 12, 1855, 2 (reprinted from the *New York Times*).

15. "Senator Sumner, 'Ida May,' and the Solid Men of Boston," *Washington Sentinel*, March 14, 1855; "Senator Sumner—Young Negroes and Daguerreotypes," *Washington Sentinel*, March 2, 1855.

16. "Boston Correspondence," *St. Albans Weekly Messenger*, March 22, 1855, 2; "Redeemed Slaves in the House," *Worcester Daily Spy*, March 12, 1855, 2; Morgan-Owens, *Girl in Black and White*, 198–99.

17. William Cooper Nell, "From Our Boston Correspondent," *Frederick Douglass' Paper*, March 16, 1855, 3; "Arrival of Senator Sumner's Proteges," *Boston Courier*, March 12, 1855; Thomas Wentworth Higginson, *Part of a Man's Life* (Boston: Houghton Mifflin, 1905), 122. Exhibitions of children, including Black children, were common. One major Boston showing took place in September 1855. See Jacqueline Jones, *No Right to an Honest Living: The Struggles of Boston's Black Workers in the Civil War Era* (New York: Basic Books, 2023), 142–43.

18. Seward, *Seward at Washington*, 250; "Mr. Sumner's Lecture," *Liberator*, April 6, 1855, 3; Morgan-Owens, *Girl in Black and White*, 1–4. Sumner delivered the "Anti-Slavery Enterprise" speech at several venues. Quotes to the speech were obtained from the published edition. See CS, *The Anti-Slavery Enterprise: Its Necessity, Practicability, and Dignity (An Address at the New York Metropolitan Theatre, May 9, 1855)* (Boston: Ticknor and Fields, 1855); Pierce, *MLCS*, 3:415.

19. Stephen Kendrick and Paul Kendrick, *Sarah's Long Walk: The Free Blacks of Boston and How Their Struggle for Equality Changed America* (Boston: Beacon Press, 2004), 217–39; Carleton Mabee, "A Negro Boycott to Integrate Boston Schools," *The New England Quarterly* 41, no. 3 (1968): 341–61. The city and statehouse reports are reprinted in Leonard W. Levy and Douglas L. Jones, eds., *Jim Crow in Boston: The Origin of the Separate but Equal Doctrine* (New York: Da Capo Press, 1974), 233–62.

20. Levy and Jones, *Jim Crow in Boston*, 280.

21. Mitchell, "The Real Ida May," 73–75; Johnson, "Charles Sumner—III, Recollections."

22. Worthington Chauncey Ford, ed., *Writings of John Quincy Adams*, vol. 4 (New York: Macmillan, 1914), 209.

23. For more on Sumner's trip west, see Pierce, *MLCS*, 3:417–20.

24. H. Edward Richardson, *Cassius Marcellus Clay: Firebrand of Freedom* (Lexington: University Press of Kentucky, 1976), 20–21 and 44–46; Cassius Clay, *History and Record of the Proceedings of the People of Lexington and Its Vicinity in the Suppression of the True American* (Lexington, Ky.: Virden, 1845), 18.

25. Forrest A. Nabors, *From Oligarchy to Republicanism: The Great Task of Reconstruction* (Columbia: University of Missouri Press, 2017), 228, 247, and 266; Clement Eaton, "The Freedom of the Press in the Upper South," *Mississippi Valley Historical Review* 18, no. 4 (1932): 479–99.

26. Pierce, *MLCS*, 3:417–19; CS, *WCS*, 4:64. The N-word was used by Sumner in the original quote about what the stagecoach driver said. For Sumner's shock at the contrast between the beauty of the land and the ugliness of slavery, see CS to William Schouler, June 14, 1855, 71/583, PCS; CS, "To the Editors of the Boston Post," *Liberator*, November 23, 1855.

27. *Nashville Union and American*, July 13, 1855, 2.

28. CS, *WCS*, 4:55–57.

29. CS to John Jay, October 18, 1855, 71/618, PCS; CS, *The Slave Oligarchy and Its Usurpations* (Washington, D.C.: Buell and Blanchard, 1855); CS to William Seward, November 11, 1855, 71/628, PCS; Allan Nevins, *Hamilton Fish* (New York: Dodd, Mead, 1936), 47; John Weiss, *Life and Correspondence of Theodore Parker*, vol. 2 (New York: Appleton, 1864), 211. At the beginning of the session, Sumner apparently told someone that "this session will not pass without the Senate Chamber's becoming the scene of some unparalleled outrage." Thomas Wentworth Higginson, *Contemporaries* (Boston: Houghton Mifflin, 1899), 283.

Chapter 11: The First Blow in a Civil War

1. Walter Stahr, *Salmon Chase: Lincoln's Vital Rival* (New York: Simon and Schuster, 2021), 226–27; Sidney Blumenthal, *All the Powers of Earth* (New York: Simon and Schuster, 2019), 98–99; William E. Gienapp, *The Origins of the Republican Party: 1852–1856* (Oxford: Oxford University Press, 1987), 250–51.

2. Shelley Hickman Clark and James W. Clark, eds., "Lawrence in 1854: Recollections of Joseph Savage," *Kansas History* 27, nos. 1/2 (2004): 34; *Address to the People of the United States, Together with the Proceedings and Resolutions of the Pro-Slavery Convention of Missouri, Held at Lexington, July, 1855* (St. Louis, Mo.: Republican Office, 1855), 23; Michael E. Woods, *Bleeding Kansas: Slavery, Sectionalism, and Civil War on the Missouri-Kansas Border* (New York: Routledge, 2017), 30–60.

3. William W. Freehling, *The Road to Disunion: Secessionists Triumphant, 1854–1861*, vol. 2 (Oxford: Oxford University Press, 1990), 72–75; Woods, *Bleeding Kansas*, 35–38.

4. Woods, *Bleeding Kansas*, 30–60.

5. CS to William Jay, May 6, 1856, 72/172, PCS.

6. For more on the speakership contest, see Jeffrey A. Jenkins and Charles Stewart, *Fighting for the Speakership: The House and the Rise of Party Government* (Princeton: Princeton University Press, 2013), 177–208. For more on the violence during the Thirty-Fourth Congress, see Joanne B. Freeman, *The Field of Blood: Violence in Congress and the Road to Civil War* (New York: Farrar, Straus & Giroux, 2018), chap. 7.

7. CS to Edward Everett Hale, March 1, 1856, 72/089, PCS; Theodore Parker to CS, May 17, 1856, 72/179, PCS; CS to Salmon Chase, May 15, 1856, 72/174, PCS. For the argument that Sumner's "The Crime Against Kansas" speech was primarily intended to defuse the political rise of the Know-Nothing Party, see William E. Gienapp, "The Crime Against Sumner: The Caning of Charles Sumner and the Rise of the Republican Party," *Civil War History* 25, no. 3 (1979): 218–45.

8. "The Nebraska Question," *The Daily Pennsylvanian*, February 1, 1854. In the original text, Douglas used the N-word.

9. "A Night in the Senate," *The Anti-Slavery Bugle*, March 18, 1854; Walter Stahr, *Seward: Lincoln's Indispensable Man* (New York: Simon and Schuster, 2012), 161; Pierce, *MLCS*, 3:459; WCS, 4:128. Sumner's letter about meeting adversaries by scorn was on a different occasion. But the sentiment equally applied to "The Crime Against Kansas." William Seward warned Sumner against including the "gratuitous assault against the honor of South Carolina." Frances Seward urged him to keep "the general tone" but remove the "cutting personal sarcasm." Frances Seward to CS, May 20, 1856, 13/220, PCS.

10. D. A. Harsha, *The Life of Charles Sumner* (New York: H. Dayton, 1858), 153–54; Pierce, *MLCS*, 3:441; "Mr. Sumner's Speech," *Clinton Republican*, May 30, 1856, 2. All quotes to Sumner's speech "The Crime Against Kansas" were obtained from the *Congressional Globe*. Cong. Globe, 34th Cong., 1st. Sess., app., 529–47 (1856) (remarks of Senator Sumner). For a published version, see CS, "The Crime Against Kansas" (Speech, U.S. Senate, May 19, 1856), WCS, 4:125.

11. For literary analyses of "The Crime Against Kansas," see Michael D. Pierson, "'All Southern Society Is Assailed by the Foulest Charges': Charles Sumner's 'The Crime Against Kansas' and the Escalation of Republican Anti-Slavery Rhetoric," *New England Quarterly* 68, no. 4 (1995): 531–57; Michael William Pfau, "Time, Tropes, and Textuality: Reading Republicanism in Charles Sumner's 'Crime Against Kansas,'" *Rhetoric and Public Affairs* 6, no. 3 (2003): 385–413; Michael William Pfau, *The Political Style of Conspiracy: Chase, Sumner, and Lincoln* (East Lansing: Michigan State University Press, 2005), chap. 3.

12. Cicero, *Verrines II.1*, trans. T. N. Mitchell (Warminster, England: Aris and Phillips, 1986), 31. For more on Cicero and Verres, see Cicero, *Against Verres, 2.1.53–86*, ed. Ingo Gildenhard (Cambridge: Open Book Publishers, 2011).

13. For Butler mocking Sumner's chastity and the probability of his having a mistress, see chapter 9.

14. Cicero, *Nine Orations and the Dream of Scipio*, trans. Palmer Bovie (New York: Mentor Books, 1967), 125. For more on Cicero's role in the Catiline Conspiracy, see Will Durant, *Caesar and Christ: A History of Roman Civilization and of Christianity from Their Beginnings to A.D. 325* (New York: Simon and Schuster, 1944), 140–45. For Sumner's admiration of Cicero, see CS, WCS, 2:22. See also numerous references to the "Ciceronian ideal" and the "Ciceronian lawyer" in Anne-Marie Taylor, *Young Charles Sumner and the Legacy of the American Enlightenment, 1811–1851* (Amherst: University of Massachusetts Press, 2001).

15. John Milton, *Paradise Lost* (London: George Routledge and Sons, 1905), 42.

16. H.R. Rep. No. 34–182, 43–44 (1856) (testimony of Bingham); H.R. Rep. No. 34–182, 42 (1856)

(testimony of Wilson); H.R. Rep. No. 34–182, 25 (1856) (testimony of Sumner); H.R. Rep. No. 34–182, 66–67 (1856) (testimony of Buffington); J. S. Pike, "Mr. Sumner's Speech," *New York Tribune*, May 21, 1856, 6; H.R. Rep. No. 34–182, 75 (1856) (testimony of Ricaud).

17. Cong. Globe, 34th Cong., 1st. Sess., 77 (1856) (remarks of Representative Brooks); Ralph Volney Harlow, *Gerrit Smith: Philanthropist and Reformer* (New York: Henry Holt, 1939), 349.

18. Daniel Walker Hollis, *University of South Carolina: South Carolina College*, vol. 1 (Columbia: University of South Carolina Press, 1951), 138–39; Alvy L. King, *Louis T. Wigfall: A Southern Fire-Eater* (Baton Rouge: Louisiana State University Press, 1970), 32–34; Cong. Globe, 33rd Cong., 1st. Sess., app., 371–75 (1854) (remarks of Representative Brooks). For more on the biography of Preston Brooks, see generally "Honorable Preston S. Brooks," *Southern Quarterly Review* 2, no. 2 (1857): 348–70; Robert Neil Mathis, "Preston Smith Brooks: The Man and His Image," *South Carolina Historical Magazine* 79, no. 4 (1978): 296–310; Stephen Puleo, *The Caning: The Assault That Drove America to Civil War* (Yardley, Pa.: Westholme Publishing, 2012), 80–98; Kenneth A. Deitreich, *The Short Life and Violent Times of Preston Smith Brooks: A Man of Mark* (Newcastle upon Tyne: Cambridge Scholars Publishing, 2019). For more on Edgefield County, see generally Orville Vernon Burton, *In My Father's House and Many Mansions: Family and Community in Edgefield, South Carolina* (Chapel Hill: University of North Carolina Press, 1985); Deitreich, *The Short Life and Violent Times of Preston Smith Brooks: A Man of Mark*. In the late 1930s, one of the people formerly enslaved on Brooks's plantation was interviewed by the Federal Writers' Project. See the interview of "Cornelius Holmes" on "Image 298 of Federal Writers' Project: Slave Narrative Project, Vol. 14, South Carolina, Part 2, Eddington-Hunter," Library of Congress, n.d., https://www.loc.gov/resource/mesn.142/?sp=298&st=image.

19. Cong. Globe, 34th Cong., 1st. Sess., 1347 (1856) (statement of Representative Brooks); Robert L. Merriwether, "Preston S. Brooks on the Caning of Charles Sumner," *South Carolina Historical and Genealogical Magazine* 52, no. 1 (January 1951): 2; Preston Brooks, "Statement by Preston S. Brooks," *Proceedings of the Massachusetts Historical Society, Oct. 1927–June 1928* 61 (1928): 221–23.

20. H.R. Rep. No. 34–182, 58–63 (1856) (testimony of Edmundson); Cong. Globe, 34th Cong., 1st. Sess., 832 (1856) (remarks of Representative Brooks); Charles S. Sydnor, "The Southerner and the Laws," *The Journal of Southern History* 6, no. 1 (1940): 17.

21. H.R. Rep. No. 34–182, 30–31 (1856) (testimony of Pearce); H.R. Rep. No. 34–182, 75 (1856) (testimony of Glossbrenner); H.R. Rep. No. 34–182, 73 (1856) (testimony of Davis); Cong. Globe, 34th Cong., 1st. Sess., 832 (1856) (remarks of Representative Brooks). For more on gutta-percha, see generally Christopher Hanlon, "Embodied Eloquence, the Sumner Assault, and the Transatlantic Cable," *American Literature* 82, no. 3 (2010); *Gutta Percha: Its Discovery, Properties, Capabilities and Uses* (New York: American Gutta Percha Company, 1848).

22. Merriwether, "Preston S. Brooks on the Caning of Charles Sumner," 2; Brooks, "Statement by Preston S. Brooks"; H.R. Rep. No. 34–182, 58–63 (1856) (testimony of Edmundson). Edmundson dubiously claimed that he told Brooks about a rumor—from Sumner's friends—that Sumner had armed himself in anticipation of an attack. The likelihood that Edmundson told Brooks about any rumor is highly doubtful, given that Sumner's friends would not have talked to Edmundson; Sumner's friends did not take any excessive precaution to protect the senator; and Brooks did not seem concerned about being shot. Southern newspapers used the implausible rumor to argue that Brooks's attack was not unprovoked. See, e.g., *Charleston Daily Courier*, July 18, 1856, 2.

23. *New York Tribune*, May 31, 1854; Freeman, *The Field of Blood*, 260. The claim that Brooks, Edmundson, and Keitt visited a restaurant looking for Sumner was made two decades later by Sumner's private secretary Arnold Johnson, who often took charge of Sumner's security. The claim is compelling because Brooks gave no explanation for what he did for the rest of the day on Wednesday and earnestly sought to avoid implicating any of his colleagues. Keitt's biographer Holt Merchant concurs that this restaurant rendezvous took place. That said, it is possible that it never occurred. See Johnson, "Recollections of Charles Sumner," 1874, 482; Holt Merchant, *South Carolina Fire-Eater: The Life of Laurence Massillon Keitt, 1824–1864* (Columbia: University of South Carolina Press, 2014), 45. For an elaborate argument that Keitt, Edmundson, and Brooks acted in concert, see Thomas John Balcerski, "Intimate Contests: Manhood, Friendship, and the Coming of the Civil War" (Ph.D. diss., Cornell University, 2014), 253–383. For more on Edmundson's biography, see Dana E. McKnight, "Henry Alonzo Edmundson" (M.A. thesis, Virginia Polytechnic Institute and State University, 1971). McKnight's thesis is stored at the Virginia Tech library and can be obtained upon request.

24. Preston Brooks to J. Ham Brooks, May 23, 1856, in Robert L. Meriwether, "Preston S. Brooks on the

Caning of Charles Sumner," *South Carolina Historical and Genealogical Magazine* 52, no. 1 (1951): 2–3; H.R. Rep. No. 34–182, 58–60 (1856) (testimony of Edmundson).

25. Brooks, "Statement by Preston S. Brooks"; H.R. Rep. No. 34–182, 43 (1856) (testimony of Wilson).

26. H.R. Rep. No. 34–182, 58–63 (1856) (testimony of Edmundson).

27. H.R. Rep. No. 34–182, 79–80 (1856) (testimony of Nicholson); H.R. Rep. No. 34–182, 60 (1856) (testimony of Edmundson); H.R. Rep. No. 34–182, 56–57 (1856) (testimony of Winslow); *New York Tribune*, May 23, 1856, 5–6. Brooks claimed that he waited to attack until after the lady in the lobby had left. But if the officer's testimony is to be believed, Brooks attacked Sumner almost instantly after the officer declined to get the lady to leave. There is little reason to give too much currency to Brooks's self-serving testimony.

28. There are variations on what Brooks said to Sumner before attacking. Sumner recalled this incomplete sentence. Brooks, for his part, recalled saying, "Mr. Sumner, I have read your last speech with care and as much impartiality as is possible under the circumstances, and I feel it my duty to say that you have libeled my State and slandered my kinsman who is aged and absent and I have come to punish you for it." See H.R. Rep. No. 34–182, 23–24 (1856) (testimony of Sumner); Brooks, "Statement by Preston S. Brooks"; H.R. Rep. No. 34–182, 80–81 (1856) (testimony of Brown); CS, WCS, 4:269 (recollection of Leader); James Watson Webb, "How It Was Done," *Buffalo Daily Republic*, May 29, 1856. For more on Sumner's chair and desk, see H.R. Rep. No. 34–182, 65 (1856) (testimony of McNair); Webb, "How It Was Done"; Johnson, "Recollections of Charles Sumner," 482; Margaret B. Klapthor, "Furniture in the Capitol: Desks and Chairs Used in the Chamber of the House of Representatives, 1819–1857," *Records of the Columbia Historical Society, Washington, D.C.* 69/70 (1969/1970): 192–93.

29. H.R. Rep. No. 34–182, 70–72 (1856) (testimony of Iverson); H.R. Rep. No. 34–182, 57–58 (1856) (testimony of Simoton); H.R. Rep. No. 34–182, 65 (1856) (testimony of McNair); Michael E. Woods, "Tracing the 'Sacred Relicts': The Strange Career of Preston Brooks's Cane," *Civil War History* 63, no. 2 (2017): 125. There are some reports that Brooks had a pistol in his pocket when he attacked Sumner, which he planned to use if the senator fought back. While the claim is plausible enough, it is unclear how anyone would have seen or known about an alleged pistol hidden in a pocket. See, e.g., "The Case of Brooks," *St. Paul Weekly Minnesotian*, July 26, 1856, 2. When the beating took place, there were reportedly shouts of "Go, Brooks!" and "Give the damned Abolitionist hell!" But only one eyewitness heard these hoots; no other eyewitness mentioned anything to this effect. See CS, WCS, 4:269 (recollection of Leader). There is also one unsubstantiated newspaper report that Brooks told friends that he was drunk when the caning took place and, for that reason, attacked more aggressively than he intended to. "Col. Preston S. Brooks," *New York Times*, January 29, 1857. Gerrit Smith seemed to think alcohol was the culprit of Brooks's crime. "Poor Brooks," Smith once wrote. "I became acquainted with him in Congress, and found him to be a frank, pleasant man. He allowed me to speak freely to him of his habit of drinking liquor. . . . But for liquor he would never have committed his enormous crime." Harlow, *Gerrit Smith*, 349.

30. While Crittenden claimed that Keitt did not try to stop him from interfering, his recollection is contradicted by many eyewitnesses. It is likely that Crittenden simply wished to avoid a dispute with a southern colleague. See H.R. Rep. No. 34–182, 47–48 (1856) (testimony of Crittenden); H.R. Rep. No. 34–182, 29 (1856) (testimony of Gorman); H.R. Rep. No. 34–182, 34 (1856) (testimony of Toombs); H.R. Rep. No. 34–182, 37 (1856) (testimony of Foster); H.R. Rep. No. 34–182, 44–47 (1856) (testimony of Holland); H.R. Rep. No. 34–182, 57–58 (1856) (testimony of Simoton). Edwin Morgan claimed two decades later that Keitt stood on one of the desks proclaiming that he would kill anyone who dared to interfere. This claim is doubtful, given that no eyewitness reported back in 1856 that Keitt acted in this manner. Morgan's own testimony at the time was that Keitt was standing *at* or *near* a desk, instead of *on top of* a desk. Morgan also did not initially mention any death threats. "The Great Crime: The Hon. Edwin B. Morgan's Description of the Assault of Brooks on Senator Sumner," *Buffalo Commercial*, May 4, 1874, 2; H.R. Rep. No. 34–182, 41 (1856) (testimony of Morgan). There is one unsubstantiated report from an eyewitness in the galleries that Keitt was holding a pistol with his other hand while waiving his cane above his head. Dr. Bunting, "Statement of an Eye-Witness," *Liberator*, June 6, 1856. Keitt implausibly claimed that his presence in the Senate during the attack was coincidental and that he had no knowledge about when or how Brooks would hit Sumner. Cong. Globe, 34th Cong., 1st. Sess., 1292 (1856) (remarks of Representative Keitt). For an argument that implicates Keitt as a co-conspirator with Brooks, see Stephen Berry and James Hill Welborn III, "The Cane of His Existence: Depression, Damage, and the Brooks-Sumner Affair," *Southern Cultures* 20, no. 4 (2014): 5–21.

31. H.R. Rep. No. 34–182, 57 (1856) (testimony of Winslow); H.R. Rep. No. 34–182, 38–39 (1856) (testimony of Murray); H.R. Rep. No. 34–182, 39–42 (1856) (testimony of Morgan); Webb, "How It Was Done." There is a report that Brooks said, "I did not intend to kill him, but I did intend to whip him." Brooks himself claimed to have said something to the effect of "I had no wish to injure him seriously, but only to flog him." H.R. Rep. No. 34–182, 30 (1856) (testimony of Pearce); Brooks, "Statement by Preston S. Brooks." Also, Brooks falsely claimed that no one interposed in his assault, declaring that he "desisted simply because I had punished him to my satisfaction." H.R. Rep. No. 34–182, 80–81 (1856) (testimony of Brown). There is one unsubstantiated report that Sumner cried out "I'm almost dead—almost dead!" after falling to the floor. "Assault on Senator Sumner in the Senate Chamber," *New York Herald*, May 23, 1856.

32. Cong. Globe, 34th Cong., 1st. Sess., 13105 (1856) (remarks of Senator Douglas); H.R. Rep. No. 34–182, 36–37 (1856) (testimony of Foster); H.R. Rep. No. 34–182, 50–54 (1856) (testimony of Boyle); H.R. Rep. No. 34–182, 66–68 (1856) (testimony of Buffinton); H.R. Rep. No. 34–182, 54–56 (1856) (testimony of Darling); Webb, "How It Was Done"; "Isaac Basett: A Senate Memoir" (U.S. Senate Historical Office), n.d., https://corpora.tika.apache.org/base/docs/govdocs1/420/420073.html. Morgan recalled that after he fell to the floor, Sumner was "laid as senseless as a corpse for several minutes, his head bleeding copiously from the frightful wounds, and the blood saturating his clothes." Edwin B. Morgan, "Speech of Edwin B. Morgan," *New York Daily Tribune*, May 31, 1856, 8. Sumner testified that after he regained consciousness, he saw Douglas and Toombs in the Senate standing next to Brooks, as if they were collaborators. He was probably wrong. Both roundly rejected their involvement, and there is no compelling evidence to implicate them. H.R. Rep. No. 34–182, 24 (1856) (testimony of Sumner); Cong. Globe, 34th Cong., 1st. Sess., 13105 (1856) (remarks of Senators Douglas and Toombs). Although one witness claimed to the press that he saw Douglas standing near Brooks with his hands in his pockets during the attack, several other eyewitnesses testified that Douglas was not in the room until afterward. Dr. Bunting, "Statement of an Eye-Witness"; H.R. Rep. No. 34–182, 31, 35, and 41 (1856) (testimony of Pearce, Toombs, and Jones). Although one report claimed Douglas had dinner with Brooks, Keitt, and other co-conspirators after the attack, this report emerged two decades later and was not corroborated. See "Reminiscences of Sumner: New and Interesting Facts About Brooks Attack," *National Republican*, March 25, 1874.

33. H.R. Rep. No. 34–182, 50–54 (1856) (testimony of Boyle); H.R. Rep. No. 34–182, 66–68 (1856) (testimony of Buffinton); H.R. Rep. No. 34–182, 54–56 (1856) (testimony of Darling); Jane G. Swisshelm, "Mr. Sumner's Health: Correspondence of the New York Tribune," *Liberator*, September 5, 1856. There are several book-length treatments of the caning, its context, and its aftermath. See T. Lloyd Benson, *The Caning of Senator Sumner* (Belmont, Calif.: Thomas Wadsworth, 2004); Williamjames Hull Hoffer, *The Caning of Charles Sumner: Honor, Idealism, and the Origins of the Civil War* (Baltimore: Johns Hopkins University Press, 2010); Puleo, *The Caning*.

34. John S. Wise, *The End of an Era* (Boston: Houghton Mifflin, 1901), 115; *Proceedings of the Bostonian Society at the Annual Meeting, January 20, 1920* (Boston: Bostonian Society, 1920), 11–14; H.R. Rep. No. 34–182, 60 (1856) (testimony of Edmundson); H.R. Rep. No. 34–182, 75 (1856) (testimony of Glossbrenner); Puleo, *The Caning*, 114–15; Brooks to Brooks, May 23, 1856. Although there is some uncertainty, the cane that passed from the Wise family to the Bostonian Society is most likely the cane that was used by Brooks. There is also uncertainty about the authenticity and location of several pieces of the cane, including the gold head, and who salvaged them. For more on the history of the artifacts, see Woods, "Tracing the 'Sacred Relicts.'"

35. "The Caning Affair," *Charlotte Democrat*, June 3, 1856; Marcus L. Martin, Kirt von Daacke, and Meghan S. Faulkner, eds., *President's Commission on Slavery and the University: Report to President Teresa A. Sullivan* (Charlottesville: University of Virginia, 2018), 38; "Another Cane for Mr. Brooks," *Richmond Enquirer*, May 30, 1856; "The Right Kind of Stuff," *Edgefield Advertiser*, July 23, 1856; "To the Editors of the Louisville Journal," *Edgefield Advertiser*, October 29, 1856; Benson, *The Caning of Senator Sumner*, 132–33; "Refuge of Oppression: From the Richmond Enquirer," *Liberator*, June 13, 1856; Hermann Eduard von Holst, *The Constitutional and Political History of the United States*, trans. John J. Lalor (Chicago: Callaghan, 1885), 350. For more on the praise Brooks received in the South, especially in South Carolina, see Harold Schultz, *Nationalism and Sectionalism in South Carolina, 1852–1860* (Durham, N.C.: Duke University Press, 1950), 115–20.

36. Pierce, *MLCS*, 3:495; "On the Chastisement of Senator Sumner," *Wilmington Daily Herald*, May 26, 1856; Freeman, *The Field of Blood*, 222; "Louisville Journal," May 28, 1856.

37. For more on the norms of congressional violence, see generally Freeman, *The Field of Blood*, chap. 7.

38. "Honorable Preston S. Brooks," *Southern Quarterly Review* 2, no. 2 (1857): 355; *New Orleans Courier*, June 28, 1856; *Buffalo Daily Republic*, June 25, 1856, 2; "From the Richmond Enquirer," *Hartford Courant*, June 5, 1856, 2. For more on the social significance of canes, see Woods, "Tracing the 'Sacred Relics.'" For more on the racialized undertones of the caning, see Manisha Sinha, "The Caning of Charles Sumner: Slavery, Race, and Ideology in the Age of the Civil War," *Journal of the Early Republic* 23, no. 2 (2003): 233–62.

39. Cong. Globe, 34th Cong., 1st. Sess., 1304–6 (1856) (remarks of Senator Butler); *New York Times*, May 22, 1856; Cong. Globe, 34th Cong., 1st. Sess., 1279–80 (1856) (remarks of Senators Wilson, Seward, and Mason); Cong. Globe, 34th Cong., 1st. Sess., 1289–92 (1856) (remarks of Representative Campbell); George H. Haynes, *Charles Sumner* (Philadelphia: George W. Jacobs, 1909), 206; Frederick W. Seward, *Seward at Washington* (New York: Derby and Miller, 1891), 272; Richard H. Sewell, *John P. Hale and the Politics of Abolition* (Cambridge, Mass.: Harvard University Press, 1965), 168; H.R. Rep. No. 34–182, 25 (1856) (testimony of Sumner). The members of the Senate committee were Lewis Cass, Augustus Dodge, Henry Geyer, James Pearce, and Philip Allen. The Republicans of the House committee were Lewis Campbell, Francis Spinner, and Alexander Pennington. The Democrats were Howell Cobb and Alfred Greenwood.

40. Cong. Globe, 34th Cong., 1st. Sess., 1304–6 (1856) (remarks of Senators Slidell, Toombs, Douglas, Wilson, and Butler); "Louisville Journal"; *Boston Courier*, May 23, 1856; Cong. Globe, 34th Cong., 1st. Sess., 1366–67 (1856) (Senate Report). Benjamin Wade was especially angry that Robert Toombs, who sat next to him, approved of the caning. In his furious desire to vindicate Sumner, Wade nearly ended up in a duel with Toombs and hoped to "put a patch on his coat the size of a dollar over his heart." Toombs, for his part, celebrated the caning. He later joined Preston Brooks for a rally in Charleston, South Carolina, and spoke jubilantly about Brooks's assault. "I saw it done, and I saw it well done!" he proclaimed to a buoyant, laughing crowd. H. L. Trefousse, *Benjamin Franklin Wade: Radical Republican from Ohio* (New York: Twayne Publishers, 1963), 102–3; "Hon. Preston S. Brooks at Home," *Charleston Courier*, October 7, 1856.

41. CS, "Finger-Point from Plymouth Rock" (Speech, Plymouth, Massachusetts, August 1, 1853), WCS, 3:269. For a study on the political impact of Sumner's caning, much of which could have been anticipated by Sumner in advance, see Gienapp, "The Crime Against Sumner."

42. Johnson, "Recollections of Charles Sumner," 482; Seward, *Seward at Washington*, 271.

43. Anna Lauren Dawes, *Charles Sumner* (New York: Dodd, Mead, 1892), 118; Cong. Globe, 34th Cong., 1st. Sess., 653 (1856) (remarks of Senator Seward).

44. Lydia Maria Child, *Letters of Lydia Maria Child* (Boston: Houghton Mifflin, 1883), 78; Puleo, *The Caning*, 129; Pierce, *MLCS*, 3:501; Horace Mann to CS, May 27, 1856, 72/191, PCS; Horace Mann to CS, September 9, 1856, 72/297, PCS; Jeremiah Chaplin and J. D. Chaplin, *Life of Charles Sumner* (Boston: D. Lothrop, 1874), 297. Though anguished and tormented, Samuel Howe did not write to Sumner at first. In line with contemporary medical knowledge, he feared that writing to him might excite Sumner's brain and nervous system when he needed to stay calm and abstain from reading letters or interacting with close friends. See Laura E. Richards, *Letters and Journals of Samuel Gridley Howe* (Boston: Dana Estes, 1909), 418–20.

45. Frederick Douglass, *Life and Times of Frederick Douglass* (Hartford: Park Publishing, 1882), 363; CS, WCS, 3:309; Ralph Waldo Emerson, *The Complete Works of Ralph Waldo Emerson*, ed. Edward W. Emerson, vol. 11 (Boston: Houghton Mifflin, 1904), 251–52. On indignation meetings after the caning, see Michael E. Woods, "'The Indignation of Freedom-Loving People': The Caning of Charles Sumner and Emotion in Antebellum Politics," *Journal of Social History* 44, no. 3 (2011): 689–705; Gienapp, "The Crime Against Sumner."

46. E. A. Warden to CS, May 25, 1856, 13/364, PCS; William Story and CS, May 26, 1856, 13/399, PCS; Gilbert Haven, "The Very Chiefest of Our Statesmen," in *Charles Sumner: Memoir and Eulogies*, ed. William M. Cornell (Boston: James H. Earle, 1874), 62; Julia Ward Howe, *Words for the Hour* (Boston: Ticknor and Fields, 1857), 15; Frances Seward to CS, July 4, 1856, 14/214, PCS. For more on the religious imagery used to describe the caning, see Joel Harlan Gradin, "'Losing Control': The Caning of Charles Sumner and the Breakdown of Antebellum Political Culture" (Ph.D. diss., University of North Carolina at Chapel Hill, 1991), 233–50.

47. Robert Morris to CS, June 11, 1860, 19/567, PCS; Sinha, "The Caning of Charles Sumner," 256; "National Convention at New Orleans, LA (Apr. 10, 1872)," Colored Conventions Project, n.d., https://omeka.coloredconventions.org/items/show/544. The Colored Conventions Proj-

ect, a remarkable digitization project of the nineteenth-century Black convention movement, has asked all researchers who cite from the collection to state and affirm its core values. Per request, "I honor CCP's commitment to a use of data that humanizes and acknowledges the Black people whose collective organizational histories are assembled here. Although the subjects of datasets are often reduced to abstract data points, I will contextualize and narrate the conditions of the people who appear as 'data' and to name them when possible." See "Introduction to CCP Corpus," Colored Conventions Project, n.d., https://omeka.coloredconventions .org/ccp-corpus.

48. "The Ruffians in the Senate," *Albany Evening Journal*, May 23, 1856; Cong. Globe, 34th Cong., 1st. Sess., 1580 (1856) (remarks of Representative Bingham); Seward, *Seward at Washington*, 272; *Liberator*, July 18, 1856.

49. Kellie Carter Jackson, *Force and Freedom: Black Abolitionists and the Politics of Violence* (Philadelphia: University of Pennsylvania Press, 2019), 118; Oswald Garrison Villard, *John Brown: A Biography Fifty Years After* (Boston: Houghton Mifflin, 1910), 154; Richard J. Hinton, *John Brown and His Men* (New York: Funk and Wagnalls, 1894), 695.

50. Pierce, *MLCS*, 3:503–4; Rev. Sir Gilbert Frankland Lewis, ed., *Letters of the Right Hon. Sir George Cornewall Lewis* (London: Longmans, Green, 1870), 315.

Chapter 12: Sumner Takes a Beating Badly

1. Frederick W. Seward, *Seward at Washington* (New York: Derby and Miller, 1891), 287; Pierce, *MLCS*, 3:484–85; Frank Preston Stearns, *The Life and Public Services of George Luther Stearns* (Philadelphia: J. B. Lippincott, 1907), 115–16, 120; Marshall S. Perry, "Case of Hon. Charles Sumner," *Boston Medical and Surgical Journal* 55, no. 21 (December 25, 1856): 417–18; Cong. Globe, 34th Cong., 1st. Sess., 1414 (1856) (remarks of Senator Butler).

2. CS to Samuel Howe, September 11, 1856, 63/697, PCS; Cong. Globe, 34th Cong., 1st. Sess., app., 1119 (1856) (remarks of Representative Giddings); CS to Richard Henry Dana Jr., June 23, 1856, 72/213, PCS.

3. CS to Samuel Howe, August 28, 1856, 63/695, PCS; CS to Joshua Giddings, August 15, 1856, 63/692, PCS; Seward, *Seward at Washington*, 282; Pierce, *MLCS*, 3:486; CS, *WCS*, 4:336.

4. Pierce, *MLCS*, 4:329, 334; Perry, "Case of Hon. Charles Sumner," 417–21; CS to Edward Pierce, January 6, 1857, 63/708, PCS; Pierce, *MLCS*, 3:505–8. Dr. Boyle dubiously testified in Brooks's trial that there was no concussion.

5. CS to Theodore Parker, March 1, 1857, 72/467, PCS. For their help in understanding Sumner's medical condition, I am grateful to Dr. Adil Asaduddin, an internist in Houston, Texas; Dr. Robert Burton, former chief of neurology at UCSF Mount Zion Hospital; and Dr. William Gaillard, chief of neurology at Children's National Hospital. All conclusions and potential errors are my own.

6. Jane G. Swisshelm, "Mr. Sumner's Health: Correspondence of the New York Tribune," *Liberator*, September 5, 1856; Mary Rosamond Dana to CS, June 1, 1856, 13/621, PCS. The young girl who wrote to Sumner was the daughter of his friend Richard Henry Dana. See CS to Richard Henry Dana Jr., June 23, 1856.

7. Ulrich B. Phillips, ed., *The Correspondence of Robert Toombs, Alexander H. Stephens, and Howell Cobb*, vol. 2 (Washington, D.C.: American Historical Association, 1913), 365; H.R. Rep. No. 34–182, 50–54 (1856) (testimony of Boyle); Cong. Globe, 34th Cong., 1st. Sess., app., 1414 (1856) (remarks of Senator Butler); *Charleston Mercury*, January 21, 1857; Manisha Sinha, "The Caning of Charles Sumner: Slavery, Race, and Ideology in the Age of the Civil War," *Journal of the Early Republic* 23, no. 2 (2003): 249; "Mr. Sumner, His Illness and His Doctor," *Richmond Enquirer*, June 20, 1856, 4. The *Richmond Enquirer* used the N-word in the original text. For more on the claim that Sumner was shamming and evidence to debunk it, see Laura A. White, "Was Charles Sumner Shamming, 1856–1859?," *New England Quarterly* 33, no. 3 (1960): 291–324. To rebut shamming claims, Republicans arranged for Sumner's doctors to publish their medical assessment of his condition. See Perry, "Case of Hon. Charles Sumner."

8. Jane Grey Swisshelm, *Half a Century* (Chicago: J. G. Swisshelm, 1880), 161; David C. Keehn, *Knights of the Golden Circle: Secret Empire, Southern Secession, Civil War* (Baton Rouge: Louisiana State University Press, 2013), 85–86, 105–6, 256; William A. Tidwell, *Confederate Covert Action in the American Civil War: April '65* (Kent, Ohio: Kent State University Press, 1995), 42, 63, 69, 76, 164, 185–86, 190; Hoffer, *The Caning of Charles Sumner*, 75.

9. Cong. Globe, 34th Cong., 1st. Sess., app., 625–35 (1856) (remarks of Senator Butler).

10. "From the National Intelligencer Yesterday: The Brooks and Sumner Case in Court," *Washington Sentinel*, July 10, 1856, 3; Pierce, *MLCS*, 3:487; *Charleston Daily Courier*, August 2, 1856, 2. The judicial proceeding against Brooks was half-hearted at best. It started after William Leader, a Pennsylvania citizen, filed a police report after witnessing the caning from only a few steps away from Sumner. Leader was in the Senate Chamber that day by coincidence and did not personally know Sumner. The prosecutor, Philip Barton Key, was a doughface Democrat—that is, a northerner who supported or sympathized with slavery. Key's uncle was the doughface chief justice Roger Taney. Key may have intentionally sought the lightest possible charge against Brooks: misdemeanor assault. He also may have entered Sumner's letters declining to participate into the record as a way to lend credence to Brooks's claims that Sumner was trying to sham his injuries. The judge, Thomas Crawford, was also a doughface. The defense counsel included Representative James Orr, who had advance knowledge of Brooks's crime. For an argument that the entire trial was essentially a farce, see Hoffer, *The Caning of Charles Sumner*, 79–85.

11. H.R. Rep. No. 34–182 (1856).

12. Cong. Globe, 34th Cong., 1st. Sess., app., 831–33 (1856) (remarks of Representative Brooks). Keitt also staged a dramatic resignation and walkout after he was censured. See Cong. Globe, 34th Cong., 1st. Sess., app., 833–38 (1856) (remarks of Representative Keitt).

13. "The Assault Case," *Alexandria Gazette*, July 16, 1856, 2; Cong. Globe, 34th Cong., 1st. Sess., 1120 (1856) (remarks of Representative Giddings).

14. "Mr. Brooks' Card," *Yorkville Enquirer*, July 24, 1856, 2; *Charleston Daily Courier*, August 2, 1856, 2.

15. "Hon. Preston S. Brooks at Home," *Charleston Courier*, October 7, 1856. For more on Brooks's disunionism, see Robert Neil Mathis, "Preston Smith Brooks: The Man and His Image," *South Carolina Historical Magazine* 79, no. 4 (1978): 307.

16. *Official Proceedings of the National Democratic Convention Held in Cincinnati* (Cincinnati: Enquirer, 1856), 26.

17. *The Republican Scrap Book* (Boston: John P. Jewett, 1856), 17.

18. *Proceedings of the First Three Republican National Conventions of 1856, 1860 and 1864* (Minneapolis: Charles W. Johnson, 1893), 33.

19. Austin Steward, *Twenty-Two Years a Slave, and Forty Years a Freeman* (Canandaigua, N.Y.: Austin Steward, 1867), 318.

20. J. G. De Roulhac Hamilton, *Papers of William Alexander Graham*, vol. 4 (Raleigh: North Carolina State Department of Archive and History, 1961), 643–44; Mary Lesley Ames, ed., *Life and Letters of Peter and Susan Lesley* (New York: G. P. Putnam's Sons, 1909), 332; *New York Tribune*, June 13, 1856, 5. For more on the Republican campaign in 1856, see Matthew Karp, "The People's Revolution of 1856," *Journal of the Civil War Era* 9, no. 4 (December 2019): 525–45.

21. CS, *WCS*, 4:368–85; "The Return of Mr. Sumner," *Boston Daily Evening Transcript*, November 1, 1856, 2; "From the Boston Bee of Tuesday: Reception of Hon. Charles Sumner," *Liberator*, November 7, 1856, 3; "From the New York Times: Senator Sumner's Reception in Boston," *Poughkeepsie Journal*, November 8, 1856, 2; "Reception of Hon. Charles Sumner at Boston," *Greenville Journal*, November 12, 1856, 2; "Charles Sumner's Reception in Boston," *Anti-Slavery Bugle*, November 15, 1856, 3; Edward Wagenknecht, ed., *Mrs. Longfellow: Selected Letters and Journals of Fanny Appleton Longfellow* (London: Longmans, Green, 1956), 206; John Weiss, *Life and Correspondence of Theodore Parker*, vol. 2 (New York: Appleton, 1864), 189–90.

22. "Dreadful Collision at Sea—Great Loss of Life," *Berkshire County Eagle*, November 21, 1856, 2; Samuel Longfellow, ed., *Life of Henry Wadsworth Longfellow: With Extracts from His Journals and Correspondence*, vol. 2 (Boston: Houghton Mifflin, 1891), 323.; "The Lyonnais Disaster," *Boston Evening Transcript*, November 21, 1856; "Frightful Collision at Sea," *Recorder*, November 24, 1856, 2; Jeremiah Chaplin and J. D. Chaplin, *Life of Charles Sumner* (Boston: D. Lothrop, 1874), 482; *National Era*, July 22, 1858, 2; "French Ship That Sank in 1856 Disaster Is Found off Massachusetts Coast," *New York Times*, September 11, 2024, https://www.nytimes.com/2024/09/11/us/le-lyonnais-shipwreck-found-massachusetts.html.

23. CS to John Jay, November 15, 1856, 72/376, PCS.

24. *New York Tribune*, January 30, 1857, 4; Cong. Globe, 34th Cong., 3rd Sess., 501–2 (1856); *Baltimore Sun*, January 30, 1857, 4; Kenneth A. Deitreich, *The Short Life and Violent Times of Preston Smith Brooks: A Man of Mark* (Newcastle upon Tyne: Cambridge Scholars Publishing, 2019), 248–63.

25. Henry Wilson to CS, January 29, 1857, 15/210, PCS; Pierce, *MLCS*, 3:524; Longfellow, *Life of Henry Wadsworth Longfellow*, 2:325; William M. Cornell, ed., *Charles Sumner: Memoir and Eulogies* (Boston: James H. Earle, 1874), 255–56.

26. Ames, *Life and Letters of Peter and Susan Lesley*, 339; Samuel Howe to CS, December 12, 1857, 72/664, PCS; Samuel Howe to CS, September 16, 1856, 72/309, PCS; Pierce, *MLCS*, 3:518.

27. CS to Theodore Parker, March 1, 1857, 72/467, PCS.

28. Pierce, *MLCS*, 3:520.

29. For more on federal judicial review, *Marbury*, and *Dred Scott*, see generally Cass R. Sunstein, "Constitutional Myth-Making: Lessons from the Dred Scott Case," *University of Chicago Law Occasional Paper*, no. 37 (1996). For a list of federal laws overturned by the Supreme Court, see "Table of Supreme Court Decisions Overruled by Subsequent Decisions," United States Congress, n.d., https://constitution.congress.gov/resources/decisions-overruled/.

30. Dred Scott v. Sandford, 60 U.S. 393 (1857).

31. "Slavery, and Not Freedom Is National," *Poughkeepsie Journal*, March 21, 1857; Harriet Martineau, "From the Westminster Review: 'Manifest Destiny' of the American Union," *Liberator*, November 6, 1857.

Chapter 13: The Man Speaks Like a Prophet

1. Pierce, *MLCS*, 3:525–55.

2. Pierce, *MLCS*, 3:525–55.

3. Alexis de Tocqueville, *Democracy in America*, trans. Henry Reeve, vol. 1 (University Park: Pennsylvania State University Press, 2002), 433.

4. Tocqueville, *Democracy in America*, 395.

5. Olivier Zunz, *The Man Who Understood Democracy: The Life of Alexis de Tocqueville* (Princeton: Princeton University Press, 2022), 349; CS, *WCS*, 12:168–72; Carl Schurz, "Eulogy Before City Authorities of Boston (Music Hall, April 29, 1874)," in *Charles Sumner: Memoir and Eulogies*, ed. William M. Cornell (Boston: James H. Earle, 1874), 125. See also CS, "Prophetic Voices Concerning America: A Monograph" (March 1874), 12:168–172, WCS; Daniel Ajootian, "Liberty and Liberation in Nineteenth-Century America: The Theory and the Practice According to John Stuart Mill, Alexis de Tocqueville, and Charles Sumner" (B.A. thesis, University of Virginia, 2019). For close studies on the centrality of equality in Sumner's political thought, see Janis L. McDonald, "The Republican Revival: Revolutionary Republicanism's Relevance for Charles Sumner's Theory of Equality and Reconstruction," *Buffalo Law Review* 38, no. 2 (April 1, 1990): 465–514; Michael W. McConnell, "Originalism and the Desegregation Decisions," *Virginia Law Review* 81, no. 4 (1995): 947–1140; Elizabeth Anderson, *The Imperative of Integration* (Princeton: Princeton University Press, 2010), 89–111; Hari Ramesh, "India, Racial Caste, and Abolition in Charles Sumner's Political Thought," *Modern Intellectual History* 19 (2022): 708–33.

6. Pierce, *MLCS*, 3:555; *Brooklyn Daily Eagle*, January 20, 1857, 2.

7. CS to Theodore Parker, December 19, 1857, 72/683, PCS; CS to Elizabeth Argyll, December 22, 1857, 72/685, PCS; Pierce, *MLCS*, 3:558–59.

8. CS to Samuel Howe, April 16, 1858, 64/012, PCS; CS to Henry Longfellow, May 10, 1858, 73/148, PCS; Pierce, *MLCS*, 3:560.

9. Pierce, *MLCS*, 3:559; Samuel Longfellow, ed., *Life of Henry Wadsworth Longfellow: With Extracts from His Journals and Correspondence*, vol. 2 (Boston: Houghton Mifflin, 1891), 351; CS, *The Best Portraits in Engraving* (New York: Frederick Keppel, 1875), 4. By the end of his life, Sumner had amassed 133 engravings, including of paintings like West's *Penn's Treaty with the Indians* and Trumbull's *The Declaration of Independence*. Most of his collection was bequeathed after his death to the Boston Museum of Fine Arts. For more on Sumner's collection, see "Charles Sumner House Floorplan," n.d., Charles Sumner Papers, Massachusetts Historical Society, Boston; Arnold B. Johnson, "Recollections of Charles Sumner: The Senator's Home and Pictures," *Scribner's Monthly* 7 (1875), 101–14; Mary S. Withington, "From the Boston Beacon: The Home of Charles Sumner," *Dorchester News-Gatherer*, January 26, 1878; W. G. Constable, "A Cranach from the Sumner Collection; with Some Notes on Charles Sumner as a Collector," *Bulletin of the Museum of Fine Arts* 41 (1943): 64–68. For a reprint of Sumner's will, see Elias Nason, *The Life and Times of Charles Sumner* (Boston: B. B. Russell, 1874), 353–55.

10. Cong. Globe, 33rd Cong., 1st. Sess., app., 269 (1854) (remarks of Senator Sumner); Cong. Globe, 34th Cong., 1st Sess., 18 (1857) (remarks of Senator Douglas).

11. L. E. Chittenden, ed., "From His Discussion of the Decision in the Dred Scott Case at Springfield, Illinois (June 26, 1857)," in *Abraham Lincoln's Speeches* (New York: Dodd, Mead, 1895), 60–70.

12. CS to John Jay, June 1, 1858, 73/182, PCS; *Boston Evening Transcript*, May 24, 1858; CS to Samuel Howe, July 22, 1858, 64/024, PCS; CS, *New York Evening Post*, May 22, 1858, 2; Henry Adams to CS, December 22, 1858, 17/356, PCS.

13. For more on Brown-Séquard, see generally Michael J. Aminoff, *Brown-Séquard: An Improbable Genius Who Transformed Medicine* (Oxford: Oxford University Press, 2011).

14. C. Edwards Lester, *Life and Public Services of Charles Sumner* (New York: United States Publishing Company, 1874), 304–5; Laura A. White, "Was Charles Sumner Shamming, 1856–1859?," *New England Quarterly* 33, no. 3 (1960): 305.

15. Nason, *The Life and Times of Charles Sumner*, 241–43. For more on moxibustion, see Hongyong Deng and Xueyong Shen, "The Mechanism of Moxibustion: Ancient Theory and Modern Research," *Evidence Based Complementary Alternative Medicine*, September 12, 2013.

16. CS to Henry Longfellow, June 27, 1858, 73/196, PCS; Charles Francis Adams to CS, August 1, 1858, 73/230, PCS; CS to Charles Francis Adams, February 5, 1859, 73/342, PCS; C. F. Nichols, ed., *The New-England Medical Gazette: A Monthly Journal of Homeopathic Medicine, Surgery, and the Collateral Sciences*, vol. 9 (Boston: Otis Clapp and Son, 1874), 183; Salmon Chase to CS, September 10, 1859, 17/719, PCS; "Hon. Charles Sumner—His Summer Rambles, Etc.," *Charleston Daily Courier*, August 11, 1858.

17. "The Operation upon Senator Sumner," *National Era*, July 22, 1858, 2; "Senator Sumner's Case (New York Tribune Correspondence)," *Berkshire County Eagle*, August 13, 1858, 2; Pierce, *MLCS*, 3:565.

18. See Lincoln's speech in Springfield on July 17, 1858, and the third, sixth, and seventh debates between him and Douglas in Abraham Lincoln and Stephen Douglas, *Political Debates Between Abraham Lincoln and Stephen Douglas* (Cleveland: Burrow Bros., 1894).

19. Franklin Benjamin Sanborn, *The Life and Letters of John Brown: Liberator of Kansas, and Martyr of Virginia* (Roberts Brothers, 1885), 585. For more on abolitionist militancy in the wake of Brown's raid, see generally LeeAnna Keith, *When It Was Grand: The Radical Republican History of the Civil War* (New York: Farrar, Straus and Giroux, 2020), chaps. 6–9.

20. CS to Edward Pierce, September 11, 1858, 64/028, PCS; CS to Edward Pierce, November 8, 1858, 64/038, PCS; CS to Samuel Howe, November 10, 1858, 64/041, PCS; CS to Edward Pierce, March 4, 1859, 64/049, PCS; CS to William Story, August 11, 1859, 73/464, PCS. For more on Sumner's time in Rome with William Story, see Andrew F. Rolle, "A Friendship Across the Atlantic: Charles Sumner and William Story," *American Quarterly* 11, no. 1 (1959): 40–57.

21. Joanne B. Freeman, *The Field of Blood: Violence in Congress and the Road to Civil War* (New York: Farrar, Straus and Giroux, 2018), 260.

22. CS to William Seward, May 20, 1860, 74/077, PCS; CS to Elizabeth Argyll, May 22, 1860, 74/080, PCS.

23. L. E. Chittenden, ed., "The 'Divided House' Speech Delivered at Springfield, Illinois, on His Nomination to the Senate of the United States (June 17, 1858)," in *Abraham Lincoln's Speeches* (New York: Dodd, Mead, 1895), 72.

24. Allan Nevins, *Hamilton Fish* (New York: Dodd, Mead, 1936), 76–77; Archibald H. Grimke, *Charles Sumner Centenary: Historical Address* (Washington, D.C.: American Negro Academy, 1911), 14. For Grimke's biography of Sumner, see Grimke, *Charles Sumner: The Scholar in Politics* (New York: Funk and Wagnalls, 1892).

25. Laura E. Richards, *Letters and Journals of Samuel Gridley Howe* (Boston: Dana Estes, 1909), 477. Upon Sumner's arrival in Boston on November 21, 1852, Henry Longfellow wrote in his diary that Sumner was "looking hale and hearty and calling himself 'a well man.'" Samuel Longfellow, ed., *Life of Henry Wadsworth Longfellow: With Extracts from His Journals and Correspondence*, vol. 2 (Boston: Houghton Mifflin, 1891), 347.

26. George H. Haynes, *The Senate of the United States: Its History and Practice*, vol. 2 (Boston: Houghton Mifflin, 1938), 917–20; "U.S. Senate: About the Senate Chamber—Historical Overview," n.d., https://www.senate.gov/about/historic-buildings-spaces/chamber/overview.htm.

27. Cong. Globe, 36th Cong., 1st Sess., 2590–604 (1860) (remarks of Senator Sumner).

28. CS to Lewis Tappan, June 25, 1860, 74/133, PCS.

29. Frederick W. Seward, *Seward at Washington* (New York: Derby and Miller, 1891), 457.

30. CS, *The Works of Charles Sumner*, vol. 5 (Boston: Lee and Shepard, 1875), 128–30; Grimke, *Charles Sumner: The Scholar in Politics*, 317.

31. CS, *WCS*, 5:267. For more on the political acumen behind Sumner's *The Barbarism of Slavery*, see Laura A. White, "Charles Sumner and the Crisis of 1860–1861," in *Essays in Honor of William E. Dodd: By His Former Students at the University of Chicago* (Chicago: University of Chicago Press, 1935), 137–46.

32. Arthur Reed Hogue, ed., *Charles Sumner: An Essay by Carl Schurz* (Urbana: University of Illinois Press, 1951), 73–74.

33. Lydia Maria Child, *Letters of Lydia Maria Child* (Boston: Houghton Mifflin, 1883), 69; David Donald, *Charles Sumner and the Coming of the Civil War* (Naperville, Ill.: Sourcebooks, 2009), 301–3; CS, *WCS*, 5:146; Joshua B. Smith to CS, June 7, 1860, 19/443, PCS; "Republican Mass Meeting at the Cooper Institute," *New York Times*, July 12, 1860. For a sample of Sumner's speeches ahead of the 1860 presidential election, see CS, *WCS*, 5:175–343. After "The Barbarism of Slavery," an effort was made by Black Bostonians to raise money for a gift to send to Sumner in gratitude. See Kathryn Grover and Janine V. da Silva, *Historic Resource Study: Boston African American National Historic Site* (Washington, D.C.: National Park Service, 2002), 129.

34. Sara Agnes Rice Pryor, *My Day: Reminiscences of a Long Life* (Macmillan, 1909), 154–55.

Chapter 14: This Is the Time That Tries Men's Souls

1. Mark J. Stegmaier, *Henry Adams in the Secession Crisis* (Baton Rouge: Louisiana State University Press, 2012), 64; Henry Wilson and Jeremiah S. Black, *Edwin M. Stanton: His Character and Public Services on the Eve of the Rebellion* (Easton, Pa.: Cole, Morwitz, 1871), 37–38; Walter Stahr, *Seward: Lincoln's Indispensable Man* (New York: Simon and Schuster, 2012), 53, 128; CS to John Andrew, January 26, 1861, 74/419, PCS; CS to John Andrew, January 28, 1861, 74/433, PCS. On the morning after his second midnight meeting with Stanton, Sumner told Frank Bird he thought the capital would ultimately be safe. "Maryland will be retained by the national capital," he wrote. "There are some who think this cannot be done; but that the revolution which carries Maryland will seize the capital. Perhaps. February will be an eventful month." CS to Francis Bird, January 28, 1861, 74/437, PCS.

2. Cong. Globe, 34th Cong., 1st Sess. app. 530 (remarks of Sen. Sumner) (1856).

3. "The Revulsion, Past and to Come," *New York Daily Herald*, December 1, 1860, 6.

4. Joseph Schafer, ed., *Intimate Letters of Carl Schurz, 1841–1869* (Madison: State Historical Society of Wisconsin, 1929), 243; Arthur Reed Hogue, ed., *Charles Sumner: An Essay by Carl Schurz* (Urbana: University of Illinois Press, 1951), 112; David M. Potter, *Lincoln and His Party in the Secession Crisis* (New Haven: Yale University Press, 1942), 222–23.

5. CS to Elizabeth Argyll, December 14, 1860, 74/320, PCS; David Donald, *Charles Sumner and the Coming of the Civil War* (Naperville, Ill.: Sourcebooks, 2009), 313; Gilbert Haven, "The Very Chiefest of Our Statesmen," in *Charles Sumner: Memoir and Eulogies*, ed. William M. Cornell (Boston: James H. Earle, 1874), 64. In January 1861, Sumner told Polish American Count Adam Gurowski that "Nobody can foresee precisely all that is in the future, but I do not doubt that any conflict will precipitate the doom of slavery. It will probably go down in blood" (Walter G. Shotwell, *Life of Charles Sumner* [New York: Thomas Y. Crowell, 1910], 407–8).

6. Joshua R. Giddings, *History of the Rebellion: Its Authors and Causes* (New York: Follet, Foster, 1864), 217–18; John Quincy Adams, *Speech of the Hon. John Quincy Adams, in the House of Representatives, on the State of the Nation: Delivered May 25, 1836* (New York: H. R. Piercy, 1836); Cong. Globe, 27th Cong., 2nd Sess., 429 (1842) (remarks of Representative Adams).

7. Joseph Story, *Commentaries on the Conflict of Laws* (Boston: Hilliard, Gray, 1834), 92, 166; CS to Joseph Story, January 20, 1834, 65/066, PCS; Brown v. United States, 12 U.S. 110, 110 (1814).

8. CS, *WCS*, 7:131.

9. *Federalist Paper* No. 23 (Alexander Hamilton); *Federalist Paper* No. 41 (James Madison); Luther v. Borden, 48 U.S. 1 (1849).

10. CS to F. W. Ballard, February 9, 1861, *MLCS* 4:17; Phillips, "Sumner (Charles)," 622.

11. Charlton Yarnall, ed., *Forty Years of Friendship: As Recorded in the Correspondence of John Duke, Lord Coleridge and Ellis Yarnall* (New York: Macmillan, 1911), 66. For more on Charles Francis Adams and his family, see generally Douglas R. Egerton, *Heirs of an Honored Name: The Decline of the Adams Family and the Rise of Modern America* (New York: Basic Books, 2019).

12. Henry Adams, *The Education of Henry Adams* (Boston: Houghton Mifflin, 1918), 31; Charles Francis Adams Jr., "Mr. Adams's Address," in *Dinner Commemorative of Charles Sumner and Complimentary to Edward L. Pierce* (Cambridge, Mass.: John Wilson and Son, 1895), 38.

13. J. C. Levenson et al., eds., *The Letters of Henry Adams*, vol. 1 (Cambridge, Mass.: Belknap Press, 1982), 222–23, 228, 232; Ernest Samuels, ed., *Henry Adams: Selected Letters* (Cambridge, Mass.: Belknap Press, 1992), 36–37.

14. Cong. Globe, 36th Cong., 2nd Sess., 341 (1861) (remarks of Senator Seward); CS to Samuel Howe, January 17, 1861, 64/161, PCS.

15. Worthington C. Ford, "Sumner's Letters to Governor Andrew, 1861," *Proceedings of the Massachusetts Historical Society, Oct. 1926–June 1927* 60 (1927): 234; James Mitchell Ashley, "Calhoun,

Seward, and Lincoln: Interesting Reminiscences of the Great Rebellion," *Magazine of Western History*, November 1890, 4; Adams, *Charles Francis Adams, 1835–1915, an Autobiography* (Boston: Houghton Mifflin, 1916), 80–82; Charles Francis Adams, *Richard Henry Dana: A Biography*, vol. 1 (Boston: Houghton Mifflin, 1890), 252–54.

16. Levenson et al., *The Letters of Henry Adams*, 1:228; David S. Brown, *The Last American Aristocrat: The Brilliant Life and Improbable Education of Henry Adams* (New York: Scribner, 2021), 63–66; Donald, *Charles Sumner and the Coming of the Civil War*, 316; Carl Schurz, *The Reminiscences of Carl Schurz*, vol. 2 (London: John Murray, 1909), 312.

17. Stahr, *Seward*, 226; Pierce, *MLCS*, 4:10; CS to Rudolph Schleiden, June 27, 1865, 79/391, PCS.

18. George E. Baker, ed., *The Works of William H. Seward*, vol. 4 (Boston: Houghton Mifflin, 1884), 399–400.

19. Eric Foner, *The Fiery Trial: Abraham Lincoln and American Slavery* (New York: W. W. Norton, 2010), 169; William E. Gienapp, "Abraham Lincoln and the Border States," *Journal of the Abraham Lincoln Association* 13 (1992): 13–46.

20. CS to Henry Pierce, January 29, 1861, 74/444, PCS; CS to John Andrew, January 17, 1861, 74/376, PCS; CS to John Andrew, January 8, 1861, 74/364, PCS; CS to Charles G. Loring, January 26, 1861, 74/423, PCS. Many of Sumner's letters to Governor Andrew and vice versa were reprinted in Worthington C. Ford, "Sumner's Letters to Governor Andrew, 1861," *Proceedings of the Massachusetts Historical Society, Oct. 1926–June 1927* 60 (1927): 193–312.

21. William Schouler, *A History of Massachusetts in the Civil War* (Boston: E. P. Dutton, 1868), 35–39; Stephen D. Engle, *In Pursuit of Justice: The Life of John Albion Andrew* (Amherst: University of Massachusetts Press, 2023), 135–47; Allan Nevins, *The War for the Union: The Improvised War (1861–1862)*, vol. 1 (New York: Charles Scribner's Sons, 1959), 79–81.

22. Stanley J. Robboy and Anita W. Robboy, "Lewis Hayden: From Fugitive Slave to Statesman," *The New England Quarterly* 46, no. 4 (1973): 609; Strangis, *Lewis Hayden and the War Against Slavery*, 117–19; Stephen Kantrowitz, *More Than Freedom: Fighting for Black Citizenship in a White Republic, 1829–1889* (New York: Penguin, 2012), 212; Brian Taylor, *Fighting for Citizenship: Black Northerners and the Debate over Military Service in the Civil War* (Chapel Hill: University of North Carolina Press, 2020), 41–42.

23. Donald, *Charles Sumner and the Coming of the Civil War*, 309; CS, *WCS*, 5:444.

24. Ephraim Douglass Adams, *Great Britain and the American Civil War* (London: Longmans, Green, 1925), 79–81; John E. Lodge to CS, March 8, 1861, 22/011, PCS; Laura A. White, "Charles Sumner and the Crisis of 1860–1861," in *Essays in Honor of William E. Dodd: By His Former Students at the University of Chicago* (Chicago: University of Chicago Press, 1935), 179–81.

25. CS to John Andrew, January 28, 1861, 74/433, PCS; L. E. Chittenden, ed., "The First Inaugural Address (March 4, 1861)," in *Abraham Lincoln's Speeches* (New York: Dodd, Mead, 1895), 240–48.

26. White, "Charles Sumner and the Crisis of 1860–1861," 168; Donald, *Charles Sumner and the Coming of the Civil War*, 320–21; Pierce, *MLCS*, 4:27–28; Edward Everett Hale, *Memories of a Hundred Years*, vol. 2 (London: Macmillan, 1904), 78; John B. Alley, "John B. Alley," in *Reminiscences of Abraham Lincoln by Distinguished Men of His Time*, ed. Allen Thorndike Rice (New York: Harper and Bros., 1909), 578–79. Unfortunately, the surviving records of the Senate Foreign Relations Committee are scant and unhelpful. Past historians have also been frustrated by these flimsy records. See David Donald, *Charles Sumner and the Rights of Man* (New York: Knopf, 1970), 14; Thomas J. Peyton Jr., "Charles Sumner and United States Foreign Relations During the American Civil War" (Ph.D. diss., Georgetown University, 1972), iii–iv. For focused studies on Charles Sumner's role in foreign affairs, see Victor H. Cohen, "Charles Sumner and Foreign Affairs" (Ph.D. diss., University of Oklahoma, 1951); Peyton, "Charles Sumner and United States Foreign Relations During the American Civil War."

27. Adams, *The Education of Henry Adams*, 102; "Douglas and Sumner," *Bristol News*, April 7, 1871, 4; CS to John Andrew, February 10, 1861, 74/494, PCS; Benjamin Perley Poore, *Perley's Reminiscences of Sixty Years in the National Metropolis*, vol. 2 (Philadelphia: Hubbard's Bros., 1886), 537.

28. William Howard Russell, *My Diary North and South* (New York: Harper and Bros., 1863), 34; Amanda Foreman, *A World on Fire: Britain's Crucial Role in the American Civil War* (New York: Random House, 2010), 75–77.

29. Stahr, *Seward*, 264–66; Frank A. Golder, "The American Civil War Through the Eyes of a Russian Diplomat," *American Historical Review* 26, no. 3 (1921): 458.

30. CS to Richard Dana, April 14, 1861, 74/640, PCS; Lord Newton, *Lord Lyons: A Record of British Diplomacy*, vol. 1 (New York: Longmans, Green, 1913), 41; Joseph A. Fry, *Lincoln, Seward, and U.S.*

Foreign Relations in the Civil War Era (Lexington: University Press of Kentucky, 2019), 50; Stahr, *Seward*, 264; Foreman, *A World on Fire*, 69–71.

31. CS, *WCS*, 6:30; James Oakes, *The Radical and the Republican: Frederick Douglass, Abraham Lincoln, and the Triumph of Antislavery Politics* (New York: W. W. Norton, 2007), 148–49. Referring to the occasion when Sumner told Lincoln about the wartime emancipation theory, Burrus Carnahan states that "Sumner's advice must have been startling to the new president. Lincoln's law practice in Illinois had not prepared him to deal with questions arising under the international laws of war." Burrus M. Carnahan, *Acts of Justice: Lincoln's Emancipation and the Law of War* (Lexington: University Press of Kentucky, 2007), 5. Writing to his secretary after the preliminary Emancipation Proclamation was released, Sumner said that "the president told me weeks ago that I was the first person who suggested the proclamation of the Acts of Congress." He was referring to the idea of Congress using its war powers to liberate enslaved people in the rebel South. CS to Benjamin Poore, September 23, 1862, 76/101, PCS.

32. Nevins, *The War for the Union*, 1:75; Ellis Yarnall, *Wordsworth and the Coleridges with Other Memories Literary and Political* (New York: Macmillan, 1899), 8; CS to Joshua Giddings, April 28, 1861, 74/677, PCS; Joshua Giddings to CS, April 30, 1861, 22/429, PCS; Samuel Howe to CS, April 16, 1861, 74/653, PCS.

33. Nevins, *The War for the Union*, 1:75; James M. McPherson, *The Struggle for Equality: Abolitionists and the Negro in the Civil War and Reconstruction* (Princeton: Princeton University Press, 1964), 47.

Chapter 15: Slavery Is the Very Goliath of the Rebellion

1. Arnold Burges Johnson, "Charles Sumner—III, Recollections," *The Cosmopolitan: A Monthly Illustrated Magazine*, October 1887, 146.

2. CS, "Beginning of the Conflict: Speech Before the Third Massachusetts Rifles" (Speech, Armory at New York, April 12, 1861), *WCS*, 5:492–96; John W. Forney, *Anecdotes of Public Men*, vol. 1 (New York: Harper and Bros., 1873), 158–60; Allan Nevins, *Ordeal of the Union*, vol. 1 (New York: Charles Scribner's Sons, 1947), 80–84.

3. David Donald, *Charles Sumner and the Rights of Man* (New York: Knopf, 1970), 124–25; Samuel Howe to CS, April 9, 1862, 064/211, PCS; Betty Boles Ellison, *The True Mary Todd Lincoln: A Biography* (Jefferson, N.C.: McFarland, 2014), 124; Jason Emerson, *Giant in the Shadows: The Life of Robert T. Lincoln* (Carbondale: Southern Illinois University Press, 2012), 70.

4. Charles Francis Adams, *Richard Henry Dana: A Biography*, vol. 2 (Boston: Houghton Mifflin, 1890), 258–59. Sumner raved about Seward to Richard Henry Dana in June upon his return from his trip to Washington. But the sentiment expressed by Dana could just as easily have applied to Sumner's state of mind in May.

5. CS to George Sumner, July 6, 1842, 62/545, PCS; John B. Alley, "John B. Alley," in *Reminiscences of Abraham Lincoln by Distinguished Men of His Time*, ed. Allen Thorndike Rice (New York: Harper and Bros., 1909), 579–80; Martin Crawford, ed., *William Howard Russell's Civil War: Private Diary and Letters, 1861–1862* (Athens: University of Georgia Press, 1992), 90.

6. Crawford, *William Howard Russell's Civil War*, 90; CS to John Andrew, May 24, 1861, 75/019, PCS; Paul Revere Frothingham, *Edward Everett: Orator and Statesman* (Boston: Houghton Mifflin, 1925), 433; Moncure D. Conway, *Autobiography: Memories and Experiences of Moncure Daniel Conway*, vol. 1 (London: Cassell, 1904), 311–12; Amanda Foreman, *A World on Fire: Britain's Crucial Role in the American Civil War* (New York: Random House, 2010), 101–2; Donald, *Charles Sumner and the Rights of Man*, 21; Edward L. Pierce, *A Diplomatic Episode: The Rejected Treaty for St. Thomas* (Boston: s.n., 1889), 7; Pierce, *MLCS*, 4:30–31. Massachusetts congressman John Alley recalled that Lincoln once told him that "he had the greatest confidence in the judgment of our Massachusetts Senator in everything pertaining to foreign relations." Alley also claimed "personal knowledge that Mr. Lincoln would not allow Mr. Seward to send any very important dispatch to England until he had first shown it to Senator Sumner." In 1864, Lincoln told Sumner, "I counselled with you twice as much as I ever did with Seward." See Alley, "John B. Alley," 579; CS to Francis Bird, April 16, 1871, 84/240, PCS. For a compilation of many statements by historians about Lincoln's dependence on Sumner for foreign affairs issues, see Lehrman Institute, "Abraham Lincoln and Foreign Affairs," *Abraham Lincoln's Classroom* (blog), n.d., https://www.abrahamlincolnsclassroom.org/abraham-lincoln-in-depth/abraham-lincoln-and-foreign-affairs/.

7. CS, *WCS*, 6:30–31; CS to Wendell Phillips, August 3, 1861, 75/112, PCS.

8. CS, *WCS*, 5:497–98; Donald, *Charles Sumner and the Rights of Man*, 47. On the State Department's confused attempts to implement *Dred Scott*, see Leon F. Litwack, *North of Slavery: The Negro in*

the Free States (Chicago: University of Chicago Press, 1961), 53–57. Robert Morris Jr. was among the first Black Americans to be issued a U.S. passport. But he was not the first. See Rebecca Sharp, "A Rare Find: Passport Applications of Free Blacks," *National Archives: Rediscovering Black History* (blog), July 22, 2020, https://rediscovering-black-history.blogs.archives.gov/2020/07/22/a-rare-find-passport-applications-of-free-blacks/. Frank Preston Stearns, whose father was a friend of Sumner's, wrote in a book that Sumner had asked Seward about issuing a passport for the son of wealthy Black businesswoman Caroline Remond Putnam. Stearns likely confused Putnam with Morris; his recollection was published more than forty years later and is uncorroborated. Frank Preston Stearns, *The Life and Public Services of George Luther Stearns* (Philadelphia: J. B. Lippincott, 1907), 267–68.

9. CS, *WCS*, 6:32.

10. CS to John Jay, August 11, 1861, 75/129, PCS; CS to Francis Lieber, September 17, 1861, 64/182, PCS; Conway, *Autobiography*, 299–303; Moncure Daniel Conway, *The Rejected Stone; or Insurrection vs. Resurrection in America* (Boston: Walker, Wise, 1862); Frank Joseph Cirillo, "'The Day of Sainthood Has Passed': Abolitionists and the Golden Moment of the Civil War, 1861–1865" (Ph.D. diss., University of Virginia, 2017), 121.

11. CS, *Union and Peace! How They Shall Be Restored* (n.p., 1861); CS to John Jay, November 10, 1861, 75/234, PCS. My interpretation of events is that Sumner intended to exert pressure on the Lincoln administration. Another way to read Sumner's state of mind is to say that he believed, in a spirit of cooperation with the White House, that he needed to prepare the public for emancipation to make Lincoln's job easier. Both interpretations are two sides of the same coin. Compare Walter G. Shotwell, *Life of Charles Sumner* (New York: Thomas Y. Crowell, 1910), 414; with Moorfield Storey, *Charles Sumner* (Boston: Houghton Mifflin, 1900), 201. For a more accessible published version of Sumner's Worcester speech, see CS, "Emancipation Our Best Weapon" (Speech, Republican State Convention at Worcester, Massachusetts, October 1, 1861), *WCS*, 6:1–29.

12. CS, *The Rebellion:—Its Origin and Main-Spring* (New York: Young Men's Republican Union, 1861); James M. McPherson, *The Struggle for Equality: Abolitionists and the Negro in the Civil War and Reconstruction* (Princeton: Princeton University Press, 1964), 78–79. For a more accessible published version of Sumner's speech, see CS, "Rebellion: Its Origin and Mainspring" (Speech, Cooper Institute, November 27, 1861), *WCS*, 6:65–118.

13. Rev. Sir Gilbert Frankland Lewis, ed., *Letters of the Right Hon. Sir George Cornewall Lewis* (London: Longmans, Green, 1870), 395. For more on European sympathies with the Confederacy, see Andre M. Fleche, *The Revolution of 1861: The American Civil War in the Age of Nationalist Conflict* (Chapel Hill: University of North Carolina Press, 2012); Donaldson Jordan and Edwin J. Pratt, *Europe and the American Civil War* (Boston: Houghton Mifflin, 1931), chaps. 8–12; Stève Sainlaude, *France and the American Civil War: A Diplomatic History* (Chapel Hill: University of North Carolina Press, 2019), chap. 6.

14. James M. McPherson, *Battle Cry of Freedom: The Civil War Era* (New York: Oxford University Press, 1988), 383. For more on British attitudes toward the North and South during secession winter and the first six months of the Civil War, see Foreman, *A World on Fire*, chaps. 3–8; Duncan Andrew Campbell, *English Opinion and the American Civil War* (Suffolk, UK: Boydell Press, 2003), chap. 1; Jordan and Pratt, *Europe and the American Civil War*, chap. 1; Ephraim Douglass Adams, *Great Britain and the American Civil War* (London: Longmans, Green, 1925), chaps. 1–6.

15. John Bright to CS, September 6, 1861, 23/185, PCS; Thomas J. Peyton Jr., "Charles Sumner and United States Foreign Relations During the American Civil War" (Ph.D. diss., Georgetown University, 1972), 120; John Morley, *The Life of Richard Cobden*, vol. 2 (London: Macmillan, 1908), 386; Richard Cobden to CS, February 12, 1862, *MLCS*, 4:157.

16. CS to Harriet Martineau, October 29, 1861, 75/225, PCS; Harriet Martineau to CS, November 14, 1861, 23/556, PCS; William Howard Russell to CS, October 14, 1861, 23/403, PCS.

17. James Chambers, *Palmerston: The People's Darling* (London: Thistle Publishing, 2004), 487; David F. Krein, *The Last Palmerston Government: Foreign Policy, Domestic Politics, and the Genesis of "Splendid Isolation"* (Ames: Iowa State University Press, 1978), 50; Robin Blackburn, *Marx and Lincoln: An Unfinished Revolution* (London: Verso, 2011), 190–91. For a compilation of letters that discuss Sumner's involvement in resolving the Trent Affair, see "The Trent Affair," *Proceedings of the Massachusetts Historical Society, Oct. 1911–June 1912* 45 (1911): 35–159; James F. Rhodes, "Bright-Sumner Letters, 1861–1872," *Proceedings of the Massachusetts Historical Society, Oct. 1912–June 1913* 46 (1912): 93–164; "Letters of the Duke and Duchess of Argyll to Charles Sumner," *Proceedings of the Massachusetts Historical Society, Oct. 1913–June 1914* 47 (1914): 66–107.

18. Richard Cobden to CS, December 12, 1861, 24/022, PCS; Kenneth Bourne, "British Preparations for War with the North, 1861–1862," *The English Historical Review* 76, no. 301 (October 1961): 600–32; Foreman, *A World on Fire*, 183–84; Gordon H. Warren, *Fountain of Discontent: The Trent Affair and Freedom of the Seas* (Boston: Northeastern University Press, 1981), 123–30.

19. Peter J. Hugill, *World Trade Since 1431: Geography, Technology, and Capitalism* (Baltimore: Johns Hopkins University Press, 1993), 128.

20. CS, "Mr. Sumner and the Cuban Flurry," *Hartford Courant*, November 22, 1873; George Sumner, *Boston Daily Evening Transcript*, November 19, 1861; CS to Richard Cobden, December 31, 1861, 75/365, PCS; Warren, *Fountain of Discontent*, 30; William James Morgan et al., eds., *Autobiography of Rear Admiral Charles Wilkes, U.S. Navy, 1798–1877* (Washington, D.C.: Naval History Division, 1978), 776; Carl Schurz, *The Reminiscences of Carl Schurz*, vol. 2 (London: John Murray, 1909), 317. Victor Cohen compellingly argues that Charles Sumner probably knew about his brother's letter to the newspaper. But Cohen overclaims when he asserts that Sumner agreed with his brother's letter. See Victor H. Cohen, "Charles Sumner and the Trent Affair," *Journal of Southern History* 22, no. 2 (May 1956): 209–10; Donald, *Charles Sumner and the Rights of Man*, 31–32; Warren, *Fountain of Discontent*, 30n10.

21. Foreman, *A World on Fire*, 193–95.

22. CS to John Bright, December 27, 1861, 75/342, PCS; *Cong. Globe*, 37th Cong., 2nd Sess., 245 (1862) (remarks of Sen. Sumner); CS, "The Trent Case and Maritime Rights" (Speech, U.S. Senate, January 9, 1862), *WCS*, 6:153–242; "The Trent Affair"; Curtis, "Eulogy Before Massachusetts State Government," in *Charles Sumner: Memoir and Eulogies*, ed. William M. Cornell (Boston: James H. Earle, 1874), 250.

23. Schurz, *The Reminiscences of Carl Schurz*, 2:309–10, 313; Hale, *Memories of a Hundred Years*, 2:191–93; CS to Wendell Phillips, December 8, 1861, 75/277, PCS.

Chapter 16: Lincoln's Bishop

1. John Forney told two different accounts of what he witnessed between Lincoln and Sumner. I have relied on both accounts to construct the dialogue of this event. In the alternative account, Forney was invited to join Sumner and the First Lady at the opera a few days later (rather than to join Sumner and the president at dinner on the same day as the argument). See Harold A. Davis, "From the Diaries of a Diplomat James S. Pike," *The New England Quarterly* 14, no. 1 (March 1941): 110–11; Rufus Rockwell Wilson, *Intimate Memories of Lincoln* (Elmira, N.Y.: The Primavera Press, 1945), 12–13. For Forney's recollections about Sumner's personality and debating ability, see John W. Forney, *Anecdotes of Public Men*, vol. 2 (New York: Harper and Bros., 1881), 253–63. For Sumner's pedantic statement to Lincoln about how emancipation would have ameliorated the administration's foreign policy follies, see Edward Everett Hale, *Memories of a Hundred Years*, vol. 2 (London: Macmillan, 1904), 192.

2. I have obtained the story of Lincoln trying to match backs with Sumner from the *Diary of a Public Man*, a treasure trove of recollections of the Civil War era published by an anonymous reporter. Historians have hotly debated the *Diary's* veracity. However, Benjamin Perley Poore—whom Sumner hired as his clerk for the Senate Foreign Relations Committee—recalled a very similar story. Thus, I am inclined to think the *Diary's* account is accurate in this case. See Anonymous, "The Diary of a Public Man: Unpublished Passages of the Secret History of the American Civil War, Part II," ed. Allen Thorndike Rice, *North American Review* 129, no. 279 (1879): 266–67; Benjamin Perley Poore, *Perley's Reminiscences of Sixty Years in the National Metropolis*, vol. 2 (Philadelphia: Hubbard's Bros., 1886), 62–63; Noah Brooks, *Men of Achievement: Statesmen* (New York: Charles Scribner's Sons, 1893), 224–25. As a starting point on the complex historiography of the *Diary*, see generally Daniel W. Crofts, *A Secession Crisis Enigma: William Henry Hurlbert and "The Diary of a Public Man"* (Baton Rouge: Louisiana State University Press, 2010).

3. Carl Schurz, *The Reminiscences of Carl Schurz*, vol. 2 (London: John Murray, 1909), 240–41; Robert Francis Lucid, ed., *The Journal of Richard Henry Dana Jr.*, vol. 1 (Cambridge, Mass.: Harvard University Press, 1968), 59; Pierce, *MLCS*, 1:164; David Donald, *Charles Sumner and the Coming of the Civil War* (Naperville, Ill.: Sourcebooks, 2009), 184; Ida M. Tarbell, *The Life of Abraham Lincoln*, vol. 2 (New York: Lincoln Memorial Association, 1895), 73; Carl Schurz to CS, June 8, 1860, 19/484, PCS. See also "Mr. Sumner and President Lincoln," *Minneapolis Daily Tribune*, January 13, 1871.

4. CS, *The Rebellion:—Its Origin and Main-Spring* (New York: Young Men's Republican Union, 1861); Linda Wheeler, "A Civil War Mystery: Who Named Lincoln the 'Great Emancipator'?," *Washington Post*, May 17, 2001; "A Letter from the President," *Daily National Intelligencer*, August 22, 1862. For some letters in which Sumner describes Lincoln as honest, slow, and inexperienced, see CS to Elizabeth Argyll, June 4, 1861, 75/039, PCS; CS to Harriet Martineau, October 29, 1861, 75/225,

PCS; CS to John Bright, December 23, 1861, 75/331, PCS; CS to John Bright, August 5, 1862, 76/040, PCS. See also CS, *WCS*, 7:116–18.

5. Auguste Laugel, "Charles Sumner," *Revue des Deux Mondes* 3, no. 4 (June 1874): 735; Evan Rowland Jones, *Lincoln, Stanton, and Grant: Historical Sketches* (London: Frederick Warne, 1875), 68–70; David Herbert Donald, *"We Are Lincoln Men": Abraham Lincoln and His Friends* (New York: Simon and Schuster, 2003), 214; Tarbell, *The Life of Abraham Lincoln*, 73; Anna Lauren Dawes, *Charles Sumner* (New York: Dodd, Mead, 1892), 180–81; Shelby M. Cullom, *Fifty Years of Public Service* (Chicago: A. C. McClurg, 1911), 152; George Rothwell Brown, ed., *Reminiscences of Senator William M. Stewart of Nevada* (New York: The Naele Publishing Company, 1908), 231; Isaac N. Arnold, *The Life of Abraham Lincoln* (Chicago: Jansen, McClurg, 1885), 411; Benjamin Quarles, *Lincoln and the Negro* (Oxford: Oxford University Press, 1962), 88–90. One of Lincoln's bodyguards, who was employed in January 1865 and had known Lincoln for less than five months, claimed forty years later that Sumner was "the only man, so far as my knowledge goes, to obtain the President's bitter dislike." His recollection is contradicted by most other reports. See William Henry Crook, "Lincoln as I Knew Him," ed. Margarita Spalding Gerry, *Harper's Magazine* 115 (June 1907): 45.

6. "Lincoln, Four Days After Son Willie's Death, Tells Sumner Mary Lincoln Needs His Help—'Can You Come?,'" *Shapell Manuscript Foundation* (blog), n.d., https://www.shapell.org/manuscript/abraham-lincoln-mary-lincoln-son-willie-dies-white-house-typhoid/.

7. Justin G. Turner and Linda Levitt, eds., *Mary Todd Lincoln: Her Life and Letters* (New York: Alfred A. Knopf, 1972), 205, 455, and 534; Thomas F. Schwartz and Kim M. Bauer, "Unpublished Mary Todd Lincoln," *Journal of the Abraham Lincoln Association* (Summer 1996): 12; David Herbert Donald, *Lincoln* (New York: Simon and Schuster, 1995), 476; Thomas F. Schwartz and Anne V. Shaughnessy, "Unpublished Mary Lincoln Letters," *Journal of the Abraham Lincoln Association* 11, no. 1 (1990): 40; Pierce, *MLCS*, 4:231; Ishbel Ross, *The President's Wife: Mary Todd Lincoln* (New York: G. P. Putnam's Sons, 1973), 206–8. According to Turner and Levitt, "Of all the distinguished gentlemen who called at the White House, Sumner was Mrs. Lincoln's overwhelming favorite" (Turner and Levitt, *Mary Todd Lincoln*, 185). According to William Barton, who claimed to have interviewed many people who knew Mary Lincoln personally, "No one who knew either Charles Sumner or Mrs. Lincoln could doubt that their relations were wholly platonic." William Eleazar Barton, *The Women Lincoln Loved* (Indianapolis: Bobbs-Merrill, 1927), 356.

8. Turner and Levitt, *Mary Todd Lincoln*, 455 and 534; Douglas L. Wilson and Rodney O. Davis, *Herndon's Informants: Letters, Interviews, and Statements About Abraham Lincoln* (Urbana: University of Illinois Press, 1998), 358–60; Ruth Painter Randall, *Mary Lincoln: Biography of a Marriage* (Boston: Little, Brown, 1953), 356–57.

9. Elizabeth Keckley, *Behind the Scenes: Thirty Years a Slave and Four Years in the White House* (New York: G. W. Carleton, 1868), 161; Randall, *Mary Lincoln*, 356–57; Catherine Clinton, *Mrs. Lincoln: A Life* (New York: HarperCollins, 2009), 198–200; "Mrs. Lincoln Again," *Weekly Star*, June 30, 1875, 6. According to Turner and Levitt, "the most potent influence on Mrs. Lincoln's political thought was her extravagant admiration for Senator Charles Sumner" (Turner and Levitt, *Mary Todd Lincoln*, 176).

10. CS to Francis Lieber, March 29, 1862, 64/207, PCS.

11. For more on the Port Royal Experiment, see Willie Lee Rose, *Rehearsal for Reconstruction: The Port Royal Experiment* (Indianapolis: Bobbs-Merrill, 1964); James Oakes, *Freedom National: The Destruction of Slavery in the United States, 1861–1865* (New York: W. W. Norton, 2012), 197–208.

12. For more on the life of Edward Pierce, see George F. Hoar, "Edward Lillie Pierce," in *Proceedings of the American Antiquarian Society* 12 (1899): 197–210; James F. Rhodes, "Memoir of Edward L. Pierce," in *Proceedings of the Massachusetts Historical Society* 18 (1904): 363–69.

13. Edward Pierce, "The Contrabands at Fortress Monroe," *The Atlantic Monthly*, November 1861.

14. Edward Pierce, *The Negroes at Port Royal: Report of E. L. Pierce, Government Agent, to the Hon. Salmon P. Chase, Secretary of the Treasury* (Boston: R. F. Wallcut, 1862); W. E. Burghardt Du Bois, *Black Reconstruction* (New York: Harcourt, Brace, 1935), 67; James M. McPherson, *The Struggle for Equality: Abolitionists and the Negro in the Civil War and Reconstruction* (Princeton: Princeton University Press, 1964), 92. Du Bois has argued that Edward Pierce's work at Fort Monroe and in the Sea Islands set the stage for the Freedmen's Bureau after the war: "It was a Pierce of Boston who pointed out the way, and thus became in a sense the founder of the Freedmen's Bureau" (W. E. Burghardt Du Bois, "The Freedmen's Bureau," *The Atlantic Monthly*, March 1901).

15. Edward Pierce to CS, March 20, 1862, 25/232, PCS; CS to Edward Pierce, February 28, 1862, 64/203, PCS; CS to Edward Pierce, June 7, 1862, 64/217, PCS; CS, *WCS*, 7:77.

16. CS, *WCS*, 7:76. Sumner's resolutions are reprinted in CS, "State Rebellion, State Suicide; Emancipation and Reconstruction: Resolutions in the Senate, February 11, 1862" (Speech, U.S. Senate, 1862), *WCS*, 6:301–18.

17. CS, *WCS*, 10:126.

18. Herman Belz, *Reconstructing the Union: Theory and Policy During the Civil War* (Ithaca, N.Y.: Cornell University Press, 1969), 51–54; Rebecca E. Zietlow, *The Forgotten Emancipator: James Mitchell Ashley and the Ideological Origins of Reconstruction* (Cambridge: Cambridge University Press, 2017), 99–100.

19. Although Members of Congress began floating legal theories about the status of seceded states from the very start of the secession crisis, historians have credited Sumner with presenting the first comprehensive theory to justify Congressional Reconstruction (also known as Radical Reconstruction). See, e.g., William A. Dunning, "The Constitution of the United States in Reconstruction," *Political Science Quarterly* 2, no. 4 (December 1887): 583; William J. Robertson, *Changing South* (New York: Boni and Liveright, 1927), 41; Du Bois, *Black Reconstruction*, 151; Donald, *Charles Sumner and the Coming of the Civil War*, 55. For more analysis of Sumner's state suicide theory, see the above sources and see also Belz, *Reconstructing the Union*, chap. 4; Diane Miller Sommerville, "'Bent on Suicide': The Political Rhetoric of Suicide in the Civil War–Era South," in *The Long Civil War: New Explanations of America's Enduring Conflict*, ed. John David Smith and Raymond Arsenault (Lexington: University Press of Kentucky, 2021), chap. 4.

20. Hale, *Memories of a Hundred Years*, 2:193–97; CS, *WCS*, 6:391–92; CS, "Emancipation Our Best Weapon," 28, *WCS*, 6:1–29; Roy P. Basler, ed., *The Collected Works of Abraham Lincoln*, vol. 5 (New Brunswick, N.J.: Rutgers University Press, 1953), 146.

21. Hale, *Memories of a Hundred Years*, 2:196; Foner, *The Fiery Trial*, 196; Irving H. Bartlett, *Wendell Phillips: Brahmin Radical* (Boston: Beacon Press, 1961), 248–49; James Brewer Stewart, *Wendell Phillips: Liberty's Hero* (Baton Rouge: Louisiana State University Press, 1986), 234–36; Edward Dicey, *Six Months in the Federal States* (London: Macmillan, 1863), 185.

22. CS, *WCS*, 6:393; *Springfield Republican*, April 25, 1873.

23. Frederick Douglass to CS, April 8, 1862, 25/324, PCS.

24. C. Edwards Lester, *Life and Public Services of Charles Sumner* (New York: United States Publishing Company, 1874), 359–60.

25. Louise M. Starr, *Bohemian Brigade: Civil War Newsmen in Action* (New York: Alfred A. Knopf, 1954), 150; CS, *WCS*, 7:215; "The Late Senator," *New York Evening Post*, March 12, 1874, 2; Lester, *Life and Public Services of Charles Sumner*, 386–87; CS to Carl Schurz, July 5, 1862, 76/006, PCS.

26. Horace Greeley, *The American Conflict: A History of the Great Rebellion*, vol. 2 (Hartford: O. D. Case, 1866), 516.

27. John G. Nicolay, *A Short Life of Abraham Lincoln* (New York: The Century Company, 1902), 327. When asked by abolitionist George Preston Stearns to push for Black enlistment in late 1861, Sumner replied, "No, I do not consider it advisable to agitate that question until the Proclamation of Emancipation has become a fact. Then we will take another step in advance" (Frank Preston Stearns, *Cambridge Sketches* [Philadelphia: J. B. Lippincott, 1905], 191).

28. CS to John Bright, October 28, 1862, 76/132, PCS.

29. Foner, *The Fiery Trial*, 184–87; Phillip W. Magness and Sebastian N. Page, *Colonization After Emancipation: Lincoln and the Movement for Black Resettlement* (Columbia: University of Missouri Press, 2011), 1–12; Schurz, *The Reminiscences of Carl Schurz*, 2:310.

30. CS, *WCS*, 6:388, 443; Dorothy Porter Wesley and Constance Porter Uzelac, eds., *William Cooper Nell: Selected Writings from 1832–1874* (Baltimore: Black Classic Press, 2002), 46–47, 623–24; Philip F. Rubio, *There's Always Work at the Post Office* (Chapel Hill: University of North Carolina Press, 2010), 20–21; Robert P. Smith, "William Cooper Nell: Crusading Black Abolitionist," *Journal of Negro History* 55, no. 3 (1970): 194; Kathryn Grover and Janine V. da Silva, *Historic Resource Study: Boston African American National Historic Site* (Washington, D.C.: National Park Service, 2002), 65.

31. Pierce, *MLCS*, 4:68. For more on the treaty, see Conway W. Henderson, "The Anglo-American Treaty of 1862 in Civil War Diplomacy," *Civil War History* 15, no. 4 (1969): 308–19; Eugene Kontorovich, "The Constitutionality of International Courts: The Forgotten Precedent of Slave Trade Tribunals," Northwestern University Faculty Working Papers, Paper 178, 2010.

32. "December 3, 1861: First Annual Message—Abraham Lincoln Presidency," Miller Center, n.d., https://millercenter.org/the-presidency/presidential-speeches/december-3-1861-first-annual-message.

33. CS, "Charles Sumner Autograph Collection, 1624–1846." For more on Charles Pinckney Sumner's visit to Haiti, see chapter 1.

34. Cong. Globe, 37th Cong., 2nd Sess., 1776 (remarks of Sen. Sumner); CS, WCS, 6:470–72; Lester, *Life and Public Services of Charles Sumner*, 391; Quarles, *Lincoln and the Negro*, 100–102; CS, WCS, 14:306–9; J. N. Leger, *Haiti: Her History and Her Detractors* (New York: Neale Publishing, 1907), 220–21; "File: Haitian Medal State Library of Massachusetts.jpg," Wikipedia, 2009, https://commons.wikimedia.org/wiki/File:Haitian_medal_state_library_of_massachusetts.jpg; "Memorial to Charles Sumner, Accompanying the Medal Presented by the Government in Behalf of the People of Hayti, May, 1871," *State Library of Massachusetts*, n.d., 2024, https://archives.lib.state.ma.us/handle/2452/862187.

35. James M. McPherson, *Battle Cry of Freedom: The Civil War Era* (New York: Oxford University Press, 1988), 506–7.

36. "Down with the Radicals," *Rutland Courier*, October 31, 1862, 2. For more on Sumner's reelection, see Pierce, *MLCS*, 4:98–106; David Donald, *Charles Sumner and the Rights of Man* (New York: Knopf, 1970), 67–86.

37. Julia Ward Howe, *Francis William Bird: A Biographical Sketch* (Boston: n.p, 1897), 60–67; *Boston Traveler*, January 3, 1863, 2.

38. CS, "The Proclamation of Emancipation: Its Policy and Necessity as a War Measure for the Suppression of the Rebellion (October 6, 1862)" (Speech, Faneuil Hall, Boston, 1862), WCS, 7:191–246.

39. For more on Sumner's unsuccessful attempts to oust Seward, see Pierce, *MLCS*, 4:110–11; Donald, *Charles Sumner and the Rights of Man*, 87–100. For Sumner's election results, see "Re-Election of Hon. Charles Sumner," *Liberator*, January 23, 1863, 2.

40. John Niven, ed., *The Salmon P. Chase Papers*, vol. 1 (Kent, Ohio: Kent State University Press, 1993), 392–93; "The First Edition of Abraham Lincoln's Preliminary Emancipation Proclamation," Library of Congress, n.d., https://www.loc.gov/resource/lprbscsm.scsm1017/?st=list.

Chapter 17: I Find the African Ready to Be Our Saviour

1. CS to Samuel Howe, December 28, 1862, 64/227, PCS; CS to John Murray Forbes, December 28, 1862, 76/285, PCS; CS to Harriet Beecher Stowe, December 25, 1862, 04/270, PCS; CS to Edward Pierce, December 3, 1862, *MLCS*, 4:113; CS to John Murray Forbes, December 30, 1862, 76/294, PCS. For a focused study on the hundred days leading up to the Emancipation Proclamation, in which Lincoln weighed whether to follow through with his promise, see Louis P. Masur, *Lincoln's Hundred Days: The Emancipation Proclamation and the War for the Union* (Cambridge, Mass.: Belknap Press, 2012).

2. John Niven, ed., *The Salmon P. Chase Papers*, vol. 3 (Kent, Ohio: Kent State University Press, 1996), 350–52.

3. CS to Abraham Lincoln, December 28, 1862, 76/289, PCS; George Livermore to CS, December 29, 1862, 27/187, PCS; George Livermore to CS, January 5, 1863, 76/314, PCS. For more on Livermore, see CS, "The Late George Livermore, Esq" (September 2, 1865), WCS, 9:433–36; Benjamin Quarles, *Lincoln and the Negro* (Oxford: Oxford University Press, 1962), 141–42, 154–55. For more on the pen, see Benson J. Lossing, *The Pictorial Field Book of the Civil War of the United States of America*, vol. 2 (Hartford: T. Belknap, 1874), 564; Benjamin Perley Poore, "Benjamin Perley Poore," in *Reminiscences of Abraham Lincoln by Distinguished Men of His Time*, ed. Allen Thorndike Rice (New York: North American Review, 1889), 230; William R. Livermore, "The Emancipation Pen," *Proceedings of the Massachusetts Historical Society, Oct. 1910–June 1911* 44 (1911): 595–604; "Pen Used by Abraham Lincoln to Sign the Emancipation Proclamation," Massachusetts Historical Society: Collections Online, n.d., http://www.masshist.org/database/4.

4. John Stauffer and Henry Louis Gates Jr., eds., *The Portable Frederick Douglass* (New York: Penguin, 2016), 324; "Emancipation Day in Boston," *Liberator*, January 16, 1863, 4; Stephen Puleo, *A City So Grand: The Rise of an American Metropolis, Boston 1850–1900* (Boston: Beacon Press, 2010), 138; Quarles, *Lincoln and the Negro*, 145.

5. John Daniels, *In Freedom's Birthplace: A Study of the Boston Negroes* (Boston: Houghton Mifflin, 1914), 57; Diane Spivey, *At the Table of Power: Food and Cuisine in the African American Struggle for Freedom, Justice, and Equality* (Pittsburgh: University of Pittsburgh Press, 2022), 202–3; Kathryn Grover and Janine V. da Silva, *Historic Resource Study: Boston African American National Historic Site* (Washington, D.C.: National Park Service, 2002), 119–20; John J. Smith to CS, August 27, 1844, 04/144, PCS.

6. CS and John Whittier, August 11, 1872, 85/037, PCS.

7. Ray Allen Billington, ed., *The Journal of Charlotte Forten: A Free Negro in the Slave Era* (New York: W. W. Norton, 1981), 115–16, 118–19.

8. Ira Berlin, Joseph R. Reidy, and Leslie S. Rowland, eds., *The Black Military Experience* (Cambridge: Cambridge University Press, 1982), 337; Stephen Kantrowitz, *More Than Freedom: Fighting for Black Citizenship in a White Republic, 1829–1889* (New York: Penguin, 2012), 282–83; Bob Luke and John David Smith, *Soldiering for Freedom: How the Union Army Recruited, Trained, and Deployed the U.S. Colored Troops* (Baltimore: Johns Hopkins University Press, 2014), 28–29; Kathryn Grover, *To Heal the Wounded Nation's Life: African Americans and the Robert Gould Shaw—54th Regiment Memorial* (Cornish, N.H.: Saint-Gaudens National Historical Park, 2021), 41–45.

9. CS to John Bright, July 21, 1863, 77/196, PCS; CS, *WCS*, 7:213, 326.

10. CS, *WCS*, 7:213–14, 268; Brian Taylor, *Fighting for Citizenship: Black Northerners and the Debate over Military Service in the Civil War* (Chapel Hill: University of North Carolina Press, 2020), 82; William Cooper Nell, *The Colored Patriots of the American Revolution* (Boston: Robert F. Wallcut, 1855); CS to John Andrew, December 28, 1862, 76/283, PCS.

11. CS, *WCS*, 7:262–65; Willie Lee Rose, *Rehearsal for Reconstruction: The Port Royal Experiment* (Indianapolis: Bobbs-Merrill, 1964), 214. For more on the enlistment of Black soldiers during the American Revolution, and the views of the Founders on their enlistment, see George Livermore, *An Historical Research Respecting the Opinion of the Founders of the Republic on Negroes as Slaves, as Citizens, and as Soldiers*, 3rd ed. (Boston: A. Williams, 1863).

12. John Andrew to CS, December 10, 1862, 27/57, PCS; CS to John Andrew, December 28, 1862, 76/283, PCS; John Hope Franklin, *From Slavery to Freedom* (New York: Alfred A. Knopf, 1947), 270–72; Frank J. Cirillo, *The Abolitionist Civil War* (New Orleans: Louisiana State University Press, 2023), 168–69; Laura E. Richards, *Letters and Journals of Samuel Gridley Howe* (Boston: Dana Estes, 1909), 502; James M. McPherson, *The Struggle for Equality: Abolitionists and the Negro in the Civil War and Reconstruction* (Princeton: Princeton University Press, 1964), 178–82; John G. Sproat, "Blueprint for Radical Reconstruction," *Journal of Southern History* 23, no. 1 (1957): 33–35; Harold Schwartz, *Samuel Gridley Howe, Social Reformer* (Cambridge, Mass.: Harvard University Press, 1956), 256–58.

13. Robert Dale Owen, James McKaye, and Samuel Howe, *Preliminary Report Touching the Condition and Management of Emancipated Refugees: Made to the Secretary of War by the American Freedmen's Inquiry Commission* (New York: John F. Trow, 1863); Sproat, "Blueprint for Radical Reconstruction." See also McPherson, *The Struggle for Equality*, 186; Rose, *Rehearsal for Reconstruction*, 208.

14. Although historians conventionally depict the Battle of Fort Wagner as a turning point in northern public opinion on Black enlistment, a recent study has argued that the battle's significance is overstated. See Glenn David Brasher, "Debating Black Manhood: The Northern Press Reports on the 54th Massachusetts at Fort Wagner," in *American Discord: The Republic and Its People in the Civil War Era*, ed. Megan L. Bever, Lesley J. Gordon, and Laura Mammina (Baton Rouge: Louisiana State University Press, 2020), 22–44.

15. CS to Edward Pierce, July 29, 1863, 64/280, PCS; Cirillo, *The Abolitionist Civil War*, 194; David Donald, *Charles Sumner and the Rights of Man* (Naperville, Ill.: Sourcebooks, 2009), 117. In one letter, Sumner referred to Shaw as "a refined brave youth, son of my friends." CS to Elizabeth Argyll, September 8, 1863, 77/274, PCS. When Sumner dined with the Shaws at some point in the 1840s, he met and befriended their then servant Joshua Smith. See chapter 23.

16. William M. Cornell, ed., *Charles Sumner: Memoir and Eulogies* (Boston: James H. Earle, 1874), 270, 280; James Ford Rhodes, *History of the United States*, vol. 5 (New York: Macmillan, 1907), 55.

17. Betty Boles Ellison, *The True Mary Todd Lincoln: A Biography* (Jefferson, N.C.: McFarland, 2014), 158; Roy P. Basler, ed., *The Collected Works of Abraham Lincoln*, vol. 6 (New Brunswick, N.J.: Rutgers University Press, 1953), 185.

18. Cong. Globe, 37th Cong., 3rd. Sess., 1020 (1863) (remarks of Senator Sumner); CS to Abraham Lincoln, March 18, 1863, 76/468, PCS.

19. CS to John Bright, August 4, 1863, 77/217, PCS; CS to John Bright, November 18, 1862, 76/176, PCS; CS to Richard Cobden, March 12, 1863, 76/460, PCS; Donald, *Charles Sumner and the Rights of Man*, 115; CS to John Bright, April 7, 1863, 76/525, PCS. For a compilation of letters that heavily discuss Sumner's involvement in the Alabama Affair, see James F. Rhodes, "Bright-Sumner Letters, 1861–1872," *Proceedings of the Massachusetts Historical Society, Oct. 1912–June 1913* 46 (1912): 93–164; "Letters of the Duke and Duchess of Argyll to Charles Sumner," *Proceedings of the Massachusetts Historical Society, Oct. 1913–June 1914* 47 (1914): 66–107.

20. CS, *Our Foreign Relations* (Boston: Wright & Potter, 1863). For a more accessible published version of the speech, see CS, "Our Foreign Relations" (Speech, Cooper Institute, September 10, 1863), WCS, 7:327.

21. Conveniently, European jurists ignored the de facto independence principle when Haiti earned its freedom in the early 1800s. European countries outright refused to recognize a so-called Black republic, and the United States did not do so until Sumner successfully campaigned for its recognition in 1862. Haiti was doubtless on Sumner's mind when he developed his theory of recognition.

22. The only jurist who came close to Sumner's rule was the Swiss luminary Emmerich de Vattel. The senator quoted from Vattel when he said, "If there be any nation that makes an open profession of trampling justice under foot, of despising and violating the rights of others, whenever it finds an opportunity, the interest of human society will authorize all others to unite in order to humble and chastise it." But Vattel's idea was extremely limited; he argued that it should not be applied in any case "where there is room for the smallest doubt." It is doubtful that Vattel was even thinking about slavery as an act of injustice so egregious that a slave country should be denied recognition. Monsieur De Vattel, *The Law of Nations*, ed. Joseph Chitty (Philadelphia: T and J. W. Johnson, 1883), 161. For a survey of the views of many eighteenth- and nineteenth-century international law jurists on the rule of recognition, see C. H. Alexandrowicz, "The Theory of Recognition in Fieri (1958)," in *The Law of Nations in Global History*, ed. David Armitage and Jennifer Pitts (Oxford: Oxford University Press, 2017), 354–74; H. Lauterpacht, "Recognition of States in International Law," *Yale Law Journal* 53, no. 3 (1944): 385–458.

23. These newspaper reports are reprinted in CS, WCS, 7:484–86.

24. Justin McCarthy, *A History of Our Own Times*, vol. 2 (London: Chatto and Windus, 1887), 372; Richard Cobden to CS, October 8, 1863, 29/336, PCS; Elizabeth Argyll to CS, September 22, 1863, 29/219, PCS; Arthur Reed Hogue, ed., *Charles Sumner: An Essay by Carl Schurz* (Urbana: University of Illinois Press, 1951), 108. After Lord Lyons returned to England, Sumner told Richard Cobden, "My relations with him for much of the time were intimate; but after my speech in New York we saw each other only accidentally. He did not call on me, & I did not call on him; & yet when we met it was in the most friendly way" (CS to Richard Cobden, March 27, 1865, 79/163, PCS).

25. Elizabeth Argyll to CS, October 26, 1863, 77/384, PCS; CS to Francis Lieber, October 24, 1863, 64/288, PCS.

26. CS to Henry Longfellow, April 29, 1863, 76/625, PCS; Johnson, "Charles Sumner—III, Recollections," 153; CS and Samuel Howe, October 7, 1863, 77/338, PCS; CS and Henry Longfellow, May 21, 1864, 78/192, PCS. For a focused study of the life of George Sumner, see Robert C. Waterston, "Memoir of George Sumner," *Proceedings of the Massachusetts Historical Society, 1880–1881* 18 (1881): 189–223. For some of his letters, see Charles S. Hamlin, "Letters of George Sumner," *Proceedings of the Massachusetts Historical Society, Oct. 1912–June 1913* 46 (1914): 341–70.

27. George F. Hoar, *Autobiography of Seventy Years*, vol. 1 (New York: Charles Scribner's Sons, 1903), 212; CS, WCS, 9:404; CS, WCS, 13:101–2.

28. Charles Sumner, "Our Domestic Relations; Or, How to Treat the Rebel States," *The Atlantic Monthly*, October 1, 1863.

29. CS, WCS, 11:411; CS, WCS, 13:43.

30. Abraham Lincoln, "Proclamation of Amnesty and Reconstruction (Dec. 8, 1863)," Office of the Historian, State Department, n.d., https://history.state.gov/historicaldocuments/frus1863p1/message1.

31. Unfortunately, Ashley's bill is available only in manuscript form at the National Archives. I have reviewed the manuscript at "38 Cong., H.R. 48" (December 21, 1863), RG 233, 38A-B1, National Archives, Washington, D.C. It is helpfully summarized in Herman Belz, *Reconstructing the Union: Theory and Policy During the Civil War* (Ithaca, N.Y.: Cornell University Press, 1969), 176–87.

32. Michael Burlingame and John R. Turner Ettlinger, eds., *Inside Lincoln's White House: The Complete Civil War Diary of John Hay* (Carbondale: Southern Illinois University Press, 1997), 124; CS to Orestes A. Brownson, December 27, 1863, 77/515, PCS; "Senator Sumner Fully Endorses the Message," *Chicago Tribune*, December 14, 1863; W. E. Burghardt Du Bois, *Black Reconstruction* (New York: Harcourt, Brace, 1935), 152–53. There is one unsubstantiated report that Sumner was upset with Lincoln's December 1863 message to Congress because it did not clearly state whether the rebel states were in or out of the Union. According to this report, which is contradicted by the bulk of the evidence, Sumner angrily slammed his books and documents upon his desk and the floor while the message was being read in the Senate. See Noah Brooks, *Washington in Lincoln's Time* (New York: The Century Company, 1895), 163–64.

33. Joshua Giddings to CS, September 15, 1863, 29/172, PCS.
34. CS to Elizabeth Argyll, April 17, 1865, *MLCS*, 4:135; CS to Elizabeth Argyll, December 29, 1863, 77/526, PCS; Edward Dicey, *Six Months in the Federal States* (London: Macmillan, 1863), 236–37; Janet Chase Hoyt, "A Woman's Memories," *New York Tribune*, April 5, 1891, 18; Benjamin Perley Poore, *Perley's Reminiscences of Sixty Years in the National Metropolis*, vol. 2 (Philadelphia: Hubbard's Bros., 1886), 141–42; Jesse R. Grant, *In the Days of My Father General Grant* (New York: Harper and Bros., 1925), 105–6; CS to Joshua Giddings, October 5, 1863, 77/324, PCS.

Chapter 18: The Prayer of One Hundred Thousand
1. William Lloyd Garrison to CS, November 12, 1863, 29/567, PCS; "The Fraternity Lectures," *Liberator*, November 20, 1863, 2; "A New Federal Constitution," *Buffalo Courier*, November 25, 1863, 2.
2. Francis Lieber to CS, December 4, 1863, 77/448, PCS. For more on Lieber's contributions to the laws of war, see generally John Fabian Witt, *Lincoln's Code: The Laws of War in American History* (New York: Free Press, 2012). For a focused study of Sumner and Lieber's relationship, see Frank Freidel, "Francis Lieber, Charles Sumner, and Slavery," *Journal of Southern History* 9, no. 1 (February 1943): 75–93.
3. CS to Charlemagne Tower, July 15, 1833, 65/051, PCS. For more on Sumner's lectures on constitutional law, see chapter 4. For the inconceivability of amending the Constitution for much of the antebellum period, see Michael Vorenberg, *Final Freedom* (London: Cambridge University Press, 2001), 10–18.
4. Harriet Beecher Stowe, *Men of Our Times; Or, Leading Patriots of the Day* (Hartford: Hartford Publishing, 1868), 229.
5. CS, *WCS*, 2:78, 140. For the connection between the Second Founding and the Declaration of Independence, see Jack M. Balkin, *Constitutional Redemption: Political Faith in an Unjust World* (Cambridge, Mass.: Harvard University Press, 2011), 18–25; Alexander Tsesis, "The Declaration of Independence and Constitutional Interpretation," *Southern California Law Review* 89 (2016): 369–98. For more on Adams's amendment, see Vorenberg, *Final Freedom*, 12, 51; Randall Woods, *John Quincy Adams* (New York: Dutton, 2024), 647–51. For Sumner's first suggestion of an abolition amendment, see CS, "Antislavery Duties of the Whig Party" (Faneuil Hall, Boston, September 23, 1846), *WCS*, 1:310–14.
6. Henry Wright to CS, May 23, 1866, 36/351, PCS; CS, *WCS*, 8:351; *Proceedings of the American Anti-Slavery Society at Its Third Decade, Held in the City of Philadelphia, Dec. 3d and 4th, 1863* (New York: American Anti-Slavery Society, 1864), 4, 16, 74–75. For more on the use of petitions by women prior to women's suffrage, see Daniel Carpenter and Colin D. Moore, "When Canvassers Became Activists: Antislavery Petitioning and the Political Mobilization of American Women," *The American Political Science Review* 108, no. 3 (2014): 479–98; Maggie Blackhawk, "Lobbying and the Petition Clause," *Stanford Law Review* 68 (2016): 1131–205.
7. "'To the Women of the Republic' (January 25, 1864)," Slavery and the Making of America, n.d., https://www.thirteen.org/wnet/slavery/experience/gender/docs2.html; Eleanor Flexner, *Century of Struggle: The Woman's Rights Movement in the United States* (New York: Atheneum, 1959), 109–12; Wendy F. Hamand, "The Woman's National Loyal League: Feminist Abolitionists and the Civil War," *Civil War History* 35, no. 1 (1989): 39–58; Wendy Hamand Venet, *Neither Ballots nor Bullets: Women Abolitionists and the Civil War* (Charlottesville: University Press of Virginia, 1991), 102–5; Faye E. Dudden, *Fighting Chance: The Struggle over Woman Suffrage and Black Suffrage in Reconstruction America* (Oxford: Oxford University Press, 2011), 51–55; Elizabeth Cady Stanton to CS, February 1, 1864, 77/640, PCS; Elizabeth Cady Stanton to CS, June 23, 1864, 31/269, PCS; Elizabeth Cady Stanton to CS, June 23, 1864, 31/275, PCS; Elizabeth Cady Stanton, Susan B. Anthony, and Matilda Joslyn Gage, eds., *History of Woman Suffrage: 1861–1876*, vol. 2 (New York: Fowler and Wells, 1882), 78. It has been reported that the petitions were rolled together with red regulation tape. However, when I examined the original petition rolls at the National Archives, all the petitions appeared to be glued together, not taped. See "Senate Petitions and Memorials Referred to the Select Committee on Slavery and Freedom," n.d., RG 46, 38A-H20, National Archives, Washington, D.C. Presumably, Wright had disclosed to Stanton and Anthony that Sumner was the senator seeking petitions.
8. Robert F. Horowitz, *The Great Impeacher: A Political Biography of James M. Ashley* (New York: Brooklyn College Press, 1979), 50–51; Rebecca E. Zietlow, *The Forgotten Emancipator: James Mitchell Ashley and the Ideological Origins of Reconstruction* (Cambridge: Cambridge University Press, 2017), 91; "The Democratic Blade," *Perrysburg Journal*, September 10, 1862; "Charles Sumner

Ashley (1864–1925)," Find a Grave, n.d., https://www.findagrave.com/memorial/44930996/charles _sumner-ashley.

9. Cong. Globe, 38th Cong., 1st. Sess., 12–21 (1863) (remarks of Representatives Ashley and Wilson).

10. CS to Elizabeth Argyll, February 8, 1864, 77/651, PCS.

11. Cong. Globe, 38th Cong., 1st. Sess., 521–23 (1864) (remarks of Senators Sumner and Trumbull); Ralph J. Roske, *His Own Counsel: The Life and Times of Lyman Trumbull* (Reno: University of Nevada Press, 1979), 105. For more on Trumbull's complex views on race and the law, see generally David B. Kopel, "Lyman Trumbull: Author of the Thirteenth Amendment, Author of the Civil Rights Act, and the First Second Amendment Lawyer," *Loyola University Chicago Law Journal* 47, no. 4 (2016): 1117–92; Paul Rego, *Lyman Trumbull and the Second Founding of the United States* (Lawrence: University Press of Kansas, 2022).

12. Cong. Globe, 38th Cong., 1st. Sess., 536 (1863) (remarks of Senator Sumner); CS, "The Prayer of One Hundred Thousand" (New York, 1864), Printed Ephemera Collection, Portfolio 125, Folder 10, Library of Congress, https://www.loc.gov/resource/rbpe.12501000/?st=gallery.

13. Cong. Globe, 38th Cong., 1st. Sess., 553 and 694 (1864) (remarks of Senator Trumbull). The many occasions that Sumner presented Loyal League petitions to the Senate floor are documented in Hamand, "The Woman's National Loyal League," 53.

14. Heather M. Butts, "Alexander Thomas Augusta—Physician, Teacher and Human Rights Activist," *Journal of the National Medical Association* 97, no. 1 (January 2005): 106–9; Karen Sarena Morris, "The Founding of the National Medical Association" (M.A. thesis, Yale University School of Medicine, 2007), 11–15; Gerald S. Henig, "The Indomitable Dr. Augusta: The First Black Physician in the U.S. Army," *Army History* 87 (2013): 22–31.

15. Cong. Globe, 38th Cong., 1st. Sess., 554 (1864) (remarks of Senator Sumner). For more on the streetcar integration movement in Washington, see Kate Masur, *An Example for All the Land: Emancipation and the Struggle over Equality in Washington, D.C.* (Chapel Hill: University of North Carolina Press, 2010), 87–90; John DeFerrari, *Capital Streetcars: Early Mass Transit in Washington, D.C.* (Charleston, S.C.: History Press, 2015), 51–55. For more on streetcar integration fights across the country during the nineteenth century, see Steve Luxenberg, *Separate: The Story of Plessy v. Ferguson and America's Journey from Slavery to Segregation* (New York: W. W. Norton, 2019).

16. Cong. Globe, 38th Cong., 1st. Sess., 3132–33 (1864) (remarks of Senators Trumbull and Sumner); Cong. Globe, 38th Cong., 2nd. Sess., 1010 (1865) (remarks of Senator Trumbull); William Lloyd Garrison to CS, April 19, 1864, 30/666, PCS.

17. CS, *WCS*, 8:110; George Downing to CS, January 31, 1867, 37/635, PCS. For more on Black Washingtonians demanding equal treatment during the second half of the Civil War, see Masur, *An Example for All the Land*, 32–37; Chris Myers Asch and George Derek Musgrove, *Chocolate City: A History of Race and Democracy in the Nation's Capital* (Chapel Hill: University of North Carolina Press, 2017), 183–89.

18. Cong. Globe, 38th Cong., 1st. Sess., 1175 (1864) (remarks of Senator Sumner); Edward McPherson, *The Political History of the United States of America During the Great Rebellion, from November 6, 1860 to July 4, 1864* (Washington, D.C.: Philp and Solomons, 1864), 242; CS, *WCS*, 8:103–17; Archibald H. Grimke, *Charles Sumner: The Scholar in Politics* (New York: Funk and Wagnalls, 1892), 359–60. A few years later, Sumner advocated for Catherine (Kate) Brown, a Black woman who worked in the ladies' retiring room in the Senate, after she was expelled from a white-only intercity railcar. Brown ultimately sued the rail company. Her case made it to the Supreme Court, where she won. See Cong. Globe, 40th Cong., 2nd Sess., 1121–25 (1868) (remarks of Senator Sumner); Washington Railroad Co. v. Brown, 84 U.S. 445 (1873); Thomas Reed Johnson, "The City on the Hill: Race Relations in Washington, D.C., 1865–1885" (Ph.D. diss., University of Maryland, 1975), 99–100; Earl M. Maltz, "Separate but Equal and the Law of Common Carriers in the Era of the Fourteenth Amendment," *Rutgers Law Journal* 17 (1986): 565–66.

19. Cong. Globe, 38th Cong., 1st. Sess., 3132 (1864) (remarks of Senator Sumner).

20. "Massachusetts Constitution (1780)—Constitution Center," National Constitution Center, n.d., https://constitutioncenter.org/the-constitution/historic-document-library/detail/massachusetts -constitution. When campaigning for his bills to integrate Washington streetcars, Sumner told a reporter that his goal was to "clean the statute-book of all support of slavery" (CS to Parke Goodwin, April 23, 1864). For more on Story's natural law views, see Joseph Story, "Natural Law," in *Encyclopaedia Americana*, ed. Francis Lieber, vol. 9 (Philadelphia: Carey and Lea, 1832), 150–58; R. Kent Newmyer, *Supreme Court Justice Joseph Story: Statesman of the Old Republic* (Chapel Hill: University of North Carolina Press, 1985), 211–15; Anne-Marie Taylor, *Young Charles Sumner and*

the Legacy of the American Enlightenment, 1811–1851 (Amherst: University of Massachusetts Press, 2001), 51–54.

21. Theodore Parker, *A Sermon of the Public Function of Woman* (Boston: Robert F. Wallcut, 1853), 12; *Proceedings of the National Women's Rights Convention Held at Cleveland, Ohio (Oct. 1853)* (Cleveland: Gray, Beardsley, Spear, 1854), 23, 32–34 (remarks of Mrs. Rose); Larry Ceplair, ed., *The Public Years of Sarah and Angelina Grimke: Selected Writings 1835–1839* (New York: Columbia University Press, 1989), 286.

22. Robin Blackburn has stated that "the modern term 'human rights' was rarely used by anti-slavery advocates." Kenneth Cmiel and Samuel Moyn, among others, have traced the term *human rights* to the 1940s. Moyn said Sumner used the term in 1870, but did not note that Sumner invoked it many times. See Robin Blackburn, *The American Crucible: Slavery, Emancipation, and Human Rights* (Brooklyn, N.Y.: Verso, 2013), 480; Kenneth Cmiel, "The Recent History of Human Rights," *The American Historical Review* 109, no. 1 (2004): 117–35; Samuel Moyn, *The Last Utopia: Human Rights in History* (Cambridge, Mass.: Belknap Press, 2010), 33. Some revisionist historians have noted the occasional use of *human rights* in the nineteenth-century abolitionist and women's rights convention movements; they have not noted that its use accelerated after Sumner started employing the term during the Civil War. See Kathryn Kish Sklar, "Human Rights Discourse in Women's Rights Conventions in the United States, 1848–1870," in *Revisiting the Origins of Human Rights*, ed. Pamela Slotte and Miia Halme-Tumisaari (Cambridge: Cambridge University Press, 2015), 163–88; Manisha Sinha, *The Slave's Cause: A History of Abolition* (New Haven: Yale University Press, 2016), 246–49; Ana Stevenson, "The 'Great Doctrine of Human Rights': Articulation and Authentication in the Nineteenth-Century U.S. Antislavery and Women's Rights Movements," *Humanity: An International Journal of Human Rights, Humanitarianism, and Development* 8, no. 3 (2017): 413–39. One historian has powerfully argued that the term *human rights* became popular—in part due to Sumner—amid the passage of the Civil Rights Act of 1875. But Sumner started regularly using the term one decade earlier. Amy Dru Stanley, "Slave Emancipation and the Revolutionizing of Human Rights," in *The World the Civil War Made*, ed. Gregory P. Downs and Kate Masur (Chapel Hill: University of North Carolina Press, 2015), 269–303. For use of the term *human rights* by John Quincy Adams and William Channing, see "Inaugural Address of John Quincy Adams (Friday, March 4, 1825)," Text, Avalon Project: Documents in Law, History and Diplomacy, n.d., https://avalon.law.yale.edu/19th_century/qadams.asp; William E. Channing, *Slavery* (Boston: James Munroe, 1835). By searching through the fifteen volumes of *WCS*, I counted nearly three hundred instances of Sumner using the term *human rights*.

23. While it is well known that antebellum lawyers often categorized rights into three or four types, there are no agreed-upon definitions in the literature of these types. For clarity, I have offered my own tentative definitions of civil, social, and political rights. For more on these categories, see, e.g., Mark Tushnet, "The Politics of Equality in Constitutional Law: The Equal Protection Clause, Dr. Du Bois, and Charles Hamilton Houston," *Journal of American History* 74, no. 3 (1987): 884–90; Mark Tushnet, "Civil Rights and Social Rights: The Future of the Reconstruction Amendments," *Loyola of Los Angeles Law Review* 25 (June 1, 1992): 1207–19; Masur, *An Example for All the Land*, 9–10; Eric Foner, *The Second Founding: How the Civil War and Reconstruction Remade the Constitution* (New York: W. W. Norton, 2019), 6–7; Pamela Brandwein, *Rethinking the Judicial Settlement of Reconstruction* (Cambridge: Cambridge University Press, 2011), 70–74; Christopher W. Schmidt, *Civil Rights in America* (Cambridge: Cambridge University Press, 2020), chaps. 1–2.

24. George E. Baker, ed., *The Works of William H. Seward*, vol. 4 (Boston: Houghton Mifflin, 1884), 302.

25. For references to "oligarchy of the skin," see, e.g., CS, *WCS*, 9:315, 322, 408, and 424. For close studies on the centrality of equality in Sumner's political thought, see Janis L. McDonald, "The Republican Revival: Revolutionary Republicanism's Relevance for Charles Sumner's Theory of Equality and Reconstruction," *Buffalo Law Review* 38, no. 2 (April 1, 1990): 465–514; Michael W. McConnell, "Originalism and the Desegregation Decisions," *Virginia Law Review* 81, no. 4 (1995): 947–1140; Elizabeth Anderson, *The Imperative of Integration* (Princeton: Princeton University Press, 2010); Hari Ramesh, "India, Racial Caste, and Abolition in Charles Sumner's Political Thought," *Modern Intellectual History* 19 (2022): 708–33; Joseph Fishkin and William E. Forbath, *The Anti-Oligarchy Constitution: Reconstructing the Economic Foundations of American Democracy* (Cambridge, Mass.: Harvard University Press, 2022), chap. 3.

26. Cong. Globe, 38th Cong., 1st. Sess., 1488 (1864) (remarks of Senators Sumner, Trumbull, and Howard).

27. Roberts v. City of Boston, 59 Mass. 198, 206 (1850). The pamphlet edition of Sumner's argument in

Roberts is CS, *Argument of Charles Sumner, Esq. Against the Constitutionality of Separate Colored Schools* (Boston: B. F. Roberts, 1849).

28. For more on Sumner's coinage of the term "equality before the law," see note 10 of chapter 7 and National Endowment for the Humanities, "Chronicling America," Text, Library of Congress, n.d., https://chroniclingamerica.loc.gov/.

29. "Eulogy on Charles Sumner by Prof. Langston," *New National Era*, April 30, 1874, 2; Phillips, "Sumner (Charles)," 621. Some years later, Professor Langston argued that Sumner read the expression "equality before the law" in its original French, then "pondered upon its meaning and finally engrafted it in the law of the United States" (John Mercer Langston, "Citizenship–Civil Rights, Supreme Court Decision," *Western Recorder* [*Lawrence, Kansas*], November 23, 1883, 2). During the movement to integrate schools in the 1950s, many legal scholars similarly argued that Sumner had effectively incorporated his principle of "equality before the law" into the Constitution. See, e.g., Edward Hirsch Levi et al., "Segregation and the Equal Protection Clause: Brief for Committee of Law Teachers Against Segregation in Legal Education," *Minnesota Law Review* 34 (1950): 293; John P. Frank and Robert F. Munro, "The Original Understanding of 'Equal Protection of the Laws,'" *Columbia Law Review* 50, no. 2 (1950): 137; Brief for Appellants in Nos. 1, 2, and 4 and for Respondents in No. 10 on Reargument, Brown v. Board of Education of Topeka, 347 U.S. 483, 1954, 70–75.

30. Cong. Globe, 38th Cong., 1st. Sess., 1482–83 (1864) (remarks of Senator Sumner); Cong. Globe, 38th Cong., 1st. Sess., 1488 (1864) (remarks of Senator Trumbull).

31. For more on the Northwest Ordinance, see Akhil Reed Amar, *America's Unwritten Constitution: The Precedents and Principles We Live By* (New York: Basic Books, 2012), 258–63.

32. For more on Sumner's involvement in the prison reform movement in the 1840s, see David Donald, *Charles Sumner and the Coming of the Civil War* (Naperville, Ill.: Sourcebooks, 2009), 101–8.

33. Cong. Globe, 37th Cong., 2nd Sess., 12 (1861) (remarks of Senator Sumner). For more on the Washington Black Codes and jail, see Henry Wilson, *History of the Rise and Fall of the Slave Power in America*, vol. 3 (Boston: Houghton Mifflin, 1877), 257–69; Kenneth J. Winkle, *Lincoln's Citadel: The Civil War in Washington, DC* (New York: W. W. Norton, 2014), chap. 13; Kate Masur, *Until Justice Be Done: America's First Civil Rights Movement, from the Revolution to Reconstruction* (New York: W. W. Norton, 2021), 292–302.

34. Cong. Globe, 39th Cong., 2nd Sess., 238 (1866) (remarks of Senator Sumner). In a letter to George William Curtis, Sumner said he gave up on trying to amend the draft because senators were impatient and wanted to vote and get dinner. "Yielding to this impatience, I forebore to press my substitutes. I regret now my forbearance," he told Curtis. Putting his hopes in the other chamber, Sumner said "there is a chance that the House will amend our proposition" (CS to George William Curtis, April 13, 1864, 78/082, PCS). For more on Sumner's views on how the "punishment for crime" clause relates to quasi-slavery institutions like peonage, see CS, WCS, 11:52–58.

35. For more on how Sumner and others understood the Enforcement Clause, see Michael W. McConnell, "Institutions and Interpretation: A Critique of City of Boerne v. Flores," *Harvard Law Review* 111 (1997): 153–95; Akhil Reed Amar, "Intratextualism," *Harvard Law Review* 126 (1999): 818–27; Steven A. Engel, "The McCulloch Theory of the Fourteenth Amendment: City of Boerne v. Flores and the Original Understanding of Section 5," *Yale Law Journal* 109 (1999): 115–54; Jack M. Balkin, "The Reconstruction Power," *New York University Law Review* 85 (February 24, 2010): 101–58; Akhil Reed Amar, "The Lawfulness of Section 5—and Thus of Section 5," *Harvard Law Review Forum* 126 (2013): 109–21; Christopher W. Schmidt, "Originalism and Congressional Power to Enforce the Fourteenth Amendment," *Washington and Lee Law Review* 75, no. 1 (2018).

36. For more on Sumner's relationship to Story and Marshall, see chapter 4. For the misconception that Sumner had drafted the Enforcement Clause of the Thirteenth Amendment, see David E. Kyvig, *Explicit and Authentic Acts: Amending the U.S. Constitution* (Lawrence: University Press of Kansas, 2008), 160. The first appearance of the Enforcement Clause in the legislative record is Cong. Globe, 38th Cong., 1st. Sess., 21 (1863) (remarks of Representative Wilson).

37. Pierce, MLCS, 4:191–92; Williamjames Hull Hoffer, *To Enlarge the Machinery of Government* (Baltimore: Johns Hopkins University Press, 2007), 128. For Sumner's national academy and civil reform bills, see CS, WCS, 8:452–57; CS, WCS, 9:51–54; Ralph Waldo Emerson to CS, December 19, 1864, 78/535, PCS. Sumner's secretary Francis Balch may have drafted the Civil Service Reform Bill for him. See "Francis V. Balch," *Boston Evening Transcript*, February 17, 1898. For more on

Sumner's role in assisting Rep. Thomas Jenckes on civil service reform, see Ari Hoogenboom, "Thomas A. Jenckes and Civil Service Reform," *The Mississippi Valley Historical Review* 47, no. 4 (1961): 636–58.

38. Cong. Globe, 38th Cong., 1st. Sess., 3334 (1864) (remarks of Senator Grimes); George R. Bentley, *A History of the Freedmen's Bureau* (New York: Octagon Books, 1974), 49; Cong. Globe, 38th Cong., 1st. Sess., 2933 (1864) (remarks of Senator Willey). For the claim that the Freedmen's Bureau Law constituted a major administrative delegation under constitutional law, see Daniel Backman, "'A Vast Labor Bureau': The Freedmen's Bureau and the Administration of Countervailing Black Labor Power," *Yale Journal on Regulation* 40 (2023): 863–65.

39. For more on the AFIC, see chapter 17.

40. Thomas Eliot to CS, March 7, 1864, 30/457, PCS. For Eliot's bill, see H.R. 51, 38th Cong. (as passed by the House, March 1, 1864), https://memory.loc.gov/cgi-bin/ampage?collId=llhb&fileName=038 /llhb038.db&recNum=188.

41. James McKaye to CS, January 20, 1864, 30/244, PCS. For more on the debates about where to place the Freedmen's Bureau, see Bentley, *A History of the Freedmen's Bureau*, 36–43; Hoffer, *To Enlarge the Machinery of Government*, chap. 3.

42. CS to John Bright, March 13, 1865, 79/121, PCS; Cong. Globe, 38th Cong., 1st. Sess., 2931 (1864) (remarks of Senator Sumner). For the argument that the Thirteenth Amendment made it constitutionally obligatory for Congress to provide "a minimal entitlement to property"—e.g., land plots—to freedpeople, see Akhil Reed Amar, "Forty Acres and a Mule: A Republican Theory of Minimal Entitlements," *Harvard Journal of Law and Public Policy* 13, no. 1 (1990): 37–43.

43. Eric Foner, *The Fiery Trial: Abraham Lincoln and American Slavery* (New York: W. W. Norton, 2010), 296.

44. Foner, *The Fiery Trial*, 292–96.

45. CS to John Andrew, August 24, 1864, 78/355, PCS; Donald, *Charles Sumner and the Rights of Man*, 187–88; David Herbert Donald, *Lincoln* (New York: Simon and Schuster, 1995), 725–26; CS to John Bright, September 27, 1864, 78/398, PCS; Stephen D. Engle, *In Pursuit of Justice: The Life of John Albion Andrew* (Amherst: University of Massachusetts Press, 2023), 282–86.

46. A close friend of Chase, Sumner often dropped by his home at breakfast to chat politics during the war. See Janet Chase Hoyt, "A Woman's Memories," *New York Tribune*, April 5, 1891.

47. Rufus Stebbins to CS, April 6, 1864, 30/604, PCS.

48. CS, "Congratulations on the Presidential Election" (Speech, Faneuil Hall, Boston, November 8, 1864), *WCS*, 9:134–36; CS to J. C. Welling, November 8, 1864, 78/465, PCS.

Chapter 19: I Was Always Honest with Mr. Lincoln

1. In the next few paragraphs about Rock's admission, I rely on: "From Washington," *Chicago Tribune*, February 2, 1865; "The World Moves," *Indiana Progress*, February 8, 1865, 2; "A Colored Lawyer Admitted to Practice in the United States Supreme Court," *Adams Sentinel*, February 14, 1865, 4; "John Rock and Tony Knapp," *Chicago Tribune*, February 19, 1865; "The Dred Scott Decision Buried in the Supreme Court—A Negro Lawyer Admitted by Chief Justice Chase," *Kansas Tribune* (Correspondence of the *New York Tribune*), February 23, 1865, 4. For more on Rock's admission to the Court and his remarkable life, see Clarence G. Contee, "The Supreme Court Bar's First Black Member," *Yearbook: Supreme Court Historical Society*, 1976, 82–85; Christopher Brooks, "Senator Charles Sumner and the Admission of John S. Rock to the Supreme Court Bar," *Journal of Supreme Court History* 48, no. 2 (2023): 139–47.

2. CS to Francis Lieber, October 12, 1864, *MLCS*, 4:207; CS to Salmon Chase, October 24, 1864, 78/447, PCS; CS, "No Bust for Author of Dred Scott Decision" (Speech, U.S. Senate, 1865), *WCS*, 9:270–310; Benjamin Perley Poore, *Perley's Reminiscences of Sixty Years in the National Metropolis*, vol. 2 (Philadelphia: Hubbard's Bros., 1886), 154–56; William H. Rehnquist, "The Supreme Court: 'The First Hundred Years Were the Hardest,'" *University of Miami Law Review* 42, no. 3 (1988): 484. On the day Taney died, Sumner wrote to Lincoln to say that "Providence has given us a victory in the death of Chief Justice Taney." Calling Taney's death "a victory for liberty and the Constitution," Sumner reiterated his request that Taney be replaced by Chase. CS to Abraham Lincoln, October 12, 1864, 78/424, PCS. See also CS to Salmon Chase, October 24, 1864, 78/447, PCS; CS to Abraham Lincoln, October 24, 1864, 78/449, PCS; CS to Abraham Lincoln, November 20, 1864, 78/476, PCS. In 1874, Congress commissioned Augustus Saint-Gaudens to make a bust of Taney, which was on display in the Old Supreme Court Chamber until 2023. The Supreme Court has separately owned, since 1854, a bust of Taney made by Horatio Stone. That bust was put on display in the Great Hall

of the modern Court around 1976 and is still there as of this book's publication date. See Matthew Hofstedt, Curator of the Supreme Court to Zaakir Tameez, March 18, 2024 (email on file with author).

3. John Rock to CS, December 17, 1864, 32/129, PCS; John Niven, ed., *The Salmon P. Chase Papers*, vol. 1 (Kent, Ohio: Kent State University Press, 1993), 593; Salmon Chase to CS, January 23, 1865, 32/362, PCS.

4. Cong. Globe, 38th Cong., 2nd Sess., 474 (1865) (remarks of Senator Sumner); Carl Schurz, "Eulogy Before City Authorities of Boston (Music Hall, April 29, 1874)," in *Charles Sumner: Memoir and Eulogies*, ed. William M. Cornell (Boston: James H. Earle, 1874), 142–43.

5. Pierce, *MLCS*, 4:290; CS, "No Names of Victories over Fellow-Citizens on Regimental Colors" (U.S. Senate, May 8, 1862), WCS, 6:499–500; CS, "Retaliation and Treatment of Prisoners of War" (U.S. Senate, January 24, 1865), WCS, 9:206–28; Cong. Globe, 38th Cong., 2nd Sess., 1126 (1865) (remarks of Senator Sumner).

6. Cong. Globe, 38th Cong., 2nd Sess., 963 (1865) (remarks of Senator Henderson); Cong. Globe, 38th Cong., 2nd Sess., 984–85 (1865) (remarks of Senators Hale and Lane); Cong. Globe, 38th Cong., 2nd Sess., 989 (1865) (remarks of Senator Sumner).

7. Cong. Globe, 38th Cong., 2nd Sess., 990 (1865); Henry Wilson, *History of the Rise and Fall of the Slave Power in America*, vol. 3 (Boston: Houghton Mifflin, 1877), 472–85. George Hoar also said, "It was a great thing for Massachusetts, a great thing for human liberty, and a great thing for Charles Sumner himself that he had Henry Wilson as a friend and ally, a disciple and a co-worker." George F. Hoar, *Autobiography of Seventy Years*, vol. 1 (New York: Charles Scribner's Sons, 1903), 217–18.

8. Herman Belz, *Reconstructing the Union: Theory and Policy During the Civil War* (Ithaca, N.Y.: Cornell University Press, 1969), 252, 256–57; CS to John Bright, January 1, 1865, 78/582, PCS; CS to Francis Lieber, December 18, 1864, 64/368, PCS; Eric Foner, *The Fiery Trial: Abraham Lincoln and American Slavery* (New York: W. W. Norton, 2010), 318–19; "Mr. Sumner and President Lincoln," *Minneapolis Daily Tribune*, January 13, 1871.

9. Cong. Globe, 38th Cong., 2nd Sess., 1007–10 (1865) (remarks of Senators Sumner and Trumbull). For a compilation of excerpts from Sumner's filibuster, see Pierce, *MLCS*, 4:223–27; CS, "No Reconstruction Without the Votes of the Blacks" (U.S. Senate, February 1865), WCS, 9:312–28.

10. Cong. Globe, 38th Cong., 2nd Sess., 1058 (1865) (remarks of Senators Conness and Sumner); Carl Sandburg, *Abraham Lincoln: The War Years*, vol. 4 (New York: Harcourt, Brace, 1939), 78; Jeremiah Chaplin and J. D. Chaplin, *Life of Charles Sumner* (Boston: D. Lothrop, 1874), 400.

11. Cong. Globe, 38th Cong., 2nd Sess., 1109, 1129 (1865) (remarks of Senator Sumner).

12. Cong. Globe, 38th Cong., 2nd Sess., 1109 (1865) (remarks of Senators Sumner and Wade).

13. Cong. Globe, 38th Cong., 2nd Sess., 1108, 1126 (1865) (remarks of Senator Sumner); Cong. Globe, 38th Cong., 2nd Sess., 1129 (1865) (remarks of Senators Sherman and Trumbull).

14. Michael Burlingame, *Abraham Lincoln: A Life*, vol. 2 (Baltimore: Johns Hopkins University Press, 2008), 775; Samuel Howe to CS, June 11, 1864, 78/234, PCS.

15. Sandburg, *Abraham Lincoln: The War Years*, 4:178; CS, WCS, 9:323–24, 327–28; Don E. Fehrenbacher and Virginia Fehrenbacher, eds., *Recollected Works of Abraham Lincoln* (Stanford: Stanford University Press, 1996), 486.

16. "Mr. Sumner and President Lincoln," *Minneapolis Daily Tribune*, January 13, 1871.

17. Abraham Lincoln to CS, March 3, 1865, 79/102, PCS; "The Inauguration Ball," *New York Herald*, March 8, 1865; "Mr. Sumner and President Lincoln," *Minneapolis Daily Tribune*, January 13, 1871.

18. "Re-Inauguration of President Lincoln," (London) *Times*, March 20, 1865, 25; Kate Masur, "Color Was a Bar to the Entrance: African American Activism and the Question of Social Equality in Lincoln's White House," *American Quarterly* 69, no. 1 (2017): 1–22; Pierce, *MLCS*, 4:232.

19. Pierce, *MLCS*, 4:233–36; CS, WCS, 9:379–80, 410; CS to Elizabeth Argyll, April 24, 1865, 79/260, PCS; Mary Lincoln to CS, April 3, 1865, 33/124, PCS; Marquis de Chambrun, "Personal Recollections of Mr. Lincoln," *Scribner's Magazine* 8 (1893): 34–35; Marquis de Chambrun, "Personal Recollections of Charles Sumner," *Scribner's Magazine* 8 (1893): 153–55; Jon Meacham, *And There Was Light: Abraham Lincoln and the American Struggle* (New York: Random House, 2022), 386; CS to Francis Bird, April 16, 1871, 84/240, PCS; Mary Lincoln to CS, July 4, 1865, 33/721, PCS.

20. Elizabeth Cady Stanton, Susan B. Anthony, and Matilda Joslyn Gage, eds., *History of Woman Suffrage: 1861–1876*, vol. 2 (New York: Fowler and Wells, 1882), 420–21.

21. Pierce, *MLCS*, 4:235–36; Marquis Adolphe de Chambrun, *Impressions of Lincoln and the Civil War: A Foreigner's Account*, trans. General Aldebert de Chambrun (New York: Random House, 1952), 108; CS to Salmon Chase, April 10, 1865, 79/217, PCS.

22. Pierce, *MLCS*, 4:232; David S. Reynolds, *Abe: Abraham Lincoln in His Times* (New York: Penguin, 2021), 896; Anthony S. Pitch, *"They Have Killed Papa Dead!": The Road to Ford's Theatre, Abraham Lincoln's Murder and the Rage for Vengeance* (Hanover, N.H.: Steerforth Press, 2018), chaps. 6–8; CS to Elizabeth Argyll, April 24, 1865, 79/260, PCS. There are more than a dozen accounts of Sumner's activity on the night of April 14 and the morning after. Given the faultiness of human memory and the emotional chaos of that night, no account is the same. In the next few paragraphs, I have reconstructed my best estimation of what exactly transpired.

23. Chaplin and Chaplin, *Life of Charles Sumner*, 413–17; George Rothwell Brown, ed., *Reminiscences of Senator William M. Stewart of Nevada* (New York: The Naele Publishing Company, 1908), 191–92; Gideon Welles, *The Diary of Gideon Welles*, vol. 2 (Boston: Houghton Mifflin, 1911), 288; Moorfield Storey, "Dickens, Stanton, Sumner, and Storey," *The Atlantic* (April 1930): 463–65. Decades later, Senator Stewart recalled that "a colored man employed by Senator Conness" told them that Lincoln and Seward had been killed. But a Treasury Department clerk testified very shortly afterward that he walked into Conness's home and informed them. The clerk's story is more credible than Stewart's recollection. See Edward Steers and William C. Edwards, eds., *The Lincoln Assassination: The Evidence* (Chicago: University of Illinois Press, 2010), 361–63. There are conflicting accounts about who told Robert Todd Lincoln first about his father's assassination. Robert's biographer has suggested that Sumner was most likely the first to inform White House staff, who thereafter told Robert, although others may have come to the White House around the same time to spread the news. See Jason Emerson, *Giant in the Shadows: The Life of Robert T. Lincoln* (Carbondale: Southern Illinois University Press, 2012), 101–3.

24. "Terrible News," *Chicago Tribune*, April 15, 1865; "Details of the Calamity," *New York Daily Herald*, April 16, 1865; "The Scene at the President's Bedside," *Chicago Tribune*, April 17, 1865; CS to Elizabeth Argyll, April 24, 1865; CS to Francis Lieber, April 17, 1865, 64/410, PCS; John G. Nicolay and John Hay, *Abraham Lincoln: A History*, vol. 10 (New York: The Century Company, 1890), 300; Storey, "Dickens, Stanton, Sumner, and Storey."

25. CS to John Bright, May 1, 1865, *MLCS*, 4:241; Storey, "Dickens, Stanton, Sumner, and Storey"; CS to Rudolph Schleiden, June 27, 1865, 79/391, PCS; "Reminiscences of Mr. Sumner," *Springfield Daily Republican*, March 17, 1874, 5; Chaplin and Chaplin, *Life of Charles Sumner*, 413–17; Johnson, "Recollections of Charles Sumner," 1875.

26. James D. Richardson, ed., "Action of Senators and Representatives in Washington," in *A Compilation of the Messages and Papers of the Presidents*, vol. 5 (Washington, D.C.: Bureau of National Literature, n.d.), 3490–91.

27. CS to John Bright, April 18, 1865, 79/248, PCS; CS to Elizabeth Argyll, April 24, 1865. For Sumner's frustration at Johnson's drunkenness at the inauguration, see "The National Disgrace," *Vermont Union*, March 17, 1865; "The Moral Exigency," *Springfield Weekly Republican*, March 18, 1865; "To Be Impeached," *Grand Haven News* (Michigan), March 22, 1865; Henry Wilson, *History of the Rise and Fall of the Slave Power in America*, vol. 3 (Boston: Houghton Mifflin, 1877), 578. Strongly believing in the dignity of public office, Sumner had even wanted to impeach California senator James McDougall for drunkenness in the Senate. See Brown, *Reminiscences of Senator William M. Stewart of Nevada*, 207.

28. Pierce, *MLCS*, 4:238–39; Mary Lincoln to CS, May 9, 1865, 33/397, PCS; Elizabeth Keckley, *Behind the Scenes: Thirty Years a Slave and Four Years in the White House* (New York: G. W. Carleton, 1868), 308.

29. CS to Francis Bird, April 25, 1865, 79/266, PCS; CS to John Bright, March 13, 1865, 79/121, PCS; Pierce, *MLCS*, 4:244; CS to George Stearns, May 4, 1865, 79/297, PCS; Carl Schurz to CS, May 9, 1865, 79/316, PCS.

30. CS, *WCS*, 9:370–71; CS to John Bright, May 1, 1865. For Sumner's eulogy of Lincoln, see CS, "Promises of the Declaration of Independence and Abraham Lincoln" (Speech, Boston Music Hall, June 1, 1865), *WCS*, 9:367–428.

31. CS to John Bright, May 1, 1865; CS to Francis Lieber, August 2, 1865, 64/424, PCS; CS to Wendell Phillips, May 1, 1865, 79/282, PCS; CS to Francis Lieber, May 2, 1865, 64/412, PCS; CS to Wendell Phillips, May 11, 1865, 79/324, PCS; CS, *WCS*, 11:22.

Chapter 20: A Magna Carta of Democracy in America

1. CS to Henry Dawes, July 20, 1865, 69/455, PCS; CS to John Bright, June 5, 1865, 79/345, PCS; CS, *WCS*, 11:22.

2. Eric Foner, *Reconstruction: America's Unfinished Revolution (1863–1877)* (New York: Harper Perennial Classics, 1988), 181–83; John Hope Franklin, *Reconstruction After the Civil War: Second Edition*

(Chicago: University of Chicago Press, 1994), 42; Hans Louis Trefousse, *Impeachment of a President: Andrew Johnson, the Blacks, and Reconstruction* (New York: Fordham University Press, 1999), 5; Annette Gordon-Reed, *Andrew Johnson* (New York: Times Books, 2011), 114–16.

3. Mark Wahlgren Summers, *The Ordeal of the Reunion: A New History of Reconstruction* (Chapel Hill: University of North Carolina Press, 2014), 69; "From Mobile; Proclamation by the Governor of Alabama," *New York Times*, July 26, 1865; Foner, *Reconstruction*, 190–92, 199–201; David W. Blight, *Race and Reunion: The Civil War in American Memory* (Cambridge, Mass.: Harvard University Press, 2001), 44–46.

4. For more on the feud between Sumner and Andrew on Reconstruction, see generally Stephen D. Engle, *In Pursuit of Justice: The Life of John Albion Andrew* (Amherst: University of Massachusetts Press, 2023), chap. 22.

5. CS to John Bright, September 26, 1865, 79/591, PCS; Thaddeus Stevens to CS, October 7, 1865, 34/384, PCS; CS, *WCS*, 9:432. For more on Sumner's campaign for Black suffrage in 1865, see Michael Les Benedict, *A Compromise of Principle: Congressional Republicans and Reconstruction, 1863–1869* (New York: W. W. Norton, 1974), 110–13.

6. These letters were reprinted in CS, "Enfranchisement and Protection of Freedmen" (Speech, U.S. Senate, December 20, 1865), *WCS*, 10:55–97.

7. For Sumner's recollection of the meeting, see CS to Francis Lieber, December 3, 1865, 64/443, PCS; CS to George Bancroft, December 2, 1865, 80/057, PCS; CS to Elizabeth Argyll, December 26, 1865, 80/082, PCS; CS to Peleg Chandler, January 3, 1866, 80/114, PCS. For Johnson's ally Lewis Campbell's recollection, see "From Lewis D. Campbell to Andrew Johnson, 1 May 1866," Papers of Andrew Johnson: Digital Edition, n.d., http://rotunda.upress.virginia.edu/founders/AWJN .html; "From Lewis D. Campbell to Andrew Johnson, 9 March 1868," Papers of Andrew Johnson: Digital Edition, n.d., http://rotunda.upress.virginia.edu/founders/AWJN.html. One day before the encounter, George Bancroft told Johnson to expect a friendly visit from Sumner. See "From George Bancroft to Andrew Johnson, 1 December, 1865," Papers of Andrew Johnson: Digital Edition, n.d., http://rotunda.upress.virginia.edu/founders/AWJN.html.

8. CS, *WCS*, 10:47–54; Carl Schurz, *Speeches, Correspondence and Political Papers of Carl Schurz*, ed. Frederic Bancroft, vol. 1 (New York: G. P. Putnam's Sons, 1913), 265–68, 274–78, 374–75; Hans L. Trefousse, *Carl Schurz: A Biography* (Knoxville: University of Tennessee Press, 1982), 153–54, 159–60; Carl Schurz, *Report on the Condition of the South*, S. Exec. Doc. No. 2 (1865).

9. CS, *WCS*, 10:56. For reprinted versions of the relevant bills and resolutions, see CS, "Impartial Jurors for Colored Persons" (Speech, U.S. Senate, December 4, 1865), *WCS*, 10:10–11; CS, "Equal Rights of Colored Persons to Be Protected by the National Courts" (Speech, U.S. Senate, December 4, 1865), *WCS*, 10:16–18; CS, "Five Conditions of Reconstruction" (Speech, U.S. Senate, December 4, 1865), *WCS*, 10:33–34; CS, "Rights of Loyal Citizens, and a Republican Government" (Speech, U.S. Senate, December 4, 1865), *WCS*, 10:35–37; CS, "Protection of the National Debt, and Rejection of Every Rebel Debt" (Speech, U.S. Senate, January 5, 1866), *WCS*, 10:99–100; CS, "Majority of Plurality in the Election of Senators" (Speech, U.S. Senate, March 23, 1866), *WCS*, 10:377–90.

10. Benedict, *A Compromise of Principle*, 38–39; Garrett Epps, *Democracy Reborn* (New York: Henry Holt, 2006), 90–92; Francis Fessenden, *Life and Public Services of William Pitt Fessenden*, vol. 2 (Boston: Houghton Mifflin, 1907), 20. Congressman James Blaine once described Sumner and Fessenden as "the two eminent New-England statemen who were so long rivals in the Senate of the United States" (James Gillespie Blaine, *Twenty Years of Congress: From Lincoln to Garfield*, vol. 2 [Norwich, Conn.: Henry Bill Publishing Company, 1886], 200).

11. Francis Lieber to CS, December 11, 1864, 78/523, PCS; CS, "Apportionment of Representatives According to Voters" (Speech, U.S. Senate, February 6, 1865), *WCS*, 10:19–20; CS, "Representation According to Voters" (Speech, U.S. Senate, December 4, 1865), *WCS*, 9:236; Benedict, *A Compromise of Principle*, 150–52; Akhil Reed Amar, *America's Constitution: A Biography* (New York: Random House, 2005), 392–95; Epps, *Democracy Reborn*, 100–113; Eric Foner, *The Second Founding: How the Civil War and Reconstruction Remade the Constitution* (New York: W. W. Norton, 2019), 57–62.

12. Cong. Globe, 39th Cong., 1st Sess., 673 (1866) (remarks of Senator Sumner); Fessenden, *Life and Public Services of William Pitt Fessenden*, 2:25, 37. Some historians have speculated that Sumner vocally opposed the Apportionment Amendment to deflect criticism from Governor John Andrew, who was potentially planning to challenge Sumner's Senate seat in the upcoming 1866 election. But I defer to Andrew's most recent biographer, who concludes that the potential 1866 Senate challenge was a rumor that Andrew never seriously entertained. See David Donald, *Charles*

Sumner and the Rights of Man (New York: Knopf, 1970), 242–46; Epps, *Democracy Reborn*, 115–16; Engle, *In Pursuit of Justice*, 358–60.

13. CS, *WCS*, 10:214; Cong. Globe, 39th Cong., 1st. Sess., 902 (1865) (remarks of Senator Sumner).

14. Cong. Globe, 39th Cong., 1st. Sess., 685 (1866) (remarks of Senator Sumner).

15. CS to John Bright, May 27, 1867, 81/086, PCS. For Sumner's doubts about voting as a birthright when he was younger, see Anne-Marie Taylor, *Young Charles Sumner and the Legacy of the American Enlightenment, 1811–1851* (Amherst: University of Massachusetts Press, 2001), 260–61.

16. David W. Blight, *Frederick Douglass: Prophet of Freedom* (New York: Simon and Schuster, 2018), 477; Philip S. Foner and George E. Walker, eds., *Proceedings of the Black National and State Conventions, 1865–1900* (Philadelphia: Temple University Press, 1986), 7, 64. For Sumner's speech calling for a national law to protect voting rights, wherein he read letters from countless Black southerners relating the failure of Johnson's white-only provisional governments to protect them, see CS, "Enfranchisement and Protection of Freedmen," (Speech, U.S. Senate, December 20, 1865), *WCS*, 10:55–97.

17. CS to John Bright, June 5, 1865, 79/345, PCS; Gordon-Reed, *Andrew Johnson*, 101–2.

18. CS to Edward Pierce, June 25, 1868, 64/556, PCS; CS, *WCS*, 11:411. For more on the Republican Guarantee Clause, see Akhil Reed Amar, "The Central Meaning of Republican Government: Popular Sovereignty, Majority Rule, and the Denominator Problem," *University of Colorado Law Review* 65 (1994): 749–86; Akhil Reed Amar, Lindsey Ohlsson Worth, and Joshua Alexander Geltzer, "Reconstructing the Republic: The Great Transition of the 1860s," in *Transitions: Legal Change, Legal Meanings*, ed. Austin Sarat (Birmingham: University of Alabama Press, 2012); Jason Mazzone, "The Incorporation of the Republican Guarantee Clause," *Notre Dame Law Review* 97 (2022): 1435–76; Carolyn Shapiro, "Democracy, Federalism, and the Guarantee Clause," *Arizona Law Review* 62 (2020).

19. CS to Francis Lieber, October 12, 1865, 64/437, PCS; CS to Francis Lieber, December 3, 1865, 64/443, PCS; W. E. Burghardt Du Bois, *Black Reconstruction* (New York: Harcourt, Brace, 1935), 192–97.

20. All quotes to Sumner's speech were obtained from Cong. Globe, 39th Cong., 1st Sess., 673–87 (1866) (remarks of Senator Sumner). For a more accessible published version, see CS, "The Equal Rights of All" (Speech, U.S. Senate, February 5, 1866), 10:115–269, *WCS*. The capacity of the Senate galleries was more than 1,500 people. See "The Senate Chamber," *Every Saturday*, February 11, 1871.

21. Excerpts from these newspapers are compiled in CS, *WCS*, 10:247–54.

22. Marian Gouverneur, *As I Remember: Recollections of American Society During the Nineteenth Century* (New York: D. Appleton, 1911), 241; George F. Hoar, *Autobiography of Seventy Years*, vol. 2 (New York: Charles Scribner's Sons, 1903), 76; Blaine, *Twenty Years of Congress*, 2:200; Salmon Chase to CS, March 9, 1866, 35/635, PCS; Thaddeus Stevens to CS, March 4, 1866, 35/586, PCS; Cong. Globe, 39th Cong., 1st. Sess., 2459 (1866) (remarks of Representative Stevens); Robert J. Cook, *Civil War Senator: William Pitt Fessenden and the Fight to Save the American Republic* (Baton Rouge: Louisiana State University Press, 2011), 201.

23. Edward McPherson, *Hand Book of Politics for 1868* (Washington City: Philp and Solomons, 1868), 52–56; *Independent Democrat* (Concord, N.H.), January 24, 1867, 2; "The Ill Manners of the President," *Burlington Times*, January 24, 1867.

24. CS to Peleg Chandler, August 17, 1867, 81/174, PCS; CS to Elizabeth Argyll, April 3, 1866, 80/229, PCS.

25. Hans L. Trefousse, *Andrew Johnson: A Biography* (New York: W. W. Norton, 1989), 245; Christopher W. Schmidt, *Civil Rights in America* (Cambridge: Cambridge University Press, 2020), 17.

26. Foner, *The Second Founding*, 63–68.

27. CS, *WCS*, 10:272; Cong. Globe, 39th Cong., 1st. Sess., 707, 765 (1866) (remarks of Senator Sumner).

28. Jeffrey A. Jenkins and Justin Peck, *Congress and the First Civil Rights Era, 1861–1918* (Chicago: University of Chicago Press, 2021), 88–95.

29. Mary Lincoln to CS, April 3, 1866, 80/233, PCS; Andrew Johnson, "Veto Message (Freedmen's Bureau Bill, Feb. 19, 1866)," American Presidency Project, n.d., https://www.presidency.ucsb.edu/documents/veto-message-437; Andrew Johnson, "Veto Message (Civil Rights Bill, Mar. 27, 1866)," n.d., https://www.presidency.ucsb.edu/documents/veto-message-438.

30. Andrew Johnson, "Remarks at a Meeting in Honor of Washington's Birthday (Feb. 22, 1866)," American Presidency Project, n.d., https://www.presidency.ucsb.edu/documents/remarks-meeting-honor-washingtons-birthday; Trefousse, *Andrew Johnson*, 244.

31. For more on how Republican centrists took a long time to understand that Andrew Johnson was guided by a primal white supremacist ideology, see Gordon-Reed, *Andrew Johnson*, 137–40.

32. CS, "Majority of Plurality in the Election of Senators"; Blaine, *Twenty Years of Congress*, 2:156–60.

33. Cook, *Civil War Senator*, 204; Fessenden, *Life and Public Services of William Pitt Fessenden*, 2:341–42.

34. For more on Sumner's influence on Section 1 of the Fourteenth Amendment, see Edward Hirsch Levi et al., "Segregation and the Equal Protection Clause: Brief for Committee of Law Teachers Against Segregation in Legal Education," *Minnesota Law Review* 34 (1950): 293; John P. Frank and Robert F. Munro, "The Original Understanding of 'Equal Protection of the Laws,'" *Columbia Law Review* 50, no. 2 (1950): 137; Brief for Appellants in Nos. 1, 2, and 4 and for Respondents in No. 10 on Reargument, Brown v. Board of Education of Topeka, 70–75.

35. Robert Dale Owen, "Political Results from the Varioloid," *The Atlantic Monthly*, June 1875, 665.

36. Susan B. Anthony to CS, May 16, 1866, 36/313, PCS.

37. *Cong. Globe*, 39th Cong., 1st. Sess., 2763–64 (1866) (remarks of Senators Sumner and Fessenden).

38. James Freeman Clarke, *Memorial and Biographical Sketches* (Boston: Houghton, Osgood, 1878), 97–98.

39. Marquis Adolphe de Chambrun, *Impressions of Lincoln and the Civil War: A Foreigner's Account*, trans. General Aldebert de Chambrun (New York: Random House, 1952), 27; CS and Theodore Tilton, April 12, 1866, 80/255, PCS; Samuel Howe to CS, February 3, 1863, 76/382, PCS.

40. Pierce, *MLCS*, 4:296; Frederick Douglass to CS, October 19, 1866, 37/082, PCS; Samuel Longfellow, ed., *Life of Henry Wadsworth Longfellow: With Extracts from His Journals and Correspondence*, vol. 3 (Boston: Houghton Mifflin, 1891), 76, 78.

41. CS to Francis Bird, August 17, 1866, 80/414, PCS.

42. David Donald, *Charles Sumner and the Coming of the Civil War* (Naperville, Ill.: Sourcebooks, 2009), 33–34; CS to George Boutwell, June 15, 1866, 80/357, PCS; Pierce, *MLCS*, 3:275; CS, *WCS*, 6:140–43; An Act to Provide for the Revision and Consolidation of the Statute Laws of the United States, 14 Stat. 74 (June 27, 1866). For the history of codification, see Margaret Wood, "The Revised Statutes of the United States: Predecessor to the U.S. Code," Library of Congress, July 2, 2015, https://blogs.loc.gov/law/2015/07/the-revised-statutes-of-the-united-states-predecessor-to-the-u-s-code; Laura Deal, "From Slip Law to United States Code: A Guide to Federal Statutes for Congressional Offices," Congressional Research Service, 2023, https://sgp.fas.org/crs/misc/R45190.pdf. For Sumner's relationship with Caleb Cushing, see Arnold Burges Johnson, "Charles Sumner—III, Recollections," *The Cosmopolitan: A Monthly Illustrated Magazine*, October 1887, 147.

43. Horatio Woodman to CS, March 18, 1866, 80/212, PCS; Henry W. Foote, *In Memory of Charles Sumner: Sermon Preached at King's Chapel* (Boston: Alfred Mudge and Sons, 1874), 35; "More Reminiscences of Charles Sumner," *Bellows Falls Times* (Vermont), April 24, 1874; CS to Elizabeth Argyll, June 25, 1866, 80/367, PCS; Pierce, *MLCS*, 4:301–2; Elias Nason, *The Life and Times of Charles Sumner* (Boston: B. B. Russell, 1874), 311; CS, *WCS*, 10:259. Sumner's utterance to Longfellow about losing his father, mother, brother, and sister at Hancock Street was recorded by Richard Henry Dana in his diary. Dana was slightly mistaken; Sumner had three sisters, not one. He had lost two of those sisters. Charles Francis Adams, *Richard Henry Dana: A Biography*, vol. 2 (Boston: Houghton Mifflin, 1890), 339. His only remaining sister, Julia, was living in California at the time and had become a bedridden invalid. See Johnson, "Charles Sumner—III, Recollections," 153.

Chapter 21: Reading, Writing, and Snoring

1. William Fessenden also used Hooper's house as an office when he became treasury secretary. See Robert J. Cook, *Civil War Senator: William Pitt Fessenden and the Fight to Save the American Republic* (Baton Rouge: Louisiana State University Press, 2011), 148. He observed that Sumner seemed interested in Alice Hooper. See Francis Fessenden, *Life and Public Services of William Pitt Fessenden*, vol. 2 (Boston: Houghton Mifflin, 1907), 341. For reports of Hooper's generosity to Chase, Johnson, McClellan, and others, see, e.g., Henry Greenleaf Parsons, *The Life of John A. Andrew*, vol. 2 (Boston: Houghton Mifflin, 1904), 188; John Niven, ed., *The Salmon P. Chase Papers*, vol. 3 (Kent, Ohio: Kent State University Press, 1996), 309–10; Benjamin Perley Poore, *Perley's Reminiscences of Sixty Years in the National Metropolis*, vol. 2 (Philadelphia: Hubbard's Bros., 1886), 181.

2. Fessenden, *Life and Public Services of William Pitt Fessenden*, 2:341; Richard Yates and Catharine Yates Pickering, *Richard Yates: Civil War Governor* (Danville, Ill.: The Interstate Printers and Publishers, 1966), 251; Leon Edel, ed., *Henry James Letters: 1875–1883*, vol. 2 (Cambridge, Mass.: Harvard University Press, 1974), 7.

3. Fessenden, *Life and Public Services of William Pitt Fessenden*, 2:341; F. B. Sanborn, *Recollections of Seventy Years*, vol. 2 (Detroit: Gale Research Company, 1967), 493; John Lothrop Motley and Susan

Margaret Stackpole Motley St. John Mildmay, *John Lothrop Motley and His Family: Further Letters and Records* (New York: John Lane, 1910), 222–23; Anna Waterston to CS, September 11, 1866, 36/700, PCS; Mary Lincoln to CS, October 1, 1866, 37/015, PCS.

4. Pierce, *MLCS*, 4:302; Elias Nason, *The Life and Times of Charles Sumner* (Boston: B. B. Russell, 1874), 312; CS to Henry Longfellow, June 24, 1866, 80/363, PCS; Marquis Adolphe de Chambrun, *Impressions of Lincoln and the Civil War: A Foreigner's Account*, trans. General Aldebert de Chambrun (New York: Random House, 1952), 28. For more on Sumner's inheritance, see David Donald, *Charles Sumner and the Rights of Man* (New York: Knopf, 1970), 272. For Sumner's friendly relationships with many wives and daughters of Washington, see previous chapters and Arnold Burges Johnson, "Charles Sumner—III, Recollections," *The Cosmopolitan: A Monthly Illustrated Magazine*, October 1887, 150–51.

5. CS to Edmund Morgan, September 3, 1866, 80/437, PCS; CS to Elizabeth Argyll, September 4, 1866, 80/441, PCS; CS to John Palfrey, September 4, 1866, 80/445, PCS; Tyler Dennett, ed., *Lincoln and the Civil War in the Diaries and Letters of John Hay* (New York: Dodd, Mead, 1939), 249.

6. Laura E. Richards and Maud Howe Elliott, *Julia Ward Howe, 1819–1910*, vol. 1 (Boston: Houghton Mifflin, 1915), 103.

7. Julia Ward Howe to CS, September 2, 1866, 36/655, PCS.

8. Allan Nevins, *Hamilton Fish* (New York: Dodd, Mead, 1936), 47; David Donald, *Charles Sumner and the Coming of the Civil War* (Naperville, Ill.: Sourcebooks, 2009), 73–75; CS to Sam Ward, January 19, 1842, 66/223, PCS.

9. Dennett, *Lincoln and the Civil War in the Diaries and Letters of John Hay*, 250; CS to Henry Longfellow, May 21, 1864, 78/192, PCS.

10. Marquis de Chambrun, *Impressions of Lincoln and the Civil War*, 28; David Donald, *Charles Sumner and the Rights of Man* (New York: Knopf, 1970), 272.

11. CS to Francis Lieber, September 22, 1866, 64/464, PCS; CS to Anna Cabot Lodge, November 1, 1866, 80/499, PCS.

12. Alice S. Hooper to CS, March 4, 1868, 41/243, PCS; "Border Gossip," *Daily Albany Argus*, October 16, 1866, 2; CS to George Bancroft, September 19, 1866, 80/453, PCS; Donald, *Charles Sumner and the Rights of Man*, 274.

13. CS to Lot Morrill, October 17, 1866, 80/486, PCS; CS to John Whittier, October 17, 1866, 80/487, PCS; Donald, *Charles Sumner and the Rights of Man*, 275; CS to Anna Cabot Lodge, November 1, 1866. For more on Sumner and Whittier's relationship, see J. Welfred Holmes, "Whittier and Sumner: A Political Friendship," *New England Quarterly* 30, no. 1 (1957): 58–72.

14. CS to Anna Cabot Lodge, January 2, 1867, 80/593, PCS; Pierce, *MLCS*, 4:304; Anna Lauren Dawes, *Charles Sumner* (New York: Dodd, Mead, 1892), 262–63; Frank Preston Stearns, *Cambridge Sketches* (Philadelphia: J. B. Lippincott, 1905), 212; "Social Life in Washington," *National Republican*, January 7, 1867, 2.

15. Dennett, *Lincoln and the Civil War in the Diaries and Letters of John Hay*, 266; Stearns, *Cambridge Sketches*, 212; *Harper's Monthly Magazine: Dec 1914 to May 1915*, vol. 80 (New York: Harper and Bros., 1914), 332; Donald, *Charles Sumner and the Rights of Man*, 275–76; James Mitchell Ashley to CS, January 13, 1867, 37/487, PCS.

16. CS, "The One Man Power vs. Congress" (Speech, Music Hall, Boston, December 20, 1865), *WCS*, 11:1.

17. Eric Foner, *Reconstruction: America's Unfinished Revolution (1863–1877)* (New York: Harper Perennial Classics, 1988), 267–68.

18. CS to Francis Bird, January 10, 1867, 080/601, PCS. For more on the Black organizing that led to the suffrage in Washington, see Kate Masur, *An Example for All the Land: Emancipation and the Struggle over Equality in Washington, D.C.* (Chapel Hill: University of North Carolina Press, 2010), chap. 4.

19. CS to William W. Story, December 16, 1866, 80/542, PCS; CS to Richard Cobden, March 27, 1865, 79/163, PCS; Peter Irons, *White Men's Law: The Roots of Systemic Racism* (Oxford: Oxford University Press, 2021), 80; Cong. Globe, 41st Cong., 2nd Sess., 1181 (1870) (remarks of Senator Sumner); W. E. Burghardt Du Bois, *Black Reconstruction* (New York: Harcourt, Brace, 1935), 197. For more on the Senate caucus that negotiated what became the First Reconstruction Act with its universal suffrage requirement, see Cong. Globe, 40th Cong., 1st. Sess., 496 (1867) (remarks of Senator Sumner); CS, *WCS*, 11:104–5; CS, *WCS*, 13:305–6, 329–30; Pierce, *MLCS*, 4:312–18; CS to John Bright, May 27, 1867, 81/086, PCS; Du Bois, *Black Reconstruction*, 332; Jeffrey A. Jenkins and Justin Peck, *Congress and the First Civil Rights Era, 1861–1918* (Chicago: University of Chicago Press, 2021), 109–19.

20. CS to Anna Cabot Lodge, July 19, 1868, 82/113, PCS; Alice S. Hooper to CS, March 4, 1868, 41/243, PCS. For the quote about Sumner snoring, see Marquis de Chambrun's comments in an interview

about Sumner's marriage in Edward Lillie Pierce, "Notes on the Separation of Charles Sumner and His Wife" (n.d.), Documents Relating to Charles Sumner, Houghton Library, Harvard University.

21. "The Sumner Scandal," *Chicago Tribune*, November 27, 1867; *Washington Star*, October 2, 1867; Norman Rich, *Friedrich Von Holstein: Politics and Diplomacy in the Era of Bismarck and Wilhelm II*, vol. 1 (Cambridge: Cambridge University Press, 1965), 292.

22. William Eleazar Barton, *The Women Lincoln Loved* (Indianapolis: Bobbs-Merrill, 1927), 357–58.

23. "Kate Chase in 1893," *Deseret Weekly* 47 (1893): 562–653; Donald, *Charles Sumner and the Rights of Man*, 292; CS to Anna Cabot Lodge, July 14, 1868, 82/109, PCS.

24. John Bigelow, *Retrospections of an Active Life*, vol. 4 (New York: Doubleday, Page, 1913), 116, 120.

25. CS to John Bright, March 13, 1865, 79/121, PCS; CS, "Further Guaranties in Reconstruction: Loyalty, Education, and a Homestead for Freedmen" (Speech, U.S. Senate, March 7, 1867), *WCS*, 11:124–36.

26. CS, "Reconstruction Again: The Ballot and Public Schools Open to All" (Speech, U.S. Senate, March 15, 1867), *WCS*, 11:141–63; Robert F. Horowitz, *The Great Impeacher: A Political Biography of James M. Ashley* (New York: Brooklyn College Press, 1979), 146; CS, *Argument of Charles Sumner, Esq. Against the Constitutionality of Separate Colored Schools* (Boston: B. F. Roberts, 1849). For more on Sumner's argument in *Roberts*, see chapter 7.

27. Donald, *Charles Sumner and the Coming of the Civil War*, 144; Cong. Globe, 41st Cong., 2nd Sess., 1183 (1870) (remarks of Sen. Stewart).

28. Johnson, "Charles Sumner—III, Recollections." In describing the behavior of the cuckoo bird, I have relied solely on ornithological reports that would have been available to Sumner. Those reports are generally consistent with the knowledge about cuckoo birds today. See Aristotle, *Aristotle's History of Animals: In Ten Books*, trans. Richard Cresswell (London: Henry G. Bohn, 1862), 146–47; James Rennie, *Bird-Architecture* (London: Charles Knight, 1844), 281–92; Wm. H. Slaney, "Do Cuckoos Take the Eggs of Other Birds as Food?," in *The Zoologist: A Popular Miscellany of Natural History*, 1856, 5321–24.

29. Cong. Globe, 40th Cong., 1st. Sess., 167 (1867) (remarks of Senator Sumner).

Chapter 22: The Imperialism of the Declaration of Independence

1. CS, *WCS*, 11:183–84; Frederick W. Seward, *Reminiscences of a War-Time Statesman and Diplomat* (New York: G. P. Putnam's Sons, 1916), 360–65; CS to Samuel Howe, March 16, 1870, 64/653, PCS.

2. Walter Stahr, *Seward: Lincoln's Indispensable Man* (New York: Simon and Schuster, 2012), 487–88; Horace Greeley, "The Russian Treaty," *New York Tribune*, April 8, 1867.

3. Benjamin Perley Poore, *Perley's Reminiscences of Sixty Years in the National Metropolis*, vol. 2 (Philadelphia: Hubbard's Bros., 1886), 242; Johnson, "Recollections of Charles Sumner," 1875, 226–27; John Bigelow, *Retrospections of an Active Life*, vol. 4 (New York: Doubleday, Page, 1913), 77; Charles Sumner, *The Cession of Russian America to the United States* (Washington, D.C.: Congressional Globe Office, 1867), 48; Lee A. Farrow, *Seward's Folly: A New Look at the Alaska Purchase* (Fairbanks: University of Alaska Press, 2016), 67–68; "Charles Sumner and the Purchase of Alaska," U.S. Senate Historical Office, n.d., https://www.senate.gov/about/powers-procedures/treaties/sumners-alaskan-project.htm.

4. CS, "Massacre of the Cheyenne Indians" (Speech, U.S. Senate, January 13, 1865), *WCS*, 9:198–99; CS, "Prohibition of Peonage" (Speech, U.S. Senate, January 3, 1867), *WCS*, 11:52–53. See also Adam J. Dahl, "Empire of the People: The Ideology of Democratic Empire in the Antebellum United States" (Ph.D. diss., University of Minnesota, 2014), 241–42.

5. William M. Cornell, ed., *Charles Sumner: Memoir and Eulogies* (Boston: James H. Earle, 1874), 281.

6. CS to Samuel Howe, February 17, 1868, 64/545, PCS.

7. Norman Rich, *Friedrich Von Holstein: Politics and Diplomacy in the Era of Bismarck and Wilhelm II*, vol. 1 (Cambridge: Cambridge University Press, 1965), 34–37; CS to Horatio Woodman, December 17, 1867, 81/306, PCS.

8. CS to Anna Cabot Lodge, July 14, 1868, 82/109, PCS; CS to Edward Pierce, August 8, 1868, 64/574, PCS; CS to Henry Longfellow, March 26, 1868, 81/510, PCS.

9. David Donald, *Charles Sumner and the Rights of Man* (New York: Knopf, 1970), 294.

10. Cong. Globe, 40th Cong., 1st. Sess., 481 (1867) (remarks of Senators Anthony, Fessenden, and Sumner).

11. James Redpath, "The Political Situation: Views of Sumner, Wilson and Butler," *Pittsburgh Commercial (Boston Advertiser)*, September 7, 1867.

12. CS, *Are We A Nation?* (New York: Young Men's Republican Union, 1867). For a more accessible

published version of the speech, see CS, "Are We a Nation?" (Speech, New York, Cooper Institute, November 19, 1867), *WCS*, 12:187–249.

13. See many references to the "Second Founding" by the Supreme Court in *Students for Fair Admissions, Inc. v. President & Fellows of Harvard Coll.*, 600 U.S. 181 (2023). For different perspectives on whether the Second Founding broke from or redeemed the original Founding, see, e.g., Jack M. Balkin, *Constitutional Redemption: Political Faith in an Unjust World* (Cambridge, Mass.: Harvard University Press, 2011); Dorothy E. Roberts, "Abolition Constitutionalism," *Harvard Law Review* 133, no. 1 (2019): 1–122; Noah Feldman, *The Broken Constitution: Lincoln, Slavery, and the Refounding of America* (New York: Farrar, Straus and Giroux, 2021); Kermit Roosevelt, *The Nation That Never Was: Reconstructing America's Story* (Chicago: University of Chicago Press, 2022); Kurt Lash, *The Fourteenth Amendment and the Privileges or Immunities of American Citizenship* (Cambridge: Cambridge University Press, 2014); Ilan Wurman, *The Second Founding: An Introduction to the Fourteenth Amendment* (Cambridge: Cambridge University Press, 2020).

14. Cornell, *Charles Sumner: Memoir and Eulogies*, 61, 281.

15. Arthur Reed Hogue, ed., *Charles Sumner: An Essay by Carl Schurz* (Urbana: University of Illinois Press, 1951), 42–43.

16. William Eleazar Barton, *The Women Lincoln Loved* (Indianapolis: Bobbs-Merrill, 1927), 345–48; CS to Anna Cabot Lodge, July 14, 1868, 82/109, PCS.

17. "The Sumner Scandal and the Truth About It," *Lancaster Intelligencer*, January 13, 1868; "The Sumner Scandal," *Wisconsin State Register*, December 7, 1867.

18. "Senator Sumner's Domestic Difficulty," *Portland Daily Press*, October 24, 1867; "The Sumner Scandal and the Truth About It," *Lancaster Intelligencer*, January 13, 1868.

19. CS to Anna Cabot Lodge, July 14, 1868, 82/109, PCS; CS to Samuel Howe, February 17, 1868, 64/545, PCS; CS to Samuel Howe, February 9, 1868, 64/540, PCS.

20. CS to Samuel Howe, February 17, 1868, 64/545, PCS; CS to Anna Cabot Lodge, July 14, 1868, 82/109, PCS.

21. Anna Cabot Lodge to CS, August 16, 1868, 43/205, PCS.

22. CS to Samuel Howe, December 15, 1867, 40/305, PCS; CS to Samuel Howe, December 18, 1867, 64/508, PCS; CS to Samuel Howe, February 17, 1868, 64/545, PCS; CS to Samuel Howe, February 18, 1868, 64/548, PCS; CS to Samuel Howe, November 17, 1867, 64/503, PCS.

23. Samuel Howe to CS, February 14, 1868, 41/073, PCS; "The Sumner Scandal's a Tissue of Lies," *North Missouri Weekly Courier*, November 7, 1867; John Bigelow, *Retrospections of an Active Life*, vol. 5 (New York: Doubleday, Page, 1913), 143.

24. For Pierce's memorandum and the interview notes, see Edward Lillie Pierce, "Notes on the Separation of Charles Sumner and His Wife" (n.d.), Documents Relating to Charles Sumner, Houghton Library, Harvard University. These notes were donated to the library by "G. B. Pierce" and were previously archived under his name. The rough notes give little information. Interviewees who claimed that Alice was pregnant and/or had an abortion appear to have included Senator Henry Anthony, Benjamin Perley Poore, "Mrs. Sprague" (probably Kate Chase Sprague), "Mrs. W. D. O'Connor" (probably Ellen Tarr O'Connor), and Senator Samuel Pomeroy and his wife, Martha. For more on the frequency of abortions and the stigma associated with it among upper-class women in the mid-nineteenth-century American North, see James C. Mohr, *Abortion in America* (New York: Oxford University Press, 1978), 89–101.

25. Samuel Hooper quoted from parts of Sumner's letter to him in his reply. See Samuel Hooper to CS, November 30, 1867, 40/199, PCS. Unfortunately, none of Sumner's letters to Hooper survive.

26. CS to Henry Longfellow, December 2, 1867, 81/276, PCS; Henry Longfellow to CS, December 8, 1867, 81/287, PCS; Samuel Hooper to CS, October 6, 1867, 39/702, PCS.

Chapter 23: Sumner's Hospitality Was Perfect

1. Anna Lauren Dawes, *Charles Sumner* (New York: Dodd, Mead, 1892), 303–4; "Charles Sumner at Home," *Chicago Tribune*, March 20, 1871; "The Desk," *Washington Chronicle*, March 14, 1874, 4; CS to Henry Longfellow, August 4, 1868, 82/146, PCS; A. Augusta Dodge, *Gail Hamilton's Life in Letters*, vol. 2 (Boston: Lee and Shepard, 1901). For more on Sumner's home and its art, see "Charles Sumner House Floorplan," n.d., Charles Sumner Papers, Massachusetts Historical Society, Boston; Elsie Dee, "Fifteen Minutes' Walk in Washington," *Boston Congregationalist*, January 26, 1871; "The Body Embalmed: The Death Chamber and a Description of the Appearance of the Remains," *National Republican*, March 12, 1874; Elias Nason, *The Life and Times of Charles Sumner* (Boston: B. B.

Russell, 1874), 334–36; Arnold B. Johnson, "Recollections of Charles Sumner: The Senator's Home and Pictures," *Scribner's Monthly* 7 (1875), 101–14; Pierce, *MLCS*, 4:338–40.

2. CS, *WCS*, 9:369. For Storey's recollections of Sumner's home and the start of his clerkship, see Moorfield Storey, "Speeches/Writing (Washington D.C., Society + Character)" n.d., Moorfield Storey Papers, Massachusetts Historical Society, Boston; M. A. De Wolfe Howe, *Portrait of an Independent: Moorfield Storey, 1845–1929* (Boston: Houghton Mifflin, 1932), 51–52; Ann Louise Leger, "Moorfield Storey: An Intellectual Biography" (Ph.D. diss., University of Iowa, 1968), 30–31; William B. Hixson Jr., *Moorfield Storey and the Abolitionist Tradition* (Oxford: Oxford University Press, 1972), 11–14. For Sumner's relationship to Kent, see chapter 4. For Kent's relationship to Hamilton, see John H. Langbein, "Chancellor Kent and the History of Legal Literature," *Columbia Law Review* 93, no. 3 (1993): 556–57. For Hamilton's attendance of the funeral of Sumner's grandfather, see chapter 1.

3. George Rothwell Brown, ed., *Reminiscences of Senator William M. Stewart of Nevada* (New York: The Naele Publishing Company, 1908), 239; Storey, "Speeches/Writing (Washington D.C., Society + Character)"; Moorfield Storey, "Charles Sumner," in *The Early Years of the Saturday Club, 1855–1870*, ed. Edward Waldo Emerson (Boston: Houghton Mifflin, 1918), 302–4; Pierce, *MLCS*, 4:342–44; Arnold B. Johnson, "Mr. Johnson's Address," in *Dinner Commemorative of Charles Sumner and Complimentary to Edward L. Pierce* (Cambridge, Mass.: John Wilson and Son, 1895); Benjamin Perley Poore, "Waifs from Washington," *Boston Journal*, October 24, 1877; Ralph Waldo Emerson, *The Letters of Ralph Waldo Emerson*, ed. Ralph L. Rusk, vol. 6 (New York: Columbia University Press, 1939), 195, 197; William M. Cornell, ed., *Charles Sumner: Memoir and Eulogies* (Boston: James H. Earle, 1874), 262.

4. Pierce, *MLCS*, 4:342; Charles Dickens, *Life, Letters, and Speeches of Charles Dickens*, vol. 2 (Boston: Houghton, Mifflin, 1894), 313–14; Walter Stahr, *Stanton: Lincoln's War Secretary* (New York: Simon and Schuster, 2017), 591–92; Storey, "Dickens, Stanton, Sumner, and Storey," 463–65. For Dickens's visit to Boston in 1842, see chapter 5.

5. Samuel Hooper to CS, October 6, 1867, 39/702, PCS; James Wormley to CS, October 8, 1867, 39/718, PCS; Pierce, *MLCS*, 4:342; J. Francis Gregory, "Charles Sumner Wormley," *Journal of Negro History* 20, no. 2 (1935): 268.

6. CS to Joshua B. Smith, February 25, 1872, 84/538, PCS; CS to James Wormley, September 28, 1871, Letters Received by James Wormley, 1868–1892, Massachusetts Historical Society, Boston; Carol Gelderman, *A Freeman of Color and His Hotel: Race, Reconstruction, and the Role of the Federal Government* (Washington, D.C.: Potomac Books, 2012), 41; Diane Spivey, *At the Table of Power: Food and Cuisine in the African American Struggle for Freedom, Justice, and Equality* (Pittsburgh: University of Pittsburgh Press, 2022), 238–41.

7. Spivey, *At the Table of Power*, 86–87; CS to George Downing, July 26, 1863, Folder 35, Box 1, Downing Papers, MSRC.

8. *A Memorial of Charles Sumner* (Boston: Wright and Porter, Printers to the Commonwealth of Massachusetts, 1874), 57–58; CS to Joshua B. Smith, January 3, 1869, 81/343, PCS; Joshua B. Smith to CS, February 12, 1869, 45/131, PCS; Spivey, *At the Table of Power*, 203–8. Smith's name appears on the official menu of the 1846 and 1847 Fourth of July Dinners in Boston. While his name is absent from the 1845 menu, the complex array of food items is nearly identical to those of the subsequent two years. I infer from this that Smith was the caterer in 1845 as well. The menus, titled "Bill of Fare, Dinner of the City Council of Boston," are available online at the American Broadsides and Ephemera Collection, series 1, nos. 16671, 16673, and 16678. For more on Smith and Sumner's collaboration to advocate for the Robert Gould Shaw Memorial, see Kathryn Grover, *To Heal the Wounded Nation's Life: African Americans and the Robert Gould Shaw—54th Regiment Memorial* (Cornish, N.H.: Saint-Gaudens National Historical Park, 2021), chap. 3.

9. Cornell, *Charles Sumner, Memoir and Eulogies*, 295–96; "Sumner's Page," *Lancaster Intelligencer*, December 22, 1869, 2; "Letter from Edwin Belcher, Augusta, Ga., to William Lloyd Garrison, April 16th, 1878," Digital Commonwealth, n.d., https://www.digitalcommonwealth.org/search /commonwealth:dv142m499. Some sources say Belcher was born in the late 1830s. For more on Belcher's biography, see Edwin Belcher to CS, December 6, 1867, 40/249, PCS; "Edwin Belcher, the Famous Colored Politician of Georgia," *Daily Knoxville Chronicle*, January 14, 1883, 3; "Edwin Belcher," *St. Louis Globe-Democrat*, January 9, 1883, 2; "A Prominent Radical Leader on Negro Emigration," *Georgia Weekly Telegraph, Journal and Messenger*, March 4, 1873, 2; Edmund L. Drago, *Black Politicians and Reconstruction in Georgia: A Splendid Failure* (Athens: University of Georgia Press, 1992), 69–70; Paul A. Cimbala, *Under the Guardianship of the Nation: The Freedmen's Bureau and the Reconstruction of Georgia, 1865–1870* (Athens: University of Georgia Press, 2003), 45–46.

10. Edwin Belcher to CS, December 6, 1867, 40/249, PCS; Edwin Belcher to CS, June 16, 1868, 42/336, PCS; Edwin Belcher to CS, June 23, 1868, 42/403, PCS.

11. "Constitution of the State of Georgia," in *Journal of the Proceedings of the Constitutional Convention of the People of Georgia* (Augusta, Ga.: E. H. Pughe, 1868), 540–62; Manisha Sinha, *The Rise and Fall of the Second American Republic: Reconstruction, 1860–1920* (New York: Liveright, 2024), 179, 227; Eric Foner, *Reconstruction: America's Unfinished Revolution (1863–1877)* (New York: Harper Perennial Classics, 1988), 385. For more on Reconstruction in Georgia during this period, see W. E. Burghardt Du Bois, *Black Reconstruction* (New York: Harcourt, Brace, 1935), 495–511.

12. Calara Mildred Thompson, *Reconstruction in Georgia: Economic, Social, Political, 1865–1872* (New York: Columbia University Press, 1915), 371.

13. Edwin Belcher to CS, July 23, 1868, 43/047, PCS; Edwin Belcher to CS, December 15, 1868, 44/095, PCS; Edwin Belcher to CS, January 19, 1869, 44/477, PCS.

14. CS to Edward Atkinson, February 27, 1868, 81/472, PCS.

15. "Secretary Stanton Again Removed by the President," *New York Times*, February 22, 1868; CS, *WCS*, 12:356; Pierce, *MLCS*, 4:350; "Sumner, Charles (1811–1874) to Edwin M. Stanton Re: (Support for Stanton over President Johnson) 'Stick!,'" Gilder-Lehrman Collection, n.d., https://www.gilderlehrman.org/collection/glc04846; Stahr, *Stanton*, 593.

16. Sumner's opinion on impeachment, which is discussed for the next several paragraphs, is reprinted in *Trial of Andrew Johnson*, vol. 2 (Washington: Government Printing Office, 1868), 247–95. For a more accessible published version, see CS, "Expulsion of the President" (Opinion, U.S. Senate, May 26, 1868), *WCS*, 12:318–413. For more on the legal debates on the impeachment proceeding and the constitutionality of the Tenure of Office Act, see generally Michael Les Benedict, *The Impeachment and Trial of Andrew Johnson* (New York: W. W. Norton, 1973); Hans Louis Trefousse, *Impeachment of a President: Andrew Johnson, the Blacks, and Reconstruction* (New York: Fordham University Press, 1999).

17. For Moorfield Storey's role in helping Sumner draft his impeachment opinion, see Howe, *Portrait of an Independent*, 115–16.

18. Trefousse, *Impeachment of a President*, 165–66; "Impeachment," *New York Herald*, May 27, 1868.

19. CS to Samuel Howe, May 21, 1868, 64/554, PCS; CS to Jonathan F. Stearns, September 25, 1831, 62/017, PCS.

20. H. L. Trefousse, *Benjamin Franklin Wade: Radical Republican from Ohio* (New York: Twayne Publishers, 1963), 74; CS to Francis Lieber, May 1868, *MLCS*, 4:351; CS to Elizabeth Argyll, June 30, 1868, 82/067, PCS.

21. CS to John Bright, August 11, 1868, 082/156, *MLCS*, 4:360.

22. "Speeches of Senator Sumner and Mr. Dana," *Springfield Daily Republican*, September 16, 1868; CS to Samuel Howe, June 30, 1868, 64/531, PCS; CS to Henry Longfellow, September 17, 1868, 82/194, PCS; CS to John Whittier, November 13, 1868, 82/221, PCS; Pierce, *MLCS*, 4:362; CS to Anna Cabot Lodge, October 14, 1868, 82/206, PCS.

23. For more on Sumner's support for the gold and silver standard, see CS, "Financial Reconstruction Through Public Faith and Specie Payments" (Speech, U.S. Senate, July 11, 1868), *WCS*, 12:443–80. For more on Fessenden's public dinner in Boston and Sumner's reelection campaign in 1868–69, see David Donald, *Charles Sumner and the Rights of Man* (New York: Knopf, 1970), 341–48. Donald overstates the possibility that John Andrew was mounting a covert Senate challenge against Sumner. See Stephen D. Engle, *In Pursuit of Justice: The Life of John Albion Andrew* (Amherst: University of Massachusetts Press, 2023), 358–60.

24. Edwin Belcher to CS, July 23, 1868, 43/046, PCS.

25. Ron Chernow, *Grant* (New York: Penguin, 2017), 798, 821; "The Political Situation," *New-Orleans Times*, September 10, 1867. Chernow notes that "Grant probably lost the majority of white votes, but hundreds of thousands of black votes made up the difference."

26. Eric Foner, *The Second Founding: How the Civil War and Reconstruction Remade the Constitution* (New York: W. W. Norton, 2019), chap. 3.

27. *Proceedings of the National Convention of the Colored Men of America Held in Washington, D.C., 1869*; Kate Masur, *An Example for All the Land: Emancipation and the Struggle over Equality in Washington, D.C.* (Chapel Hill: University of North Carolina Press, 2010), 181.

28. Elizabeth Cady Stanton, Susan B. Anthony, and Matilda Joslyn Gage, eds., *History of Woman Suffrage: 1861–1876*, vol. 2 (New York: Fowler and Wells, 1882), 348–55; "Woman Suffrage Convention," *National Republican*, January 21, 1869, 4; Masur, *An Example for All the Land*, 181; Sinha, *The Rise and Fall of the Second American Republic*, 219–20, 223–24.

29. Cong. Globe, 39th Cong., 1st. Sess., 107, 952 (1866) (remarks of Senator Sumner); Wendy Hamand Venet, *Neither Ballots nor Bullets: Women Abolitionists and the Civil War* (Charlottesville: University Press of Virginia, 1991), 153.

30. Susan B. Anthony to CS, April 19, 1869, 46/317, PCS; Susan B. Anthony to CS, February 8, 1870, 49/595, PCS.

31. CS, "Powers of Congress to Prohibit Inequality, Caste, and Oligarchy of the Skin (with Susan B. Anthony's Annotations)" (1869), Charles Sumner Papers (Folder 1860–1869), Library of Congress, Washington, D.C.; Susan B. Anthony, "Image 50 of Susan B. Anthony Papers: Daybook and Diaries, 1856–1906; Diaries; 1874," Library of Congress, Washington, D.C., n.d., https://www.loc.gov/resource/mss11049.mss11049-002_00107_00307/?sp=50&st=image.

32. Laura E. Richards and Maud Howe Elliott, *Julia Ward Howe, 1819–1910*, vol. 1 (Boston: Houghton Mifflin, 1915), 206; James Harvey Young, "Anna Elizabeth Dickinson and the Civil War: For and Against Lincoln," *Journal of American History* 31, no. 1 (June 1, 1944): 68; Stanton, Anthony, and Gage, eds., *History of Woman Suffrage*, 2:434–35. Sumner also introduced Anna Dickinson before she gave remarks at the Lincoln Hall in Washington in 1871. Pierce, *MLCS*, 4:464.

33. Thomas Wentworth Higginson, *Contemporaries* (Boston: Houghton Mifflin, 1899), 291.

34. All quotes are obtained from CS, "Powers of Congress to Prohibit Inequality, Caste, and Oligarchy of the Skin," 13:34–52.

35. Both Anthony and Stanton would invoke Sumner's phrase "anything for human rights is constitutional" in their advocacy for Congress and the courts to recognize a woman's right to vote under the Fourteenth Amendment. See, e.g., Elizabeth Cady Stanton, *The Selected Papers of Elizabeth Cady Stanton and Susan B. Anthony*, vol. 2 (New Brunswick, N.J.: Rutgers University Press, 1997), 583; Ann D. Gordon, *The Selected Papers of Elizabeth Cady Stanton and Susan B. Anthony*, vol. 6 (New Brunswick, N.J.: Rutgers University Press, 2013), 93.

36. CS, *WCS*, 13:50.

Chapter 24: Grawnt

1. *New York Herald*, December 15, 1867; "The Political Situation: Views of Sumner, Wilson and Butler," *New York Times*, September 5, 1867, 1/8.

2. Sumner, *The True Grandeur of Nations: An Oration Delivered Before the Authorities of the City of Boston, July 4, 1845* (Boston: American Peace Society, 1845), 55. For more on Sumner's speech "The True Grandeur of Nations," see chapter 5.

3. "The First Nomination of Gen. Grant for the Presidency," *Chicago Tribune*, July 22, 1891, 9; CS to Benjamin Hall Wright, March 12, 1869, 82/354, PCS.

4. CS to Francis Lieber, November 4, 1868, 64/591, PCS; David Donald, *Charles Sumner and the Rights of Man* (New York: Knopf, 1970), 370.

5. George William Curtis, ed., *The Correspondence of John Lothrop Motley*, vol. 2 (New York: Harper and Bros., 1889), 302; Gideon Welles, *The Diary of Gideon Welles*, vol. 3 (Boston: Houghton Mifflin, 1911), 548.

6. Pierce, *MLCS*, 4:374; CS, *"Republicanism vs. Grantism": Speech of Hon. Charles Sumner (May 31, 1872)* (Boston: Lee and Shepard, 1872), 26.

7. "New Cabinet," *Daily Nonpareil*, March 7, 1869; Pierce, *MLCS*, 4:377–78; Allan Nevins, *Hamilton Fish* (New York: Dodd, Mead, 1936), 46–47.

8. Hamilton Fish to CS, March 13, 1869, 45/497, PCS.

9. Pierce, *MLCS*, 4:381; James T. Fields to CS, January 14, 1869, 44/389, PCS; Henry Bowen Anthony to CS, May 24, 1869, 47/095, PCS.

10. CS to Samuel Howe, April 5, 1869, 64/613, PCS; James Penny Boyd, *Military and Civil Life of Gen. Ulysses S. Grant* (Philadelphia: P. W. Ziegler, 1885), 596; CS to Francis Lieber, April 22, 1869, 64/615, PCS; Donald, *Charles Sumner and the Rights of Man*, 373.

11. CS to Whitelaw Reid, January 12, 1871, 84/096, PCS; CS to Elizabeth Argyll, May 18, 1869, 82/472, PCS; John Y. Simon, ed., *The Papers of Ulysses S. Grant*, vol. 19 (Carbondale: Southern Illinois University Press, 1995), 212; Nevins, *Hamilton Fish*, 156–57; *New York Herald*, September 25, 1877; Pierce, *MLCS*, 4:409.

12. Robert H. Ferrell, *American Diplomacy: A History* (New York: W. W. Norton, 1959), 155. For more on the Treaty of Washington negotiations, which involved a great deal of infighting among Sumner, Fish, Motley, and Grant, see Nevins, *Hamilton Fish*, 159–75, 470–93; Donald, *Charles Sumner and the Rights of Man*, 374–413.

13. CS, *The Question of Caste* (Boston: Wright & Potter, 1869). For a more accessible published ver-

sion, see CS, "The Question of Caste" (Speech, Boston Music Hall, October 21, 1869), *WCS*, 13:134–83. For a list of places where Sumner delivered the speech, see Pierce, *MLCS*, 4:415. For a study on how Sumner understood the Indian caste system, see Hari Ramesh, "India, Racial Caste, and Abolition in Charles Sumner's Political Thought," *Modern Intellectual History* 19 (2022): 708–33.

14. For more on phrenology and how it was practiced by Agassiz and Howe, see, e.g., Susan Branson, "Phrenology and the Science of Race in Antebellum America," *Early American Studies* 15, no. 1 (2017): 164–93; Edward Lurie, "Louis Agassiz and the Races of Man," *Isis* 45, no. 3 (1954): 227–42; Matthew Furrow, "Samuel Gridley Howe, the Black Population of Canada West, and the Racial Ideology of the 'Blueprint for Radical Reconstruction,'" *Journal of American History* 97, no. 2 (2010): 344–70.

15. CS, "Naturalization Laws: No Discrimination on Account of Color" (Speech, U.S. Senate, July 2, 1870), *WCS*, 13:474–98; Xi Wang, *The Trial of Democracy: Black Suffrage and Northern Republicans, 1860–1910* (Athens: University of Georgia Press, 1997), 68–78; Jeffrey A. Jenkins and Justin Peck, *Congress and the First Civil Rights Era, 1861–1918* (Chicago: University of Chicago Press, 2021), 138–43; Frederick Douglass to CS, July 6, 1870, 51/227, PCS. For more on Sumner's attitude toward Chinese naturalization, see Dale Baum, "Woman Suffrage and the 'Chinese Question': The Limits of Radical Republicanism in Massachusetts, 1865–1876," *The New England Quarterly* 56, no. 1 (1983): 60–77.

16. Pierce, *MLCS*, 4:369–70; CS to Samuel Howe, December 7, 1868, 64/597, PCS; William M. Armstrong, ed., *The Gilded Age: Letters of E. L. Godkin* (Albany: State University of New York Press), 136; CS to Henry Longfellow, July 8, 1869, 82/557, PCS; Donald, *Charles Sumner and the Rights of Man*, 330; Schurz, "Eulogy Before City Authorities of Boston (Music Hall, April 29, 1874)," in *Charles Sumner: Memoir and Eulogies*, ed. William M. Cornell (Boston: James H. Earle, 1874), 161.

17. George Sewall Boutwell, *Reminiscences of Sixty Years in Public Affairs: Governor of Massachusetts, 1851–1852*, vol. 2 (New York: McClure, Phillips, 1902), 215.

18. Donald, *Charles Sumner and the Rights of Man*, 369.

19. Charles W. Calhoun, *The Presidency of Ulysses S. Grant* (Lawrence: University Press of Kansas, 2017), 61; Charles Eliot Norton, ed., *Letters of James Russell Lowell*, vol. 2 (New York: Harper and Bros., 1894), 233; Arthur Reed Hogue, ed., *Charles Sumner: An Essay by Carl Schurz* (Urbana: University of Illinois Press, 1951), 81.

20. For a survey of nineteenth-century Dominican history, see Frank Moya Pons, *The Dominican Republic: A National History* (Princeton: Markus Wiener Publishers, 1995), chaps. 6–11; Anne Eller, *We Dream Together: Dominican Independence, Haiti, and the Fight for Caribbean Freedom* (Durham, N.C.: Duke University Press, 2016).

21. CS to George Bemis, December 24, 1866, 80/566, PCS; CS, *WCS*, 14:187–88.

22. For a focused study on Grant's effort to annex San Domingo and the role that Báez, Babcock, and other actors played, see John B. Crume, "President Grant and His Santo Domingo Annexation Project—A Study of Ill Judgment" (Ph.D. diss., Florida Atlantic University, 1972).

23. Benjamin Perley Poore, "Waifs from Washington," *Boston Journal*, October 24, 1877; Benjamin Perley Poore, *Perley's Reminiscences of Sixty Years in the National Metropolis*, vol. 1 (Philadelphia: Hubbard's Bros., 1886), 279–81. My account of Grant's visit to Sumner's home relies largely on Poore's recollection, which differs somewhat from Sumner's retelling. In a Senate speech one year later, Sumner said that Grant brought up the Santo Domingo treaty almost immediately after coming to his home, and Sumner later switched the subject to James Ashley's removal afterward. I do not rely much on Sumner's account because he failed to mention that Poore and John Forney were present in the room, probably wishing to avoid implicating them in his controversy. See Charles Sumner, "Naboth's Vineyard" (Speech, U.S. Senate, December 21, 1870), 125–26, *WCS*, 14:89–131; Donald, *Charles Sumner and the Rights of Man*, 435.

24. Simon, *The Papers of Ulysses S. Grant*, 19:368–71; Robert F. Horowitz, *The Great Impeacher: A Political Biography of James M. Ashley* (New York: Brooklyn College Press, 1979), 161–63; Clark C. Spence, "Spoilsman in Montana: James M. Ashley," *Montana: The Magazine of Western History* 18, no. 2 (1968): 24–35.

25. On Hamilton Fish, see Jacob Dolson Cox, "How Judge Hoar Ceased to Be Attorney-General," *The Atlantic* 6 (August 1895): 167. On Orville Babcock, see Chernow, *Grant*, 848–49, 888–89.

26. John Y. Simon, ed., *The Papers of Ulysses S. Grant*, vol. 28 (Carbondale: Southern Illinois University Press, 2005), 308n8; CS, "Naboth's Vineyard," 14:126; Americus, "The Annexation of San Domingo," *The Galaxy* 11 (January 1871): 414–15; A. J. Langguth, *After Lincoln: How the North Won the Civil War and Lost the Peace* (New York: Simon and Schuster, 2014), 271; Poore, "Waifs from Washington"; Benjamin Perley Poore, *Perley's Reminiscences of Sixty Years in the National Metropolis*, vol. 2 (Philadelphia: Hubbard's Bros., 1886), 279–81.

27. For Sumner's work on Mexico, the Danish West Indies, and Cuba, see Donald, *Charles Sumner and the Rights of Man*, 101–3, 354–58, 417–19. Moorfield Storey, who was Sumner's secretary at the time of Grant's visit, observed that it would be incredible for Sumner to have "pledged himself to support the treaties without having seen them." After all, "in such matters he was extremely cautious, and where the 'Black Republic' was concerned, he would have been especially so." Moorfield Storey, *Charles Sumner* (Boston: Houghton Mifflin, 1900), 383.

28. CS to Hamilton Fish, March 20, 1870, 83/339, PCS; Nevins, *Hamilton Fish*, 313–16; Pierce, *MLCS*, 4:438; CS to William Lloyd Garrison, April 26, 1871, 84/256, PCS; CS, *WCS*, 14:179–80.

29. "Grant Interview in Hamburg (July 6, 1878)," Papers of Ulysses S. Grant: Digital Edition, n.d., http://rotunda.upress.virginia.edu/founders/AWJN.html; Joseph Hawley to CS, March 25, 1870, 50/246, PCS; Chernow, *Grant*, 662.

30. Eric T. L. Love, "Santo Domingo," in *Race over Empire: Racism and U.S. Imperialism, 1865–1900* (Chapel Hill: University of North Carolina Press, 2004), 43–52; Chernow, *Grant*, 846–47; "Grant and the San Domingo Treaty," *Spirit of Democracy* (Woodsfield, Ohio), March 29, 1870, 2.

31. Donald, *Charles Sumner and the Rights of Man*, 441; Charles Francis Adams, *Richard Henry Dana: A Biography*, vol. 1 (Boston: Houghton Mifflin, 1890), 659; CS to William Lloyd Garrison, April 26, 1871, 84/256, PCS.

32. Because Senators Sumner and Morton spoke extemporaneously during executive session, there is no published account of their speeches in the *Congressional Globe* or elsewhere. I relied on brief summaries of their speeches in the *New York Tribune*, March 25, 1870; "Debate on the San Domingo Treaty in the Senate," *Chicago Tribune*, March 25, 1870, 10; "Sumner's Argument Against Ratification," *New York Daily Herald*, March 25, 1870; "Long Debate on the San Domingo Treaty in the Senate," *Chicago Republican* (*Daily Inter Ocean*), March 25, 1870; "Arguments on the San Domingo Treaty," *Boston Advertiser*, March 26, 1870.

33. Cong. Globe, 42nd Cong., 1st Sess., 36–37 (1871) (remarks of Senator Schurz).

34. Calhoun, *The Presidency of Ulysses S. Grant*, 234; CS, *WCS*, 14:258–60; "An Interview with Ex-Secretary Fish," *Boston Evening Transcript*, October 19, 1877.

35. "From Ulysses S. Grant to Hamilton Fish, 1 July 1870," Papers of Ulysses S. Grant: Digital Edition, n.d., http://rotunda.upress.virginia.edu/founders/AWJN.html; Pierce, *MLCS*, 4:446; Cox, "How Judge Hoar Ceased to Be Attorney-General," 172; *New York Herald*, September 25, 1877; Calhoun, *The Presidency of Ulysses S. Grant*, 258; Mary Lincoln to CS, September 7, 1870, 51/468, PCS.

36. CS to George Bemis, July 22, 1870, 83/515, PCS; Donald, *Charles Sumner and the Rights of Man*, 369; Sara Norton and M. A. De Wolfe Howe, *Letters of Charles Eliot Norton*, vol. 2 (Boston: Houghton Mifflin, 1913), 42–43.

Chapter 25: Law-givers Are Among the Most God-like Characters

1. "Fifteenth Amendment: Grand Demonstration Last Night," *Washington Daily Chronicle*, April 2, 1870; Steven Hahn, *A Nation Under Our Feet: Black Political Struggles in the Rural South from Slavery to the Great Migration* (Cambridge, Mass.: Belknap Press, 2003), 216–17; Cong. Globe, 38th Cong., 1st Sess., 1363 (1864) (remarks of Sen. Sumner); Hiram Revels to CS, March 1870, 50/288, PCS; Hiram Revels to CS, April 9, 1870, 50/351, PCS. On the constitutional questions around Revels's admission into the Senate, see Richard A. Primus, "The Riddle of Hiram Revels," *Harvard Law Review* 119, no. 6 (2006): 1680–734.

2. I have not found the original copy of Sumner's letter to Langston asking him to draw up the first draft of the Civil Rights Bill. An unpublished, comprehensive finding aid for Langston's papers, available in the finding aid shelves of the Amistad Research Center in New Orleans, has also noted that the original copy does not appear to have survived. That said, there is little reason to doubt the letter's authenticity. Langston had the letter published in the *National Era* during Sumner's lifetime, and Sumner never denied working with Langston, whom he often invited to his home to discuss strategy on passing the Civil Rights Bill up until his very death. For the next two decades, African Americans often credited Langston with authorship of the original Civil Rights Bill. See, e.g., "Equality Before the Law: Address of Professor John M. Langston," *New National Era*, August 7, 1873; "Questions of the Hour: Speech of Hon. J. S. Hinton," *North Vernon Plain Dealer*, September 29, 1874; "A Letter from John M. Langston on the Subject," *Petersburg Index*, October 9, 1874, 2; "Interviews: Hon. John M. Langston," *National Republican*, October 17, 1883, 2; "John Mercer Langston," *Appeal*, April 26, 1890.

3. A modern biography of Langston's full life is needed. For more on his life, see John Mercer Langston, *From the Virginia Plantation to the National Capitol* (Hartford: American Publishing Company,

1894); William Francis Cheek, "Forgotten Prophet: The Life of John Mercer Langston" (Ph.D. diss., University of Virginia, 1961); William Cheek and Aimee Lee Cheek, *John Mercer Langston and the Fight for Black Freedom, 1829–1865* (Urbana: University of Illinois Press, 1989); Kenneth W. Mack, *Representing the Race: The Creation of the Civil Rights Lawyer* (Cambridge, Mass.: Harvard University Press, 2012), 13–26. Langston's career is also discussed at many points in David W. Blight, *Frederick Douglass: Prophet of Freedom* (New York: Simon and Schuster, 2018).

4. "Mass Meeting of Colored Citizens," *Washington Chronicle*, April 25, 1872, 4; Langston, *From the Virginia Plantation to the National Capitol*, 523; "John Mercer Langston."

5. Nat Brandt, *The Town That Started the Civil War* (Syracuse: Syracuse University Press, 1990), 186; John Mercer Langston, *Freedom and Citizenship: Selected Lectures and Addresses* (Washington, D.C.: R. H. Darby, 1883), 15, 170; Langston, *From the Virginia Plantation to the National Capitol*, 187; CS, *WCS*, 1:265.

6. S. 916, 41st Cong. (May 13, 1870).

7. Christopher W. Schmidt, *Civil Rights in America* (Cambridge: Cambridge University Press, 2020), 33.

8. Amy Dru Stanley, "Slave Emancipation and the Revolutionizing of Human Rights," in *The World the Civil War Made*, ed. Gregory P. Downs and Kate Masur (Chapel Hill: University of North Carolina Press, 2015), 283.

9. For more on the common law right-of-access doctrine and how it relates to Sumner's civil rights work, see Frederick W. Peirsol, "An Innkeepers 'Right' to Discriminate," *Florida Law Review* 15 (1962); Alfred Avins, "What Is a Place of 'Public' Accommodation?," *Marquette Law Review* 52, no. 1 (1968); Randy E. Barnett and Evan D. Bernick, *The Original Meaning of the Fourteenth Amendment: Its Letter and Spirit* (Cambridge, Mass.: Harvard University Press, 2021), 185–93. Sumner discussed the history of the common law right-of-access doctrine in CS, *WCS*, 14:388–98.

10. CS, *WCS*, 14:392. For more on the theater provision of Sumner's Civil Rights Supplement and the right to seek amusement, see generally Stanley, "Slave Emancipation and the Revolutionizing of Human Rights."

11. Langston, *Freedom and Citizenship*, 170; "Senator Sumner Serenaded," *Boston Journal*, December 2, 1873, 4; CS, *WCS*, 10:7; CS, *WCS*, 9:109–17; CS, *WCS*, 11:414–17; *Argument of Charles Sumner, Esq., Before the Supreme Court of Massachusetts in the Case of Sarah C. Roberts vs. the City of Boston (December 4, 1849)* (Washington, D.C.: F. and J. Rives and Geo. A. Bailey, 1870). For more on the Charles Sumner School and Museum, see Nancy C. Curtis, *Black Heritage Sites: The South* (New York: The New Press, 1996), 71–72; "Charles Sumner School," DC Historic Sites, n.d., https://historicsites.dcpreservation.org/items/show/578.

12. S. J. Bowen to CS, July 23, 1869, 47/540, PCS; J. Sella Martin to CS, April 4, 1869, 46/054, PCS. For more on the effort to integrate the Washington schools, see James H. Whyte, *The Uncivil War: Washington During the Reconstruction: 1865–1878* (New York: Twayne Publishers, 1958), 76–79, 164–66; Thomas Reed Johnson, "The City on the Hill: Race Relations in Washington, D.C., 1865–1885" (Ph.D. diss., University of Maryland, 1975), 109–28; Clare Hennigan, "The 'Last Ditch' of Oppression: Charles Sumner and Public Schools in the District of Columbia," *Washington History* 28, no. 1 (2016): 56–66.

13. Cong. Globe, 41st Cong., 2nd Sess., 1677 (1870) (remarks of Senator Sumner); Karen Sarena Morris, "The Founding of the National Medical Association" (M.A. thesis, Yale University School of Medicine, 2007), 29; David Chanoff and Louis W. Sullivan, *We'll Fight It Out Here: A History of the Ongoing Struggle for Health Equity* (Baltimore: Johns Hopkins University Press, 2022), 13–17. For more on Alexander Augusta's effort to penalize a streetcar company that separated its cars by race, see chapter 18. For Black medical doctors, the privilege to inclusion within medical societies was seen as a core feature of what it meant to be an American citizen. See Michael Vorenberg, "Citizenship and the Thirteenth Amendment," in *The Promises of Liberty: The History and Contemporary Relevance of the Thirteenth Amendment*, ed. Alexander Tsesis (New York: Columbia University Press, 2010), 58–77.

14. Alfred H. Kelly, "The Congressional Controversy over School Segregation, 1867–1875," *American Historical Review* 64, no. 3 (April 1959): 543; Gregory Downs, *The Second American Revolution* (Chapel Hill: University of North Carolina Press, 2019), 11.

15. "The Charleston Platform," *Spirit of Jefferson*, June 21, 1870, 2; "The Jeffersonian and Col. Mungen," *Hancock Courier*, March 3, 1870, 2; "Yankee Congress," *Southern Home*, June 2, 1870, 3; "Patriotism," *Weekly Caucasian*, February 12, 1870, 2; "Local and State," *Argus and Patriot*, May 20, 1869, 2.

16. "From Washington: Mungen's Speech," *Georgia Weekly Telegraph, Journal and Messenger*, March 8, 1870; "Mungen on Sumner," *Selma Morning Times*, March 3, 1870.

17. On the decline of influence of Sumner and other Radicals within the Republican Party, see Hans L. Trefousse, *The Radical Republicans: Lincoln's Vanguard for Racial Justice* (New York: Alfred A. Knopf, 1969), chap. 13.

18. Ruth Painter Randall, *Mary Lincoln: Biography of a Marriage* (Boston: Little, Brown, 1953), 375–78; Betty Boles Ellison, *The True Mary Todd Lincoln: A Biography* (Jefferson, N.C.: McFarland, 2014), 203–6; Sally Orne to CS, September 12, 1869, 48/147, PCS.

19. Cong. Globe, 41st Cong., 2nd Sess., 5397–98, 5559 (1870) (remarks of Senators Yates and Morrill); William Eleazar Barton, *The Women Lincoln Loved* (Indianapolis: Bobbs-Merrill, 1927), 360–61.

20. Pierce, *MLCS*, 4:450; "Sumner on Grant and Motley—An Interview with the Senator," *Chicago Republican*, November 19, 1870.

21. "Sumner on Grant and Motley—An Interview with the Senator"; Cong. Globe, 41st Cong., 3rd Sess., 247 (1870) (remarks of Senator Sumner); "By Telegraph from Washington," *Boston Journal*, December 21, 1870.

22. "December 5, 1870: Second Annual Message—Ulysses S. Grant Presidency," Miller Center, n.d., https://millercenter.org/the-presidency/presidential-speeches/december-5-1870-second-annual-message; Gerald Horne, *Confronting Black Jacobins: The U.S., the Haitian Revolution, and the Origins of the Dominican Republic* (New York: Monthly Review Press, 2015), 294; "San Domingo: Extracts from Recent Diplomatic Correspondence," *New York Times*, January 26, 1871, 2; Fritz Daguillard, *A Jewel in the Crown: Charles Sumner and the Struggle for Haiti's Recognition* (Washington, D.C.: Haitian Embassy, 1999), 44–45; Stephen Preston to CS, February 10, 1871, 51/508, PCS; Stephen Preston to CS, June 23, 1870, 51/126, PCS; CS to Samuel Howe, December 30, 1870, 64/674, PCS; CS, WCS, 14:179–80. Preston's letters to Sumner are in French. In reading and translating his letters, I received help from two native speakers, Sabrine Djemil and Vardy Amusan. All conclusions and potential errors are my own.

23. "Frederick Douglass Papers: Lecture on Haiti (Jan. 2, 1893)," Library of Congress, n.d., https://www.loc.gov/item/mss11879000475/; CS to Samuel Howe, August 3, 1871, 64/705, PCS; CS to Gerrit Smith, August 20, 1871, 84/399, PCS; CS to Gerrit Smith, July 9, 1872, 84/628, PCS. For more on Sumner's effort to secure diplomatic recognition for Haiti, see chapter 16.

24. CS to Gerrit Smith, August 20, 1871, 84/399, PCS; CS to Gerrit Smith, July 9, 1872, 84/628, PCS.

25. Cong. Globe, 41st Cong., 3rd Sess., 228 (remarks of Senator Sumner), 237 and 239 (1870) (remarks of Senators Morton and Nye).

26. Frederick Douglass to CS, December 12, 1870, 52/001, PCS; Ron Chernow, *Grant* (New York: Penguin, 2017), 913.

27. "Communications," *The Journal of Negro History* 21, no. 1 (1936): 56–60; George T. Downing, "Do Not Douglass and Downing Agree?," *The New National Era*, June 22, 1871.

28. Hiram Revels to CS, March 30, 1870, 50/288, PCS.

29. CS to Samuel Howe, August 3, 1871, 64/205, PCS; Harold Schwartz, *Samuel Gridley Howe, Social Reformer* (Cambridge, Mass.: Harvard University Press, 1956), 290, 296–97.

30. Frederick Douglass, *Life and Times of Frederick Douglass* (Hartford: Park Publishing, 1882), 500; "Life on the Frigate," *New York Tribune*, February 21, 1871.

31. Carl Schurz, "Speech: Annexation of San Domingo, January 11th, 1871," in Carl Schurz, *Speeches, Correspondence and Political Papers of Carl Schurz*, ed. Frederic Bancroft, vol. 2 (New York: G. P. Putnam's Sons, 1913), 71–121; Pierce, *MLCS*, 4:457. For focused studies on how different actors understood race and the question of Dominican annexation, see Eric T. L. Love, "Santo Domingo," in *Race over Empire: Racism and U.S. Imperialism, 1865–1900* (Chapel Hill: University of North Carolina Press, 2004); and Nicholas Guyatt, "America's Conservatory: Race, Reconstruction, and the Santo Domingo Debate," *The Journal of American History* 97, no. 4 (2011): 974–1000.

32. Andrew L. Slap, *The Doom of Reconstruction: The Liberal Republicans in the Civil War Era* (New York: Fordham University Press, 2006), chap. 1; Heather Cox Richardson, *West from Appomattox: The Reconstruction of America After the Civil War* (New Haven: Yale University Press, 2007), 107–10.

33. Schurz, *Speeches, Correspondence and Political Papers of Carl Schurz*, 2:60.

34. CS, WCS, 14:134.

35. Schurz, *Speeches, Correspondence and Political Papers of Carl Schurz*, 2:311; CS to Carl Schurz, September 30, 1871, 55/366, PCS; CS to Carl Schurz, August 1, 1871, 84/384, PCS.

Chapter 26: The Dignity of a Black People

1. John Mercer Langston, *From the Virginia Plantation to the National Capitol* (Hartford: American Publishing Company, 1894), 300, 303–4; "Howard University: Commencement Exercises of the

Law Department," *Daily Patriot*, February 4, 1871, 4; "Commencement: Exercises of the Law Class of Howard University," *Washington Chronicle*, February 4, 1871, 4; CS, *WCS*, 14:146–50.

2. Cong. Globe, 41st Cong., 3rd Sess., 1055 (1871) (remarks of Sen. Sumner); CS, "Colored Schools in Washington" (Speech, U.S. Senate, February 8, 1871), *WCS*, 14:153–63; *Report of the Board of Trustees of Colored Schools of Washington and Georgetown, D.C.* (Washington, D.C.: M'Gill and Witherow, 1871); Clare Hennigan, "The 'Last Ditch' of Oppression: Charles Sumner and Public Schools in the District of Columbia," *Washington History* 28, no. 1 (2016): 56–66.

3. "Illness of Mr. Sumner," *North Star*, February 24, 1871; *Reading Times* (Pennsylvania), February 21, 1871; "Senator Sumner's Illness," *Daily Patriot*, February 20, 1871; James A. Garfield to CS, February 19, 1871, 52/563, PCS; CS to Charles Edward Brown-Séquard, February 5, 1871, 64/680, PCS; Pierce, *MLCS*, 4:463; Moorfield Storey, *Charles Sumner* (Boston: Houghton Mifflin, 1900), 392.

4. Cong. Globe, 40th Cong., 2nd Sess., 3249, 3391 (1868) (remarks of Sen. Conkling); Cong. Globe, 41st Cong., 2nd Sess., 1145 (1870) (remarks of Sen. Conkling); Cong. Globe, 41st Cong., 3rd Sess., 246 (1870) (remarks of Sen. Conkling); Elizabeth Adams, "George William Curtis and His Friends," *More Books* 14 (1939): 357

5. CS to William Lloyd Garrison, December 29, 1870, 84/033, PCS; Stafford H. Northcote, "Diaries, 1869, 1870, 1871, 1875, 1882, of the First Earl of Iddesleigh" (1907), 187, Hathi Trust Digital Library.

6. Cong. Globe, 42nd Cong., 1st Sess., 34 (1871) (remarks of Senator Sumner); Pierce, *MLCS*, 4:469–70; Allan Nevins, *Hamilton Fish* (New York: Dodd, Mead, 1936), 461–62; James Gillespie Blaine, *Twenty Years of Congress: From Lincoln to Garfield*, vol. 2 (Norwich, Conn.: Henry Bill Publishing Company, 1886, 503–4; Pierce, *MLCS*, 4:463; Anna Lauren Dawes, *Charles Sumner* (New York: Dodd, Mead, 1892), 305–6; David Donald, *Charles Sumner and the Rights of Man* (New York: Knopf, 1970), 491.

7. Cong. Globe, 42nd Cong., 1st Sess., 35, 43, and 49–50, (1871) (remarks of Senators Wilson, Trumbull, and Tipton); Ralph J. Roske, *His Own Counsel: The Life and Times of Lyman Trumbull* (Reno: University of Nevada Press, 1979), 158–59.

8. Cong. Globe, 42nd Cong., 1st Sess., 37 (1871) (remarks of Senator Schurz).

9. "Discussion on Mr. Sumner's Removal," *Boston Evening Transcript*, March 11, 1871, 4; Nevins, *Hamilton Fish*, 461–63.

10. "Senator Sumner," *Pittsburgh Weekly Post*, March 18, 1871, 2; Donald, *Charles Sumner and the Rights of Man*, 500; "The Sumner Case," *Chicago Tribune*, March 15, 1871, 2; "Effect of Sumner's Displacement on the Republican Majority," *New York Daily Herald*, March 13, 1871, 3; "Senator Sumner and the Republican Party," *Daily Evening Telegraph*, March 11, 1871, 2; Charles W. Calhoun, *The Presidency of Ulysses S. Grant* (Lawrence: University Press of Kansas, 2017), 305.

11. "Senator Howe on the Removal of Mr. Sumner," *Bangor Daily Whig*, April 1, 1871.

12. "Mr. Sumner in the Senate," (London) *Daily Telegraph*, April 12, 1871, 5; "Mr. Sumner's Speech on His San Domingo Resolutions," *Oquawka Spectator*, April 6, 1871, 3; "Washington," *States and Union*, April 5, 1871, 2.

13. Cong. Globe, 42nd Cong., 1st Sess., 294–305 (1871) (Sen. Sumner); "Sumner and 1872," *Springfield Daily Republican*, April 5, 1871.

14. "The Feeling of Annexation," *New York Herald*, March 17, 1871; Franklin Benjamin Sanborn, *Dr. S. G. Howe, the Philanthropist* (New York: Funk and Wagnalls, 1891), 330. While I am quoting from a letter from Howe in Santo Domingo in 1874, his reaction must have been the same on his first trip in 1871.

15. Ron Chernow, *Grant* (New York: Penguin, 2017), 914.

16. Laurent Dubois, *Haiti: The Aftershocks of History* (New York: Metropolitan Books, 2012), 177; Frederick Douglass, *Life and Times of Frederick Douglass* (Hartford: Park Publishing, 1882), 496. For a study on Douglass's opinion of annexation, see Lauren Whitney Hammond, "Outpost of Empire, Endpost of Blackness: African Americans, the Dominican Republic, and U.S. Foreign Policy, 1869–1965" (Ph.D. diss., University of Texas, 2014), chap. 1.

17. Harold Schwartz, *Samuel Gridley Howe, Social Reformer* (Cambridge, Mass.: Harvard University Press, 1956), 313; Henry Garnet to CS, December 23, 1871, 55/726, PCS; "Fred Douglass on Sumner," *Columbia Herald-Statesman*, April 7, 1871, 2.

18. CS to Samuel Howe, August 3, 1871, 64/705, PCS; "Dr. Howe, the Santo Domingo Commissioner," *New National Era*, April 27, 1871, 3; CS to Samuel Howe, January 9, 1871, 64/724, PCS. For more on Howe's journeys to Santo Domingo, see Schwartz, *Samuel Gridley Howe: Social Reformer*, chap. 19; James W. Trent Jr., *The Manliest Man: Samuel G. Howe and the Contours of Nineteenth-Century American Reform* (Amherst: University of Massachusetts Press, 2012), chap. 8. CS to Samuel Howe, August 3, 1871; "Dr. Howe, the Santo Domingo Commissioner," 3; CS to Samuel Howe, January 9, 1871.

19. *Sycamore True Republican*, April 1, 1871.

20. "Sumner Interviewed," *Richmond Independent*, March 25, 1871.

21. Schwartz, *Samuel Gridley Howe, Social Reformer*, 309; "Grant Interview in Hamburg (July 6, 1878)," Papers of Ulysses S. Grant: Digital Edition, n.d., http://rotunda.upress.virginia.edu/founders /AWJN.html.

22. CS, *WCS*, 14:306–9; J. N. Leger, *Haiti: Her History and Her Detractors* (New York: Neale Publishing, 1907), 220–21; Fritz Daguillard, *A Jewel in the Crown: Charles Sumner and the Struggle for Haiti's Recognition* (Washington, D.C.: Haitian Embassy, 1999), 49; "File: Haitian Medal State Library of Massachusetts.Jpg," Wikipedia, 2009, https://commons.wikimedia.org/wiki/File:Haitian_medal_state _library_of_massachusetts.jpg; "Memorial to Charles Sumner, Accompanying the Medal Presented by the Government in Behalf of the People of Hayti, May, 1871," State Library of Massachusetts, n.d., 22, 2024, https://archives.lib.state.ma.us/handle/2452/862187.

23. James Freeman Clarke, *Memorial and Biographical Sketches* (Boston: Houghton, Osgood, 1878), 98; Storey, *Charles Sumner*, 399; CS to Edward Pierce, May 12, 1871, 64/692, PCS; CS, *WCS*, 14:246.

24. George Downing, "Caste," *New National Era*, October 20, 1870, 1; George Downing, "A Bivalvular Boomerang," *New National Era*, June 8, 1871, 3.

25. George Downing to CS, February 7, 1871, 52/479, PCS; George Downing to CS, March 10, 1871, 53/034, PCS.

26. Edwin Belcher to CS, March 10, 1870, 50/146, PCS.

27. Cong. Globe, 42nd Cong., 1st Sess., 21 (1871) (remarks of Sen. Sumner); CS, *WCS*, 14:358.

28. CS, "Rights and Duties of Our Colored Fellow-Citizens" (Letter, National Convention of Colored Citizens at Columbia, South Carolina, October 12, 1871), *WCS*, 14:316–319; "A Word of Mr. Downing's Letter," *New National Era*, June 8, 1871, 2.

29. Carl Schurz, *Speeches, Correspondence and Political Papers of Carl Schurz*, ed. Frederic Bancroft, vol. 2 (New York: G. P. Putnam's Sons, 1913), 398.

30. "December 4, 1871: Third Annual Message—Ulysses S. Grant Presidency," Miller Center, n.d., https://millercenter.org/the-presidency/presidential-speeches/december-4-1871-third-annual -message.

31. Carl Schurz to CS, September 30, 1871, 55/366, PCS; CS to Carl Schurz, September 25, 1871, 84/429, PCS.

Chapter 27: The Constitution Is Not Mean, Stingy, and Pettifogging

1. "The Obstacles to Reunion," in *The Saturday Review of Politics, Literature, Science and Art*, vol. 13 (London: Saturday Review, 1862), 87–88; CS to John G. Whittier, August 11, 1872, 85/037, PCS.

2. For Sumner's interest in universal amnesty in 1865, see Pierce, *MLCS*, 4:289–90. For the other examples of Sumner's leniency toward the South, see previous chapters.

3. Edwin Belcher to CS, February 1, 1869, 44/677, PCS. For the story of the visit by the Georgians to Sumner's home, see *A Memorial of Charles Sumner* (Boston: Wright and Porter, Printers to the Commonwealth of Massachusetts, 1874), 58.

4. Cong. Globe, 42nd Cong., 2nd Sess., 240, 244 (1871) (remarks of Senator Sumner); Cong. Globe, 42nd Cong., 2nd Sess., 434 (1872) (remarks of Senator Sumner). For an overview of the strategy to latch civil rights onto amnesty, see Robert W. Burg, "Amnesty, Civil Rights, and the Meaning of Liberal Republicanism, 1862–1872," *American Nineteenth Century History* 4, no. 3 (2003). For the text of Sumner's civil rights amendment, see Alan Friedlander and Richard Allan Gerber, *Welcoming Ruin: The Civil Rights Act of 1875* (Leiden, Netherlands: Brill, 2020), app. B.

5. Cong. Globe, 42nd Cong., 2nd Sess., 278 (1871) (remarks of Senator Sumner).

6. CS to George William Curtis, December 30, 1871, 84/482, PCS; CS to George Downing, April 8, 1872, Box 1, Folder 21, Degrasse-Howard Papers, Massachusetts Historical Society, Boston, https:// www.masshist.org/collection-guides/digitized/fa0153/b1-f21#22; CS to Henry Longfellow, February 25, 1872, 84/536, PCS.

7. Patricia W. Romero, ed., *I Too Am America: Documents from 1619 to the Present* (The Association for the Study of Negro Life and History, 1968), 144; "Mr. Sumner Complimented for His Labors in Behalf of the Blacks," *Boston Journal*, January 2, 1872; "Delegation of Colored Men," *New National Era*, January 18, 1872; CS, *WCS*, 14:438.

8. Cong. Globe, 42nd Cong., 2nd Sess., 245 (1871) (remarks of Senator Sumner); Cong. Globe, 42nd Cong., 2nd Sess., 434 (1872) (remarks of Senator Sumner).

9. Cong. Globe, 42nd Cong., 2nd Sess., 244–45 (1871) (remarks of Senator Sumner); Cong. Globe,

42nd Cong., 2nd Sess., 430, 431, 434 (1872) (remarks of Senator Sumner); "Petition from Women of the District of Columbia Asking for the Passage of the Sumner Civil Rights Bill (January 15, 1872)," National Archives NextGen Catalog, accessed June 20, 2024, https://catalog.archives.gov /id/306406.

10. Cong. Globe, 42nd Cong., 2nd Sess., 434, 726, 729 (1872) (remarks of Senator Sumner). For all the letters and petitions from Black Americans that Sumner read in support of the civil rights amendment, see Cong. Globe, 42nd Cong., 2nd Sess., 36, 84, 158, 244–45 (1871); Cong. Globe, 42nd Cong., 2nd Sess., 293–94, 429–34, 480, 662, 726–29, 824, 2247, 3258, 3361 (1872). Some of these letters and petitions were reprinted in CS, "Equality Before the Law Protected by National Statute" (Speech, U.S. Senate, 1872), WCS, 14:355–473.

11. Cong. Globe, 42nd Cong., 2nd Sess., 764, 3631 (1872) (remarks of Senators Davis and Trumbull).

12. For helpful secondary literature on the congressional debate about the constitutionality of Sumner's bill, see Bertram Wyatt-Brown, "The Civil Rights Act of 1875," The Western Political Quarterly 18, no. 4 (1965): 764–69; S. G. F. Spackman, "American Federalism and the Civil Rights Act of 1875," Journal of American Studies 10, no. 3 (1976); Earl M. Maltz, "The Civil Rights Act and the Civil Rights Cases: Congress, Court, and Constitution," Florida Law Review 44 (1992): 612–25; Pamela Brandwein, Rethinking the Judicial Settlement of Reconstruction (Cambridge: Cambridge University Press, 2011), 61–86.

13. Cong. Globe, 42nd Cong., 2nd Sess., 764 (1872) (remarks of Senator Davis).

14. CS, WCS, 14:472–73.

15. Cong. Globe, 42nd Cong., 2nd Sess., 3361–62 (1872) (remarks of Senator Trumbull); Christopher W. Schmidt, Civil Rights in America (Cambridge: Cambridge University Press, 2020), 36; Brandwein, Rethinking the Judicial Settlement of Reconstruction, 78.

16. CS, Argument of Charles Sumner, Esq. Against the Constitutionality of Separate Colored Schools (Boston: B. F. Roberts, 1849); Cong. Globe, 42nd Cong., 2nd Sess., 823 (1872) (remarks of Senator Sumner).

17. Cong. Globe, 42nd Cong., 2nd Sess., 294, 431 (1872) (remarks of Senator Sumner).

18. Cong. Globe, 42nd Cong., 2nd Sess., 726 (1872) (remarks of Senator Sumner); Cong. Globe, 42nd Cong., 2nd Sess., app., 1–5 (1872) (remarks of Senator Morrill).

19. Cong. Globe, 39th Cong., 1st. Sess., 570 (1866) (remarks of Senator Morrill).

20. CS, WCS, 7:216; Cong. Globe, 42nd Cong., 2nd Sess., 726–30 (1872) (remarks of Senator Sumner). Eric Foner described Reconstruction as an "unfinished revolution" in the subtitle of Foner, Reconstruction.

21. Cong. Globe, 42nd Cong., 2nd Sess., 825 (1872) (remarks of Senator Sumner). For a study on how Sumner and other Radicals understood the Declaration's interpretive role in constitutional law, see Alexander Tsesis, "The Declaration of Independence and Constitutional Interpretation," Southern California Law Review 89 (2016): 369–98; Sebastián J. Delgado, "The Utopian Liberal: Continuity and Change in the Philosophy of Charles Sumner," Law and History Review: The Docket, 2023, https://lawandhistoryreview.org/article/sebastian-j-delgado-the-utopian-liberal -continuity-and-change-in-the-philosophy-of-charles-sumner-undergraduate-focus/.

22. Edwin Bruce Thompson, Matthew Hale Carpenter: Webster of the West (Madison: State Historical Society of Wisconsin, 1954), 120; Benjamin Perley Poore, Perley's Reminiscences of Sixty Years in the National Metropolis, vol. 2 (Philadelphia: Hubbard's Bros., 1886), 310–11; Alexander McDonald Thomson, A Political History of Wisconsin (n.p.: Brookhaven Press, 1900), 192; Frank Abial Flower, Life of Matthew Hale Carpenter (Madison, Wisc.: D. Atwood, 1883), 402.

23. Cong. Globe, 41st Cong., 2nd Sess., 2424–25, 2750 (1870) (remarks of Senator Carpenter).

24. Cong. Globe, 42nd Cong., 2nd Sess., 758–63 (1872) (remarks of Senator Carpenter).

25. George Hoar, "Introduction," in Charles Sumner: His Complete Works, by Charles Sumner, vol. 1 (Boston: Lee and Shepard, 1900), xvi–xvii.

26. Thomson, A Political History of Wisconsin, 191.

27. Cong. Globe, 42nd Cong., 2nd Sess., 822–25 (1872) (remarks of Senator Sumner).

28. Cong. Globe, 42nd Cong., 2nd Sess., 827–28 (1872) (remarks of Senator Sumner).

29. Cong. Globe, 42nd Cong., 2nd Sess., 826, 919 (1872) (remarks of Senator Carpenter).

30. Cong. Globe, 42nd Cong., 2nd Sess., 826 (1872) (remarks of Senator Sumner); Cong. Globe, 42nd Cong., 2nd Sess., 919, 929 (1872).

31. CS to Henry Longfellow, February 25, 1872, 84/536, PCS. CS to Longfellow, February 25, 1872.

32. Francis Lieber to CS, March 2, 1872, MLCS, 4:510–11; Wendell Phillips to CS, March 3, 1872, MLCS, 4:511.

33. Pierce, *MLCS*, 4:504–10; CS, "Reform and Purity in Government: Neutral Duties, Sale of Arms to Belligerent France" (Speech, U.S. Senate, February 28, 1872), *WCS*, 15:5–44.

34. CS, "Parliamentary Law on the Appointment of Special Committees of the Senate" (Speech, U.S. Senate, March 1872), *WCS*, 15:45–60; "Threatened Arrest of Sumner," *Cincinnati Enquirer*, March 27, 1872. On the day that Sumner was expected to testify or be arrested, Frank Bird sent him a one-word telegram: "Stick." It was a reference to Sumner's famous note to Edwin Stanton when Stanton had been fired by President Johnson.

35. "Pen and Ink Portrait," *Brooklyn Union*, February 23, 1872, 4.

36. "David Ames Wells to Carl Schurz, March 15, 1877, Papers of Carl Schurz (Microfilm), 1876–1881" (n.d.), Film No. 158, Reel 2 (Volume 31), Yale University; David Ames Wells to CS, April 14, 1872, 57/155, PCS; Hans L. Trefousse, *The Radical Republicans: Lincoln's Vanguard for Racial Justice* (New York: Alfred A. Knopf, 1969), 508–9; CS to George Downing, April 8, 1872.

37. Francis Bird, April 15, 1872, 57/159, PCS; Francis Bird, April 23, 1872, 57/217, PCS; Pierce, *MLCS*, 4:517.

38. Henry Wilson to CS, March 17, 1872, 55/645, PCS.

39. Donald, *Charles Sumner and the Rights of Man*, 544; PCS; Francis Bird to CS, May 1, 1872, 57/269, PCS.

40. Cong. Globe, 41st Cong., 2nd Sess., 759 (1870) (remarks of Senator Carpenter).

41. "Liberal Republican Platform of 1872 | The American Presidency Project," accessed July 2, 2024, https://www.presidency.ucsb.edu/documents/liberal-republican-platform-1872.

42. For more on Greeley's nomination, see James M. McPherson, "Grant or Greeley? The Abolitionist Dilemma in the Election of 1872," *American Historical Review* 71 (October 1965): 43–61; Matthew T. Downey, "Horace Greeley and the Politicians: The Liberal Republican Convention in 1872," *The Journal of American History* 53, no. 4 (March 1967); David W. Blight, *Race and Reunion: The Civil War in American Memory* (Cambridge, Mass.: Harvard University Press, 2001), 124–29; Andrew L. Slap, *The Doom of Reconstruction: The Liberal Republicans in the Civil War Era* (New York: Fordham University Press, 2006), chap. 7.

43. Richard White, *The Republic for Which It Stands: The United States During Reconstruction and the Gilded Age, 1865–1896* (Oxford: Oxford University Press, 2017), 210–11. For Greeley's biography, see Robert C. Williams, *Horace Greeley: Champion of American Freedom* (New York: New York University Press, 2006); Adam Tuchinsky, *Horace Greeley's New-York Tribune: Civil War–Era Socialism and the Crisis of Free Labor* (Ithaca, N.Y.: Cornell University Press, 2009).

44. CS to Charles W. Slack, May 12, 1872, 84/680, PCS.

45. John Y. Simon, ed., *The Papers of Ulysses S. Grant*, vol. 23 (Carbondale: Southern Illinois University Press, 2000), 99; *Daily Patriot*, May 10, 1872, 4.

46. For an account of the messy procedural journey of Sumner's Civil Rights Bill in May 1872, see Jeffrey A. Jenkins and Justin Peck, *Congress and the First Civil Rights Era, 1861–1918* (Chicago: University of Chicago Press, 2021), 182–86.

47. Cong. Globe, 42nd Cong., 2nd Sess., 3729 and 3735 (1872) (remarks of Senators Thurman and Spencer).

48. Cong. Globe, 42nd Cong., 2nd Sess., 3735–36 (1872) (remarks of Senators Spencer, Frelinghuysen, and Carpenter). For the lobbying effort to remove the schools provision from Sumner's bill, see Alfred H. Kelly, "The Congressional Controversy over School Segregation, 1867–1875," *American Historical Review* 64, no. 3 (April 1959): 537–63; James M. McPherson, "Abolitionists and the Civil Rights Act of 1875," *The Journal of American History* 52, no. 3 (1965): 493–510.

49. Cong. Globe, 42nd Cong., 2nd Sess., 3737–39 (1872) (remarks of Senator Sumner).

Chapter 28: You Are the Jesus of the Negro Race

1. *Washington Chronicle*, March 13, 1874, 4; Elias Nason, *The Life and Times of Charles Sumner* (Boston: B. B. Russell, 1874), 312; Pierce, *MLCS*, 4:96.

2. CS, *WCS*, 15:198–99; William Lloyd Garrison to CS, May 27, 1872, 57/440, PCS; Pierce, *MLCS*, 4:539–40; Edward Pierce to CS, October 17, 1873, 64/749, PCS; CS to James Freeman Clarke, June 7, 1872, 84/610, PCS; Samuel Howe to CS, November 30, 1854, 71/484, PCS; Harold Schwartz, *Samuel Gridley Howe, Social Reformer* (Cambridge, Mass.: Harvard University Press, 1956), 311.

3. George William Curtis, "Charles Sumner: A Eulogy," *Harper's Weekly*, June 20, 1874; CS, *Republicanism vs. Grantism: Speech of Hon. Charles Sumner (May 31, 1872)* (Boston: Lee and Shepard, 1872); David Donald, *Charles Sumner and the Rights of Man* (New York: Knopf, 1970), 548.

4. Francis Hickox Smith, *Presidential Election, 1872: Proceedings of the National Union Republican Convention Held at Philadelphia, June 5 and 6, 1872* (Washington, D.C.: Gibson Bros., 1872), 14.

5. George William Curtis, *Orations and Addresses of George William Curtis*, vol. 3 (New York: Harper and Bros., 1894), 246–47.

6. CS to Sarah J. Luce, August 11, 1872, 85/035, PCS; Ron Chernow, *Grant* (New York: Penguin, 2017), 798; James Parton, *The Life of Horace Greeley, Editor of "The New York Tribune": From His Birth to the Present Time* (Boston: Houghton Mifflin, 1889), 552; Horace Greeley, *New York Tribune*, April 12, 1872. For more on Greeley's 1872 campaign, see James M. McPherson, "Grant or Greeley? The Abolitionist Dilemma in the Election of 1872," *American Historical Review* 71 (October 1965): 43–61; Matthew T. Downey, "Horace Greeley and the Politicians: The Liberal Republican Convention in 1872," *The Journal of American History* 53, no. 4 (March 1967); Andrew L. Slap, *The Doom of Reconstruction: The Liberal Republicans in the Civil War Era* (New York: Fordham University Press, 2006), chaps. 8–9.

7. George M. Arnold to CS, May 20, 1872, 57/382, PCS; Frederick Douglass to CS, July 19, 1872, 58/492, PCS; Joshua Smith to CS, July 22, 1872, 58/536, PCS; Joshua Smith to CS, July 29, 1872, 58/657, PCS.

8. "A Colored Gentleman: Prominent Colored Lawyer of Boston for Greeley," *Tennessean*, July 24, 1872; Millington W. Bergeson-Lockwood, *Race over Party: Black Politics and Partisanship in Late Nineteenth-Century Boston* (Chapel Hill: University of North Carolina Press, 2018), 49.

9. "Mr. Sumner to the Colored Voters," *Missouri Republican*, July 31, 1872, 3; "Sumner's Apology," *Washington Chronicle*, September 5, 1872, 2.

10. "Campaign Documents," *Leavenworth Daily Commercial*, August 21, 1872, 2; "Senator Sumner's Position," *New York Tribune*, July 31, 1872; CS, "Interest and Duty of Colored Citizens in the Presidential Election" (July 29, 1872), WCS, 15:83–172.

11. "Blaine to Sumner," *New York Daily Herald*, August 3, 1872, 6; "A New Reason for Sumner's and Greeley's Apostacy," *Boston Evening Transcript*, August 3, 1872, 4. For more on Robert Harlan and his white half brother James Harlan, see generally Peter S. Canellos, *The Great Dissenter: The Story of John Marshall Harlan, America's Judicial Hero* (New York: Simon and Schuster, 2022).

12. James Wilson to CS, August 10, 1872, 59/294, PCS; J. S. Frisbie to CS, August 3, 1872, 59/110, PCS; Edwin Belcher to CS, August 5, 1872, 59/135, PCS; Robert Morris to CS, August 1, 1872, 59/018, PCS; CS, "Retrospect and Promise: Address at a Serenade" (Speech, Sumner's House in Washington, August 9, 1872), WCS, 15:202–4.

13. "Charles Sumner: His Sudden Departure for Europe—Ill-Health the Cause," *Chicago Evening Post*, September 7, 1872; "Mr. Sumner in London," *Daily Albany Argus*, October 15, 1872.

14. David W. Blight, *Race and Reunion: The Civil War in American Memory* (Cambridge, Mass.: Harvard University Press, 2001), 127; Thomas Nast, "It Is Only a Truce to Regain Power ('Playing Possum')," Library of Congress, 1872, https://www.loc.gov/item/89712269/.

15. For Sumner's speech that was printed but not delivered, see CS, "Greeley or Grant?" (Speech, Cooper Institute, September 3, 1872), WCS, 15:209–54.

16. Pierce, MLCS, 4:534–36; "Charles Sumner in Europe," *Morning Democrat*, September 16, 1872; CS to Frank Bird, September 15, 1872, 85/062, PCS; CS to Nathaniel P. Banks and Edward Avery, October 6, 1872, 85/080, PCS; "Massachusetts Coalition," *Boston Globe*, September 12, 1872, 4.

17. "Sumner: His Departure for Europe Yesterday," *New York Daily Herald*, September 4, 1872, 4; "A New Departure: From the Boston Journal," *Burlington Free Press*, September 5, 1872, 2; "Charles Sumner: His Sudden Departure for Europe—Ill-Health the Cause"; "Mr. Sumner's Health and Departure for Europe," *Springfield Daily Republican*, September 5, 1872, 4; "Gone to Europe," *Elk County Advocate*, September 12, 1872; Frank Abial Flower, *Life of Matthew Hale Carpenter* (Madison, Wisc.: D. Atwood, 1883), 274; David Donald, *Charles Sumner and the Rights of Man* (Naperville, Ill.: Sourcebooks, 2009), 554. It is not clear who leaked Sumner's departure to the press.

18. John Bigelow, *Retrospections of an Active Life*, vol. 5 (New York: Doubleday, Page, 1913), 80–82; Charles-Édouard Brown-Séquard to CS, July 1, 1858, MLCS, 3:565; George H. Haynes, *Charles Sumner* (Philadelphia: George W. Jacobs, 1909), 201; Edward Waldo Emerson and Waldo Emerson Forbes, eds., *Journals of Ralph Waldo Emerson with Annotations*, vol. 10 (Boston: Houghton Mifflin, 1913), 293.

19. "Charles Sumner's Position," *New York Daily Herald*, December 2, 1872, 10; CS to Henry Longfellow, September 27, 1872, 85/074, PCS; CS to Matilde Lieber, October 15, 1872, 85/082, PCS.

20. CS to Elizabeth Argyll, November 14, 1872, 85/087, PCS; George Smalley, "Sumner," *Chicago Evening Mail*, December 2, 1872.

21. CS to Edwin Denison Morgan, May 5, 1873, 85/201, PCS.

22. "Address of D. A. Straker, Esq.," *New National Era*, March 26, 1874.

23. Pierce, MLCS, 4:535; "Political," *Chicago Evening Post*, October 28, 1872.

24. Pierce, *MLCS*, 4:541–43. For more on Sumner's Europe trip, see Moncure D. Conway, "Senator Sumner in London," *Boston Journal*, October 11, 1872; George Smalley, "Mr. Sumner in London," *Boston Advertiser*, October 14, 1872; George Smalley, "Mr. Sumner's Health," *Boston Journal*, November 23, 1872.

25. CS to William Story, August 2, 1852, *MLCS*, 3:333; Pierce, *MLCS*, 4:541–2. For more on William Story and Sumner's relationship, see Andrew F. Rolle, "A Friendship Across the Atlantic: Charles Sumner and William Story," *American Quarterly* 11, no. 1 (1959): 40–57.

26. George Smalley, "Mr. Sumner in London," *Boston Advertiser*, October 14, 1872; "White Star Line of Steamers Between New York and Liverpool: Baltic," Royal Museums Greenwich, accessed July 6, 2024, https://www.rmg.co.uk/collections/objects/rmgc-object-156596; "Senator Sumner's Vivid Description of His Trip in the 'Baltic,'" *Chicago Tribune*, November 27, 1872, 8; "Rescue of a Wrecked Crew," *Richwood Gazette*, December 19, 1872, 4.

27. "Mr. Sumner's Sufferings," *Perrysburg Journal*, April 3, 1874, 4; CS to Henry Longfellow, December 2, 1872, 85/095, PCS; Charles Edward Brown-Séquard to CS, December 3, 1872, 60/089, PCS; Benjamin Perley Poore, "Charles Sumner: His Death Yesterday," *Washington Chronicle*, March 12, 1874, 5.

28. CS, *WCS*, 15:275; CS to Anna Cabot Lodge, January 11, 1873, 85/130, PCS.

29. "Charles Sumner's Position—An Attitude of Observation," *New York Daily Herald*, December 2, 1872, 4.

30. "Charles Sumner's Position—His Civil Rights Bill and the Abolition of the Electoral College," *New Orleans Republican*, December 9, 1872.

31. CS, "The One Man Power vs. Congress," *WCS*, 11:1.

32. Eric Foner, *The Fiery Trial: Abraham Lincoln and American Slavery* (New York: W. W. Norton, 2010), 296.

33. CS, "A Single Term for the President, and Choice by Direct Vote of the People" (Speech, U.S. Senate, February 11, 1867), *WCS*, 11:98–101; CS, "One Term for President" (Speech, U.S. Senate, December 21, 1871), *WCS*, 14:320–26; "Electing President by the Vote of the People," *Reading Times* (Pennsylvania), June 4, 1872. For more on Sumner and Ashley's amendments for a direct popular vote, see Alexander Keyssar, *Why Do We Still Have the Electoral College?* (Cambridge, Mass.: Harvard University Press, 2020), 180–85.

34. Pierce, *MLCS*, 4:530.

Chapter 29: I Have a Toothache in My Heart

1. CS, "No Names of Battles with Fellow-Citizens on the Army-Register or the Regimental Colors of the United States" (Bill, U.S. Senate, December 2, 1872), *WCS*, 15:255; Chas. H. Taylor, ed., *Journal of the House of Representatives of the Commonwealth of Massachusetts for the Year 1873 and for the Extra Session of 1872* (Boston: Wright and Potter, 1873), 54–55. As early as 1847, long before the Civil War, Sumner had believed that "no success over brethren of the same country could be the foundation of honor." He noted that in Republican Rome, "no thanksgiving or religious ceremony was allowed by the Senate in commemoration of such success" of civil war. See CS, *WCS*, 2:38.

2. "Committee Hearing: The National Battle Flags," *Boston Evening Transcript*, December 14, 1872, 2; "The Raid upon Charles Sumner," *Springfield Daily Republican*, December 18, 1872, 4–5.

3. Pierce, *MLCS*, 4:550–52. For a careful procedural review of the censure resolution, see Edward Pierce, "Charles Sumner and the Battle-Flags: An Historical Statement: First Paper," *Boston Commonwealth*, July 25, 1874; Edward Pierce, "Charles Sumner and the Battle-Flags: An Historical Statement: Second Paper," *Boston Commonwealth*, August 1, 1874; Edward Pierce, "Charles Sumner and the Battle-Flags: An Historical Statement: Third Paper," *Boston Commonwealth*, August 8, 1874.

4. James Freeman Clarke, *Memorial and Biographical Sketches* (Boston: Houghton, Osgood, 1878), 109; *New York Herald*, March 6, 1873, 3; *Springfield Daily Republican*, March 6, 7, 8, 10; Julia Ward Howe, *Words for the Hour* (Boston: Ticknor and Fields, 1857), 14–15; Julia Ward Howe, *Diary of Julia Ward Howe* (March 5), 1873, 168, https://www.juliawardhowe.org/genealogy/journals/; "Garrison on Sumner," *New York Times*, March 10, 1873; Charles W. Durham, "'Suffering for Truth's Sake': The Conflict Between Abdiel and Satan in *Paradise Lost*," *CEA Critic* 68, no. 1/2 (2005): 60–66.

5. *Springfield Daily Republican*, March 8, 1873.

6. CS to Wendell Phillips, December 16, 1872, 85/99, PCS; CS to Willard P. Phillips, March 16, 1873, 85/167, PCS; CS to William Lloyd Garrison, December 30, 1872, 85/118, PCS.

7. Pierce, *MLCS*, 4:556; CS to Henry Longfellow, December 30, 1872, 85/118, PCS; CS to Henry Longfellow, January 25, 1874, 85/347, PCS; David Donald, *Charles Sumner and the Rights of Man*, 583.

8. Frederick Douglass to CS, April 26, 1869, 46/459, PCS.

9. CS, *Fame and Glory: An Address Before the Literary Societies of Amherst College* (Boston: William D. Ticknor, 1847).

10. Pierce, *MLCS*, 4:562; Henry Wilson, *History of the Rise and Fall of the Slave Power in America*, 3 vols. (Boston: Houghton Mifflin, 1872–77); *A Memorial of Charles Sumner* (Boston: Wright and Porter, Printers to the Commonwealth of Massachusetts, 1874), 61–62.

11. Pierce, *MLCS*, 4:562, 556–57; David Donald, *Charles Sumner and the Rights of Man* (New York: Knopf, 1970), 571–73.

12. Pierce, *MLCS*, 4:569; Clarke, *Memorial and Biographical Sketches*, 104–5. Throughout this book, Reverend Clarke frequently mixed up dates of past events. Clarke recalled that Sumner attended the church in December 1873, but he probably visited in November 1873 or earlier.

13. "Senator Sumner's Serenade," *National Republican*, December 2, 1873; "The Sumner Serenade," *St. Louis Republican*, December 2, 1873.

14. "Mr. Douglass' Views," *New National Era*, April 6, 1871, 2; David W. Blight, *Frederick Douglass: Prophet of Freedom* (New York: Simon and Schuster, 2018), 322; Frederic May Holland, *Frederick Douglass: The Colored Orator* (Funk and Wagnalls, 1891), 326–27.

15. "Sumner Repudiated by Fred. Douglass," *Richmond Whig*, April 4, 1871; "Speech of Hon. Frederick Douglass," *New National Era*, May 2, 1872; Booker T. Washington, *Frederick Douglass* (Philadelphia: G. W. Jacobs, 1907), 285. See also Frederick Douglass, *Life and Times of Frederick Douglass* (Hartford: Park Publishing, 1882), 499.

16. *Cong. Rec.*, 43rd Cong., 1st Sess., 325 (1873) (remarks of Senator Sumner); Alan Friedlander and Richard Allan Gerber, *Welcoming Ruin: The Civil Rights Act of 1875* (Leiden, Netherlands: Brill, 2020), 57–59; *Cong. Rec.*, 43rd Cong., 1st Sess., 11 (1873) (remarks of Senator Ferry).

17. George T. Downing, *Memorial of the National Convention of Colored Persons, Praying to Be Protected in Their Civil Rights* (National Civil Rights Convention, 1877).

18. "An Extraordinary Statement," *Georgia Weekly Telegraph, Journal and Messenger*, December 26, 1873; "Alexander Stephens on Civil Rights," *Charleston News and Courier*, December 24, 1874.

19. *Cong. Rec.*, 43rd Cong., 1st Sess., 378–86 (1873) (remarks of Representative Stephens).

20. For a survey of the responses by Black congressmen to Alexander Stephens, see Friedlander and Gerber, *Welcoming Ruin*, 71–78; "Neglected Voices: Speeches of African-American Representatives Addressing the Civil Rights Bill of 1875," New York University School of Law, n.d., https://www.law.nyu.edu/sites/default/files/civilrightsactspeeches.pdf.

21. J. L. M. Curry, *A Brief Sketch of George Peabody and a History of the Peabody Education Fund* (Cambridge University Press, John Wilson & Son, 1898), 65. For more on the Peabody Education Fund's role in lobbying against Sumner's bill, see F. Bruce Rosen, "The Influence of the Peabody Fund on Education in Reconstruction Florida," *Florida Historical Quarterly* 55, no. 3 (1976): 310–20; Earle H. West, "The Peabody Education Fund and Negro Education, 1867–1880," *History of Education Quarterly* 6, no. 2 (1966): 3–21; Friedlander and Gerber, *Welcoming Ruin*, 115–17, 502–3.

22. *Cong. Rec.*, 43rd Cong., 1st Sess., 948–50 (1873) (remarks of Senator Sumner); CS, "Supplementary Civil-Rights Bill: The Last Appeal" (Speech, U.S. Senate, January 27, 1874), *WCS*, 3:301–14.

23. Pierce, "Charles Sumner and the Battle-Flags: An Historical Statement: Third Paper."

24. Joshua Smith to CS, December 2, 1872, 60/080, PCS; Joshua Smith to CS, January 7, 1873, 60/345, PCS.

25. *A Memorial of Charles Sumner*, 60; Wendell Phillips, "Judge Hoar, Mr. Sumner and the Civil Rights Bill," *Springfield Daily Republican*, April 7, 1874; "Address of the Hon. Joshua B. Smith (Colored)," *New York Tribune*, March 16, 1874, 2.

26. Joseph Taber Johnson, "Angina Pectoris, Illustrated by the Case of Charles Sumner," *Boston Medical and Surgical Journal* 91, no. 16 (October 15, 1874): 372; George Sewall Boutwell, *Reminiscences of Sixty Years in Public Affairs: Governor of Massachusetts, 1851–1852*, vol. 2 (New York: McClure, Phillips, 1902), 217–18; Donald, *Charles Sumner and the Rights of Man*, 585; "Death of Charles Sumner," *New York Tribune*, March 12, 1874.

Epilogue

1. There are many reports about Sumner's death scene. In constructing my account, based on my best judgment of the contradictory recollections, I relied on and obtained quotes from the following sources: "Death of Charles Sumner," *New York Tribune*, March 12, 1874; Benjamin Perley Poore, "Charles Sumner: His Death Yesterday," *Washington Chronicle*, March 12, 1874, 5; "The Great Statesman Gone to His Rest," *Boston Globe*, March 12, 1874; "Death of Senator Sumner," *Boston Post*, March 12, 1874; *A Memorial of Charles Sumner* (Boston: Wright & Porter, Printers to the Commonwealth of Massachusetts, 1874), 10–13; Arnold B. Johnson, "Recollections of Charles Sumner," *Scribner's Monthly* 8 (1874), 486–90; "Letter from George T. Downing of Washington to Wendell Phillips," *Boston Globe*, April 6, 1874; "Newspaper Clippings and Printed Matter About the Downing Family, Box 1, Folder 23, Image 19," Degrasse-Howard Papers, Massachusetts Historical Society, accessed July 23, 2024, https://www.masshist.org/collection-guides/digitized/fa0153/b1-f23#19; "Frederick Douglass Papers: Subject File, 1845–1939; Sumner, Charles," Library of Congress, accessed July 21, 2024, https://www.loc.gov/resource/mss11879.20002/; Edward Pierce, *Memoir and Letters of Charles Sumner*, vol. 4 (Boston: Roberts Bros., 1877), 596–99; George F. Hoar, "Some Political Reminiscences," *Scribner's Magazine* 25 (1899), 555–57.

2. For more on electric baths in this era, see George M. Schweig, *The Electric Bath, Its Medical Uses, Effects and Appliance* (New York: G. P. Putnam's Sons, 1877).

3. John 14:1–15 (New International Version).

4. There are different variations of Hoar's reply. I relied on "Death of Charles Sumner," *New York Tribune*, March 12, 1874. In an alternative account, Hoar replied, "He said of you once that he never knew so *white* a soul." See Ralph Waldo Emerson, *Journals of Ralph Waldo Emerson: With Annotations*, vol. 10 (Boston: Houghton Mifflin, 1914), 430.

5. "Charles Sumner: Mourning in Washington," *New National Era*, March 19, 1874; "Charles Sumner: His Mortal Remains in Boston," *Boston Evening Transcript*, March 16, 1874; "A Statesman's Funeral," *New York Tribune*, March 14, 1874; "The Dead Statesman," *Washington Evening Star*, March 13, 1874; "Charles Sumner," *Harper's Weekly*, April 4, 1874. For a sample of other newspapers that compared Sumner's funeral to that of Lincoln, see, e.g., "Massachusetts' Dead," *New York Daily Herald*, March 16, 1874, 3; "The Death of Sumner," *Boston Globe*, Mar. 16, 1874, 2; "Charles Sumner," *Lamoille Newsdealer*, March 18, 1874, 2; "Death of Senator Sumner," *Bolivar Free Press*, March 19, 1874.

6. "The Journey from Washington," *New York Tribune*, March 14, 1874; "Charles Sumner: Funeral of the Late Senator," *Morning Republican*, March 14, 1874; "Obsequies: America's Greatest Statesman," *Washington Chronicle*, March 14, 1874, 5; "Charles Sumner," *New National Era*, March 19, 1874, 2.

7. "The Funeral," *Boston Daily Globe*, March 14, 1874, 1, 5; "Charles Sumner," *Boston Post*, March 14, 1874, 4; "Charles Sumner: His Mortal Remains in Boston," *Boston Evening Transcript*, March 16, 1874, 2; "The Dead Statesman," *Springfield Daily Republican*, March 17, 1874, 5; "Charles Sumner," *Harper's Weekly* 18, no. 901 (April 4, 1874): 296.

8. George F. Hoar, "Some Political Reminiscences," 558. On the passage of the Civil Rights Act of 1875, see Alan Friedlander and Richard Allan Gerber, *Welcoming Ruin: The Civil Rights Act of 1875* (Leiden: Brill, 2020), chaps. 4–6, 14.

9. On the Clinton massacre, see Michael F. Holt, *By One Vote: The Disputed Presidential Election of 1876* (Lawrence: University Press of Kansas, 2008), 45–48; Ron Chernow, *Grant* (New York: Penguin, 2017), 813–18.

10. Carol Gelderman, *A Freeman of Color and His Hotel: Race, Reconstruction, and the Role of the Federal Government* (Washington, D.C.: Potomac, 2012), 47. On the alleged Compromise of 1877, see C. Vann Woodward, *Reunion and Reaction: The Compromise of 1877 and the End of Reconstruction* (New York: Oxford University Press, 1966); Allan Peskin, "Was There a Compromise of 1877?," *The Journal of American History* 60, no. 1 (1973): 63–75; C. Vann Woodward, "Communication: Yes, There Was a Compromise of 1877," *The Journal of American History* 60, no. 1 (1973): 215–23; Michael Les Benedict, "Southern Democrats in the Crisis of 1876–1877: A Reconsideration of Reunion and Reaction," *The Journal of Southern History* 46, no. 4 (1980): 489–524.

11. On the *Civil Rights Cases* and Conkling's role in establishing corporate personhood under the Fourteenth Amendment, see Marianne L. Engelman Lado, "A Question of Justice: African-American Legal Perspectives on the 1883 Civil Rights Cases," *Chicago Kent Law Review* 70 (1995): 1123–95; Adam Winkler, *We the Corporations: How American Businesses Won Their Civil Rights* (New York: Liveright, 2018), chap. 4.

12. Plessy v. Ferguson, 163 U.S. 537, 552 (1896); W. E. Burghardt Du Bois, *Black Reconstruction* (New

York: Harcourt, Brace, 1935), 26. For more on Black Codes and *Plessy*, see Steve Luxenberg, *Separate: The Story of* Plessy v. Ferguson, *and America's Journey from Slavery to Segregation* (New York: W. W. Norton, 2019), pts. 4–5.

13. On the conventional narrative of American racial progress, see Jennifer A. Richeson, "Americans Are Determined to Believe in Black Progress," *The Atlantic*, July 27, 2020, https://www.theatlantic.com/magazine/archive/2020/09/the-mythology-of-racial-progress/614173/.

14. Charles Flint Kellogg, *NAACP: A History of the National Association for the Advancement of Colored People*, vol. 1 (Baltimore: Johns Hopkins University Press, 1967), 6, 55–57; David Levering Lewis, *W. E. B. Du Bois, 1868–1919: Biography of a Race* (New York: Henry Holt, 1993), 264, 432–33; William B. Hixson Jr., *Moorfield Storey and the Abolitionist Tradition* (Oxford: Oxford University Press, 1972), chaps. 3–4.

15. "Emancipation," *Washington Daily Chronicle*, April 18, 1873, 4; Frederick Douglass, *Oration, Delivered in Corinthian Hall, Rochester, July 5th, 1852* (Rochester: Lee, Mann, 1852), 14; Ginger Thompson, "Quake Leaves Cracks in Washington Monument, Closing It for Now," *New York Times*, August 24, 2011, https://www.nytimes.com/2011/08/25/us/25monument.html; CS, "Mr. Sumner's Eulogy," in *A Memorial of Abraham Lincoln* (Boston: J. E. Farwell, 1865), 151.

IMAGE CREDITS

1. Sumner in his thirties: Edward L. Pierce, *The Memoirs and Letters of Charles Sumner*, vol. 1 (Boston: Roberts Brothers, 1877).

2. Samuel Gridley Howe: Courtesy of the Miriam and Ira D. Wallach Division of Art, Prints and Photographs: Print Collection, The New York Public Library.

3. Robert Morris: Courtesy of the Social Law Library, Willard Collection.

4. Mary and Oscar Williams: Courtesy of the Massachusetts Historical Society.

5. Preston Brooks: Courtesy of the Library of Congress, Prints and Photographs Division, LC-DIG-ds-11107.

6. Illustration of Sumner's caning: D. A. Harsha, *The Life of Charles Sumner* (New York: Dayton & Burdick, 1856).

7. Sumner holding Proclamation: Courtesy of the National Portrait Gallery, Smithsonian Institution.

8. Emancipation petition: Courtesy of the National Archives, Records of the U.S. Senate, SEN38A-H20.

9. Sumner in his old age: *Harper's Weekly*, March 24, 1866.

10. Alice Mason Hooper: Courtesy of the Boston Athenaeum.

11. Sumner in his study: *Frank Leslie's Illustrated Newspaper*, March 28, 1874.

12. "Execution in the U.S. Senate" cartoon: *Puck*, no. 2 (1871).

13. John Mercer Langston: Courtesy of the Library of Congress, Prints and Photographs Division, LC-B5-35340.

14. Frederick Douglass notecard: Courtesy of the Library of Congress, Manuscript Division, The Frederick Douglass Papers.

15. Sumner's casket at the United States Capitol: *Frank Leslie's Illustrated Newspaper*, March 28, 1874.

16. Sumner's casket at the Massachusetts State House: *Harper's Weekly*, April 4, 1874.

17. Sumner Avenue in Haiti: Courtesy of Rita Daguillard. Thanks are also due to Robert Daguillard and Ambassador Harold Joseph.

ACKNOWLEDGMENTS

I AM THANKFUL TO EVERYONE WHO CONTRIBUTED TO THIS LABOR OF love. The credit for anything beneficial in this book ought to go to them; any factual errors or defects in reasoning are entirely my own.

Many scholars shaped this work, beginning with my teachers at Yale Law School. Akhil Reed Amar opened my eyes to Reconstruction's legal significance through a transformative class on constitutional law. He educates, challenges, and inspires me every day. I will never cease to be grateful for his generous stewardship of this project. Anthony Kronman gifted me with his boundless enthusiasm and read half the manuscript. John Fabian Witt and Reva Siegel offered thoughtful advice on how to frame the book. Samuel Moyn helped me balance my courses with writing and explained the world of history publishing to me. Monica Bell and Claire Priest welcomed me into their respective writing workshops, where they and fellow participants critiqued parts of the manuscript and grounded me in my writing.

My deepest thanks go to the Yale History Department. Joanne Freeman kindly spent time with me to share her perspective on Sumner's caning. John Gaddis extended his advice on the best practices in biography. And David Blight was friendly, gracious, and hilarious in numerous impromptu conversations.

Jack Balkin pulled me out of the Yale bubble and invited me to present my book proposal to Jonathan Gienapp, Mark Graber, Steve Griffin, Andrew Koppelman, and Sanford Levinson, all of whom offered incisive advice. Graber even read this manuscript with his careful eye. Thanks to Griffin, I attended the Second Founding Conference at Tulane University, where I benefited from the wisdom of Evan Bernick, Jamelle Bouie, Pamela Brandwein, Kate Masur, Rachel Shelden, Alexander Tsesis, and

Rebecca Zietlow, among others. Thanks to Akhil Amar, I met Tom Donnelly, who has generously helped with this project long before a single word was written. I also spoke to Michael Vorenberg, who offered warm encouragement and illuminating thoughts.

I'm grateful to several scholars at the University of Virginia, my alma mater. Louis Nelson, a vice provost and a brilliant historian, kindly gave me some advice. Risa Goluboff, the dean of Virginia Law, found time in her busy schedule to help me navigate the NAACP papers. Ian Solomon, the dean of the Frank Batten School of Leadership and Public Policy, has an invigorating love for Sumner and was the first person to read a chapter of this book. I must also thank President Emerita Teresa Sullivan, who has been a gracious mentor of many years; Garry Gabison, who taught me how to conduct research; Michael Smith, who taught me how to love and read; and Kenneth Elzinga, who taught me how to keep the faith and write. Finally, I am grateful to President Jim Ryan and the wonderful, funny, and passionate members of his entire team.

Some mentors in the legal profession helped me to chart my schooling and career as I wrote this unwieldy manuscript. Thank you to Brianne Gorod, Deepak Gupta, Ashwin Phatak, and Arjun Ramamurti.

My thanks are also due to a few tour guides and companions. Meaghan Michel, a learned historian and National Park Ranger, showed me around Beacon Hill and shared her thoughts on Sumner's sexuality. Steve Livengood of the U.S. Capitol Historical Society took me to the Old Supreme Court Chamber and the Old Senate Chamber, where Sumner was caned. Patricia Silberman and Stephen Klineberg were wonderful company on the Capitol tour and also invited me to watch a riveting oral argument at the Supreme Court. Thanks to Samir Doshi, I visited the Court's inner chambers and saw the bust of Roger Taney in the Great Hall.

Some physicians reviewed Sumner's medical records to help me understand Sumner's heart disease and his health conditions after the caning. Thank you to Dr. Adil Asaduddin, an internist in Houston, Texas; Dr. Robert Burton, former chief of neurology at UCSF Mount Zion Hospital; and Dr. William Gaillard, chief of neurology at Children's National Hospital.

Librarians are the heroes behind every biography. I'm grateful to the staff of the Amistad Research Center, the Anne T. and Robert M. Bass Library, the Beinecke Rare Book & Manuscript Library, the Boston Athenaeum, the Harvard University Archives, the Houghton Library, the Library of Congress, the Lillian Goldman Law Library, the Louis Jefferson Long Library, the Massachusetts Historical Society, the Moorland-Spingarn Research Center, the New York Public Library, and the U.S. National Archives in Washington and Boston.

Some librarians deserve special recognition. At Yale, Alison Burke helped me locate over a hundred documents and never took longer than a few hours to reply to an email. Mary Ellen Budney helped me find several political cartoons. John Nann was a fabulous, patient recipient of my incessant questions. Jason Eiseman introduced me to several digital humanities tools; he also helped me win a research grant from the Oscar M. Ruebhausen Fund, for which I am grateful. In Massachusetts, I'm especially thankful to Nathaniel Wiltzen and Jessica Shrey. Finally, in Washington, my thanks go to Matthew Hofstedt, the curator of the U.S. Supreme Court; Mary Baumann, Josh Howard, and Daniel S. Holt at the Senate Historical Office; and the staff at the House Historical Office.

Many brilliant students contributed to this book, especially several undergraduate research assistants. Yale student Rachel Zhu has been my thought partner and lieutenant. She deserves credit for many findings, including the discovery that Sumner's wife, Alice, was accused of being "enceinte," a French word for pregnant. The talented Yale student Areeb Gani built a machine learning model on Sumner's handwriting and created a searchable database of his letters on Transkribus. Daniel Patel, an inventive student at Harvard, gathered some library materials that weren't available to me. Finally, several fabulous Yale students digitized microfilm and transcribed letters: Danish Khan, Kamal Mahamud, Krishna Tewatia, and Laiqa Walli.

I was blessed with some wonderful classmates at Yale Law School. I owe my deepest thanks to Shreyas Gandlur for editing more than four hundred pages of this book with intoxicating enthusiasm. I couldn't have enjoyed law school without the exuberance of Ayesha Durrani, Philsan Isaak, Melisa Olgun, and Saif Zihiri. I'm grateful to the generous souls who pressure tested this book's ideas: Cameron Averill, Al Brady, Matt Buck, Avi Feinsod, Jaewon Kim, Reshard Kolabhai, Isaac May, Demi Moore, Daniel Moraff, Melissa Muller, Jack Sadler, Grace Watkins, and Isabelle Zaslavsky, to name just a few. I'm thankful to three honorary law students—Leanne Fan, Kelly Martin, and Sol-Marie Quintero—for their help as well. Most of all, I'm grateful to my Orange Street roommates, who endured my bizarre sleep schedule and let me take over a big spot in our common area for well over a year. Thank you to Robert Codio, Jamil Rahman, and Areeb Siddiqui, the dearest of friends, and our two cats, Sim Sim and Manju.

Remarkable friends lent their help. Helen Kramer, whose faith and brilliance inspire me so much, edited this book assiduously. Her rich ideas were woven into these pages. Ronnie Kuriakose hosted me in Boston, commissioned a look-alike of Preston Brooks's cane, and even gifted me a gutta-percha pen. Several others helped in different ways. Thank you to Mikayel Hussayn Aakil, Mazin Ahmad, Qadir Ahmad, Maarya Akmal, Afsah Ali, Saad Awan, Eileen Chen, Amy Fan, Zainab Khan, Farooq Rizvi, Nolan Shah, Andrew Sokulski, Mariam Syed, Rana Thabata, David Valerio, and Sara Zahir.

To learn about publishing, I turned to Timothy McMahan King and Kimberley Meyer, two authors who graciously lent me their wisdom. I deeply appreciate Kyle O'Connor, who improved my book proposal. I also benefited from David Hopen, a fellow young author whose tweaks to my draft pitch made a world of a difference. I'm grateful to Nika Jonas, who seemingly knew everything about publishers and became a warm friend. And I can't thank enough Haroon K. Ullah, who coached me through the process with boundless energy and believed in this project before I believed in it myself.

After the contract was signed and the book was written, no one helped more than Judith Goldstein, who held my hand through the editing process and expanded my vision for what this book could be. The organization she founded, Humanity in Action, changed my life years ago and instilled in me and many others a dedication to pluralism and democracy.

My agent, Andrew Stuart, has been the best shepherd and advocate any young author could dream of working with. He reached out to me within forty-five minutes of my pitch, grilled me over the phone, asked me to rewrite the proposal, and helped mold the project into what it has become. I so admire his searing intellect, generosity with his time, and willingness to take a chance on me.

My editor, Tim Duggan, invested more time and money into this book than I expected in my wildest dreams. He saw right away how important Sumner was to American history and modern law, and he has been a gracious and patient editor ever since. I'm equally grateful to the impeccable editorial assistant Zoë Affron, production editor Hannah Campbell, publicist Catryn Silbersack, marketers Sarah Bode and Alyssa Weinberg, and the entire team at Henry Holt for championing this project. Thanks as well to Jenna Dolan, a copyeditor par excellence, and fact-checkers Elizabeth Bergman, Ateeb

Gul, and Nicola Slater-Arnold for their vigilant and astute work. Slater-Arnold was especially pivotal in the final stretch of this project.

I end in the beginning. Andrew Dewey, my high school history teacher at Carnegie Vanguard in Houston, inspired my love for the Civil War and Reconstruction period. Kathryn Eaker, Juliet Stipeche, and the late Billy Reagan were among the warmest mentors growing up and instilled in me the values of empathy, rigor, and service. Deborah Bial and the Posse Foundation sent me far away to college while reminding me and my posse to stay true to our roots. In college, Andrus Ashoo and Kimberley Bassett kept me grounded.

The ultimate thanks go to my family. Noor Ghafoor has been a bedrock source of support, the funnest of friends, and the warmest of confidantes. Asra Hussain and Hamaad Raza joyously opened their door (and sofa) to me so often. Azra Asaduddin taught me to love reading at an early age, and, along with Adil Khan, has given me a place to eat, sleep, decompress, and read books ever since. Saad Raza convinced me to love history as a young kid and was one of the first people I talked to about the book. Nuha Khan has been my youngest and most beloved reader. Her energy and curiosity, from the very first car ride where I told her about this project, gave me the power to push through. I'm so grateful to my brothers for putting up with me and my parents for all that they have given me. Most of all, I owe my life to the prayers, reminders, and love of my grandmothers: Sroor Asaduddin, Sara Ghafoor, and the late Shaheen Tameez.

In the Islamic tradition, classical scholars ended their books by saying *Allāhu a'lam*, an Arabic expression that acknowledges the limitations of human knowledge. Studying the past proved to me how little I will ever know. For every stone I turned during my research, I discovered more stones that I couldn't. I seek the reader's forgiveness for what I missed. As the scholars used to say, "God knows better."

INDEX

ABOUT THE AUTHOR

Zaakir Tameez is a scholar of antitrust and constitutional law. A graduate of Yale Law School and the University of Virginia, he has published award-winning scholarship and coauthored amicus briefs before the Texas and United States Supreme Courts. He is a Fulbright Scholar and Humanity in Action Senior Fellow from Houston, Texas.